WORDSWORTH CLASSICS
OF WORLD LITERATURE

General Editor: Tom Griffith

THE ESSENTIAL
PHILOSOPHICAL WORKS

D1638568

THE ESSENTIAL PHILOSOPHICAL WORKS

◆

David Hume

with an introduction
by Charlotte R. Brown and
William Edward Morris

WORDSWORTH CLASSICS
OF WORLD LITERATURE

For my husband
Anthony John Ranson
with love from your wife, the publisher
Eternally grateful for your unconditional
love, not just for me but for our children
Simon, Andrew and Nichola Trayler

1

Readers who are interested in other titles from
Wordsworth Editions are invited to visit our website at
www.wordsworth-editions.com

For our latest list and a full mail order service contact
Bibliophile Books, Unit 5 Datapoint,
South Crescent, London E16 4TL
Tel: +44 020 74 74 24 74
Fax: +44 020 74 74 85 89
orders@bibliophilebooks.com

This edition published 2011 by Wordsworth Editions Limited
8B East Street, Ware, Hertfordshire SG12 9HJ

ISBN 978 1 84022 666 9

Typeset in Great Britain by Roperford Editorial
Printed and bound by Clays Ltd, St Ives plc

CONTENTS

INTRODUCTION

The most important philosopher ever to write in English, David Hume was also well known in his own time as an historian and essayist. A master stylist in any genre, his major philosophical works – *A Treatise of Human Nature* (1739–1740), the *Enquiries concerning Human Understanding* (1748) and *concerning the Principles of Morals* (1751), as well as his posthumously published *Dialogues concerning Natural Religion* (1779) – remain widely and deeply influential.

Hume was the outstanding philosopher of what we now call the Scottish Enlightenment, the extraordinary outburst of Scottish intellectual and scientific activity in the eighteenth century that was pivotal in creating the modern world. Edinburgh was the epicenter of the Scottish Enlightenment, and Hume was one of the leading lights in this 'hotbed of genius'.

Although Hume's more conservative contemporaries denounced his writings as works of scepticism and atheism, his influence is evident in the moral philosophy and economic writings of his close friend Adam Smith. Hume also awakened Immanuel Kant from his 'dogmatic slumbers' and 'caused the scales to fall' from Jeremy Bentham's eyes. Charles Darwin counted Hume as a central influence, as did 'Darwin's bulldog', Thomas Henry Huxley. The diverse directions in which these writers took what they gleaned from reading Hume reflect not only the richness of their sources but also the wide range of his empiricism. Today, philosophers recognize Hume as a precursor of contemporary cognitive science, as well as one of the most thoroughgoing exponents of philosophical naturalism.

Life and Works
Born in Edinburgh, Scotland's capital, in 1711, Hume's family was socially well connected, but not wealthy. His mother realized that he was 'uncommonly wake-minded' or precocious, so when

his older brother went up to Edinburgh University, Hume went with him, although he was only 10 or 11. There he studied Latin and Greek language and culture and read widely in history, literature and philosophy. He was supposed to pursue a legal career, but found the law 'nauseous' and decided instead to become a 'Scholar & Philosopher'. He followed a rigorous program of reading and reflection for several years until there 'open'd up to me a New Scene of Thought'. The intensity of developing his philosophical vision precipitated a psychological crisis in the isolated scholar. But the crisis passed, and Hume remained intent on developing his 'new scene of thought'. As a second son, his inheritance was meager, so he moved to France, where he could live cheaply. In 1734, when he was only 23, he began writing *A Treatise of Human Nature*.

Hume returned to England in 1737 to ready the *Treatise* for the press. In hopes of receiving the favorable opinion of a leading philosopher and theologian, he 'castrated' his manuscript, deleting his controversial discussion of miracles, along with other 'nobler parts'. Book 1, 'Of the Understanding', and Book 2, 'Of the Passions', appeared anonymously in 1739. The next year saw the publication of Book 3, 'Of Morals' and his anonymous 'Abstract' of Books 1 and 2, which features a clear, succinct account of 'one simple argument' concerning causation.

The *Treatise*'s poor reception prompted Hume to recast it. In 1748, *An Enquiry concerning Human Understanding* appeared, covering the central ideas of Book 1 of the *Treatise* and his discussion of free will from Book 2. He also included material he had excised from the *Treatise*. In 1751 *An Enquiry concerning the Principles of Morals* was published, a rewritten version of Book 3 of the *Treatise* which Hume described as 'incomparably the best' of all his work.

From time to time Hume made forays into the wider world. He served as a secretary in several diplomatic missions, was the librarian of the law library in Edinburgh, and held important diplomatic posts in France. During his stay in Paris, he became the rage of its salons, enjoying the company of famous European intellectuals.

Hume's reputation as an atheist and sceptic dogged him throughout his life. Twice turned down for professorships, he never held an academic post. As a librarian, one of his orders for 'indecent

Books' prompted a move for his dismissal and excommunication. Friends and publishers persuaded him to hold off publishing some of his more controversial writings, especially those on religion, during his lifetime.

In 1775, Hume was diagnosed with intestinal cancer. He died in 1776, just after writing his short autobiography, 'My Own Life'. There was much curiosity about how 'the great infidel' would face his death, but his friends agreed that he prepared himself with the same peaceful cheer that characterized his life.

In addition to the *Treatise* and the *Enquiries*, Hume's other writings include collections of his popular essays on politics, economics, history and aesthetics. During his stint as law librarian, he used the library's resources to research his six-volume *History of England*, which was a bestseller well into the next century. He also wrote extensively on topics in the philosophy of religion. His most controversial work, *Dialogues concerning Natural Religion*, posthumously published in 1779, is a devastating critique of the argument from design.

This volume contains the *Treatise*, the *Abstract* and the *Enquiries*, in addition to his autobiographical essay. The relation between the *Treatise* and the *Enquiries*, however, presents a problem for Hume scholars, since he seems to disavow the *Treatise* in an advertisement he attached to late editions of his works. Should we take his statement literally and let the *Enquiries* represent his considered view? Or is the *Treatise* the best statement of his position?

Both options presuppose that there are substantial enough differences between the two works to warrant our taking one or the other as best representing Hume's position. But there are good reasons to doubt this. Hume himself claims that the 'philosophical principles are the same in both'. His project in the *Enquiries* was to 'cast the whole anew . . . where some negligences in his former reasoning and more in the expression, are . . . corrected', since he believed that the *Treatise*'s lack of success 'proceeded more from the manner than the matter'. Perhaps Hume's recasting of the *Treatise* was designed to correct its 'manner' of presentation – its structure – more than its 'matter' – its philosophical content, which suggests that we might understand him best by reading both works, despite their differences, together.

Hume is a major player in two important debates of the modern period, the debates about causation and the foundation of ethics. After briefly sketching the philosophical background to these debates, we look at his criticisms of his predecessors, his understanding of the problems that need to be solved, as well as his radically innovative solutions to them.

Hume's Project, Method and Machinery

Before we look at Hume's contributions to these debates, we need to understand how he conceives of his philosophical project. What are its aims? What methodology should it employ? He answers these questions in his 'Introduction' to the *Treatise*, in the *Abstract*, and in the first sections of both *Enquiries*.

As the title of the *Treatise* proclaims, Hume's subject is human nature. He summarizes his project in its subtitle: 'an attempt to introduce the experimental method of reasoning into moral subjects'. In Hume's day, 'moral' meant anything concerned with human beings, not just morality or ethics. Moral philosophy contrasts with natural philosophy, or what we now call natural science. Hume aims to bring the scientific method to the study of human nature.

Hume's reading convinced him that the philosophical study of human nature was in a sorry state. While he had reservations about the ancient philosophers for depending 'more on Invention than Experience', he found modern philosophers – his contemporaries and immediate predecessors – disturbing. Their theories were too speculative, paying too little attention to what human nature was actually like. Instead of helping us understand ourselves, they were mired in interminable debates about inadequately supported suppositions.

He begins by asking why philosophers haven't made the spectacular progress in trying to understand human nature that natural scientists have recently achieved in the physical sciences. His answer is that scientists have cured themselves of their 'passion for hypotheses and systems', which in Hume's day was code for any theory that depended more on speculative conjecture than experience and observation. In studying human nature, philosophers haven't yet purged themselves of this temptation.

To make progress, Hume says, we need first to 'reject every system . . . however subtle or ingenious, which is not founded on fact and observation'. These 'systems' cover a wide range of entrenched and influential philosophical and theological views. They have in common that they attempt to discover the 'ultimate original principles' – principles that purport to give us a deeper and more certain knowledge of ultimate reality – of human nature. But Hume argues that in attempting to go beyond anything we can possibly experience, these metaphysical theories try to 'penetrate into subjects utterly inaccessible to the understanding'. As a result, their claims to have found the 'ultimate principles' of human nature are unintelligible. In its incoherent efforts to go deeper, metaphysics loses any claim to be a science. These 'airy sciences' only have the 'air' of science.

Worse still, these metaphysical systems serve as smokescreens for 'popular superstitions' that attempt to overwhelm us with religious fears and prejudices. Although 'superstition' was code during this period for Catholicism, Hume was confident that his readers, most of whom were Protestants, would know that organized religion in general is his real target.

The only way to resist the allure of these pseudo-sciences is to engage with them, countering their 'abstruse philosophy and metaphysical jargon' with 'accurate and just reasoning'. Thus the initial phase of Hume's project is essentially *critical*. It aims to eliminate metaphysics by showing that these theories are not just false, but unintelligible.

Until recently, scholars emphasized this *critical phase* at the expense of the rest of Hume's project, which encouraged the charge that he was a negative sceptic. But while Hume is indeed sceptical about the possibility of metaphysical insights that go deeper than science can, he is not at all sceptical about the prospect of a science of human nature. His critique of metaphysics clears the way for the *constructive phase* of his project: an investigation of 'the proper province of human reason', which Hume believes will lead to the development of an empirical science of human nature based on 'the only solid foundation' of experiment and observation.

Metaphysics tempts us to think we can find principles that show us the ultimate nature of reality. Hume shows us how to resist that temptation. His project takes us away from an incoherent search for 'ultimate principles' to the principles that actually govern human nature. Hume believes that his proposed descriptive 'delineation of the distinct parts and powers of the mind', offers a genuine alternative to the unintelligible speculations of previous philosophies. His preferred terms, 'mental geography' and 'anatomy of the mind', aptly characterize the way he thinks we should pursue the science of human nature.

By answering empirical questions in the only way they can be intelligibly answered, Hume thinks we shall finally achieve a clear understanding of how we think, feel, and act, of our various powers and capacities as well as our limitations.

He proposes to explain how we think, feel and act by accounting for 'all effects from the simplest and fewest causes'. He believes that if he follows the same caution Newton displayed in developing his physics, he will be able to explain the workings of our minds in an equally economical manner. To do so, he introduces the minimal amount of machinery necessary to account for the operations of our understanding, all of which is warranted by our experience of how our minds work.

He begins with an account of *perceptions*, because he believes that any intelligible philosophical question can be asked and answered in those terms. Although every modern philosopher held some version of this 'theory of ideas', Hume's version is distinctive for three reasons. First, he distinguishes between impressions and ideas. Next, he bases his account of the cognitive content or meaning of our ideas on that distinction; and finally, he uses the principles of association to account for the connections among perceptions.

Hume uses the term *perception* to designate any mental content. He divides perceptions into two categories, *impressions* and *ideas*. Impressions include sensations as well as passions, desires and sentiments. Ideas are 'faint images of these in thinking and reasoning'. He thinks everyone is familiar with his distinction, since it is simply the difference between feeling something (the present pain of sun-burn) and thinking of something (recalling a painful childhood sunburn). Hume also distinguishes between *impressions of sensation* ('outward sentiment' or 'original impressions') and *impressions of reflection* ('inward sentiment' or 'secondary impressions'). Impressions of sensation include the feelings that come from our five senses as well as sensations of pain and pleasure, all of which arise 'from unknown causes'. Impressions of reflection include desires, emotions, passions, and sentiments. They are so called because most are caused by our reactions to ideas, as when remembering a very unpleasant experience causes the strong desire to avoid further experiences like it.

Although we may freely separate and combine ideas to form complex ideas of things we haven't experienced (adding my idea of a bull's horn to my idea of a horse to form an idea of a unicorn), our creative powers extend no farther than what we're given in experience. *Complex ideas* are composed of *simple ideas*, which are fainter copies of the simple impressions from which they are ultimately derived, to which they correspond and which they exactly represent.

Hume offers this claim as his 'first principle . . . in the science of human nature', presenting it as an empirical thesis. Usually called the 'Copy Principle', it is most often identified with his distinctive brand of *empiricism*. His use of the principle's reverse in his account of *definition*, however, is perhaps the most innovative element of his system.

Hume touts his account of definition as 'a new microscope or species of optics', with which we will surmount 'the chief obstacle . . . to our improvement in the moral or metaphysical sciences . . . the obscurity of the ideas, and ambiguity of the terms'.

It is a device for determining the cognitive content of words and ideas, using a simple series of tests. Begin with a term. Ask what idea is annexed to it. If there is no such idea, then the term has no cognitive content, however prominently it figures in philosophy or theology. If there is an idea annexed to the term, and it is complex, break it down into the simple ideas that compose it, and trace them back to their original impressions. If the process fails at any point, the idea in question lacks cognitive content. When carried through successfully, however, it yields a 'just definition' – a precise account of the troublesome idea or term.

Hume uses his account of definition in his project's *critical phase* to show that the central concepts of traditional metaphysics lack any intelligible content. He also uses it in its *constructive phase* to determine the precise meaning of our terms and ideas.

Our ideas are also regularly connected, and a science of human nature should account for this 'secret tie or union' among them. Hume explained this 'union' in terms of the mind's natural ability to *associate* certain ideas. Association is 'a gentle force, which commonly prevails', by means of which one idea or impression naturally introduces another. Hume locates three principles of association: *resemblance* (a photo calls up your idea of its subject), *contiguity* (passing a church reminds you of the theater that once stood next to it), and *causation* (someone's son makes you think of his father).

Causation is the strongest associative principle, and the only one that takes us 'beyond our senses', establishing a link between our past and present experiences and our expectations about the future. It is also the least understood, but Hume intimates that he will soon rectify this deficiency.

Hume regarded his use of the principles of association as his most distinctive contribution, one that entitled him to call himself an '*inventor*'. He advertised the associative principles as the philosophical equivalent of Newton's Law of Gravitation: 'Here is a kind of Attraction, which in the mental world will be found to have as extraordinary effects as in the natural.' Like the inverse square law, its 'effects are every where conspicuous' but their causes 'are mostly unknown, and must be resolv'd into *original* qualities of human nature, which I pretend not to explain.' Trying to account for them further would take us illegitimately beyond the bounds of experience. Nonetheless, since the associative principles 'are the only ties of our thoughts, they are really *to us* the cement of the universe, and all the operations of the mind must, in great measure, depend on them.'

Causation

The medieval synthesis Thomas Aquinas (1224–1274) forged between Christian theology and Aristotle's science and metaphysics set the terms for the early modern causation debate. Aristotle (384–322 BCE) believed there was an absolute categorical distinction between scientific knowledge (*scientia*) and belief (*opinio*). Scientific knowledge was knowledge of causes and scientific explanation was an activity of intellect consisting in *demonstration* – proving the *necessary connection* between a cause and its effect from intuitively obvious premises independently of experience.

Modern philosophers thought of themselves as scientific revolutionaries because they rejected Aristotle's account of causation. Even so, they accepted his distinction between knowledge and belief, and regarded causal inference as an exercise of reason, which aimed at demonstrating the necessary connection between cause and effect. Nicholas Malebranche (1638–1715) and others following Descartes (1596–1650) were optimistic about the possibility of obtaining demonstrative scientific knowledge, while those in the British experimental tradition were more pessimistic. John Locke (1632–1704) was sufficiently sceptical about what knowledge we could attain that he constructed one of the first accounts of probable inference.

When Hume enters the debate, he translates the traditional distinction between knowledge and belief into his own terms, dividing 'all the objects of human reason or enquiry' into two categories: *relations of ideas* and *matters of fact*. Propositions concerning *relations of ideas* are intuitively or demonstratively certain. They are known a priori – discoverable independently of experience by 'the mere operation of thought', so their truth doesn't depend on anything actually existing. *That the interior angles of a Euclidean triangle sum to 180 degrees* is true whether or not there are any Euclidean triangles to be found in nature.

In sharp contrast, the truth of propositions concerning *matters of fact* depends on the way the world is. Their contraries are always possible, and their denials never imply contradictions. Matters of fact can't be the subjects of demonstration, and can't have the certainty demonstrations provide. However certain it may be that *the sun will rise tomorrow*, it can't be demonstrated, and however false, the claim that it won't involves no contradiction.

Hume's method dictates his strategy. He begins with the *causal inferences* we make. In the *critical phase*, he argues that his predecessors were wrong: our causal inferences aren't determined by 'reason or any other operation of the understanding'. He supplies an alternative in the *constructive phase*: the associative principles are their basis. He then examines the idea of *necessary connection*. While he agrees with his predecessors that that idea is an essential part of our idea of causation, in the *critical phase*, he argues that their various attempts to characterize it are unintelligible. In the *constructive phase*, he offers his own positive account of that idea, by determining its source in impressions.

Hume's contributions to the critical phase of the causation debate are contained in *Treatise* 1.3.6 and in Section 4 of the first *Enquiry*, appropriately titled 'Sceptical doubts concerning the operations of the understanding'. The constructive phase in the *Enquiry* is in the following section, also appropriately titled, 'Sceptical solution of these doubts', while his constructive account in the *Treatise* stretches from 1.3.7 through 1.3.10. His critical and constructive accounts of our idea of necessary connection are found in single sections of both works: *Treatise* 1.3.14 and *Enquiry* 8. Even though his discussion of causation is neither 'simple' nor a 'single argument', Hume summarizes it in the *Abstract* as the 'one simple argument' he showcases.

Causal Inference: the critical phase. Causal inferences are the only way we can go beyond the evidence of our senses and memories. In making them, we suppose there is some *connection* between present facts and what we infer from them. But what is this connection? How is it established?

If the connection is established by reasoning, it must concern either *relations of ideas* or *matters of fact*.

Hume argues that the connection can't involve relations of ideas. Effects are distinct events from their causes, so there is no contradiction in conceiving of a cause occurring, and its usual effect not occurring. Ordinary causal judgments are so familiar that we tend to overlook this; they seem immediate and intuitive. But suppose you were suddenly brought into the world as an adult, armed with the intellectual firepower of an Einstein. Could you, simply by examining an aspirin tablet, determine that it will relieve your headache?

If causal inferences don't involve a priori reasoning about relations of ideas, they must concern matters of fact and experience. When we've had many experiences of one kind of event constantly conjoined with another, we begin to think of them as cause and effect and infer the one from the other. This describes what we all *do*, but what is the *foundation* of our inferences?

Hume argues that even after we've had many experiences of a cause being conjoined with its effect, our inferences aren't determined by reason, or by any other process of the understanding.

In the past my headaches have been relieved by taking aspirin, so I believe taking aspirin will relieve the headache I'm having now. My inference is based on the superficial sensible qualities of the aspirin – its size, shape, color, and taste, which have nothing to do with headache relief. Even if I assume that the aspirin has 'secret powers' – powers unknown to me and not accessible through my senses – that are doing the heavy lifting in relieving my headache, these qualities are unknown, so they can't be the basis of my inference.

How, then, do I draw the conclusions I draw from the constant conjunction of objects in my experience?

When I infer that this aspirin will cure my present headache, I'm doing *more* than just citing remembered constant conjunctions. I'm *projecting* my past experience into the future, to objects that may only appear similar.

These two propositions are clearly different:

(1) I've found that taking aspirin has always been followed by headache relief and

(2) Taking aspirin similar to the ones I've taken in the past will relieve my present headache.

We do infer propositions like (2) from propositions like (1). But if our inferences are determined by reason, then what chain of reasoning takes me from (1) to (2), since Hume has shown that their connection obviously isn't intuitive?

Notice that while (1) summarizes my past experience, (2) makes a claim about what will happen in the immediate future. The chain of reasoning I need must show me how my past experience is relevant to my future experience. I need some proposition or propositions that will establish an appropriate *link* between past and future, and take me from (1) to (2) using either *demonstrative reasoning*, concerning relations of ideas, or *probable reasoning*, concerning matters of fact.

From Hume's earlier points about demonstrative reasoning, we can see that it won't establish the link we need. However unlikely it may be, we can always intelligibly conceive of a change in the course of nature. Even though aspirin relieved my past headaches, it implies no contradiction to suppose that it won't relieve the one I'm having now, so it can't be proven false by any reasoning involving relations of ideas.

That leaves probable reasoning. But probable reasoning can't establish the connection, either, since it is based on the relation of cause and effect. What we understand about the relation of cause and effect is based on experience, and our inferences from experience are based on the principle that nature is uniform – that the future will be like the past.

But this Uniformity Principle isn't intuitive, either, and trying to prove it by probable arguments is either viciously circular or question-begging. For any such appeal must assume some version of the Uniformity Principle itself – the very principle we need to justify.

This exhausts the ways reason might establish a connection between cause and effect, and so completes the critical phase of Hume's project. Hume insists that he offers his remarks not as 'discouragement, but rather an incitement . . . to attempt something more full and satisfactory'. Having cleared a space for his constructive account, he is ready to do just that.

Causal Inference: the constructive phase. We make causal inferences all the time. If they aren't determined by reason, then 'some principle of equal weight and authority' must lead us to make them. 'What that principle is may well be worth the pains of enquiry'. We've discovered that we make them only after we've experienced the regular conjunction of different kinds of events, and 'whenever the repetition of any particular act or operation produces a propensity to renew the same act or operation, without being impelled by any reasoning or process of the understanding, we always say, that this propensity is the effect of *Custom.*'

Custom and *habit* are general names for the principles of association. It is therefore custom, and not reason, that 'determines the mind . . . to suppose the future conformable to the past'. Since causation is the operative associative principle here, Hume is presenting a causal account of causal inference. It is only because our minds are governed by the associative principles that we're able to draw an inference from many cases that we can't from one exactly similar case.

Causal inference leads us not only to *conceive* of the effect, but also to *expect* it. When I expect the aspirin will relieve my headache, I'm not just thinking about headache relief, I *believe* that aspirin will relieve it. What more is involved in my belief that my headache will be relieved by taking aspirin than in my conceiving that it will be?

It can't be that there is some additional idea that beliefs have – the idea of belief, perhaps – that conceptions lack. If there were, given our ability to freely combine ideas, we could by an act of will, just add that idea to any conception whatsoever, and believe anything we like.

Hume concludes that belief must be some sentiment or feeling aroused in us independently of our wills, which accompanies those ideas that constitute them. It is a particular way or manner of conceiving an idea that is generated by the circumstances in which we find ourselves.

We've been focusing on the background circumstances – experienced constant conjunctions. But if only constant conjunctions were involved, my thoughts about aspirin and headaches would only be hypothetical. For belief, one of the conjoined objects must be present to my senses or memories; I must be taking, or just have taken, the aspirin. In these circumstances, believing that my headache will soon be relieved is as unavoidable as feeling affection for a close friend, or anger when someone harms us. 'All these operations are a species of natural instincts, which no reasoning . . . is able either to produce or to prevent'.

Defining this sentiment may well be impossible, just as difficult as it is to define how cold or anger feels to someone who has never experienced those feelings. But Hume thinks we can describe belief, if only by analogy, although he was never completely satisfied with his efforts to do so. Belief is a livelier, firmer, more vivid, steady and intense conception of an object. His characterizations are intended to go beyond merely recording intensity of feeling in order to capture 'that act of the mind, which renders realities . . . more present to us than fictions, causes them to weigh more in the thought, and gives them a superior influence on the passions and imagination.'

But how does an idea come to be conceived in such a manner that it constitutes a belief?

Hume's explanation is that as I become accustomed to aspirin's relieving my headaches, I develop a propensity – a tendency – to expect headache relief to follow taking aspirin. That propensity is due to the associative bond that my repeated experiences of taking aspirin and headache relief have formed. My present impressions of taking an aspirin are as forceful and vivid as anything could be, and some of their force and vivacity transfer through the associative path to the idea of headache relief, enlivening it with enough force and vivacity to give it the 'strength and solidity' that constitutes belief.

Since I don't know how aspirin relieves headaches, it is fortunate that there is 'a kind of pre-established harmony between the course of nature and the succession of our ideas' that teaches me to take aspirin when I have a headache. Custom, Hume maintains, in language that anticipates and influenced Darwin, 'is that principle by which this correspondence has been effected; so necessary to the subsistence of our species, and the regulation of our conduct, in every circumstance and occurrence of human life'. Better to rely on 'the ordinary wisdom of nature', which ensures that beliefs are formed 'by some instinct or mechanical tendency', than trust it to 'the fallacious deductions of our reason'.

The Idea of Necessary Connection

The early modern causation debate revolved around a family of 'nearly synonymous' key ideas, the most prominent of which were *power* and *necessary connection*. For Hume, 'there are no ideas, which occur in metaphysics, more obscure and uncertain.' He showcases the critical and constructive uses of his theory of definition as he attempts 'to fix . . . the precise meaning of these terms, and thereby remove some part of that obscurity, which is so much complained of in this species of philosophy.'

Necessary Connection: the critical phase. To get clear about the idea of power or necessary connection, we need to determine the impressions that are its source. He finds in his predecessors three possible sources for that idea: Locke thought we get our idea of power secondarily from *external impressions* of the interactions of physical objects, and primarily from *internal impressions* of our ability to move our bodies and to call up ideas. Malebranche argued that what we take to be causes of either bodily motion or mental activity aren't really causes at all. They are only *occasions* for God, the only source of necessary connection, to act in the world. Hume rejects all three possible sources.

He argues that *external impressions* of the interactions of bodies can't give rise to our idea of power. We only observe bodies' sensible qualities, which tell us nothing about what power they might have. While we see that the motion of one billiard ball follows another, we only observe their *conjunction*, but never their *connection*.

Attending to the *internal impressions* of the operations of our minds doesn't improve matters. We don't get our idea of power from our ability to move our bodies. Although voluntary bodily movements follow our willing that those movements occur, this is a matter of fact I learn through experience, not from some internal impression of my will's power. When I decide to type, my fingers move over the keyboard. When I decide to stop, they stop, but I have no idea how any of this happens. I can't move my fingers directly, nor can I move my pancreas with equal ease. If I were aware of the power of my will, I'd know both the physical details involved and my will's limitations.

Our ability to control our thoughts doesn't give us an impression of power, either. We don't have a clue about how we call up our ideas. Our command over them is limited and varies from time to time. We learn about these limitations and variations only through experience. The mechanisms by which they operate are totally unknown and incomprehensible. If I decide to think about Istanbul, the idea of that city generally comes to mind, but I experience only the succession of decision followed by the idea's appearance, and never the power itself.

When ordinary people can't determine what caused some event, they attribute it to some 'invisible intelligent principle'. Malebranche and the occasionalists do the same thing, except they apply this principle across the boards. They argue that true causes aren't powers or forces, either in the physical world or in human minds. The only true cause is God's willing that certain objects should always be conjoined with certain others.

Anyone aware of our minds' narrow limits should realize that Malebranche's theory takes us into 'fairyland'. It goes so far beyond our experience that we have no way of intelligibly assessing it. It also capitalizes on how little we know about the interactions of bodies, but since our idea of God is based on extrapolations from our faculties, our ignorance in this regard should also apply to him.

Hume admits that since we've canvassed the leading contenders for the source of our idea of necessary connection, it might *seem* that we have no such idea.

Necessary Connection: the constructive phase. But that, Hume maintains, would be too hasty. In our discussion of causal inference, we saw that when we've found that one kind of event is constantly conjoined with another, we begin to expect the one to occur when the other does. We don't hesitate to call the first, the *cause*, and the second, the *effect*. We suppose there's some connection between them.

But we also saw that there's nothing different in the repetition of constantly conjoined cases from the exactly similar single case, *except* that after we've experienced their constant conjunction, habit determines us to expect the effect when the cause occurs.

Hume concludes that it is just this felt connection – our awareness of this customary transition from one associated object to another – that is the source of our idea of power or necessary connection. When we say that one object is necessarily connected to another, what we really mean is that they have acquired an associative connection in our thoughts that gives rise to this inference.

Having finally located the missing ingredient, Hume is now ready to offer a definition of *cause*. He in fact gives us two. The first,

> A cause is an object, followed by another, where all the objects similar to the first are followed by objects similar to the second,

gives the relevant *external impressions*, while the second,

> A cause is an object followed by another, and whose appearance always conveys the thought to that other,

captures the *internal impression* – our awareness of being determined by custom to move from cause to effect. Both are definitions on Hume's account, but his 'just definition' of our idea of cause is the conjunction of the two, for only together do they capture *all* the relevant impressions involved.

Conclusion. Hume's contribution to the early modern causation debate is revolutionary in at least three respects. First, he differs radically from previous philosophers by arguing that our causal inferences aren't based on any exercise of reason. Second, in basing our causal inferences on the associative principles, he is giving a causal explanation of causal inference. Finally, his account of our idea of necessary connection locates that idea *in us*, not in the connection between our ideas of the objects we regard as causes and effect. In all these respects, Hume radically changed the course of the causation debate. His account was controversial in his day, and it remains so in ours. Every subsequent account of causation must begin by confronting the challenges Hume posed for traditional ways of looking at causation.

Hume's discussion of causation is his flagship illustration of his method at work, and in his subsequent work he goes on to apply not only his method, but also the concrete results he has achieved, to other debates and problems prominent in the modern period: probable inference, liberty and necessity, testimony for miracles, the question of intelligent design, and as we shall see in the next section, the debate about the foundations of ethics.

Moral Sentimentalism

Hume steps into an ongoing debate about the foundations of ethics, often called the British Moralists debate, that began in the mid-seventeenth century and continued until the end of the eighteenth. Three types of theories are represented in this debate: self-interest theories, rationalist theories and sentimentalist theories. Hume became the most famous proponent of sentimentalism. He uses the same method here as he did in the causation debate: there is a *critical phase* in which he argues against his opponents, and a *constructive phase* in which he develops his version of sentimentalism.

Thomas Hobbes's (1588–1679) brilliant but shocking attempt to derive moral and political obligation from motives of self-interest initiated the British Moralists debate. Hobbes, as his contemporaries understood him, characterized us as being naturally self-centered and power-hungry creatures, concerned above all with our own preservation. In the state of nature, a pre-moral and pre-legal condition, we seek to preserve ourselves by trying to dominate others. Since we are equally powerful, the result is a state of 'war of all against all' in which life is 'nasty, short and brutish'. The way out is to make a compact with one another. We agree to hand over our power and freedom to a sovereign, who makes the laws necessary for us to live together peacefully and has the power to enforce them. Acting morally requires that we comply with the laws the sovereign establishes, but the basis of morality is self-interest.

Two kinds of moral theories developed in reaction to Hobbes – rationalism and sentimentalism. While both object to Hobbes's moral theory, they do so on different grounds. As the eighteenth century progressed, they began to argue less with Hobbes and more with each other. In the *Treatise*, Hume strategically assumes that Hobbes's theory was no longer on the table, so there were only two possibilities for him to consider – moral rationalism and sentimentalism. If one falls, the other stands. By the time Hume wrote the second *Enquiry*, however, he had dropped the crucial strategic assumption he made in the *Treatise*. His primary opponents now are self-interest theories, especially Hobbes's self-interest theory. While he continues to oppose moral rationalism in the second *Enquiry*, he consigns his arguments against them to an appendix.

Moral Rationalism: critical phase. Hume offers a battery of arguments against moral rationalism, but two are especially important. In *Treatise* 2.3.3, he challenges the long-cherished rationalist belief about reason's right and even obligation to govern us. Nothing is more common, Hume says, than for philosophers and even ordinary people to talk about a combat between reason and passion. They say that we ought to govern our conduct by our reason rather than our passions. If our passions are not in line with reason's commands, we ought to restrain them or bring them into conformity with reason.

Hume argues that this picture is mistaken, since reason alone is incapable of moving us. The main type of reasoning that bears on action is causal reasoning, which informs us of the means to our ends. But the belief that there is a causal connection between two things will never move us by itself. When causal reasoning figures in the production of action, it always presupposes some pre-existing desire or want. Noticing a causal connection between exercising and losing weight will only move you if you want to lose weight. If reasoning is to have practical force, it must be tied to a desire or want.

Hume's other main argument, the first of several in *Treatise* 3.1.1, is the argument from motivation. This argument concerns the source of our moral concepts. Does the idea of 'moral goodness' or 'virtue' spring from reason or sentiment? His specific target is the rationalist, Samuel Clarke (1675–1729), who believes that there are demonstrable moral relations – relations of fitness and unfitness – that we discover a priori by means of reason alone. Gratitude, for example, is a fitting or suitable response to kindness, while ingratitude is an unfitting response. Clarke also thinks that the rational intuition that an action is fitting has the power to obligate us and to move us. This argument, like the last one, has implications for a much wider audience of philosophers as well as ordinary people.

Hume argues that reason by itself is incapable of giving rise to moral ideas and offers two supporting premises. One is that moral ideas have pervasive practical effects. Experience shows that people are motivated to perform an action because they think it is obligatory and refrain because they think it is unjust. They try to cultivate the virtues in themselves and are proud when they succeed and ashamed when they fail. If moral ideas didn't have these practical effects, moral rules would be pointless. The second premise, as Hume just argued, is simply that reason by itself is incapable of having these practical effects. By itself, reason can't excite passions or produce actions. If moral ideas are capable of exciting passions and producing or preventing actions, but reason alone is incapable of doing these things, moral ideas can't spring from reason alone.

Reason, then, gives rise neither to new motives nor to moral ideas. It is essentially passive and inert. If it is incapable of giving rise to new motives or moral ideas, the rationalist claim that we ought to act in conformity with reason's dictates is nonsensical. Having exposed reason's pretensions to rule, Hume inverts the rationalist's picture and provocatively concludes 'reason is, and ought only to be the slave of the passions.' Reason's role is to 'serve and obey' the passions.

Sentimentalism: constructive phase. Taking the defeat of rationalism to be the triumph of sentimentalism, Hume concludes that 'morality . . . is more properly felt.' The moral sentiments are feelings of praise or blame, approval or disapproval that arise when we survey a person's character. In several key passages, he describes them as calm forms of love and hatred. When we evaluate our own character traits, pride and humility replace love and hatred.

Hume's view of morality rests on two assumptions. One is that he identifies the moral point of view with the point of view of a spectator. The central moral concepts are those spectators use to assess their own or other people's characters and actions rather than those agents use to deliberate about what they ought to do. The other is that what we approve and disapprove of in the first instance are people's character traits and the motives that typically spring from them. He offers a theory about what character traits are morally good and bad – a theory of virtue and vice. Virtue is loveable and vice hateful in the eyes of beholders.

According to Hume, the moral project in its *constructive phase* consists in discovering the fundamental principles of the mind that explain the origin of our moral ideas. The explanation must be naturalistic, consistent with the scientific picture of the world. Francis Hutcheson (1694–1746), Hume's sentimentalist predecessor, claimed that God gave us a special moral sense, which disposes us to approve and disapprove. Hume rejects this view since it is unscientific.

Hume traces the moral sentiments to the operation of more fundamental principles in human nature, in particular, to sympathy. In Book 2 of the *Treatise*, he describes sympathy as our capacity to receive the passions, sentiments, and even beliefs of others. It is not itself a passion, and should not be confused with feelings of empathy, compassion, or pity. It is a mechanism that explains why we are able to feel what others are feeling – feeling miserable when your friend feels miserable or cheerful when she is cheerful. It explains a wide range of phenomena: our interest in history and current affairs, our ability to enjoy literature, movies, novels, and, more generally, our sociability. It is central to Hume's account of the passions, the sense of beauty and morality.

Hume explains sympathy in terms of the same associative principles that explain our ability to engage in causal reasoning – resemblance, contiguity and causality. In Book 2 of the *Treatise*, he maintains that our ability to sympathize varies with variations in these relations. We sympathize more strongly and easily with people who resemble us, are contiguous to us, or are family members. Sympathy and the associative principles that explain it are deep-seated principles in human nature. Without sympathy and the associative principles that explain it, we would be unimaginably different.

In *Treatise* 3.3.1, Hume develops his account of moral evaluation in response to two objections to his claim that the moral sentiments spring from sympathy. One is that the moral sentiments can't be based in sympathy because the loves and hatreds that result from the natural and spontaneous workings of sympathy vary, but our moral approval doesn't vary. The second objection is that 'virtue in rags' is still valued. Sympathy works by looking at the actual effects of a person's character traits, but sometimes misfortune prevents people from exercising their good character traits, yet we still admire them.

Hume argues that moral love and hatred spring from sympathy, but only when we regulate our sympathetic reactions by taking up the general point of view. There are two regulatory features to the general point of view. The first is that we survey a person's character from the perspective of the person and his usual associates – friends, family, neighbors, and co-workers. We sympathize with the person and the people with whom that person regularly interacts and we judge character traits in terms of whether they are good or bad for these people. Second, we regulate sympathy further by relying on general rules that specify the general effects and tendencies of character traits rather than sympathizing with their actual effects.

The general point of view is, for Hume, the moral perspective. Its regulative features define a perspective we can share with everyone, from which we may survey a person's character traits. When we occupy the general point of view, we sympathize with the person herself and the people with whom she interacts, and come to love the person for those traits that normally are useful and pleasant for everyone.

Even though Hume bases morality in sentiment, he is able to show that moral judgments are impartial and objective. The regulation of sympathy ensures that we set aside considerations of self-interest and considerations derived from the special ways we may be related to others, ensuring that our moral judgments are impartial. The general point of view also explains why we tend to agree about which character traits are morally good and which are bad. The regulatory features define a perspective we share with others from which we survey a person's character.

Hume argues that we love and admire four sorts of character traits – those that are useful or immediately agreeable to the agent or to others. He thinks that experience confirms this hypothesis, a task he takes up in his discussion of individual virtues.

On Hume's view, morality is entirely a product of human nature. First-order sentiments, the passions and affections that motivate people to act, and actions expressive of them are what have moral value. Second-order, reflective sentiments we have about our own or other people's sentiments are what make them valuable. Both the locus and source of morality are rooted in our nature.

Self-interest theories: critical phase. On Hume's understanding of self-interest theories, self-interest plays two distinct roles in their explanations of morality: first, moral approval and disapproval spring from a concern for our own interest and, second, the motive of which we ultimately approve is self-interest. Hume rejects both claims. He takes Hobbes's self-interest theory to be the most powerful and philosophically interesting self-interest theory.

In Appendix 2 of the *Enquiry*, Hume opposes the idea that self-interest is the motive of which we approve. On his reading of Hobbes, while we approve of kindness, friendship, and other benevolent affections, any desire to benefit others really springs from self-interest, although we may not be conscious of its influence on those desires. Hume argues that this 'selfish hypothesis' is empirically implausible, since we can point to 'thousands' of instances in which people are motivated by a genuine concern for others, even when it could not possibly benefit them and might even harm them. An individual may grieve when his friend dies, even if the friend relied on his patronage. How could his grief spring from self-interest? Parents regularly sacrifice their own interests for the sake of their children. Non-human animals care about members of their own species and us. Is their concern a 'deduction' of self-interest? We are by nature social and sympathetic creatures that care about others for their own sake.

Hume also borrows an argument from Joseph Butler (1692–1752). Happiness consists in the pleasures that arise from the satisfaction of our particular appetites and desires. It is because we want food, fame and other things that we take pleasure in getting them. If you don't have any particular appetites or desires, you won't want anything and there will be no pleasures available to you. In order to get the pleasures that self-love aims at, you must want something other than happiness itself.

Hume is equally adamant that selfish accounts of approval and disapproval are mistaken. He opposes them beginning in Section 2 and ending in Part 1 of the 'Conclusion' of the *Enquiry*. The question, he says, is whether moral approval arises from an interested or disinterested source. He looks at each type of virtue in turn and argues that in each case approval does not spring from self-interest.

Hume first discusses benevolence, justice and the other social virtues that are useful to others and society as a whole. He agrees with Hobbes that justice and the other social virtues make it possible for us to live together peacefully, which is in our interest. Our own good is bound up with the good of society. But he argues against Hobbes that we do not approve of justice and the other social virtues on grounds of self-interest. If the moral sentiments were based on thoughts about their advantages and disadvantages to us, we would never approve or disapprove of people from 'distant ages and remote countries', since they cannot possibly affect us. We would never admire the good deeds of our enemies or rivals, since they are hurtful to us. We approve of the social virtues not because they benefit us, but because we sympathize with the benefits they bestow on others or society.

Hume next examines virtues that are useful to the agent (industriousness), agreeable to the agent (cheerfulness) and agreeable to others (politeness, decency). He argues that we approve of them not because they are advantageous to us, but because we sympathize with the benefits they confer on others. This provides further support for his theory against Hobbes's.

Although Hume argues, as he did in the *Treatise*, that approval and disapproval arise from sympathy, there is some controversy about whether he changes his account of sympathy in the *Enquiry*, replacing it with feelings of humanity or even benevolence. On either reading, Hume traces the moral sentiments to a disinterested basis in human nature.

Justice: constructive phase. In both the *Treatise* and the second *Enquiry*, Hume rightly showcases his pioneering account of justice. In the *Treatise*, he emphasizes the distinction between the natural virtues and the artificial virtues. The natural virtues are character traits and patterns of behavior that human beings would exhibit in their natural condition, even if there were no social order. They include such character traits as being humane, kind and charitable. The artificial virtues are dispositions based on social practices and institutions that we agree to create because they are useful to us. They include justice, fidelity in keeping promises and contracts, and allegiance to government. In saying that justice and the other practices are artificial, Hume doesn't mean to imply that they are fake or unreal. Rather, his point is that they result from conventions or agreements we make with each other. We approve of just people because we sympathize with the benefits they bestow on others and society as a whole.

After arguing in *Treatise* 3.2.1 that justice is artificial, in *Treatise* 3.2.2 he explains why we establish the institution of justice and why we approve of people who comply with its rules. Hume thinks of the institution of justice quite narrowly as concerned with establishing and maintaining property rights. He argues that justice is a solution to a problem. The problem is that since we care most about our family and close friends and since material goods are scarce and portable, we are tempted to take goods from others to give to our family and friends. Since we are bound to fight over these goods, we aren't able to reap the benefits of increased power, ability and security that result from living together in society. The solution is to establish property rights.

We agree that some things are yours, others are mine, and that we will keep our hands off each other's goods. Hume was one of the first to see that what is useful is the practice or institution of justice, rather than individual acts of justice.

Conclusion. Sentimentalism is enjoying a revival. New versions of the theory have been produced during the end of the last century and the start of this one, the most prominent of which are those of Annette Baier and Simon Blackburn. Hume's insight that justice and the other artificial virtues are based in conventions and that they are solutions to problems we face is still held in high regard. John Rawls draws heavily on Hume in his masterpiece, *A Theory of Justice.*

CHARLOTTE R. BROWN
WILLIAM EDWARD MORRIS
Illinois Wesleyan University

FURTHER READING

Work by Hume's immediate predecessors and contemporaries available in accessible, inexpensive editions:

Rationalism
René Descartes, *Meditations*. Cambridge University Press, PB

Moral Rationalism and Sentimentalism
Readings from Thomas Hobbes, Samuel Clarke and other moral rationalists, as well as from Hume's sentimentalist predecessor, Francis Hutcheson, can be found in *British Moralists*, edited by D. D. Raphael, Hackett, PB, 2 volumes

Empiricism
Locke's *Essay concerning Human Understanding* is available in an abridged form (which even Locke thought desirable) from Hackett, edited by Kenneth Winkler
British Natural Philosophy: Newton, Philosophical Writings, edited by Andrew Janiak, Cambridge University Press, PB

There is a great deal of work on various aspects of Hume's philosophy and its relation to problems in contemporary philosophy. Some of the most accessible are:

Simon Blackburn, *How to Read Hume*. Granta, PB
Terence Penelhum, *Hume: Philosophers in Perspective*. Macmillan
Barry Stroud, *Hume*. Routledge, PB

A more detailed introduction to Hume from the authors of the introduction to this volume will be available early in 2012:

Charlotte R. Brown and William Edward Morris, *Starting with Hume*. Continuum, PB

A TREATISE OF
HUMAN NATURE

ADVERTISEMENT

My design in the present work is sufficiently explained in the Introduction. *The reader must only observe, that all the subjects I have there planned out to myself, are not treated of in these two volumes. The subjects of the* understanding *and* passions *make a compleat chain of reasoning by themselves; and I was willing to take advantage of this natural division, in order to try the taste of the public. If I have the good fortune to meet with success, I shall proceed to the examination of* morals, politics, *and* criticism; *which will compleat this* Treatise of human Nature. *The approbation of the public I consider as the greatest reward of my labours; but am determined to regard its judgment, whatever it be, as my best instruction.*

INTRODUCTION

Nothing is more usual and more natural for those, who pretend to discover anything new to the world in philosophy and the sciences, than to insinuate the praises of their own systems, by decrying all those, which have been advanced before them. And indeed were they content with lamenting that ignorance, which we still lie under in the most important questions, that can come before the tribunal of human reason, there are few, who have an acquaintance with the sciences, that would not readily agree with them. It is easy for one of judgment and learning, to perceive the weak foundation even of those systems, which have obtained the greatest credit, and have carried their pretensions highest to accurate and profound reasoning. Principles taken upon trust, consequences lamely deduced from them, want of coherence in the parts, and of evidence in the whole, these are every where to be met with in the systems of the most eminent philosophers, and seem to have drawn disgrace upon philosophy itself.

Nor is there required such profound knowledge to discover the present imperfect condition of the sciences, but even the rabble without doors may judge from the noise and clamour, which they hear, that all goes not well within. There is nothing which is not the subject of debate, and in which men of learning are not of contrary opinions. The most trivial question escapes not our controversy, and in the most momentous we are not able to give any certain decision. Disputes are multiplied, as if every thing was uncertain; and these disputes are managed with the greatest warmth, as if every thing was certain. Amidst all this bustle it is not reason, which carries the prize, but eloquence; and no man needs ever despair of gaining proselytes to the most extravagant hypothesis, who has art enough to represent it in any favourable colours. The victory is not gained by the men at arms, who manage the pike and the sword; but by the trumpeters, drummers, and musicians of the army.

From hence in my opinion arises that common prejudice against metaphysical reasonings of all kinds, even amongst those, who profess themselves scholars, and have a just value for every other part of literature. By metaphysical reasonings, they do not understand those on any particular branch of science, but every kind of argument, which is any way abstruse, and requires some attention to be comprehended. We have so often lost our labour in such researches, that we commonly reject them without hesitation, and resolve, if we must for ever be a prey to errors and delusions, that they shall at least be natural and entertaining. And indeed nothing but the most determined scepticism, along with a great degree of indolence, can justify this aversion to metaphysics. For if truth be at all within the reach of human capacity, it is certain it must lie very deep and abstruse: and to hope we shall arrive at it without pains, while the greatest geniuses have failed with the utmost pains, must certainly be esteemed sufficiently vain and presumptuous. I pretend to no such advantage in the philosophy I am going to unfold, and would esteem it a strong presumption against it, were it so very easy and obvious.

It is evident, that all the sciences have a relation, greater or less, to human nature: and that however wide any of them may seem to run from it, they still return back by one passage or another. Even *Mathematics, Natural Philosophy, and Natural Religion*, are in some measure dependent on the science of MAN; since they lie under the cognizance of men, and are judged of by their powers and faculties. It is impossible to tell what changes and improvements we might make in these sciences were we thoroughly acquainted with the extent and force of human understanding, and could explain the nature of the ideas we employ, and of the operations we perform in our reasonings. And these improvements are the more to be hoped for in natural religion, as it is not content with instructing us in the nature of superior powers, but carries its views farther, to their disposition towards us, and our duties towards them; and consequently we ourselves are not only the beings, that reason, but also one of the objects, concerning which we reason.

If therefore the sciences of Mathematics, Natural Philosophy, and Natural Religion, have such a dependence on the knowledge of man, what may be expected in the other sciences, whose connexion with human nature is more close and intimate? The sole end of logic is to explain the principles and operations of our reasoning faculty, and the nature of our ideas: morals and criticism regard our tastes and sentiments: and politics consider men as united in society, and dependent on each other. In these four sciences of *Logic, Morals, Criticism, and Politics*, is comprehended almost everything, which it can any way import us to be acquainted with, or which can tend either to the improvement or ornament of the human mind.

Here then is the only expedient, from which we can hope for success in our philosophical researches, to leave the tedious lingering method, which we have hitherto followed, and instead of taking now and then a castle or village on the frontier, to march up directly to the capital or center of these sciences, to human nature itself; which being once masters of, we may every where else hope for an easy victory. From this station we may extend our conquests over all those sciences, which more intimately concern human life, and may afterwards proceed at leisure to discover more fully those, which are the objects of pure curiosity. There is no question of importance, whose decision is not comprised in the science of man; and there is none, which can be decided with any certainty, before we become acquainted with that science. In pretending, therefore, to explain the principles of human nature, we in effect propose a complete system of the sciences, built on a foundation almost entirely new, and the only one upon which they can stand with any security.

And as the science of man is the only solid foundation for the other sciences, so the only solid foundation we can give to this science itself must be laid on experience and observation. It is no astonishing reflection to consider, that the application of experimental philosophy to moral subjects should come after that to natural at the distance of above a whole century; since we find in fact, that there was about the same interval betwixt the origins of these sciences; and that reckoning from THALES to SOCRATES, the space of time is nearly equal to that betwixt my Lord Bacon and some late philosophers* in England, who have begun to put the science of man on a new footing, and have engaged the

* Mr *Locke*, my Lord *Shaftesbury*, Dr *Mandeville*, Mr *Hutchinson*, Dr *Butler*, etc.

attention, and excited the curiosity of the public. So true it is, that however other nations may rival us in poetry, and excel us in some other agreeable arts, the improvements in reason and philosophy can only be owing to a land of toleration and of liberty.

Nor ought we to think, that this latter improvement in the science of man will do less honour to our native country than the former in natural philosophy, but ought rather to esteem it a greater glory, upon account of the greater importance of that science, as well as the necessity it lay under of such a reformation. For to me it seems evident, that the essence of the mind being equally unknown to us with that of external bodies, it must be equally impossible to form any notion of its powers and qualities otherwise than from careful and exact experiments, and the observation of those particular effects, which result from its different circumstances and situations. And though we must endeavour to render all our principles as universal as possible, by tracing up our experiments to the utmost, and explaining all effects from the simplest and fewest causes, it is still certain we cannot go beyond experience; and any hypothesis, that pretends to discover the ultimate original qualities of human nature, ought at first to be rejected as presumptuous and chimerical.

I do not think a philosopher, who would apply himself so earnestly to the explaining the ultimate principles of the soul, would show himself a great master in that very science of human nature, which he pretends to explain, or very knowing in what is naturally satisfactory to the mind of man. For nothing is more certain, than that despair has almost the same effect upon us with enjoyment, and that we are no sooner acquainted with the impossibility of satisfying any desire, than the desire itself vanishes. When we see, that we have arrived at the utmost extent of human reason, we sit down contented, though we be perfectly satisfied in the main of our ignorance, and perceive that we can give no reason for our most general and most refined principles, beside our experience of their reality; which is the reason of the mere vulgar, and what it required no study at first to have discovered for the most particular and most extraordinary phenomenon. And as this impossibility of making any farther progress is enough to satisfy the reader, so the writer may derive a more delicate satisfaction from the free confession of his ignorance, and from his prudence in avoiding that error, into which so many have fallen, of imposing their conjectures and hypotheses on the world for the most certain principles. When this mutual contentment and satisfaction can be obtained betwixt the master and scholar, I know not what more we can require of our philosophy.

But if this impossibility of explaining ultimate principles should be esteemed a defect in the science of man, I will venture to affirm, that it is a defect common to it with all the sciences, and all the arts, in which we can employ ourselves, whether they be such as are cultivated in the schools of the philosophers, or practised in the shops of the meanest artizans. None of them can go beyond experience, or establish any principles which are not founded on that authority. Moral philosophy has, indeed, this peculiar disadvantage, which is not found in natural, that in collecting its experiments, it cannot make them purposely, with premeditation, and after such a manner as to satisfy itself concerning every particular difficulty which may be. When I am at a loss to know the effects of one body upon another in any situation, I need only put them in that situation, and observe what results from it. But should I endeavour to clear up after the same manner any doubt in moral philosophy, by placing myself in the same case with that which I consider, it is evident this reflection and premeditation would so disturb the operation of my natural principles, as must render it impossible to form any just conclusion from the phenomenon. We must therefore glean up our experiments in this science from a cautious observation of human life, and take them as they appear in the common course of the world, by men's behaviour in company, in affairs, and in their pleasures. Where experiments of this kind are judiciously collected and compared, we may hope to establish on them a science which will not be inferior in certainty, and will be much superior in utility to any other of human comprehension.

BOOK ONE

OF THE UNDERSTANDING

PART ONE

*Of Ideas, their Origin, Composition,
Connexion, Abstraction, etc.*

SECTION ONE

Of the origin of our ideas

All the perceptions of the human mind resolve themselves into
two distinct kinds, which I shall call IMPRESSIONS and IDEAS. The
difference betwixt these consists in the degrees of force and
liveliness, with which they strike upon the mind, and make their
way into our thought or consciousness. Those perceptions, which
enter with most force and violence, we may name *impressions*: and
under this name I comprehend all our sensations, passions and
emotions, as they make their first appearance in the soul. By *ideas*
I mean the faint images of these in thinking and reasoning; such
as, for instance, are all the perceptions excited by the present
discourse, excepting only those which arise from the sight and
touch, and excepting the immediate pleasure or uneasiness it may
occasion. I believe it will not be very necessary to employ many
words in explaining this distinction. Every one of himself will
readily perceive the difference betwixt feeling and thinking. The
common degrees of these are easily distinguished; though it is
not impossible but in particular instances they may very nearly
approach to each other. Thus in sleep, in a fever, in madness, or in
any very violent emotions of soul, our ideas may approach to our
impressions, As on the other hand it sometimes happens, that our
impressions are so faint and low, that we cannot distinguish them

from our ideas. But notwithstanding this near resemblance in a few instances, they are in general so very different, that no-one can make a scruple to rank them under distinct heads, and assign to each a peculiar name to mark the difference.*

There is another division of our perceptions, which it will be convenient to observe, and which extends itself both to our impressions and ideas. This division is into SIMPLE and COMPLEX. Simple perceptions or impressions and ideas are such as admit of no distinction nor separation. The complex are the contrary to these, and may be distinguished into parts. Though a particular colour, taste, and smell, are qualities all united together in this apple, it is easy to perceive they are not the same, but are at least distinguishable from each other.

Having by these divisions given an order and arrangement to our objects, we may now apply ourselves to consider with the more accuracy their qualities and relations. The first circumstance, that strikes my eye, is the great resemblance betwixt our impressions and ideas in every other particular, except their degree of force and vivacity. The one seem to be in a manner the reflexion of the other; so that all the perceptions of the mind are double, and appear both as impressions and ideas. When I shut my eyes and think of my chamber, the ideas I form are exact representations of the impressions I felt; nor is there any circumstance of the one, which is not to be found in the other. In running over my other perceptions, I find still the same resemblance and representation. Ideas and impressions appear always to correspond to each other. This circumstance seems to me remarkable, and engages my attention for a moment.

Upon a more accurate survey I find I have been carried away too far by the first appearance, and that I must make use of the distinction of perceptions into *simple* and *complex*, to limit this general decision, *that all our ideas and impressions are resembling*. I

---

* I here make use of these terms, *impression* and *idea*, in a sense different from what is usual, and I hope this liberty will be allowed me. Perhaps I rather restore the word, idea, to its original sense, from which Mr *Locke* had perverted it, in making it stand for all our perceptions. By the terms of impression I would not be understood to express the manner, in which our lively perceptions are produced in the soul, but merely the perceptions themselves; for which there is no particular name either in the *English* or any other language, that I know of.

observe, that many of our complex ideas never had impressions, that corresponded to them, and that many of our complex impressions never are exactly copied in ideas. I can imagine to myself such a city as the *New Jerusalem*, whose pavement is gold and walls are rubies, though I never saw any such. I have seen *Paris*; but shall I affirm I can form such an idea of that city, as will perfectly represent all its streets and houses in their real and just proportions?

I perceive, therefore, that though there is in general a great resemblance betwixt our *complex* impressions and ideas, yet the rule is not universally true, that they are exact copies of each other. We may next consider how the case stands with our *simple* perceptions. After the most accurate examination, of which I am capable, I venture to affirm, that the rule here holds without any exception, and that every simple idea has a simple impression, which resembles it, and every simple impression a correspondent idea. That idea of red, which we form in the dark, and that impression which strikes our eyes in sun-shine, differ only in degree, not in nature. That the case is the same with all our simple impressions and ideas, it is impossible to prove by a particular enumeration of them. Every one may satisfy himself in this point by running over as many as he pleases. But if any one should deny this universal resemblance, I know no way of convincing him, but by desiring him to shew a simple impression, that has not a correspondent idea, or a simple idea, that has not a correspondent impression. If he does not answer this challenge, as it is certain he cannot, we may from his silence and our own observation establish our conclusion.

Thus we find, that all simple ideas and impressions resemble each other; and as the complex are formed from them, we may affirm in general, that these two species of perception are exactly correspondent. Having discovered this relation, which requires no farther examination, I am curious to find some other of their qualities. Let us consider how they stand with regard to their existence, and which of the impressions and ideas are causes, and which effects.

The *full* examination of this question is the subject of the present treatise; and therefore we shall here content ourselves with establishing one general proposition, *That all our simple ideas in their first appearance are derived from simple impressions, which are correspondent to them, and which they exactly represent.*

In seeking for phenomena to prove this proposition, I find only those of two kinds; but in each kind the phenomena are obvious, numerous, and conclusive. I first make myself certain, by a new review, of what I have already asserted, that every simple impression is attended with a correspondent idea, and every simple idea with a correspondent impression. From this constant conjunction of resembling perceptions I immediately conclude, that there is a great connexion betwixt our correspondent impressions and ideas, and that the existence of the one has a considerable influence upon that of the other. Such a constant conjunction, in such an infinite number of instances, can never arise from chance; but clearly proves a dependence of the impressions on the ideas, or of the ideas on the impressions. That I may know on which side this dependence lies, I consider the order of their *first appearance*; and find by constant experience, that the simple impressions always take the precedence of their correspondent ideas, but never appear in the contrary order. To give a child an idea of scarlet or orange, of sweet or bitter, I present the objects, or in other words, convey to him these impressions; but proceed not so absurdly, as to endeavour to produce the impressions by exciting the ideas. Our ideas upon their appearance produce not their correspondent impressions, nor do we perceive any colour, or feel any sensation merely upon thinking of them. On the other hand we find, that any impression either of the mind or body is constantly followed by an idea, which resembles it, and is only different in the degrees of force and liveliness. The constant conjunction of our resembling perceptions, is a convincing proof, that the one are the causes of the other; and this priority of the impressions is an equal proof, that our impressions are the causes of our ideas, not our ideas of our impressions.

To confirm this I consider another plain and convincing phenomenon; which is, that, where-ever by any accident the faculties, which give rise to any impressions, are obstructed in their operations, as when one is born blind or deaf; not only the impressions are lost, but also their correspondent ideas; so that there never appear in the mind the least traces of either of them. Nor is this only true, where the organs of sensation are entirely destroyed, but likewise where they have never been put in action to produce a particular impression. We cannot form to ourselves a just idea of the taste of a pine apple, without having actually tasted it.

There is however one contradictory phenomenon, which may prove, that it is not absolutely impossible for ideas to go before their correspondent impressions. I believe it will readily be allowed that the several distinct ideas of colours, which enter by the eyes, or those of sounds, which are conveyed by the hearing, are really different from each other, though at the same time resembling. Now if this be true of different colours, it must be no less so of the different shades of the same colour, that each of them produces a distinct idea, independent of the rest. For if this should be denied, it is possible, by the continual gradation of shades, to run a colour insensibly into what is most remote from it; and if you will not allow any of the means to be different, you cannot without absurdity deny the extremes to be the same. Suppose therefore a person to have enjoyed his sight for thirty years, and to have become perfectly well acquainted with colours of all kinds, excepting one particular shade of blue, for instance, which it never has been his fortune to meet with. Let all the different shades of that colour, except that single one, be placed before him, descending gradually from the deepest to the lightest; it is plain, that he will perceive a blank, where that shade is wanting, said will be sensible, that there is a greater distance in that place betwixt the contiguous colours, than in any other. Now I ask, whether it is possible for him, from his own imagination, to supply this deficiency, and raise up to himself the idea of that particular shade, though it had never been conveyed to him by his senses? I believe there are few but will be of opinion that he can; and this may serve as a proof, that the simple ideas are not always derived from the correspondent impressions; though the instance is so particular and singular, that it is scarce worth our observing, and does not merit that for it alone we should alter our general maxim.

But besides this exception, it may not be amiss to remark on this head, that the principle of the priority of impressions to ideas must be understood with another limitation, *viz.*, that as our ideas are images of our impressions, so we can form secondary ideas, which are images of the primary; as appears from this very reasoning concerning them. This is not, properly speaking, an exception to the rule so much as an explanation of it. Ideas produce the images of themselves in new ideas; but as the first ideas are supposed to be derived from impressions, it still remains true, that all our simple ideas proceed either mediately or immediately, from their correspondent impressions.

This then is the first principle I establish in the science of human nature; nor ought we to despise it because of the simplicity of its appearance. For it is remarkable, that the present question concerning the precedency of our impressions or ideas, is the same with what has made so much noise in other terms, when it has been disputed whether there be any *innate ideas*, or whether all ideas be derived from sensation and reflexion. We may observe, that in order to prove the ideas of extension and colour not to be innate, philosophers do nothing but shew that they are conveyed by our senses. To prove the ideas of passion and desire not to be innate, they observe that we have a preceding experience of these emotions in ourselves. Now if we carefully examine these arguments, we shall find that they prove nothing but that ideas are preceded by other more lively perceptions, from which they are derived, and which they represent. I hope this clear stating of the question will remove all disputes concerning it, and win render this principle of more use in our reasonings, than it seems hitherto to have been.

SECTION TWO

Division of the subject

Since it appears, that our simple impressions are prior to their correspondent ideas, and that the exceptions are very rare, method seems to require we should examine our impressions, before we consider our ideas. Impressions way be divided into two kinds, those of SENSATION and those of REFLEXION. The first kind arises in the soul originally, from unknown causes. The second is derived in a great measure from our ideas, and that in the following order. An impression first strikes upon the senses, and makes us perceive heat or cold, thirst or hunger, pleasure or pain of some kind or other. Of this impression there is a copy taken by the mind, which remains after the impression ceases;

and this we call an idea. This idea of pleasure or pain, when it returns upon the soul, produces the new impressions of desire and aversion, hope and fear, which may properly be called impressions of reflexion, because derived from it. These again are copied by the memory and imagination, and become ideas; which perhaps in their turn give rise to other impressions and ideas. So that the impressions of reflexion are only antecedent to their correspondent ideas; but posterior to those of sensation, and derived from them. The examination of our sensations belongs more to anatomists and natural philosophers than to moral; and therefore shall not at present be entered upon. And as the impressions of reflexion, *viz.* passions, desires, and emotions, which principally deserve our attention, arise mostly from ideas, it will be necessary to reverse that method, which at first sight seems most natural; and in order to explain the nature and principles of the human mind, give a particular account of ideas, before we proceed to impressions. For this reason I have here chosen to begin with ideas.

SECTION THREE

Of the ideas of the memory and the imagination

We find by experience, that when any impression has been present with the mind, it again makes its appearance there as an idea; and this it may do after two different ways: either when in its new appearance it retains a considerable degree of its first vivacity, and is somewhat intermediate betwixt an impression and an idea: or when it entirely loses that vivacity, and is a perfect idea. The faculty, by which we repeat our impressions in the first manner, is called the MEMORY, and the other the IMAGINATION. It is evident at first sight, that the ideas of the memory are much more lively and strong than those of the imagination, and that the former faculty paints its objects in more distinct colours, than any which are employed by the latter. When we remember any past event, the idea of it flows in upon the mind in a forcible manner; whereas in the imagination the perception is faint and languid, and cannot without difficulty be preserved by the mind steady and uniform for any considerable time. Here then is a sensible difference betwixt one species of ideas and another. But of this more fully hereafter.*

There is another difference betwixt these two kinds of ideas, which is no less evident, namely that though neither the ideas of the memory nor imagination, neither the lively nor faint ideas can make their appearance in the mind, unless their correspondent impressions have gone before to prepare the way for them, yet the imagination is not restrained to the same order and form with the original impressions; while the memory is in a manner tied down in that respect, without any power of variation.

It is evident, that the memory preserves the original form, in which its objects were presented, and that where-ever we depart from it in recollecting any thing, it proceeds from some defect or imperfection in that faculty. An historian may, perhaps, for the more convenient carrying on of his narration, relate an event before another, to which it was in fact posterior; but then he takes notice of this disorder, if he be exact; and by that means replaces the idea in its due position. It is the same case in our recollection of those places and persons, with which we were formerly acquainted. The chief exercise of the memory is not to preserve the simple ideas, but their order and position. In short, this principle is supported by such a number of common and vulgar phenomena, that we may spare ourselves the trouble of insisting on it any farther.

The same evidence follows us in our second principle, *of the liberty of the imagination to transpose and change its ideas.* The fables we meet with in poems and romances put this entirely out of the question. Nature there is totally confounded, and nothing mentioned but winged horses, fiery dragons, and monstrous giants. Nor will this liberty of the fancy appear strange, when we consider, that all our ideas are copied from our impressions, and that there are not any two impressions which are perfectly inseparable. Not to mention, that this is an evident consequence of the division of ideas into simple and complex. Where-ever the imagination perceives a difference among ideas, it can easily produce a separation.

* Part 3, Section 5.

SECTION FOUR

Of the connexion or association of ideas

As all simple ideas may be separated by the imagination, and may be united again in what form it pleases, nothing would be more unaccountable than the operations of that faculty, were it not guided by some universal principles, which render it, in some measure, uniform with itself in all times and places. Were ideas entirely loose and unconnected, chance alone would join them; and it is impossible the same simple ideas should fall regularly into complex ones (as they commonly do) without some bond of union among them, some associating quality, by which one idea naturally introduces another. This uniting principle among ideas is not to be considered as an inseparable connexion; for that has been already excluded from the imagination: nor yet are we to conclude, that without it the mind cannot join two ideas; for nothing is more free than that faculty: but we are only to regard it as a gentle force, which commonly prevails, and is the cause why, among other things, languages so nearly correspond to each other; nature in a manner pointing out to every one those simple ideas, which are most proper to be united in a complex one. The qualities, from which this association arises, and by which the mind is after this manner conveyed from one idea to another, are three, *viz.* RESEMBLANCE, CONTIGUITY in time or place, and CAUSE and EFFECT.

I believe it will not be very necessary to prove, that these qualities produce an association among ideas, and upon the appearance of one idea naturally introduce another. It is plain, that in the course of our thinking, and in the constant revolution of our ideas, our imagination runs easily from one idea to any other that *resembles* it, and that this quality alone is to the fancy a sufficient bond and association. It is likewise evident that as the senses, in changing their objects, are necessitated to change them regularly, and take them as they lie *contiguous* to each other, the imagination must by long custom acquire the same method of thinking, and run along the parts of space and time in conceiving its objects. As to the connexion, that is made by the relation of *cause and effect*, we shall have occasion afterwards to examine it to the bottom, and therefore shall not at present insist upon it. It is sufficient to observe, that there is no relation, which produces a stronger connexion in the fancy, and makes one idea more readily recall another, than the relation of cause and effect betwixt their objects.

That we may understand the full extent of these relations, we must consider, that two objects are connected together in the imagination, not only when the one is immediately resembling, contiguous to, or the cause of the other, but also when there is interposed betwixt them a third object, which bears to both of them any of these relations. This may be carried on to a great length; though at the same time we may observe, that each remove considerably weakens the relation. Cousins in the fourth degree are connected by *causation*, if I may be allowed to use that term; but not so closely as brothers, much less as child and parent. In general we may observe, that all the relations of blood depend upon cause and effect, and are esteemed near or remote, according to the number of connecting causes interposed betwixt the persons.

Of the three relations above-mentioned this of causation is the most extensive. Two objects may be considered as placed in this relation, as well when one is the cause of any of the actions or motions of the other, as when the former is the cause of the existence of the latter. For as that action or motion is nothing but the object itself, considered in a certain light, and as the object continues the same in all its different situations, it is easy to imagine how such an influence of objects upon one another may connect them in the imagination.

We may carry this farther, and remark, not only that two objects are connected by the relation of cause and effect, when the one produces a motion or any action in the other, but also when it has a power of producing it. And this we may observe to be the source of all the relations of interest and duty, by which men influence each other in society, and are placed in the ties of government and subordination. A master is such-a-one as by his situation, arising either from force or agreement, has a power of directing in certain particulars the actions of another, whom we call servant. A judge is one, who in all disputed cases can fix by his opinion the possession or property of any thing betwixt any members of the society. When a person is possessed of any power, there is no more required to convert it into action, but the exertion of the will; and that in every case is considered as possible, and in many as probable; especially in the case of authority, where the obedience of the subject is a pleasure and advantage to the superior.

These are therefore the principles of union or cohesion among our simple ideas, and in the imagination supply the place of that inseparable connexion, by which they are united in our memory. Here is a kind of ATTRACTION, which in the mental world will be found to have as extraordinary effects as in the natural, and to shew itself in as many and as various forms. Its effects are every where conspicuous; but as to its causes, they are mostly unknown, and must be resolved into *original* qualities of human nature, which I pretend not to explain. Nothing is more requisite for a true philosopher, than to restrain the intemperate desire of searching into causes, and having established any doctrine upon a sufficient number of experiments, rest contented with that, when he sees a farther examination would lead him into obscure and uncertain speculations. In that case his enquiry would be much better employed in examining the effects than the causes of his principle.

Amongst the effects of this union or association of ideas, there are none more remarkable, than those complex ideas, which are the common subjects of our thoughts and reasoning, and generally arise from some principle of union among our simple ideas. These complex ideas may be divided into *Relations*, *Modes*, and *Substances*. We shall briefly examine each of these in order, and shall subjoin some considerations concerning our *general* and *particular* ideas, before we leave the present subject, which may be considered as the elements of this philosophy.

SECTION FIVE
Of relations

The word RELATION is commonly used in two senses considerably different from each other. Either for that quality, by which two ideas are connected together in the imagination, and the one naturally introduces the other, after the manner above-explained: or for that particular circumstance, in which, even upon the arbitrary union of two ideas in the fancy, we may think proper to compare them. In common language the former is always the sense, in which we use the word, relation; and it is only in philosophy, that we extend it to mean any particular subject of comparison, without a connecting principle. Thus distance will be allowed by philosophers to be a true relation, because we acquire an idea of it by the comparing of objects: but in a common way we say, *that nothing can be more distant than such or such things from each other, nothing can have less relation*: as if distance and relation were incompatible.

It may perhaps be esteemed an endless task to enumerate all those qualities, which make objects admit of comparison, and by which the ideas of *philosophical* relation are produced. But if we diligently consider them, we shall find that without difficulty they may be comprised under seven general heads, which may be considered as the sources of all *philosophical* relation.

(1) The first is *resemblance*: and this is a relation, without which no philosophical relation can exist; since no objects will admit of comparison, but what have some degree of resemblance. But though resemblance be necessary to all philosophical relation, it does not follow, that it always produces a connexion or association of ideas. When a quality becomes very general, and is common to a great many individuals, it leads not the mind directly to any one of them; but by presenting at once too great a choice, does thereby prevent the imagination from fixing on any single object.

(2) *Identity* may be esteemed a second species of relation. This relation I here consider as applied in its strictest sense to constant and unchangeable objects; without examining the nature and foundation of personal identity, which shall find its place afterwards. Of all relations the most universal is that of identity, being common to every being whose existence has any duration.

(3) After identity the most universal and comprehensive relations are those of *Space* and *Time*, which are the sources of an infinite number of comparisons, such as *distant, contiguous, above, below, before, after*, etc.

(4) All those objects, which admit of *quantity*, or *number*, may be compared in that particular; which is another very fertile source of relation.

(5) When any two objects possess the same *quality* in common, the *degrees*, in which they possess it, form a fifth species of relation.

Thus of two objects, which are both heavy, the one may be either of greater, or less weight than the other. Two colours, that are of the same kind, may yet be of different shades, and in that respect admit of comparison.

(6) The relation of *contrariety* may at first sight be regarded as an exception to the rule, *that no relation of any kind can subsist without some degree of resemblance*. But let us consider, that no two ideas are in themselves contrary, except those of existence and non-existence, which are plainly resembling, as implying both of them an idea of the object; though the latter excludes the object from all times and places, in which it is supposed not to exist.

(7) All other objects, such as fire and water, heat and cold, are only found to be contrary from experience, and from the contrariety of their *causes* or *effects*; which relation of cause and effect is a seventh philosophical relation, as well as a natural one. The resemblance implied in this relation, shall be explained afterwards.

It might naturally be expected, that I should join *difference* to the other relations. But that I consider rather as a negation of relation, than as anything real or positive. Difference is of two kinds as opposed either to identity or resemblance. The first is called a difference of *number*; the other of *kind*.

SECTION SIX

Of modes and substances

I would fain ask those philosophers, who found so much of their reasonings on the distinction of substance and accident, and imagine we have clear ideas of each, whether the idea of *substance* be derived from the impressions of sensation or of reflection? If it be conveyed to us by our senses, I ask, which of them; and after what manner? If it be perceived by the eyes, it must be a colour; if by the ears, a sound; if by the palate, a taste; and so of the other senses. But I believe none will assert, that substance is either a colour, or sound, or a taste. The idea of substance must therefore be derived from an impression of reflection, if it really exist. But the impressions of reflection resolve themselves into our passions and emotions: none of which can possibly represent a substance. We have therefore no idea of substance, distinct from that of a collection of particular qualities, nor have we any other meaning when we either talk or reason concerning it.

The idea of a substance as well as that of a mode, is nothing but a collection of simple ideas, that are united by the imagination, and have a particular name assigned them, by which we are able to recall, either to ourselves or others, that collection. But the difference betwixt these ideas consists in this, that the particular qualities, which form a substance, are commonly referred to an unknown *something*, in which they are supposed to inhere; or granting this fiction should not take place, are at least supposed to be closely and inseparably connected by the relations of contiguity and causation. The effect of this is, that whatever new simple quality we discover to have the same connexion with the rest, we immediately comprehend it among them, even though it did not enter into the first conception of the substance. Thus our idea of gold may at first be a yellow colour, weight, malleableness, fusibility; but upon the discovery of its dissolubility in *aqua regia*, we join that to the other qualities, and suppose it to belong to the substance as much as if its idea had from the beginning made a part of the compound one. The principle of union being regarded as the chief part of the complex idea, gives entrance to whatever quality afterwards occurs, and is equally comprehended by it, as are the others, which first presented themselves.

That this cannot take place in modes, is evident from considering their mature. The simple ideas of which modes are formed, either represent qualities, which are not united by contiguity and causation, but are dispersed in different subjects; or if they be all united together, the uniting principle is not regarded as the foundation of the complex idea. The idea of a dance is an instance of the first kind of modes; that of beauty of the second. The reason is obvious, why such complex ideas cannot receive any new idea, without changing the name, which distinguishes the mode.

SECTION SEVEN

Of abstract ideas

A very material question has been started concerning *abstract* or *general* ideas, *whether they be general or particular in the mind's conception of them.* A great philosopher[*] has disputed the received opinion in this particular, and has asserted, that all general ideas are nothing but particular ones, annexed to a certain term, which gives them a more extensive signification, and makes them recall upon occasion other individuals, which are similar to them. As I look upon this to be one of the greatest and most valuable discoveries that has been made of late years in the republic of letters, I shall here endeavour to confirm it by some arguments, which I hope will put it beyond all doubt and controversy.

It is evident, that in forming most of our general ideas, if not all of them, we abstract from every particular degree of quantity and quality, and that an object ceases not to be of any particular species on account of every small alteration in its extension, duration and other properties. It may therefore be thought, that here is a plain dilemma, that decides concerning the nature of those abstract ideas, which have afforded so much speculation to philosophers. The abstract idea of a man represents men of all sizes and all qualities; which it is concluded it cannot do, but either by representing at once all possible sizes and all possible qualities, or by representing no particular one at all. Now it having been esteemed absurd to defend the former proposition, as implying an infinite capacity in the mind, it has been commonly inferred in favour of the latter: and our abstract ideas have been supposed to represent no particular degree either of quantity or quality. But that this inference is erroneous, I shall endeavour to make appear, *first*, by proving, that it is utterly impossible to conceive any quantity or quality, without forming a precise notion of its degrees: and *secondly* by showing, that though the capacity of the mind be not infinite, yet we can at once form a notion of all possible degrees of quantity and quality, in such a manner at least, as, however imperfect, may serve all the purposes of reflection and conversation.

[*] Dr Berkeley.

To begin with the first proposition, *that the mind cannot form any notion of quantity or quality without forming a precise notion of degrees of each*; we may prove this by the three following arguments. First, We have observed, that whatever objects are different are distinguishable, and that whatever objects are distinguishable are separable by the thought and imagination. And we may here add, that these propositions are equally true in the *inverse*, and that whatever objects are separable are also distinguishable, and that whatever objects are distinguishable, are also different. For how is it possible we can separate what is not distinguishable, or distinguish what is not different? In order therefore to know, whether abstraction implies a separation, we need only consider it in this view, and examine, whether all the circumstances, which we abstract from in our general ideas, be such as are distinguishable and different from those, which we retain as essential parts of them. But it is evident at first sight, that the precise length of a line is not different nor distinguishable from the line itself; nor the precise degree of any quality from the quality. These ideas, therefore, admit no more of separation than they do of distinction and difference. They are consequently conjoined with each other in the conception; and the general idea of a line, notwithstanding all our abstractions and refinements, has in its appearance in the mind a precise degree of quantity and quality; however it may be made to represent others, which have different degrees of both.

Secondly, it is confessed, that no object can appear to the senses; or in other words, that no impression can become present to the mind, without being determined in its degrees both of quantity and quality. The confusion, in which impressions are sometimes involved, proceeds only from their faintness and unsteadiness, not from any capacity in the mind to receive any impression, which in its real existence has no particular degree nor proportion. That is a contradiction in terms; and even implies the flattest of all contradictions, *viz.* that it is possible for the same thing both to be and not to be.

Now since all ideas are derived from impressions, and are nothing but copies and representations of them, whatever is true of the one must be acknowledged concerning the other. Impressions and ideas differ only in their strength and vivacity. The foregoing conclusion is not founded on any particular degree of vivacity. It cannot therefore be affected by any variation in that particular. An idea is a weaker impression; and as a strong impression must necessarily have a determinate quantity and quality, the case must be the same with its copy or representative.

Thirdly, it is a principle generally received in philosophy that everything in nature is individual, and that it is utterly absurd to suppose a triangle really existent, which has no precise proportion of sides and angles. If this therefore be absurd in *fact and reality*, it must also be absurd *in idea*; since nothing of which we can form a clear and distinct idea is absurd and impossible. But to form the idea of an object, and to form an idea simply, is the same thing; the reference of the idea to an object being an extraneous denomination, of which in itself it bears no mark or character. Now as it is impossible to form an idea of an object, that is possessed of quantity and quality, and yet is possessed of no precise degree of either; it follows that there is an equal impossibility of forming an idea, that is not limited and confined in both these particulars. Abstract ideas are therefore in themselves individual, however they may become general in their representation. The image in the mind is only that of a particular object, though the application of it in our reasoning be the same, as if it were universal.

This application of ideas beyond their nature proceeds from our collecting all their possible degrees of quantity and quality in such an imperfect manner as may serve the purposes of life, which is the second proposition I proposed to explain. When we have found a resemblance* among several objects, that often occur to us, we apply the same name to all of them, whatever differences we may observe in the degrees of their quantity and quality, and whatever other differences may appear among them. After we have acquired a custom of this kind, the hearing of that name revives the idea of one of these objects, and makes the imagination conceive it with all its particular circumstances and proportions. But as the same word is supposed to have been frequently applied to other individuals, that are different in many respects from that idea, which is immediately present to the mind; the word not being able to revive the idea of all these individuals, only touches the soul, if I may be allowed so to speak, and revives that custom,

[* see Appendix to the *Treatise*.]

which we have acquired by surveying them. They are not really and in fact present to the mind, but only in power; nor do we draw them all out distinctly in the imagination, but keep ourselves in a readiness to survey any of them, as we may be prompted by a present design or necessity. The word raises up an individual idea, along with a certain custom; and that custom produces any other individual one, for which we may have occasion. But as the production of all the ideas, to which the name may be applied, is in most cases impossible, we abridge that work by a more partial consideration, and find but few inconveniences to arise in our reasoning from that abridgment.

For this is one of the most extraordinary circumstances in the present affair, that after the mind has produced an individual idea, upon which we reason, the attendant custom, revived by the general or abstract term, readily suggests any other individual, if by chance we form any reasoning, that agrees not with it. Thus should we mention the word triangle, and form the idea of a particular equilateral one to correspond to it, and should we afterwards assert, *that the three angles of a triangle are equal to each other*, the other individuals of a scalenum and isosceles, which we overlooked at first, immediately crowd in upon us, and make us perceive the falsehood of this proposition, though it be true with relation to that idea, which we had formed. If the mind suggests not always these ideas upon occasion, it proceeds from some imperfection in its faculties; and such a one as is often the source of false reasoning and sophistry. But this is principally the case with those ideas which are abstruse and compounded. On other occasions the custom is more entire, and it is seldom we run into such errors.

Nay so entire is the custom, that the very same idea may be annexed to several different words, and may be employed in different reasonings, without any danger of mistake. Thus the idea of an equilateral triangle of an inch perpendicular may serve us in talking of a figure, of a rectilinear figure, of a regular figure, of a triangle, and of an equilateral triangle. All these terms, therefore, are in this case attended with the same idea; but as they are wont to be applied in a greater or lesser compass, they excite their particular habits, and thereby keep the mind in a readiness to observe, that no conclusion be formed contrary to any ideas, which are usually comprized under them.

Before those habits have become entirely perfect, perhaps the mind may not be content with forming the idea of only one individual, but may run over several, in order to make itself comprehend its own meaning, and the compass of that collection, which it intends to express by the general term. That we may fix the meaning of the word, figure, we may revolve in our mind the ideas of circles, squares, parallelograms, triangles of different sizes and proportions, and may not rest on one image or idea. However this may be, it is certain *that* we form the idea of individuals, whenever we use any general term; *that* we seldom or never can exhaust these individuals; and *that* those, which remain, are only represented by means of that habit, by which we recall them, whenever any present occasion requires it. This then is the nature of our abstract ideas and general terms; and it is after this manner we account for the foregoing paradox, *that some ideas are particular in their nature, but general in their representation.* A particular idea becomes general by being annexed to a general term; that is, to a term, which from a customary conjunction has a relation to many other particular ideas, and readily recalls them in the imagination.

The only difficulty, that can remain on this subject, must be with regard to that custom, which so readily recalls every particular idea, for which we may have occasion, and is excited by any word or sound, to which we commonly annex it. The most proper method, in my opinion, of giving a satisfactory explication of this act of the mind, is by producing other instances, which are analogous to it, and other principles, which facilitate its operation. To explain the ultimate causes of our mental actions is impossible. It is sufficient, if we can give any satisfactory account of them from experience and analogy.

First then I observe, that when we mention any great number, such as a thousand, the mind has generally no adequate idea of it, but only a power of producing such an idea, by its adequate idea of the decimals, under which the number is comprehended. This imperfection, however, in our ideas, is never felt in our reasonings; which seems to be an instance parallel to the present one of universal ideas.

Secondly, we have several instances of habits, which may be revived by one single word; as when a person, who has by rote any periods of a discourse, or any number of verses, will be put in remembrance of the whole, which he is at a loss to recollect, by that single word or expression, with which they begin.

Thirdly, I believe every one, who examines the situation of his mind in reasoning will agree with me, that we do not annex distinct and complete ideas to every term we make use of, and that in talking of *government*, *church*, *negotiation*, *conquest*, we seldom spread out in our minds all the simple ideas, of which these complex ones are composed. It is however observable, that notwithstanding this imperfection we may avoid talking nonsense on these subjects, and may perceive any repugnance among the ideas, as well as if we had a full comprehension of them. Thus if instead of saying, *that in war the weaker have always recourse to negotiation*, we should say, *that they have always recourse to conquest*, the custom, which we have acquired of attributing certain relations to ideas, still follows the words, and makes us immediately perceive the absurdity of that proposition; in the same manner as one particular idea may serve us in reasoning concerning other ideas, however different from it in several circumstances.

Fourthly, As the individuals are collected together, said placed under a general term with a view to that resemblance, which they bear to each other, this relation must facilitate their entrance in the imagination, and make them be suggested more readily upon occasion. And indeed if we consider the common progress of the thought, either in reflection or conversation, we shall find great reason to be satisfied in this particular. Nothing is more admirable, than the readiness, with which the imagination suggests its ideas, and presents them at the very instant, in which they become necessary or useful. The fancy runs from one end of the universe to the other in collecting those ideas, which belong to any subject. One would think the whole intellectual world of ideas was at once subjected to our view, and that we did nothing but pick out such as were most proper for our purpose. There may not, however, be any present, beside those very ideas, that are thus collected by a kind of magical faculty in the soul, which, though it be always most perfect in the greatest geniuses, and is properly what we call a genius, is however inexplicable by the utmost efforts of human understanding.

Perhaps these four reflections may help to remove all difficulties to the hypothesis I have proposed concerning abstract ideas, so contrary to that, which has hitherto prevailed in philosophy, But, to tell the truth I place my chief confidence in what I have already proved concerning the impossibility of general ideas, according to the common method of explaining them. We must certainly seek some new system on this head, and there plainly is none beside what I have proposed. If ideas be particular in their nature, and at the same time finite in their number, it is only by custom they can become general in their representation, and contain an infinite number of other ideas under them.

Before I leave this subject I shall employ the same principles to explain that *distinction of reason*, which is so much talked of, and is so little understood, in the schools. Of this kind is the distinction betwixt figure and the body figured; motion and the body moved. The difficulty of explaining this distinction arises from the principle above explained, *that all ideas, which are different, are separable.* For it follows from thence, that if the figure be different from the body, their ideas must be separable as well as distinguishable: if they be not different, their ideas can neither be separable nor distinguishable. What then is meant by a distinction of reason, since it implies neither a difference nor separation?

To remove this difficulty we must have recourse to the foregoing explication of abstract ideas. It is certain that the mind would never have dreamed of distinguishing a figure from the body figured, as being in reality neither distinguishable, nor different, nor separable; did it not observe, that even in this simplicity there might be contained many different resemblances and relations. Thus when a globe of white marble is presented, we receive only the impression of a white colour disposed in a certain form, nor are we able to separate and distinguish the colour from the form. But observing afterwards a globe of black marble and a cube of white, and comparing them with our former object, we find two separate resemblances, in what formerly seemed, and really is, perfectly inseparable. After a little more practice of this kind, we begin to distinguish the figure from the colour by a *distinction of reason*; that is, we consider the figure and colour together, since they are in effect the same and undistinguishable; but still view them in different aspects, according to the resemblances, of which they are susceptible. When we would consider only the figure of the globe of white marble, we form in reality an idea both of the figure and colour, but tacitly carry our eye to its resemblance with the globe of black marble: and in the same manner, when we would consider its colour only, we turn our view to its resemblance with the cube of white marble. By this means we accompany our ideas with a kind of reflection, of which custom renders us, in a great measure, insensible. A person, who desires us to consider the figure of a globe of white marble without thinking on its colour, desires an impossibility; but his meaning is, that we should consider the figure and colour together, but still keep in our eye the resemblance to the globe of black marble, or that to any other globe of whatever colour or substance.

PART TWO

Of the Ideas of Space and Time

Whatever has the air of a paradox, and is contrary to the first and most unprejudiced notions of mankind, is often greedily embraced by philosophers, as shewing the superiority of their science, which could discover opinions so remote from vulgar conception. On the other hand, anything proposed to us, which causes surprize and admiration, gives such a satisfaction to the mind, that it indulges itself in those agreeable emotions, and will never be persuaded that its pleasure is entirely without foundation. From these dispositions in philosophers and their disciples arises that mutual complaisance betwixt them; while the former furnish such plenty of strange and unaccountable opinions, and the latter so readily believe them. Of this mutual complaisance I cannot give a more evident instance than in the doctrine of infinite divisibility, with the examination of which I shall begin this subject of the ideas of space and time.

It is universally allowed, that the capacity of the mind is limited, and can never attain a full and adequate conception of infinity: and though it were not allowed, it would be sufficiently evident from the plainest observation and experience. It is also obvious, that whatever is capable of being divided *in infinitum*, must consist of an infinite number of parts, and that it is impossible to set any bounds to the number of parts, without setting bounds at the same time to the division. It requires scarce any induction to conclude from hence, that the *idea*, which we form of any finite quality, is not infinitely divisible, but that by proper distinctions and separations we may run up this idea to inferior ones, which will be perfectly simple and indivisible. In rejecting the infinite capacity of the mind, we suppose it may arrive at an end in the division of its ideas; nor are there any possible means of evading the evidence of this conclusion.

It is therefore certain, that the imagination reaches a *minimum*, and may raise up to itself an idea, of which it cannot conceive any sub-division, and which cannot be diminished without a total annihilation. When you tell me of the thousandth and ten thousandth part of a grain of sand, I have a distinct idea of these numbers and of their different proportions; but the images, which I form in my mind to represent the things themselves, are nothing different from each other, nor inferior to that image, by which I represent the grain of sand itself, which is supposed so vastly to exceed them. What consists of parts is distinguishable into them, and what is distinguishable is separable. But whatever we may imagine of the thing, the idea of a grain of sand is not distinguishable, nor separable into twenty, much less into a thousand, ten thousand, or an infinite number of different ideas.

It is the same case with the impressions of the senses as with the ideas of the imagination. Put a spot of ink upon paper, fix your eye upon that spot, and retire to such a distance, that at last you lose sight of it; it is plain, that the moment before it vanished the image or impression was perfectly indivisible. It is not for want of rays of light striking on our eyes, that the minute parts of distant bodies convey not any sensible impression; but because they are removed beyond that distance, at which their impressions were reduced to a minimum, and were incapable of any farther diminution. A microscope or telescope, which renders them visible, produces not any new rays of light, but only spreads those, which always flowed from them; and by that means both gives parts to impressions, which to the naked eye appear simple and uncompounded, and advances to a *minimum*, what was formerly imperceptible.

We may hence discover the error of the common opinion, that the capacity of the mind is limited on both sides, and that it is impossible for the imagination to form an adequate idea, of what goes beyond a certain degree of minuteness as well as of greatness. Nothing can be more minute, than some ideas, which we form in the fancy; and images, which appear to the senses; since there are ideas and images perfectly simple and indivisible. The only defect of our senses is, that they give us disproportioned images of things, and represent as minute and uncompounded what is really great and composed of a vast number of parts. This mistake we are not sensible of: but taking the impressions of those minute objects, which appear to the senses, to be equal or nearly equal to the objects, and finding by reason, that there are other objects vastly more minute, we too hastily conclude, that these are inferior to any idea of our imagination or impression of our senses. This however is certain, that we can form ideas, which shall be no greater than the smallest atom of the animal spirits of an insect a thousand times less than a mite: and we ought rather to conclude, that the difficulty lies in enlarging our conceptions so much as to form a just notion of a mite, or even of an insect a thousand times less than a mite. For in order to form a just notion of these animals, we must have a distinct idea representing every part of them, which, according to the system of infinite divisibility, is utterly impossible, and, according to that of indivisible parts or atoms, is extremely difficult, by reason of the vast number and multiplicity of these parts.

SECTION TWO

Of the infinite divisibility of space and time

Wherever ideas are adequate representations of objects, the relations, contradictions and agreements of the ideas are all applicable to the objects; and this we may in general observe to be the foundation of all human knowledge. But our ideas are adequate representations of the most minute parts of extension; and through whatever divisions and subdivisions we may suppose these parts to be arrived at, they can never become inferior to some ideas, which we form. The plain consequence is, that whatever *appears* impossible and contradictory upon the comparison of these ideas, must be *really* impossible and contradictory, without any farther excuse or evasion.

Every thing capable of being infinitely divided contains an infinite number of parts; otherwise the division would be stopped short by the indivisible parts, which we should immediately arrive at. If therefore any finite extension be infinitely divisible, it can be no contradiction to suppose, that a finite extension contains an infinite number of parts: and *vice versa*, if it be a contradiction to suppose, that a finite extension contains an infinite number of parts, no finite extension can be infinitely divisible. But that this latter supposition is absurd, I easily convince myself by the consideration of my clear ideas. I first take the least idea I can form of a part of extension, and being certain that there is nothing more minute than this idea, I conclude, that whatever I discover by its means must be a real quality of extension. I then repeat this idea once, twice, thrice, &c., and find the compound idea of extension, arising from its repetition, always to augment, and become double, triple, quadruple, &c., till at last it swells up to a considerable bulk, greater or smaller, in proportion as I repeat more or less the same idea. When I stop in the addition of parts, the idea of extension ceases to augment; and were I to carry on the addition *in infinitum*, I clearly perceive, that the idea of extension must also become infinite. Upon the whole, I conclude, that the idea of an infinite number of parts is individually the same idea with that of an infinite extension; that no finite extension is capable of containing an infinite number of parts; and consequently that no finite extension is infinitely divisible.*

I may subjoin another argument proposed by a noted author,† which seems to me very strong and beautiful. It is evident, that existence in itself belongs only to unity, and is never applicable to number, but on account of the units, of which the number is composed. Twenty men may be said to exist; but it is only because one, two, three, four, &c. are existent, and if you deny the existence of the latter, that of the former falls of course. It is therefore utterly absurd to suppose any number to exist, and yet deny the existence of units; and as extension is always a number, according to the common sentiment of metaphysicians, and never resolves itself into any unit or indivisible quantity, it follows, that extension can

---

* It has been objected to me, that infinite divisibility supposes only an infinite number of *proportional* not of *aliquot* parts, and that an infinite number of proportional parts does not form an infinite extension. But this distinction is entirely frivolous. Whether these parts be called *aliquot* or *proportional*, they cannot be inferior to those minute parts we conceive; and therefore cannot form a less extension by their conjunction.

† Mons. *Malezieu.*

never at all exist. It is in vain to reply, that any determinate quantity of extension is an unit; but such-a-one as admits of an infinite number of fractions, and is inexhaustible in its sub-divisions. For by the same rule these twenty men *may be considered as an unit*. The whole globe of the earth, nay the whole universe, *may be considered as an unit*. That term of unity is merely a fictitious denomination, which the mind may apply to any quantity of objects it collects together; nor can such an unity any more exist alone than number can, as being in reality a true number. But the unity, which can exist alone, and whose existence is necessary to that of all number, is of another kind, and must be perfectly indivisible, and incapable of being resolved into any lesser unity.

All this reasoning takes place with regard to time; along with an additional argument, which it may be proper to take notice of. It is a property inseparable from time, and which in a manner con-stitutes its essence, that each of its parts succeeds another, and that none of them, however contiguous, can ever be co-existent. For the same reason, that the year 1737 cannot concur with the present year 1738, every moment must be distinct from, and posterior or antecedent to another. It is certain then, that time, as it exists, must be composed of indivisible moments. For if in time we could never arrive at an end of division, and if each moment, as it succeeds another, were not perfectly single and indivisible, there would be an infinite number of co-existent moments, or parts of time; which I believe will be allowed to be an arrant contradiction.

The infinite divisibility of space implies that of time, as is evident from the nature of motion. If the latter, therefore, be impossible, the former must be equally so.

I doubt not but it will readily be allowed by the most obstinate defender of the doctrine of infinite divisibility, that these argu-ments are difficulties, and that it is impossible to give any answer to them which will be perfectly clear and satisfactory. But here we may observe, that nothing can be more absurd, than this custom of calling a *difficulty* what pretends to be a *demonstration*, and endeavouring by that means to elude its force and evidence. It is not in demonstrations as in probabilities, that difficulties can take place, and one argument counter-balance another, and diminish its authority. A demonstration, if just, admits of no opposite difficulty; and if not just, it is a mere sophism, and consequently can never be a difficulty. It is either irresistible, or has no manner of force. To talk therefore of objections and replies, and balancing of arguments in such a question as this, is to confess, either that human reason is nothing but a play of words, or that the person himself, who talks so, has not a capacity equal to such subjects. Demonstrations may be difficult to be comprehended, because of abstractedness of the subject; but can never have such difficulties as will weaken their authority, when once they are comprehended.

It is true, mathematicians are wont to say, that there are here equally strong arguments on the other side of the question, and that the doctrine of indivisible points is also liable to unanswerable objections. Before I examine these arguments and objections in detail, I will here take them in a body, and endeavour by a short and decisive reason to prove at once, that it is utterly impossible they can have any just foundation.

It is an established maxim in metaphysics, *That whatever the mind clearly conceives, includes the idea of possible existence*, or in other words, *that nothing we imagine is absolutely impossible*. We can form the idea of a golden mountain, and from thence conclude that such a mountain may actually exist. We can form no idea of a mountain without a valley, and therefore regard it as impossible.

Now it is certain we have an idea of extension; for otherwise why do we talk and reason concerning it? It is likewise certain that this idea, as conceived by the imagination, though divisible into parts or inferior ideas, is not infinitely divisible, nor consists of an infinite number of parts: for that exceeds the comprehension of our limited capacities. Here then is an idea of extension, which consists of parts or inferior ideas, that are perfectly indivisible: consequently this idea implies no contradiction: consequently it is possible for extension really to exist conformable to it: and consequently all the arguments employed against the possibility of mathematical points are mere scholastick quibbles, and unworthy of our attention.

These consequences we may carry one step farther, and conclude that all the pretended demonstrations for the infinite divisibility of extension are equally sophistical; since it is certain these demonstrations cannot be just without proving the impossibility of mathematical points; which it is an evident absurdity to pretend to.

SECTION THREE

Of the other qualities of our idea of space and time

No discovery could have been made more happily for deciding all controversies concerning ideas, than that above-mentioned, that impressions always take the precedency of them, and that every idea, with which the imagination is furnished, first makes its appearance in a correspondent impression. These latter perceptions are all so clear and evident, that they admit of no controversy; though many of our ideas are so obscure, that it is almost impossible even for the mind, which forms them, to tell exactly their nature and composition. Let us apply this principle, in order to discover farther the nature of our ideas of space and time.

Upon opening my eyes, and turning them to the surrounding objects, I perceive many visible bodies; and upon shutting them again, and considering the distance betwixt these bodies, I acquire the idea of extension. As every idea is derived from some impression, which is exactly similar to it, the impressions similar to this idea of extension, must either be some sensations derived from the sight, or some internal impressions arising from these sensations.

Our internal impressions are our passions, emotions, desires and aversions; none of which, I believe, will ever be asserted to be the model, from which the idea of space is derived. There remains therefore nothing but the senses, which can convey to us this original impression. Now what impression do our senses here convey to us? This is the principal question, and decides without appeal concerning the nature of the idea.

The table before me is alone sufficient by its view to give me the idea of extension. This idea, then, is borrowed from, and represents some impression, which this moment appears to the senses. But my senses convey to me only the impressions of coloured points, disposed in a certain manner. If the eye is sensible of any thing farther, I desire it may be pointed out to me. But if it be impossible to shew any thing farther, we may conclude with certainty, that the idea of extension is nothing but a copy of these coloured points, and of the manner of their appearance.

Suppose that in the extended object, or composition of coloured points, from which we first received the idea of extension, the points were of a purple colour; it follows, that in every repetition of that idea we would not only place the points in the same order with respect to each other, but also bestow on them that precise colour, with which alone we are acquainted. But afterwards having experience of the other colours of violet, green, red, white, black, and of all the different compositions of these, and finding a resemblance in the disposition of coloured points, of which they are composed, we omit the peculiarities of colour, as far as possible, and found an abstract idea merely on that disposition of points, or manner of appearance, in which they agree. Nay even when the resemblance is carried beyond the objects of one sense, and the impressions of touch are found to be similar to those of sight in the disposition of their parts; this does not hinder the abstract idea from representing both, upon account of their resemblance. All abstract ideas are really nothing but particular ones, considered in a certain light; but being annexed to general terms, they are able to represent a vast variety, and to comprehend objects, which, as they are alike in some particulars, are in others vastly wide of each other.

The idea of time, being derived from the succession of our perceptions of every kind, ideas as well as impressions, and impressions of reflection as well as of sensation, will afford us an instance of an abstract idea, which comprehends a still greater variety than that of space, and yet is represented in the fancy by some particular individual idea of a determinate quantity and quality.

As it is from the disposition of visible and tangible objects we receive the idea of space, so from the succession of ideas and impressions we form the idea of time, nor is it possible for time alone ever to make its appearance, or be taken notice of by the mind. A man in a sound sleep, or strongly occupied with one thought, is insensible of time; and according as his perceptions succeed each other with greater or less rapidity, the same duration appears longer or shorter to his imagination. It has been remarked by a great philosopher,* that our perceptions have certain bounds in this particular, which are fixed by the original nature and constitution of the mind, and beyond which no influence of external objects on the senses is ever able to hasten or retard our thought. If you wheel about a burning coal with rapidity, it will present to the senses an image of a circle of fire; nor will there

* Mr *Locke.*

seem to be any interval of time betwixt its revolutions; merely because it is impossible for our perceptions to succeed each other with the same rapidity, that motion may be communicated to external objects. Wherever we have no successive perceptions, we have no notion of time, even though there be a real succession in the objects. From these phenomena, as well as from many others, we may conclude, that time cannot make its appearance to the mind, either alone, or attended with a steady unchangeable object, but is always discovered by some *perceivable* succession of changeable objects.

To confirm this we may add the following argument, which to me seems perfectly decisive and convincing. It is evident, that time or duration consists of different parts: for otherwise we could not conceive a longer or shorter duration. It is also evident, that these parts are not co-existent: for that quality of the co-existence of parts belongs to extension, and is what distinguishes it from duration. Now as time is composed of parts, that are not coexistent; an unchangeable object, since it produces none but coexistent impressions, produces none that can give us the idea of time; and consequently that idea must be derived from a succession of changeable objects, and time in its first appearance can never be severed from such a succession.

Having therefore found, that time in its first appearance to the mind is always conjoined with a succession of changeable objects, and that otherwise it can never fall under our notice, we must now examine whether it can be *conceived* without our conceiving any succession of objects, and whether it can alone form a distinct idea in the imagination.

In order to know whether any objects, which are joined in impression, be separable in idea, we need only consider, if they be different from each other; in which case, it is plain they may be conceived apart. Every thing, that is different, is distinguishable: and everything, that is distinguishable, may be separated, according to the maxims above-explained. If on the contrary they be not different, they are not distinguishable: and if they be not distinguishable, they cannot be separated. But this is precisely the case with respect to time, compared with our successive perceptions. The idea of time is not derived from a particular impression mixed up with others, and plainly distinguishable from them; but arises altogether from the manner, in which impressions appear to the mind, without making one of the number. Five notes played on a flute give us the impression and idea of time; though time be not a sixth impression, which presents itself to the hearing or any other of the senses. Nor is it a sixth impression, which the mind by reflection finds in itself. These five sounds making their appearance in this particular manner, excite no emotion in the mind, nor produce an affection of any kind, which being observed by it can give rise to a new idea. For *that* is necessary to produce a new idea of reflection, nor can the mind, by revolving over a thousand times all its ideas of sensation, ever extract from them any new original idea, unless nature has so framed its faculties, that it feels some new original impression arise from such a contemplation. But here it only takes notice of the *manner*, in which the different sounds make their appearance; and that it may afterwards consider without considering these particular sounds, but may conjoin it with any other objects. The ideas of some objects it certainly must have, nor is it possible for it without these ideas ever to arrive at any conception of time; which since it appears not as any primary distinct impression, can plainly be nothing but different ideas, or impressions, or objects disposed in a certain manner, that is, succeeding each other.

I know there are some who pretend, that the idea of duration is applicable in a proper sense to objects, which are perfectly unchangeable; and this I take to be the common opinion of philosophers as well as of the vulgar. But to be convinced of its falsehood we need but reflect on the foregoing conclusion, that the idea of duration is always derived from a succession of changeable objects, and can never be conveyed to the mind by any thing stedfast and unchangeable. For it inevitably follows from thence, that since the idea of duration cannot be derived from such an object, it can never in any propriety or exactness be applied to it, nor can any thing unchangeable be ever said to have duration. Ideas always represent the objects or impressions, from which they are derived, and can never without a fiction represent or be applied to any other. By what fiction we apply the idea of time, even to what is unchangeable, and suppose, as is common, that duration is a measure of rest as well as of motion, we shall consider* afterwards.

* Section 5.

There is another very decisive argument, which establishes the present doctrine concerning our ideas of space and time, and is founded only on that simple principle, *that our ideas of them are compounded of parts, which are indivisible*. This argument may be worth the examining.

Every idea, that is distinguishable, being also separable, let us take one of those simple indivisible ideas, of which the compound one of *extension* is formed, and separating it from all others, and considering it apart, let us form a judgment of its nature and qualities.

It is plain it is not the idea of extension. For the idea of extension consists of parts; and this idea, according to the supposition, is perfectly simple and indivisible. Is it therefore nothing? That is absolutely impossible. For as the compound idea of extension, which is real, is composed of such ideas; were these so many non-entities, there would be a real existence composed of non-entities; which is absurd. Here therefore I must ask, *What is our idea of a simple and indivisible point*? No wonder if my answer appear somewhat new, since the question itself has scarce ever yet been thought of. We are wont to dispute concerning the nature of mathematical points, but seldom concerning the nature of their ideas.

The idea of space is conveyed to the mind by two senses, the sight and touch; nor does anything ever appear extended, that is not either visible or tangible. That compound impression, which represents extension, consists of several lesser impressions, that are indivisible to the eye or feeling, and may be called impressions of atoms or corpuscles endowed with colour and solidity. But this is not all. It is not only requisite, that these atoms should be coloured or tangible, in order to discover themselves to our senses; it is also necessary we should preserve the idea of their colour or tangibility in order to comprehend them by our imagination. There is nothing but the idea of their colour or tangibility, which can render them conceivable by the mind. Upon the removal of the ideas of these sensible qualities, they are utterly annihilated to the thought or imagination.

Now such as the parts are, such is the whole. If a point be not considered as coloured or tangible, it can convey to us no idea; and consequently the idea of extension, which is composed of the ideas of these points, can never possibly exist. But if the idea of extension really can exist, as we are conscious it does, its parts must also exist; and in order to that, must be considered as coloured or tangible. We have therefore no idea of space or extension, but when we regard it as an object either of our sight or feeling.

The same reasoning will prove, that the indivisible moments of time must be filled with some real object or existence, whose succession forms the duration, and makes it be conceivable by the mind.

SECTION FOUR
Objections answered

Our system concerning space and time consists of two parts, which are intimately connected together. The first depends on this chain of reasoning. The capacity of the mind is not infinite; consequently no idea of extension or duration consists of an infinite number of parts or inferior ideas, but of a finite number, and these simple and indivisible: it is therefore possible for space and time to exist conformable to this idea: and if it be possible, it is certain they actually do exist conformable to it; since their infinite divisibility is utterly impossible and contradictory.

The other part of our system is a consequence of this. The parts, into which the ideas of space and time resolve themselves, become at last indivisible; and these indivisible parts, being nothing in themselves, are inconceivable when not filled with something real and existent. The ideas of space and time are therefore no separate or distinct ideas, but merely those of the manner or order, in which objects exist: or in other words, it is impossible to conceive either a vacuum and extension without matter, or a time, when there was no succession or change in any real existence. The intimate connexion betwixt these parts of our system is the reason why we shall examine together the objections, which have been urged against both of them, beginning with those against the finite divisibility of extension.

I. The first of these objections, which I shall take notice of, is more proper to prove this connexion and dependence of the one part upon the other, than to destroy either of them. It has often been maintained in the schools, that extension must be divisible, *in infinitum*, because the system of mathematical points is absurd; and that system is absurd, because a mathematical point is a non-entity, and consequently can never by its conjunction with others form a real existence. This would be perfectly decisive, were there no medium betwixt the infinite divisibility of matter, and the non-entity of mathematical points. But there is evidently a medium, *viz.* the bestowing a colour or solidity on these points; and the absurdity of both the extremes is a demonstration of the truth and reality of this medium. The system of *physical* points, which is another medium, is too absurd to need a refutation. A real extension, such as a physical point is supposed to be, can never exist without parts, different from each other; and wherever objects are different, they are distinguishable and separable by the imagination.

II. The second objection is derived from the necessity there would be of *penetration*, if extension consisted of mathematical points. A simple and indivisible atom, that touches another, must necessarily penetrate it; for it is impossible it can touch it by its external parts, from the very supposition of its perfect simplicity, which excludes all parts. It must therefore touch it intimately, and in its whole essence, *secundum se, tota, et totaliter*; which is the very definition of penetration. But penetration is impossible: mathematical points are of consequence equally impossible.

I answer this objection by substituting a juster idea of penetration. Suppose two bodies containing no void within their circumference, to approach each other, and to unite in such a manner that the body, which results from their union, is no more extended than either of them; it is this we must mean when we talk of penetration. But it is evident this penetration is nothing but the annihilation of one of these bodies, and the preservation of the other, without our being able to distinguish particularly which is preserved and which annihilated. Before the approach we have the idea of two bodies. After it we have the idea only of one. It is impossible for the mind to preserve any notion of difference betwixt two bodies of the same nature existing in the same place at the same time.

Taking then penetration in this sense, for the annihilation of one body upon its approach to another, I ask any one, if he sees a necessity, that a coloured or tangible point should be annihilated upon the approach of another coloured or tangible point? On the contrary, does he not evidently perceive, that from the union of these points there results an object, which is compounded and divisible, and may be distinguished into two parts, of which each preserves its existence distinct and separate, notwithstanding its contiguity to the other? Let him aid his fancy by conceiving these points to be of different colours, the better to prevent their coalition and confusion. A blue and a red point may surely lie contiguous without any penetration or annihilation. For if they cannot, what possibly can become of them? Whether shall the red or the blue be annihilated? Or if these colours unite into one, what new colour will they produce by their union?

What chiefly gives rise to these objections, and at the same time renders it so difficult to give a satisfactory answer to them, is the natural infirmity and unsteadiness both of our imagination and senses, when employed on such minute objects. Put a spot of ink upon paper, and retire to such a distance, that the spot becomes altogether invisible; you will find, that upon your return and nearer approach the spot first becomes visible by short intervals; and afterwards becomes always visible; and afterwards acquires only a new force in its colouring without augmenting its bulk; and afterwards, when it has increased to such a degree as to be really extended, it is still difficult for the imagination to break it into its component parts, because of the uneasiness it finds in the conception of such a minute object as a single point. This infirmity affects most of our reasonings on the present subject, and makes it almost impossible to answer in an intelligible manner, and in proper expressions, many questions which may arise concerning it.

III. There have been many objections drawn from the *mathematics* against the indivisibility of the parts of extension: though at first sight that science seems rather favourable to the present doctrine; and if it be contrary in its *demonstrations*, it is perfectly conformable in its *definitions*. My present business then must be to defend the definitions, and refute the demonstrations.

A surface is *defined* to be length and breadth without depth: a line to be length without breadth or depth: a point to be what has neither length, breadth nor depth. It is evident that all this is perfectly unintelligible upon any other supposition than that of the composition of extension by indivisible points or atoms. How else could any thing exist without length, without breadth, or without depth?

Two different answers, I find, have been made to this argument; neither of which is in my opinion satisfactory. The first is, that the objects of geometry, those surfaces, lines and points, whose proportions and positions it examines, are mere ideas in the mind; and not only never did, but never can exist in nature. They never did exist; for no one will pretend to draw a line or make a surface entirely conformable to the definition: they never can exist; for we may produce demonstrations from these very ideas to prove, that they are impossible.

But can anything be imagined more absurd and contradictory than this reasoning? Whatever can be conceived by a clear and distinct idea necessarily implies the possibility of existence; and he who pretends to prove the impossibility of its existence by any argument derived from the clear idea, in reality asserts, that we have no clear idea of it, because we have a clear idea. It is in vain to search for a contradiction in any thing that is distinctly conceived by the mind. Did it imply any contradiction, it is impossible it could ever be conceived.

There is therefore no medium betwixt allowing at least the possibility of indivisible points, and denying their idea; and it is on this latter principle, that the second answer to the foregoing argument is founded. It has been pretended,* that though it be impossible to conceive a length without any breadth, yet by an abstraction without a separation, we can consider the one without regarding the other; in the same manner as we may think of the length of the way betwixt two towns, and overlook its breadth. The length is inseparable from the breadth both in nature and in our minds; but this excludes not a partial consideration, and a *distinction of reason*, after the manner above explained.

In refuting this answer I shall not insist on the argument, which I have already sufficiently explained, that if it be impossible for the mind to arrive at a *minimum* in its ideas, its capacity must be infinite, in order to comprehend the infinite number of parts, of which its idea of any extension would be composed. I shall here endeavour to find some new absurdities in this reasoning.

* *L'Art de penser.*

A surface terminates a solid; a line terminates a surface; a point terminates a line; but I assert, that if the *ideas* of a point, line or surface were not indivisible, it is impossible we should ever conceive these terminations: for let these ideas be supposed infinitely divisible; and then let the fancy endeavour to fix itself on the idea of the last surface, line or point; it immediately finds this idea to break into parts; and upon its seizing the last of these parts, it loses its hold by a new division, and so on *in infinitum*, without any possibility of its arriving at a concluding idea. The number of fractions bring it no nearer the last division, than the first idea it formed. Every particle eludes the grasp by a new fraction; like quicksilver, when we endeavour to seize it. But as in fact there must be something, which terminates the idea of every finite quantity; and as this terminating idea cannot itself consist of parts or inferior ideas; otherwise it would be the last of its parts, which finished the idea, and so on; this is a clear proof, that the ideas of surfaces, lines and points admit not of any division; those of surfaces in depth; of lines in breadth and depth; and of points in any dimension.

The schoolmen were so sensible of the force of this argument, that some of them maintained, that nature has mixed among those particles of matter, which are divisible *in infinitum*, a number of mathematical points, in order to give a termination to bodies; and others eluded the force of this reasoning by a heap of unintelligible cavils and distinctions. Both these adversaries equally yield the victory. A man who hides himself, confesses as evidently the superiority of his enemy, as another, who fairly delivers his arms.

Thus it appears, that the definitions of mathematics destroy the pretended demonstrations; and that if we have the idea of indivisible points, lines and surfaces conformable to the definition, their existence is certainly possible: but if we have no such idea, it is impossible we can ever conceive the termination of any figure; without which conception there can be no geometrical demonstration.

But I go farther, and maintain, that none of these demonstrations can have sufficient weight to establish such a principle, as this of infinite divisibility; and that because with regard to such minute objects, they are not properly demonstrations, being built on ideas, which are not exact, and maxims, which are not precisely true.

When geometry decides any thing concerning the proportions of quantity, we ought not to look for the utmost *precision* and exactness. None of its proofs extend so far. It takes the dimensions and proportions of figures justly; but roughly, and with some liberty. Its errors are never considerable; nor would it err at all, did it not aspire to such an absolute perfection.

I first ask mathematicians, what they mean when they say one line or surface is EQUAL to, or GREATER, or LESS than another? Let any of them give an answer, to whatever sect he belongs, and whether he maintains the composition of extension by indivisible points, or by quantities divisible *in infinitum*. This question will embarrass both of them.

There are few or no mathematicians, who defend the hypothesis of indivisible points; and yet these have the readiest and justest answer to the present question. They need only reply, that lines or surfaces are equal, when the numbers of points in each are equal; and that as the proportion of the numbers varies, the proportion of the lines and surfaces is also varied. But though this answer be *just*, as well as obvious; yet I may affirm, that this standard of equality is entirely *useless*, and that it never is from such a comparison we determine objects to be equal or unequal with respect to each other. For as the points, which enter into the composition of any line or surface, whether perceived by the sight or touch, are so minute and so confounded with each other, that it is utterly impossible for the mind to compute their number, such a computation will never afford us a standard by which we may judge of proportions. No one will ever be able to determine by an exact numeration, that an inch has fewer points than a foot, or a foot fewer than an ell or any greater measure: for which reason we seldom or never consider this as the standard of equality or inequality.

As to those, who imagine, that extension is divisible *in infinitum*, it is impossible they can make use of this answer, or fix the equality of any line or surface by a numeration of its component parts. For since, according to their hypothesis, the least as well as greatest figures contain an infinite number of parts; and since infinite numbers, properly speaking, can neither be equal nor unequal with respect to each other; the equality or inequality of any portions of space can never depend on any proportion in the number of their parts. It is true, it may be said, that the inequality of an ell and a yard consists in the different numbers of the feet, of which they are composed; and that of a foot and a yard in the number of the inches. But as that quantity we call an inch in the one is supposed equal to what we call an inch in the other, and as it is impossible for the mind to find this equality by proceeding *in infinitum* with these references to inferior quantities: it is evident, that at last we must fix some standard of equality different from an enumeration of the parts.

There are some,* who pretend, that equality is best defined by *congruity*, and that any two figures are equal, when upon the placing of one upon the other, all their parts correspond to and touch each other. In order to judge of this definition let us consider, that since equality is a relation, it is not, strictly speaking, a property in the figures themselves, but arises merely from the comparison, which the mind makes betwixt them. If it consists, therefore, in this imaginary application and mutual contact of parts, we must at least have a distinct notion of these parts, and must conceive their contact. Now it is plain, that in this conception we would run up these parts to the greatest minuteness, which can possibly be conceived; since the contact of large parts would never render the figures equal. But the minutest parts we can conceive are mathematical points; and consequently this standard of equality is the same with that derived from the equality of the number of points; which we have already determined to be a just but an useless standard. We must therefore look to some other quarter for a solution of the present difficulty.†

It is evident, that the eye, or rather the mind is often able at one view to determine the proportions of bodies, and pronounce them equal to, or greater or less than each other, without examining or comparing the number of their minute parts. Such judgments are not only common,but in many cases certain andinfallible. Whenthe measure of a yard and that of a foot are presented, the mind can no more question, that the first is longer than the second, than it can doubt of those principles, which are the most clear and self-evident.

There are therefore three proportions, which the mind distinguishes in the general appearance of its objects, and calls by the

* See Dr *Barrow*'s mathematical lectures.
[† see Appendix to the *Treatise*.]

names of *greater, less* and *equal*. But though its decisions concerning these proportions be sometimes infallible, they are not always so; nor are our judgments of this kind more exempt from doubt and error than those on any other subject. We frequently correct our first opinion by a review and reflection; and pronounce those objects to be equal, which at first we esteemed unequal; and regard an object as less, though before it appeared greater than another. Nor is this the only correction, which these judgments of our senses undergo; but we often discover our error by a juxta-position of the objects; or where that is impracticable, by the use of some common and invariable measure, which being success-ively applied to each, informs us of their different proportions. And even this correction is susceptible of a new correction, and of different degrees of exactness, according to the nature of the instrument, by which we measure the bodies, and the care which we employ in the comparison.

When therefore the mind is accustomed to these judgments and their corrections, and finds that the same proportion which makes two figures have in the eye that appearance, which we call *equality*, makes them also correspond to each other, and to any common measure, with which they are compared, we form a mixed notion of equality derived both from the looser and stricter methods of comparison. But we are not content with this. For as sound reason convinces us that there are bodies *vastly* more minute than those, which appear to the senses; and as a false reason would persuade us, that there are bodies *infinitely* more minute; we clearly per-ceive, that we are not possessed of any instrument or art of measuring, which can secure us from all error and uncertainty. We are sensible, that the addition or removal of one of these minute parts, is not discernible either in the appearance or measuring; and as we imagine, that two figures, which were equal before, cannot be equal after this removal or addition, we therefore suppose some imaginary standard of equality, by which the appearances and measuring are exactly corrected, and the figures reduced entirely to that proportion. This standard is plainly imaginary. For as the very idea of equality is that of such a particular appearance corrected by juxtaposition or a common measure, the notion of any correction beyond what we have instruments and art to make, is a mere fiction of the mind, and useless as well as incomprehensible. But though this standard be only imaginary, the fiction however is very natural; nor is anything more usual, than for the mind to proceed after this manner with any action, even after the reason has ceased, which first determined it to begin. This appears very conspicuously with regard to time; where though it is evident we have no exact method of determining the proportions of parts, not even so exact as in extension, yet the various corrections of our measures, and their different degrees of exactness, have given as an obscure and implicit notion of a perfect and entire equality. The case is the same in many other subjects. A musician finding his ear becoming every day more delicate, and correcting himself by reflection and attention, proceeds with the same act of the mind, even when the subject fails him, and entertains a notion of a complete *tierce* or *octave*, without being able to tell whence he derives his standard. A painter forms the same fiction with regard to colours. A mechanic with regard to motion. To the one *light* and *shade*; to the other *swift* and *slow* are imagined to be capable of an exact comparison and equality beyond the judgments of the senses.

We may apply the same reasoning to CURVE and RIGHT lines. Nothing is more apparent to the senses, than the distinction betwixt a curve and a right line; nor are there any ideas we more easily form than the ideas of these objects. But however easily we may form these ideas, it is impossible to produce any definition of them, which will fix the precise boundaries betwixt them. When we draw lines upon paper, or any continued surface, there is a certain order, by which the lines run along from one point to another, that they may produce the entire impression of a curve or right line; but this order is perfectly unknown, and nothing is observed but the united appearance. Thus even upon the system of indivisible points, we can only form a distant notion of some unknown standard to these objects. Upon that of infinite divisibility we cannot go even this length; but are reduced merely to the general appearance, as the rule by which we determine lines to be either curve or right ones. But though we can give no perfect definition of these lines, nor produce any very exact method of distinguishing the one from the other; yet this hinders us not from correcting the first appearance by a more accurate consideration, and by a comparison with some rule, of whose rectitude from repeated trials we have a greater assurance. And it is from these corrections, and by carrying on the same action of the mind, even when its reason fails us, that we form the loose idea of a perfect standard to these figures, without being able to explain or comprehend it.

It is true, mathematicians pretend they give an exact definition of a right line, when they say, *it is the shortest way betwixt two points.* But in the first place I observe, that this is more properly the discovery of one of the properties of a right line, than a just definition of it. For I ask any one, if upon mention of a right line he thinks not immediately on such a particular appearance, and if it is not by accident only that he considers this property? A right line can be comprehended alone; but this definition is unintelligible without a comparison with other lines, which we conceive to be more extended. In common life it is established as a maxim, that the straightest way is always the shortest; which would be as absurd as to say, the shortest way is always the shortest, if our idea of a right line was not different from that of the shortest way betwixt two points.

Secondly, I repeat what I have already established, that we have no precise idea of equality and inequality, shorter and longer, more than of a right line or a curve; and consequently that the one can never afford us a perfect standard for the other. An exact idea can never be built on such as are loose and undetermined.

The idea of a *plain surface* is as little susceptible of a precise standard as that of a right line; nor have we any other means of distinguishing such a surface, than its general appearance. It is in vain, that mathematicians represent a plain surface as produced by the flowing of a right line. It will immediately be objected, that our idea of a surface is as independent of this method of forming a surface, as our idea of an ellipse is of that of a cone; that the idea of a right line is no more precise than that of a plain surface; that a right line may flow irregularly, and by that means form a figure quite different from a plane; and that therefore we must suppose it to flow along two right lines, parallel to each other, and on the same plane; which is a description, that explains a thing by itself, and returns in a circle.

It appears, then, that the ideas which are most essential to geometry, *viz.* those of equality and inequality, of a right line and a plain surface, are far from being exact and determinate, according to our common method of conceiving them. Not only we are incapable of telling, if the case be in any degree doubtful, when such particular figures are equal; when such a line is a right one, and such a surface a plain one; but we can form no idea of that proportion, or of these figures, which is firm and invariable. Our appeal is still to the weak and fallible judgment, which we make from the appearance of the objects, and correct by a compass or common measure; and if we join the supposition of any farther correction, it is of such-a-one as is either useless or imaginary. In vain should we have recourse to the common topic, and employ the supposition of a deity, whose omnipotence may enable him to form a perfect geometrical figure, and describe a right line without any curve or inflexion. As the ultimate standard of these figures is derived from nothing but the senses and imagination, it is absurd to talk of any perfection beyond what these faculties can judge of; since the true perfection of any thing consists in its conformity to its standard.

Now since these ideas are so loose and uncertain, I would fain ask any mathematician what infallible assurance he has, not only of the more intricate, and obscure propositions of his science, but of the most vulgar and obvious principles? How can he prove to me, for instance, that two right lines cannot have one common segment? Or that it is impossible to draw more than one right line betwixt any two points? Should he tell me, that these opinions are obviously absurd, and repugnant to our clear ideas; I would answer, that I do not deny, where two right lines incline upon each other with a sensible angle, but it is absurd to imagine them to have a common segment. But supposing these two lines to approach at the rate of an inch in twenty leagues, I perceive no absurdity in asserting, that upon their contact they become one. For, I beseech you, by what rule or standard do you judge, when you assert, that the line, in which I have supposed them to concur, cannot make the same right line with those two, that form so small an angle betwixt them? You must surely have some idea of a right line, to which this line does not agree. Do you therefore mean that it takes not the points in the same order and by the same rule, as is peculiar and essential to a right line? If so, I must inform you, that besides that in judging after this manner you allow, that extension is composed of indivisible points (which, perhaps, is more than you intend) besides this, I say, I must inform you, that neither is this the standard from which we form the idea of a right line; nor, if it were, is there any such firmness in our senses or imagination, as to determine when such an order is violated or preserved. The original standard of a right line is in reality nothing but a certain general appearance; and it is evident right lines may be made to concur with each other, and yet correspond to this standard, though corrected by all the means either practicable or imaginable.*

This may open our eyes a little, and let us see, that no geometrical demonstration for the infinite divisibility of extension can have so much force as what we naturally attribute to every argument, which is supported by such magnificent pretensions. At the same time we may learn the reason, why geometry fails of evidence in this single point, while all its other reasonings command our fullest assent and approbation. And indeed it seems more requisite to give the reason of this exception, than to shew, that we really must make such an exception, and regard all the mathematical arguments for infinite divisibility as utterly sophistical. For it is evident, that as no idea of quantity is infinitely divisible, there cannot be imagined a more glaring absurdity, than to endeavour to prove, that quantity itself admits of such a division; and to prove this by means of ideas, which are directly opposite in that particular. And as this absurdity is very glaring in itself, so there is no argument founded on it which is not attended with a new absurdity, and involves not an evident contradiction.

I might give as instances those arguments for infinite divisibility, which are derived from the *point of contact*. I know there is no mathematician, who will not refuse to be judged by the diagrams he describes upon paper, these being loose draughts, as he will tell us, and serving only to convey with greater facility certain ideas, which are the true foundation of all our reasoning. This I am satisfied with, and am willing to rest the controversy merely upon these ideas. I desire therefore our mathematician to form, as accurately as possible, the ideas of a circle and a right line; and I then ask, if upon the conception of their contact he can conceive them as touching in a mathematical point, or if he must necessarily imagine them to concur for some space. Whichever side he

[* see Appendix to the *Treatise*.]

chooses, he runs himself into equal difficulties. If he affirms, that in tracing these figures in his imagination, he can imagine them to touch only in a point, he allows the possibility of that idea, and consequently of the thing. If he says, that in his conception of the contact of those lines he must make them concur, he thereby acknowledges the fallacy of geometrical demonstrations, when carried beyond a certain degree of minuteness; since it is certain he has such demonstrations against the concurrence of a circle and a right line; that is, in other words, he can prove an idea, *viz.* that of concurrence, to be *incompatible* with two other ideas, *viz.* those of a circle and right line; though at the same time he acknowledges these ideas to be *inseparable*.

SECTION FIVE

The same subject continued

If the second part of my system be true, *that the idea of space or extension is nothing but the idea of visible or tangible points distributed in a certain order;* it follows, that we can form no idea of a vacuum, or space, where there is nothing visible or tangible. This gives rise to three objections, which I shall examine together, because the answer I shall give to one is a consequence of that which I shall make use of for the others.

First, It may be said, that men have disputed for many ages concerning a vacuum and a plenum, without being able to bring the affair to a final decision; and philosophers, even at this day, think themselves at liberty to take part on either side, as their fancy leads them. But whatever foundation there may be for a controversy concerning the things themselves, it may be pretended, that the very dispute is decisive concerning the idea, and that it is impossible men could so long reason about a vacuum, and either refute or defend it, without having a notion of what they refuted or defended.

Secondly, If this argument should be contested, the reality or at least the possibility of the *idea* of a vacuum may be proved by the following reasoning. Every idea is possible, which is a necessary and infallible consequence of such as are possible. Now though we allow the world to be at present a plenum, we may easily conceive it to be deprived of motion; and this idea will certainly be allowed possible. It must also be allowed possible, to conceive the annihilation of any part of matter by the omnipotence of the deity, while the other parts remain at rest. For as every idea, that is distinguishable, is separable by the imagination; and as every idea, that is separable by the imagination, may be conceived to be separately existent; it is evident, that the existence of one particle of matter, no more implies the existence of another, than a square figure in one body implies a square figure in every one. This being granted, I now demand what results from the concurrence of these two possible ideas of *rest* and *annihilation*, and what must we conceive to follow upon the annihilation of all the air and subtile matter in the chamber, supposing the walls to remain the same, without any motion or alteration? There are some metaphysicians, who answer, that since matter and extension are the same, the annihilation of one necessarily implies that of the other; and there being now no distance betwixt the walls of the chamber, they touch each other; in the same manner as my hand touches the paper, which is immediately before me. But though this answer be very common, I defy these metaphysicians to conceive the matter according to their hypothesis, or imagine the floor and roof, with all the opposite sides of the chamber, to touch each other, while they continue in rest, and preserve the same position. For how can the two walls, that run from south to north, touch each other, while they touch the opposite ends of two walls, that run from east to west? And how can the floor and roof ever meet, while they are separated by the four walls, that lie in a contrary position? If you change their position, you suppose a motion. If you conceive any thing betwixt them, you suppose a new creation. But keeping strictly to the two ideas of *rest* and *annihilation*, it is evident, that the idea, which results from them, is not that of a contact of parts, but something else; which is concluded to be the idea of a vacuum.

The third objection carries the matter still farther, and not only asserts, that the idea of a vacuum is real and possible, but also necessary and unavoidable. This assertion is founded on the motion we observe in bodies, which, it is maintained, would be impossible and inconceivable without a vacuum, into which one body must move in order to make way for another. I shall not enlarge upon this objection, because it principally belongs to natural philosophy, which lies without our present sphere.

In order to answer these objections, we must take the matter pretty deep, and consider the nature and origin of several ideas, lest we dispute without understanding perfectly the subject of the controversy. It is evident the idea of darkness is no positive idea, but merely the negation of light, or more properly speaking, of coloured and visible objects. A man, who enjoys his sight, receives no other perception from turning his eyes on every side, when entirely deprived of light, than what is common to him with one born blind; and it is certain such-a-one has no idea either of light or darkness. The consequence of this is, that it is not from the mere removal of visible objects we receive the impression of extension without matter; and that the idea of utter darkness can never be the same with that of vacuum.

Suppose again a man to be supported in the air, and to be softly conveyed along by some invisible power; it is evident he is sensible of nothing, and never receives the idea of extension, nor indeed any idea, from this invariable motion. Even supposing he moves his limbs to and fro, this cannot convey to him that idea. He feels in that case a certain sensation or impression, the parts of which are successive to each other, and may give him the idea of time: but certainly are not disposed in such a manner, as is necessary to convey the idea of space or extension.

Since then it appears, that darkness and motion, with the utter removal of every thing visible and tangible, can never give us the idea of extension without matter, or of a vacuum; the next question is, whether they can convey this idea, when mixed with something visible and tangible?

It is commonly allowed by philosophers, that all bodies, which discover themselves to the eye, appear as if painted on a plain surface, and that their different degrees of remoteness from ourselves are discovered more by reason than by the senses. When I hold up my hand before me, and spread my fingers, they are separated as perfectly by the blue colour of the firmament, as they could be by any visible object, which I could place betwixt them. In order, therefore, to know whether the sight can convey the impression and idea of a vacuum, we must suppose, that amidst an entire darkness, there are luminous bodies presented to us, whose light discovers only these bodies themselves, without giving us any impression of the surrounding objects.

We must form a parallel supposition concerning the objects of our feeling. It is not proper to suppose a perfect removal of all tangible objects: we must allow something to be perceived by the feeling; and after an interval and motion of the hand or other organ of sensation, another object of the touch to be met with; and upon leaving that, another; and so on, as often as we please. The question is, whether these intervals do not afford us the idea of extension without body?

To begin with the first case; it is evident, that when only two luminous bodies appear to the eye, we can perceive, whether they be conjoined or separate: whether they be separated by a great or small distance; and if this distance varies, we can perceive its increase or diminution, with the motion of the bodies. But as the distance is not in this case any thing coloured or visible, it may be thought that there is here a vacuum or pure extension, not only intelligible to the mind, but obvious to the very senses.

This is our natural and most familiar way of thinking; but which we shall learn to correct by a little reflection. We may observe, that when two bodies present themselves, where there was formerly an entire darkness, the only change, that is discoverable, is in the appearance of these two objects, and that all the rest continues to be as before, a perfect negation of light, and of every coloured or visible object. This is not only true of what may be said to be remote from these bodies, but also of the very distance, which is interposed betwixt them; *that* being nothing but darkness, or the negation of light; without parts, without composition, invariable and indivisible. Now since this distance causes no perception different from what a blind man receives from his eyes, or what is conveyed to us in the darkest night, it must partake of the same properties: and as blindness and darkness afford us no ideas of extension, it is impossible that the dark and undistinguishable distance betwixt two bodies can ever produce that idea.

The sole difference betwixt an absolute darkness and the appearance of two or more visible luminous objects consists, as I said, in the objects themselves, and in the manner they affect our senses. The angles, which the rays of light flowing from them, form with each other; the motion that is required in the eye, in its passage from one to the other; and the different parts of the organs, which are affected by them; these produce the only perceptions, from which we can judge of the distance. But as these perceptions are each of them simple and indivisible, they can never give us the idea of extension.

We may illustrate this by considering the sense of feeling, and the imaginary distance or interval interposed betwixt tangible or solid objects. I suppose two cases, *viz.* that of a man supported in the air, and moving his limbs to and fro, without meeting any thing tangible; and that of a man, who feeling something tangible, leaves it, and after a motion, of which he is sensible, perceives another tangible object; and I then ask, wherein consists the difference betwixt these two cases? No one will make any scruple to affirm, that it consists merely in the perceiving those objects, and that the sensation, which arises from the motion, is in both cases the same: and as that sensation is not capable of conveying to us an idea of extension, when unaccompanied with some other perception, it can no more give us that idea, when mixed with the impressions of tangible objects; since that mixture produces no alteration upon it.

But though motion and darkness, either alone, or attended with tangible and visible objects, convey no idea of a vacuum or extension without matter, yet they are the causes why we falsely imagine we can form such an idea. For there is a close relation betwixt that motion and darkness, and a real extension, or composition of visible and tangible objects.

First, We may observe, that two visible objects appearing in the midst of utter darkness, affect the senses in the same manner, and form the same angle by the rays, which flow from them, and meet in the eye, as if the distance betwixt them were filled with visible objects, that give us a true idea of extension. The sensation of motion is likewise the same, when there is nothing tangible interposed betwixt two bodies, as when we feel a compounded body, whose different parts are placed beyond each other.

Secondly, We find by experience, that two bodies, which are so placed as to affect the senses in the same manner with two others, that have a certain extent of visible objects interposed betwixt them, are capable of receiving the same extent, without any sensible impulse or penetration, and without any change on that angle, under which they appear to the senses. In like manner, where there is one object, which we cannot feel after another without an interval, and the perceiving of that sensation we call motion in our hand or organ of sensation; experience shews us, that it is possible the same object may be felt with the same sensation of motion, along with the interposed impression of solid and tangible objects, attending the sensation. That is, in other words, an invisible and intangible distance may be converted into a visible and tangible one, without any change on the distant objects.

Thirdly, We may observe, as another relation betwixt these two kinds of distance, that they have nearly the same effects on every natural phenomenon. For as all qualities, such as heat, cold, light, attraction, &c. diminish in proportion to the distance; there is but little difference observed, whether this distance be marked out by compounded and sensible objects, or be known only by the manner, in which the distant objects affect the senses.

Here then are three relations betwixt that distance, which conveys the idea of extension, and that other, which is not filled with any coloured or solid object. The distant objects affect the senses in the same manner, whether separated by the one distance or the other; the second species of distance is found capable of receiving the first; and they both equally diminish the force of every quality.

These relations betwixt the two kinds of distance will afford us an easy reason, why the one has so often been taken for the other, and why we imagine we have an idea of extension without the idea of any object either of the sight or feeling. For we may establish it as a general maxim in this science of human nature, that wherever there is a close relation betwixt two ideas, the mind is very apt to mistake them, and in all its discourses and reasonings to use the one for the other. This phenomenon occurs on so many occasions, and is of such consequence, that I cannot forbear stopping a moment to examine its causes. I shall only premise, that we must distinguish exactly betwixt the phenomenon itself, and the causes, which I shall assign for it; and must not imagine from any uncertainty in the latter, that the former is also uncertain. The phenomenon may be real, though my explication be chimerical. The falsehood of the one is no consequence of that of the other;

though at the same time we may observe, that it is very natural for us to draw such a consequence; which is an evident instance of that very principle, which I endeavour to explain.

When I received the relations of *resemblance, contiguity* and *causation*, as principles of union among ideas, without examining into their causes, it was more in prosecution of my first maxim, that we must in the end rest contented with experience, than for want of something specious and plausible, which I might have displayed on that subject. It would have been easy to have made an imaginary dissection of the brain, and have shewn, why upon our conception of any idea, the animal spirits run into all the contiguous traces, and rouse up the other ideas, that are related to it. But though I have neglected any advantage, which I might have drawn from this topic in explaining the relations of ideas, I am afraid I must here have recourse to it, in order to account for the mistakes that arise from these relations. I shall therefore observe, that as the mind is endowed with a power of exciting any idea it pleases; whenever it dispatches the spirits into that region of the brain, in which the idea is placed; these spirits always excite the idea, when they run precisely into the proper traces, and rummage that cell, which belongs to the idea. But as their motion is seldom direct, and naturally turns a little to the one side or the other; for this reason the animal spirits, falling into the contiguous traces, present other related ideas in lieu of that, which the mind desired at first to survey. This change we are not always sensible of; but continuing still the same train of thought, make use of the related idea, which is presented to us, and employ it in our reasoning, as if it were the same with what we demanded. This is the cause of many mistakes and sophisms in philosophy; as will naturally be imagined, and as it would be easy to show, if there was occasion.

Of the three relations above-mentioned that of resemblance is the most fertile source of error; and indeed there are few mistakes in reasoning, which do not borrow largely from that origin. Resembling ideas are not only related together, but the actions of the mind, which we employ in considering them, are so little different, that we are not able to distinguish them. This last circumstance is of great consequence, and we may in general observe, that wherever the actions of the mind in forming any two ideas are the same or resembling, we are very apt to confound these ideas, and take the one for the other. Of this we shall see many instances in the progress of this treatise. But though resemblance be the relation, which most readily produces a mistake in ideas, yet the others of causation and contiguity may also concur in the same influence. We might produce the figures of poets and orators, as sufficient proofs of this, were it as usual, as it is reasonable, in metaphysical subjects to draw our arguments from that quarter. But lest metaphysicians should esteem this below their dignity, I shall borrow a proof from an observation, which may be made on most of their own discourses, *viz.* that it is usual for men to use words for ideas, and to talk instead of thinking in their reasonings. We use words for ideas, because they are commonly so closely connected that the mind easily mistakes them. And this likewise is the reason, why we substitute the idea of a distance, which is not considered either as visible or tangible, in the room of extension, which is nothing but a composition of visible or tangible points disposed in a certain order. In causing this mistake there concur both the relations of *causation* and *resemblance*. As the first species of distance is found to be convertible into the second, it is in this respect a kind of cause; and the similarity of their manner of affecting the senses, and diminishing every quality, forms the relation of resemblance.

After this chain of reasoning and explication of my principles, I am now prepared to answer all the objections that have been offered, whether derived from *metaphysics* or *mechanics*. The frequent disputes concerning a vacuum, or extension without matter prove not the reality of the idea, upon which the dispute turns; there being nothing more common, than to see men deceive themselves in this particular; especially when by means of any close relation, there is another idea presented, which may be the occasion of their mistake.

We may make almost the same answer to the second objection, derived from the conjunction of the ideas of rest and annihilation. When every thing is annihilated in the chamber, and the walls continue immoveable, the chamber must be conceived much in the same manner as at present, when the air that fills it, is not an object of the senses. This annihilation leaves to the *eye*, that fictitious distance, which is discovered by the different parts of the organ, that are affected, and by the degrees of light and shade – and to the *feeling*, that which consists in a sensation of motion in the hand, or other member of the body. In vain should we search any farther. On whichever side we turn this subject, we shall find that these are the only impressions such an object can produce after the supposed annihilation; and it has already been remarked, that impressions can give rise to no ideas, but to such as resemble them.

Since a body interposed betwixt two others may be supposed to be annihilated, without producing any change upon such as lie on each hand of it, it is easily conceived, how it may be created anew, and yet produce as little alteration. Now the motion of a body has much the same effect as its creation. The distant bodies are no more affected in the one case, than in the other. This suffices to satisfy the imagination, and proves there is no repugnance in such a motion. Afterwards experience comes in play to persuade us that two bodies, situated in the manner above-described, have really such a capacity of receiving body betwixt them, and that there is no obstacle to the conversion of the invisible and intangible distance into one that is visible and tangible. However natural that conversion may seem, we cannot be sure it is practicable, before we have had experience of it.

Thus I seem to have answered the three objections above-mentioned; though at the same time I am sensible, that few will be satisfied with these answers, but will immediately propose new objections and difficulties. It will probably be said, that my reasoning makes nothing to the matter in hand, and that I explain only the manner in which objects affect the senses, without endeavouring to account for their real nature and operations. Though there be nothing visible or tangible interposed betwixt two bodies, yet we find *by experience*, that the bodies may be placed in the same manner, with regard to the eye, and require the same motion of the hand in passing from one to the other, as if divided by something visible and tangible. This invisible and intangible distance is also found *by experience* to contain a capacity of receiving body, or of becoming visible and tangible. Here is the whole of my system; and in no part of it have I endeavoured to explain the cause, which separates bodies after this manner, and gives them a capacity of receiving others betwixt them, without any impulse or penetration.

I answer this objection, by pleading guilty, and by confessing that my intention never was to penetrate into the nature of bodies, or explain the secret causes of their operations. For besides that this belongs not to my present purpose, I am afraid, that such an enterprize is beyond the reach of human understanding, and that we can never pretend to know body otherwise than by those external properties, which discover themselves to the senses. As to those who attempt any thing farther, I cannot approve of their ambition, till I see, in some one instance at least, that they have met with success. But at present I content myself with knowing perfectly the manner in which objects affect my senses, and their connections with each other, as far as experience informs me of them. This suffices for the conduct of life; and this also suffices for my philosophy, which pretends only to explain the nature and causes of our perceptions, or impressions and ideas.*

I shall conclude this subject of extension with a paradox, which will easily be explained from the foregoing reasoning. This paradox is, that if you are pleased to give to the invisible and intangible distance, or in other words, to the capacity of becoming a visible and tangible distance, the name of a vacuum, extension and matter are the same, and yet there is a vacuum. If you will not give it that name, motion is possible in a plenum, without any impulse *in infinitum*, without returning in a circle, and without penetration. But however we may express ourselves, we must always confess, that we have no idea of any real extension without filling it with sensible objects, and conceiving its parts as visible or tangible.

As to the doctrine, that time is nothing but the manner, in which some real objects exist; we may observe, that it is liable to the same objections as the similar doctrine with regard to extension. If it be a sufficient proof, that we have the idea of a vacuum, because we dispute and reason concerning it; we must for the same reason have the idea of time without any changeable existence; since there is no subject of dispute more frequent and common. But that we really have no such idea, is certain. For whence should it be derived? Does it arise from an impression of sensation or of reflection? Point it out distinctly to us, that we may know its nature and qualities. But if you cannot point out *any such impression*, you may be certain you are mistaken, when you imagine you have *any such idea*.

[* see Appendix to the *Treatise*.]

But though it be impossible to shew the impression, from which the idea of time without a changeable existence is derived; yet we can easily point out those appearances, which make us fancy we have that idea. For we may observe, that there is a continual succession of perceptions in our mind; so that the idea of time being for ever present with us, when we consider a stedfast object at five-a-clock, and regard the same at six, we are apt to apply to it that idea in the same manner as if every moment were distinguished by a different position, or an alteration of the object. The first and second appearances of the object, being compared with the succession of our perceptions, seem equally removed as if the object had really changed. To which we may add, what experience shews us, that the object was susceptible of such a number of changes betwixt these appearances; as also that the unchangeable or rather fictitious duration has the same effect upon every quality, by increasing or diminishing it, as that succession, which is obvious to the senses. From these three relations we are apt to confound our ideas, and imagine we can form the idea of a time and duration, without any change or succession.

SECTION SIX

Of the idea of existence, and of external existence

It may not be amiss, before we leave this subject, to explain the ideas of *existence* and of *external existence*; which have their difficulties, as well as the ideas of space and time. By this means we shall be the better prepared for the examination of knowledge and probability, when we understand perfectly all those particular ideas, which may enter into our reasoning.

There is no impression nor idea of any kind, of which we have any consciousness or memory, that is not conceived as existent; and it is evident, that from this consciousness the most perfect idea and assurance of *being* is derived. From hence we may form a dilemma, the most clear and conclusive that can be imagined, *viz.* that since we never remember any idea or impression without attributing existence to it, the idea of existence must either be derived from a distinct impression, conjoined with every perception or object of our thought, or must be the very same with the idea of the perception or object.

As this dilemma is an evident consequence of the principle, that every idea arises from a similar impression, so our decision betwixt the propositions of the dilemma is no more doubtful. So far from there being any distinct impression, attending every impression and every idea, that I do not think there are any two distinct impressions, which are inseparably conjoined. Though certain sensations may at one time be united, we quickly find they admit of a separation, and may be presented apart. And thus, though every impression and idea we remember be considered as existent, the idea of existence is not derived from any particular impression.

The idea of existence, then, is the very same with the idea of what we conceive to be existent. To reflect on any thing simply, and to reflect on it as existent, are nothing different from each other. That idea, when conjoined with the idea of any object, makes no addition to it. Whatever we conceive, we conceive to be existent. Any idea we please to form is the idea of a being; and the idea of a being is any idea we please to form.

Whoever opposes this, must necessarily point out that distinct impression, from which the idea of entity is derived, and must prove, that this impression is inseparable from every perception we believe to be existent. This we may without hesitation conclude to be impossible.

Our foregoing reasoning* concerning the *distinction* of ideas without any real *difference* will not here serve us in any stead. That kind of distinction is founded on the different resemblances, which the same simple idea may have to several different ideas. But no object can be presented resembling some object with respect to its existence, and different from others in the same particular; since every object, that is presented, must necessarily be existent.

A like reasoning will account for the idea of *external existence*. We may observe, that it is universally allowed by philosophers, and is besides pretty obvious of itself, that nothing is ever really present with the mind but its perceptions or impressions and ideas, and that external objects become known to us only by those perceptions they occasion. To hate, to love, to think, to feel, to see; all this is nothing but to perceive.

* Part 1, Section 7.

Now since nothing is ever present to the mind but perceptions, and since all ideas are derived from something antecedently present to the mind; it follows, that it is impossible for us so much as to conceive or form an idea of any thing specifically different from ideas and impressions. Let us fix our attention out of ourselves as much as possible: let us chase our imagination to the heavens, or to the utmost limits of the universe; we never really advance a step beyond ourselves, nor can conceive any kind of existence, but those perceptions, which have appeared in that narrow compass. This is the universe of the imagination, nor have we any idea but what is there produced.

The farthest we can go towards a conception of external objects, when supposed *specifically* different from our perceptions, is to form a relative idea of them, without pretending to comprehend the related objects. Generally speaking we do not suppose them specifically different; but only attribute to them different relations, connections and durations. But of this more fully hereafter.*

* Part 4, Section 2.

PART THREE

Of Knowledge and Probability

SECTION ONE

Of knowledge

There are seven* different kinds of philosophical relation, *viz.* *resemblance, identity, relations of time and place, proportion in quantity or number, degrees in any quality, contrariety* and *causation*. These relations may be divided into two classes: into such as depend entirely on the ideas, which we compare together, and such as may be changed without any change in the ideas. It is from the idea of a triangle, that we discover the relation of equality, which its three angles bear to two right ones; and this relation is invariable, as long as our idea remains the same. On the contrary, the relations of *contiguity* and *distance* betwixt two objects may be changed merely by an alteration of their place, without any change on the objects themselves or on their ideas; and the place depends on a hundred different accidents, which cannot be foreseen by the mind. It is the same case with *identity* and *causation*. Two objects, though perfectly resembling each other, and even appearing in the same place at different times, may be numerically different: and as the power, by which one object produces another, is never discoverable merely from their idea, it is evident *cause* and *effect* are relations, of which we receive information from experience, and not from any abstract reasoning or reflection. There is no single phenomenon, even the most simple, which can be accounted for from the qualities of the objects, as they appear to us; or which we could foresee without the help of our memory and experience.

It appears, therefore, that of these seven philosophical relations, there remain only four, which depending solely upon ideas, can

* Part 1, Section 5.

be the objects of knowledge and certainty. These four are *resemblance, contrariety, degrees in quality*, and *proportions in quantity or number*. Three of these relations are discoverable at first sight, and fall more properly under the province of intuition than demonstration. When any objects *resemble* each other, the resemblance will at first strike the eye, or rather the mind; and seldom requires a second examination. The case is the same with *contrariety*, and with the *degrees* of any *quality*. No one can once doubt but existence and non-existence destroy each other, and are perfectly incompatible and contrary. And though it be impossible to judge exactly of the degrees of any quality, such as colour, taste, heat, cold, when the difference betwixt them is very small: yet it is easy to decide, that any of them is superior or inferior to another, when their difference is considerable. And this decision we always pronounce at first sight, without any enquiry or reasoning.

We might proceed, after the same manner, in fixing the *proportions* of *quantity* or *number*, and might at one view observe a superiority or inferiority betwixt any numbers, or figures; especially where the difference is very great and remarkable. As to equality or any exact proportion, we can only guess at it from a single consideration; except in very short numbers, or very limited portions of extension; which are comprehended in an instant, and where we perceive an impossibility of falling into any considerable error. In all other cases we must settle the proportions with some liberty, or proceed in a more *artificial* manner.

I have already observed, that geometry, or the *art*, by which we fix the proportions of figures; though it much excels both in universality and exactness, the loose judgments of the senses and imagination; yet never attains a perfect precision and exactness. Its first principles are still drawn from the general appearance of the objects; and that appearance can never afford us any security, when we examine the prodigious minuteness of which nature is susceptible. Our ideas seem to give a perfect assurance, that no two right lines can have a common segment; but if we consider these ideas, we shall find, that they always suppose a sensible inclination of the two lines, and that where the angle they form is extremely small, we have no standard of a right line so precise as to assure us of the truth of this proposition. It is the same case with most of the primary decisions of the mathematics.

There remain, therefore, algebra and arithmetic as the only sciences, in which we can carry on a chain of reasoning to any degree of intricacy, and yet preserve a perfect exactness and certainty. We are possessed of a precise standard, by which we can judge of the equality and proportion of numbers; and according as they correspond or not to that standard, we determine their relations, without any possibility of error. When two numbers are so combined, as that the one has always an unit answering to every unit of the other, we pronounce them equal; and it is for want of such a standard of equality in extension, that geometry can scarce be esteemed a perfect and infallible science.

But here it may not be amiss to obviate a difficulty, which may arise from my asserting, that though geometry falls short of that perfect precision and certainty, which are peculiar to arithmetic and algebra, yet it excels the imperfect judgments of our senses and imagination. The reason why I impute any defect to geometry, is, because its original and fundamental principles are derived merely from appearances; and it may perhaps be imagined, that this defect must always attend it, and keep it from ever reaching a greater exactness in the comparison of objects or ideas, than what our eye or imagination alone is able to attain. I own that this defect so far attends it, as to keep it from ever aspiring to a full certainty: but since these fundamental principles depend on the easiest and least deceitful appearances, they bestow on their consequences a degree of exactness, of which these consequences are singly incapable. It is impossible for the eye to determine the angles of a chiliagon to be equal to 1996 right angles, or make any conjecture, that approaches this proportion; but when it determines, that right lines cannot concur; that we cannot draw more than one right line between two given points; its mistakes can never be of any consequence. And this is the nature and use of geometry, to run us up to such appearances, as, by reason of their simplicity, cannot lead us into any considerable error.

I shall here take occasion to propose a second observation concerning our demonstrative reasonings, which is suggested by the same subject of the mathematics. It is usual with mathematicians, to pretend, that those ideas, which are their objects, are of so refined and spiritual a nature, that they fall not under the conception of the fancy, but must be comprehended by a pure and intellectual view, of which the superior faculties of the soul are alone capable. The same notion runs through most parts of philosophy, and is principally made use of to explain oar abstract ideas, and to shew how we can form an idea of a triangle, for instance, which shall neither be an isoceles nor scalenum, nor be confined to any particular length and proportion of sides. It is easy to see, why philosophers are so fond of this notion of some spiritual and refined perceptions; since by that means they cover many of their absurdities, and may refuse to submit to the decisions of clear ideas, by appealing to such as are obscure and uncertain. But to destroy this artifice, we need but reflect on that principle so oft insisted on, *that all our ideas are copied from our impressions*. For from thence we may immediately conclude, that since all impressions are clear and precise, the ideas, which are copied from them, must be of the same nature, and can never, but from our fault, contain any thing so dark and intricate. An idea is by its very nature weaker and fainter than an impression; but being in every other respect the same, cannot imply any very great mystery. If its weakness render it obscure, it is our business to remedy that defect, as much as possible, by keeping the idea steady and precise; and till we have done so, it is in vain to pretend to reasoning and philosophy.

SECTION TWO

Of probability, and of the idea of cause and effect

This is all I think necessary to observe concerning those four relations, which are the foundation of science; but as to the other three, which depend not upon the idea, and may be absent or present even while *that* remains the same, it will be proper to explain them more particularly. These three relations are *identity, the situations in time and place, and causation.*

All kinds of reasoning consist in nothing but a *comparison*, and a discovery of those relations, either constant or inconstant, which two or more objects bear to each other. This comparison we may make, either when both the objects are present to the senses, or when neither of them is present, or when only one. When both the objects are present to the senses along with the relation, we call *this* perception rather than reasoning; nor is there in this case any exercise of the thought, or any action, properly speaking, but a mere passive admission of the impressions through the organs of sensation. According to this way of thinking, we ought not to receive as reasoning any of the observations we may make concerning *identity*, and the *relations* of *time* and *place*; since in none of them the mind can go beyond what is immediately present to the senses, either to discover the real existence or the relations of objects. It is only *causation*, which produces such a connexion, as to give us assurance from the existence or action of one object, that it was followed or preceded by any other existence or action; nor can the other two relations be ever made use of in reasoning, except so far as they either affect or are affected by it. There is nothing in any objects to persuade us, that they are either always *remote* or always *contiguous*; and when from experience and observation we discover, that their relation in this particular is invariable, we always conclude there is some secret *cause*, which separates or unites them. The same reasoning extends to *identity*. We readily suppose an object may continue individually the same, though several times absent from and present to the senses; and ascribe to it an identity, notwithstanding the interruption of the perception, whenever we conclude, that if we had kept our eye or hand constantly upon it, it would have conveyed an invariable and uninterrupted perception. But this conclusion beyond the impressions of our senses can be founded only on the connexion of *cause and effect*; nor can we otherwise have any security, that the object is not changed upon us, however much the new object may resemble that which was formerly present to the senses. Whenever we discover such a perfect resemblance, we consider, whether it be common in that species of objects; whether possibly or probably any cause could operate in producing the change and resemblance; and according as we determine concerning these causes and effects, we form our judgment concerning the identity of the object.

Here then it appears, that of those three relations, which depend not upon the mere ideas, the only one, that can be traced beyond our senses and informs us of existences and objects, which we do not see or feel, is *causation*. This relation, therefore, we shall endeavour to explain fully before we leave the subject of the understanding.

To begin regularly, we must consider the idea of *causation*, and see from what origin it is derived. It is impossible to reason justly, without understanding perfectly the idea concerning which we reason; and it is impossible perfectly to understand any idea, without tracing it up to its origin, and examining that primary impression, from which it arises. The examination of the impression bestows a clearness on the idea; and the examination of the idea bestows a like clearness on all our reasoning.

Let us therefore cast our eye on any two objects, which we call cause and effect, and turn them on all sides, in order to find that impression, which produces an idea of such prodigious consequence. At first sight I perceive, that I must not search for it in any of the particular qualities of the objects; since which-ever of these *qualities* I pitch on, I find some object, that is not possessed of it, and yet falls under the denomination of cause or effect. And indeed there is nothing existent, either externally or internally, which is not to be considered either as a cause or an effect; though it is plain there is no one quality, which universally belongs to all beings, and gives them a title to that denomination.

The idea, then, of causation must be derived from some *relation* among objects; and that relation we must now endeavour to discover. I find in the first place, that whatever objects are considered as causes or effects, are *contiguous*; and that nothing can operate in a time or place, which is ever so little removed from those of its existence. Though distant objects may sometimes seem productive of each other, they are commonly found upon examination to be linked by a chain of causes, which are contiguous among themselves, and to the distant objects; and when in any particular instance we cannot discover this connexion, we still presume it to exist. We may therefore consider the relation of CONTIGUITY as essential to that of causation; at least may suppose it such, according to the general opinion, till we can find a more proper occasion* to clear up this matter, by examining what objects are or are not susceptible of juxtaposition and conjunction.

The second relation I shall observe as essential to causes and effects, is not so universally acknowledged, but is liable to some controversy. It is that of PRIORITY of time in the cause before the effect. Some pretend that it is not absolutely necessary a cause

* Part 4, Section 5.

should precede its effect; but that any object or action, in the very first moment of its existence, may exert its productive quality, and give rise to another object or action, perfectly co-temporary with itself. But beside that experience in most instances seems to contradict this opinion, we may establish the relation of priority by a kind of inference or reasoning. It is an established maxim both in natural and moral philosophy, that an object, which exists for any time in its full perfection without producing another, is not its sole cause; but is assisted by some other principle, which pushes it from its state of inactivity, and makes it exert that energy, of which it was secretly possessed. Now if any cause may be perfectly co-temporary with its effect, it is certain, according to this maxim, that they must all of them be so; since any one of them, which retards its operation for a single moment, exerts not itself at that very individual time, in which it might have operated; and therefore is no proper cause. The consequence of this would be no less than the destruction of that succession of causes, which we observe in the world; and indeed, the utter annihilation of time. For if one cause were co-temporary with its effect, and this effect with *its* effect, and so on, it is plain there would be no such thing as succession, and all objects must be co-existent.

If this argument appear satisfactory, it is well. If not, I beg the reader to allow me the same liberty, which I have used in the preceding case, of supposing it such. For he shall find, that the affair is of no great importance.

Having thus discovered or supposed the two relations of *contiguity* and *succession* to be essential to causes and effects, I find I am stopped short, and can proceed no farther in considering any single instance of cause and effect. Motion in one body is regarded upon impulse as the cause of motion in another. When we consider these objects with utmost attention, we find only that the one body approaches the other; and that the motion of it precedes that of the other, but without any sensible interval. It is in vain to rack ourselves with *farther* thought and reflection upon this subject. We can go no *farther* in considering this particular instance.

Should any one leave this instance, and pretend to define a cause, by saying it is something productive of another, it is evident he would say nothing. For what does he mean by *production*? Can he give any definition of it, that will not be the same with that of causation? If he can, I desire it may be produced. If he cannot, he here runs in a circle, and gives a synonimous term instead of a definition.

Shall we then rest contented with these two relations of contiguity and succession, as affording a complete idea of causation? By no means. An object may be contiguous and prior to another, without being considered as its cause. There is a NECESSARY CONNEXION to be taken into consideration; and that relation is of much greater importance, than any of the other two above-mentioned.

Here again I turn the object on all sides, in order to discover the nature of this necessary connexion, and find the impression, or impressions, from which its idea may be derived. When I cast my eye on the *known qualities* of objects, I immediately discover that the relation of cause and effect depends not in the least on *them*. When I consider their *relations*, I can find none but those of contiguity and succession; which I have already regarded as imperfect and unsatisfactory. Shall the despair of success make me assert, that I am here possessed of an idea, which is not preceded by any similar impression? This would be too strong a proof of levity and inconstancy; since the contrary principle has been already so firmly established, as to admit of no farther doubt; at least, till we have more fully examined the present difficulty.

We must, therefore, proceed like those, who being in search of any thing, that lies concealed from them, and not finding it in the place they expected, beat about all the neighbouring fields, without any certain view or design, in hopes their good fortune will at last guide them to what they search for. It is necessary for us to leave the direct survey of this question concerning the nature of that *necessary connexion*, which enters into our idea of cause and effect; and endeavour to find some other questions, the examination of which will perhaps afford a hint, that may serve to clear up the present difficulty. Of these questions there occur two, which I shall proceed to examine, *viz*.

First, For what reason we pronounce it *necessary*, that every thing whose existence has a beginning, should also have a cause.

Secondly, Why we conclude, that such particular causes must *necessarily* have such particular effects; and what is the nature of that *inference* we draw from the one to the other, and of the *belief* we repose in it?

I shall only observe before I proceed any farther, that though the ideas of cause and effect be derived from the impressions of reflection as well as from those of sensation, yet for brevity's sake, I commonly mention only the latter as the origin of these ideas; though I desire that whatever I say of them may also extend to the former. Passions are connected with their objects and with one another; no less than external bodies are connected together. The same relation, then, of cause and effect, which belongs to one, must be common to all of them.

SECTION THREE

Why a cause is always necessary

To begin with the first question concerning the necessity of a cause: It is a general maxim in philosophy, that *whatever begins to exist, must have a cause of existence.* This is commonly taken for granted in all reasonings, without any proof given or demanded. It is supposed to be founded on intuition, and to be one of those maxims, which though they may be denied with the lips, it is impossible for men in their hearts really to doubt of. But if we examine this maxim by the idea of knowledge above-explained, we shall discover in it no mark of any such intuitive certainty; but on the contrary shall find, that it is of a nature quite foreign to that species of conviction.

All certainty arises from the comparison of ideas, and from the discovery of such relations as are unalterable, so long as the ideas continue the same. These relations are *resemblance, proportions in quantity and number, degrees of any quality, and contrariety;* none of which are implied in this proposition, *Whatever has a beginning has also a cause of existence.* That proposition therefore is not intuitively certain. At least any one, who would assert it to be intuitively certain, must deny these to be the only infallible relations, and must find some other relation of that kind to be implied in it; which it will then be time enough to examine.

But here is an argument, which proves at once, that the foregoing proposition is neither intuitively nor demonstrably certain. We can never demonstrate the necessity of a cause to every new existence, or new modification of existence, without shewing at the same time the impossibility there is, that any thing can ever begin to exist without some productive principle; and where the latter proposition cannot be proved, we must despair of ever being able to prove the former. Now that the latter proposition is utterly incapable of a demonstrative proof, we may satisfy ourselves by considering that as all distinct ideas are separable from each other, and as the ideas of cause and effect are evidently distinct, it will be easy for us to conceive any object to be non-existent this moment, and existent the next, without conjoining to it the distinct idea of a cause or productive principle. The separation, therefore, of the idea of a cause from that of a beginning of existence, is plainly possible for the imagination; and consequently the actual separation of these objects is so far possible, that it implies no contradiction nor absurdity; and is therefore incapable of being refuted by any reasoning from mere ideas; without which it is impossible to demonstrate the necessity of a cause.

Accordingly we shall find upon examination, that every demonstration, which has been produced for the necessity of a cause, is fallacious and sophistical. All the points of time and place, say some philosophers,* in which we can suppose any object to begin to exist, are in themselves equal; and unless there be some cause, which is peculiar to one time and to one place, and which by that means determines and fixes the existence, it must remain in eternal suspense; and the object can never begin to be, for want of something to fix its beginning. But I ask; Is there any more difficulty in supposing the time and place to be fixed without a cause, than to suppose the existence to be determined in that manner? The first question that occurs on this subject is always, *whether* the object shall exist or not: the next, *when* and *where* it shall begin to exist. If the removal of a cause be intuitively absurd in the one case, it must be so in the other: and if that absurdity be not clear without a proof in the one case, it will equally require one in the other. The absurdity, then, of the one supposition can never be a proof of that of the other; since they are both upon the same footing, and must stand or fall by the same reasoning.

The second argument,† which I find used on this head, labours under an equal difficulty. Every thing, it is said, must have a cause;

* Mr *Hobbes*.
† Dr *Clarke* and others.

for if any thing wanted a cause, *it* would produce *itself*; that is, exist before it existed; which is impossible. But this reasoning is plainly unconclusive; because it supposes, that in our denial of a cause we still grant what we expressly deny, *viz.* that there must be a cause; which therefore is taken to be the object itself; and *that*, no doubt, is an evident contradiction. But to say that any thing is produced, or to express myself more properly, comes into existence, without a cause, is not to affirm, that it is itself its own cause; but on the contrary in excluding all external causes, excludes *a fortiori* the thing itself, which is created. An object, that exists absolutely without any cause, certainly is not its own cause; and when you assert, that the one follows from the other, you suppose the very point in question, and take it for granted, that it is utterly impossible any thing can ever begin to exist without a cause, but that, upon the exclusion of one productive principle, we must still have recourse to another.

It is exactly the same case with the third argument,* which has been employed to demonstrate the necessity of a cause. Whatever is produced without any cause, is produced by *nothing*; or in other words, has nothing for its cause. But nothing can never be a cause, no more than it can be something, or equal to two right angles. By the same intuition, that we perceive nothing not to be equal to two right angles, or not to be something, we perceive, that it can never be a cause; and consequently must perceive, that every object has a real cause of its existence.

I believe it will not be necessary to employ many words in shewing the weakness of this argument, after what I have said of the foregoing. They are all of them founded on the same fallacy, and are derived from the same turn of thought. It is sufficient only to observe, that when we exclude all causes we really do exclude them, and neither suppose nothing nor the object itself to be the causes of the existence; and consequently can draw no argument from the absurdity of these suppositions to prove the absurdity of that exclusion. If every thing must have a cause, it follows, that upon the exclusion of other causes we must accept of the object itself or of nothing as causes. But it is the very point in question, whether every thing must have a cause or not; and therefore, according to all just reasoning, it ought never to be taken for granted.

* Mr *Locke*.

They are still more frivolous, who say, that every effect must have a cause, because it is implied in the very idea of effect. Every effect necessarily pre-supposes a cause; effect being a relative term, of which cause is the correlative. But this does not prove, that every being must be preceded by a cause; no more than it follows, because every husband must have a wife, that therefore every man must be married. The true state of the question is, whether every object, which begins to exist, must owe its existence to a cause: and this I assert neither to be intuitively nor demonstratively certain, and hope to have proved it sufficiently by the foregoing arguments.

Since it is not from knowledge or any scientific reasoning, that we derive the opinion of the necessity of a cause to every new production, that opinion must necessarily arise from observation and experience. The next question, then, should naturally be, *how experience gives rise to such a principle?* But as I find it will be more convenient to sink this question in the following, *Why we conclude, that such particular causes must necessarily have such particular effects, and why we form an inference from one to another?* we shall make that the subject of our future enquiry. It will, perhaps, be found in the end, that the same answer will serve for both questions.

SECTION FOUR

Of the component parts of our reasonings concerning cause and effect

Though the mind in its reasonings from causes or effects carries its view beyond those objects, which it sees or remembers, it must never lose sight of them entirely, nor reason merely upon its own ideas, without some mixture of impressions, or at least of ideas of the memory, which are equivalent to impressions. When we infer effects from causes, we must establish the existence of these causes; which we have only two ways of doing, either by an immediate perception of our memory or senses, or by an inference from other causes; which causes again we must ascertain in the same manner, either by a present impression, or by an inference from their causes, and so on, till we arrive at some object, which we see or remember. It is impossible for us to carry on our inferences *in infinitum*; and the only thing, that can stop them, is an impression of the memory or senses, beyond which there is no room for doubt or enquiry.

To give an instance of this, we may choose any point of history, and consider for what reason we either believe or reject it. Thus we believe that CAESAR was killed in the senate-house on the *Ides of March*; and that because this fact is established on the unanimous testimony of historians, who agree to assign this precise time and place to that event. Here are certain characters and letters present either to our memory or senses; which characters we likewise remember to have been used as the signs of certain ideas; and these ideas were either in the minds of such as were immediately present at that action, and received the ideas directly from its existence; or they were derived from the testimony of others, and that again from another testimony, by a visible gradation, till we arrive at those who were eyewitnesses and spectators of the event. It is obvious all this chain of argument or connexion of causes and effects, is at first founded on those characters or letters, which are seen or remembered, and that without the authority either of the memory or senses our whole reasoning would be chimerical and without foundation. Every link of the chain would in that case hang upon another; but there would not be any thing fixed to one end of it, capable of sustaining the whole; and consequently there would be no belief nor evidence. And this actually is the case with all *hypothetical* arguments, or reasonings upon a supposition; there being in them, neither any present impression, nor belief of a real existence.

I need not observe, that it is no just objection to the present doctrine, that we can reason upon our past conclusions or principles, without having recourse to those impressions, from which they first arose. For even supposing these impressions should be entirely effaced from the memory, the conviction they produced may still remain; and it is equally true, that all reasonings concerning causes and effects are originally derived from some impression; in the same manner, as the assurance of a demonstration proceeds always from a comparison of ideas, though it may continue after the comparison is forgot.

SECTION FIVE
Of the impressions of the senses and memory

In this kind of reasoning, then, from causation, we employ materials, which are of a mixed and heterogeneous nature, and which, however connected, are yet essentially different from each other. All our arguments concerning causes and effects consist both of an impression of the memory or senses, and of the idea of that existence, which produces the object of the impression, or is produced by it. Here therefore we have three things to explain, *viz*. *First*, The original impression. *Secondly*, The transition to the idea of the connected cause or effect. *Thirdly*, The nature and qualities of that idea.

As to those *impressions*, which arise from the *senses*, their ultimate cause is, in my opinion, perfectly inexplicable by human reason, and it will always be impossible to decide with certainty, whether they arise immediately from the object, or are produced by the creative power of the mind, or are derived from the author of our being. Nor is such a question any way material to our present purpose. We may draw inferences from the coherence of our perceptions, whether they be true or false; whether they represent nature justly, or be mere illusions of the senses.

When we search for the characteristic, which distinguishes the memory from the imagination, we must immediately perceive, that it cannot lie in the simple ideas it presents to us; since both these faculties borrow their simple ideas from the impressions, and can never go beyond these original perceptions. These faculties are as little distinguished from each other by the arrangement of their complex ideas. For though it be a peculiar property of the memory to preserve the original order and position of its ideas, while the imagination transposes and changes them, as it pleases; yet this difference is not sufficient to distinguish them in their operation, or make us know the one from the other; it being impossible to recall the past impressions, in order to compare them with our present ideas, and see whether their arrangement be exactly similar. Since therefore the memory is known, neither by the order of its *complex* ideas, nor the nature of its *simple* ones; it follows, that the difference betwixt it and the imagination lies in its superior force and vivacity. A man may indulge his fancy in feigning any past scene of adventures; nor would there be any possibility of distinguishing this from a remembrance of a like kind, were not the ideas of the imagination fainter and more obscure.*

A painter, who intended to represent a passion or emotion of any kind, would endeavour to get a sight of a person actuated by a like emotion, in order to enliven his ideas, and give them a force and vivacity superior to what is found in those, which are mere fictions of the imagination. The more recent this memory is, the clearer is the idea; and when after a long interval he would return to the contemplation of his object, he always finds its idea to be much decayed, if not wholly obliterated. We are frequently in doubt concerning the ideas of the memory, as they become very weak and feeble; and are at a loss to determine whether any image proceeds from the fancy or the memory, when it is not drawn in such lively colours as distinguish that latter faculty. I think I remember such an event, says one; but am not sure. A long tract of time has almost worn it out of my memory, and leaves me uncertain whether or not it be the pure offspring of my fancy.

And as an idea of the memory, by losing its force and vivacity, may degenerate to such a degree, as to be taken for an idea of the imagination; so on the other hand an idea of the imagination may acquire such a force and vivacity, as to pass for an idea of the memory, and counterfeit its effects on the belief and judgment. This is noted in the case of liars; who by the frequent repetition of their lies, come at last to believe and remember them, as realities; custom and habit having in this case, as in many others, the same influence on the mind as nature, and infixing the idea with equal force and vigour.

Thus it appears, that the *belief* or *assent*, which always attends the memory and senses, is nothing but the vivacity of those perceptions they present; and that this alone distinguishes them from the imagination. To believe is in this case to feel an immediate impression of the senses, or a repetition of that impression in the memory. It is merely the force and liveliness of the perception, which constitutes the first act of the judgment, and lays the foundation of that reasoning, which we build upon it, when we trace the relation of cause and effect.

[* see Appendix to the *Treatise*.]

SECTION SIX

Of the inference from the impression to the idea

It is easy to observe, that in tracing this relation, the inference we draw from cause to effect, is not derived merely from a survey of these particular objects, and from such a penetration into their essences as may discover the dependance of the one upon the other. There is no object, which implies the existence of any other if we consider these objects in themselves, and never look beyond the ideas which we form of them. Such an inference would amount to knowledge, and would imply the absolute contradiction and impossibility of conceiving any thing different. But as all distinct ideas are separable, it is evident there can be no impossibility of that kind. When we pass from a present impression to the idea of any object, we might possibly have separated the idea from the impression, and have substituted any other idea in its room.

It is therefore by EXPERIENCE only, that we can infer the existence of one object from that of another. The nature of experience is this. We remember to have had frequent instances of the existence of one species of objects; and also remember, that the individuals of another species of objects have always attended them, and have existed in a regular order of contiguity and succession with regard to them. Thus we remember, to have seen that species of object we call *flame*, and to have felt that species of sensation we call *heat*. We likewise call to mind their constant conjunction in all past instances. Without any farther ceremony, we call the one *cause* and the other *effect*, and infer the existence of the one from that of the other. In all those instances, from which we learn the conjunction of particular causes and effects, both the causes and effects have been perceived by the senses, and are remembered But in all cases, wherein we reason concerning them, there is only one perceived or remembered, and the other is supplied in conformity to our past experience.

Thus in advancing we have insensibly discovered a new relation betwixt cause and effect, when we least expected it, and were entirely employed upon another subject. This relation is their CONSTANT CONJUNCTION. Contiguity and succession are not sufficient to make us pronounce any two objects to be cause and effect, unless we perceive, that these two relations are preserved in several instances. We may now see the advantage of quitting the direct survey of this relation, in order to discover the nature of that *necessary connexion*, which makes so essential a part of it. There are hopes, that by this means we may at last arrive at our proposed end; though to tell the truth, this new-discovered relation of a constant conjunction seems to advance us but very little in our way. For it implies no more than this, that like objects have always been placed in like relations of contiguity and succession; and it seems evident, at least at first sight, that by this means we can never discover any new idea, and can only multiply, but not enlarge the objects of our mind. It may be thought, that what we learn not from one object, we can never learn from a hundred, which are all of the same kind, and are perfectly resembling in every circumstance. As our senses shew us in one instance two bodies, or motions, or qualities in certain relations of success and contiguity; so our memory presents us only with a multitude of instances, wherein we always find like bodies, motions, or qualities in like relations. From the mere repetition of any past impression, even to infinity, there never will arise any new original idea, such as that of a necessary connexion; and the number of impressions has in this case no more effect than if we confined ourselves to one only. But though this reasoning seems just and obvious; yet as it would be folly to despair too soon, we shall continue the thread of our discourse; and having found, that after the discovery of the constant conjunction of any objects, we always draw an inference from one object to another, we shall now examine the nature of that inference, and of the transition from the impression to the idea. Perhaps it will appear in the end, that the necessary connexion depends on the inference, instead of the inference's depending on the necessary connexion.

Since it appears, that the transition from an impression present to the memory or senses to the idea of an object, which we call cause or effect, is founded on past *experience*, and on our remembrance of their *constant conjunction*, the next question is, Whether experience produces the idea by means of the understanding or imagination; whether we are determined by reason to make the transition, or by a certain association and relation of perceptions. If reason determined us, it would proceed upon that principle, *that instances, of which we have had no experience, must resemble those, of which we have had experience, and that the course of nature continues always uniformly the same.* In order therefore to clear up this matter, let us consider all the arguments, upon which such a proposition may be supposed to be founded; and as these must be derived either from *knowledge* or *probability*, let us cast our eye on each of these degrees of evidence, and see whether they afford any just conclusion of this nature.

Our foregoing method of reasoning will easily convince us, that there can be no demonstrative arguments to prove, *that those instances, of which we have had no experience, resemble those, of which we have had experience.* We can at least conceive a change in the course of nature; which sufficiently proves, that such a change is not absolutely impossible. To form a clear idea of any thing, is an undeniable argument for its possibility, and is alone a refutation of any pretended demonstration against it.

Probability, as it discovers not the relations of ideas, considered as such, but only those of objects, must in some respects be founded on the impressions of our memory and senses, and in some respects on our ideas. Were there no mixture of any impression in our probable reasonings, the conclusion would be entirely chimerical: and were there no mixture of ideas, the action of the mind, in observing the relation, would, properly speaking, be sensation, not reasoning. It is therefore necessary, that in all probable reasonings there be something present to the mind, either seen or remembered; and that from this we infer something connected with it, which is not seen nor remembered.

The only connexion or relation of objects, which can lead us beyond the immediate impressions of our memory and senses, is that of cause and effect; and that because it is the only one, on which we can found a just inference from one object to another. The idea of cause and effect is derived from *experience*, which informs us, that such particular objects, in all past instances, have been constantly conjoined with each other: and as an object similar to one of these is supposed to be immediately present in its impression, we thence presume on the existence of one similar to its usual attendant. According to this account of things, which is, I think, in every point unquestionable, probability is founded on the presumption of a resemblance betwixt those objects, of which we have had experience, and those, of which we have had none; and therefore it is impossible this presumption can arise from probability. The same principle cannot be both the cause and effect of another; and this is, perhaps, the only proposition concerning that relation, which is either intuitively or demonstratively certain.

Should any one think to elude this argument; and without determining whether our reasoning on this subject be derived from demonstration or probability, pretend that all conclusions from causes and effects are built on solid reasoning: I can only desire, that this reasoning may be produced, in order to be exposed to our examination. It may, perhaps, be said, that after experience of the constant conjunction of certain objects, we reason in the following manner. Such an object is always found to produce another. It is impossible it could have this effect, if it was not endowed with a power of production. The power necessarily implies the effect; and therefore there is a just foundation for drawing a conclusion from the existence of one object to that of its usual attendant. The past production implies a power: the power implies a new production: and the new production is what we infer from the power and the past production.

It were easy for me to shew the weakness of this reasoning, were I willing to make use of those observations, I have already made, that the idea of *production* is the same with that of *causation*, and that no existence certainly and demonstratively implies a power in any other object; or were it proper to anticipate what I shall have occasion to remark afterwards concerning the idea we form of *power* and *efficacy*. But as such a method of proceeding may seem either to weaken my system, by resting one part of it on another, or to breed a confusion in my reasoning, I shall endeavour to maintain my present assertion without any such assistance.

It shall therefore be allowed for a moment, that the production of one object by another in any one instance implies a power; and that this power is connected with its effect. But it having been already proved, that the power lies not in the sensible qualities of the cause; and there being nothing but the sensible qualities present to us; I ask, why in other instances you presume that the same power still exists, merely upon the appearance of these qualities? Your appeal to past experience decides nothing in the present case; and at the utmost can only prove, that that very object, which produced any other, was at that very instant endowed with such a power; but can never prove, that the same power must continue in the same object or collection of sensible qualities; much less, that a like power is always conjoined with like sensible qualities. Should it be said, that we have experience, that the same power continues united with the same object, and that like objects are endowed with like powers, I would renew my question, *why from this experience we form any conclusion beyond those past instances, of which we have had experience.* If you answer this question in the same manner as the preceding, your answer gives still occasion to a new question of the same kind, even *in infinitum*; which clearly proves, that the foregoing reasoning had no just foundation.

Thus not only our reason fails us in the discovery of the *ultimate connexion* of causes and effects, but even after experience has informed us of their *constant conjunction*, it is impossible for us to satisfy ourselves by our reason, why we should extend that experience beyond those particular instances, which have fallen under our observation. We suppose, but are never able to prove, that there must be a resemblance betwixt those objects, of which we have had experience, and those which lie beyond the reach of our discovery.

We have already taken notice of certain relations, which make us pass from one object to another, even though there be no reason to determine us to that transition; and this we may establish for a general rule, that wherever the mind constantly and uniformly makes a transition without any reason, it is influenced by these relations. Now this is exactly the present case. Reason can never shew us the connexion of one object with another, though aided by experience, and the observation of their constant conjunction in all past instances. When the mind, therefore, passes from the idea or impression of one object to the idea or belief of another, it is not determined by reason, but by certain principles, which associate together the ideas of these objects, and unite them in the imagination. Had ideas no more union in the fancy than objects seem to have to the understanding, we could never draw any inference from causes to effects, nor repose belief in any matter of fact. The inference, therefore, depends solely on the union of ideas.

The principles of union among ideas, I have reduced to three general ones, and have asserted, that the idea or impression of any object naturally introduces the idea of any other object, that is resembling, contiguous to, or connected with it. These principles I allow to be neither the *infallible* nor the *sole* causes of an union among ideas. They are not the infallible causes. For one may fix his attention during some time on any one object without looking farther. They are not the sole causes. For the thought has evidently a very irregular motion in running along its objects, and may leap from the heavens to the earth, from one end of the creation to the other, without any certain method or order. But though I allow this weakness in these three relations, and this irregularity in the imagination; yet I assert that the only *general* principles, which associate ideas, are resemblance, contiguity and causation.

There is indeed a principle of union among ideas, which at first sight may be esteemed different from any of these, but will be found at the bottom to depend on the same origin. When every individual of any species of objects is found by experience to be constantly united with an individual of another species, the appearance of any new individual of either species naturally conveys the thought to its usual attendant. Thus because such a particular idea is commonly annexed to such a particular word, nothing is required but the hearing of that word to produce the correspondent idea; and it will scarce be possible for the mind, by its utmost efforts, to prevent that transition. In this case it is not absolutely necessary, that upon hearing such a particular sound we should reflect on any past experience, and consider what idea has been usually connected with the sound. The imagination of itself supplies the place of this reflection, and is so accustomed to pass from the word to the idea, that it interposes not a moment's delay betwixt the hearing of the one, and the conception of the other.

But though I acknowledge this to be a true principle of association among ideas, I assert it to be the very same with that betwixt the ideas of cause and effect, and to be an essential part in all our reasonings from that relation. We have no other notion of cause and effect, but that of certain objects, which have been *always conjoined* together, and which in all past instances have been found inseparable. We cannot penetrate into the reason of the conjunction. We only observe the thing itself, and always find that from the constant conjunction the objects acquire an union in the imagination. When the impression of one becomes present to us, we immediately form an idea of its usual attendant; and consequently we may establish this as one part of the definition of an opinion or belief, that it is *an idea related to or associated with a present impression*.

Thus though causation be a *philosophical* relation, as implying contiguity, succession, and constant conjunction, yet it is only so far as it is a *natural* relation, and produces an union among our ideas, that we are able to reason upon it, or draw any inference from it.

SECTION SEVEN
Of the nature of the idea or belief

The idea of an object is an essential part of the belief of it, but not the whole. We conceive many things, which we do not believe. In order then to discover more fully the nature of belief, or the qualities of those ideas we assent to, let us weigh the following considerations.

It is evident, that all reasonings from causes or effects terminate in conclusions, concerning matter of fact; that is, concerning the existence of objects or of their qualities. It is also evident, that the idea of existence is nothing different from the idea of any object, and that when after the simple conception of any thing we would conceive it as existent, we in reality make no addition to or alteration on our first idea. Thus when we affirm, that God is existent, we simply form the idea of such a being, as he is represented to us; nor is the existence, which we attribute to him, conceived by a particular idea, which we join to the idea of his other qualities, and can again separate and distinguish from them. But I go farther; and not content with asserting, that the conception of the existence of any object is no addition to the simple conception of it, I likewise maintain, that the belief of the existence joins no new ideas to those which compose the idea of the object. When I think of God, when I think of him as existent, and when I believe him to be existent, my idea of him neither increases nor diminishes. But as it is certain there is a great diff-erence betwixt the simple conception of the existence of an object, and the belief of it, and as this difference lies not in the parts or composition of the idea, which we conceive; it follows, that it must lie in the *manner*, in which we conceive it.

Suppose a person present with me, who advances propositions, to which I do not assent, *that Caesar died in his bed, that silver is more fusible than lead, or mercury heavier than gold*; it is evident, that notwithstanding my incredulity, I clearly understand his meaning, and form all the same ideas, which he forms. My imagination is endowed with the same powers as his; nor is it possible for him to conceive any idea, which I cannot conceive; nor conjoin any, which I cannot conjoin. I therefore ask, Wherein consists the difference betwixt believing and disbelieving any proposition? The answer is easy with regard to propositions, that are proved by intuition or demonstration. In that case, the person, who assents, not only conceives the ideas according to the proposition, but is necessarily determined to conceive them in that particular manner, either immediately or by the interposition of other ideas. Whatever is absurd is unintelligible; nor is it possible for the imagination to conceive any thing contrary to a demonstration. But as in reasonings from causation, and concerning matters of fact, this absolute necessity cannot take place, and the imagination is free to conceive both sides of the question, I still ask, *Wherein consists the difference betwixt incredulity and belief*? since in both cases the conception of the idea is equally possible and requisite.

It will not be a satisfactory answer to say, that a person, who does not assent to a proposition you advance, after having conceived the object in the same manner with you, immediately conceives it in a different manner, and has different ideas of it. This answer is unsatisfactory; not because it contains any falsehood, but because it discovers not all the truth. It is confessed, that in all cases, wherein we dissent from any person, we conceive both sides of the question; but as we can believe only one, it evidently follows, that the belief must make some difference betwixt that conception to which we assent, and that from which we dissent. We may mingle, and unite, and separate, and confound, and vary our ideas in a hundred different ways; but until there appears some principle, which fixes one of these different situations, we have in reality no opinion: and this principle, as it plainly makes no addition to our precedent ideas, can only change the *manner* of our conceiving them.

All the perceptions of the mind are of two kinds, *viz*. impressions and ideas, which differ from each other only in their different degrees of force and vivacity. Our ideas are copied from our impressions, and represent them in all their parts. When you would any way vary the idea of a particular object, you can only increase or diminish its force and vivacity. If you make any other change on it, it represents a different object or impression. The case is the same as in colours. A particular shade of any colour may acquire a new degree of liveliness or brightness without any other variation. But when you produce any other variation, it is no longer the same shade or colour. So that as belief does nothing but vary the manner, in which we conceive any object, it can only bestow on our ideas an additional force and vivacity. An opinion, therefore, or belief may be most accurately defined, A LIVELY IDEA RELATED TO OR ASSOCIATED WITH A PRESENT IMPRESSION.*

* We may here take occasion to observe a very remarkable error, which being frequently inculcated in the schools, has become a kind of establishd maxim, and is universally received by all logicians. This error consists in the vulgar division of the acts of the understanding, into *conception*, *judgment* and *reasoning*, and in the definitions we give of them. Conception is defined to be the simple survey of one or more ideas: Judgment to be the separating or uniting of different ideas: Reasoning to be the separating or uniting of different ideas by the interposition of others, which show the relation they bear to each other. But these distinctions and definitions are faulty in very considerable articles. For *first*, it is far from being true, that in every judgment, which we form, we unite two different ideas; since in that proposition, *God is*, or indeed any other, which regards existence, the idea of existence is no distinct idea, which we unite with that of the object, and which is capable of forming a compound idea by the union. *Secondly*, As we can thus form a proposition, which contains only one idea, so we may exert our reason without employing more than two ideas, and without having recourse to a third to serve as a medium betwixt them. We infer a cause immediately from its effect; and this inference is not only a true species of reasoning, but the strongest of all others, and more convincing than when we interpose another idea to connect the two extremes. What we may in general affirm concerning these three acts of the understanding is, that taking them in a proper light, they all resolve themselves into the first, and are nothing but particular ways of conceiving our objects. Whether we consider a single object, or several; whether we dwell on these objects, or run from them to others; and in whatever form or order we survey them, the act of the mind exceeds not a simple conception; and the only remarkable difference, which occurs on this occasion, is, when we join belief to the conception, and are persuaded of the truth of what we conceive. This act of the mind has never yet been explaind by any philosopher; and therefore I am at liberty to propose my hypothesis concerning it; which is, that it is only a strong and steady conception of any idea, and such as approaches in some measure to an immediate impression.

Here are the heads of those arguments, which lead us to this conclusion. When we infer the existence of an object from that of others, some object must always be present either to the memory or senses, in order to be the foundation of our reasoning; since the mind cannot run up with its inferences *in infinitum*. Reason can never satisfy us that the existence of any one object does ever imply that of another; so that when we pass from the impression of one to the idea or belief of another, we are not determined by reason, but by custom or a principle of association. But belief is somewhat more than a simple idea. It is a particular manner of forming an idea: and as the same idea can only be varied by a variation of its degrees of force and vivacity; it follows upon the whole, that belief is a lively idea produced by a relation to a present impression, according to the foregoing definition.*

This definition will also be found to be entirely conformable to every one's feeling and experience. Nothing is more evident, than that those ideas, to which we assent, are more strong, firm and vivid, than the loose reveries of a castle-builder. If one person sits down to read a book as a romance, and another as a true history, they plainly receive the same ideas, and in the same order; nor does the incredulity of the one, and the belief of the other hinder them from putting the very same sense upon their author. His words produce the same ideas in both; though his testimony has not the same influence on them. The latter has a more lively conception of all the incidents. He enters deeper into the concerns of the persons: represents to himself their actions, and characters, and friendships, and enmities: he even goes so far as to form a notion of their features, and air, and person. While the former, who gives no credit to the testimony of the author, has a more faint and languid conception of all these particulars; and except on account of the style and ingenuity of the composition, can receive little entertainment from it.

[* see Appendix to the *Treatise*.]

Of the causes of belief

Having thus explained the nature of belief, and shewn that it consists in a lively idea related to a present impression; let us now proceed to examine from what principles it is derived, and what bestows the vivacity on the idea.

I would willingly establish it as a general maxim in the science of human nature, *that when any impression becomes present to us, it not only transports the mind to such ideas as are related to it, but likewise communicates to them a share of its force and vivacity.* All the operations of the mind depend in a great measure on its disposition, when it performs them; and according as the spirits are more or less elevated, and the attention more or less fixed, the action will always have more or less vigour and vivacity. When therefore any object is presented, which elevates and enlivens the thought, every action, to which the mind applies itself, will be more strong and vivid, as long as that disposition continues, Now it is evident the continuance of the disposition depends entirely on the objects, about which the mind is employed; and that any new object naturally gives a new direction to the spirits, and changes the disposition; as on the contrary, when the mind fixes constantly on the same object, or passes easily and insensibly along related objects, the disposition has a much longer duration. Hence it happens, that when the mind is once enlivened by a present impression, it proceeds to form a more lively idea of the related objects, by a natural transition of the disposition from the one to the other. The change of the objects is so easy, that the mind is scarce sensible of it, but applies itself to the conception of the related idea with all the force and vivacity it acquired from the present impression.

If in considering the nature of relation, and that facility of transition, which is essential to it, we can satisfy ourselves concerning the reality of this phenomenon, it is well: but I must confess I place my chief confidence in experience to prove so material a principle. We may, therefore, observe, as the first experiment to our present purpose, that upon the appearance of the picture of an absent friend, our idea of him is evidently enlivened by the *resemblance*, and that every passion, which that idea occasions, whether of joy or sorrow, acquires new force and vigour. In producing this effect there concur both a relation and a present impression. Where the picture bears him no resemblance, or at least was not intended for him, it never so much as conveys our thought to him: and where it is absent, as well as the person; though the mind may pass from the thought of the one to that of the other; it feels its idea to be rather weakened than enlivened by that transition. We take a pleasure in viewing the picture of a friend, when it is set before us; but when it is removed, rather choose to consider him directly, than by reflexion in an image, which is equally distinct and obscure.

The ceremonies of the *Roman Catholic* religion may be considered as experiments of the same nature. The devotees of that strange superstition usually plead in excuse of the mummeries, with which they are upbraided, that they feel the good effect of those external motions, and postures, and actions, in enlivening their devotion, and quickening their fervour, which otherwise would decay away, if directed entirely to distant and immaterial objects. We shadow out the objects of our faith, say they, in sensible types and images, and render them more present to us by the immediate presence of these types, than it is possible for us to do, merely by an intellectual view and contemplation. Sensible objects have always a greater influence on the fancy than any other; and this influence they readily convey to those ideas, to which they are related, and which they resemble. I shall only infer from these practices, and this reasoning, that the effect of resemblance in enlivening the idea is very common; and as in every case a resemblance and a present impression must concur, we are abundantly supplied with experiments to prove the reality of the foregoing principle.

We may add force to these experiments by others of a different kind, in considering the effects of *contiguity*, as well as of *resemblance*. It is certain, that distance diminishes the force of every idea, and that upon our approach to any object, though it does not discover itself to our senses, it operates upon the mind with an influence that imitates an immediate impression.* The thinking on any object readily transports the mind to what is contiguous; but it is only the actual presence of an object, that transports it with a

[* see Appendix to the *Treatise*.]

superior vivacity. When I am a few miles from home, whatever relates to it touches me more nearly than when I am two hundred leagues distant; though even at that distance the reflecting on any thing in the neighbourhood of my friends and family naturally produces an idea of them. But as in this latter case, both the objects of the mind are ideas; notwithstanding there is an easy transition betwixt them; that transition alone is not able to give a superior vivacity to any of the ideas, for want of some immediate impression.

No one can doubt but causation has the same influence as the other two relations; of resemblance and contiguity. Superstitious people are fond of the relicks of saints and holy men, for the same reason that they seek after types and images, in order to enliven their devotion, and give them a more intimate and strong conception of those exemplary lives, which they desire to imitate. Now it is evident, one of the best relicks a devotee could procure, would be the handywork of a saint; and if his clothes and furniture are ever to be considered in this light, it is because they were once at his disposal, and were moved and affected by him; in which respect they are to be considered as imperfect effects, and as connected with him by a shorter chain of consequences than any of those, from which we learn the reality of his existence. This phenomenon clearly proves, that a present impression with a relation of causation may enliven any idea, and consequently produce belief or assent, according to the precedent definition of it.

But why need we seek for other arguments to prove, that a present impression with a relation or transition of the fancy may enliven any idea, when this very instance of our reasonings from cause and effect will alone suffice to that purpose? It is certain we must have an idea of every matter of fact, which we believe. It is certain, that this idea arises only from a relation to a present impression. It is certain, that the belief super-adds nothing to the idea, but only changes our manner of conceiving it, and renders it more strong and lively. The present conclusion concerning the influence of relation is the immediate consequence of all these steps; and every step appears to me sure and infallible. There enters nothing into this operation of the mind but a present impression, a lively idea, and a relation or association in the fancy betwixt the impression and idea; so that there can be no suspicion of mistake.

In order to put this whole affair in a fuller light, let us consider it as a question in natural philosophy, which we must determine by experience and observation. I suppose there is an object presented, from which I draw a certain conclusion, and form to myself ideas, which I am said to believe or assent to. Here it is evident, that however that object, which is present to my senses, and that other, whose existence I infer by reasoning, may be thought to influence each other by their particular powers or qualities; yet as the phenomenon of belief, which we at present examine, is merely internal, these powers and qualities, being entirely unknown, can have no hand in producing it. It is the present impression, which is to be considered as the true and real cause of the idea, and of the belief which attends it. We must therefore endeavour to discover by experiments the particular qualities, by which it is enabled to produce so extraordinary an effect.

First then I observe, that the present impression has not this effect by its own proper power and efficacy, and when considered alone, as a single perception, limited to the present moment. I find, that an impression, from which, on its first appearance, I can draw no conclusion, may afterwards become the foundation of belief, when I have had experience of its usual consequences. We must in every case have observed the same impression in past instances, and have found it to be constantly conjoined with some other impression. This is confirmed by such a multitude of experiments, that it admits not of the smallest doubt.

From a second observation I conclude, that the belief, which attends the present impression, and is produced by a number of past impressions and conjunctions; that this belief, I say, arises immediately, without any new operation of the reason or imagination. Of this I can be certain, because I never am conscious of any such operation, and find nothing in the subject, on which it can be founded. Now as we call every thing CUSTOM, which proceeds from a past repetition, without any new reasoning or conclusion, we may establish it as a certain truth, that all the belief, which follows upon any present impression, is derived solely from that origin. When we are accustomed to see two impressions conjoined together, the appearance or idea of the one immediately carries us to the idea of the other.

Being fully satisfied on this head, I make a third set of experiments, in order to know, whether any thing be requisite, beside the customary transition, towards the production of this phenomenon of belief. I therefore change the first impression into an idea; and observe, that though the customary transition to the correlative idea still remains, yet there is in reality no belief nor persuasion. A present impression, then, is absolutely requisite to this whole operation; and when after this I compare an impression with an idea, and find that their only difference consists in their different degrees of force and vivacity, I conclude upon the whole, that belief is a more vivid and intense conception of an idea, proceeding from its relation to a present impression.

Thus all probable reasoning is nothing but a species of sensation. It is not solely in poetry and music, we must follow our taste and sentiment, but likewise in philosophy. When I am convinced of any principle, it is only an idea, which strikes more strongly upon me. When I give the preference to one set of arguments above another, I do nothing but decide from my feeling concerning the superiority of their influence. Objects have no discoverable connexion together; nor is it from any other principle but custom operating upon the imagination, that we can draw any inference from the appearance of one to the existence of another.

It will here be worth our observation, that the past experience, on which all our judgments concerning cause and effect depend, may operate on our mind in such an insensible manner as never to be taken notice of, and may even in some measure be unknown to us. A person, who stops short in his journey upon meeting a river in his way, foresees the consequences of his proceeding forward; and his knowledge of these consequences is conveyed to him by past experience, which informs him of such certain conjunctions of causes and effects. But can we think, that on this occasion he reflects on any past experience, and calls to remembrance instances, that he has seen or heard of, in order to discover the effects of water on animal bodies? No surely; this is not the method, in which he proceeds in his reasoning. The idea of sinking is so closely connected with that of water, and the idea of suffocating with that of sinking, that the mind makes the transition without the assistance of the memory. The custom operates before we have time for reflection. The objects seem so inseparable, that we interpose not a moment's delay in passing from the one to the other. But as this transition proceeds from experience, and not from any primary connexion betwixt the ideas, we must necessarily acknowledge, that experience may produce a belief and a judgment of causes and effects by a secret operation, and without being once thought of. This removes all pretext, if there yet remains any, for asserting that the mind is convinced by reasoning of that principle, *that instances of which we have no experience, must necessarily resemble those, of which we have*. For we here find, that the understanding or imagination can draw inferences from past experience, without reflecting on it; much more without forming any principle concerning it, or reasoning upon that principle.

In general we may observe, that in all the most established and uniform conjunctions of causes and effects, such as those of gravity, impulse, solidity, &c. the mind never carries its view expressly to consider any past experience: though in other associations of objects, which are more rare and unusual, it may assist the custom and transition of ideas by this reflection. Nay we find in some cases, that the reflection produces the belief without the custom; or more properly speaking, that the reflection produces the custom in an *oblique* and *artificial* manner. I explain myself. It is certain, that not only in philosophy, but even in common life, we may attain the knowledge of a particular cause merely by one experiment, provided it be made with judgment, and after a careful removal of all foreign and superfluous circumstances. Now as after one experiment of this kind, the mind, upon the appearance either of the cause or the effect, can draw an inference concerning the existence of its correlative; and as a habit can never be acquired merely by one instance; it may be thought, that belief cannot in this case be esteemed the effect of custom. But this difficulty will vanish, if we consider, that though we are here supposed to have had only one experiment of a particular effect, yet we have many millions to convince us of this principle; *that like objects placed in like circumstances, will always produce like effects*; and as this principle has established itself by a sufficient custom, it bestows an evidence and firmness on any opinion, to which it can be applied. The connexion of the ideas is not habitual after one experiment: but this connexion is comprehended under another principle, that is habitual; which brings us back to our hypothesis. In all cases we transfer our experience to instances, of which we have no experience, either *expressly* or *tacitly*, either *directly* or *indirectly*.

I must not conclude this subject without observing, that it is very difficult to talk of the operations of the mind with perfect propriety and exactness; because common language has seldom made any very nice distinctions among them, but has generally called by the same term all such as nearly resemble each other. And as this is a source almost inevitable of obscurity and confusion in the author; so it may frequently give rise to doubts and objections in the reader, which otherwise he would never have dreamed of. Thus my general position, that an opinion or belief is *nothing but a strong and lively idea derived from a present impression related to it*, maybe liable to the following objection, by reason of a little ambiguity in those words *strong and lively*. It may be said, that not only an impression may give rise to reasoning, but that an idea may also have the same influence; especially upon my principle, *that all our ideas are derived from correspondent impressions*. For suppose I form at present an idea, of which I have forgot the correspondent impression, I am able to conclude from this idea, that such an impression did once exist; and as this conclusion is attended with belief, it may be asked, from whence are the qualities of force and vivacity derived, which constitute this belief? And to this I answer very readily, *from the present idea*. For as this idea is not here considered, as the representation of any absent object, but as a real perception in the mind, of which we are intimately conscious, it must be able to bestow on whatever is related to it the same quality, call it *firmness, or solidity, or force, or vivacity*, with which the mind reflects upon it, and is assured of its present existence. The idea here supplies the place of an impression, and is entirely the same, so far as regards our present purpose.

Upon the same principles we need not be surprized to hear of the remembrance of an idea: that is, of the idea of an idea, and of its force and vivacity superior to the loose conceptions of the imagination. In thinking of our past thoughts we not only delineate out the objects, of which we were thinking, but also conceive the action of the mind in the meditation, that certain *je-ne-scai-quoi*, of which it is impossible to give any definition or description, but which every one sufficiently understands. When the memory offers an idea of this, and represents it as past, it is easily conceived how that idea may have more vigour and firmness, than when we think of a past thought, of which we have no remembrance.

After this any one will understand how we may form the idea of an impression and of an idea, and how we way believe the existence of an impression and of an idea.

SECTION NINE

Of the effects of other relations and other habits

However convincing the foregoing arguments may appear, we must not rest contented with them, but must turn the subject on every side, in order to find some new points of view, from which we may illustrate and confirm such extraordinary, and such fundamental principles. A scrupulous hesitation to receive any new hypothesis is so laudable a disposition in philosophers, and so necessary to the examination of truth, that it deserves to be complied with, and requires that every argument be produced, which may tend to their satisfaction, and every objection removed, which may stop them in their reasoning.

I have often observed, that, beside cause and effect, the two relations of resemblance and contiguity, are to be considered as associating principles of thought, and as capable of conveying the imagination from one idea to another. I have also observed, that when of two objects connected together by any of these relations, one is immediately present to the memory or senses, not only the mind is conveyed to its co-relative by means of the associating principle; but likewise conceives it with an additional force and vigour, by the united operation of that principle, and of the present impression. All this I have observed, in order to confirm by analogy, my explication of our judgments concerning cause and effect. But this very argument may, perhaps, be turned against me, and instead of a confirmation of my hypothesis, may become an objection to it. For it may be said, that if all the parts of that hypothesis be true, *viz. that* these three species of relation are derived from the same principles; *that* their effects in informing and enlivening our ideas are the same; and *that* belief is nothing but a more forcible and vivid conception of an idea; it should follow, that that action of the mind may not only be derived from the relation of cause and effect, but also from those of contiguity and resemblance. But as we find by experience, that belief arises only from causation, and that we can draw no inference from one object to another, except they be connected by this relation, we may conclude, that there is some error in that reasoning, which leads us into such difficulties.

This is the objection; let us now consider its solution. It is evident, that whatever is present to the memory, striking upon the mind with a vivacity, which resembles an immediate impression, must become of considerable moment in all the operations of the mind, and must easily distinguish itself above the mere fictions of the imagination. Of these impressions or ideas of the memory we form a kind of system, comprehending whatever we remember to have been present, either to our internal perception or senses; and every particular of that system, joined to the present impressions, we are pleased to call a *reality*. But the mind stops not here. For finding, that with this system of perceptions, there is another connected by custom, or if you will, by the relation of cause or effect, it proceeds to the consideration of their ideas; and as it feels that it is in a manner necessarily determined to view these particular ideas, and that the custom or relation, by which it is determined, admits not of the least change, it forms them into a new system, which it likewise dignifies with the title of *realities*. The first of these systems is the object of the memory and senses; the second of the judgment.

It is this latter principle, which peoples the world, and brings us acquainted with such existences, as by their removal in time and place, lie beyond the reach of the senses and memory. By means of it I paint the universe in my imagination, and fix my attention on any part of it I please. I form an idea of ROME, which I neither see nor remember; but which is connected with such impressions as I remember to have received from the conversation and books of travellers and historians. This idea of *Rome* I place in a certain situation on the idea of an object, which I call the globe. I join to it the conception of a particular government, and religion, and manners. I look backward and consider its first foundation; its several revolutions, successes, and misfortunes. All this, and every-thing else, which I believe, are nothing but ideas; though by their force and settled order, arising from custom and the relation of cause and effect, they distinguish themselves from the other ideas, which are merely the offspring of the imagination.

As to the influence of contiguity and resemblance, we may observe, that if the contiguous and resembling object be com-prehended in this system of realities, there is no doubt but these two relations will assist that of cause and effect, and infix the related idea with more force in the imagination. This I shall enlarge upon presently. Mean while I shall carry my observation a step farther, and assert, that even where the related object is but feigned, the relation will serve to enliven the idea, and increase its influence. A poet, no doubt, will be the better able to form a strong description of the *Elysian* fields, that he prompts his imagination by the view of a beautiful meadow or garden; as at another time he may by his fancy place himself in the midst of these fabulous regions, that by the feigned contiguity he may enliven his imagination.

But though I cannot altogether exclude the relations of resem-blance and contiguity from operating on the fancy in this manner, it is observable that, when single, their influence is very feeble and uncertain. As the relation of cause and effect is requisite to persuade us of any real existence, so is this persuasion requisite to give force to these other relations. For where upon the appearance of an impression we not only feign another object, but likewise arbitrarily, and of our mere good-will and pleasure give it a particular relation to the impression, this can have but a small effect upon the mind; nor is there any reason, why, upon the return of the same impression, we should be determined to place the same object in the same relation to it. There is no manner of necessity for the mind to feign any resembling and contiguous objects; and if it feigns such, there is as little necessity for it always to confine itself to the same, without any difference or variation. And indeed such a fiction is founded on so little reason, that nothing but pure *caprice* can determine the mind to form it; and that principle being fluctuating and uncertain, it is impossible it can ever operate with any considerable degree of force and con-stancy. The mind foresees and anticipates the change; and even from the very first instant feels the looseness of its actions, and the weak hold it has of its objects. And as this imperfection is very sensible in every single instance, it still increases by experience and observation, when we compare the several instances we may remember, and form a *general rule* against the reposing any assurance in those momentary glimpses of light, which arise in the imagination from a feigned resemblance and contiguity.

The relation of cause and effect has all the opposite advantages. The objects it presents are fixed and unalterable. The impressions of the memory never change in any considerable degree; and each impression draws along with it a precise idea, which takes its place in the imagination as something solid and real, certain and invariable. The thought is always determined to pass from the impression to the idea, and from that particular impression to that particular idea, without any choice or hesitation.

But not content with removing this objection, I shall endeavour to extract from it a proof of the present doctrine. Contiguity and resemblance have an effect much inferior to causation; but still have some effect, and augment the conviction of any opinion, and the vivacity of any conception. If this can be proved in several new instances, beside what we have already observed, it will be allowed no inconsiderable argument, that belief is nothing but a lively idea related to a present impression.

To begin with contiguity; it has been remarked among the *Mahometans* as well as *Christians*, that those *pilgrims*, who have seen MECCA or the HOLY LAND, are ever after more faithful and zealous believers, than those who have not had that advantage. A man, whose memory presents him with a lively image of the *Red-Sea, and the Desert, and Jerusalem, and Galilee*, can never doubt of any miraculous events, which are related either by *Moses or the Evangelists*. The lively idea of the places passes by an easy transition to the facts, which are supposed to have been related to them by contiguity, and increases the belief by increasing the vivacity of the conception. The remembrance of these fields and rivers has the same influence on the vulgar as a new argument; and from the same causes.

We may form a like observation concerning *resemblance*. We have remarked, that the conclusion, which we draw from a present object to its absent cause or effect, is never founded on any qualities, which we observe in that object, considered in itself, or, in other words, that it is impossible to determine, otherwise than by experience, what will result from any phenomenon, or what has preceded it. But though this be so evident in itself, that it seemed not to require any proof; yet some philosophers have imagined that there is an apparent cause for the communication of motion, and that a reasonable man might immediately infer the motion of one body from the impulse of another, without having recourse to any past observation. That this opinion is false will admit of an easy proof. For if such an inference may be drawn merely from the ideas of body, of motion, and of impulse, it must amount to a demonstration, and must imply the absolute impossibility of any contrary supposition. Every effect, then, beside the communication of motion, implies a formal contradiction; and it is impossible not only that it can exist, but also that it can be conceived. But we may soon satisfy ourselves of the contrary, by forming a clear and consistent idea of one body's moving upon another, and of its rest immediately upon the contact, or of its returning back in the same line in which it came; or of its annihilation; or circular or elliptical motion: and in short, of an infinite number of other changes, which we may suppose it to undergo. These suppositions are all consistent and natural; and the reason, Why we imagine the communication of motion to be more consistent and natural not only than those suppositions, but also than any other natural effect, is founded on the relation of *resemblance* betwixt the cause and effect, which is here united to experience, and binds the objects in the closest and most intimate manner to each other, so as to make us imagine them to be absolutely inseparable. Resemblance, then, has the same or a parallel influence with experience; and as the only immediate effect of experience is to associate our ideas together, it follows, that all belief arises from the association of ideas, according to my hypothesis.

It is universally allowed by the writers on optics, that the eye at all times sees an equal number of physical points, and that a man on the top of a mountain has no larger an image presented to his senses, than when he is cooped up in the narrowest court or chamber. It is only by experience that he infers the greatness of the object from some peculiar qualities of the image; and this inference of the judgment he confounds with sensation, as is common on other occasions. Now it is evident, that the inference of the judgment is here much more lively than what is usual in our common reasonings, and that a man has a more vivid conception of the vast extent of the ocean from the image he receives by the eye, when he stands on the top of the high promontory, than merely from hearing the roaring of the waters. He feels a more sensible pleasure from its magnificence; which is a proof of a more lively idea: and he confounds his judgment with sensation, which is another proof of it. But as the inference is equally certain and immediate in both cases, this superior vivacity of our conception in one case can proceed from nothing but this, that in drawing an inference from the sight, beside the customary conjunction, there is also a resemblance betwixt the image and the object we infer; which strengthens the relation, and conveys the vivacity of the impression to the related idea with an easier and more natural movement.

No weakness of human nature is more universal and conspicuous than what we commonly call CREDULITY, or a too easy faith in the testimony of others; and this weakness is also very naturally accounted for from the influence of resemblance. When we receive any matter of fact upon human testimony, our faith arises from the very same origin as our inferences from causes to effects, and from effects to causes; nor is there anything but our *experience* of the governing principles of human nature, which can give us any assurance of the veracity of men. But though experience be the true standard of this, as well as of all other judgments, we seldom regulate ourselves entirely by it; but have a remarkable propensity to believe whatever is reported, even concerning apparitions, enchantments, and prodigies, however contrary to daily experience and observation. The words or discourses of others have an intimate connexion with certain ideas in their mind; and these ideas have also a connexion with the facts or objects, which they represent. This latter connexion is generally much over-rated, and commands our assent beyond what experience will justify; which can proceed from nothing beside the resemblance betwixt the ideas and the facts. Other effects only point out their causes in an oblique manner; but the testimony of men does it directly, and is to be considered as an image as well as an effect. No wonder, therefore, we are so rash in drawing our inferences from it, and are less guided by experience in our judgments concerning it, than in those upon any other subject.

As resemblance, when conjoined with causation, fortifies our reasonings; so the want of it in any very great degree is able almost entirely to destroy them. Of this there is a remarkable instance in the universal carelessness and stupidity of men with regard to a future state, where they show as obstinate an incredulity, as they do a blind credulity on other occasions. There is not indeed a more ample matter of wonder to the studious, and of regret to the pious man, than to observe the negligence of the bulk of mankind concerning their approaching condition; and it is with reason, that many eminent theologians have not scrupled to affirm, that though the vulgar have no formal principles of infidelity, yet they are really infidels in their hearts, and have nothing like what we can call a belief of the eternal duration of their souls. For let us consider on the one hand what divines have displayed with such eloquence concerning the importance of eternity; and at the same time reflect, that though in matters of rhetoric we ought to lay our account with some exaggeration, we must in this case allow, that the strongest figures are infinitely inferior to the subject: and after this let us view on the other hand, the prodigious security of men in this particular: I ask, if these people really believe what is inculcated on them, and what they pretend to affirm; and the answer is obviously in the negative. As belief is an act of the mind arising from custom, it is not strange the want of resemblance should overthrow what custom has established, and diminish the force of the idea, as much as that latter principle increases it. A future state is so far removed from our comprehension, and we have so obscure an idea of the manner, in which we shall exist after the dissolution of the body, that all the reasons we can invent, however strong in themselves, and however much assisted by education, are never able with slow imaginations to surmount this difficulty, or bestow a sufficient authority and force on the idea. I rather choose to ascribe this incredulity to the faint idea we form of our future condition, derived from its want of resemblance to the present life, than to that derived from its remoteness. For I observe, that men are everywhere concerned about what may happen after their death, provided it regard this world; and that there are few to whom their name, their family, their friends, and their country are in any period of time entirely indifferent.

And indeed the want of resemblance in this case so entirely destroys belief, that except those few, who upon cool reflection on the importance of the subject, have taken care by repeated meditation to imprint in their minds the arguments for a future state, there scarce are any, who believe the immortality of the soul with a true and established judgment; such as is derived from the testimony of travellers and historians. This appears very conspicuously wherever men have occasion to compare the pleasures and pains, the rewards and punishments of this life with those of a future; even though the case does not concern themselves, and there is no violent passion to disturb their judgment. The *Roman Catholicks* are certainly the most zealous of any sect in the Christian world; and yet you'll find few among the more sensible people of that communion who do not blame the *Gunpowder-treason*, and the massacre of *St Bartholomew*, as cruel and barbarous, though projected or executed against those very people, whom without any scruple they condemn to eternal and infinite punishments. All we can say in excuse for this inconsistency is, that they really do not believe what they affirm concerning a future state; nor is there any better proof of it than the very inconsistency.

We may add to this a remark; that in matters of religion men take a pleasure in being terrified, and that no preachers are so popular, as those who excite the most dismal and gloomy passions. In the common affairs of life, where we feel and are penetrated with the solidity of the subject, nothing can be more disagreeable than fear and terror; and it is only in dramatic performances and in religious discourses, that they ever give pleasure. In these latter cases the imagination reposes itself indolently on the idea; and the passion, being softened by the want of belief in the subject, has no more than the agreeable effect of enlivening the mind, and fixing the attention.

The present hypothesis will receive additional confirmation, if we examine the effects of other kinds of custom, as well as of other relations. To understand this we must consider, that custom, to which I attribute all belief and reasoning, may operate upon the mind in invigorating an idea after two several ways. For supposing that in all past experience we have found two objects to have been always conjoined together, it is evident, that upon the appearance of one of these objects in an impression, we must from custom make an easy transition to the idea of that object, which usually attends it; and by means of the present impression and easy transition must conceive that idea in a stronger and more lively manner, than we do any loose floating image of the fancy. But let us next suppose, that a mere idea alone, without any of this curious and almost artificial preparation, should frequently make its appearance in the mind, this idea must by degrees acquire a facility and force; and both by its firm hold and easy introduction distinguish itself from any new and unusual idea. This is the only particular, in which these two kinds of custom agree; and if it appear, that their effects on the judgment, are similar and proportionable, we may certainly conclude, that the foregoing explication of that faculty is satisfactory. But can we doubt of this agreement in their influence on the judgment, when we consider the nature and effects of EDUCATION?

All those opinions and notions of things, to which we have been accustomed from our infancy, take such deep root, that it is impossible for us, by all the powers of reason and experience, to eradicate them; and this habit not only approaches in its influence, but even on many occasions prevails over that which arises from the constant and inseparable union of causes and effects. Here we most not be contented with saying, that the vividness of the idea produces the belief: we must maintain that they are individually the same. The frequent repetition of any idea infixes it in the imagination; but could never possibly of itself produce belief, if that act of the mind was, by the original constitution of our natures, annexed only to a reasoning and comparison of ideas. Custom may lead us into some false comparison of ideas. This is the utmost effect we can conceive of it. But it is certain it could never supply the place of that comparison, nor produce any act of the mind, which naturally belonged to that principle.

A person, that has lost a leg or an arm by amputation, endeavours for a long time afterwards to serve himself with them. After the death of any one, it is a common remark of the whole family, but especially of the servants, that they can scarce believe him to be dead, but still imagine him to be in his chamber or in any other place, where they were accustomed to find him. I have often heard in conversation, after talking of a person, that is any way celebrated, that one, who has no acquaintance with him, will say, *I have never seen such-a-one, but almost fancy I have; so often have I heard talk of him*. All these are parallel instances.

If we consider this argument from *education* in a proper light, it will appear very convincing; and the more so, that it is founded on one of the most common phenomena, that is any where to be met with. I am persuaded, that upon examination we shall find more than one half of those opinions, that prevail among mankind, to be owing to education, and that the principles, which are thus implicitely embraced, overbalance those, which are owing either to abstract reasoning or experience. As liars, by the frequent repetition of their lies, come at last to remember them; so the judgment, or rather the imagination, by the like means, may have ideas so strongly imprinted on it, and conceive them in so full a light, that they may operate upon the mind in the same manner with those, which the senses, memory or reason present to us. But as education is an artificial and not a natural cause, and as its maxims are frequently contrary to reason, and even to themselves in different times and places, it is never upon that account recognized by philosophers; though in reality it be built almost on the same foundation of custom and repetition as our reasonings from causes and effects.*

---

* In general we may observe, that as our assent to all probable reasonings is founded on the vivacity of ideas, it resembles many of those whimsies and prejudices, which are rejected under the opprobrious character of being the offspring of the imagination. By this expression it appears that the word, imagination, is commonly usd in two different senses; and though nothing be more contrary to true philosophy, than this inaccuracy, yet in the following reasonings I have often been obligd to fall into it. When I oppose the imagination to the memory, I mean the faculty, by which we form our fainter ideas. When I oppose it to reason, I mean the same faculty, excluding only our demonstrative and probable reasonings. When I oppose it to neither, it is indifferent whether it be taken in the larger or more limited sense, or at least the context will sufficiently explain the meaning.

Of the influence of belief

But though education be disclaimed by philosophy, as a fallacious ground of assent to any opinion, it prevails nevertheless in the world, and is the cause why all systems are apt to be rejected at first as new and unusual. This perhaps will be the fate of what I have here advanced concerning *belief*, and though the proofs I have produced appear to me perfectly conclusive, I expect not to make many proselytes to my opinion. Men will scarce ever be persuaded, that effects of such consequence can flow from principles, which are seemingly so inconsiderable, and that the far greatest part of our reasonings with all our actions and passions, can be derived from nothing but custom and habit. To obviate this objection, I shall here anticipate a little what would more properly fall under our consideration afterwards, when we come to treat of the passions and the sense of beauty.

There is implanted in the human mind a perception of pain and pleasure, as the chief spring and moving principle of all its actions. But pain and pleasure have two ways of making their appearance in the mind; of which the one has effects very different from the other. They may either appear in impression to the actual feeling, or only in idea, as at present when I mention them. It is evident the influence of these upon our actions is far from being equal. Impressions always actuate the soul, and that in the highest degree; but it is not every idea which has the same effect. Nature has proceeded with caution in this case, and seems to have carefully avoided the inconveniences of two extremes. Did impressions alone influence the will, we should every moment of our lives be subject to the greatest calamities; because, though we foresaw their approach, we should not be provided by nature with any principle of action, which might impel us to avoid them. On the other hand, did every idea influence our actions, our condition would not be much mended. For such is the unsteadiness and activity of thought, that the images of every thing, especially of goods and evils, are always wandering in the mind; and were it moved by every idle conception of this kind, it would never enjoy a moment's peace and tranquillity.

Nature has, therefore, chosen a medium, and has neither bestowed on every idea of good and evil the power of actuating the will, nor yet has entirely excluded them from this influence. Though an idle fiction has no efficacy, yet we find by experience, that the ideas of those objects, which we believe either are or will be existent, produce in a lesser degree the same effect with those impressions, which are immediately present to the senses and perception. The effect, then, of belief is to raise up a simple idea to an equality with our impressions, and bestow on it a like influence on the passions. This effect it can only have by making an idea approach an impression in force and vivacity. For as the different degrees of force make all the original difference betwixt an impression and an idea, they must of consequence be the source of all the differences in the effects of these perceptions, and their removal, in whole or in part, the cause of every new resemblance they acquire. Wherever we can make an idea approach the impressions in force and vivacity, it will likewise imitate them in its influence on the mind; and *vice versa*, where it imitates them in that influence, as in the present case, this must proceed from its approaching them in force and vivacity. Belief, therefore, since it causes an idea to imitate the effects of the impressions, must make it resemble them in these qualities, and is nothing but *a more vivid and intense conception of any idea*. This, then, may both serve as an additional argument for the present system, and may give us a notion after what manner our reasonings from causation are able to operate on the will and passions.

As belief is almost absolutely requisite to the exciting our passions, so the passions in their turn are very favourable to belief; and not only such facts as convey agreeable emotions, but very often such as give pain, do upon that account become more readily the objects of faith and opinion. A coward, whose fears are easily awakened, readily assents to every account of danger he meets with; as a person of a sorrowful and melancholy disposition is very credulous of every thing, that nourishes his prevailing passion. When any affecting object is presented, it gives the alarm, and excites immediately a degree of its proper passion; especially in persons who are naturally inclined to that passion. This emotion passes by an easy transition to the imagination; and diffusing itself over our idea of the affecting object, makes us form that idea with greater force and vivacity, and consequently assent to it, according to the precedent system. Admiration and surprize have the same effect as the other passions; and accordingly we may observe, that among the vulgar, quacks and projectors meet with a more easy faith upon account of their magnificent pretensions, than if they kept themselves within the bounds of moderation. The first astonishment, which naturally attends their miraculous relations, spreads itself over the whole soul, and so vivifies and enlivens the idea, that it resembles the inferences we draw from experience. This is a mystery, with which we may be already a little acquainted, and which we shall have farther occasion to be let into in the progress of this treatise.

After this account of the influence of belief on the passions, we shall find less difficulty in explaining its effects on the imagination, however extraordinary they may appear. It is certain we cannot take pleasure in any discourse, where our judgment gives no assent to those images which are presented to our fancy. The conversation of those who have acquired a habit of lying, though in affairs of no moment, never gives any satisfaction; and that because those ideas they present to us, not being attended with belief, make no impression upon the mind. Poets themselves, though liars by profession, always endeavour to give an air of truth to their fictions; and where that is totally neglected, their performances, however ingenious, will never be able to afford much pleasure. In short, we may observe, that even when ideas have no manner of influence on the will and passions, truth and reality are still requisite, in order to make them entertaining to the imagination.

But if we compare together all the phenomena that occur on this head, we shall find, that truth, however necessary it may seem in all works of genius, has no other effect than to procure an easy reception for the ideas, and to make the mind acquiesce in them with satisfaction, or at least without reluctance. But as this is an effect, which may easily be supposed to flow from that solidity and force, which, according to my system, attend those ideas that are established by reasonings from causation; it follows, that all the influence of belief upon the fancy may be explained from that system. Accordingly we may observe, that wherever that influence arises from any other principles beside truth or reality, they supply its place, and give an equal entertainment to the imagination.

Poets have formed what they call a poetical system of things, which though it be believed neither by themselves nor readers, is commonly esteemed a sufficient foundation for any fiction. We have been so much accustomed to the names of MARS, JUPITER, VENUS, that in the same manner as education infixes any opinion, the constant repetition of these ideas makes them enter into the mind with facility, and prevail upon the fancy, without influencing the judgment. In like manner tragedians always borrow their fable, or at least the names of their principal actors, from some known passage in history; and that not in order to deceive the spectators; for they will frankly confess, that truth is not in any circumstance inviolably observed: but in order to procure a more easy reception into the imagination for those extraordinary events, which they represent. But this is a precaution, which is not required of comic poets, whose personages and incidents, being of a more familiar kind, enter easily into the conception, and are received without any such formality, even though at first sight they be known to be fictitious, and the pure offspring of the fancy.

This mixture of truth and falsehood in the fables of tragic poets not only serves our present purpose, by shewing, that the imagination can be satisfied without any absolute belief or assurance; but may in another view be regarded as a very strong confirmation of this system. It is evident, that poets make use of this artifice of borrowing the names of their persons, and the chief events of their poems, from history, in order to procure a more easy reception for the whole, and cause it to make a deeper impression on the fancy and affections. The several incidents of the piece acquire a kind of relation by being united into one poem or representation; and if any of these incidents be an object of belief, it bestows a force and vivacity on the others, which are related to it. The vividness of the first conception diffuses itself along the relations, and is conveyed, as by so many pipes or canals, to every idea that has any communication with the primary one. This, indeed, can never amount to a perfect assurance; and that because the union among the ideas is, in a manner, accidental: but still it approaches so near, in its influence, as may convince us, that they are derived from the same origin. Belief must please the imagination by means of the force and vivacity which attends it; since every idea, which has force and vivacity, is found to be agreeable to that faculty.

To confirm this we may observe, that the assistance is mutual betwixt the judgment and fancy, as well as betwixt the judgment and passion; and that belief not only gives vigour to the imagination, but that a vigorous and strong imagination is of all talents the most proper to procure belief and authority. It is difficult for us to withhold our assent from what is painted out to us in all the colours of eloquence; and the vivacity produced by the fancy is in many cases greater than that which arises from custom and experience. We are hurried away by the lively imagination of our author or companion; and even he himself is often a victim to his own fire and genius.

Nor will it be amiss to remark, that as a lively imagination very often degenerates into madness or folly, and bears it a great resemblance in its operations; so they influence the judgment after the same manner, and produce belief from the very same principles. When the imagination, from any extraordinary ferment of the blood and spirits, acquires such a vivacity as disorders all its powers and faculties, there is no means of distinguishing betwixt truth and falsehood; but every loose fiction or idea, having the same influence as the impressions of the memory, or the conclusions of the judgment, is received on the same footing, and operates with equal force on the passions. A present impression and a customary transition are now no longer necessary to enliven our ideas. Every chimera of the brain is as vivid and intense as any of those inferences, which we formerly dignified with the name of conclusions concerning matters of fact, and sometimes as the present impressions of the senses.*

We may observe the same effect of poetry in a lesser degree; only with this difference, that the least reflection dissipates the illusions of poetry, and places the objects in their proper light. It is however certain, that in the warmth of a poetical enthusiasm, a poet has a counterfeit belief, and even a kind of vision of his objects: and if there be any shadow of argument to support this belief, nothing contributes more to his full conviction than a blaze of poetical figures and images, which have their effect upon the poet himself, as well as upon his readers.

[* see Appendix to the *Treatise*.]

SECTION ELEVEN

Of the probability of chances

But in order to bestow on this system its full force and evidence, we must carry our eye from it a moment to consider its consequences, and explain from the same principles some other species of reasoning, which are derived from the same origin.

Those philosophers, who have divided human reason into *knowledge and probability*, and have defined the first to be *that evidence, which arises from the comparison of ideas*, are obliged to comprehend all our arguments from causes or effects under the general term of probability. But though every one be free to use his terms in what sense he pleases; and accordingly in the precedent part of this discourse, I have followed this method of expression; it is however certain, that in common discourse we readily affirm, that many arguments from causation exceed probability, and may be received as a superior kind of evidence. One would appear ridiculous, who would say, that it is only probable the sun will rise tomorrow, or that all men must die; though it is plain we have no further assurance of these facts, than what experience affords us. For this reason, it would perhaps be more convenient, in order at once to preserve the common signification of words, and mark the several degrees of evidence, to distinguish human reason into three kinds, *viz. that from knowledge, from proofs, and from probabilities.* By knowledge, I mean the assurance arising from the comparison of ideas. By proofs, those arguments, which are derived from the relation of cause and effect, and which are entirely free from doubt and uncertainty. By probability, that evidence, which is still attended with uncertainty. It is this last species of reasoning, I proceed to examine.

Probability or reasoning from conjecture may be divided into two kinds, *viz.* that which is founded on *chance*, and that which arises from *causes*. We shall consider each of these in order.

The idea of cause and effect is derived from experience, which presenting us with certain objects constantly conjoined with each other, produces such a habit of surveying them in that relation, that we cannot without a sensible violence survey them in any other. On the other hand, as chance is nothing real in itself, and, properly speaking, is merely the negation of a cause, its influence on the mind is contrary to that of causation; and it is essential to it, to leave the imagination perfectly indifferent, either to consider the existence or non-existence of that object, which is regarded as contingent. A cause traces the way to our thought, and in a manner forces us to survey such certain objects, in such certain relations. Chance can only destroy this determination of the thought, and leave the mind in its native situation of indifference; in which, upon the absence of a cause, it is instantly re-instated.

Since therefore an entire indifference is essential to chance, no one chance can possibly be superior to another, otherwise than as it is composed of a superior number of equal chances. For if we affirm that one chance can, after any other manner, be superior to another, we must at the same time affirm, that there is something, which gives it the superiority, and determines the event rather to that side than the other: that is, in other words, we must allow of a cause, and destroy the supposition of chance; which we had before established. A perfect and total indifference is essential to chance, and one total indifference can never in itself be either superior or inferior to another. This truth is not peculiar to my system, but is acknowledged by every one, that forms calculations concerning chances.

And here it is remarkable, that though chance and causation be directly contrary, yet it is impossible for us to conceive this combination of chances, which is requisite to render one hazard superior to another, without supposing a mixture of causes among the chances, and a conjunction of necessity in some particulars, with a total indifference in others. Where nothing limits the chances, every notion, that the most extravagant fancy can form, is upon a footing of equality; nor can there be any circumstance to give one the advantage above another. Thus unless we allow, that there are some causes to make the dice fall, and preserve their form in their fall, and lie upon some one of their sides, we can form no calculation concerning the laws of hazard. But supposing these causes to operate, and supposing likewise all the rest to be indifferent and to be determined by chance, it is easy to arrive at a notion of a superior combination of chances. A die that has four sides marked with a certain number of spots, and only two with another, affords us an obvious and easy instance of this superiority.

The mind is here limited by the causes to such a precise number and quality of the events; and at the same time is undetermined in its choice of any particular event.

Proceeding then in that reasoning, wherein we have advanced three steps; *that* chance is merely the negation of a cause, and produces a total indifference in the mind; *that* one negation of a cause and one total indifference can never be superior or inferior to another; and *that* there must always be a mixture of causes among the chances, in order to be the foundation of any reasoning: we are next to consider what effect a superior combination of chances can have upon the mind, and after what manner it influences our judgment and opinion. Here we may repeat all the same arguments we employed in examining that belief, which arises from causes; and may prove, after the same manner, that a superior number of chances produces our assent neither by *demonstration* nor *probability*. It is indeed evident that we can never by the comparison of mere ideas make any discovery, which can be of consequence in this affair, and that it is impossible to prove with certainty, that any event must fall on that side where there is a superior number of chances. To suppose in this case any certainty, were to overthrow what we have established concerning the opposition of chances, and their perfect equality and indifference.

Should it be said, that though in an opposition of chances it is impossible to determine with *certainty*, on which side the event will fall, yet we can pronounce with certainty, that it is more likely and probable, it will be on that side where there is a superior number of chances, than where there is an inferior: should this be said, I would ask, what is here meant by *likelihood and probability*? The likelihood and probability of chances is a superior number of equal chances; and consequently when we say it is likely the event will fall on the side, which is superior, rather than on the inferior, we do no more than affirm, that where there is a superior number of chances there is actually a superior, and where there is an inferior there is an inferior; which are identical propositions, and of no consequence. The question is, by what means a superior number of equal chances operates upon the mind, and produces belief or assent; since it appears, that it is neither by arguments derived from demonstration, nor from probability.

In order to clear up this difficulty, we shall suppose a person to take a die, formed after such a manner as that four of its sides are marked with one figure, or one number of spots, and two with another; and to put this die into the box with an intention of throwing it: it is plain, he must conclude the one figure to be more probable than the other, and give the preference to that which is inscribed on the greatest number of sides. He in a manner believes, that this will lie uppermost; though still with hesitation and doubt, in proportion to the number of chances, which are contrary: and according as these contrary chances diminish, and the superiority increases on the other side, his belief acquires new degrees of stability and assurance. This belief arises from an operation of the mind upon the simple and limited object before us; and therefore its nature will be the more easily discovered and explained. We have nothing but one single die to contemplate, in order to comprehend one of the most curious operations of the understanding.

This die, formed as above, contains three circumstances worthy of our attention. *First*, Certain causes, such as gravity, solidity, a cubical figure, &c. which determine it to fall, to preserve its form in its fall, and to turn up one of its sides. *Secondly*, A certain number of sides, which are supposed indifferent. *Thirdly*, A certain figure inscribed on each side. These three particulars form the whole nature of the die, so far as relates to our present purpose; and consequently are the only circumstances regarded by the mind in its forming a judgment concerning the result of such a throw. Let us, therefore, consider gradually and carefully what must be the influence of these circumstances on the thought and imagination.

First, We have already observed, that the mind is determined by custom to pass from any cause to its effect, and that upon the appearance of the one, it is almost impossible for it not to form an idea of the other. Their constant conjunction in past instances has produced such a habit in the mind, that it always conjoins them in its thought, and infers the existence of the one from that of its usual attendant. When it considers the die as no longer supported by the box, it can not without violence regard it as suspended in the air; but naturally places it on the table, and views it as turning up one of its sides. This is the effect of the intermingled causes, which are requisite to our forming any calculation concerning chances.

Secondly, It is supposed, that though the die be necessarily determined to fall, and turn up one of its sides, yet there is nothing to fix the particular side, but that this is determined entirely by chance. The very nature and essence of chance is a negation of causes, and the leaving the mind in a perfect indifference among those events, which are supposed contingent. When therefore the thought is determined by the causes to consider the die as falling and turning up one of its sides, the chances present all these sides as equal, and make us consider every one of them, one after another, as alike probable and possible. The imagination passes from the cause, *viz.* the throwing of the die, to the effect, *viz.* the turning up one of the six sides; and feels a kind of impossibility both of stopping short in the way, and of forming any other idea. But as all these six sides are incompatible, and the die cannot turn up above one at once, this principle directs us not to consider all of them at once as lying uppermost; which we look upon as impossible: neither does it direct us with its entire force to any particular side; for in that case this side would be considered as certain and inevitable; but it directs us to the whole six sides after such a manner as to divide its force equally among them. We conclude in general, that some one of them must result from the throw: we run all of them over in our minds: the determination of the thought is common to all; but no more of its force falls to the share of any one, than what is suitable to its proportion with the rest. It is after this manner the original impulse, and consequently the vivacity of thought, arising from the causes, is divided and split in pieces by the intermingled chances.

We have already seen the influence of the two first qualities of the die, *viz.* the *causes*, and the *number* and *indifference* of the sides, and have learned how they give an impulse to the thought, and divide that impulse into as many parts as there are units in the number of sides. We must now consider the effects of the third particular, *viz.* the *figures* inscribed on each side. It is evident that where several sides have the same figure inscribed on them, they must concur in their influence on the mind, and must unite upon one image or idea of a figure all those divided impulses, that were dispersed over the several sides, upon which that figure is inscribed. Were the question only what side will be turned up, these are all perfectly equal, and no one could ever have any advantage above another. But as the question is concerning the figure, and as the same figure is presented by more than one side: it is evident, that the impulses belonging to all these sides must re-unite in that one figure, and become stronger and more forcible by the union. Four sides are supposed in the present case to have the same figure inscribed on them, and two to have another figure. The impulses of the former are, therefore, superior to those of the latter. But as the events are contrary, and it is impossible both these figures can be turned up; the impulses likewise become contrary, and the inferior destroys the superior, as far as its strength goes. The vivacity of the idea is always proportionable to the degrees of the impulse or tendency to the transition; and belief is the same with the vivacity of the idea, according to the precedent doctrine.

SECTION TWELVE
Of the probability of causes

What I have said concerning the probability of chances can serve to no other purpose, than to assist us in explaining the probability of causes; since it is commonly allowed by philosophers, that what the vulgar call chance is nothing but a secret and concealed cause. That species of probability, therefore, is what we must chiefly examine.

The probabilities of causes are of several kinds; but are all derived from the same origin, *viz. the association of ideas to a present impression*. As the habit, which produces the association, arises from the frequent conjunction of objects, it must arrive at its perfection by degrees, and must acquire new force from each instance, that falls under our observation. The first instance has little or no force: the second makes some addition to it: the third becomes still more sensible; and it is by these slow steps, that our judgment arrives at a full assurance. But before it attains this pitch of perfection, it passes through several inferior degrees, and in all of them is only to be esteemed a presumption or probability. The gradation, therefore, from probabilities to proofs is in many cases insensible; and the difference betwixt these kinds of evidence is more easily perceived in the remote degrees, than in the near and contiguous.

It is worthy of remark on this occasion, that though the species of probability here explained be the first in order, and naturally takes place before any entire proof can exist, yet no one, who is arrived at the age of maturity, can any longer be acquainted with it. It is true, nothing is more common than for people of the most advanced knowledge to have attained only an imperfect experience of many particular events; which naturally produces only an imperfect habit and transition: but then we must consider, that the mind, having formed another observation concerning the connexion of causes and effects, gives new force to its reasoning from that observation; and by means of it can build an argument on one single experiment, when duly prepared and examined. What we have found once to follow from any object, we conclude will for ever follow from it; and if this maxim be not always built upon as certain, it is not for want of a sufficient number of experiments, but because we frequently meet with instances to the contrary; which leads us to the second species of probability, where there is a *contrariety* in our experience and observation.

It would be very happy for men in the conduct of their lives and actions, were the same objects always conjoined together, and we had nothing to fear but the mistakes of our own judgment, without having any reason to apprehend the uncertainty of nature. But as it is frequently found, that one observation is contrary to another, and that causes and effects follow not in the same order, of which we have had experience, we are obliged to vary our reasoning on account of this uncertainty, and take into consideration the contrariety of events. The first question, that occurs on this head, is concerning the nature and causes of the contrariety.

The vulgar, who take things according to their first appearance, attribute the uncertainty of events to such an uncertainty in the causes, as makes them often fail of their usual influence, though they meet with no obstacle nor impediment in their operation. But philosophers observing, that almost in every part of nature there is contained a vast variety of springs and principles, which are hid, by reason of their minuteness or remoteness, find that it is at least possible the contrariety of events may not proceed from any contingency in the cause, but from the secret operation of contrary causes. This possibility is converted into certainty by farther observation, when they remark, that upon an exact scrutiny, a contrariety of effects always betrays a contrariety of causes, and proceeds from their mutual hindrance and opposition. A peasant can give no better reason for the stopping of any clock or watch than to say, that commonly it does not go right: but an artizan easily perceives, that the same force in the spring or pendulum has always the same influence on the wheels; but fails of its usual effect, perhaps by reason of a grain of dust, which puts a stop to the whole movement. From the observation of several parallel instances, philosophers form a maxim, that the connexion betwixt all causes and effects is equally necessary, and that its seeming uncertainty in some instances proceeds from the secret opposition of contrary causes.

But however philosophers and the vulgar may differ in their explication of the contrariety of events, their inferences from it are always of the same kind, and founded on the same principles. A contrariety of events in the past may give us a kind of hesitating belief for the future after two several ways. *First*, By producing an imperfect habit and transition from the present impression to the related idea. When the conjunction of any two objects is frequent, without being entirely constant, the mind is determined to pass from one object to the other; but not with so entire a habit, as when the union is uninterrupted, and all the instances we have ever met with are uniform and of a piece. We find from common experience, in our actions as well as reasonings, that a constant perseverance in any course of life produces a strong inclination and tendency to continue for the future; though there are habits of inferior degrees of force, proportioned to the inferior degrees of steadiness and uniformity in our conduct.

There is no doubt but this principle sometimes takes place, and produces those inferences we draw from contrary phenomena: though I am persuaded, that upon examination we shall not find it to be the principle, that most commonly influences the mind in this species of reasoning. When we follow only the habitual determination of the mind, we make the transition without any reflection, and interpose not a moment's delay betwixt the view of one object and the belief of that, which is often found to attend it. As the custom depends not upon any deliberation, it operates immediately, without allowing any time for reflection. But this method of proceeding we have but few instances of in our probable reasonings; and even fewer than in those, which are derived from the uninterrupted conjunction of objects. In the former species of reasoning we commonly take knowingly into consideration the contrariety of past events; we compare the different sides of the contrariety, and carefully weigh the experiments, which we have on each side: whence we may conclude, that our reasonings of this kind arise not *directly* from the habit, but in an *oblique* manner; which we must now endeavour to explain.

It is evident, that when an object is attended with contrary effects, we judge of them only by our past experience, and always consider those as possible, which we have observed to follow from it. And as past experience regulates our judgment concerning the possibility of these effects, so it does that concerning their probability; and that effect, which has been the most common, we always esteem the most likely. Here then are two things to be considered, *viz.* the *reasons* which determine us to make the past a standard for the future, and the *manner* how we extract a single judgment from a contrariety of past events.

First we may observe, that the supposition, *that the future resembles the past*, is not founded on arguments of any kind, but is derived entirely from habit, by which we are determined to expect for the future the same train of objects, to which we have been accustomed. This habit or determination to transfer the past to the future is full and perfect; and consequently the first impulse of the imagination in this species of reasoning is endowed with the same qualities.

But, *secondly*, when in considering past experiments we find them of a contrary nature, this determination, though full and perfect in itself, presents us with no steady object, but offers us a number of disagreeing images in a certain order and proportion. The first impulse, therefore, is here broke into pieces, and diffuses itself over all those images, of which each partakes an equal share of that force and vivacity, that is derived from the impulse. Any of these past events may again happen; and we judge, that when they do happen, they will be mixed in the same proportion as in the past.

If our intention, therefore, be to consider the proportions of contrary events in a great number of instances, the images presented by our past experience must remain in their *first form*, and preserve their first proportions. Suppose, for instance, I have found by long observation, that of twenty ships, which go to sea, only nineteen return. Suppose I see at present twenty ships that leave the port: I transfer my past experience to the future, and represent to myself nineteen of these ships as returning in safety, and one as perishing. Concerning this there can be no difficulty. But as we frequently run over those several ideas of past events, in order to form a judgment concerning one single event, which appears uncertain; this consideration must change the *first form* of our ideas, and draw together the divided images presented by experience; since it is to *it* we refer the determination of that particular event, upon which we reason. Many of these images are supposed to concur, and a superior number to concur on one side. These agreeing images unite together, and render the idea more strong and lively, not only than a mere fiction of the imagination, but also than any idea, which is supported by a lesser number of experiments. Each new experiment is as a new stroke of the pencil, which bestows an additional vivacity on the colours without either multiplying or enlarging the figure. This operation of the mind has been so fully explained in treating of the probability of chance, that I need not here endeavour to render it more intelligible. Every past experiment may be considered as a kind of chance; it being uncertain to us, whether the object will exist conformable to one experiment or another. And for this reason every thing that has been said on the one subject is applicable to both.

Thus upon the whole, contrary experiments produce an imperfect belief, either by weakening the habit, or by dividing and afterwards joining in different parts, that *perfect* habit, which makes us conclude in general, that instances, of which we have no experience, must necessarily resemble those of which we have.

To justify still farther this account of the second species of probability, where we reason with knowledge and reflection from a contrariety of past experiments, I shall propose the following considerations, without fearing to give offence by that air of subtilty, which attends them. Just reasoning ought still, perhaps, to retain its force, however subtile; in the same manner as matter preserves its solidity in the air, and fire, and animal spirits, as well as in the grosser and more sensible forms.

First, We may observe, that there is no probability so great as not to allow of a contrary possibility; because otherwise it would cease to be a probability, and would become a certainty. That probability of causes, which is most extensive, and which we at present examine, depends on a contrariety of experiments: and it is evident an experiment in the past proves at least a possibility for the future.

Secondly, The component parts of this possibility and probability are of the same nature, and differ in number only, but not in kind. It has been observed, that all single chances are entirely equal, and that the only circumstance, which can give any event, that is contingent, a superiority over another is a superior number of chances. In like manner, as the uncertainty of causes is discovery by experience, which presents us with a view of contrary events, it is plain, that when we transfer the past to the future, the known to the unknown, every past experiment has the same weight, and that it is only a superior number of them, which can throw the balance on any side. The possibility, therefore, which enters into every reasoning of this kind, is composed of parts, which are of the same nature both among themselves, and with those, that compose the opposite probability.

Thirdly, We may establish it as a certain maxim, that in all moral as well as natural phenomena, wherever any cause consists of a number of parts, and the effect increases or diminishes, according to the variation of that number, the effect, properly speaking, is a compounded one, and arises from the union of the several effects, that proceed from each part of the cause. Thus, because the gravity of a body increases or diminishes by the increase or diminution of its parts, we conclude that each part contains this quality and contributes to the gravity of the whole. The absence or presence of a part of the cause is attended with that of a proportionable part of the effect. This connexion or constant conjunction sufficiently proves the one part to be the cause of the other. As the belief which we have of any event, increases or diminishes according to the number of chances or past experiments, it is to be considered as a compounded effect, of which each part arises from a proportionable number of chances or experiments.

Let us now join these three observations, and see what conclusion we can draw from them. To every probability there is an opposite possibility. This possibility is composed of parts, that are entirely of the same nature with those of the probability; and consequently have the same influence on the mind and understanding. The belief, which attends the probability, is a compounded effect, and is formed by the concurrence of the several effects, which proceed from each part of the probability. Since therefore each part of the probability contributes to the production of the belief, each part of the possibility must have the same influence on the opposite side; the nature of these parts being entirely the same. The contrary belief, attending the possibility, implies a view of a certain object, as well as the probability does an opposite view. In this particular both these degrees of belief are alike. The only manner then, in which the superior number of similar component parts in the one can exert its influence, and prevail above the inferior in the other, is by producing a stronger and more lively view of its object. Each part presents a particular view; and all these views uniting together produce one general view, which is fuller and more distinct by the greater number of causes or principles, from which it is derived.

The component parts of the probability and possibility, being alike in their nature, must produce like effects; and the likeness of their effects consists in this, that each of them presents a view of a particular object. But though these parts be alike in their nature, they are very different in their quantity and number; and this difference must appear in the effect as well as the similarity. Now as the view they present is in both cases full and entire, and comprehends the object in all its parts, it is impossible that in this particular there can be any difference; nor is there any thing but a superior vivacity in the probability, arising from the concurrence of a superior number of views, which can distinguish these effects.

Here is almost the same argument in a different light. All our reasonings concerning the probability of causes are founded on the transferring of past to future. The transferring of any past experiment to the future is sufficient to give us a view of the object; whether that experiment be single or combined with others of the same kind; whether it be entire, or opposed by others of a contrary kind. Suppose, then, it acquires both these qualities of combination and opposition, it loses not upon that account its former power of presenting a view of the object, but only concurs with and opposes other experiments, that have a like influence. A question, therefore, may arise concerning the manner both of the concurrence and opposition. As to the *concurrence*, there is only the choice left betwixt these two hypotheses. *First*, That the view of the object, occasioned by the transference of each past experiment, preserves itself entire, and only multiplies the number of views. Or, *secondly*, That it runs into the other similar and correspondent views, and gives them a superior degree of force and vivacity. But that the first hypothesis is erroneous, is evident from experience, which informs us, that the belief, attending any reasoning, consists in one conclusion, not in a multitude of similar ones, which would only distract the mind, and in many cases would be too numerous to be comprehended distinctly by any finite capacity. It remains, therefore, as the only reasonable opinion, that these similar views run into each other, and unite their forces; so as to produce a stronger and clearer view, than what arises from any one alone. This is the manner, in which past experiments concur, when they are transferred to any future event. As to the manner of their *opposition*, it is evident, that as the contrary views are incompatible with each other, and it is impossible the object can at once exist conformable to both of them, their influence becomes mutually destructive, and the mind is determined to the superior only with that force, which remains, after subtracting the inferior.

I am sensible how abstruse all this reasoning must appear to the generality of readers, who not being accustomed to such profound reflections on the intellectual faculties of the mind, will be apt to reject as chimerical whatever strikes not in with the common received notions, and with the easiest and most obvious principles of philosophy. And no doubt there are some pains required to enter into these arguments; though perhaps very little are necessary to perceive the imperfection of every vulgar hypothesis on this subject, and the little light, which philosophy can yet afford us in such sublime and such curious speculations. Let men be once fully persuaded of these two principles, *That there is nothing in any object, considered in itself, which can afford us a reason for drawing a conclusion beyond it;* and, *That even after the observation of the frequent or constant conjunction of objects, we have no reason to draw any inference concerning any object beyond those of which we have had experience*; I say, let men be once fully convinced of these two principles, and this will throw them so loose from all common systems, that they will make no difficulty of receiving any, which may appear the most extraordinary. These principles we have found to be sufficiently convincing, even with regard to our most certain reasonings from causation: but I shall venture to affirm, that with regard to these conjectural or probable reasonings they still acquire a new degree of evidence.

First, It is obvious, that in reasonings of this kind, it is not the object presented to us, which, considered in itself, affords us any reason to draw a conclusion concerning any other object or event. For as this latter object is supposed uncertain, and as the uncertainty is derived from a concealed contrariety of causes in the former, were any of the causes placed in the known qualities of that object, they would no longer be concealed, nor would our conclusion be uncertain.

But, *secondly*, it is equally obvious in this species of reasoning, that if the transference of the past to the future were founded merely on a conclusion of the understanding, it could never occasion any belief or assurance. When we transfer contrary experiments to the future, we can only repeat these contrary experiments with their particular proportions; which could not produce assurance in any single event, upon which we reason, unless the fancy melted together all those images that concur, and extracted from them one single idea or image, which is intense and lively in proportion to the number of experiments from which it is derived, and their superiority above their antagonists. Our past experience presents no determinate object; and as our belief, however faint, fixes itself on a determinate object, it is evident that the belief arises not merely from the transference of past to future, but from some operation of the *fancy* conjoined with it. This may lead us to conceive the manner, in which that faculty enters into all our reasonings.

I shall conclude this subject with two reflections, which may deserve our attention. The *first* may be explained after this manner. When the mind forms a reasoning concerning any matter of fact, which is only probable, it casts its eye backward upon past experience, and transferring it to the future, is presented with so many contrary views of its object, of which those that are of the same kind uniting together, and running into one act of the mind, serve to fortify and enliven it. But suppose that this multitude of views or glimpses of an object proceeds not from experience, but from a voluntary act of the imagination; this effect does not follow, or at least, follows not in the same degree. For though custom and education produce belief by such a repetition, as is not derived from experience, yet this requires a long tract of time, along with a very frequent and *undesigned* repetition. In general we may pronounce, that a person who would *voluntarily* repeat any idea in his mind, though supported by one past experience, would be no more inclined to believe the existence of its object, than if he had contented himself with one survey of it. Beside the effect of design; each act of the mind, being separate and independent, has a separate influence, and joins not its force with that of its fellows. Not being united by any common object, producing them, they have no relation to each other; and consequently make no transition or union of forces. This phenomenon we shall understand better afterwards.

My *second* reflection is founded on those large probabilities, which the mind can judge of, and the minute differences it can observe betwixt them. When the chances or experiments on one side amount to ten thousand, and on the other to ten thousand and one, the judgment gives the preference to the latter, upon account of that superiority; though it is plainly impossible for the mind to run over every particular view, and distinguish the superior vivacity of the image arising from the superior number, where the difference is so inconsiderable. We have a parallel instance in the affections. It is evident, according to the principles above-mentioned, that when an object produces any passion in us, which varies according to the different quantity of the object; I say, it is evident, that the passion, properly speaking, is not a simple emotion, but a compounded one, of a great number of weaker passions, derived from a view of each part of the object.

For otherwise it were impossible the passion should increase by the increase of these parts. Thus a man, who desires a thousand pound, has in reality a thousand or more desires which uniting together, seem to make only one passion; though the composition evidently betrays itself upon every alteration of the object, by the preference he gives to the larger number, if superior only by an unit. Yet nothing can be more certain, than that so small a difference would not be discernible in the passions, nor could render them distinguishable from each other. The difference, therefore, of our conduct in preferring the greater number depends not upon our passions, but upon custom, and *general rules*. We have found in a multitude of instances, that the augmenting the numbers of any sum augments the passion, where the numbers are precise and the difference sensible. The mind can perceive from its immediate feeling, that three guineas produce a greater passion than two; and *this* it transfers to larger numbers, because of the resemblance; and by a general rule assigns to a thousand guineas, a stronger passion than to nine hundred and ninety nine. These general rules we shall explain presently.

But beside these two species of probability, which are derived from an *imperfect* experience and from *contrary* causes, there is a third arising from ANALOGY, which differs from them in some material circumstances. According to the hypothesis above explained all kinds of reasoning from causes or effects are founded on two particulars, *viz*., the constant conjunction of any two objects in all past experience, and the resemblance of a present object to any one of them. The effect of these two particulars is, that the present object invigorates and enlivens the imagination; and the resemblance, along with the constant union, conveys this force and vivacity to the related idea; which we are therefore said to believe, or assent to. If you weaken either the union or resemblance, you weaken the principle of transition, and of consequence that belief, which arises from it. The vivacity of the first impression cannot be fully conveyed to the related idea, either where the conjunction of their objects is not constant, or where the present impression does not perfectly resemble any of those, whose union we are accustomed to observe. In those probabilities of chance and causes above-explained, it is the constancy of the union, which is diminished; and in the probability derived from analogy, it is the resemblance only, which is affected. Without some degree of resemblance, as well as union, it is impossible there can be any reasoning: but as this resemblance admits of many different degrees, the reasoning becomes proportionably more or less firm and certain. An experiment loses of its force, when transferred to instances, which are not exactly resembling; though it is evident it may still retain as much as may be the foundation of probability, as long as there is any resemblance remaining.

SECTION THIRTEEN

Of unphilosophical probability

All these kinds of probability are received by philosophers, and allowed to be reasonable foundations of belief and opinion. But there are others, that are derived from the same principles, though they have not had the good fortune to obtain the same sanction. The *first* probability of this kind may be accounted for thus. The diminution of the union, and of the resemblance, as above explained, diminishes the facility of the transition, and by that means weakens the evidence; and we may farther observe, that the same diminution of the evidence will follow from a diminution of the impression, and from the shading of those colours, under which it appears to the memory or senses. The argument, which we found on any matter of fact we remember, is more or less convincing according as the fact is recent or remote; and though the difference in these degrees of evidence be not received by philosophy as solid and legitimate; because in that case an argument must have a different force to day, from what it shall have a month hence; yet notwithstanding the opposition of philosophy, it is certain, this circumstance has a considerable influence on the understanding, and secretly changes the authority of the same argument, according to the different times, in which it is proposed to us. A greater force and vivacity in the impression naturally conveys a greater to the related idea; and it is on the degrees of force and vivacity, that the belief depends, according to the foregoing system.

There is a *second* difference, which we may frequently observe in our degrees of belief and assurance, and which never fails to take place, though disclaimed by philosophers. An experiment, that is recent and fresh in the memory, affects us more than one that is in some measure obliterated; and has a superior influence on the judgment, as well as on the passions. A lively impression produces more assurance than a faint one; because it has more original force to communicate to the related idea, which thereby acquires a greater force and vivacity. A recent observation has a like effect; because the custom and transition is there more entire, and preserves better the original force in the communication. Thus a drunkard, who has seen his companion die of a debauch, is struck with that instance for some time, and dreads a like accident for himself: but as the memory of it decays away by degrees, his former security returns, and the danger seems less certain and real.

I add, as a *third* instance of this kind, that though our reasonings from proofs and from probabilities be considerably different from each other, yet the former species of reasoning often degenerates insensibly into the latter, by nothing but the multitude of connected arguments. It is certain, that when an inference is drawn immediately from an object, without any intermediate cause or effect, the conviction is much stronger, and the persuasion more lively, than when the imagination is carried through a long chain of connected arguments, however infallible the connexion of each link may be esteemed. It is from the original impression, that the vivacity of all the ideas is derived, by means of the customary transition of the imagination; and it is evident this vivacity must gradually decay in proportion to the distance, and must lose somewhat in each transition. Sometimes this distance has a greater influence than even contrary experiments would have; and a man may receive a more lively conviction from a probable reasoning, which is close and immediate, than from a long chain of consequences, though just and conclusive in each part. Nay it is seldom such reasonings produce any conviction; and one must have a very strong and firm imagination to preserve the evidence to the end, where it passes through so many stages.

But here it may not be amiss to remark a very curious phenomenon, which the present subject suggests to us. It is evident there is no point of ancient history, of which we can have any assurance, but by passing through many millions of causes and effects, and through a chain of arguments of almost an immeasurable length. Before the knowledge of the fact could come to the first historian, it must be conveyed through many mouths; and after it is committed to writing, each new copy is a new object, of which the connexion with the foregoing is known only by experience and observation. Perhaps, therefore, it may be concluded from the precedent reasoning, that the evidence of all ancient history must now be lost; or at least, will be lost in time, as the chain of causes increases, and runs on to a greater length. But as it seems contrary to common sense to think, that if the republic of letters, and the art of printing continue on the same footing as at present, our posterity, even after a thousand ages, can ever doubt if there has been such a man as JULIUS CAESAR; this may be considered as an objection to the present system. If belief consisted only in a certain vivacity, conveyed from an original impression, it would decay by the length of the transition, and must at last be utterly extinguished: and *vice versa*, if belief on some occasions be not capable of such an extinction; it must be something different from that vivacity.

Before I answer this objection I shall observe, that from this topic there has been borrowed a very celebrated argument against the *Christian Religion*; but with this difference, that the connexion betwixt each link of the chain in human testimony has been there supposed not to go beyond probability, and to be liable to a degree of doubt and uncertainty. And indeed it must be confessed, that in this manner of considering the subject, (which however is not a true one) there is no history or tradition, but what must in the end lose all its force and evidence. Every new probability diminishes the original conviction; and however great that conviction may be supposed, it is impossible it can subsist under such re-iterated diminutions. This is true in general; though we shall find afterwards,* that there is one very memorable exception, which is of vast consequence in the present subject of the understanding.

Mean while to give a solution of the preceding objection upon the supposition, that historical evidence amounts at first to an entire proof; let us consider, that though the links are innumerable, that connect any original fact with the present impression, which is the

---

* Part 4. Section 1.

foundation of belief; yet they are all of the same kind, and depend on the fidelity of Printers and Copyists. One edition passes into another, and that into a third, and so on, till we come to that volume we peruse at present. There is no variation in the steps. After we know one we know all of them; and after we have made one, we can have no scruple as to the rest. This circumstance alone preserves the evidence of history, and will perpetuate the memory of the present age to the latest posterity. If all the long chain of causes and effects, which connect any past event with any volume of history, were composed of parts different from each other, and which it were necessary for the mind distinctly to conceive, it is impossible we should preserve to the end any belief or evidence. But as most of these proofs are perfectly resembling, the mind runs easily along them, jumps from one part to another with facility, and forms but a confused and general notion of each link. By this means a long chain of argument, has as little effect in diminishing the original vivacity, as a much shorter would have, if composed of parts, which were different from each other, and of which each required a distinct consideration.

A fourth unphilosophical species of probability is that derived from *general rules*, which we rashly form to ourselves, and which are the source of what we properly call PREJUDICE. An *Irishman* cannot have wit, and a *Frenchman* cannot have solidity; for which reason, though the conversation of the former in any instance be visibly very agreeable, and of the latter very judicious, we have entertained such a prejudice against them, that they must be dunces or fops in spite of sense and reason. Human nature is very subject to errors of this kind; and perhaps this nation as much as any other.

Should it be demanded why men form general rules, and allow them to influence their judgment, even contrary to present observation and experience, I should reply, that in my opinion it proceeds from those very principles, on which all judgments concerning causes and effects depend. Our judgments concerning cause and effect are derived from habit and experience; and when we have been accustomed to see one object united to another, our imagination passes from the first to the second, by a natural transition, which precedes reflection, and which cannot be prevented by it. Now it is the nature of custom not only to operate with its full force, when objects are presented, that are exactly the same with those to which we have been accustomed; but also to operate in an inferior degree, when we discover such as are similar; and though the habit loses somewhat of its force by every difference, yet it is seldom entirely destroyed, where any considerable circumstances remain the same. A man, who has contracted a custom of eating fruit by the use of pears or peaches, will satisfy himself with melons, where he cannot find his favourite fruit; as one, who has become a drunkard by the use of red wines, will be carried almost with the same violence to white, if presented to him. From this principle I have accounted for that species of probability, derived from analogy, where we transfer our experience in past instances to objects which are resembling, but are not exactly the same with those concerning which we have had experience. In proportion as the resemblance decays, the probability diminishes; but still has some force as long as there remain any traces of the resemblance.

This observation we may carry farther; and may remark, that though custom be the foundation of all our judgments, yet sometimes it has an effect on the imagination in opposition to the judgment, and produces a contrariety in our sentiments concerning the same object. I explain myself. In almost all kinds of causes there is a complication of circumstances, of which some are essential, and others superfluous; some are absolutely requisite to the production of the effect, and others are only conjoined by accident. Now we may observe, that when these superfluous circumstances are numerous, and remarkable, and frequently conjoined with the essential, they have such an influence on the imagination, that even in the absence of the latter they carry us on to the conception of the usual effect, and give to that conception a force and vivacity, which make it superior to the mere fictions of the fancy. We may correct this propensity by a reflection on the nature of those circumstances: but it is still certain, that custom takes the start, and gives a bias to the imagination.

To illustrate this by a familiar instance, let us consider the case of a man, who, being hung out from a high tower in a cage of iron cannot forbear trembling, when he surveys the precipice below him, though he knows himself to be perfectly secure from falling, by his experience of the solidity of the iron, which supports him;

and though the ideas of fall and descent, and harm and death, be derived solely from custom and experience. The same custom goes beyond the instances, from which it is derived, and to which it perfectly corresponds; and influences his ideas of such objects as are in some respect resembling, but fall not precisely under the same rule. The circumstances of depth and descent strike so strongly upon him, that their influence cannot be destroyed by the contrary circumstances of support and solidity, which ought to give him a perfect security. His imagination runs away with its object, and excites a passion proportioned to it. That passion returns back upon the imagination and enlivens the idea; which lively idea has a new influence on the passion, and in its turn augments its force and violence; and both his fancy and affections, thus mutually supporting each other, cause the whole to have a very great influence upon him.

But why need we seek for other instances, while the present subject of [un]philosophical probabilities offers us so obvious an one, in the opposition betwixt the judgment and imagination arising from these effects of custom? According to my system, all reasonings are nothing but the effects of custom; and custom has no influence, but by enlivening the imagination, and giving us a strong conception of any object. It may, therefore, be concluded, that our judgment and imagination can never be contrary, and that custom cannot operate on the latter faculty after such a manner, as to render it opposite to the former. This difficulty we can remove after no other manner, than by supposing the influence of general rules. We shall afterwards* take notice of some general rules, by which we ought to regulate our judgment concerning causes and effects; and these rules are formed on the nature of our understanding, and on our experience of its operations in the judgments we form concerning objects. By them we learn to distinguish the accidental circumstances from the efficacious causes; and when we find that an effect can be produced without the concurrence of any particular circumstance, we conclude that that circumstance makes not a part of the efficacious cause, however frequently conjoined with it. But as this frequent conjunction necessarily makes it have some effect on the imagination, in spite of the opposite conclusion from

* Section 15.

general rules, the opposition of these two principles produces a contrariety in our thoughts, and causes us to ascribe the one inference to our judgment, and the other to our imagination. The general rule is attributed to our judgment; as being more extensive and constant. The exception to the imagination, as being more capricious and uncertain.

Thus our general rules are in a manner set in opposition to each other. When an object appears, that resembles any cause in very considerable circumstances, the imagination naturally carries us to a lively conception of the usual effect, though the object be different in the most material and most efficacious circumstances from that cause. Here is the first influence of general rules. But when we take a review of this act of the mind, and compare it with the more general and authentic operations of the understanding, we find it to be of an irregular nature, and destructive of all the most established principles of reasonings; which is the cause of our rejecting it. This is a second influence of general rules, and implies the condemnation of the former. Sometimes the one, sometimes the other prevails, according to the disposition and character of the person. The vulgar are commonly guided by the first, and wise men by the second. Mean while the sceptics may here have the pleasure of observing a new and signal contradiction in our reason, and of seeing all philosophy ready to be subverted by a principle of human nature, and again saved by a new direction of the very same principle. The following of general rules is a very unphilosophical species of probability; and yet it is only by following them that we can correct this, and all other unphilosophical probabilities.

Since we have instances, where general rules operate on the imagination even contrary to the judgment, we need not be surprized to see their effects increase, when conjoined with that latter faculty, and to observe that they bestow on the ideas they present to us a force superior to what attends any other. Every one knows, there is an indirect manner of insinuating praise or blame, which is much less shocking than the open flattery or censure of any person. However he may communicate his sentiments by such secret insinuations, and make them known with equal certainty as by the open discovery of them, it is certain that their influence is not equally strong and powerful. One who lashes me with concealed strokes of satire, moves not my indignation to such a degree, as if he flatly told me I was a fool and coxcomb; though I equally understand his meaning, as if he did. This difference is to be attributed to the influence of general rules.

Whether a person openly abuses me, or slyly intimates his contempt, in neither case do I immediately perceive his sentiment or opinion; and it is only by signs, that is, by its effects, I become sensible of it. The only difference, then, betwixt these two cases consists in this, that in the open discovery of his sentiments he makes use of signs, which are general and universal; and in the secret intimation employs such as are more singular and uncommon. The effect of this circumstance is, that the imagination, in running from the present impression to the absent idea, makes the transition with greater facility, and consequently conceives the object with greater force, where the connexion is common and universal, than where it is more rare and particular. Accordingly we may observe, that the open declaration of our sentiments is called the taking off the mask, as the secret intimation of our opinions is said to be the veiling of them. The difference betwixt an idea produced by a general connexion, and that arising from a particular one is here compared to the difference betwixt an impression and an idea. This difference in the imagination has a suitable effect on the passions; and this effect is augmented by another circumstance. A secret intimation of anger or contempt shews that we still have some consideration for the person, and avoid the directly abusing him. This makes a concealed satire less disagreeable; but still this depends on the same principle. For if an idea were not more feeble, when only intimated, it would never be esteemed a mark of greater respect to proceed in this method than in the other.

Sometimes scurrility is less displeasing than delicate satire, because it revenges us in a manner for the injury at the very time it is committed, by affording us a just reason to blame and contemn the person, who injures us. But this phenomenon likewise depends upon the same principle. For why do we blame all gross and injurious language, unless it be, because we esteem it contrary to good breeding and humanity? And why is it contrary, unless it be more shocking than any delicate satire? The rules of good breeding condemn whatever is openly disobliging, and gives a sensible pain and confusion to those, with whom we converse. After this is once established, abusive language is universally blamed, and gives less pain upon account of its coarseness and incivility, which render the person despicable, that employs it. It becomes less disagreeable, merely because originally it is more so; and it is more disagreeable, because it affords an inference by general and common rules, that are palpable and undeniable.

To this explication of the different influence of open and concealed flattery or satire, I shall add the consideration of another phenomenon, which is analogous to it. There are many particulars in the point of honour both of men and women, whose violations, when open and avowed, the world never excuses, but which it is more apt to overlook, when the appearances are saved, and the transgression is secret and concealed. Even those, who know with equal certainty, that the fault is committed, pardon it more easily, when the proofs seem in some measure oblique and equivocal, than when they are direct and undeniable. The same idea is presented in both cases, and, properly speaking, is equally assented to by the judgment; and yet its influence is different, because of the different manner, in which it is presented.

Now if we compare these two cases, of the *open* and *concealed* violations of the laws of honour, we shall find, that the difference betwixt them consists in this, that in the first case the sign, from which we infer the blameable action, is single, and suffices alone to be the foundation of our reasoning and judgment; whereas in the latter the signs are numerous, and decide little or nothing when alone and unaccompanied with many minute circumstances, which are almost imperceptible. But it is certainly true, that any reasoning is always the more convincing, the more single and united it is to the eye, and the less exercise it gives to the imagination to collect all its parts, and run from them to the correlative idea, which forms the conclusion. The labour of the thought disturbs the regular progress of the sentiments, as we shall observe presently.* The idea strikes not on us with such vivacity; and consequently has no such influence on the passion and imagination.

From the same principles we may account for those observations of the CARDINAL DE RETZ, *that there are many things, in which the world wishes to be deceived; and that it more easily excuses a*

---

* Part 4, Section 1.

person in acting than in talking contrary to the decorum of his profession and character. A fault in words is commonly more open and distinct than one in actions, which admit of many palliating excuses, and decide not so clearly concerning the intention and views of the actor.

Thus it appears upon the whole, that every kind of opinion or judgment, which amounts not to knowledge, is derived entirely from the force and vivacity of the perception, and that these qualities constitute in the mind, what we call the BELIEF of the existence of any object. This force and this vivacity are most conspicuous in the memory; and therefore our confidence in the veracity of that faculty is the greatest imaginable, and equals in many respects the assurance of a demonstration. The next degree of these qualities is that derived from the relation of cause and effect; and this too is very great, especially when the conjunction is found by experience to be perfectly constant, and when the object, which is present to us, exactly resembles those, of which we have had experience. But below this degree of evidence there are many others, which have an influence on the passions and imagination, proportioned to that degree of force and vivacity, which they communicate to the ideas. It is by habit we make the transition from cause to effect; and it is from some present impression we borrow that vivacity, which we diffuse over the correlative idea. But when we have not observed a sufficient number of instances, to produce a strong habit; or when these instances are contrary to each other; or when the resemblance is not exact; or the present impression is faint and obscure; or the experience in some measure obliterated from the memory; or the connexion dependent on a long chain of objects; or the inference derived from general rules, and yet not conformable to them: in all these cases the evidence diminishes by the diminution of the force and intenseness of the idea. This therefore is the nature of the judgment and probability.

What principally gives authority to this system is, beside the undoubted arguments, upon which each part is founded, the agreement of these parts, and the necessity of one to explain another. The belief, which attends our memory, is of the same nature with that, which is derived from our judgments: nor is there any difference betwixt that judgment, which is derived from a constant and uniform connexion of causes and effects, and that which depends upon an interrupted and uncertain. It is indeed evident, that in all determinations, where the mind decides from contrary experiments, it is first divided within itself, and has an inclination to either side in proportion to the number of experiments we have seen and remember. This contest is at last determined to the advantage of that side, where we observe a superior number of these experiments; but still with a diminution of force in the evidence correspondent to the number of the opposite experiments. Each possibility, of which the probability is composed, operates separately upon the imagination; and it is the larger collection of possibilities, which at last prevails, and that with a force proportionable to its superiority. All these phenomena lead directly to the precedent system; nor will it ever be possible upon any other principles to give a satisfactory and consistent explication of them. Without considering these judgments as the effects of custom on the imagination, we shall lose ourselves in perpetual contradiction and absurdity.

SECTION FOURTEEN
Of the idea of necessary connexion

Having thus explained the manner, *in which we reason beyond our immediate impressions, and conclude that such particular causes must have such particular effects*; we must now return upon our footsteps to examine that question, which* first occurred to us, and which we dropped in our way, *viz. What is our idea of necessity, when we say that two objects are necessarily connected together.* Upon this head I repeat what I have often had occasion to observe, that as we have no idea, that is not derived from an impression, we must find some impression, that gives rise to this idea of necessity, if we assert we have really such an idea. In order to this I consider, in what objects necessity is commonly supposed to lie; and finding that it is always ascribed to causes and effects, I turn my eye to two objects supposed to be placed in that relation; and examine them in all the situations, of which they are susceptible. I immediately perceive, that they are *contiguous* in time and place, and that the object we

---

* Section 2.

call cause *precedes* the other we call effect. In no one instance can I go any farther, nor is it possible for me to discover any third relation betwixt these objects. I therefore enlarge my view to comprehend several instances; where I find like objects always existing in like relations of contiguity and succession. At first sight this seems to serve but little to my purpose. The reflection on several instances only repeats the same objects; and therefore can never give rise to a new idea. But upon farther enquiry I find, that the repetition is not in every particular the same, but produces a new impression, and by that means the idea, which I at present examine. For after a frequent repetition, I find, that upon the appearance of one of the objects, the mind is *determined* by custom to consider its usual attendant, and to consider it in a stronger light upon account of its relation to the first object. It is this impression, then, or *determination*, which affords me the idea of necessity.

I doubt not but these consequences will at first sight be received without difficulty, as being evident deductions from principles, which we have already established, and which we have often employed in our reasonings. This evidence both in the first principles, and in the deductions, may seduce us unwarily into the conclusion, and make us imagine it contains nothing extraordinary, nor worthy of our curiosity. But though such an inadvertence may facilitate the reception of this reasoning, it will make it be the more easily forgot; for which reason I think it proper to give warning, that I have just now examined one of the most sublime questions in philosophy, *viz. that concerning the power and efficacy of causes*; where all the sciences seem so much interested. Such a warning will naturally rouse up the attention of the reader, and make him desire a more full account of my doctrine, as well as of the arguments, on which it is founded. This request is so reasonable, that I cannot refuse complying with it; especially as I am hopeful that these principles, the more they are examined, will acquire the more force and evidence.

There is no question, which on account of its importance, as well as difficulty, has caused more disputes both among ancient and modern philosophers, than this concerning the efficacy of causes, or that quality which makes them be followed by their effects. But before they entered upon these disputes, methinks it would not have been improper to have examined what idea we have of that efficacy, which is the subject of the controversy. This is what I find principally wanting in their reasonings, and what I shall here endeavour to supply.

I begin with observing that the terms of *efficacy, agency, power, force, energy, necessity, connexion*, and *productive quality*, are all nearly synonymous; and therefore it is an absurdity to employ any of them in defining the rest. By this observation we reject at once all the vulgar definitions, which philosophers have given of power and efficacy; and instead of searching for the idea in these definitions, must look for it in the impressions, from which it is originally derived. If it be a compound idea, it must arise from compound impressions. If simple, from simple impressions.

I believe the most general and most popular explication of this matter, is to say,* that finding from experience, that there are several new productions in matter, such as the motions and variations of body, and concluding that there must somewhere be a power capable of producing them, we arrive at last by this reasoning at the idea of power and efficacy. But to be convinced that this explication is more popular than philosophical, we need but reflect on two very obvious principles. *First*, That reason alone can never give rise to any original idea, and *secondly*, that reason, as distinguished from experience, can never make us conclude, that a cause or productive quality is absolutely requisite to every beginning of existence. Both these considerations have been sufficiently explained: and therefore shall not at present be any farther insisted on.

I shall only infer from them, that since reason can never give rise to the idea of efficacy, that idea must be derived from experience, and from some particular instances of this efficacy, which make their passage into the mind by the common channels of sensation or reflection. Ideas always represent their objects or impressions; and *vice versa*, there are some objects necessary to give rise to every idea. If we pretend, therefore, to have any just idea of this efficacy, we must produce some instance, wherein the efficacy is plainly discoverable to the mind, and its operations obvious to our consciousness or sensation. By the refusal of this, we acknowledge, that the idea is impossible and imaginary, since the principle of innate ideas, which alone can save us from this dilemma, has been

* See Mr *Locke*, chapter of power.

already refuted, and is now almost universally rejected in the learned world. Our present business, then, must be to find some natural production, where the operation and efficacy of a cause can be clearly conceived and comprehended by the mind, without any danger of obscurity or mistake.

In this research we meet with very little encouragement from that prodigious diversity, which is found in the opinions of those philosophers, who have pretended to explain the secret force and energy of causes.* There are some, who maintain, that bodies operate by their substantial form; others, by their accidents or qualities; several, by their matter and form; some, by their form and accidents; others, by certain virtues and faculties distinct from all this. All these sentiments again are mixed and varied in a thousand different ways; and form a strong presumption, that none of them have any solidity or evidence, and that the supposition of an efficacy in any of the known qualities of matter is entirely without foundation. This presumption must increase upon us, when we consider, that these principles of substantial forms, and accidents, and faculties, are not in reality any of the known properties of bodies, but are perfectly unintelligible and inexplicable. For it is evident philosophers would never have had recourse to such obscure and uncertain principles, had they met with any satisfaction in such as are clear and intelligible; especially in such an affair as this, which must be an object of the simplest understanding, if not of the senses. Upon the whole, we may conclude, that it is impossible in any one instance to shew the principle, in which the force and agency of a cause is placed; and that the most refined and most vulgar understandings are equally at a loss in this particular. If any one think proper to refute this assertion, he need not put himself to the trouble of inventing any long reasonings: but may at once shew us an instance of a cause, where we discover the power or operating principle. This defiance we are obliged frequently to make use of, as being almost the only means of proving a negative in philosophy.

The small success, which has been met with in all the attempts to fix this power, has at last obliged philosophers to conclude, that the ultimate force and efficacy of nature is perfectly unknown to us, and that it is in vain we search for it in all the known qualities of

---

* See Father *Malbranche*, Book vi, Part 2, chap. 3; and the illustrations upon it.

matter. In this opinion they are almost unanimous; and it is only in the inference they draw from it, that they discover any difference in their sentiments. For some of them, as the *Cartesians* in particular, having established it as a principle, that we are perfectly acquainted with the essence of matter, have very naturally inferred, that it is endowed with no efficacy, and that it is impossible for it of itself to communicate motion, or produce any of those effects, which we ascribe to it. As the essence of matter consists in extension, and as extension implies not actual motion, but only mobility; they conclude, that the energy, which produces the motion, cannot lie in the extension.

This conclusion leads them into another, which they regard as perfectly unavoidable. Matter, say they, is in itself entirely unactive, and deprived of any power, by which it may produce, or continue, or communicate motion: but since these effects are evident to our senses, and since the power, that produces them, must be placed somewhere, it must lie in the DEITY, or that divine being, who contains in his nature all excellency and perfection. It is the deity, therefore, who is the prime mover of the universe, and who not only first created matter, and gave it its original impulse, but likewise by a continued exertion of omnipotence, supports its existence, and successively bestows on it all those motions, and configurations, and qualities, with which it is endowed.

This opinion is certainly very curious, and well worth our attention; but it will appear superfluous to examine it in this place, if we reflect a moment on our present purpose in taking notice of it. We have established it as a principle, that as all ideas are derived from impressions, or some precedent *perceptions*, it is impossible we can have any idea of power* and efficacy, unless some instances can be produced, wherein this power is *perceived* to exert itself. Now, as these instances can never be discovered in body, the *Cartesians*, proceeding upon their principle of innate ideas, have had recourse to a supreme spirit or deity, whom they consider as the only active being in the universe, and as the immediate cause of every alteration in matter. But the principle of innate ideas being allowed to be false, it follows, that the supposition of a deity can serve us in no stead, in accounting for that idea of agency, which we search for in vain in all the objects, which are presented

[* see Appendix to the *Treatise*.]

to our senses, or which we are internally conscious of in our own minds. For if every idea be derived from an impression, the idea of a deity proceeds from the same origin; and if no impression, either of sensation or reflection, implies any force or efficacy, it is equally impossible to discover or even imagine any such active principle in the deity. Since these philosophers, therefore, have concluded, that matter cannot be endowed with any efficacious principle, because it is impossible to discover in it such a principle; the same course of reasoning should determine them to exclude it from the supreme being. Or if they esteem that opinion absurd and impious, as it really is, I shall tell them how they may avoid it; and that is, by concluding from the very first, that they have no adequate idea of power or efficacy in any object; since neither in body nor spirit, neither in superior nor inferior natures, are they able to discover one single instance of it.

The same conclusion is unavoidable upon the hypothesis of those, who maintain the efficacy of second causes, and attribute a derivative, but a real power and energy to matter. For as they confess, that this energy lies not in any of the known qualities of matter, the difficulty still remains concerning the origin of its idea. If we have really an idea of power, we may attribute power to an unknown quality: but as it is impossible, that that idea can be derived from such a quality, and as there is nothing in known qualities, which can produce it; it follows that we deceive ourselves, when we imagine we are possessd of any idea of this kind, after the manner we commonly understand it. All ideas are derived from, and represent impressions. We never have any impression, that contains any power or efficacy. We never therefore have any idea of power.

It has been established as a certain principle, that general or abstract ideas are nothing but individual ones taken in a certain light, and that, in reflecting on any object, it is as impossible to exclude from our thought all particular degrees of quantity and quality as from the real nature of things. If we be possessed, therefore, of any idea of power in general, we must also be able to conceive some particular species of it; and as power cannot subsist alone, but is always regarded as an attribute of some being or existence, we must be able to place this power in some particular being, and conceive that being as endowed with a real force and energy, by which such a particular effect necessarily results from its operation. We must distinctly and particularly conceive the connexion betwixt the cause and effect, and be able to pronounce, from a simple view of the one, that it must be followed or preceded by the other. This is the true manner of conceiving a particular power in a particular body: and a general idea being impossible without an individual; where the latter is impossible, it is certain the former can never exist. Now nothing is more evident, than that the human mind cannot form such an idea of two objects, as to conceive any connexion betwixt them, or comprehend distinctly that power or efficacy, by which they are united. Such a connexion would amount to a demonstration, and would imply the absolute impossibility for the one object not to follow, or to be conceived not to follow upon the other: which kind of connexion has already been rejected in all cases. If any one is of a contrary opinion, and thinks he has attained a notion of power in any particular object, I desire he may point out to me that object. But till I meet with such-a-one, which I despair of, I cannot forbear concluding, that since we can never distinctly conceive how any particular power can possibly reside in any particular object, we deceive ourselves in imagining we can form any such general idea.

Thus upon the whole we may infer, that when we talk of any being, whether of a superior or inferior nature, as endowed with a power or force, proportioned to any effect; when we speak of a necessary connexion betwixt objects, and suppose, that this connexion depends upon an efficacy or energy, with which any of these objects are endowed; in all these expressions, *so applied*, we have really no distinct meaning, and make use only of common words, without any clear and determinate ideas. But as it is more probable, that these expressions do here lose their true meaning by being *wrong applied*, than that they never have any meaning; it will be proper to bestow another consideration on this subject, to see if possibly we can discover the nature and origin of those ideas, we annex to them.

Suppose two objects to be presented to us, of which the one is the cause and the other the effect; it is plain, that from the simple consideration of one, or both these objects we never shall perceive the tie by which they are united, or be able certainly to pronounce, that there is a connexion betwixt them. It is not, therefore, from any one instance, that we arrive at the idea of cause and effect, of a necessary connexion of power, of force, of energy, and of efficacy. Did we never see any but particular conjunctions of objects, entirely different from each other, we should never be able to form any such ideas.

But again; suppose we observe several instances, in which the same objects are always conjoined together, we immediately conceive a connexion betwixt them, and begin to draw an inference from one to another. This multiplicity of resembling instances, therefore, constitutes the very essence of power or connexion, and is the source from which the idea of it arises. In order, then, to understand the idea of power, we must consider that multiplicity; nor do I ask more to give a solution of that difficulty, which has so long perplexed us. For thus I reason. The repetition of perfectly similar instances can never *alone* give rise to an original idea, different from what is to be found in any particular instance, as has been observed, and as evidently follows from our fundamental principle, *that all ideas are copied from impressions*. Since therefore the idea of power is a new original idea, not to be found in any one instance, and which yet arises from the repetition of several instances, it follows, that the repetition *alone* has not that effect, but must either *discover* or *produce* something new, which is the source of that idea. Did the repetition neither discover nor produce anything new, our ideas might be multiplied by it, but would not be enlarged above what they are upon the observation of one single instance. Every enlargement, therefore, (such as the idea of power or connexion) which arises from the multiplicity of similar instances, is copied from some effects of the multiplicity, and will be perfectly understood by understanding these effects. Wherever we find anything new to be discovered or produced by the repetition, there we must place the power, and must never look for it in any other object.

But it is evident, in the first place, that the repetition of like objects in like relations of succession and contiguity *discovers* nothing new in any one of them: since we can draw no inference from it, nor make it a subject either of our demonstrative or probable reasonings; as has been already* proved. Nay suppose we

* Section 6.

could draw an inference, it would be of no consequence in the present case; since no kind of reasoning can give rise to a new idea, such as this of power is; but wherever we reason, we must antecedently be possessed of clear ideas, which may be the objects of our reasoning. The conception always precedes the understanding; and where the one is obscure, the other is uncertain; where the one fails, the other must fail also.

Secondly, It is certain that this repetition of similar objects in similar situations *produces* nothing new either in these objects, or in any external body. For it will readily be allowed, that the several instances we have of the conjunction of resembling causes and effects are in themselves entirely independent, and that the communication of motion, which I see result at present from the shock of two billiard-balls, is totally distinct from that which I saw result from such an impulse a twelve-month ago. These impulses have no influence on each other. They are entirely divided by time and place; and the one might have existed and communicated motion, though the other never had been in being.

There is, then, nothing new either discovered or produced in any objects by their constant conjunction, and by the uninterrupted resemblance of their relations of succession and contiguity. But it is from this resemblance, that the ideas of necessity, of power, and of efficacy, are derived. These ideas, therefore, represent not anything, that does or can belong to the objects, which are constantly conjoined. This is an argument, which, in every view we can examine it, will be found perfectly unanswerable. Similar instances are still the first source of our idea of power or necessity; at the same time that they have no influence by their similarity either on each other, or on any external object. We must, therefore, turn ourselves to some other quarter to seek the origin of that idea.

Though the several resembling instances, which give rise to the idea of power, have no influence on each other, and can never produce any new quality in the *object*, which can be the model of that idea, yet the *observation* of this resemblance produces a new impression *in the mind*, which is its real model. For after we have observed the resemblance in a sufficient number of instances, we immediately feel a determination of the mind to pass from one object to its usual attendant, and to conceive it in a stronger light upon account of that relation. This determination is the only effect of the resemblance; and therefore must be the same with power or efficacy, whose idea is derived from the resemblance. The several instances of resembling conjunctions lead us into the notion of power and necessity. These instances are in themselves totally distinct from each other, and have no union but in the mind, which observes them, and collects their ideas. Necessity, then, is the effect of this observation, and is nothing but an internal impression of the mind, or a determination to carry our thoughts from one object to another. Without considering it in this view, we can never arrive at the most distant notion of it, or be able to attribute it either to external or internal objects, to spirit or body, to causes or effects.

The necessary connexion betwixt causes and effects is the foundation of our inference from one to the other. The foundation of our inference is the transition arising from the accustomed union. These are, therefore, the same.

The idea of necessity arises from some impression. There is no impression conveyed by our senses, which can give rise to that idea. It must, therefore, be derived from some internal impression, or impression of reflection. There is no internal impression, which has any relation to the present business, but that propensity, which custom produces, to pass from an object to the idea of its usual attendant. This therefore is the essence of necessity. Upon the whole, necessity is something, that exists in the mind, not in objects; nor is it possible for us ever to form the most distant idea of it, considered as a quality in bodies. Either we have no idea of necessity, or necessity is nothing but that determination of the thought to pass from causes to effects, and from effects to causes, according to their experienced union.

Thus as the necessity, which makes two times two equal to four, or three angles of a triangle equal to two right ones, lies only in the act of the understanding, by which we consider and compare these ideas; in like manner the necessity or power, which unites causes and effects, lies in the determination of the mind to pass from the one to the other. The efficacy or energy of causes is neither placed in the causes themselves, nor in the deity, nor in the concurrence of these two principles; but belongs entirely to the soul, which considers the union of two or more objects in all past instances. It is here that the real power of causes is placed along with their connexion and necessity.

I am sensible, that of all the paradoxes, which I have had, or shall hereafter have occasion to advance in the course of this treatise, the present one is the most violent, and that it is merely by dint of solid proof and reasoning I can ever hope it will have admission, and overcome the inveterate prejudices of mankind. Before we are reconciled to this doctrine, how often must we repeat to ourselves, *that* the simple view of any two objects or actions, however related, can never give us any idea of power, or of a connexion betwixt them: *that* this idea arises from the repetition of their union: *that* the repetition neither discovers nor causes any thing in the objects, but has an influence only on the mind, by that customary transition it produces: *that* this customary transition is, therefore, the same with the power and necessity; which are consequently qualities of perceptions, not of objects, and are internally felt by the soul, and not perceived externally in bodies? There is commonly an astonishment attending every thing extraordinary; and this astonishment changes immediately into the highest degree of esteem or contempt, according as we approve or disapprove of the subject. I am much afraid, that though the foregoing reasoning appears to me the shortest and most decisive imaginable; yet with the generality of readers the bias of the mind will prevail, and give them a prejudice against the present doctrine.

This contrary bias is easily accounted for. It is a common observation, that the mind has a great propensity to spread itself on external objects, and to conjoin with them any internal impressions, which they occasion, and which always make their appearance at the same time that these objects discover themselves to the senses. Thus as certain sounds and smells are always found to attend certain visible objects, we naturally imagine a conjunction, even in place, betwixt the objects and qualities, though the qualities be of such a nature as to admit of no such conjunction, and really exist no where. But of this more fully hereafter.* Mean while it is sufficient to observe, that the same propensity is the reason, why we suppose necessity and power to lie in the objects we consider, not in our mind that considers them; notwithstanding it is not possible for us to form the most distant idea of that quality, when it is not taken for the determination of the mind, to pass from the idea of an object to that of its usual attendant.

* Part 4, Section 5.

But though this be the only reasonable account we can give of necessity, the contrary notion is so riveted in the mind from the principles above-mentioned, that I doubt not but my sentiments will be treated by many as extravagant and ridiculous. What! the efficacy of causes lie in the determination of the mind! As if causes did not operate entirely independent of the mind, and would not continue their operation, even though there was no mind existent to contemplate them, or reason concerning them. Thought may well depend on causes for its operation, but not causes on thought. This is to reverse the order of nature, and make that secondary, which is really primary, To every operation there is a power proportioned; and this power must be placed on the body, that operates. If we remove the power from one cause, we must ascribe it to another: but to remove it from all causes, and bestow it on a being, that is no ways related to the cause or effect, but by perceiving them, is a gross absurdity, and contrary to the most certain principles of human reason.

I can only reply to all these arguments, that the case is here much the same, as if a blind man should pretend to find a great many absurdities in the supposition, that the colour of scarlet is not the same with the sound of a trumpet, nor light the same with solidity. If we have really no idea of a power or efficacy in any object, or of any real connexion betwixt causes and effects, it will be to little purpose to prove, that an efficacy is necessary in all operations. We do not understand our own meaning in talking so, but ignorantly confound ideas, which are entirely distinct from each other. I am, indeed, ready to allow, that there may be several qualities both in material and immaterial objects, with which we are utterly unacquainted; and if we please to call these *power* or *efficacy*, it will be of little consequence to the world. But when, instead of meaning these unknown qualities, we make the terms of power and efficacy signify something, of which we have a clear idea, and which is incompatible with those objects, to which we apply it, obscurity and error begin then to take place, and we are led astray by a false philosophy. This is the case, when we transfer the determination of the thought to external objects, and suppose any real intelligible connexion betwixt them; that being a quality, which can only belong to the mind that considers them.

As to what may be said, that the operations of nature are independent of our thought and reasoning, I allow it; and accordingly have observed, that objects bear to each other the relations of contiguity and succession: that like objects may be observed in several instances to have like relations; and that all this is independent of, and antecedent to the operations of the understanding. But if we go any farther, and ascribe a power or necessary connexion to these objects; this is what we can never observe in them, but must draw the idea of it from what we feel internally in contemplating them. And this I carry so far, that I am ready to convert my present reasoning into an instance of it, by a subtility, which it will not be difficult to comprehend.

When any object is presented to us, it immediately conveys to the mind a lively idea of that object, which is usually found to attend it; and this determination of the mind forms the necessary connexion of these objects. But when we change the point of view, from the objects to the perceptions; in that case the impression is to be considered as the cause, and the lively idea as the effect; and their necessary connexion is that new determination, which we feel to pass from the idea of the one to that of the other. The uniting principle among our internal perceptions is as unintelligible as that among external objects, and is not known to us any other way than by experience. Now the nature and effects of experience have been already sufficiently examined and explained. It never gives us any insight into the internal structure or operating principle of objects, but only accustoms the mind to pass from one to another.

It is now time to collect all the different parts of this reasoning, and by joining them together form an exact definition of the relation of cause and effect, which makes the subject of the present enquiry. This order would not have been excusable, of first examining our inference from the relation before we had explained the relation itself, had it been possible to proceed in a different method. But as the nature of the relation depends so much on that of the inference, we have been obliged to advance in this seemingly preposterous manner, and make use of terms before we were able exactly to define them, or fix their meaning. We shall now correct this fault by giving a precise definition of cause and effect.

There may two definitions be given of this relation, which are only different, by their presenting a different view of the same object, and making us consider it either as a *philosophical* or as a *natural* relation; either as a comparison of two ideas, or as an association betwixt them. We may define a CAUSE to be 'An object precedent and contiguous to another, and where all the objects resembling the former are placed in like relations of precedency and contiguity to those objects that resemble the latter'. If this definition be esteemed defective, because drawn from objects foreign to the cause, we may substitute this other definition in its place, *viz.* A CAUSE is 'an object precedent and contiguous to another, and so united with it, that the idea of the one determines the mind to form the idea of the other, and the impression of the one to form a more lively idea of the other.' Should this definition also be rejected for the same reason, I know no other remedy, than that the persons, who express this delicacy, should substitute a juster definition in its place. But for my part I must own my incapacity for such an undertaking. When I examine with the utmost accuracy those objects, which are commonly denominated causes and effects, I find, in considering a single instance, that the one object is precedent and contiguous to the other; and in enlarging my view to consider several instances, I find only, that like objects are constantly placed in like relations of succession and contiguity. Again, when I consider the influence of this constant conjunction, I perceive, that such a relation can never be an object of reasoning, and can never operate upon the mind, but by means of custom, which determines the imagination to make a transition from the idea of one object to that of its usual attendant, and from the impression of one to a more lively idea of the other. However extraordinary these sentiments may appear, I think it fruitless to trouble myself with any farther enquiry or reasoning upon the subject, but shall repose myself on them as on established maxims.

It will only be proper, before we leave this subject, to draw some corollaries from it, by which we may remove several prejudices and popular errors, that have very much prevailed in philosophy. First, We may learn from the foregoing doctrine, that all causes are of the same kind, and that in particular there is no foundation for that distinction, which we sometimes make betwixt efficient causes and causes *sine qua non*; or betwixt efficient causes, and formal, and material, and exemplary, and final causes. For as our idea of efficiency is derived from the constant conjunction of two objects, wherever this is observed, the cause is efficient; and where it is not, there can never be a cause of any kind. For the same reason we must reject the distinction betwixt *cause* and *occasion*, when supposed to signify any thing essentially different from each other. If constant conjunction be implied in what we call occasion, it is a real cause. If not, it is no relation at all, and cannot give rise to any argument or reasoning.

Secondly, The same course of reasoning will make us conclude, that there is but one kind of *necessity*, as there is but one kind of cause, and that the common distinction betwixt *moral* and *physical* necessity is without any foundation in nature. This clearly appears from the precedent explication of necessity. It is the constant conjunction of objects, along with the determination of the mind, which constitutes a physical necessity: and the removal of these is the same thing with *chance*. As objects must either be conjoined or not, and as the mind must either be determined or not to pass from one object to another, it is impossible to admit of any medium betwixt chance and an absolute necessity. In weakening this conjunction and determination you do not change the nature of the necessity; since even in the operation of bodies, these have different degrees of constancy and force, without producing a different species of that relation.

The distinction, which we often make betwixt *power* and the *exercise* of it, is equally without foundation.

Thirdly, We may now be able fully to overcome all that repugnance, which it is so natural for us to entertain against the foregoing reasoning, by which we endeavoured to prove, that the necessity of a cause to every beginning of existence is not founded on any arguments either demonstrative or intuitive. Such an opinion will not appear strange after the foregoing definitions. If we define a cause to be *an object precedent and contiguous to another, and where all the objects resembling the former are placed in a like relation of priority and contiguity to those objects, that resemble the latter*; we may easily conceive, that there is no absolute nor metaphysical necessity, that every beginning of existence should be attended with such an object. If we define a cause to be, *an object precedent and contiguous to another, and so united with it in the imagination, that the idea of the one determines the mind to form the idea of the other, and the impression of the one to form a more lively idea of the other*, we shall make still less difficulty of assenting to this opinion. Such an influence on the mind is in itself perfectly extraordinary and incomprehensible; nor can we be certain of its reality, but from experience and observation.

I shall add as a fourth corollary that we can never have reason to believe that any object exists, of which we cannot form an idea. For as all our reasonings concerning existence are derived from causation, and as all our reasonings concerning causation are derived from the experienced conjunction of objects, not from any reasoning or reflection, the same experience must give us a notion of these objects, and must remove all mystery from our conclusions. This is so evident, that it would scarce have merited our attention, were it not to obviate certain objections of this kind, which might arise against the following reasonings concerning *matter* and *substance*. I need not observe, that a full knowledge of the object is not requisite, but only of those qualities of it, which we believe to exist.

SECTION FIFTEEN
Rules by which to judge of causes and effects

According to the precedent doctrine, there are no objects which by the mere survey, without consulting experience, we can determine to be the causes of any other; and no objects, which we can certainly determine in the same manner not to be the causes. Any thing may produce any thing. Creation, annihilation, motion, reason, volition; all these may arise from one another, or from any other object we can imagine. Nor will this appear strange, if we compare two principles explained above, *that the constant conjunction of objects determines their causation,* and * *that properly speaking, no objects are contrary to one another but existence and non-existence.* Where objects are not contrary, nothing hinders them from having that constant conjunction, on which the relation of cause and effect totally depends.

Since therefore it is possible for all objects to become causes or effects to each other, it may be proper to fix some general rules, by which we may know when they really are so.

* Part 1, Section 5.

1. The cause and effect must be contiguous in space and time.

2. The cause must be prior to the effect.

3. There must be a constant union betwixt the cause and effect. It is chiefly this quality, that constitutes the relation.

4. The same cause always produces the same effect, and the same effect never arises but from the same cause. This principle we derive from experience, and is the source of most of our philosophical reasonings. For when by any clear experiment we have discovered the causes or effects of any phenomenon, we immediately extend our observation to every phenomenon of the same kind, without waiting for that constant repetition, from which the first idea of this relation is derived.

5. There is another principle, which hangs upon this, *viz.* that where several different objects produce the same effect, it must be by means of some quality, which we discover to be common amongst them. For as like effects imply like causes, we must always ascribe the causation to the circumstance, wherein we discover the resemblance.

6. The following principle is founded on the same reason. The difference in the effects of two resembling objects must proceed from that particular, in which they differ. For as like causes always produce like effects, when in any instance we find our expectation to be disappointed, we must conclude that this irregularity proceeds from some difference in the causes.

7. When any object increases or diminishes with the increase or diminution of its cause, it is to be regarded as a compounded effect, derived from the union of the several different effects, which arise from the several different parts of the cause. The absence or presence of one part of the cause is here supposed to be always attended with the absence or presence of a proportionable part of the effect. This constant conjunction sufficiently proves, that the one part is the cause of the other. We must, however, beware not to draw such a conclusion from a few experiments. A certain degree of heat gives pleasure; if you diminish that heat, the pleasure diminishes; but it does not follow, that if you augment it beyond a certain degree, the pleasure will likewise augment; for we find that it degenerates into pain.

8. The eighth and last rule I shall take notice of is, that an object, which exists for any time in its full perfection without any effect,

is not the sole cause of that effect, but requires to be assisted by some other principle, which may forward its influence and operation. For as like effects necessarily follow from like causes, and in a contiguous time and place, their separation for a moment shews, that these causes are not complete ones.

Here is all the LOGIC I think proper to employ in my reasoning; and perhaps even this was not very necessary, but might have been supplied by the natural principles of our understanding. Our scholastic head-pieces and logicians shew no such superiority above the mere vulgar in their reason and ability, as to give us any inclination to imitate them in delivering a long system of rules and precepts to direct our judgment, in philosophy. All the rules of this nature are very easy in their invention, but extremely difficult in their application; and even experimental philosophy, which seems the most natural and simple of any, requires the utmost stretch of human judgment. There is no phenomenon in nature, but what is compounded and modified by so many different circumstances, that in order to arrive at the decisive point, we must carefully separate whatever is superfluous, and enquire by new experiments, if every particular circumstance of the first experiment was essential to it. These new experiments are liable to a discussion of the same kind; so that the utmost constancy is required to make us persevere in our enquiry, and the utmost sagacity to choose the right way among so many that present themselves. If this be the case even in natural philosophy, how much more in moral, where there is a much greater complication of circumstances, and where those views and sentiments, which are essential to any action of the mind, are so implicit and obscure, that they often escape our strictest attention, and are not only unaccountable in their causes, but even unknown in their existence? I am much afraid lest the small success I meet with in my enquiries will make this observation bear the air of an apology rather than of boasting.

If any thing can give me security in this particular, it will be the enlarging of the sphere of my experiments as much as possible; for which reason it may be proper in this place to examine the reasoning faculty of brutes, as well as that of human creatures.

SECTION SIXTEEN
Of the reason of animals

Next to the ridicule of denying an evident truth, is that of taking much pains to defend it; and no truth appears to me more evident, than that beasts are endowed with thought and reason as well as men. The arguments are in this case so obvious, that they never escape the most stupid and ignorant.

We are conscious, that we ourselves, in adapting means to ends, are guided by reason and design, and that it is not ignorantly nor casually we perform those actions, which tend to self-preservation, to the obtaining pleasure, and avoiding pain. When therefore we see other creatures, in millions of instances, perform like actions, and direct them to like ends, all our principles of reason and probability carry us with an invincible force to believe the existence of a like cause. It is needless in my opinion to illustrate this argument by the enumeration of particulars. The smallest attention will supply us with more than are requisite. The resemblance betwixt the actions of animals and those of men is so entire in this respect, that the very first action of the first animal we shall please to pitch on, will afford us an incontestable argument for the present doctrine.

This doctrine is as useful as it is obvious, and furnishes us with a kind of touchstone, by which we may try every system in this species of philosophy. It is from the resemblance of the external actions of animals to those we ourselves perform, that we judge their internal likewise to resemble ours; and the same principle of reasoning, carried one step farther, will make us conclude that since our internal actions resemble each other, the causes, from which they are derived, must also be resembling. When any hypothesis, therefore, is advanced to explain a mental operation, which is common to men and beasts, we must apply the same hypothesis to both; and as every true hypothesis will abide this trial, so I may venture to affirm, that no false one will ever be able to endure it. The common defect of those systems, which philosophers have employed to account for the actions of the mind, is, that they suppose such a subtility and refinement of thought, as not only exceeds the capacity of mere animals, but even of children and the common people in our own species; who are notwithstanding susceptible of the same emotions and affections as persons of the most accomplished genius and understanding. Such a subtility is a dear proof of the falsehood, as the contrary simplicity of the truth, of any system.

Let us therefore put our present system concerning the nature of the understanding to this decisive trial, and see whether it will equally account for the reasonings of beasts as for these of the human species.

Here we must make a distinction betwixt those actions of animals, which are of a vulgar nature, and seem to be on a level with their common capacities, and those more extraordinary instances of sagacity, which they sometimes discover for their own preservation, and the propagation of their species. A dog, that avoids fire and precipices, that shuns strangers, and caresses his master, affords us an instance of the first kind. A bird, that chooses with such care and nicety the place and materials of her nest, and sits upon her eggs for a due time, and in suitable season, with all the precaution that a chymist is capable of in the most delicate projection, furnishes us with a lively instance of the second.

As to the former actions, I assert they proceed from a reasoning, that is not in itself different, nor founded on different principles, from that which appears in human nature. It is necessary in the first place, that there be some impression immediately present to their memory or senses, in order to be the foundation of their judgment. From the tone of voice the dog infers his master's anger, and foresees his own punishment. From a certain sensation affecting his smell, he judges his game not to be far distant from him.

Secondly, The inference he draws from the present impression is built on experience, and on his observation of the conjunction of objects in past instances. As you vary this experience, he varies his reasoning. Make a beating follow upon one sign or motion for some time, and afterwards upon another; and he will successively draw different conclusions, according to his most recent experience.

Now let any philosopher make a trial, and endeavour to explain that act of the mind, which we call *belief*, and give an account of the principles, from which it is derived, independent of the influence of custom on the imagination, and let his hypothesis be equally applicable to beasts as to the human species; and after he has done this, I promise to embrace his opinion. But at the same time I demand as an equitable condition, that if my system be the only one, which can answer to all these terms, it may be received as entirely satisfactory and convincing. And that it is the only one, is evident almost without any reasoning. Beasts certainly never perceive any real connexion among objects. It is therefore by experience they infer one from another. They can never by any arguments form a general conclusion, that those objects, of which they have had no experience, resemble those of which they have. It is therefore by means of custom alone, that experience operates upon them. All this was sufficiently evident with respect to man. But with respect to beasts there cannot be the least suspicion of mistake; which must be owned to be a strong confirmation, or rather an invincible proof of my system.

Nothing shews more the force of habit in reconciling us to any phenomenoun, than this, that men are not astonished at the operations of their own reason, at the same time, that they admire the instinct of animals, and find a difficulty in explaining it, merely because it cannot be reduced to the very same principles. To consider the matter aright, reason is nothing but a wonderful and unintelligible instinct in our souls, which carries us along a certain train of ideas, and endows them with particular qualities, according to their particular situations and relations. This instinct, it is true, arises from past observation and experience; but can any one give the ultimate reason, why past experience and observation produces such an effect, any more than why nature alone should produce it? Nature may certainly produce whatever can arise from habit: nay, habit is nothing but one of the principles of nature, and derives all its force from that origin.

PART FOUR

Of the Sceptical and other Systems of Philosophy

In all demonstrative sciences the rules are certain and infallible; but when we apply them, our fallible and uncertain faculties are very apt to depart from them, and fall into error. We must, therefore, in every reasoning form a new judgment, as a check or control on our first judgment or belief; and must enlarge our view to comprehend a kind of history of all the instances, wherein our understanding has deceived us, compared with those, wherein its testimony was just and true. Our reason must be considered as a kind of cause, of which truth is the natural effect; but such-a-one as by the irruption of other causes, and by the inconstancy of our mental powers, may frequently be prevented. By this means all knowledge degenerates into probability; and this probability is greater or less, according to our experience of the veracity or deceitfulness of our understanding, and according to the simplicity or intricacy of the question.

There is no Algebraist nor Mathematician so expert in his science, as to place entire confidence in any truth immediately upon his discovery of it, or regard it as any thing, but a mere probability. Every time he runs over his proofs, his confidence increases; but still more by the approbation of his friends; and is raised to its utmost perfection by the universal assent and applauses of the learned world. Now it is evident, that this gradual increase of assurance is nothing but the addition of new probabilities, and is derived from the constant union of causes and effects, according to past experience and observation.

In accounts of any length or importance, Merchants seldom trust to the infallible certainty of numbers for their security; but by the artificial structure of the accounts, produce a probability beyond what is derived from the skill and experience of the accountant. For that is plainly of itself some degree of probability; though uncertain and variable, according to the degrees of his experience and length of the account. Now as none will maintain, that our assurance in a long numeration exceeds probability, I may safely affirm, that there scarce is any proposition concerning numbers, of which we can have a fuller security. For it is easily possible, by gradually diminishing the numbers, to reduce the longest series of addition to the most simple question, which can be formed, to an addition of two single numbers; and upon this supposition we shall find it impracticable to shew the precise limits of knowledge and of probability, or discover that particular number, at which the one ends and the other begins. But knowledge and probability are of such contrary and disagreeing natures, that they cannot well run insensibly into each other, and that because they will not divide, but must be either entirely present, or entirely absent. Besides, if any single addition were certain, every one would be so, and consequently the whole or total sum; unless the whole can be different from all its parts. I had almost said, that this was certain; but I reflect that it must reduce *itself*, as well as every other reasoning, and from knowledge degenerate into probability.

Since therefore all knowledge resolves itself into probability, and becomes at last of the same nature with that evidence, which we employ in common life, we must now examine this latter species of reasoning, and see on what foundation it stands.

In every judgment, which we can form concerning probability, as well as concerning knowledge, we ought always to correct the first judgment, derived from the nature of the object, by another judgment, derived from the nature of the understanding. It is certain a man of solid sense and long experience ought to have, and usually has, a greater assurance in his opinions, than one that is foolish and ignorant, and that our sentiments have different degrees of authority, even with ourselves, in proportion to the degrees of our reason and experience. In the man of the best sense and longest experience, this authority is never entire; since even such-a-one must be conscious of many errors in the past, and must still dread the like for the future. Here then arises a new species of probability to correct and regulate the first, and fix its just standard and proportion. As demonstration is subject to the control of probability, so is probability liable to a new correction by a reflex act of the mind, wherein the nature of our understanding, and our reasoning from the first probability become our objects.

Having thus found in every probability, beside the original uncertainty inherent in the subject, a new uncertainty derived from the weakness of that faculty, which judges, and having adjusted these two together, we are obliged by our reason to add a new doubt derived from the possibility of error in the estimation we make of the truth and fidelity of our faculties. This is a doubt, which immediately occurs to us, and of which, if we would closely pursue our reason, we cannot avoid giving a decision. But this decision, though it should be favourable to our preceding judgment, being founded only on probability, must weaken still further our first evidence, and must itself be weakened by a fourth doubt of the same kind, and so on *in infinitum*: till at last there remain nothing of the original probability, however great we may suppose it to have been, and however small the diminution by every new uncertainty. No finite object can subsist under a decrease repeated *in infinitum*; and even the vastest quantity, which can enter into human imagination, must in this manner be reduced to nothing. Let our first belief be never so strong, it must infallibly perish by passing through so many new examinations, of which each diminishes somewhat of its force and vigour. When I reflect on the natural fallibility of my judgment, I have less confidence in my opinions, than when I only consider the objects concerning which I reason; and when I proceed still farther, to turn the scrutiny against every successive estimation I make of my faculties, all the rules of logic require a continual diminution, and at last a total extinction of belief and evidence.

Should it here be asked me, whether I sincerely assent to this argument, which I seem to take such pains to inculcate, and whether I be really one of those sceptics, who hold that all is uncertain, and that our judgment is not in any thing possessed of *any* measures of truth and falsehood; I should reply, that this question is entirely superfluous, and that neither I, nor any other person was ever sincerely and constantly of that opinion. Nature, by an absolute and uncontrollable necessity has determined us to judge as well as to breathe and feel; nor can we any more forbear viewing certain objects in a stronger and fuller light, upon account of their customary connexion with a present impression, than we can hinder ourselves from thinking as long as we are awake, or seeing the surrounding bodies, when we turn our eyes towards them in broad sunshine. Whoever has taken the pains to refute the cavils of this *total* scepticism, has really disputed without an antagonist, and endeavoured by arguments to establish a faculty, which nature has antecedently implanted in the mind, and rendered unavoidable.

My intention then in displaying so carefully the arguments of that fantastic sect, is only to make the reader sensible of the truth of my hypothesis, *that all our reasonings concerning causes and effects are derived from nothing but custom; and that belief is more properly an act of the sensitive, than of the cogitative part of our natures.* I have here proved, that the very same principles, which make us form a decision upon any subject, and correct that decision by the consideration of our genius and capacity, and of the situation of our mind, when we examined that subject; I say, I have proved, that these same principles, when carried farther, and applied to every new reflex judgment, must, by continually diminishing the original evidence, at last reduce it to nothing, and utterly subvert all belief and opinion. If belief, therefore, were a simple act of the thought, without any peculiar manner of conception, or the addition of a force and vivacity, it must infallibly destroy itself, and in every case terminate in a total suspense of judgment. But as experience will sufficiently convince any one, who thinks it worth while to try, that though he can find no error in the foregoing arguments, yet he still continues to believe, and think, and reason as usual, he may safely conclude, that his reasoning and belief is some sensation or peculiar manner of conception, which it is impossible for mere ideas and reflections to destroy.

But here, perhaps, it may be demanded, how it happens, even upon my hypothesis, that these arguments above-explained produce not a total suspense of judgment, and after what manner the mind ever retains a degree of assurance in any subject? For as these new probabilities, which by their repetition perpetually diminish the original evidence, are founded on the very same principles, whether of thought or sensation, as the primary judgment, it may seem unavoidable, that in either case they must equally subvert it, and by the opposition, either of contrary thoughts or sensations, reduce the mind to a total uncertainty. I suppose, there is some question proposed to me, and that after revolving over the impressions of my memory and senses, and carrying my thoughts from them to such objects, as are commonly conjoined with them, I feel a stronger and more forcible conception on the one side, than on the other. This strong conception forms my first decision. I suppose, that afterwards I examine my judgment itself, and observing from experience, that it is sometimes just and sometimes erroneous, I consider it as regulated by contrary principles or causes, of which some lead to truth, and some to error; and in balancing these contrary causes, I diminish by a new probability the assurance of my first decision. This new probability is liable to the same diminution as the foregoing, and so on, *in infinitum*. It is therefore demanded, *how it happens, that even after all we retain a degree of belief, which is sufficient for our purpose, either in philosophy or common life.*

I answer, that after the first and second decision; as the action of the mind becomes forced and unnatural, and the ideas faint and obscure; though the principles of judgment, and the balancing of opposite causes be the same as at the very beginning; yet their influence on the imagination, and the vigour they add to, or diminish from the thought, is by no means equal. Where the mind reaches not its objects with easiness and facility, the same principles have not the same effect as in a more natural conception of the ideas; nor does the imagination feel a sensation, which holds any proportion with that which arises from its common judgments and opinions. The attention is on the stretch: the posture of the mind is uneasy; and the spirits being diverted from their natural course, are not governed in their movements by the same laws, at least not to the same degree, as when they flow in their usual channel.

If we desire similar instances, it will not be very difficult to find them. The present subject of metaphysics will supply us abundantly. The same argument, which would have been esteemed convincing in a reasoning concerning history or politics, has little or no influence in these abstruser subjects, even though it be perfectly comprehended; and that because there is required a study and an effort of thought, in order to its being comprehended: and this effort of thought disturbs the operation of our sentiments, on which the belief depends. The case is the same in other subjects. The straining of the imagination always hinders the regular flowing of the passions and sentiments. A tragic poet, that would represent his heroes as very ingenious and witty in their misfortunes, would never touch the passions. As the emotions of the soul prevent any subtile reasoning and reflection, so these latter actions of the mind are equally prejudicial to the former. The mind, as well as the body, seems to be endowed with a certain precise degree of force and activity, which it never employs in one action, but at the expense of all the rest. This is more evidently true, where the actions are of quite different natures; since in that case the force of the mind is not only diverted, but even the disposition changed, so as to render us incapable of a sudden transition from one action to the other, and still more of performing both at once. No wonder, then, the conviction, which arises from a subtile reasoning, diminishes in proportion to the efforts, which the imagination makes to enter into the reasoning, and to conceive it in all its parts. Belief, being a lively conception, can never be entire, where it is not founded on something natural and easy.

This I take to be the true state of the question, and cannot approve of that expeditious way, which some take with the sceptics, to reject at once all their arguments without enquiry or examination. If the sceptical reasonings be strong, say they, it is a proof, that reason may have some force and authority: if weak, they can never be sufficient to invalidate all the conclusions of our understanding. This argument is not just; because the sceptical reasonings, were it possible for them to exist, and were they not destroyed by their subtility, would be successively both strong and weak, according to the successive dispositions of the mind. Reason first appears in possession of the throne, prescribing laws, and imposing maxims, with an absolute sway and authority. Her enemy, therefore, is obliged to take shelter under her protection, and by making use of rational arguments to prove the fallaciousness and imbecility of reason, produces, in a manner, a patent under her band and seal. This patent has at first an authority, proportioned to the present and immediate authority of reason, from which it is derived. But as it is supposed to be contradictory to reason, it gradually diminishes the force of that governing power and its own at the same time; till at last they both vanish away into nothing, by a regular and just diminution. The sceptical and dogmatical reasons are of the same kind, though contrary in their operation and tendency; so that where the latter is strong, it has an enemy of equal force in the former to encounter; and as their forces were at first equal, they still continue so, as long as either of them subsists; nor does one of them lose any force in the contest, without taking as much from its antagonist. It is happy, therefore, that nature breaks the force of all sceptical arguments in time, and keeps them from having any considerable influence on the understanding. Were we to trust entirely to their self-destruction, that can never take place, until they have first subverted all conviction, and have totally destroyed human reason.

SECTION TWO

Of scepticism with regard to the senses

Thus the sceptic still continues to reason and believe, even though be asserts, that he cannot defend his reason by reason; and by the same rule he must assent to the principle concerning the existence of body, though he cannot pretend by any arguments of philosophy to maintain its veracity. Nature has not left this to his choice, and has doubtless, esteemed it an affair of too great importance to be trusted to our uncertain reasonings and speculations. We may well ask, *What causes induce us to believe in the existence of body?* but it is in vain to ask, *Whether there be body or not?* That is a point, which we must take for granted in all our reasonings.

The subject, then, of our present enquiry is concerning the *causes* which induce us to believe in the existence of body: and my reasonings on this head I shall begin with a distinction, which at first sight may seem superfluous, but which will contribute very much to the perfect understanding of what follows. We ought to examine apart those two questions, which are commonly confounded together, *viz.* Why we attribute a CONTINUED existence to objects, even when they are not present to the senses; and why we suppose them to have an existence DISTINCT from the mind and perception. Under this last head I comprehend their situation as well as relations, their *external* position as well as the *independence* of their existence and operation. These two questions concerning the continued and distinct existence of body are intimately connected together. For if the objects of our senses continue to exist, even when they are not perceived, their existence is of course independent of and distinct from the perception: and *vice versa*, if their existence be independent of the perception and distinct from it, they must continue to exist, even though they be not perceived. But though the decision of the one question decides the other; yet that we may the more easily discover the principles of human nature, from whence the decision arises, we shall carry along with us this distinction, and shall consider, whether it be the *senses*, *reason*, or the *imagination*, that produces the opinion of a *continued* or of a *distinct* existence. These are the only questions, that are intelligible on the present subject. For as to the notion of external existence, when taken for something specially different from our perceptions, we have already shewn* its absurdity.

To begin with the SENSES, it is evident these faculties are incapable of giving rise to the notion of the *continued* existence of their objects, after they no longer appear to the senses. For that is a contradiction in terms, and suppose that the senses continue to operate, even after they have ceased all manner of operation. These faculties, therefore, if they have any influence in the present case, must produce the opinion of a distinct, not of a continued existence; and in order to that, must present their impressions either as images and representations, or as these very distinct and external existences.

That our senses offer not their impressions as the images of something *distinct*, or *independent*, and *external*, is evident; because they convey to us nothing but a single perception, and never give us the least intimation of any thing beyond. A single perception can never produce the idea of a double existence, but by some inference either of the reason or imagination. When the mind looks farther than what immediately appears to it, its conclusions can never be put to the account of the senses; and it certainly looks farther, when from a single perception it infers a double

* Part 2, Section 6.

existence, and supposes the relations of resemblance and causation betwixt them.

If our senses, therefore, suggest any idea of distinct existences,
they must convey the impressions as those very existences, by a
kind of fallacy and illusion. Upon this head we may observe, that
all sensations are felt by the mind, such as they really are, and that
when we doubt, whether they present themselves as distinct
objects, or as mere impressions, the difficulty is not concerning
their nature, but concerning their relations and situation. Now if
the senses presented our impressions as external to, and independent of ourselves, both the objects and ourselves must be obvious
to our senses, otherwise they could not be compared by these
faculties. The difficulty, then, is how far we are *ourselves* the
objects of our senses.

It is certain there is no question in philosophy more abstruse
than that concerning identity, and the nature of the uniting
principle, which constitutes a person. So far from being able by
our senses merely to determine this question, we must have
recourse to the most profound metaphysics to give a satisfactory
answer to it; and in common life it is evident these ideas of self and
person are never very fixed nor determinate. It is absurd, therefore, to imagine the senses can ever distinguish betwixt ourselves
and external objects.

Add to this, that every impression, external and internal, passions,
affections, sensations, pains and pleasures, are originally on the
same footing; and that whatever other differences we may observe
among them, they appear, all of them, in their true colours, as
impressions or perceptions. And indeed, if we consider the matter
aright, it is scarce possible it should be otherwise, nor is it conceivable that our senses should be more capable of deceiving us in
the situation and relations, than in the nature of our impressions.
For since all actions and sensations of the mind are known to us by
consciousness, they must necessarily appear in every particular what
they are, and be what they appear. Every thing that enters the mind,
being in *reality* a perception, it is impossible any thing should to
feeling appear different. This were to suppose, that even where we
are most intimately conscious, we might be mistaken.

But not to lose time in examining, whether it is possible for our
senses to deceive us, and represent our perceptions as distinct from

ourselves, that is as *external* to and *independent* of us; let us consider whether they really do so, and whether this error proceeds from an immediate sensation, or from some other causes.

To begin with the question concerning *external* existence, it may perhaps be said, that setting aside the metaphysical question of the identity of a thinking substance, our own body evidently belongs to us; and as several impressions appear exterior to the body, we suppose them also exterior to ourselves. The paper, on which I write at present, is beyond my hand. The table is beyond the paper. The walls of the chamber beyond the table. And in casting my eye towards the window, I perceive a great extent of fields and buildings beyond my chamber. From all this it may be inferred, that no other faculty is required, beside the senses, to convince us of the external existence of body. But to prevent this inference, we need only weigh the three following considerations. *First*, That, properly speaking, it is not our body we perceive, when we regard our limbs and members, but certain impressions, which enter by the senses; so that the ascribing a real and corporeal existence to these impressions, or to their objects, is an act of the mind as difficult to explain, as that which we examine at present. *Secondly*, Sounds, and tastes, and smells, though commonly regarded by the mind as continued independent qualities, appear not to have any existence in extension, and consequently cannot appear to the senses as situated externally to the body. The reason, why we ascribe a place to them, shall be considered afterwards. *Thirdly*, Even our sight informs us not of distance or outness (so to speak) immediately and without a certain reasoning and experience, as is acknowledged by the most rational philosophers.

As to the *independency* of our perceptions on ourselves, this can never be an object of the senses; but any opinion we form concerning it, must be derived from experience and observation: and we shall see afterwards, that our conclusions from experience are far from being favourable to the doctrine of the independency of our perceptions. Mean while we may observe that when we talk of real distinct existences, we have commonly more in our eye their independency than external situation in place, and think an object has a sufficient reality, when its Being is uninterrupted, and independent of the incessant revolutions, which we are conscious of in ourselves.

Thus to resume what I have said concerning the senses; they give us no notion of continued existence, because they cannot operate beyond the extent, in which they really operate. They as little produce the opinion of a distinct existence, because they neither can offer it to the mind as represented, nor as original. To offer it as represented, they must present both an object and an image. To make it appear as original, they must convey a falsehood; and this falsehood must lie in the relations and situation: in order to which they must be able to compare the object with ourselves; and even in that case they do not, nor is it possible they should, deceive us. We may, therefore, conclude with certainty, that the opinion of a continued and of a distinct existence never arises from the senses.

To confirm this we may observe, that there are three different kinds of impressions conveyed by the senses. The first are those of the figure, bulk, motion and solidity of bodies. The second those of colours, tastes, smells, sounds, heat and cold. The third are the pains and pleasures, that arise from the application of objects to our bodies, as by the cutting of our flesh with steel, and such like. Both philosophers and the vulgar suppose the first of these to have a distinct continued existence. The vulgar only regard the second as on the same footing. Both philosophers and the vulgar, again, esteem the third to be merely perceptions and consequently interrupted and dependent beings.

Now it is evident, that, whatever may be our philosophical opinion, colours, sounds, heat and cold, as far as appears to the senses, exist after the same manner with motion and solidity, and that the difference we make betwixt them in this respect, arises not from the mere perception. So strong is the prejudice for the distinct continued existence of the former qualities, that when the contrary opinion is advanced by modern philosophers, people imagine they can almost refute it from their feeling and experience, and that their very senses contradict this philosophy. It is also evident, that colours, sounds, &c. are originally on the same footing with the pain that arises from steel, and pleasure that proceeds from a fire; and that the difference betwixt them is founded neither on perception nor reason, but on the imagination. For as they are confessed to be, both of them, nothing but perceptions arising from the particular configurations and motions of the parts of body, wherein possibly can their difference consist? Upon the whole, then, we may conclude, that as far as the senses are judges, all perceptions are the same in the manner of their existence.

We may also observe in this instance of sounds and colours, that we can attribute a distinct continued existence to objects without ever consulting REASON, or weighing our opinions by any philosophical principles. And indeed, whatever convincing arguments philosophers may fancy they can produce to establish the belief of objects independent of the mind, it is obvious these arguments are known but to very few, and that it is not by them, that children, peasants, and the greatest part of mankind are induced to attribute objects to some impressions, and deny them to others. Accordingly we find, that all the conclusions, which the vulgar form on this head, are directly contrary to those, which are confirmed by philosophy. For philosophy informs us, that every thing, which appears to the mind, is nothing but a perception, and is interrupted, and dependent on the mind: whereas the vulgar confound perceptions and objects, and attribute a distinct continued existence to the very things they feel or see. This sentiment, then, as it is entirely unreasonable, must proceed from some other faculty than the understanding. To which we may add, that as long as we take our perceptions and objects to be the same, we can never infer the existence of the one from that of the other, nor form any argument from the relation of cause and effect; which is the only one that can assure us of matter of fact. Even after we distinguish our perceptions from our objects, it will appear presently, that we are still incapable of reasoning from the existence of one to that of the other: so that upon the whole our reason neither does, nor is it possible it ever should, upon any supposition, give us an assurance of the continued and distinct existence of body. That opinion must be entirely owing to the IMAGINATION: which must now be the subject of our enquiry.

Since all impressions are internal and perishing existences, and appear as such, the notion of their distinct and continued existence must arise from a concurrence of some of their qualities with the qualities of the imagination, and since this notion does not extend to all of them, it must arise from certain qualities peculiar to some impressions. It will therefore be easy for us to discover these qualities by a comparison of the impressions, to which we attribute a distinct and continued existence, with those, which we regard as internal and perishing.

We may observe, then, that it is neither upon account of the involuntariness of certain impressions, as is commonly supposed, nor of their superior force and violence, that we attribute to them a reality, and continued existence, which we refuse to others, that are voluntary or feeble. For it is evident our pains and pleasures, our passions and affections, which we never suppose to have any existence beyond our perception, operate with greater violence, and are equally involuntary, as the impressions of figure and extension, colour and sound, which we suppose to be permanent beings. The heat of a fire, when moderate, is supposed to exist in the fire; but the pain, which it causes upon a near approach, is not taken to have any being, except in the perception.

These vulgar opinions, then, being rejected, we must search for some other hypothesis, by which we may discover those peculiar qualities in our impressions, which makes us attribute to them a distinct and continued existence.

After a little examination, we shall find, that all those objects, to which we attribute a continued existence, have a peculiar *constancy*, which distinguishes them from the impressions, whose existence depends upon our perception. Those mountains, and houses, and trees, which lie at present under my eye, have always appeared to me in the same order; and when I lose sight of them by shutting my eyes or turning my head, I soon after find them return upon me without the least alteration. My bed and table, my books and papers, present themselves in the same uniform manner, and change not upon account of any interruption in my seeing or perceiving them. This is the case with all the impressions, whose objects are supposed to have an external existence; and is the case with no other impressions, whether gentle or violent, voluntary or involuntary.

This constancy, however, is not so perfect as not to admit of very considerable exceptions. Bodies often change their position and qualities, and after a little absence or interruption may become hardly knowable. But here it is observable, that even in these changes they preserve a *coherence*, and have a regular dependence on each other; which is the foundation of a kind of reasoning from causation, and produces the opinion of their continued existence. When I return to my chamber after an hour's absence, I find not my fire in the same situation, in which I left it: but then I am accustomed in other instances to see a like alteration produced in a like time, whether I am present or absent, near or remote. This coherence, therefore, in their changes is one of the characteristics of external objects, as well as their constancy.

Having found that the opinion of the continued existence of body depends on the COHERENCE, and CONSTANCY of certain impressions, I now proceed to examine after what manner these qualities give rise to so extraordinary an opinion. To begin with the coherence; we may observe, that though those internal impressions, which we regard as fleeting and perishing, have also a certain coherence or regularity in their appearances, yet it is of somewhat a different nature, from that which we discover in bodies. Our passions are found by experience to have a mutual connexion with and dependence on each other; but on no occasion is it necessary to suppose, that they have existed and operated, when they were not perceived, in order to preserve the same dependence and connexion, of which we have had experience. The case is not the same with relation to external objects. Those require a continued existence, or otherwise lose, in a great measure, the regularity of their operation. I am here seated in my chamber with my face to the fire; and all the objects, that strike my senses, are contained in a few yards around me. My memory, indeed, informs me of the existence of many objects; but then this information extends not beyond their past existence, nor do either my senses or memory give any testimony to the continuance of their being. When therefore I am thus seated, and revolve over these thoughts, I hear on a sudden a noise as of a door turning upon its hinges; and a little after see a porter, who advances towards me. This gives occasion to many new reflections and reasonings. First, I never have observed, that this noise could proceed from any thing but the motion of a door; and therefore conclude, that the present phenomenon is a contradiction to all past experience, unless the door, which I remember on the other side the chamber, be still in being. Again, I have always found, that a human body was possessed of a quality, which I call gravity, and which hinders it from mounting in the air, as this porter must have done to arrive at my chamber, unless the stairs I remember be not annihilated by my absence. But this is not all. I receive a letter, which upon opening it I perceive by the hand-writing and subscription to have come from a friend, who says he is two hundred leagues distant. It is evident I can never account for this phenomenon, conformable to my experience in other instances, without spreading out in my mind the whole sea and continent between us, and supposing the effects and continued existence of posts and ferries, according to my memory and observation. To consider these phenomena of the porter and letter in a certain light, they are contradictions to common experience, and may be regarded as objections to those maxims, which we form concerning the connexions of causes and effects. I am accustomed to hear such a sound, and see such an object in motion at the same time. I have not received in this particular instance both these perceptions. These observations are contrary, unless I suppose that the door still remains, and that it was opened without my perceiving it: and this supposition, which was at first entirely arbitrary and hypothetical, acquires a force and evidence by its being the only one, upon which I can reconcile these contradictions. There is scarce a moment of my life, wherein there is not a similar instance presented to me, and I have not occasion to suppose the continued existence of objects, in order to connect their past and present appearances, and give them such an union with each other, as I have found by experience to be suitable to their particular natures and circumstances. Here then I am naturally led to regard the world, as something real and durable, and as preserving its existence, even when it is no longer present to my perception.

But though this conclusion from the coherence of appearances may seem to be of the same nature with our reasonings concerning causes and effects; as being derived from custom, and regulated by past experience; we shall find upon examination, that they are at the bottom considerably different from each other, and that this inference arises from the understanding, and from custom in an indirect and oblique manner. For it will readily be allowed, that since nothing is ever really present to the mind, besides its own perceptions, it is not only impossible, that any habit should ever be acquired otherwise than by the regular succession of these perceptions, but also that any habit should ever exceed that degree of regularity. Any degree, therefore, of regularity in our perceptions, can never be a foundation for us to infer a greater degree of regularity in some objects, which are not perceived; since this supposes a contradiction, *viz*. a habit acquired by what was never present to the mind. But it is evident, that whenever we infer the continued existence of the objects of sense from their coherence, and the frequency of their union, it is in order to bestow on the objects a greater regularity than what is observed in our mere perceptions. We remark a connexion betwixt two kinds of objects in their past appearance to the senses, but are not able to observe this connexion to be perfectly constant, since the turning about of our head or the shutting of our eyes is able to break it. What then do we suppose in this case, but that these objects still continue their usual connexion, notwithstanding their apparent interruption, and that the irregular appearances are joined by something, of which we are insensible? But as all reasoning concerning matters of fact arises only from custom, and custom can only be the effect of repeated perceptions, the extending of custom and reasoning beyond the perceptions can never be the direct and natural effect of the constant repetition and connexion, but must arise from the co-operation of some other principles.

I have already observed,* in examining the foundation of mathematics, that the imagination, when set into any train of thinking, is apt to continue, even when its object fails it, and like a galley put in motion by the oars, carries on its course without any new impulse. This I have assigned for the reason, why, after considering several loose standards of equality, and correcting them by each other, we proceed to imagine so correct and exact a standard of that relation, as is not liable to the least error or variation. The same principle makes us easily entertain this opinion of the continued existence of body. Objects have a certain coherence even as they appear to our senses; but this coherence is much greater and more uniform, if we suppose the objects to have a continued existence; and as the mind is once in the train of observing an uniformity among objects, it naturally continues, till it renders the uniformity as complete as possible. The simple supposition of their continued existence suffices for this purpose, and gives us a notion

* Part 2, Section 4.

of a much greater regularity among objects, than what they have when we look no farther than our senses.

But whatever force we may ascribe to this principle, I am afraid it is too weak to support alone so vast an edifice, as is that of the continued existence of all external bodies; and that we must join the *constancy* of their appearance to the *coherence*, in order to give a satisfactory account of that opinion. As the explication of this will lead me into a considerable compass of very profound reasoning; I think it proper, in order to avoid confusion, to give a short sketch or abridgment of my system, and afterwards draw out all its parts in their full compass. This inference from the constancy of our perceptions, like the precedent from their coherence, gives rise to the opinion of the *continued* existence of body, which is prior to that of its *distinct* existence, and produces that latter principle.

When we have been accustomed to observe a constancy in certain impressions, and have found, that the perception of the sun or ocean, for instance, returns upon us after an absence or annihilation with like parts and in a like order, as at its first appearance, we are not apt to regard these interrupted perceptions as different (which they really are), but on the contrary consider them as individually the same, upon account of their resemblance. But as this interruption of their existence is contrary to their perfect identity, and makes us regard the first impression as annihilated, and the second as newly created, we find ourselves somewhat at a loss, and are involved in a kind of contradiction. In order to free ourselves from this difficulty, we disguise, as much as possible, the interruption, or rather remove it entirely, by supposing that these interrupted perceptions are connected by a real existence, of which we are insensible. This supposition, or idea of continued existence, acquires a force and vivacity from the memory of these broken impressions, and from that propensity, which they give us, to suppose them the same; and according to the precedent reasoning, the very essence of belief consists in the force and vivacity of the conception.

In order to justify this system, there are four things requisite. *First*, To explain the *principium individuationis*, or principle of identity. *Secondly*, Give a reason, why the resemblance of our broken and interrupted perceptions induces us to attribute an identity to them. *Thirdly*, Account for that propensity, which this illusion gives, to unite these broken appearances by a continued existence. *Fourthly* and lastly, Explain that force and vivacity of conception, which arises from the propensity.

First, As to the principle of individuation; we may observe, that the view of any one object is not sufficient to convey the idea of identity. For in that proposition, *an object is the same with itself*, if the idea expressed by the word, *object*, were no ways distinguished from that meant by *itself*, we really should mean nothing, nor would the proposition contain a predicate and a subject, which however are implied in this affirmation. One single object conveys the idea of unity, not that of identity.

On the other hand, a multiplicity of objects can never convey this idea, however resembling they may be supposed. The mind always pronounces the one not to be the other, and considers them as forming two, three, or any determinate number of objects, whose existences are entirely distinct and independent.

Since then both number and unity are incompatible with the relation of identity, it must lie in something that is neither of them. But to tell the truth, at first sight this seems utterly impossible. Betwixt unity and number there can be no medium; no more than betwixt existence and nonexistence. After one object is supposed to exist, we must either suppose another also to exist; in which case we have the idea of number: or we must suppose it not to exist; in which case the first object remains at unity.

To remove this difficulty, let us have recourse to the idea of time or duration. I have already observed,* that time, in a strict sense, implies succession, and that when we apply its idea to any unchangeable object, it is only by a fiction of the imagination, by which the unchangeable object is supposd to participate of the changes of the co-existent objects, and in particular of that of our perceptions. This fiction of the imagination almost universally takes place; and it is by means of it, that a single object, placed before us, and surveyed for any time without our discovering in it any interruption or variation, is able to give us a notion of identity. For when we consider any two points of this time, we may place them in different lights: we may either survey them at the very same instant; in which case they give us the idea of number, both by themselves and by the object; which must be

---

* Part 2, Section 5.

multiplied, in order to be conceivd at once, as existent in these two different points of time. Or on the other hand, we may trace the succession of time by a like succession of ideas, and conceiving first one moment, along with the object then existent, imagine afterwards a change in the time without any *variation* or *interruption* in the object; in which case it gives us the idea of unity. Here then is an idea, which is a medium betwixt unity and number; or more properly speaking, is either of them, according to the view, in which we take it: and this idea we call that of identity. We cannot, in any propriety of speech, say, that an object is the same with itself, unless we mean, that the object existent at one time is the same with itself existent at another. By this means we make a difference, betwixt the idea meant by the word, *object*, and that meant by *itself*, without going the length of number, and at the same time without restraining ourselves to a strict and absolute unity.

Thus the principle of individuation is nothing but the *invariableness* and *uninterruptedness* of any object, through a supposd variation of time, by which the mind can trace it in the different periods of its existence, without any break of the view, and without being obliged to form the idea of multiplicity or number.

I now proceed to explain the *second* part of my system, and shew why the constancy of our perceptions makes us ascribe to them a perfect numerical identity, though there be very long intervals betwixt their appearance, and they have only one of the essential qualities of identity, *viz*, *invariableness*. That I may avoid all ambiguity and confusion on this head, I shall observe, that I here account for the opinions and belief of the vulgar with regard to the existence of body; and therefore must entirely conform myself to their manner of thinking and of expressing themselves. Now we have already observed, that however philosophers may distinguish betwixt the objects and perceptions of the senses; which they suppose co-existent and resembling; yet this is a distinction, which is not comprehended by the generality of mankind, who as they perceive only one being, can never assent to the opinion of a double existence and representation. Those very sensations, which enter by the eye or ear, are with them the true objects, nor can they readily conceive that this pen or paper, which is immediately perceived, represents another, which is different from, but resembling it. In order, therefore, to accommodate myself to their notions, I shall at first suppose; that there is only a single existence, which I shall call indifferently *object* or *perception*, according as it shall seem best to suit my purpose, understanding by both of them what any common man means by a hat, or shoe, or stone, or any other impression, conveyed to him by his senses. I shall be sure to give warning, when I return to a more philosophical way of speaking and thinking.

To enter, therefore, upon the question concerning the source of the error and deception with regard to identity, when we attribute it to our resembling perceptions, notwithstanding their interruption; I must here recall an observation, which I have already proved and explained.* Nothing is more apt to make us mistake one idea for another, than any relation betwixt them, which associates them together in the imagination, and makes it pass with facility from one to the other. Of all relations, that of resemblance is in this respect the most efficacious; and that because it not only causes an association of ideas, but also of dispositions, and makes us conceive the one idea by an act or operation of the mind, similar to that by which we conceive the other. This circumstance I have observed to be of great moment; and we may establish it for a general rule, that whatever ideas place the mind in the same disposition or in similar ones, are very apt to be confounded. The mind readily passes from one to the other, and perceives not the change without a strict attention, of which, generally speaking, it is wholly incapable.

In order to apply this general maxim, we must first examine the disposition of the mind in viewing any object which preserves a perfect identity, and then find some other object, that is confounded with it, by causing a similar disposition. When we fix our thought on any object, and suppose it to continue the same for some time; it is evident we suppose the change to lie only in the time, and never exert ourselves to produce any new image or idea of the object. The faculties of the mind repose themselves in a manner, and take no more exercise, than what is necessary to continue that idea, of which we were formerly possessed, and which subsists without variation or interruption. The passage from one moment to another is scarce felt, and distinguishes not

* Part 2, Section 5.

itself by a different perception or idea, which may require a different direction of the spirits, in order to its conception.

Now what other objects, beside identical ones, are capable of placing the mind in the same disposition, when it considers them, and of causing the same uninterrupted passage of the imagination from one idea to another? This question is of the last importance. For if we can find any such objects, we may certainly conclude, from the foregoing principle, that they are very naturally confounded with identical ones, and are taken for them in most of our reasonings. But though this question be very important, it is not very difficult nor doubtful. For I immediately reply, that a succession of related objects places the mind in this disposition, and is considered with the same smooth and uninterrupted progress of the imagination, as attends the view of the same invariable object. The very nature and essence of relation is to connect our ideas with each other, and upon the appearance of one, to facilitate the transition to its correlative. The passage betwixt related ideas is, therefore, so smooth and easy, that it produces little alteration on the mind, and seems like the continuation of the same action; and as the continuation of the same action is an effect of the continued view of the same object, it is for this reason we attribute sameness to every succession of related objects. The thought slides along the succession with equal facility, as if it considered only one object; and therefore confounds the succession with the identity.

We shall afterwards see many instances of this tendency of relation to make us ascribe an *identity* to *different* objects; but shall here confine ourselves to the present subject. We find by experience, that there is such a *constancy* in almost all the impressions of the senses, that their interruption produces no alteration on them, and hinders them not from returning the same in appearance and in situation as at their first existence. I survey the furniture of my chamber; I shut my eyes, and afterwards open them; and find the new perceptions to resemble perfectly those, which formerly struck my senses. This resemblance is observed in a thousand instances, and naturally connects together our ideas of these interrupted perceptions by the strongest relation, and conveys the mind with an easy transition from one to another. An easy transition or passage of the imagination, along the ideas of these different and interrupted perceptions, is almost the same disposition of mind with that in which we consider one constant and uninterrupted perception. It is therefore very natural for us to mistake the one for the other.*

The persons, who entertain this opinion concerning the identity of our resembling perceptions, are in general all the unthinking and unphilosophical part of mankind, (that is, all of us, at one time or other) and consequently such as suppose their perceptions to be their only objects, and never think of a double existence internal and external, representing and represented. The very image, which is present to the senses, is with us the real body; and it is to these interrupted images we ascribe a perfect identity. But as the interruption of the appearance seems contrary to the identity, and naturally leads us to regard these resembling perceptions as different from each other, we here find ourselves at a loss how to reconcile such opposite opinions. The smooth passage of the imagination along the ideas of the resembling perceptions makes us ascribe to them a perfect identity. The interrupted manner of their appearance makes us consider them as so many resembling, but still distinct beings, which appear after certain intervals. The perplexity arising from this contradiction produces a propension to unite these broken appearances by the fiction of a continued existence, which is the *third* part of that hypothesis I proposed to explain.

Nothing is more certain from experience, than that any contradiction either to the sentiments or passions gives a sensible uneasiness, whether it proceeds from without or from within; from the opposition of external objects, or from the combat of internal principles. On the contrary, whatever strikes in with the natural propensities, and either externally forwards their

---

* This reasoning, it must be confessed, is somewhat abstruse, and difficult to be comprehended; but it is remarkable, that this very difficulty may be converted into a proof of the reasoning. We may observe, that there are two relations, and both of them resemblances, which contribute to our mistaking the succession of our interrupted perceptions for an identical object. The first is, the resemblance of the perceptions: the second is the resemblance, which the act of the mind in surveying a succession of resembling objects bears to that in surveying an identical object. Now these resemblances we are apt to confound with each other; and it is natural we should, according to this very reasoning. But let us keep them distinct, and we shall find no difficulty in conceiving the precedent argument.

satisfaction, or internally concurs with their movements, is sure to give a sensible pleasure. Now there being here an opposition betwixt the notion of the identity of resembling perceptions, and the interruption of their appearance, the mind must be uneasy in that situation, and will naturally seek relief from the uneasiness. Since the uneasiness arises from the opposition of two contrary principles, it must look for relief by sacrificing the one to the other. But as the smooth passage of our thought along our resembling perceptions makes us ascribe to them an identity, we can never without reluctance yield up that opinion. We must, therefore, turn to the other side, and suppose that our perceptions are no longer interrupted, but preserve a continued as well as an invariable existence, and are by that means entirely the same. But here the interruptions in the appearance of these perceptions are so long and frequent, that it is impossible to overlook them; and as the *appearance* of a perception in the mind and its *existence* seem at first sight entirely the same, it may be doubted, whether we can ever assent to so palpable a contradiction, and suppose a perception to exist without being present to the mind. In order to clear up this matter, and learn how the interruption in the appearance of a perception implies not necessarily an interruption in its existence, it will be proper to touch upon some principles, which we shall have occasion to explain more fully afterwards.*

We may begin with observing, that the difficulty in the present case is not concerning the matter of fact, or whether the mind forms such a conclusion concerning the continued existence of its perceptions, but only concerning the manner in which the conclusion is formed, and principles from which it is derived. It is certain, that almost all mankind, and even philosophers themselves, for the greatest part of their lives, take their perceptions to be their only objects, and suppose, that the very being, which is intimately present to the mind, is the real body or material existence. It is also certain, that this very perception or object is supposed to have a continued uninterrupted being, and neither to be annihilated by our absence, nor to be brought into existence by our presence. When we are absent from it, we say it still exists, but that we do not feel, we do not see it. When we are present, we say

* Section 6.

we feel, or see it. Here then may arise two questions; *First*, How we can satisfy ourselves in supposing a perception to be absent from the mind without being annihilated. *Secondly*, After what manner we conceive an object to become present to the mind, without some new creation of a perception or image; and what we mean by this *seeing*, and *feeling*, and *perceiving*.

As to the first question; we may observe, that what we call a *mind*, is nothing but a heap or collection of different perceptions, united together by certain relations, and supposed, though falsely, to be endowed with a perfect simplicity and identity. Now as every perception is distinguishable from another, and may be considered as separately existent; it evidently follows, that there is no absurdity in separating any particular perception from the mind; that is, in breaking off all its relations, with that connected mass of perceptions, which constitute a thinking being.

The same reasoning affords us an answer to the second question. If the name of *perception* renders not this separation from a mind absurd and contradictory, the name of *object*, standing for the very same thing, can never render their conjunction impossible. External objects are seen, and felt, and become present to the mind; that is, they acquire such a relation to a connected heap of perceptions, as to influence them very considerably in augmenting their number by present reflections and passions, and in storing the memory with ideas. The same continued and uninterrupted Being may, therefore, be sometimes present to the mind, and sometimes absent from it, without any real or essential change in the Being itself. An interrupted appearance to the senses implies not necessarily an interruption in the existence. The supposition of the continued existence of sensible objects or perceptions involves no contradiction. We may easily indulge our inclination to that supposition. When the exact resemblance of our perceptions makes us ascribe to them an identity, we may remove the seeming interruption by feigning a continued being, which may fill those intervals, and preserve a perfect and entire identity to our perceptions.

But as we here not only *feign* but *believe* this continued existence, the question is, *from whence arises such a belief*; and this question leads us to the *fourth* member of this system. It has been proved already, that belief in general consists in nothing, but the vivacity of an idea; and that an idea may acquire this vivacity by its relation to some present impression. Impressions are naturally the most vivid perceptions of the mind; and this quality is in part conveyed by the relation to every connected idea. The relation causes a smooth passage from the impression to the idea, and even gives a propensity to that passage. The mind falls so easily from the one perception to the other, that it scarce perceives the change, but retains in the second a considerable share of the vivacity of the first. It is excited by the lively impression; and this vivacity is conveyed to the related idea, without any great diminution in the passage, by reason of the smooth transition and the propensity of the imagination.

But suppose, that this propensity arises from some other principle, besides that of relation; it is evident it must still have the same effect, and convey the vivacity from the impression to the idea. Now this is exactly the present case. Our memory presents us with a vast number of instances of perceptions perfectly resembling each other, that return at different distances of time, and after considerable interruptions. This resemblance gives us a propension to consider these interrupted perceptions as the same; and also a propension to connect them by a continued existence, in order to justify this identity, and avoid the contradiction, in which the interrupted appearance of these perceptions seems necessarily to involve us. Here then we have a propensity to feign the continued existence of all sensible objects; and as this propensity arises from some lively impressions of the memory, it bestows a vivacity on that fiction: or in other words, makes us believe the continued existence of body. If sometimes we ascribe a continued existence to objects, which are perfectly new to us, and of whose constancy and coherence we have no experience, it is because the manner, in which they present themselves to our senses, resembles that of constant and coherent objects; and this resemblance is a source of reasoning and analogy, and leads us to attribute the same qualities to similar objects.

I believe an intelligent reader will find less difficulty to assent to this system, than to comprehend it fully and distinctly, and will allow, after a little reflection, that every part carries its own proof along with it. It is indeed evident, that as the vulgar *suppose* their perceptions to be their only objects, and at the same time *believe* the continued existence of matter, we must account for the origin of the belief upon that supposition. Now upon that supposition, it is a false opinion that any of our objects, or perceptions, are identically the same after an interruption; and consequently the opinion of their identity can never arise from reason, but must arise from the imagination. The imagination is seduced into such an opinion only by means of the resemblance of certain perceptions; since we find they are only our resembling perceptions, which we have a propension to suppose the same. This propension to bestow an identity on our resembling perceptions, produces the fiction of a continued existence; since that fiction, as well as the identity, is really false, as is acknowledged by all philosophers, and has no other effect than to remedy the interruption of our perceptions, which is the only circumstance that is contrary to their identity. In the last place this propension causes belief by means of the present impressions of the memory; since without the remembrance of former sensations, it is plain we never should have any belief of the continued existence of body. Thus in examining all these parts, we find that each of them is supported by the strongest proofs: and that all of them together form a consistent system, which is perfectly convincing. A strong propensity or inclination alone, without any present impression, will sometimes cause a belief or opinion. How much more when aided by that circumstance?

But though we are led after this manner, by the natural propensity of the imagination, to ascribe a continued existence to those sensible objects or perceptions, which we find to resemble each other in their interrupted appearance; yet a very little reflection and philosophy is sufficient to make us perceive the fallacy of that opinion. I have already observed, that there is an intimate connexion betwixt those two principles, of a *continued* and of a *distinct* or *independent* existence, and that we no sooner establish the one than the other follows, as a necessary consequence. It is the opinion of a continued existence, which first takes place, and without much study or reflection draws the other along with it, wherever the mind follows its first and most natural tendency. But when we compare experiments, and reason a little upon them, we quickly perceive, that the doctrine of the independent existence of our sensible perceptions is contrary to the plainest experience. This leads us backward upon our footsteps to perceive our error in attributing a continued existence to our perceptions, and is the origin of many very curious opinions, which we shall here endeavour to account for.

It will first be proper to observe a few of those experiments, which convince us, that our perceptions are not possessed of any independent existence. When we press one eye with a finger, we immediately perceive all the objects to become double, and one half of them to be removed from their common and natural position. But as we do not attribute a continued existence to both these perceptions, and as they are both of the same nature, we clearly perceive, that all our perceptions are dependent on our organs, and the disposition of our nerves and animal spirits. This opinion is confirmed by the seeming increase and diminution of objects, according to their distance; by the apparent alterations in their figure; by the changes in their colour and other qualities from our sickness and distempers: and by an infinite number of other experiments of the same kind; from all which we learn, that our sensible perceptions are not possessed of any distinct or independent existence.

The natural consequence of this reasoning should be, that our perceptions have no more a continued than an independent existence; and indeed philosophers have so far run into this opinion, that they change their system, and distinguish (as we shall do for the future) betwixt perceptions and objects, of which the former are supposed to be interrupted, and perishing, and different at every different return; the latter to be uninterrupted, and to preserve a continued existence and identity. But however philosophical this new system may be esteemed, I assert that it is only a palliative remedy, and that it contains all the difficulties of the vulgar system, with some others, that are peculiar to itself. There are no principles either of the understanding or fancy, which lead us directly to embrace this opinion of the double existence of perceptions and objects, nor can we arrive at it but by passing through the common hypothesis of the identity and continuance of our interrupted perceptions. Were we not first persuaded, that our perceptions are our only objects, and continue to exist even when they no longer make their appearance to the senses, we should never be led to think, that our perceptions and objects are different, and that our objects alone preserve a continued existence. The latter hypothesis has no primary recommendation either to reason or the imagination, but acquires all its influence on the imagination from the former. This proposition contains two parts, which we shall endeavour to prove as distinctly and clearly, as such abstruse subjects will permit.

As to the first part of the proposition, *that this philosophical hypothesis has no primary recommendation, either to reason or the imagination*, we may soon satisfy ourselves with regard to *reason* by the following reflections. The only existences, of which we are certain, are perceptions, which being immediately present to us by consciousness, command our strongest assent, and are the first foundation of all our conclusions. The only conclusion we can draw from the existence of one thing to that of another, is by means of the relation of cause and effect, which shews, that there is a connexion betwixt them, and that the existence of one is dependent on that of the other. The idea of this relation is derived from past experience, by which we find, that two beings are constantly conjoined together, and are always present at once to the mind. But as no beings are ever present to the mind but perceptions; it follows that we may observe a conjunction or a relation of cause and effect between different perceptions, but can never observe it between perceptions and objects. It is impossible, therefore, that from the existence or any of the qualities of the former, we can ever form any conclusion concerning the existence of the latter, or ever satisfy our reason in this particular.

It is no less certain, that this philosophical system has no primary recommendation to the *imagination*, and that that faculty would never, of itself, and by its original tendency, have fallen upon such a principle. I confess it will be somewhat difficult to prove this to the full satisfaction of the reader; because it implies a negative, which in many cases will not admit of any positive proof. If any one would take the pains to examine this question, and would invent a system, to account for the direct origin of this opinion from the imagination, we should be able, by the examination of that system, to pronounce a certain judgment in the present subject. Let it be taken for granted, that our perceptions are broken, and interrupted, and however like, are still different from each other; and let any one upon this supposition shew why the fancy, directly and immediately, proceeds to the belief of another existence, resembling these perceptions in their nature, but yet continued, and uninterrupted, and identical; and after he has done this to my satisfaction, I promise to renounce my present opinion. Mean while I cannot forbear concluding, from the very abstractedness and difficulty of the first supposition, that it is an improper subject for the fancy to work upon. Whoever would explain the origin of the *common* opinion concerning the continued and distinct existence of body, must take the mind in its *common* situation, and must proceed upon the supposition, that our perceptions are our only objects, and continue to exist even when they are not perceived. Though this opinion be false, it is the most natural of any, and has alone any primary recommendation to the fancy.

As to the second part of the proposition, *that the philosophical system acquires all its influence on the imagination from the vulgar one;* we may observe, that this is a natural and unavoidable consequence of the foregoing conclusion, *that it has no primary recommendation to reason or the imagination.* For as the philosophical system is found by experience to take hold of many minds, and in particular of all those, who reflect ever so little on this subject, it must derive all its authority from the vulgar system; since it has no original authority of its own. The manner, in which these two systems, though directly contrary, are connected together, may be explained, as follows.

The imagination naturally runs on in this train of thinking. Our perceptions are our only objects: resembling perceptions are the same, however broken or uninterrupted in their appearance: this appearing interruption is contrary to the identity: the interruption consequently extends not beyond the appearance, and the perception or object really continues to exist, even when absent from us: our sensible perceptions have, therefore, a continued and uninterrupted existence. But as a little reflection destroys this conclusion, that our perceptions have a continued existence, by shewing that they have a dependent one, it would naturally be expected, that we must altogether reject the opinion, that there is such a thing in nature as a continued existence, which is preserved even when it no longer appears to the senses. The case, however, is otherwise. Philosophers are so far from rejecting the opinion of a continued existence upon rejecting that of the independence and continuance of our sensible perceptions, that though all sects agree in the latter sentiment, the former, which is, in a manner, its necessary consequence, has been peculiar to a few extravagant sceptics; who after all maintained that opinion in words only, and were never able to bring themselves sincerely to believe it.

There is a great difference betwixt such opinions as we form after a calm and profound reflection, and such as we embrace by a kind of instinct or natural impulse, on account of their suitableness and conformity to the mind. If these opinions become contrary, it is not difficult to foresee which of them will have the advantage. As long as our attention is bent upon the subject, the philosophical and studied principle may prevail; but the moment we relax our thoughts, nature will display herself, and draw us back to our former opinion. Nay she has sometimes such an influence, that she can stop our progress, even in the midst of our most profound reflections, and keep us from running on with all the consequences of any philosophical opinion. Thus though we clearly perceive the dependence and interruption of our perceptions, we stop short in our career, and never upon that account reject the notion of an independent and continued existence. That opinion has taken such deep root in the imagination, that it is impossible ever to eradicate it, nor will any strained metaphysical conviction of the dependence of our perceptions be sufficient for that purpose.

But though our natural and obvious principles here prevail above our studied reflections, it is certain there must be some struggle and opposition in the case: at least so long as these rejections retain any force or vivacity. In order to set ourselves at ease in this particular, we contrive a new hypothesis, which seems to comprehend both these principles of reason and imagination. This hypothesis is the philosophical, one of the double existence of perceptions and objects; which pleases our reason, in allowing, that our dependent perceptions are interrupted and different; and at the same time is agreeable to the imagination, in attributing a continued existence to something else, which we call *objects*. This philosophical system, therefore, is the monstrous offspring of two principles, which are contrary to each other, which are both at once embraced by the mind, and which are unable mutually to destroy each other. The imagination tells us, that our resembling perceptions have a continued and uninterrupted existence, and are not annihilated by their absence. Reflection tells us, that even our resembling perceptions are interrupted in their existence, and different from each other. The contradiction betwixt these opinions we elude by a new fiction, which is conformable to the hypotheses both of reflection and fancy, by ascribing these contrary qualities to different existences; the *interruption* to perceptions, and the *continuance* to objects. Nature is obstinate, and will not quit the field, however strongly attacked by reason; and at the same time reason is so clear in the point, that there is no possibility of disguising her. Not being able to reconcile these two enemies, we endeavour to set ourselves at ease as much as possible, by successively granting to each whatever it demands, and by feigning a double existence, where each may find something, that has all the conditions it desires. Were we fully convinced, that our resembling perceptions are continued, and identical, and independent, we should never run into this opinion of a double existence, since we should find satisfaction in our first supposition, and would not look beyond. Again, were we fully convinced, that our perceptions are dependent, and interrupted, and different, we should be as little inclined to embrace the opinion of a double existence; since in that case we should clearly perceive the error of our first supposition of a continued existence, and would never regard it any farther. It is therefore from the intermediate situation of the mind, that this opinion arises, and from such an adherence to these two contrary principles, as makes us seek some pretext to justify our receiving both; which happily at last is found in the system of a double existence.

Another advantage of this philosophical system is its similarity to the vulgar one; by which means we can humour our reason for a moment, when it becomes troublesome and sollicitous; and yet upon its least negligence or inattention, can easily return to our vulgar and natural notions. Accordingly we find, that philosophers neglect not this advantage; but immediately upon leaving their closets, mingle with the rest of mankind in those exploded opinions, that our perceptions are our only objects, and continue identically and uninterruptedly the same in all their interrupted appearances.

There are other particulars of this system, wherein we may remark its dependence on the fancy, in a very conspicuous manner. Of these, I shall observe the two following. *First*, We suppose external objects to resemble internal perceptions. I have already shewn, that the relation of cause and effect can never afford us any just conclusion from the existence or qualities of our perceptions to the existence of external continued objects: and I shall farther add, that even though they could afford such a conclusion, we should never have any reason to infer, that our objects resemble our perceptions. That opinion, therefore, is derived from nothing but the quality of the fancy above-explained, *that it borrows all its ideas from some precedent perception.* We never can conceive any thing but perceptions, and therefore must make every thing resemble them.

Secondly, As we suppose our objects in general to resemble our perceptions, so we take it for granted, that every particular object resembles that perception, which it causes. The relation of cause and effect determines us to join the other of resemblance; and the ideas of these existences being already united together in the fancy by the former relation, we naturally add the latter to complete the union. We have a strong propensity to complete every union by joining new relations to those which we have before observed betwixt any ideas, as we shall have occasion to observe presently.[*]

Having thus given an account of all the systems both popular and philosophical, with regard to external existences, I cannot forbear giving vent to a certain sentiment, which arises upon reviewing those systems. I begun this subject with premising, that we ought to have an implicit faith in our senses, and that this would be the conclusion, I should draw from the whole of my reasoning. But to be ingenuous, I feel myself *at present* of a quite contrary sentiment, and am more inclined to repose no faith at all in my senses, or rather imagination, than to place in it such an implicit confidence. I cannot conceive how such trivial qualities of the fancy, conducted by such false suppositions, can ever lead to any solid and rational system. They are the coherence and con-stancy of our perceptions, which produce the opinion of their continued existence; though these qualities of perceptions have no perceivable connexion with such an existence. The constancy of our perceptions has the most considerable effect, and yet is attended with the greatest difficulties. It is a gross illusion to

[*] Section 5.

suppose, that our resembling perceptions are numerically the same; and it is this illusion, which leads us into the opinion, that these perceptions are uninterrupted, and are still existent, even when they are not present to the senses. This is the case with our popular system. And as to our philosophical one, it is liable to the same difficulties; and is over-and-above loaded with this absurdity, that it at once denies and establishes the vulgar supposition. Philosophers deny our resembling perceptions to be identically the same, and uninterrupted; and yet have so great a propensity to believe them such, that they arbitrarily invent a new set of perceptions, to which they attribute these qualities. I say, a new set of perceptions: for we may well suppose in general, but it is impossible for us distinctly to conceive, objects to be in their nature any thing but exactly the same with perceptions. What then can we look for from this confusion of groundless and extraordinary opinions but error and falsehood? And how can we justify to ourselves any belief we repose in them?

This sceptical doubt, both with respect to reason and the senses, is a malady, which can never be radically cured, but must return upon us every moment, however we may chase it away, and sometimes may seem entirely free from it. It is impossible upon any system to defend either our understanding or senses; and we but expose them farther when we endeavour to justify them in that manner. As the sceptical doubt arises naturally from a profound and intense reflection on those subjects, it always increases, the farther we carry our reflections, whether in opposition or conformity to it. Carelessness and in-attention alone can afford us any remedy. For this reason I rely entirely upon them; and take it for granted, whatever may be the reader's opinion at this present moment, that an hour hence he will be persuaded there is both an external and internal world; and going upon that supposition, I intend to examine some general systems both ancient and modern, which have been proposed of both, before I proceed to a more particular enquiry concerning our impressions. This will not, perhaps, in the end be found foreign to our present purpose.

SECTION THREE
Of the ancient philosophy

Several moralists have recommended it as an excellent method of becoming acquainted with our own hearts, and knowing our progress in virtue, to recollect our dreams in a morning, and examine them with the same rigour, that we would our most serious and most deliberate actions. Our character is the same throughout, say they, and appears best where artifice, fear, and policy have no place, and men can neither be hypocrites with themselves nor others. The generosity, or baseness of our temper, our meekness or cruelty, our courage or pusillanimity, influence the fictions of the imagination with the most unbounded liberty, and discover themselves in the most glaring colours. In like manner, I am persuaded, there might be several useful discoveries made from a criticism of the fictions of the ancient philosophy, concerning *substances, and substantial forms, and accidents, and occult qualities*; which, however unreasonable and capricious, have a very intimate connexion with the principles of human nature.

It is confessed by the most judicious philosophers, that our ideas of bodies are nothing but collections formed by the mind of the ideas of the several distinct sensible qualities, of which objects are composed, and which we find to have a constant union with each other. But however these qualities may in themselves be entirely distinct, it is certain we commonly regard the compound, which they form, as ONE thing, and as continuing the SAME under very considerable alterations. The acknowledged composition is evidently contrary to this supposed *simplicity*, and the variation to the *identity*. It may, therefore, be worth while to consider the causes, which make us almost universally fall into such evident contradictions, as well as the *means* by which we endeavour to conceal them.

It is evident, that as the ideas of the several distinct, *successive* qualities of objects are united together by a very close relation, the mind, in looking along the succession, must be carried from one part of it to another by an easy transition, and will no more perceive the change, than if it contemplated the same unchangeable object.

This easy transition is the effect, or rather essence of relation; and as the imagination readily takes one idea for another, where their influence on the mind is similar; hence it proceeds, that any such succession of related qualities is readily considered as one continued object, existing without any variation. The smooth and uninterrupted progress of the thought, being alike in both cases, readily deceives the mind, and makes us ascribe an identity to the changeable succession of connected qualities.

But when we alter our method of considering the succession, and instead of traceing it gradually through the successive points of time, survey at once any two distinct periods of its duration, and compare the different conditions of the successive qualities; in that case the variations, which were insensible when they arose gradually, do now appear of consequence, and seem entirely to destroy the identity. By this means there arises a kind of contrariety in our method of thinking, from the different points of view, in which we survey the object, and from the nearness or remoteness of those instants of time, which we compare together. When we gradually follow an object in its successive changes, the smooth progress of the thought makes us ascribe an identity to the succession; because it is by a similar act of the mind we consider an unchangeable object. When we compare its situation after a considerable change the progress of the thought is broke; and consequently we are presented with the idea of diversity: in order to reconcile which contradictions the imagination is apt to feign something unknown and invisible, which it supposes to continue the same under all these variations; and this unintelligible something it calls a *substance, or original and first matter.*

We entertain a like notion with regard to the *simplicity* of substances, and from like causes. Suppose an object perfectly simple and indivisible to be presented, along with another object, whose *co-existent* parts are connected together by a strong relation, it is evident the actions of the mind, in considering these two objects, are not very different. The imagination conceives the simple object at once, with facility, by a single effort of thought, without change or variation. The connexion of parts in the compound object has almost the same effect, and so unites the object within itself, that the fancy feels not the transition in passing from one part to another. Hence the colour, taste, figure, solidity, and other qualities, combined in a peach or melon, are conceived to form one thing; and that on account of their close relation, which makes them affect the thought in the same manner, as if perfectly uncompounded. But the mind rests not here. Whenever it views the object in another light, it finds that all these qualities are different, and distinguishable, and separable from each other; which view of things being destructive of its primary and more natural notions, obliges the imagination to feign an unknown something, or *original* substance and matter, as a principle of union or cohesion among these qualities, and as what may give the compound object a title to be called one thing, notwithstanding its diversity and composition.

The peripatetic philosophy asserts the *original* matter to be perfectly homogeneous in all bodies, and considers fire, water, earth, and air, as of the very same substance; on account of their gradual revolutions and changes into each other. At the same time it assigns to each of these species of objects a distinct *substantial form*, which it supposes to be the source of all those different qualities they possess, and to be a new foundation of simplicity and identity to each particular species. All depends on our manner of viewing the objects. When we look along the insensible changes of bodies, we suppose all of them to be of the same substance or essence. When we consider their sensible differences, we attribute to each of them a substantial and essential difference. And in order to indulge ourselves in both these ways of considering our objects, we suppose all bodies to have at once a substance and a substantial form.

The notion of *accidents* is an unavoidable consequence of this method of thinking with regard to substances and substantial forms; nor can we forbear looking upon colours, sounds, tastes, figures, and other properties of bodies, as existences, which cannot subsist apart, but require a subject of inhesion to sustain and support them. For having never discovered any of these sensible qualities, where, for the reasons above-mentioned, we did not likewise fancy a substance to exist; the same habit, which makes us infer a connexion betwixt cause and effect, makes us here infer a dependence of every quality on the unknown substance. The custom of imagining a dependence has the same effect as the custom of observing it would have. This conceit, however, is no more reasonable than any of the foregoing. Every quality being a distinct thing from another, may be conceived to exist apart, and may exist apart, not only from every other quality, but from that unintelligible chimera of a substance.

But these philosophers carry their fictions still farther in their sentiments concerning *occult qualities*, and both suppose a substance supporting, which they do not understand, and an accident supported, of which they have as imperfect an idea. The whole system, therefore, is entirely incomprehensible, and yet is derived from principles as natural as any of these above-explained.

In considering this subject we may observe a gradation of three opinions, that rise above each other, according as the persons, who form them, acquire new degrees of reason and knowledge. These opinions are that of the vulgar, that of a false philosophy, and that of the true; where we shall find upon enquiry, that the true philosophy approaches nearer to the sentiments of the vulgar, than to those of a mistaken knowledge. It is natural for men, in their common and careless way of thinking, to imagine they perceive a connexion betwixt such objects as they have constantly found united together; and because custom has rendered it difficult to separate the ideas, they are apt to fancy such a separation to be in itself impossible and absurd. But philosophers, who abstract from the effects of custom, and compare the ideas of objects, immediately perceive the falsehood of these vulgar sentiments, and discover that there is no known connexion among objects. Every different object appears to them entirely distinct and separate; and they perceive, that it is not from a view of the nature and qualities of objects we infer one from another, but only when in several instances we observe them to have been constantly conjoined. But these philosophers, instead of drawing a just inference from this observation, and concluding, that we have no idea of power or agency, separate from the mind, and belonging to causes; I say, instead of drawing this conclusion, they frequently search for the qualities, in which this agency consists, and are displeased with every system, which their reason suggests to them, in order to explain it. They have sufficient force of genius to free them from the vulgar error, that there is a natural and perceivable connexion betwixt the several sensible qualities and actions of matter; but not sufficient to keep them from ever seeking for this connexion in matter, or causes. Had they fallen upon the just conclusion, they would have returned back to the situation of the vulgar, and would have regarded all these disquisitions with indolence and indifference. At present they seem to be in a very lamentable condition, and such as the poets have given us but a faint notion of in their descriptions of the punishment of *Sisyphus* and *Tantalus*. For what can be imagined more tormenting, than to seek with eagerness, what for ever flies us; and seek for it in a place, where it is impossible it can ever exist?

But as nature seems to have observed a kind of justice and compensation in every thing, she has not neglected philosophers more than the rest of the creation; but has reserved them a consolation amid all their disappointments and afflictions. This consolation principally consists in their invention of the words: *faculty* and *occult quality*. For it being usual, after the frequent use of terms, which are really significant and intelligible, to omit the idea, which we would express by them, and to preserve only the custom, by which we recall the idea at pleasure; so it naturally happens, that after the frequent use of terms, which are wholly insignificant and unintelligible, we fancy them to be on the same footing with the precedent, and to have a secret meaning, which we might discover by reflection. The resemblance of their appearance deceives the mind, as is usual, and makes us imagine a thorough resemblance and conformity. By this means these philosophers set themselves at ease, and arrive at last, by an illusion, at the same indifference, which the people attain by their stupidity, and true philosophers by their moderate scepticism. They need only say, that any phenomenon, which puzzles them, arises from a faculty or an occult quality, and there is an end of all dispute and enquiry upon the matter.

But among all the instances, wherein the Peripatetics have shewn they were guided by every trivial propensity of the imagination, no one is more-remarkable than their *sympathies, antipathies, and horrors of a vacuum*. There is a very remarkable inclination in human nature, to bestow on external objects the same emotions, which it observes in itself; and to find every where those ideas, which are most present to it. This inclination, it is true, is suppressed by a little reflection, and only takes place in children, poets, and the ancient philosophers. It appears in children, by their desire of beating the stones, which hurt them: in poets, by their readiness to personify every thing: and in the ancient philosophers, by these fictions of sympathy and antipathy. We must pardon children, because of their age; poets, because they profess to follow implicitly the suggestions of their fancy: but what excuse shall we find to justify our philosophers in so signal a weakness?

SECTION FOUR

Of the modern philosophy

But here it may be objected, that the imagination, according to my own confession, being the ultimate judge of all systems of philosophy, I am unjust in blaming the ancient philosophers for making use of that faculty, and allowing themselves to be entirely guided by it in their reasonings. In order to justify myself, I must distinguish in the imagination betwixt the principles which are permanent, irresistible, and universal; such as the customary transition from causes to effects, and from effects to causes: and the principles, which are changeable, weak, and irregular; such as those I have just now taken notice of. The former are the foundation of all our thoughts and actions, so that upon their removal human nature must immediately perish and go to ruin. The latter are neither unavoidable to mankind, nor necessary, or so much as useful in the conduct of life; but on the contrary are observed only to take place in weak minds, and being opposite to the other principles of custom and reasoning, may easily be subverted by a due contrast and opposition. For this reason the former are received by philosophy, and the latter rejected. One who concludes somebody to be near him, when he hears an articulate voice in the dark, reasons justly and naturally; though that conclusion be derived from nothing but custom, which infixes and enlivens the idea of a human creature, on account of his usual conjunction with the present impression. But one, who is tormented he knows not why, with the apprehension of spectres in the dark, may, perhaps, be said to reason, and to reason naturally too: but then it must be in the same sense, that a malady is said to be natural; as arising from natural causes, though it be contrary to health, the most agreeable and most natural situation of man.

The opinions of the ancient philosophers, their fictions of substance and accident, and their reasonings concerning substantial forms and occult qualities, are like the spectres in the dark, and are derived from principles, which, however common, are neither universal nor unavoidable in human nature. The *modern philosophy* pretends to be entirely free from this defect, and to arise only from the solid, permanent, and consistent principles of the imagination. Upon what grounds this pretension is founded must now be the subject of our enquiry.

The fundamental principle of that philosophy is the opinion concerning colours, sounds, tastes, smells, heat and cold; which it asserts to be nothing but impressions in the mind, derived from the operation of external objects, and without any resemblance to the qualities of the objects. Upon examination, I find only one of the reasons commonly produced for this opinion to be satisfactory, *viz.* that derived from the variations of those impressions, even while the external object, to all appearance, continues the same. These variations depend upon several circumstances. Upon the different situations of our health: a man in a malady feels a disagreeable taste in meats, which before pleased him the most. Upon the different complexions and constitutions of men: that seems bitter to one, which is sweet to another. Upon the difference of their external situation and position: colours reflected from the clouds change according to the distance of the clouds, and according to the angle they make with the eye and luminous body. Fire also communicates the sensation of pleasure at one distance, and that of pain at another. Instances of this kind are very numerous and frequent.

The conclusion drawn from them, is likewise as satisfactory as can possibly be imagined. It is certain, that when different impressions of the same sense arise from any object, every one of these impressions has not a resembling quality existent in the object. For as the same object cannot, at the same time, be endowed with different qualities of the same sense, and as the same quality cannot resemble impressions entirely different; it evidently follows, that many of our impressions have no external model or archetype. Now from like effects we presume like causes. Many of the impressions of colour, sound, &c. are confessed to be nothing but internal existences, and to arise from causes, which no ways resemble them. These impressions are in appearance nothing different from the other impressions of colour, sound, &c. We conclude, therefore, that they are, all of them, derived from a like origin.

This principle being once admitted, all the other doctrines of that philosophy seem to follow by an easy consequence. For upon the removal of sounds, colours, heat, cold, and other sensible qualities, from the rank of continued independent existences, we are reduced merely to what are called primary qualities, as the only *real* ones, of which we have any adequate notion. These primary qualities are extension and solidity, with their different mixtures and modifications; figure, motion, gravity, and cohesion. The generation, increase, decay, and corruption of animals and vegetables, are nothing but changes of figure and motion; as also the operations of all bodies on each other; of fire, of light, water, air, earth, and of all the elements and powers of nature. One figure and motion produces another figure and motion; nor does there remain in the material universe any other principle, either active or passive, of which we can form the most distant idea.

I believe many objections might be made to this system: but at present I shall confine myself to one, which is in my opinion very decisive. I assert, that instead of explaining the operations of external objects by its means, we utterly annihilate all these objects, and reduce ourselves to the opinions of the most extravagant scepticism concerning them. If colours, sounds, tastes, and smells be merely perceptions, nothing we can conceive is possessed of a real, continued, and independent existence; not even motion, extension and solidity, which are the primary qualities chiefly insisted on.

To begin with the examination of motion; it is evident this is a quality altogether inconceivable alone, and without a reference to some other object. The idea of motion necessarily supposes that of a body moving. Now what is our idea of the moving body, without which motion is incomprehensible? It must resolve itself into the idea of extension or of solidity; and consequently the reality of motion depends upon that of these other qualities.

This opinion, which is universally acknowledged concerning motion, I have proved to be true with regard to extension; and have shewn that it is impossible to conceive extension, but as composed of parts, endowed with colour or solidity. The idea of extension is a compound idea; but as it is not compounded of an infinite number of parts or inferior ideas, it must at last resolve itself into such as are perfectly simple and indivisible. These simple and indivisible parts, not being ideas of extension, must be non-entities, unless conceived as coloured or solid. Colour is excluded from any real existence. The reality, therefore, of our idea of extension depends upon the reality of that of solidity, nor can the former be just while the latter is chimerical. Let us, then, lend our attention to the examination of the idea of solidity.

The idea of solidity is that of two objects, which being impelled by the utmost force, cannot penetrate each other; but still maintain a separate and distinct existence. Solidity, therefore, is perfectly incomprehensible alone, and without the conception of some bodies, which are solid, and maintain this separate and distinct existence. Now what idea have we of these bodies? The ideas of colours, sounds, and other secondary qualities are excluded. The idea of motion depends on that of extension, and the idea of extension on that of solidity. It is impossible, therefore, that the idea of solidity can depend on either of them. For that would be to run in a circle, and make one idea depend on another, while at the same time the latter depends on the former. Our modern philosophy, therefore, leaves us no just nor satisfactory idea of solidity; nor consequently of matter.

This argument will appear entirely conclusive to every one that comprehends it; but because it may seem abstruse and intricate to the generality of readers, I hope to be excused, if I endeavour to render it more obvious by some variation of the expression. In order to form an idea of solidity, we must conceive two bodies pressing on each other without any penetration; and it is impossible to arrive at this idea, when we confine ourselves to one object, much more without conceiving any. Two non-entities cannot exclude each other from their places; because they never possess any place, nor can be endowed with any quality. Now I ask, what idea do we form of these bodies or objects, to which we suppose solidity to belong? To say, that we conceive them merely as solid, is to run on *in infinitum*. To affirm, that we paint them out to ourselves as extended, either resolves all into a false idea, or returns in a circle. Extension must necessarily be considered either as coloured, which is a false idea; or as solid, which brings us back to the first question. We may make the same observation concerning mobility and figure; and upon the whole must conclude, that after the exclusion of colours, sounds, heat and cold from the rank of external existences, there remains nothing, which can afford us a just and constituent idea of body.

Add to this, that, properly speaking, solidity or impenetrability is nothing, but an impossibility of annihilation, as has been* already observed: for which reason it is the more necessary for us to form some distinct idea of that object, whose annihilation we suppose impossible. An impossibility of being annihilated cannot exist, and can never be conceived to exist, by itself: but necessarily requires some object or real existence, to which it may belong. Now the difficulty still remains, how to form an idea of this object or existence, without having recourse to the secondary and sensible qualities.

Nor must we omit on this occasion our accustomed method of examining ideas by considering those impressions, from which they are derived. The impressions, which enter by the sight and hearing, the smell and taste, are affirmed by modern philosophy to be without any resembling objects; and consequently the idea of solidity, which is supposed to be real, can never be derived from any of these senses. There remains, therefore, the feeling as the only sense, that can convey the impression, which is original to the idea of solidity; and indeed we naturally imagine, that we feel the solidity of bodies, and need but touch any object in order to perceive this quality. But this method of thinking is more popular than philosophical; as will appear from the following reflections.

First, It is easy to observe, that though bodies are felt by means of their solidity, yet the feeling is a quite different thing from the solidity; and that they have not the least resemblance to each other. A man, who has the palsy in one hand, has as perfect an idea of impenetrability, when he observes that hand to be

* Part 2, Section 4.

supported by the table, as when he feels the same table with the other hand. An object, that presses upon any of our members, meets with resistance; and that resistance, by the motion it gives to the nerves and animal spirits, conveys a certain sensation to the mind; but it does not follow, that the sensation, motion, and resistance are any ways resembling.

Secondly, The impressions of touch are simple impressions, except when considered with regard to their extension; which makes nothing to the present purpose: and from this simplicity I infer, that they neither represent solidity, nor any real object. For let us put two cases, *viz.* that of a man, who presses a stone, or any solid body, with his hand, and that of two stones, which press each other; it will readily be allowed, that these two cases are not in every respect alike, but that in the former there is conjoined with the solidity, a feeling or sensation, of which there is no appearance in the latter. In order, therefore, to make these two cases alike, it is necessary to remove some part of the impression, which the man feels by his hand, or organ of sensation; and that being impossible in a simple impression, obliges us to remove the whole, and proves that this whole impression has no archetype or model in external objects. To which we may add, that solidity necessarily supposes two bodies, along with contiguity and impulse; which being a compound object, can never be represented by a simple impression. Not to mention, that though solidity continues always invariably the same, the impressions of touch change every moment upon us; which is a clear proof that the latter are not representations of the former.

Thus there is a direct and total opposition betwixt our reason and our senses; or more properly speaking, betwixt those conclusions we form from cause and effect, and those that persuade us of the continued and independent existence of body. When we reason from cause and effect, we conclude, that neither colour, sound, taste, nor smell have a continued and independent existence. When we exclude these sensible qualities there remains nothing in the universe, which has such an existence.

SECTION FIVE

Of the immateriality of the soul

Having found such contradictions and difficulties in every system concerning external objects, and in the idea of matter, which we fancy so clear and determinate, we shall naturally expect still greater difficulties and contradictions in every hypothesis concerning our internal perceptions, and the nature of the mind, which we are apt to imagine so much more obscure, and uncertain. But in this we should deceive ourselves. The intellectual world, though involved in infinite obscurities, is not perplexed with any such contradictions, as those we have discovered in the natural. What is known concerning it, agrees with itself; and what is unknown, we must be contented to leave so.

It is true, would we hearken to certain philosophers, they promise to diminish our ignorance; but I am afraid it is at the hazard of running us into contradictions, from which the subject is of itself exempted. These philosophers are the curious reasoners concerning the material or immaterial substances, in which they suppose our perceptions to inhere. In order to put a stop to these endless cavils on both sides, I know no better method, than to ask these philosophers in a few words, *What they mean by substance and inhesion?* And after they have answered this question, it will then be reasonable, and not till then, to enter seriously into the dispute.

This question we have found impossible to be answered with regard to matter and body: but besides that in the case of the mind, it labours under all the same difficulties, it is burthened with some additional ones, which are peculiar to that subject. As every idea is derived from a precedent impression, had we any idea of the substance of our minds, we must also have an impression of it; which is very difficult, if not impossible, to be conceived. For how can an impression represent a substance, otherwise than by resembling it? And how can an impression resemble a substance, since, according to this philosophy, it is not a substance, and has none of the peculiar qualities or characteristics of a substance?

But leaving the question of *what may or may not be*, for that other *what actually is*, I desire those philosophers, who pretend that we have an idea of the substance of our minds, to point out the impression that produces it, and tell distinctly after what manner that impression operates, and from what object it is derived. Is it an impression of sensation or of reflection? Is it pleasant, or painful, or indifferent? Does it attend us at all times, or does it only return at intervals? If at intervals, at what times principally does it return, and by what causes is it produced?

If instead of answering these questions, any one should evade the difficulty, by saying, that the definition of a substance is *something which may exist by itself*; and that this definition ought to satisfy us: should this be said, I should observe, that this definition agrees to every thing, that can possibly be conceived; and never will serve to distinguish substance from accident, or the soul from its perceptions. For thus I reason. Whatever is clearly conceived may exist; and whatever is clearly conceived, after any manner, may exist after the same manner. This is one principle, which has been already acknowledged. Again, every thing, which is different, is distinguishable, and every thing which is distinguishable, is separable by the imagination. This is another principle. My conclusion from both is, that since all our perceptions are different from each other, and from every thing else in the universe, they are also distinct and separable, and may be considered as separately existent, and may exist separately, and have no need of any thing else to support their existence. They are, therefore, substances, as far as this definition explains a substance.

Thus neither by considering the first origin of ideas, nor by means of a definition are we able to arrive at any satisfactory notion of substance; which seems to me a sufficient reason for abandoning utterly that dispute concerning the materiality and immateriality of the soul, and makes me absolutely condemn even the question itself. We have no perfect idea of any thing but of a perception. A substance is entirely different from a perception. We have, therefore, no idea of a substance. Inhesion in something is supposed to be requisite to support the existence of our perceptions. Nothing appears requisite to support the existence of a perception. We have, therefore, no idea of inhesion. What possibility then of answering that question, *Whether perceptions inhere in a material or immaterial substance*, when we do not so much as understand the meaning of the question?

There is one argument commonly employed for the immateriality of the soul, which seems to me remarkable. Whatever is extended consists of parts; and whatever consists of parts is divisible, if not in reality, at least in the imagination. But it is impossible anything divisible can be *conjoined* to a thought or perception, which is a being altogether inseparable and indivisible. For supposing such a conjunction, would the indivisible thought exist on the left or on the right hand of this extended divisible body? On the surface or in the middle? On the back or fore side of it? If it be conjoined with the extension, it must exist somewhere within its dimensions. If it exist within its dimensions, it must either exist in one particular part; and then that particular part is indivisible, and the perception is conjoined only with it, not with the extension: or if the thought exists in every part, it must also be extended, and separable, and divisible, as well as the body; which is utterly absurd and contradictory. For can any one conceive a passion of a yard in length, a foot in breadth, and an inch in thickness? Thought, therefore, and extension are qualities wholly incompatible, and never can incorporate together into one subject.

This argument affects not the question concerning the *substance* of the soul, but only that concerning its *local conjunction* with matter; and therefore it may not be improper to consider in general what objects are, or are not susceptible of a local conjunction. This is a curious question, and may lead us to some discoveries of considerable moment.

The first notion of space and extension is derived solely from the senses of sight and feeling; nor is there any thing, but what is coloured or tangible, that has parts disposed after such a manner, as to convey that idea. When we diminish or increase a relish, it is not after the same manner that we diminish or increase any visible object; and when several sounds strike our hearing at once, custom and reflection alone make us form an idea of the degrees of the distance and contiguity of those bodies, from which they are derived. Whatever marks the place of its existence either must be extended, or must be a mathematical point, without parts or composition. What is extended must have a particular figure, as square, round, triangular; none of which will agree to a desire, or indeed to any impression or idea, except to these two senses above-mentioned. Neither ought a desire, though indivisible, to be considered as a mathematical point. For in that case it would be possible, by the addition of others, to make two, three, four desires, and these disposed and situated in such a manner, as to have a determinate length, breadth and thickness; which is evidently absurd.

It will not be surprising after this, if I deliver a maxim, which is condemned by several metaphysicians, and is esteemed contrary to the most certain principles of human reason. This maxim is *that an object may exist, and yet be no where*: and I assert, that this is not only possible, but that the greatest part of beings do and must exist after this manner. An object may be said to be no where, when its parts are not so situated with respect to each other, as to form any figure or quantity; nor the whole with respect to other bodies so as to answer to our notions of contiguity or distance. Now this is evidently the case with all our perceptions and objects, except those of the sight and feeling. A moral reflection cannot be placed on the right or on the left hand of a passion, nor can a smell or sound be either of a circular or a square figure. These objects and perceptions, so far from requiring any particular place, are absolutely incompatible with it, and even the imagination cannot attribute it to them. And as to the absurdity of supposing them to be no where, we may consider, that if the passions and sentiments appear to the perception to have any particular place, the idea of extension might be derived from them, as well as from the sight and touch; contrary to what we have already established. If they *appear* not to have any particular place, they may possibly *exist* in the same manner; since whatever we conceive is possible.

It will not now be necessary to prove, that those perceptions, which are simple, and exist no where, are incapable of any conjunction in place with matter or body, which is extended and divisible; since it is impossible to found a relation* but on some common quality. It may be better worth our while to remark, that this question of the local conjunction of objects does not only occur in metaphysical disputes concerning the nature of the soul, but that even in common life we have every moment occasion to examine it. Thus supposing we consider a fig at one end of the table, and an olive at the other, it is evident, that in forming the

---

* Part 1, Section 5.

complex ideas of these substances, one of the most obvious is that of their different relishes; and it is as evident, that we incorporate and conjoin these qualities with such as are coloured and tangible. The bitter taste of the one, and sweet of the other are supposed to lie in the very visible body, and to be separated from each other by the whole length of the table. This is so notable and so natural an illusion, that it may be proper to consider the principles, from which it is derived.

Though an extended object be incapable of a conjunction in place with another, that exists without any place or extension, yet are they susceptible of many other relations. Thus the taste and smell of any fruit are inseparable from its other qualities of colour and tangibility; and whichever of them be the cause or effect, it is certain they are always co-existent. Nor are they only co-existent in general, but also co-temporary in their appearance in the mind; and it is upon the application of the extended body to our senses we perceive its particular taste and smell. These relations, then, of *causation, and contiguity in the time of their appearance*, betwixt the extended object and the quality, which exists without any particular place, must have such an effect on the mind, that upon the appearance of one it will immediately turn its thought to the conception of the other. Nor is this all. We not only turn our thought from one to the other upon account of their relation, but likewise endeavour to give them a new relation, *viz.* that of a *conjunction in place*, that we may render the transition more easy and natural. For it is a quality, which I shall often have occasion to remark in human nature, and shall explain more fully in its proper place, that when objects are united by any relation, we have a strong propensity to add some new relation to them, in order to complete the union. In our arrangement of bodies we never fail to place such as are resembling, in contiguity to each other, or at least in correspondent points of view: why, but because we feel a satisfaction in joining the relation of contiguity to that of resemblance, or the resemblance of situation to that of qualities? The effects of this propensity have been* already observed in that resemblance, which we so readily suppose betwixt particular impressions and their external causes. But we shall not find a more evident effect of it, than in the present instance, where from the relations of causation and contiguity in time betwixt two

---

* Section 2, towards the end.

objects, we feign likewise that of a conjunction in place, in order to strengthen the connexion.

But whatever confused notions we may form of an union in place betwixt an extended body, as a fig, and its particular taste, it is certain that upon reflection we must observe in this union something altogether unintelligible and contradictory. For should we ask ourselves one obvious question, *viz.* if the taste, which we conceive to be contained in the circumference of the body, is in every part of it or in one only, we must quickly find ourselves at a loss, and perceive the impossibility of ever giving a satisfactory answer. We cannot rely, that it is only in one part: for experience convinces us, that every part has the same relish. We can as little reply, that it exists in every part: for then we must suppose it figured and extended; which is absurd and incomprehensible. Here then we are influenced by two principles directly contrary to each other, *viz.* that *inclination* of our fancy by which we are determined to incorporate the taste with the extended object, and our *reason*, which shows us the impossibility of such an union. Being divided betwixt these opposite principles, we renounce neither one nor the other, but involve the subject in such confusion and obscurity, that we no longer perceive the opposition. We suppose, that the taste exists within the circumference of the body, but in such a manner, that it fills the whole without extension, and exists entire in every part without separation. In short, we use in our most familiar way of thinking, that scholastic principle, which, when crudely proposed, appears so shocking, of *totum in toto & totum in qualibet parte*: which is much the same, as if we should say, that a thing is in a certain place, and yet is not there.

All this absurdity proceeds from our endeavouring to bestow a place on what is utterly incapable of it; and that endeavour again arises from our inclination to complete an union, which is founded on causation, and a contiguity of time, by attributing to the objects a conjunction in place. But if ever reason be of sufficient force to overcome prejudice, it is certain, that in the present case it must prevail. For we have only this choice left, either to suppose that some beings exist without any place; or that they are figured and extended; or that when they are incorporated with extended objects, the whole is in the whole, and the whole in every part. The absurdity of the two last suppositions proves sufficiently the veracity of the first. Nor is there any fourth opinion. For as to the supposition of their existence in the manner of mathematical points, it resolves itself into the second opinion, and supposes, that several passions may be placed in a circular figure, and that a certain number of smells, conjoined with a certain number of sounds, may make a body of twelve cubic inches; which appears ridiculous upon the bare mentioning of it.

But though in this view of things we cannot refuse to condemn the materialists, who conjoin all thought with extension; yet a little reflection will show us equal reason for blaming their antagonists, who conjoin all thought with a simple and indivisible substance. The most vulgar philosophy informs us, that no external object can make itself known to the mind immediately, and without the interposition of an image or perception. That table, which just now appears to me, is only a perception, and all its qualities are qualities of a perception. Now the most obvious of all its qualities is extension. The perception consists of parts. These parts are so situated, as to afford us the notion of distance and contiguity; of length, breadth, and thickness. The termination of these three dimensions is what we call figure. This figure is moveable, separable, and divisible. Mobility, and separability are the distinguishing properties of extended objects. And to cut short all disputes, the very idea of extension is copied from nothing but an impression, and consequently must perfectly agree to it. To say the idea of extension agrees to any thing, is to say it is extended.

The free-thinker may now triumph in his turn; and having found there are impressions and ideas really extended, may ask his antagonists, how they can incorporate a simple and indivisible subject with an extended perception? All the arguments of Theologians may here be retorted upon them. Is the indivisible subject, or immaterial substance, if you will, on the left or on the right hand of the perception? Is it in this particular part, or in that other? Is it in every part without being extended? Or is it entire in any one part without deserting the rest? It is impossible to give any answer to these questions, but what will both be absurd in itself, and will account for the union of our indivisible perceptions with an extended substance.

This gives me an occasion to take a-new into consideration the question concerning the substance of the soul; and though I have condemned that question as utterly unintelligible, yet I cannot forbear proposing some farther reflections concerning it. I assert, that the doctrine of the immateriality, simplicity, and indivisibility of a thinking substance is a true atheism, and will serve to justify all those sentiments, for which *Spinoza* is so universally infamous. From this topic, I hope at least to reap one advantage, that my adversaries will not have any pretext to render the present doctrine odious by their declamations, when they see that they can be so easily retorted on them.

The fundamental principle of the atheism of *Spinoza* is the doctrine of the simplicity of the universe, and the unity of that substance, in which he supposes both thought and matter to inhere. There is only one substance, says he, in the world; and that substance is perfectly simple and indivisible, and exists every where, without any local presence. Whatever we discover externally by sensation; whatever we feel internally by reflection; all these are nothing but modifications of that one, simple, and necessarily existent being, and are not possessed of any separate or distinct existence. Every passion of the soul; every configuration of matter, however different and various, inhere in the same substance, and preserve in themselves their characters of distinction, without communicating them to that subject, in which they inhere. The same *substratum*, if I may so speak, supports the most different modifications, without any difference in itself; and varies them, without any variation. Neither time, nor place, nor all the diversity of nature are able to produce any composition or change in its perfect simplicity and identity.

I believe this brief exposition of the principles of that famous atheist will be sufficient for the present purpose, and that without entering farther into these gloomy and obscure regions, I shall be able to shew, that this hideous hypothesis is almost the same with that of the immateriality of the soul, which has become so popular. To make this evident, let us remember,* that as every idea is derived from a preceding perception, it is impossible our idea of a perception, and that of an object or external existence can ever represent what are specifically different from each other. Whatever difference we may suppose betwixt them, it is still incomprehensible to us; and we are obliged either to conceive an

---

* Part 2, Section 6.

external object merely as a relation without a relative, or to make it the very same with a perception or impression.

The consequence I shall draw from this may, at first sight, appear a mere sophism; but upon the least examination will be found solid and satisfactory. I say then, that since we may suppose, but never can conceive a specific difference betwixt an object and impression; any conclusion we form concerning the connexion and repugnance of impressions, will not be known certainly to be applicable to objects; but that on the other hand, whatever conclusions of this kind we form concerning objects, will most certainly be applicable to impressions. The reason is not difficult. As an object is supposed to be different from an impression, we cannot be sure, that the circumstance, upon which we found our reasoning, is common to both, supposing we form the reasoning upon the impression. It is still possible, that the object may differ from it in that particular. But when we first form our reasoning concerning the object, it is beyond doubt, that the same reasoning must extend to the impression: and that because the quality of the object, upon which the argument is founded, must at least be conceived by the mind; and could not be conceived, unless it were common to an impression; since we have no idea but what is derived from that origin. Thus we may establish it as a certain maxim, that we can never, by any principle, but by an irregular kind* of reasoning from experience, discover a connexion or repugnance betwixt objects, which extends not to impressions; though the inverse proposition may not be equally true, that all the discoverable relations of impressions are common to objects.

To apply this to the present case; there are two different systems of being presented, to which I suppose myself under necessity of assigning some substance, or ground of inhesion. I observe first the universe of objects or of body: the sun, moon and stars; the earth, seas, plants, animals, men, ships, houses, and other productions either of art or nature. Here *Spinoza* appears, and tells me, that these are only modifications; and that the subject, in which they inhere, is simple, incompounded, and indivisible. After this I consider the other system of beings, *viz.* the universe of thought, or my impressions and ideas. There I observe another sun, moon and stars; an earth, and seas, covered and inhabited by plants and

---

* Such as that of Section 2, from the coherence of our perceptions.

animals; towns, houses, mountains, rivers; and in short every thing I can discover or conceive in the first system. Upon my enquiring concerning these, Theologians present themselves, and tell me, that these also are modifications, and modifications of one simple, uncompounded, and indivisible substance. Immediately upon which I am deafened with the noise of a hundred voices, that treat the first hypothesis with detestation and scorn, and the second with applause and veneration. I turn my attention to these hypotheses to see what may be the reason of so great a partiality; and find that they have the same fault of being unintelligible, and that as far as we can understand them, they are so much alike, that it is impossible to discover any absurdity in one, which is not common to both of them. We have no idea of any quality in an object, which does not agree to, and may not represent a quality in an impression; and that because all our ideas are derived from our impressions. We can never, therefore, find any repugnance betwixt an extended object as a modification, and a simple uncompounded essence, as its substance, unless that repugnance takes place equally betwixt the perception or impression of that extended object, and the same uncompounded essence. Every idea of a quality in an object passes through an impression; and therefore every *perceivable* relation, whether of connexion or repugnance, must be common both to objects and impressions.

But though this argument, considered in general, seems evident beyond all doubt and contradiction, yet to make it more clear and sensible, let us survey it in detail; and see whether all the absurdities, which have been found in the system of *Spinoza*, may not likewise be discovered in that of Theologians.*

First, It has been said against *Spinoza*, according to the scholastic way of talking, rather than thinking, that a mode, not being any distinct or separate existence, must be the very same with its substance, and consequently the extension of the universe, must be in a manner identified with that, simple, uncompounded essence, in which the universe is supposed to inhere. But this, it may be pretended, is utterly impossible and inconceivable unless the indivisible substance expand itself, so as to correspond to the extension, or the extension contract itself, so as to answer to the indivisible substance. This argument seems just, as far as we can understand it;

---

* See *Bayle's* dictionary, article of *Spinoza*.

and it is plain nothing is required, but a change in the terms, to apply the same argument to our extended perceptions, and the simple essence of the soul; the ideas of objects and perceptions being in every respect the same, only attended with the supposition of a difference, that is unknown and incomprehensible.

Secondly, It has been said, that we have no idea of substance, which is not applicable to matter; nor any idea of a distinct substance, which is not applicable to every distinct portion of matter. Matter, therefore, is not a mode but a substance, and each part of matter is not a distinct mode, but a distinct substance. I have already proved, that we have no perfect idea of substance; but that taking it for *something, that can exist by itself*, it is evident every perception is a substance, and every distinct part of a perception a distinct substance: and consequently the one hypothesis labours under the same difficulties in this respect with the other.

Thirdly, It has been objected to the system of one simple substance in the universe, that this substance being the support or *substratum* of every thing, must at the very same instant be modified into forms, which are contrary and incompatible. The round and square figures are incompatible in the same substance at the same time. How then is it possible, that the same substance can at once be modified into that square table, and into this round one? I ask the same question concerning the impressions of these tables; and find that the answer is no more satisfactory in one case than in the other.

It appears, then, that to whatever side we turn, the same difficulties follow us, and that we cannot advance one step towards the establishing the simplicity and immateriality of the soul, without preparing the way for a dangerous and irrecoverable atheism. It is the same case, if instead of calling thought a modification of the soul, we should give it the more ancient, and yet more modish name of an *action*. By an action we mean much the same thing, as what is commonly called an abstract mode; that is, something which, properly speaking, is neither distinguishable, nor separable from its substance, and is only conceived by a distinction of reason, or an abstraction. But nothing is gained by this change of the term of modification, for that of action; nor do we free ourselves from one single difficulty by its means; as will appear from the two following reflexions.

First, I observe, that the word, action, according to this explication of it, can never justly be applied to any perception, as derived from a mind or thinking substance. Our perceptions are all really different, and separable, and distinguishable from each other, and from everything else, which we can imagine: and therefore it is impossible to conceive, how they can be the action or abstract mode of any substance. The instance of motion, which is commonly made use of to shew after what manner perception depends, as an action, upon its substance, rather confounds than instructs us. Motion to all appearance induces no real nor essential change on the body, but only varies its relation to other objects. But betwixt a person in the morning walking in a garden with company, agreeable to him; and a person in the afternoon enclosed in a dungeon, and full of terror, despair, and resentment, there seems to be a radical difference, and of quite another kind, than what is produced on a body by the change of its situation. As we conclude from the distinction and separability of their ideas, that external objects have a separate existence from each other; so when we make these ideas themselves our objects, we must draw the same conclusion concerning *them*, according to the precedent reasoning. At least it must be confessed, that having no idea of the substance of the soul, it is impossible for us to tell how it can admit of such differences, and even contrarieties of perception without any fundamental change; and consequently can never tell in what sense perceptions are actions of that substance. The use, therefore, of the word, *action*, unaccompanied with any meaning, instead of that of modification, makes no addition to our knowledge, nor is of any advantage to the doctrine of the immateriality of the soul.

I add in the second place, that if it brings any advantage to that cause, it must bring an equal to the cause of atheism. For do our Theologians pretend to make a monopoly of the word, *action*, and may not the atheists likewise take possession of it, and affirm that plants, animals, men, &c. are nothing but particular actions of one simple universal substance, which exerts itself from a blind and absolute necessity? This you'll say is utterly absurd. I own it is unintelligible; but at the same time assert, according to the principles above-explained, that it is impossible to discover any absurdity in the supposition, that all the various objects in nature are actions of one simple substance, which absurdity will not be applicable to a like supposition concerning impressions and ideas.

From these hypotheses concerning the *substance* and *local conjunction* of our perceptions, we may pass to another, which is more intelligible than the former, and more important than the latter, *viz.* concerning the *cause* of our perceptions. Matter and motion, it is commonly said in the schools, however varied, are still matter and motion, and produce only a difference in the position and situation of objects. Divide a body as often as you please, it is still body. Place it in any figure, nothing ever results but figure, or the relation of parts. Move it in any manner, you still find motion or a change of relation. It is absurd to imagine, that motion in a circle, for instance, should be nothing but merely motion in a circle; while motion in another direction, as in an ellipse, should also be a passion or moral reflection: that the shocking of two globular particles should become a sensation of pain, and that the meeting of two triangular ones should afford a pleasure. Now as these different shocks, and variations, and mixtures are the only changes, of which matter is susceptible, and as these never afford us any idea of thought or perception, it is concluded to be impossible, that thought can ever be caused by matter.

Few have been able to withstand the seeming evidence of this argument; and yet nothing in the world is more easy than to refute it. We need only reflect on what has been proved at large, that we are never sensible of any connexion betwixt causes and effects, and that it is only by our experience of their constant conjunction, we can arrive at any knowledge of this relation. Now as all objects, which are not contrary, are susceptible of a constant conjunction, and as no real objects are contrary;* I have inferred from these principles, that to consider the matter *a priori*, any thing may produce any thing, and that we shall never discover a reason, why any object may or may not be the cause of any other, however great, or however little the resemblance may be betwixt them. This evidently destroys the precedent reasoning concerning the cause of thought or perception. For though there appear no manner of connexion betwixt motion or thought, the case is the same with all other causes and effects. Place one body of a pound weight on one end of a lever, and another body of the same

* Part 3, Section 15.

weight on another end; you will never find in these bodies any principle of motion dependent on their distances from the center, more than of thought and perception. If you pretend, therefore, to prove *a priori*, that such a position of bodies can never cause thought; because turn it which way you will, it is nothing but a position of bodies; you must by the same course of reasoning conclude, that it can never produce motion; since there is no more apparent connexion in the one case than in the other. But as this latter conclusion is contrary to evident experience, and as it is possible we may have a like experience in the operations of the mind, and may perceive a constant conjunction of thought and motion; you reason too hastily, when from the mere consideration of the ideas, you conclude that it is impossible motion can ever produce thought, or a different position of parts give rise to a different passion or reflection. Nay it is not only possible we may have such an experience, but it is certain we have it; since every one may perceive, that the different dispositions of his body change his thoughts and sentiments. And should it be said, that this depends on the union of soul and body; I would answer, that we must separate the question concerning the substance of the mind from that concerning the cause of its thought; and that confining ourselves to the latter question we find by the comparing their ideas, that thought and motion are different from each other, and by experience, that they are constantly united; which being all the circumstances, that enter into the idea of cause and effect, when applied to the operations of matter, we may certainly conclude, that motion may be, and actually is, the cause of thought and perception.

There seems only this dilemma left us in the present case; either to assert, that nothing can be the cause of another, but where the mind can perceive the connexion in its idea of the objects: or to maintain, that all objects, which we find constantly conjoined, are upon that account to be regarded as causes and effects. If we choose the first part of the dilemma, these are the consequences. *First*, We in reality affirm, that there is no such thing in the universe as a cause or productive principle, not even the deity himself; since our idea of that supreme Being is derived from particular impressions, none of which contain any efficacy, nor seem to have *any* connexion with *any* other existence. As to what may be said, that the connexion betwixt the idea of an infinitely powerful being, and that of any effect, which he wills, is necessary and unavoidable; I answer, that we have no idea of a being endowed with any power, much less of one endowed with infinite power. But if we will change expressions, we can only define power by connexion; and then in saying, that the idea, of an infinitely powerful being is connected with that of every effect, which he wills, we really do no more than assert, that a being, whose volition is connected with every effect, is connected with every effect: which is an identical proposition, and gives us no insight into the nature of this power or connexion. But, *secondly*, supposing, that the deity were the great and efficacious principle, which supplies the deficiency of all causes, this leads us into the grossest impieties and absurdities. For upon the same account, that we have recourse to him in natural operations, and assert that matter cannot of itself communicate motion, or produce thought, *viz.* because there is no apparent connexion betwixt these objects; I say, upon the very same account, we must acknowledge that the deity is the author of all our volitions and perceptions; since they have no more apparent connexion either with one another, or with the supposed but unknown substance of the soul. This agency of the supreme Being we know to have been asserted by several philosophers* with relation to all the actions of the mind, except volition, or rather an inconsiderable part of volition; though it is easy to perceive, that this exception is a mere pretext, to avoid the dangerous consequences of that doctrine. If nothing be active but what has an apparent power, thought is in no case any more active than matter; and if this inactivity must make us have recourse to a deity, the supreme being is the real cause of all our actions, bad as well as good, vicious as well as virtuous.

Thus we are necessarily reduced to the other side of the dilemma, *viz..* that all objects, which are found to be constantly conjoined, are upon that account only to be regarded as causes and effects. Now as all objects, which are not contrary, are susceptible of a constant conjunction, and as no real objects are contrary: it follows, that for aught we can determine by the mere ideas, any thing may be the cause or effect of any thing; which evidently gives the advantage to the materialists above their antagonists.

* As father *Malebranche* and other *Cartesians*.

To pronounce, then, the final decision upon the whole; the question concerning the substance of the soul is absolutely unintelligible: all our perceptions are not susceptible of a local union, either with what is extended or unextended: there being some of them of the one kind, and some of the other: and as the constant conjunction of objects constitutes the very essence of cause and effect, matter and motion may often be regarded as the causes of thought, as far as we have any notion of that relation.

It is certainly a kind of indignity to philosophy, whose sovereign authority ought every where to be acknowledged, to oblige her on every occasion to make apologies for her conclusions, and justify herself to every particular art and science, which may be offended at her. This puts one in mind of a king arraigned for high-treason against his subjects. There is only one occasion, when philosophy will think it necessary and even honourable to justify herself, and that is, when religion may seem to be in the least offended; whose rights are as dear to her as her own, and are indeed the same. If any one, therefore, should imagine that the foregoing arguments are any ways dangerous to religion, I hope the following apology will remove his apprehensions.

There is no foundation for any conclusion *a priori*, either concerning the operations or duration of any object, of which it is possible for the human mind to form a conception. Any object may be imagined to become entirely inactive, or to be annihilated in a moment; and it is an evident principle, *that whatever we can imagine, is possible*. Now this is no more true of matter, than of spirit; of an extended compounded substance, than of a simple and unextended. In both cases the metaphysical arguments for the immortality of the soul are equally inconclusive: and in both cases the moral arguments and those derived from the analogy of nature are equally strong and convincing. If my philosophy, therefore, makes no addition to the arguments for religion, I have at least the satisfaction to think it takes nothing from them, but that every thing remains precisely as before.

SECTION SIX

Of personal identity

There are some philosophers who imagine we are every moment intimately conscious of what we call our SELF; that we feel its existence and its continuance in existence; and are certain, beyond the evidence of a demonstration, both of its perfect identity and simplicity. The strongest sensation, the most violent passion, say they, instead of distracting us from this view, only fix it the more intensely, and make us consider their influence on *self* either by their pain or pleasure. To attempt a farther proof of this were to weaken its evidence; since no proof can be derived from any fact, of which we are so intimately conscious; nor is there any thing, of which we can be certain, if we doubt of this.

Unluckily all these positive assertions are contrary to that very experience, which is pleaded for them, nor have we any idea of *self*, after the manner it is here explained. For from what impression could this idea be derived? This question it is impossible to answer without a manifest contradiction and absurdity; and yet it is a question, which must necessarily be answered, if we would have the idea of self pass for clear and intelligible. It must be some one impression, that gives rise to every real idea. But self or person is not any one impression, but that to which our several impressions and ideas are supposed to have a reference. If any impression gives rise to the idea of self, that impression must continue invariably the same, through the whole course of our lives; since self is supposed to exist after that manner. But there is no impression constant and invariable. Pain and pleasure, grief and joy, passions and sensations succeed each other, and never all exist at the same time. It cannot, therefore, be from any of these impressions, or from any other, that the idea of self is derived; and consequently there is no such idea.

But farther, what must become of all our particular perceptions upon this hypothesis? All these are different, and distinguishable, and separable from each other, and may be separately considered, and may exist separately, and have no need of any thing to support their existence. After what manner, therefore, do they belong to self; and how are they connected with it? For my part, when I enter most intimately into what I call *myself*, I always stumble on some particular perception or other, of heat or cold, light or shade, love or hatred, pain or pleasure. I never can catch *myself* at any time without a perception, and never can observe any thing but the perception. When my perceptions are removed for any time, as by sound sleep; so long am I insensible of *myself*, and may truly be said not to exist. And were all my perceptions removed by death, and could I neither think, nor feel, nor see, nor love, nor hate after the dissolution of my body, I should be entirely annihilated, nor do I conceive what is farther requisite to make me a perfect non-entity. If any one, upon serious and unprejudiced reflection thinks he has a different notion of *himself*, I must confess I can reason no longer with him. All I can allow him is, that he may be in the right as well as I, and that we are essentially different in this particular. He may, perhaps, perceive something simple and continued, which he calls *himself*; though I am certain there is no such principle in me.

But setting aside some metaphysicians of this kind, I may venture to affirm of the rest of mankind, that they are nothing but a bundle or collection of different perceptions, which succeed each other with an inconceivable rapidity, and are in a perpetual flux and movement. Our eyes cannot turn in their sockets without varying our perceptions. Our thought is still more variable than our sight; and all our other senses and faculties contribute to this change; nor is there any single power of the soul, which remains unalterably the same, perhaps for one moment. The mind is a kind of theatre, where several perceptions successively make their appearance; pass, re-pass, glide away, and mingle in an infinite variety of postures and situations. There is properly no *simplicity* in it at one time, nor *identity* in different; whatever natural propension we may have to imagine that simplicity and identity. The comparison of the theatre must not mislead us. They are the successive perceptions only, that constitute the mind; nor have we the most distant notion of the place, where these scenes are represented, or of the materials, of which it is composed.

What then gives us so great a propension to ascribe an identity to these successive perceptions, and to suppose ourselves possessed of an invariable and uninterrupted existence through the whole course of our lives? In order to answer this question, we must distinguish betwixt personal identity, as it regards our thought or imagination, and as it regards our passions or the concern we take in ourselves. The first is our present subject; and to explain it perfectly we must take the matter pretty deep, and account for that identity, which we attribute to plants and animals; there being a great analogy betwixt it, and the identity of a self or person.

We have a distinct idea of an object, that remains invariable and uninterrupted through a supposed variation of time; and this idea we call that of *identity* or *sameness*. We have also a distinct idea of several different objects existing in succession, and connected together by a close relation; and this to an accurate view affords as perfect a notion of *diversity*, as if there was no manner of relation among the objects. But though these two ideas of identity, and a succession of related objects be in themselves perfectly distinct, and even contrary, yet it is certain, that in our common way of thinking they are generally confounded with each other. That action of the imagination, by which we consider the uninterrupted and invariable object, and that by which we reflect on the succession of related objects, are almost the same to the feeling, nor is there much more effort of thought required in the latter case than in the former. The relation facilitates the transition of the mind from one object to another, and renders its passage as smooth as if it contemplated one continued object. This resemblance is the cause of the confusion and mistake, and makes us substitute the notion of identity, instead of that of related objects. However at one instant we may consider the related succession as variable or interrupted, we are sure the next to ascribe to it a perfect identity, and regard it as enviable and uninterrupted. Our propensity to this mistake is so great from the resemblance above-mentioned, that we fall into it before we are aware; and though we incessantly correct ourselves by reflection, and return to a more accurate method of thinking, yet we cannot long sustain our philosophy, or take off this bias from the imagination. Our last resource is to yield to it, and boldly assert that these different related objects are in effect the same, however interrupted and variable. In order to justify to ourselves this absurdity, we often feign some new and unintelligible principle, that connects the objects together, and prevents their interruption or variation. Thus we feign the continued existence of the perceptions of our senses, to remove the interruption: and run into the notion of a *soul*, and *self*, and *substance*, to disguise the variation. But we may farther observe, that where we do not give rise to such a fiction, our propension to confound identity with relation is so great, that we are apt to imagine* something unknown and mysterious, connecting the parts, beside their relation; and this I take to be the case with regard to the identity we ascribe to plants and vegetables. And even when this does not take place, we still feel a propensity to confound these ideas, though we are not able fully to satisfy ourselves in that particular, nor find any thing invariable and uninterrupted to justify our notion of identity.

Thus the controversy concerning identity is not merely a dispute of words. For when we attribute identity, in an improper sense, to variable or interrupted objects, our mistake is not confined to the expression, but is commonly attended with a fiction, either of something invariable and uninterrupted, or of something myst-erious and inexplicable, or at least with a propensity to such fictions. What will suffice to prove this hypothesis to the satis-faction of every fair enquirer, is to shew from daily experience and observation, that the objects, which are variable or interrupted, and yet are supposed to continue the same, are such only as consist of a succession of parts, connected together by resemblance, contiguity, or causation. For as such a succession answers evid-ently to our notion of diversity, it can only be by mistake we ascribe to it an identity; and as the relation of parts, which leads us into this mistake, is really nothing but a quality, which produces an association of ideas, and an easy transition of the imagination from one to another, it can only be from the resemblance, which this act of the mind bears to that, by which we contemplate one continued object, that the error arises. Our chief business, then, must be to prove, that all objects, to which we ascribe identity, without observing their invariableness and uninterruptedness, are such as consist of a succession of related objects.

In order to this, suppose any mass of matter, of which the parts are contiguous and connected, to be placed before us; it is plain

---

* If the reader is desirous to see how a great genius may be influencd by these seemingly trivial principles of the imagination, as well as the mere vulgar, let him read my Lord *Shaftsbury's* reasonings concerning the uniting principle of the universe, and the identity of plants and animals. See his *Moralists: or, Philosophical Rhapsody*.

we must attribute a perfect identity to this mass, provided all the parts continue uninterruptedly and invariably the same, whatever motion or change of place we may observe either in the whole or in any of the parts. But supposing some very *small* or *inconsiderable* part to be added to the mass, or subtracted from it; though this absolutely destroys the identity of the whole, strictly speaking; yet as we seldom think so accurately, we scruple not to pronounce a mass of matter the same, where we find so trivial an alteration. The passage of the thought from the object before the change to the object after it, is so smooth and easy, that we scarce perceive the transition, and are apt to imagine, that it is nothing but a continued survey of the same object.

There is a very remarkable circumstance, that attends this experiment; which is, that though the change of any considerable part in a mass of matter destroys the identity of the whole, yet we must measure the greatness of the part, not absolutely, but by its *proportion* to the whole. The addition or diminution of a mountain would not be sufficient to produce a diversity in a planet: though the change of a very few inches would be able to destroy the identity of some bodies. It will be impossible to account for this, but by reflecting that objects operate upon the mind, and break or interrupt the continuity of its actions not according to their real greatness, but according to their proportion to each other: and therefore, since this interruption makes an object cease to appear the same, it must be the uninterrupted progress of the thought, which constitutes the imperfect identity.

This may be confirmed by another phenomenon. A change in any considerable part of a body destroys its identity; but it is remarkable, that where the change is produced *gradually* and *insensibly* we are less apt to ascribe to it the same effect. The reason can plainly be no other, than that the mind, in following the successive changes of the body, feels an easy passage from the surveying its condition in one moment to the viewing of it in another, and at no particular time perceives any interruption in its actions. From which continued perception, it ascribes a continued existence and identity to the object.

But whatever precaution we may use in introducing the changes gradually, and making them proportionable to the whole, it is certain, that where the changes are at last observed to become considerable, we make a scruple of ascribing identity to such different objects. There is, however, another artifice, by which we may induce the imagination to advance a step farther; and that is, by producing a reference of the parts to each other, and a combination to some common end or purpose. A ship, of which a considerable part has been changed by frequent reparations, is still considered as the same; nor does the difference of the materials hinder us from ascribing an identity to it. The common end, in which the parts conspire, is the same under all their variations, and affords an easy transition of the imagination from one situation of the body to another.

But this is still more remarkable, when we add a *sympathy* of parts to their *common end*, and suppose that they bear to each other, the reciprocal relation of cause and effect in all their actions and operations. This is the case with all animals and vegetables; where not only the several parts have a reference to some general purpose, but also a mutual dependence on, and connexion with each other. The effect of so strong a relation is, that though every one must allow, that in a very few years both vegetables and animals endure a total change, yet we still attribute identity to them, while their form, size, and substance are entirely altered. An oak, that grows from a small plant to a large tree, is still the same oak; though there be not one particle of matter, or figure of its parts the same. An infant becomes a man, and is sometimes fat, sometimes lean, without any change in his identity.

We may also consider the two following phenomena, which are remarkable in their kind. The first is, that though we commonly be able to distinguish pretty exactly betwixt numerical and specific identity, yet it sometimes happens, that we confound them, and in our thinking and reasoning employ the one for the other. Thus a man, who hears a noise, that is frequently interrupted and renewed, says, it is still the same noise; though it is evident the sounds have only a specific identity or resemblance, and there is nothing numerically the same, but the cause, which produced them. In like manner it may be said without breach of the propriety of language, that such a church, which was formerly of brick, fell to ruin, and that the parish rebuilt the same church of free-stone, and according to modern architecture. Here neither the form nor materials are the same, nor is there any thing common to the two objects, but their relation to the inhabitants of the parish; and yet this alone is sufficient to make us denominate them the same. But we must observe, that in these cases the first object is in a manner annihilated before the second comes into existence; by which means, we are never presented in any one point of time with the idea of difference and multiplicity: and for that reason are less scrupulous in calling them the same.

Secondly, We may remark, that though in a succession of related objects, it be in a manner requisite, that the change of parts be not sudden nor entire, in order to preserve the identity, yet where the objects are in their nature changeable and inconstant, we admit of a more sudden transition, than would otherwise be consistent with that relation. Thus as the nature of a river consists in the motion and change of parts; though in less than four and twenty hours these be totally altered; this hinders not the river from continuing the same during several ages. What is natural and essential to any thing is, in a manner, expected; and what is expected makes less impression, and appears of less moment, than what is unusual and extraordinary. A considerable change of the former kind seems really less to the imagination, than the most trivial alteration of the latter; and by breaking less the continuity of the thought, has less influence in destroying the identity.

We now proceed to explain the nature of *personal identity*, which has become so great a question in philosophy, especially of late years in *England*, where all the abstruser sciences are studied with a peculiar ardour and application. And here it is evident, the same method of reasoning must be continued which has so successfully explained the identity of plants, and animals, and ships, and houses, and of all the compounded and changeable productions either of art or nature. The identity, which we ascribe to the mind of man, is only a fictitious one, and of a like kind with that which we ascribe to vegetables and animal bodies. It cannot, therefore, have a different origin, but must proceed from a like operation of the imagination upon like objects.

But lest this argument should not convince the reader; though in my opinion perfectly decisive; let him weigh the following reasoning, which is still closer and more immediate. It is evident, that the identity, which we attribute to the human mind, however perfect we may imagine it to be, is not able to run the several different perceptions into one, and make them lose their characters of distinction and difference, which are essential to them. It is still true, that every distinct perception, which enters into the composition of the mind, is a distinct existence, and is different, and distinguishable, and separable from every other perception, either contemporary or successive. But as, notwithstanding this distinction and separability, we suppose the whole train of perceptions to be united by identity, a question naturally arises concerning this relation of identity; whether it be something that really binds our several perceptions together, or only associates their ideas in the imagination. That is, in other words, whether in pronouncing concerning the identity of a person, we observe some real bond among his perceptions, or only feel one among the ideas we form of them. This question we might easily decide, if we would recollect what has been already proved at large, that the understanding never observes any real connexion among objects, and that even the union of cause and effect, when strictly examined, resolves itself into a customary association of ideas. For from thence it evidently follows, that identity is nothing really belonging to these different perceptions, and uniting them together; but is merely a quality, which we attribute to them, because of the union of their ideas in the imagination, when we reflect upon them. Now the only qualities, which can give ideas an union in the imagination, are these three relations above-mentioned. These are the uniting principles in the ideal world, and without them every distinct object is separable by the mind, and may be separately considered, and appears not to have any more connexion with any other object, than if disjoined by the greatest difference and remoteness. It is, therefore, on some of these three relations of resemblance, contiguity and causation, that identity depends; and as the very essence of these relations consists in their producing an easy transition of ideas; it follows, that our notions of personal identity, proceed entirely from the smooth and uninterrupted progress of the thought along a train of connected ideas, according to the principles above-explained.

The only question, therefore, which remains, is, by what relations this uninterrupted progress of our thought is produced, when we consider the successive existence of a mind or thinking person. And here it is evident we must confine ourselves to resemblance and causation, and must drop contiguity, which has little or no influence in the present case.

To begin with *resemblance*; suppose we could see clearly into the breast of another, and observe that succession of perceptions, which constitutes his mind or thinking principle, and suppose that he always preserves the memory of a considerable part of past perceptions; it is evident that nothing could more contribute to the bestowing a relation on this succession amidst all its variations. For what is the memory but a faculty, by which we raise up the images of past perceptions? And as an image necessarily resembles its object, must not the frequent placing of these resembling perceptions in the chain of thought, convey the imagination more easily from one link to another, and make the whole seem like the continuance of one object? In this particular, then, the memory not only discovers the identity, but also contributes to its production, by producing the relation of resemblance among the perceptions. The case is the same whether we consider ourselves or others.

As to *causation*; we may observe, that the true idea of the human mind, is to consider it as a system of different perceptions or different existences, which are linked together by the relation of cause and effect, and mutually produce, destroy, influence, and modify each other. Our impressions give rise to their correspondent ideas; and these ideas in their turn produce other impressions. One thought chases another, and draws after it a third, by which it is expelled in its turn. In this respect, I cannot compare the soul more properly to any thing than to a republic or commonwealth, in which the several members are united by the reciprocal ties of government and subordination, and give rise to other persons, who propagate the same republic in the incessant changes of its parts. And as the same individual republic may not only change its members, but also its laws and constitutions; in like manner the same person may vary his character and disposition, as well as his impressions and ideas, without losing his identity. Whatever changes he endures, his several parts are still connected by the relation of causation. And in this view our identity with regard to the passions serves to corroborate that with regard to the imagination, by the making our distant perceptions influence each other, and by giving us a present concern for our past or future pains or pleasures.

As memory alone acquaints us with the continuance and extent of this succession of perceptions, it is to be considered, upon that account chiefly, as the source of personal identity. Had we no memory, we never should have any notion of causation, nor consequently of that chain of causes and effects, which constitute our self or person. But having once acquired this notion of causation from the memory, we can extend the same chain of causes, and consequently the identity of our persons beyond our memory, and can comprehend times, and circumstances, and actions, which we have entirely forgot, but suppose in general to have existed. For how few of our past actions are there, of which we have any memory? Who can tell me, for instance, what were his thoughts and actions on the 1st of *January* 1715, the 11th of *March* 1719, and the 3rd of *August* 1733? Or will he affirm, because he has entirely forgot the incidents of these days, that the present self is not the same person with the self of that time; and by that means overturn all the most established notions of personal identity? In this view, therefore, memory does not so much *produce* as *discover* personal identity, by shewing us the relation of cause and effect among our different perceptions. It will be incumbent on those, who affirm that memory produces entirely our personal identity, to give a reason why we can thus extend our identity beyond our memory.

The whole of this doctrine leads us to a conclusion, which is of great importance in the present affair, *viz.* that all the nice and subtile questions concerning personal identity can never possibly be decided, and are to be regarded rather as grammatical than as philosophical difficulties. Identity depends on the relations of ideas; and these relations produce identity, by means of that easy transition they occasion. But as the relations, and the easiness of the transition may diminish by insensible degrees, we have no just standard, by which we can decide any dispute concerning the time, when they acquire or lose a title to the name of identity. All the disputes concerning the identity of connected objects are merely verbal, except so far as the relation of parts gives rise to some fiction or imaginary principle of union, as we have already observed.

What I have said concerning the first origin and uncertainty of our notion of identity, as applied to the human mind, may be extended with little or no variation to that of *simplicity*. An object, whose different co-existent parts are bound together by a close relation, operates upon the imagination after much the same manner as one perfectly simple and indivisible, and requires not a much greater stretch of thought in order to its conception. From this similarity of operation we attribute a simplicity to it, and feign a principle of union as the support of this simplicity, and the center of all the different parts and qualities of the object.

Thus we have finished our examination of the several systems of philosophy, both of the intellectual and natural world; and in our miscellaneous way of reasoning have been led into several topics; which will either illustrate and confirm some preceding part of this discourse, or prepare the way for our following opinions. It is now time to return to a more close examination of our subject, and to proceed in the accurate anatomy of human nature, having fully explained the nature of our judgment and understandings.

SECTION SEVEN
Conclusion of this book

But before I launch out into those immense depths of philosophy, which lie before me, I find myself inclined to stop a moment in my present station, and to ponder that voyage, which I have undertaken, and which undoubtedly requires the utmost art and industry to be brought to a happy conclusion. Methinks I am like a man, who having struck on many shoals, and having narrowly escaped shipwreck in passing a small frith, has yet the temerity to put out to sea in the same leaky weather-beaten vessel, and even carries his ambition so far as to think of compassing the globe under these disadvantageous circumstances. My memory of past errors and perplexities, makes me diffident for the future. The wretched condition, weakness, and disorder of the faculties, I must employ in my enquiries, increase my apprehensions. And the impossibility of amending or correcting these faculties, reduces me almost to despair, and makes me resolve to perish on the barren rock, on which I am at present, rather than venture myself upon that boundless ocean, which runs out into immensity. This sudden view of my danger strikes me with melancholy; and as it is usual for that passion, above all others, to indulge itself; I cannot forbear feeding my despair, with all those desponding reflections, which the present subject furnishes me with in such abundance.

I am first affrighted and confounded with that forlorn solitude, in which I am placed in my philosophy, and fancy myself some strange uncouth monster, who not being able to mingle and unite in society, has been expelled all human commerce, and left utterly abandoned and disconsolate. Fain would I run into the crowd for shelter and warmth; but cannot prevail with myself to mix with such deformity. I call upon others to join me, in order to make a company apart; but no one will hearken to me. Every one keeps at a distance, and dreads that storm, which beats upon me from every side. I have exposed myself to the enmity of all metaphysicians, logicians, mathematicians, and even theologians; and can I wonder at the insults I must suffer? I have declared my disapprobation of their systems; and can I be surprized, if they should express a hatred of mine and of my person? When I look abroad, I foresee on every side, dispute, contradiction, anger, calumny and detraction. When I turn my eye inward, I find nothing but doubt and ignorance. All the world conspires to oppose and contradict me; though such is my weakness, that I feel all my opinions loosen and fall of themselves, when unsupported by the approbation of others. Every step I take is with hesitation, and every new reflection makes me dread an error and absurdity in my reasoning.

For with what confidence can I venture upon such bold enterprizes, when beside those numberless infirmities peculiar to myself, I find so many which are common to human nature? Can I be sure, that in leaving all established opinions I am following truth; and by what criterion shall I distinguish her, even if fortune should at last guide me on her foot-steps? After the most accurate and exact of my reasonings, I can give no reason why I should assent to it; and feel nothing but a *strong* propensity to consider objects *strongly* in that view, under which they appear to me. Experience is a principle, which instructs me in the several conjunctions of objects for the past. Habit is another principle, which determines me to expect the same for the future; and both of them conspiring to operate upon the imagination, make me form certain ideas in a more intense and lively manner, than others, which are not attended with the same advantages. Without this quality, by which the mind enlivens some ideas beyond others (which seemingly is so trivial, and so little founded on reason) we could never assent to any argument, nor carry our view beyond those few objects, which are present to our senses. Nay, even to these objects we could never attribute any existence, but what was dependent on the senses; and must comprehend them entirely in that succession of perceptions, which constitutes our self or person. Nay farther, even with relation to that succession, we could only admit of those perceptions, which are immediately present to our consciousness, nor could those lively images, with which the memory presents us, be ever received as true pictures of past perceptions. The memory, senses, and understanding are, therefore, all of them founded on the imagination, or the vivacity of our ideas.

No wonder a principle so inconstant and fallacious should lead us into errors, when implicitly followed (as it must be) in all its variations. It is this principle, which makes us reason from causes and effects; and it is the same principle, which convinces us of the continued existence of external objects, when absent from the senses. But though these two operations be equally natural and necessary in the human mind, yet in some circumstances* they are directly contrary, nor is it possible for us to reason justly and regularly from causes and effects, and at the same time believe the continued existence of matter. How then shall we adjust those principles together? Which of them shall we prefer? Or in case we prefer neither of them, but successively assent to both, as is usual among philosophers, with what confidence can we afterwards usurp that glorious title, when we thus knowingly embrace a manifest contradiction?

This contradiction† would be more excusable, were it compensated by any degree of solidity and satisfaction in the other parts of our reasoning. But the case is quite contrary. When we trace up the human understanding to its first principles, we find it to lead us into such sentiments, as seem to turn into ridicule all our past pains and industry, and to discourage us from future enquiries. Nothing is more curiously enquired after by the mind of man, than the causes of every phenomenon; nor are we content with knowing the immediate causes, but push on our enquiries, till we arrive at the original and ultimate principle. We would not willingly stop

* Section 4.
† Part 3, Section 14.

before we are acquainted with that energy in the cause, by which it operates on its effect; that tie, which connects them together; and that efficacious quality, on which the tie depends. This is our aim in all our studies and reflections: and how must we be disappointed, when we learn, that this connexion, tie, or energy lies merely in ourselves, and is nothing but that determination of the mind, which is acquired by custom, and causes us to make a transition from an object to its usual attendant, and from the impression of one to the lively idea of the other? Such a discovery not only cuts off all hope of ever attaining satisfaction, but even prevents our very wishes; since it appears, that when we say we desire to know the ultimate and operating principle, as something, which resides in the external object, we either contradict ourselves, or talk without a meaning.

This deficiency in our ideas is not, indeed, perceived in common life, nor are we sensible, that in the most usual conjunctions of cause and effect we are as ignorant of the ultimate principle, which binds them together, as in the most unusual and extraordinary. But this proceeds merely from an illusion of the imagination; and the question is, how far we ought to yield to these illusions. This question is very difficult, and reduces us to a very dangerous dilemma, whichever way we answer it. For if we assent to every trivial suggestion of the fancy; beside that these suggestions are often contrary to each other; they lead us into such errors, absurdities, and obscurities, that we must at last become ashamed of our credulity. Nothing is more dangerous to reason than the flights of the imagination, and nothing has been the occasion of more mistakes among philosophers. Men of bright fancies may in this respect be compared to those angels, whom the scripture represents as covering their eyes with their wings. This has already appeared in so many instances, that we may spare ourselves the trouble of enlarging upon it any farther.

But on the other hand, if the consideration of these instances makes us take a resolution to reject all the trivial suggestions of the fancy, and adhere to the understanding, that is, to the general and more established properties of the imagination; even this resolution, if steadily executed, would be dangerous, and attended with the most fatal consequences. For I have already shewn,* that

* Section 1.

the understanding, when it acts alone, and according to its most general principles, entirely subverts itself, and leaves not the lowest degree of evidence in any proposition, either in philosophy or common life. We save ourselves from this total scepticism only by means of that singular and seemingly trivial property of the fancy, by which we enter with difficulty into remote views of things, and are not able to accompany them with so sensible an impression, as we do those, which are more easy and natural. Shall we, then, establish it for a general maxim, that no refined or elaborate reasoning is ever to be received? Consider well the consequences of such a principle. By this means you cut off entirely all science and philosophy: you proceed upon one singular quality of the imagination, and by a parity of reason must embrace all of them: and you expressly contradict yourself; since this maxim must be built on the preceding reasoning, which will be allowed to be sufficiently refined and metaphysical. What party, then, shall we choose among these difficulties? If we embrace this principle, and condemn all refined reasoning, we run into the most manifest absurdities. If we reject it in favour of these reasonings, we subvert entirely the human understanding. We have, therefore, no choice left but betwixt a false reason and none at all. For my part, I know not what ought to be done in the present case. I can only observe what is commonly done; which is, that this difficulty is seldom or never thought of; and even where it has once been present to the mind, is quickly forgot, and leaves but a small impression behind it. Very refined reflections have little or no influence upon us; and yet we do not, and cannot establish it for a rule, that they ought not to have any influence; which implies a manifest contradiction.

But what have I here said, that reflections very refined and metaphysical have little or no influence upon us? This opinion I can scarce forbear retracting, and condemning from my present feeling and experience. The *intense* view of these manifold contradictions and imperfections in human reason has so wrought upon me, and heated my brain, that I am ready to reject all belief and reasoning, and can look upon no opinion even as more probable or likely than another. Where am I, or what? From what causes do I derive my existence, and to what condition shall I return? Whose favour shall I court, and whose anger must I dread? What beings surround me? and on whom have I any influence, or who have any influence on me? I am confounded with all these questions, and begin to fancy myself in the most deplorable condition imaginable, invironed with the deepest darkness, and utterly deprived of the use of every member and faculty.

Most fortunately it happens, that since reason is incapable of dispelling these clouds, nature herself suffices to that purpose, and cures me of this philosophical melancholy and delirium, either by relaxing this bent of mind, or by some avocation, and lively impression of my senses, which obliterate all these chimeras. I dine, I play a game of backgammon, I converse, and am merry with my friends; and when after three or four hours' amusement, I would return to these speculations, they appear so cold, and strained, and ridiculous, that I cannot find in my heart to enter into them any farther.

Here then I find myself absolutely and necessarily determined to live, and talk, and act like other people in the common affairs of life. But notwithstanding that my natural propensity, and the course of my animal spirits and passions reduce me to this indolent belief in the general maxims of the world, I still feel such remains of my former disposition, that I am ready to throw all my books and papers into the fire, and resolve never more to renounce the pleasures of life for the sake of reasoning and philosophy. For those are my sentiments in that splenetic humour, which governs me at present. I may, nay I must yield to the current of nature, in submitting to my senses and understanding; and in this blind submission I shew most perfectly my sceptical disposition and principles. But does it follow, that I must strive against the current of nature, which leads me to indolence and pleasure; that I must seclude myself, in some measure, from the commerce and society of men, which is so agreeable; and that I must torture my brains with subtilities and sophistries, at the very time that I cannot satisfy myself concerning the reasonableness of so painful an application, nor have any tolerable prospect of arriving by its means at truth and certainty. Under what obligation do I lie of making such an abuse of time? And to what end can it serve either for the service of mankind, or for my own private interest? No: if I must be a fool, as all those who reason or believe any thing *certainly* are, my follies shall at least be natural and agreeable. Where I strive against my inclination, I shall have a good reason for my resistance; and will no more be led a-wandering into such dreary solitudes, and rough passages, as I have hitherto met with.

These are the sentiments of my spleen and indolence; and indeed I must confess, that philosophy has nothing to oppose to them, and expects a victory more from the returns of a serious good-humoured disposition, than from the force of reason and conviction. In all the incidents of life we ought still to preserve our scepticism. If we believe, that fire warms, or water refreshes, it is only because it costs us too much pains to think otherwise. Nay if we are philosophers, it ought only to be upon sceptical principles, and from an inclination, which we feel to the employing ourselves after that manner. Where reason is lively, and mixes itself with some propensity, it ought to be assented to. Where it does not, it never can have any title to operate upon us.

At the time, therefore, that I am *tired* with amusement and company, and have indulged a *reverie* in my chamber, or in a solitary walk by a river-side, I feel my mind all collected within itself, and am naturally *inclined* to carry my view into all those subjects, about which I have met with so many disputes in the course of my reading and conversation. I cannot forbear having a curiosity to be acquainted with the principles of moral good and evil, the nature and foundation of government, and the cause of those several passions and inclinations, which actuate and govern me. I am uneasy to think I approve of one object, and disapprove of another; call one thing beautiful, and another deformed; decide concerning truth and falsehood, reason and folly, without knowing upon what principles I proceed. I am concerned for the condition of the learned world, which lies under such deplorable ignorance in all these particulars. I feel an ambition to arise in me of contributing to the instruction of mankind, and of acquiring a name by my inventions and discoveries. These sentiments spring up naturally in my present disposition; and should I endeavour to banish them, by attaching myself to any other business or diversion, I *feel* I should be a loser in point of pleasure; and this is the origin of my philosophy.

But even suppose this curiosity and ambition should not transport me into speculations without the sphere of common life, it would necessarily happen, that from my very weakness I must be led into such enquiries. It is certain, that superstition is much more bold in its systems and hypotheses than philosophy; and while the latter contents itself with assigning new causes and principles to the phenomena, which appear in the visible world, the former opens a world of its own, and presents us with scenes, and beings, and objects, which are altogether new. Since therefore it is almost impossible for the mind of man to rest, like those of beasts, in that narrow circle of objects, which are the subject of daily conversation and action, we ought only to deliberate concerning the choice of our guide, and ought to prefer that which is safest and most agreeable. And in this respect I make bold to recommend philosophy, and shall not scruple to give it the preference to superstition of every kind or denomination. For as superstition arises naturally and easily from the popular opinions of mankind, it seizes more strongly on the mind, and is often able to disturb us in the conduct of our lives and actions. Philosophy on the contrary, if just, can present us only with mild and moderate sentiments; and if false and extravagant, its opinions are merely the objects of a cold and general speculation, and seldom go so far as to interrupt the course of our natural propensities. The CYNICS are an extraordinary instance of philosophers, who from reasonings purely philosophical ran into as great extravagancies of conduct as any *Monk* or *Dervise* that ever was in the world. Generally speaking, the errors in religion are dangerous; those in philosophy only ridiculous.

I am sensible, that these two cases of the strength and weakness of the mind will not comprehend all mankind, and that there are in *England*, in particular, many honest gentlemen, who being always employed in their domestic affairs, or amusing themselves in common recreations, have carried their thoughts very little beyond those objects, which are every day exposed to their senses. And indeed, of such as these I pretend not to make philosophers, nor do I expect them either to be associates in these researches or auditors of these discoveries. They do well to keep themselves in their present situation; and instead of refining them into philosophers, I wish we could communicate to our founders of systems, a share of this gross earthy mixture, as an ingredient, which they commonly stand much in need of, and which would serve to temper those fiery particles, of which they are composed. While a warm imagination is allowed to enter into philosophy, and hypotheses embraced merely for being specious and agreeable, we can never have any steady principles, nor any sentiments, which will suit with common practice and experience. But were these hypotheses once removed, we might hope to establish a system or set of opinions, which if not true (for that, perhaps, is too much to be hoped for) might at least be satisfactory to the human mind, and might stand the test of the most critical examination. Nor should we despair of attaining this end, because of the many chimerical systems, which have successively arisen and decayed away among men, would we consider the shortness of that period, wherein these questions have been the subjects of enquiry and reasoning. Two thousand years with such long interruptions, and under such mighty discouragements are a small space of time to give any tolerable perfection to the sciences; and perhaps we are still in too early an age of the world to discover any principles, which will bear the examination of the latest posterity. For my part, my only hope is, that I may contribute a little to the advancement of knowledge, by giving in some particulars a different turn to the speculations of philosophers, and pointing out to them more distinctly those subjects, where alone they can expect assurance and conviction. Human Nature is the only science of man; and yet has been hitherto the most neglected. It will be sufficient for me, if I can bring it a little more into fashion; and the hope of this serves to compose my temper from that spleen, and invigorate it from that indolence, which sometimes prevail upon me. If the reader finds himself in the same easy disposition, let him follow me in my future speculations. If not, let him follow his inclination, and wait the returns of application and good humour. The conduct of a man, who studies philosophy in this careless manner, is more truly sceptical than that of one, who feeling in himself an inclination to it, is yet so overwhelmed with doubts and scruples, as totally to reject it. A true sceptic will be diffident of his philosophical doubts, as well as of his philosophical conviction; and will never refuse any innocent satisfaction, which offers itself, upon account of either of them.

Nor is it only proper we should in general indulge our inclination in the most elaborate philosophical researches, notwithstanding our sceptical principles, but also that we should yield to that propensity, which inclines us to be positive and certain in *particular points*, according to the light, in which we survey them in any *particular instant*. It is easier to forbear all examination and enquiry, than to check ourselves in so natural a propensity, and guard against that assurance, which always arises from an exact and full survey of an object. On such an occasion we are apt not only to forget our scepticism, but even our modesty too; and make use of such terms as these, *it is evident, it is certain, it is undeniable*; which a due deference to the public ought, perhaps, to prevent. I may have fallen into this fault after the example of others; but I here enter a *caveat* against any objections, which may be offered on that head; and declare that such expressions were extorted from me by the present view of the object, and imply no dogmatical spirit, nor conceited idea of my own judgment, which are sentiments that I am sensible can become no body, and a sceptic still less than any other.

BOOK TWO

OF THE PASSIONS

PART ONE

Of Pride and Humility

SECTION ONE

Division of the subject

As all the perceptions of the mind may be divided into *impressions* and *ideas,* so the impressions admit of another division into *original* and *secondary.* This division of the impressions is the same with that which I formerly* made use of when I distinguished them into impressions of *sensation* and *reflection.* Original impressions or impressions of sensation are such as without any antecedent perception arise in the soul, from the constitution of the body, from the animal spirits, or from the application of objects to the external organs. Secondary, or reflective impressions are such as proceed from some of these original ones, either immediately or by the interposition of its idea. Of the first kind are all the impressions of the senses, and all bodily pains and pleasures: of the second are the passions, and other emotions resembling them.

It is certain, that the mind, in its perceptions, must begin somewhere; and that since the impressions precede their correspondent ideas, there must be some impressions, which without any introduction make their appearance in the soul. As these depend upon natural and physical causes, the examination of them would lead me too far from my present subject, into the sciences of anatomy and natural philosophy. For this reason I shall here confine myself to those other impressions, which I have called secondary and

* Book 1, Part 1, Section 2.

reflective, as arising either from the original impressions, or from their ideas. Bodily pains and pleasures are the source of many passions, both when felt and considered by the mind; but arise originally in the soul, or in the body, whichever you please to call it, without any preceding thought or perception. A fit of the gout produces a long train of passions, as grief, hope, fear; but is not derived immediately from any affection or idea.

The reflective impressions may be divided into two kinds, *viz.* the *calm* and the *violent*. Of the first kind is the sense of beauty and deformity in action, composition, and external objects. Of the second are the passions of love and hatred, grief and joy, pride and humility. This division is far from being exact. The raptures of poetry and music frequently rise to the greatest height; while those other impressions, properly called *passions*, may decay into so soft an emotion, as to become, in a manner, imperceptible. But as in general the passions are more violent than the emotions arising from beauty and deformity, these impressions have been commonly distinguished from each other. The subject of the human mind being so copious and various, I shall here take advantage of this vulgar and specious division, that I may proceed with the greater order; and having said all I thought necessary concerning our ideas, shall now explain those violent emotions or passions, their nature, origin, causes, and effects.

When we take a survey of the passions, there occurs a division of them into *direct* and *indirect*. By direct passions I understand such as arise immediately from good or evil, from pain or pleasure. By indirect such as proceed from the same principles, but by the conjunction of other qualities. This distinction I cannot at present justify or explain any farther. I can only observe in general, that under the indirect passions I comprehend pride, humility, ambition, vanity, love, hatred, envy, pity, malice, generosity, with their dependants. And under the direct passions, desire, aversion, grief, joy, hope, fear, despair and security. I shall begin with the former.

SECTION TWO

Of pride and humility, their objects and causes

The passions of PRIDE and HUMILITY being simple and uniform impressions, it is impossible we can ever, by a multitude of words, give a just definition of them, or indeed of any of the passions. The utmost we can pretend to is a description of them, by an enumeration of such circumstances, as attend them: but as these words, *pride* and *humility*, are of general use, and the impressions they represent the most common of any, every one, of himself, will be able to form a just idea of them, without any danger of mistake. For which reason, not to lose time upon preliminaries, I shall immediately enter upon the examination of these passions.

It is evident, that pride and humility, though directly contrary, have yet the same OBJECT. This object is self, or that succession of related ideas and impressions, of which we have an intimate memory and consciousness. Here the view always fixes when we are actuated by either of these passions. According as our idea of ourself is more or less advantageous, we feel either of those opposite affections, and are elated by pride, or dejected with humility. Whatever other objects may be comprehended by the mind, they are always considered with a view to ourselves; otherwise they would never be able either to excite these passions, or produce the smallest increase or diminution of them. When self enters not into the consideration, there is no room either for pride or humility.

But though that connected succession of perceptions, which we call *self*, be always the object of these two passions, it is impossible it can be their CAUSE, or be sufficient alone to excite them. For as these passions are directly contrary, and have the same object in common; were their object also their cause; it could never produce any degree of the one passion, but at the same time it must excite an equal degree of the other; which opposition and contrariety must destroy both. It is impossible a man can at the same time be both proud and humble; and where he has different reasons for these passions, as frequently happens, the passions either take place alternately; or if they encounter, the one annihilates the other, as far as its strength goes, and the remainder only of that, which is superior, continues to operate upon the mind. But in the present case neither of the passions could ever become superior; because supposing it to be the view only of ourself, which excited them, that being perfectly indifferent to either, must produce both in the very same proportion; or in other words, can produce neither. To excite any passion, and at the same time raise an equal share of its antagonist, is immediately to undo what was done, and must leave the mind at last perfectly calm and indifferent.

We must therefore, make a distinction betwixt the cause and the object of these passions; betwixt that idea, which excites them, and that to which they direct their view, when excited. Pride and humility, being once raised, immediately turn our attention to ourself, and regard that as their ultimate and final object; but there is something farther requisite in order to raise them: something, which is peculiar to one of the passions, and produces not both in the very same degree. The first idea, that is presented to the mind, is that of the cause or productive principle. This excites the passion, connected with it; and that passion, when excited, turns our view to another idea, which is that of self. Here then is a passion placed betwixt two ideas, of which the one produces it, and the other is produced by it. The first idea, therefore, represents the *cause*, the second the *object* of the passion.

To begin with the causes of pride and humility; we may observe, that their most obvious and remarkable property is the vast variety of *subjects*, on which they may be placed. Every valuable quality of the mind, whether of the imagination, judgment, memory or disposition; wit, good-sense, learning, courage, justice, integrity; all these are the cause of pride; and their opposites of humility. Nor are these passions confined to the mind but extend their view to the body likewise. A man may be proud of his beauty, strength, agility, good mien, address in dancing, riding, and of his dexterity in any manual business or manufacture. But this is not all. The passions looking farther, comprehend whatever objects are in the least allied or related to us. Our country, family, children, relations, riches, houses, gardens, horses, dogs, clothes; any of these may become a cause either of pride or of humility.

From the consideration of these causes, it appears necessary we should make a new distinction in the causes of the passion, betwixt that *quality*, which operates, and the *subject*, on which it is placed. A man, for instance, is vain of a beautiful house, which belongs to him, or which he has himself built and contrived. Here the object of the passion is himself, and the cause is the beautiful house: which cause again is sub-divided into two parts, *viz*. the quality, which operates upon the passion, and the subject in which the quality inheres. The quality is the beauty, and the subject is the house, considered as his property or contrivance. Both these parts are essential, nor is the distinction vain and chimerical. Beauty, considered merely as such, unless placed upon something related to us, never produces any pride or vanity; and the strongest relation alone, without beauty, or something else in its place, has as little influence on that passion. Since, therefore, these two particulars are easily separated and there is a necessity for their conjunction, in order to produce the passion, we ought to consider them as component parts of the cause; and infix in our minds an exact idea of this distinction.

SECTION THREE

Whence these objects and causes are derived

Being so far advanced as to observe a difference betwixt the *object* of the passions and their *cause*, and to distinguish in the cause the *quality*, which operates on the passions, from the *subject*, in which it inheres; we now proceed to examine what determines each of them to be what it is, and assigns such a particular object, and quality, and subject to these affections. By this means we shall fully understand the origin of pride and humility.

It is evident in the first place, that these passions are determined to have self for their *object*, not only by a natural but also by an original property. No one can doubt but this property is *natural* from the constancy and steadiness of its operations. It is always self, which is the object of pride and humility; and whenever the passions look beyond, it is still with a view to ourselves, nor can any person or object otherwise have any influence upon us.

That this proceeds from an *original* quality or primary impulse, will likewise appear evident, if we consider that it is the distinguishing characteristic of these passions. Unless nature had given some original qualities to the mind, it could never have any secondary ones; because in that case it would have no foundation for action, nor could ever begin to exert itself. Now these qualities, which we must consider as original, are such as are most inseparable from the soul, and can be resolved into no other: and such is the quality, which determines the object of pride and humility.

We may, perhaps, make it a greater question, whether the *causes*, that produce the passion, be as *natural* as the object, to which it is directed, and whether all that vast variety proceeds from caprice or from the constitution of the mind. This doubt we shall soon remove, if we cast our eye upon human nature, and consider that in all nations and ages, the same objects still give rise to pride and humility; and that upon the view even of a stranger, we can know pretty nearly, what will either increase or diminish his passions of this kind. If there be any variation in this particular, it proceeds from nothing but a difference in the tempers and complexions of men; and is besides very inconsiderable. Can we imagine it possible, that while human nature remains the same, men will ever become entirely indifferent to their power, riches, beauty or personal merit, and that their pride and vanity will not be affected by these advantages?

But though the causes of pride and humility be plainly *natural*, we shall find upon examination, that they are not *original*, and that it is utterly impossible they should each of them be adapted to these passions by a particular provision, and primary constitution of nature, Beside their prodigious number, many of them are the effects of art, and arise partly from the industry, partly from the caprice, and partly from the good fortune of men. Industry produces houses, furniture, clothes. Caprice determines their particular kinds and qualities. And good fortune frequently contributes to all this, by discovering the effects that result from the different mixtures and combinations of bodies. It is absurd, therefore, to imagine, that each of these was foreseen and provided for by nature, and that every new production of art, which causes pride or humility; instead of adapting itself to the passion by partaking of some general quality, that naturally operates on the mind; is itself the object of an original principle, which till then lay concealed in the soul, and is only by accident at last brought to light. Thus the first mechanic, that invented a fine scritoire, produced pride in him, who became possessedd of it, by principles different from those, which made him proud of handsome chairs and tables. As this appears evidently ridiculous, we must conclude, that each cause of pride and humility is not adapted to the passions by a distinct original quality; but that there are some one or more circumstances common to all of them, on which their efficacy depends.

Besides, we find in the course of nature, that though the effects be many, the principles, from which they arise, are commonly but few and simple, and that it is the sign of an unskilful naturalist to have recourse to a different quality, in order to explain every different operation. How much more must this be true with regard to the human mind, which being so confined a subject may justly be thought incapable of containing such a monstrous heap of principles, as would be necessary to excite the passions of pride and humility, were each distinct cause adapted to the passion by a distinct set of principles?

Here, therefore, moral philosophy is in the same condition as natural, with regard to astronomy before the time of *Copernicus*. The ancients, though sensible of that maxim, *that nature does nothing in vain*, contrived such intricate systems of the heavens, as seemed inconsistent with true philosophy, and gave place at last to something more simple and natural. To invent without scruple a new principle to every new phenomenon, instead of adapting it to the old; to overload our hypotheses with a variety of this kind; are certain proofs, that none of these principles is the just one, and that we only desire, by a number of falsehoods, to cover our ignorance of the truth.

SECTION FOUR

Of the relations of impressions and ideas

Thus we have established two truths without any obstacle or difficulty, *that it is from natural principles this variety of causes excites pride and humility*, and *that it is not by a different principle each different cause is adapted to its passion*. We shall now proceed to enquire how we may reduce these principles to a lesser number, and find among the causes something common, on which their influence depends.

In order to this we must reflect on certain properties of human nature, which though they have a mighty influence on every operation both of the understanding and passions, are not commonly much insisted on by philosophers. The *first* of these is the association of ideas, which I have so often observed and explained. It is impossible for the mind to fix itself steadily upon one idea for any considerable time; nor can it by its utmost efforts ever arrive at such a constancy. But however changeable our thoughts may be, they are not entirely without rule and method in their changes. The rule, by which they proceed, is to pass from one object to what is resembling, contiguous to, or produced by it. When one idea is present to the imagination, any other, united by these relations, naturally follows it, and enters with more facility by means of that introduction.

The *second* property I shall observe in the human mind is a like association of impressions. All resembling impressions are connected together, and no sooner one arises than the rest immediately follow. Grief and disappointment give rise to anger, anger to envy, envy to malice, and malice to grief again, till the whole circle be compleated. In like manner our temper, when elevated with joy, naturally throws itself into love, generosity, pity, courage, pride, and the other resembling affections. It is difficult for the mind, when actuated by any passion, to confine itself to that passion alone, without any change or variation. Human nature is too inconstant to admit of any such regularity. Changeableness is essential to it. And to what can it so naturally change as to affections or emotions, which are suitable to the temper, and agree with that set of passions, which then prevail? It is evident, then, there is an attraction or association among impressions, as well as among ideas; though with this remarkable difference, that ideas are associated by resemblance, contiguity, and causation; and impressions only by resemblance.

In the *third* place, it is observable of these two kinds of association, that they very much assist and forward each other, and that the transition is more easily made where they both concur in the same object. Thus a man, who, by any injury from another, is very much discomposed and ruffled in his temper, is apt to find a hundred subjects of discontent, impatience, fear, and other uneasy passions; especially if he can discover these subjects in or near the person, who was the cause of his first passion. Those principles, which forward the transition of ideas, here concur with those, which operate on the passions; and both uniting in one action, bestow on the mind a double impulse. The new passion, there-fore, must arise with so much greater violence, and the transition to it must be rendered so much more easy and natural.

Upon this occasion I may cite the authority of an elegant writer, who expresses himself in the following manner: 'As the fancy delights in every thing that is great, strange, or beautiful, and is still more pleased the more it finds of these perfections in the *same* object, so it is capable of receiving a new satisfaction by the assistance of another sense. Thus any continued sound, as the music of birds, or a fall of waters, awakens every moment the mind of the beholder, and makes him more attentive to the several beauties of the place, that lie before him. Thus if there arises a fragrancy of smells or perfumes, they heighten the pleasure of the imagination, and make even the colours and verdure of the landscape appear more agreeable; for the ideas of both senses recommend each other, and are pleasanter together than when they enter the mind separately: as the different colours of a picture, when they are well disposed, set off one another, and receive an additional beauty from the advantage of the situation.'* In this phenomenon we may remark the association both of impressions and ideas, as well as the mutual assistance they lend each other.

SECTION FIVE

Of the influence of these relations on pride and humility

These principles being established on unquestionable experience, I begin to consider how we shall apply them, by revolving over all the causes of pride and humility, whether these causes be regarded, as the qualities, that operate, or as the subjects, on which the *qualities* are placed. In examining these qualities I immediately find many of them to concur in producing the sensation of pain and pleasure, independent of those affections, which I here endeavour to explain. Thus the beauty of our person, of itself, and by its very appearance, gives pleasure, as well as pride; and its deformity, pain as well as humility. A magnificent feast delights us, and a sordid one displeases. What I discover to be true in some instances, I *suppose* to be so in all; and take it for granted at present, without any

[* Addison, *Spectator* 412, final paragraph.]

farther proof, that every cause of pride, by its peculiar qualities, produces a separate pleasure, and of humility a separate uneasiness.

Again, in considering the *subjects*, to which these qualities adhere, I make a new *supposition*, which also appears probable from many obvious instances, *viz*, that these subjects are either parts of ourselves, or something nearly related to us. Thus the good and bad qualities of our actions and manners constitute virtue and vice, and determine our personal character, than which nothing operates more strongly on these passions. In like manner, it is the beauty or deformity of our person, houses, equipage, or furniture, by which we are rendered either vain or humble. The same qualities, when transferred to subjects, which bear us no relation, influence not in the smallest degree either of these affections.

Having thus in a manner supposed two properties of the causes of these affections, *viz*, that the *qualities* produce a separate pain or pleasure, and that the *subjects*, on which the qualities are placed, are related to self; I proceed to examine the passions themselves, in order to find something in them, correspondent to the supposed properties of their causes. *First*, I find, that the peculiar object of pride and humility is determined by an original and natural instinct, and that it is absolutely impossible, from the primary constitution of the mind, that these passions should ever look beyond self, or that individual person, of whose actions and sentiments each of us is intimately conscious. Here at last the view always rests, when we are actuated by either of these passions; nor can we, in that situation of mind, ever lose sight of this object. For this I pretend not to give any reason; but consider such a peculiar direction of the thought as an original quality.

The *second* quality, which I discover in these passions, and which I likewise consider an an original quality, is their sensations, or the peculiar emotions they excite in the soul, and which constitute their very being and essence. Thus pride is a pleasant sensation, and humility a painful; and upon the removal of the pleasure and pain, there is in reality no pride nor humility. Of this our very feeling convinces us; and beyond our feeling, it is here in vain to reason or dispute.

If I compare, therefore, these two *established* properties of the passions, *viz*, their object, which is self, and their sensation, which is either pleasant or painful, to the two *supposed* properties of the causes, *viz*, their relation to self, and their tendency to produce a pain or pleasure, independent of the passion; I immediately find, that taking these suppositions to be just, the true system breaks in upon me with an irresistible evidence. That cause, which excites the passion, is related to the object, which nature has attributed to the passion; the sensation, which the cause separately produces, is related to the sensation of the passion: from this double relation of ideas and impressions, the passion is derived. The one idea is easily converted into its correlative; and the one impression into that, which resembles and corresponds to it: with how much greater facility must this transition be made, where these movements mutually assist each other, and the mind receives a double impulse from the relations both of its impressions and ideas?

That we may comprehend this the better, we must suppose, that nature has given to the organs of the human mind, a certain disposition fitted to produce a peculiar impression or emotion, which we call *pride*: to this emotion she has assigned a certain idea, *viz*, that of *self*, which it never fails to produce. This contrivance of nature is easily conceived. We have many instances of such a situation of affairs. The nerves of the nose and palate are so disposed, as in certain circumstances to convey such peculiar sensations to the mind: the sensations of lust and hunger always produce in us the idea of those peculiar objects, which are suitable to each appetite. These two circumstances are united in pride. The organs are so disposed as to produce the passion; and the passion, after its production, naturally produces a certain idea. All this needs no proof. It is evident we never should be possessed of that passion, were there not a disposition of mind proper for it; and it is as evident, that the passion always turns our view to ourselves, and makes us think of our own qualities and circumstances.

This being fully comprehended, it may now be asked, *Whether nature produces the passion immediately, of herself; or whether she must be assisted by the co-operation of other causes?* For it is observable, that in this particular her conduct is different in the different passions and sensations. The palate must be excited by an external object, in order to produce any relish: but hunger arises internally, without the concurrence of any external object. But however the case may stand with other passions and impressions, it is certain, that pride requires the assistance of some foreign object, and that the organs, which produce it, exert not themselves like the heart and arteries, by an original internal movement. For *first*, daily experience convinces us, that pride requires certain causes to excite it, and languishes when unsupported by some excellency in the character, in bodily accomplishments, in clothes, equipage or fortune. *Secondly*, it is evident pride would be perpetual, if it arose immediately from nature; since the object is always the same, and there is no disposition of body peculiar to pride, as there is to thirst and hunger. *Thirdly*, Humility is in the very same situation with pride; and therefore, either must, upon this supposition, be perpetual likewise, or must destroy the contrary passion from the very first moment; so that none of them could ever make its appearance. Upon the whole, we may rest satisfied with the foregoing conclusion, that pride must have a cause, as well as an object, and that the one has no influence without the other.

The difficulty, then, is only to discover this cause, and find what it is that gives the first motion to pride, and sets those organs in action, which are naturally fitted to produce that emotion. Upon my consulting experience, in order to resolve this difficulty, I immediately find a hundred different causes, that produce pride; and upon examining these causes, I suppose, what at first I perceive to be probable, that all of them concur in two circumstances; which are, that of themselves they produce an impression, allied to the passion, and are placed on a subject, allied to the object of the passion. When I consider after this the nature of *relation*, and its effects both on the passions and ideas, I can no longer doubt, upon these suppositions, that it is the very principle, which gives rise to pride, and bestows motion on those organs, which being naturally disposed to produce that affection, require only a first impulse or beginning to their action. Any thing, that gives a pleasant sensation, and is related to self, excites the passion of pride, which is also agreeable, and has self for its object.

What I have said of pride is equally true of humility. The sensation of humility is uneasy, as that of pride is agreeable; for which reason the separate sensation, arising from the causes, must be reversed, while the relation to self continues the same. Though pride and humility are directly contrary in their effects, and in their sensations, they have notwithstanding the same object; so that it is requisite only to change the relation of impressions, without making any change upon that of ideas. Accordingly we find, that a beautiful house, belonging to ourselves, produces pride; and that the same house, still belonging to ourselves, produces humility, when by any accident its beauty is changed into deformity, and thereby the sensation of pleasure, which corresponded to pride, is transformed into pain, which is related to humility. The double relation between the ideas and impressions subsists in both cases, and produces an easy transition from the one emotion to the other.

In a word, nature has bestowed a kind of attraction on certain impressions and ideas, by which one of them, upon its appearance, naturally introduces its correlative. If these two attractions or associations of impressions and ideas concur on the same object, they mutually assist each other, and the transition of the affections and of the imagination is made with the greatest ease and facility. When an idea produces an impression, related to an impression, which is connected with an idea, related to the first idea, these two impressions must be in a manner inseparable, nor will the one in any case be unattended with the other. It is after this manner, that the particular causes of pride and humility are determined. The quality, which operates on the passion, produces separately an impression resembling it; the subject, to which the quality adheres, is related to self, the object of the passion: no wonder the whole cause, consisting of a quality and of a subject, does so unavoidably give rise to the passion.

To illustrate this hypothesis we may compare it to that, by which I have already explained the belief attending the judgments, which we form from causation. I have observed, that in all judgments of this kind, there is always a present impression and a related idea; and that the present impression gives a vivacity to the fancy, and the relation conveys this vivacity, by an easy transition, to the related idea. Without the present impression, the attention is not fixed, nor the spirits excited. Without the relation, this attention rests on its first object, and has no farther consequence. There is evidently a great analogy betwixt that hypothesis and our present one of an impression and idea, that transfuse themselves into another impression and idea by means of their double relation: which analogy must be allowed to be no despicable proof of both hypotheses.

SECTION SIX

Limitations of this system

But before we proceed farther in this subject, and examine particularly all the causes of pride and humility, it will be proper to make some limitations to the general system, *that all agreeable objects, related to ourselves, by an association of ideas and impressions, produce pride, and disagreeable ones, humility*: and these limitations are derived from the very nature of the subject.

I. Suppose an agreeable object to acquire a relation to self, the first passion, that appears on this occasion, is joy; and this passion discovers itself upon a slighter relation than pride and vain-glory. We may feel joy upon being present at a feast, where our senses are regaled with delicacies of every kind: but it is only the master of the feast, who, beside the same joy, has the additional passion of self-applause and vanity. It is true, men sometimes boast of a great entertainment, at which they have only been present; and by so small a relation convert their pleasure into pride: but however, this must in general be owned, that joy arises from a more inconsiderable relation than vanity, and that many things, which are too foreign to produce pride, are yet able to give us a delight and pleasure, The reason of the difference may be explained thus. A relation is requisite to joy, in order to approach the object to us, and make it give us any satisfaction. But beside this, which is common to both passions, it is requisite to pride, in order to produce a transition from one passion to another, and convert the satisfaction into vanity. As it has a double task to perform, it must be endowed with double force and energy. To which we may add, that where agreeable objects bear not a very close relation to ourselves, they commonly do to some other person; and this latter relation not only excels, but even diminishes, and sometimes destroys the former, as we shall see afterwards.*

Here then is the first limitation, we must make to our general position, *that every thing related to us, which produces pleasure or pain, produces likewise pride or humility*. There is not only a relation required, but a close one, and a closer than is required to joy.

II. The second limitation is, that the agreeable or disagreeable object be not only closely related, but also peculiar to ourselves, or

* Part 2, Section 4.

at least common to us with a few persons. It is a quality observable in human nature, and which we shall endeavour to explain afterwards, that every thing, which is often presented and to which we have been long accustomed, loses its value in our eyes, and is in a little time despised and neglected. We likewise judge of objects more from comparison than from their real and intrinsic merit; and where we cannot by some contrast enhance their value, we are apt to overlook even what is essentially good in them. These qualities of the mind have an effect upon joy as well as pride; and it is remarkable, that goods which are common to all mankind, and have become familiar to us by custom, give us little satisfaction; though perhaps of a more excellent kind, than those on which, for their singularity, we set a much higher value. But though this circumstance operates on both these passions, it has a much greater influence on vanity. We are rejoiced for many goods, which, on account of their frequency, give us no pride. Health, when it returns after a long absence, affords us a very sensible satisfaction; but is seldom regarded as a subject of vanity, because it is shared with such vast numbers.

The reason, why pride is so much more delicate in this particular than joy, I take to be, as follows. In order to excite pride, there are always two objects we must contemplate, *viz*. the *cause* or that object which produces pleasure; and self, which is the real object of the passion. But joy has only one object necessary to its production, *viz*. that which gives pleasure; and though it be requisite, that this bear some relation to self, yet that is only requisite in order to render it agreeable; nor is self, properly speaking, the object of this passion. Since, therefore, pride has in a manner two objects, to which it directs our view; it follows, that where neither of them have any singularity, the passion must be more weakened upon that account, than a passion, which has only one object. Upon comparing ourselves with others, as we are every moment apt to do, we find we are not in the least distinguished; and upon comparing the object we possess, we discover still the same unlucky circumstance. By two comparisons so disadvantageous the passion must be entirely destroyed.

III. The third limitation is, that the pleasant or painful object be very discernible and obvious, and that not only to ourselves, but to others also. This circumstance, like the two foregoing, has an effect upon joy, as well as pride. We fancy ourselves more happy, as well as more virtuous or beautiful, when we appear so to others; but are still more ostentatious of our virtues than of our pleasures. This proceeds from causes, which I shall endeavour to explain afterwards.

IV. The fourth limitation is derived from the inconstancy of the cause of these passions, and from the short duration of its connexion with ourselves. What is casual and inconstant gives but little joy, and less pride. We are not much satisfied with the thing itself; and are still less apt to feel any new degrees of self-satisfaction upon its account. We foresee and anticipate its change by the imagination; which makes us little satisfied with the thing: we compare it to ourselves, whose existence is more durable; by which means its inconstancy appears still greater. It seems ridiculous to infer an excellency in ourselves from an object, which is of so much shorter duration, and attends us during so small a part of our existence. It will be easy to comprehend the reason, why this cause operates not with the same force in joy as in pride; since the idea of self is not so essential to the former passion as to the latter.

V. I may add as a fifth limitation, or rather enlargement of this system, that *general rules* have a great influence upon pride and humility, as well as on all the other passions. Hence we form a notion of different ranks of men, suitable to the power of riches they are possessed of; and this notion we change not upon account of any peculiarities of the health or temper of the persons, which may deprive them of all enjoyment in their possessions. This may be accounted for from the same principles, that explained the influence of general rules on the understanding. Custom readily carries us beyond the just bounds in our passions, as well as in our reasonings.

It may not be amiss to observe on this occasion, that the influence of general rules and maxims on the passions very much contributes to facilitate the effects of all the principles, which we shall explain in the progress of this treatise. For it is evident, that if a person full-grown, and of the same nature with ourselves, were on a sudden transported into our world, he would be very much embarrassed with every object, and would not readily find what degree of love or hatred, pride or humility, or any other passion he ought to attribute to it. The passions are often varied by very inconsiderable principles; and these do not always play with a perfect regularity, especially on the first trial. But as custom and practice have brought to light all these principles, and have settled the just value of every thing; this must certainly contribute to the easy production of the passions, and guide us, by means of general established maxims, in the proportions we ought to observe in preferring one object to another. This remark may, perhaps, serve to obviate difficulties, that may arise concerning some causes, which I shall hereafter ascribe to particular passions, and which may be esteemed too refined to operate so universally and certainly, as they are found to do.

I shall close this subject with a reflection derived from these five limitations. This reflection is, that the persons, who are proudest, and who in the eye of the world have most reason for their pride, are not always the happiest; nor the most humble always the most miserable, as may at first sight be imagined from this system. An evil may be real, though its cause has no relation to us: it may be real, without being peculiar: it may be real, without shewing itself to others: it may be real, without being constant: and it may be real, without falling under the general rules. Such evils as these will not fail to render us miserable, though they have little tendency to diminish pride: and perhaps the most real and the most solid evils of life will be found of this nature.

SECTION SEVEN
Of vice and virtue

Taking these limitations along with us, let us proceed to examine the causes of pride and humility; and see, whether in every case we can discover the double relations, by which they operate on the passions. If we find that all these causes are related to self, and produce a pleasure or uneasiness separate from the passion, there will remain no farther scruple with regard to the present system. We shall principally endeavour to prove the latter point; the former being in a manner self-evident.

To begin with VICE and VIRTUE; which are the most obvious causes of these passions; it would be entirely foreign to my present purpose to enter upon the controversy, which of late years has so much excited the curiosity of the publick, *whether these moral distinctions be founded on natural and original principless, or arise from interest and education*. The examination of this I reserve for the following book; and in the mean time I shall endeavour to show, that my system maintains its ground upon either of these hypotheses; which will be a strong proof of its solidity.

For granting that morality had no foundation in nature, it must still be allowed, that vice and virtue, either from self-interest or the prejudices of education, produce in us a real pain and pleasure; and this we may observe to be strenuously asserted by the defenders of that hypothesis. Every passion, habit, or turn of character (say they) which has a tendency to our advantage or prejudice, gives a delight or uneasiness; and it is from thence the approbation or disapprobation arises. We easily gain from the liberality of others, but are always in danger of losing by their avarice: courage defends us, but cowardice lays us open to every attack: justice is the support of society, but injustice, unless checked would quickly prove its ruin: humility exalts; but pride mortifies us. For these reasons the former qualities are esteemed virtues, and the latter regarded as vices. Now since it is granted there is a delight or uneasiness still attending merit or demerit of every kind, this is all that is requisite for my purpose.

But I go farther, and observe, that this moral hypothesis and my present system not only agree together, but also that, allowing the former to be just, it is an absolute and invincible proof of the latter. For if all morality be founded on the pain or pleasure, which arises from the prospect of any loss or advantage, that may result from our own characters, or from those of others, all the effects of morality must be derived from the same pain or pleasure, and among the rest, the passions of pride and humility. The very essence of virtue, according to this hypothesis, is to produce pleasure and that of vice to give pain. The virtue and vice must be part of our character in order to excite pride or humility. What farther proof can we desire for the double relation of impressions and ideas?

The same unquestionable argument may be derived from the opinion of those, who maintain that morality is something real, essential, and founded on nature. The most probable hypothesis, which has been advanced to explain the distinction betwixt vice and virtue, and the origin of moral rights and obligations, is, that from a primary constitution of nature certain characters and passions, by the very view and contemplation, produce a pain, and others in like manner excite a pleasure. The uneasiness and satisfaction are not only inseparable from vice and virtue, but constitute their very nature and essence. To approve of a character is to feel an original delight upon its appearance. To disapprove of it is to be sensible of an uneasiness. The pain and pleasure, therefore, being the primary causes of vice and virtue, must also be the causes of all their effects, and consequently of pride and humility, which are the unavoidable attendants of that distinction.

But supposing this hypothesis of moral philosophy should be allowed to be false, it is still evident, that pain and pleasure, if not the causes of vice and virtue, are at least inseparable from them. A generous and noble character affords a satisfaction even in the survey; and when presented to us, though only in a poem or fable, never fails to charm and delight us. On the other hand cruelty and treachery displease from their very nature; nor is it possible ever to reconcile us to these qualities, either in ourselves or others. Thus one hypothesis of morality is an undeniable proof of the foregoing system, and the other at worst agrees with it.

But pride and humility arise not from these qualities alone of the mind, which, according to the vulgar systems of ethics, have been comprehended as parts of moral duty, but from any other that has a connexion with pleasure and uneasiness. Nothing flatters our vanity more than the talent of pleasing by our wit, good humour, or any other accomplishment; and nothing gives us a more sensible mortification than a disappointment in any attempt of that nature. No one has ever been able to tell what *wit* is, and to shew why such a system of thought must be received under that denomination, and such another rejected. It is only by taste we can decide concerning it, nor are we possessed of any other standard, upon which we can form a judgment of this kind. Now what is this *taste*, from which true and false wit in a manner receive their being, and without which no thought can have a title to either of these denominations? It is plainly nothing but a sensation of pleasure from true wit, and of uneasiness from false, without our being able to tell the reasons of that pleasure or uneasiness. The power of bestowing these opposite sensations is, therefore, the very essence of true and false wit; and consequently the cause of that pride or humility, which arises from them.

There may, perhaps, be some, who being accustomed to the style of the schools and pulpit, and having never considered human nature in any other light, than that in which *they* place it, may here be surprized to hear me talk of virtue as exciting pride, which they look upon as a vice; and of vice as producing humility, which they have been taught to consider as a virtue. But not to dispute about words, I observe, that by *pride* I understand that agreeable impression, which arises in the mind, when the view either of our virtue, beauty, riches or power makes us satisfied with ourselves: and that by *humility* I mean the opposite impression. It is evident the former impression is not always vicious, nor the latter virtuous. The most rigid morality allows us to receive a pleasure from reflecting on a generous action; and it is by none esteemed a virtue to feel any fruitless remorses upon the thoughts of past villainy and baseness. Let us, therefore, examine these impressions, considered in themselves; and enquire into their causes, whether placed on the mind or body, without troubling ourselves at present with that merit or blame, which may attend them.

SECTION EIGHT
Of beauty and deformity

Whether we consider the body as a part of ourselves, or assent to those philosophers, who regard it as something external, it must still be allowed to be near enough connected with us to form one of these double relations, which I have asserted to be necessary to the causes of pride and humility. Wherever, therefore, we can find the other relation of impressions to join to this of ideas, we may expect with assurance either of these passions, according as the impression is pleasant or uneasy. But *beauty* of all kinds gives us a peculiar delight and satisfaction; as *deformity* produces pain, upon whatever subject it may be placed, and whether surveyed in an animate or inanimate object. If the beauty or deformity, therefore, be placed upon our own bodies, this pleasure or uneasiness must be converted into pride or humility, as having in this case all the circumstances requisite to produce a perfect transition of impressions and ideas. These opposite sensations are related to the opposite passions. The beauty or deformity is closely related to self, the object of both these passions. No wonder, then, our own beauty becomes an object of pride, and deformity of humility.

But this effect of personal and bodily qualities is not only a proof of the present system, by shewing that the passions arise not in this case without all the circumstances I have required, but may be employed as a stronger and more convincing argument. If we consider all the hypotheses, which have been formed either by philosophy or common reason, to explain the difference betwixt beauty and deformity, we shall find that all of them resolve into this, that beauty is such an order and construction of parts, as either by the *primary constitution* of our nature, by *custom*, or by *caprice*, is fitted to give a pleasure and satisfaction to the soul. This is the distinguishing character of beauty, and forms all the difference betwixt it and deformity, whose natural tendency is to produce uneasiness. Pleasure and pain, therefore, are not only necessary attendants of beauty and deformity, but constitute their very essence. And indeed, if we consider, that a great part of the beauty, which we admire either in animals or in other objects, is derived from the idea of convenience and utility, we shall make no scruple to assent to this opinion. That shape, which produces strength, is beautiful in one animal; and that which is a sign of agility in another. The order and convenience of a palace are no less essential to its beauty, than its mere figure and appearance. In like manner the rules of architecture require, that the top of a pillar should be more slender than its base, and that because such a figure conveys to us the idea of security, which is pleasant; whereas the contrary form gives us the apprehension of danger, which is uneasy. From innumerable instances of this kind, as well as from considering that beauty like wit, cannot be defined, but is discerned only by a taste or sensation, we may conclude, that beauty is nothing but a form, which produces pleasure, as deformity is a structure of parts, which conveys pain; and since the power of producing pain and pleasure make in this manner the essence of beauty and deformity, all the effects of these qualities must be derived from the sensation; and among the rest pride and humility, which of all their effects are the most common and remarkable.

This argument I esteem just and decisive; but in order to give greater authority to the present reasoning, let us suppose it false for a moment, and see what will follow. It is certain, then, that if the power of producing pleasure and pain forms not the essence of beauty and deformity, the sensations are at least inseparable from the qualities, and it is even difficult to consider them apart. Now there is nothing common to natural and moral beauty, (both of which are the causes of pride) but this power of producing pleasure; and as a common effect supposes always a common cause, it is plain the pleasure must in both cases be the real and influencing cause of the passion. Again; there is nothing originally different betwixt the beauty of our bodies and the beauty of external and foreign objects, but that the one has a near relation to ourselves, which is wanting in the other. This original difference, therefore, must be the cause of all their other differences, and among the rest, of their different influence upon the passion of pride, which is excited by the beauty of our person, but is not affected in the least by that of foreign and external objects. Placing, then, these two conclusions together, we find they compose the preceding system betwixt them, *viz*, that pleasure, as a related or resembling impression, when placed on a related object by a natural transition, produces pride; and its contrary, humility. This system, then, seems already sufficiently confirmed by experience; though we have not yet exhausted all our arguments.

It is not the beauty of the body alone that produces pride, but also its strength and force. Strength is a kind of power; and therefore the desire to excel in strength is to be considered as an inferior species of *ambition*. For this reason the present phenomenon will be sufficiently accounted for, in explaining that passion.

Concerning all other bodily accomplishments we may observe in general, that whatever in ourselves is either useful, beautiful, or surprising, is an object of pride; and its contrary, of humility. Now it is obvious, that every thing useful, beautiful or surprising, agrees in producing a separate pleasure and agrees in nothing else. The pleasure, therefore, with the relation to self must be the cause of the passion.

Though it should be questioned, whether beauty be not something real, and different from the power of producing pleasure, it can never be disputed, that as surprize is nothing but a pleasure arising from novelty, it is not, properly speaking, a quality in any object, but merely a passion or impression in the soul. It must, therefore, be from that impression, that pride by a natural transition arises. And it arises so naturally, that there is nothing *in us or belonging to us*, which produces surprize, that does not at the same time excite that other passion. Thus we are vain of the surprising adventures we have met with, the escapes we have made, and dangers we have been exposed to. Hence the origin of vulgar lying; where men without any interest, and merely out of vanity, heap up a number of extraordinary events, which are either the fictions of their brain, or if true, have at least no connexion with themselves. Their fruitful invention supplies them with a variety of adventures; and where that talent is wanting, they appropriate such as belong to others, in order to satisfy their vanity.

In this phenomenon are contained two curious experiments, which if we compare them together, according to the known rules, by which we judge of cause and effect in anatomy, natural philosophy, and other sciences, will be an undeniable argument for that influence of the double relations above-mentioned. By one of these experiments we find, that an object produces pride merely by the interposition of pleasure; and that because the quality, by which it produces pride, is in reality nothing but the power of producing pleasure. By the other experiment we find, that the pleasure produces the pride by a transition along related ideas; because when we cut off that relation the passion is immediately destroyed.. A surprising adventure, in which we have been ourselves engaged, is related to us, and by that means produces pride: but the adventures of others, though they may cause pleasure, yet for want of this relation of ideas, never excite that passion. What farther proof can be desired for the present system?

There is only one objection to this system with regard to our body: which is, that though nothing be more agreeable than health, and more painful than sickness, yet commonly men are neither proud of the one, nor mortified with the other. This will easily be accounted for, if we consider the *second* and *fourth* limitations, proposed to our general system. It was observed, that no object ever produces pride or humility, if it has not something *peculiar* to ourself; as also, that every cause of that passion must be in some measure *constant*, and hold some proportion to the duration of our self, which is its object. Now as health and sickness vary incessantly to all men, and there is none, who is *solely* or *certainly* fixed in either, these accidental blessings and calamities are in a manner separated from us, and are never considered as connected with our being and existence. And that this account is just appears hence, that wherever a malady of any kind is so rooted in our constitution, that we no longer entertain any hopes of recovery, from that moment it becomes an object of humility; as is evident in old men, whom nothing mortifies more than the consideration of their age and infirmities. They endeavour, as long as possible, to conceal their blindness and deafness, their rheums and gouts; nor do they ever confess them without reluctance and uneasiness. And though young men are not ashamed of every head-ache or cold they fall into, yet no topic is so proper to mortify human pride, and make us entertain a mean opinion of our nature, than this, that we are every moment of our lives subject to such infirmities. This sufficiently proves that bodily pain and sickness are in themselves proper causes of humility; though the custom of estimating every thing by comparison more than by its intrinsic worth and value, makes us overlook these calamities, which we find to be incident to every one, and causes us to form an idea of our merit and character independent of them.

We are ashamed of such maladies as affect others, and are either dangerous or disagreeable to them. Of the epilepsy; because it gives a horror to every one present: of the itch; because it is infectious: of the king's-evil; because it commonly goes to posterity. Men always consider the sentiments of others in their judgment of themselves. This has evidently appeared in some of the foregoing reasonings; and will appear still more evidently, and be more fully explained afterwards.

SECTION NINE
Of external advantages and disadvantages

But though pride and humility have the qualities of our mind and body, that is *self*, for their natural and more immediate causes, we find by experience, that there are many other objects, which produce these affections, and that the primary one is, in some measure, obscured and lost by the multiplicity of foreign and extrinsic. We found a vanity upon houses, gardens, equipages, as well as upon personal merit and accomplishments; and though these external advantages be in themselves widely distant from thought or a person, yet they considerably influence even a passion, which is directed to that as its ultimate object, This happens when external objects acquire any particular relation to ourselves, and are associated or connected with us. A beautiful fish in the ocean, an animal in a desert, and indeed any thing that neither belongs, nor is related to us, has no manner of influence on our vanity, whatever extraordinary qualities it may be endowed with, and whatever degree of surprize and admiration it may naturally occasion. It must be some way associated with us in order to touch our pride. Its idea must hang in a manner, upon that of ourselves; and the transition from the one to the other must be easy and natural.

But here it is remarkable, that though the relation of *resemblance* operates upon the mind in the same manner as contiguity and causation, in conveying us from one idea to another, yet it is seldom a foundation either of pride or of humility. If we resemble a person in any of the valuable parts of his character, we must, in some degree, possess the quality, in which we resemble him; and this quality we always choose to survey directly in ourselves rather than by reflexion in another person, when we would found upon it any degree of vanity. So that though a likeness may occasionally produce that passion by suggesting a more advantageous idea of ourselves, it is there the view fixes at last, and the passion finds its ultimate and final cause.

There are instances, indeed, wherein men shew a vanity in resembling a great man in his countenance, shape, air, or other minute circumstances, that contribute not in any degree to his reputation; but it must be confessed that this extends not very far, nor is of any considerable moment in these affections. For this I assign the following reason. We can never have a vanity of resembling in trifles any person, unless he be possessed of very shining qualities, which give us a respect and veneration for him. These qualities, then, are, properly speaking, the causes of our vanity, by means of their relation to ourselves. Now after what manner are they related to ourselves? They are parts of the person we value, and consequently connected with these trifles; which are also supposed to be parts of him. These trifles are connected with the resembling qualities in us; and these qualities in us, being parts, are connected with the whole; and by that means form a chain of several links of the person we resemble. But besides that this multitude of relations must weaken the connexion; it is evident the mind, in passing from the shining qualities to the trivial ones, must by that contrast the better perceive the minuteness of the latter, and be in some measure ashamed of the comparison and resemblance.

The relation, therefore, of contiguity, or that of causation, betwixt the cause and object of pride and humility, is alone requisite to give rise to these passions; and these relations are nothing else but qualities, by which the imagination is conveyed from one idea to another. Now let us consider what effect these can possibly have upon the mind, and by what means they become so requisite to the production of the passions. It is evident, that the association of ideas operates in so silent and imperceptible a manner, that we are scarce sensible of it, and discover it more by its effects than by any immediate feeling or perception. It produces no emotion, and gives rise to no new impression of any kind, but only modifies those ideas, of which the mind was formerly possessed, and which it could recall upon occasion. From this reasoning, as well as from undoubted experience, we may conclude, that an association of ideas, however necessary, is not alone sufficient to give rise to any passion.

It is evident, then, that when the mind feels the passion either of pride or humility upon the appearance of a related object, there is, beside the relation or transition of thought, an emotion or original impression produced by some other principle. The question is, whether the emotion first produced be the passion itself, or some other impression related to it. This question we cannot be long in deciding. For besides all the other arguments, with which this subject abounds, it must evidently appear, that the relation of ideas, which experience shews to be so requisite a circumstance to the production of the passion, would be entirely superfluous, were it not to second a relation of affections, and facilitate the transition from one impression to another. If nature produced immediately the passion of pride or humility, it would be compleated in itself, and would require no farther addition or increase from any other affection. But supposing the first emotion to be only related to pride or humility, it is easily conceived to what purpose the relation of objects may serve, and how the two different associations, of impressions and ideas, by uniting their forces, may assist each other's operation. This is not only easily conceived, but I will venture to affirm it is the only manner, in which we can conceive this subject. An easy transition of ideas, which, of itself, causes no emotion, can never be necessary, or even useful to the passions, but by forwarding the transition betwixt some related impressions. Not to mention, that the same object causes a greater or smaller degree of pride, not only in proportion to the increase or decrease of its qualities, but also to the distance or nearness of the relation; which is a clear argument for the transition of affections along the relation of ideas; since every change in the relation produces a proportionable change in the passion. Thus one part of the preceding system, concerning the relations of ideas is a sufficient proof of the other, concerning that of impressions; and is itself so evidently founded on experience, that it would be lost time to endeavour farther to prove it.

This will appear still more evidently in particular instances. Men are vain of the beauty of their country, of their county, of their parish. Here the idea of beauty plainly produces a pleasure. This pleasure is related to pride. The object or cause of this pleasure is, by the supposition, related to self, or the object of pride. By this double relation of impressions and ideas, a transition is made from the one impression to the other.

Men are also vain of the temperature of the climate, in which they were born; of the fertility of their native soil; of the goodness of the wines, fruits or victuals, produced by it; of the softness or force of their language; with other particulars of that kind. These objects have plainly a reference to the pleasures of the senses, and are originally considered as agreeable to the feeling, taste or hearing. How is it possible they could ever become objects of pride, except by means of that transition above-explained?

There are some, that discover a vanity of an opposite kind, and affect to depreciate their own country, in comparison of those, to which they have travelled. These persons find, when they are at home, and surrounded with their countrymen, that the strong relation betwixt them and their own nation is shared with so many, that it is in a manner lost to them; whereas their distant relation to a foreign country, which is formed by their having seen it and lived in it, is augmented by their considering how few there are who have done the same. For this reason they always admire the beauty, utility and rarity of what is abroad, above what is at home.

Since we can be vain of a country, climate or any inanimate object, which bears a relation to us, it is no wonder we are vain of the qualities of those, who are connected with us by blood or friendship. Accordingly we find, that the very same qualities, which in ourselves produce pride, produce also in a lesser degree the same affection, when discovered in persons related to us. The beauty, address, merit, credit and honours of their kindred are carefully displayed by the proud, as some of the most considerable sources of their vanity.

As we are proud of riches in ourselves, so to satisfy our vanity we desire that every one, who has any connexion with us, should likewise be possessed of them, and are ashamed of any one, that is mean or poor, among our friends and relations. For this reason we remove the poor as far from us as possible; and as we cannot prevent poverty in some distant collaterals, and our forefathers are taken to be our nearest relations; upon this account every one affects to be of a good family, and to be descended from a long succession of rich and honourable ancestors.

I have frequently observed, that those, who boast of the antiquity of their families, are glad when they can join this circumstance, that their ancestors for many generations have been uninterrupted proprietors of the same portion of land, and that their family has never changed its possessions, or been transplanted into any other county or province. I have also observed, that it is an additional subject of vanity, when they can boast, that these possessions have been transmitted through a descent composed entirely of males, and that the honour, and fortune have never passed through any female. Let us endeavour to explain these phenomena by the foregoing system.

It is evident, that when any one boasts of the antiquity of his family, the subjects of his vanity are not merely the extent of time and number of ancestors, but also their riches and credit, which are supposed to reflect a lustre on himself on account of his relation to them. He first considers these objects; is affected by them in an agreeable manner; and then returning back to himself, through the relation of parent and child, is elevated with the passion of pride, by means of the double relation, of impressions and ideas. Since therefore the passion depends on these relations, whatever strengthens any of the relations must also increase the passion, and whatever weakens the relations must diminish the passion. Now it is certain the identity of the possession strengthens the relation of ideas arising from blood and kindred, and conveys the fancy with greater facility from one generation to another, from the remote ancestors to their posterity, who are both their heirs and their descendants. By this facility the impression is transmitted more entire, and excites a greater degree of pride and vanity.

The case is the same with the transmission of the honours and fortune through a succession of males without their passing through any female. It is a quality of human nature, which we shall consider* afterwards, that the imagination naturally turns to whatever is important and considerable; and where two objects are presented to it, a small and a great one, usually leaves the former, and dwells entirely upon the latter. As in the society of marriage, the male sex has the advantage above the female, the husband first engages our attention; and whether we consider him directly, or reach him by passing through related objects, the thought both rests upon him with greater satisfaction, and arrives at him with greater facility than his consort. It is easy to see, that this property must strengthen the child's relation to the father, and weaken that to the mother. For as all relations are nothing but a propensity to pass from one idea to another, whatever strengthens the propensity strengthens the relation; and as we have a stronger propensity to pass from the idea of the children to that of the

* Part 2, Section 2.

father, than from the same idea to that of the mother, we ought to regard the former relation as the closer and more considerable. This is the reason why children commonly bear their father's name, and are esteemed to be of nobler or baser birth, according to *his* family. And though the mother should be possessed of a superior spirit and genius to the father, as often happens, the *general rule* prevails, notwithstanding the exception, according to the doctrine above-explained. Nay even when a superiority of any kind is so great, or when any other reasons have such an effect, as to make the children rather represent the mother's family than the father's, the general rule still retains such an efficacy that it weakens the relation, and makes a kind of break in the line of ancestors. The imagination runs not along them with facility, nor is able to transfer the honour and credit of the ancestors to their posterity of the same name and family so readily, as when the transition is conformable to the general rules, and passes from father to son, or from brother to brother.

SECTION TEN

Of property and riches

But the relation, which is esteemed the closest, and which of all others produces most commonly the passion of pride, is that of *property*. This relation it will be impossible for me fully to explain before I come to treat of justice and the other moral virtues. It is sufficient to observe on this occasion, that property may be defined, *such a relation betwixt a person and an object as permits him, but forbids any other, the free use and possession of it, without violating the laws of justice and moral equity.* If justice, therefore, be a virtue, which has a natural and original influence on the human mind, property may be looked upon as a particular species of *causation*; whether we consider the liberty it gives the proprietor to operate as he please upon the object or the advantages, which he reaps from it. It is the same case, if justice, according to the system of certain philosophers, should be esteemed an artificial and not a natural virtue. For then honour, and custom, and civil laws supply the place of natural conscience, and produce, in some degree, the same effects. This in the mean time is certain, that the mention of the property naturally carries our thought to the proprietor, and of the proprietor to the property; which being a proof of a perfect relation of ideas is all that is requisite to our present purpose. A relation of ideas, joined to that of impressions, always produces a transition of affections; and therefore, whenever any pleasure or pain arises from an object, connected with us by property, we may be certain, that either pride or humility must arise from this conjunction of relations; if the foregoing system be solid and satisfactory. And whether it be so or not, we may soon satisfy ourselves by the most cursory view of human life.

Every thing belonging to a vain man is the best that is any where to be found. His houses, equipage, furniture, clothes, horses, hounds, excel all others in his conceit; and it is easy to observe, that from the least advantage in any of these, he draws a new subject of pride and vanity. His wine, if you'll believe him, has a finer flavour than any other; his cookery is more exquisite; his table more orderly; his servants more expert; the air, in which he lives, more healthful; the soil he cultivates more fertile; his fruits ripen earlier and to greater perfection: such a thing is remarkable for its novelty; such another for its antiquity: this is the workmanship of a famous artist; that belonged once to such a prince or great man: all objects, in a word, that are useful, beautiful or surprising, or are related to such, may, by means of property, give rise to this passion. These agree in giving pleasure, and agree in nothing else. This alone is common to them; and therefore must be the quality that produces the passion, which is their common effect. As every new instance is a new argument, and as the instances are here without number, I may venture to affirm, that scarce any system was ever so fully proved by experience, as that which I have here advanced.

If the property of any thing, that gives pleasure either by its utility, beauty or novelty, produces also pride by a double relation of impressions and ideas; we need not be surprized, that the power of acquiring this property, should have the same effect. Now riches are to be considered as the power of acquiring the property of what pleases; and it is only in this view they have any influence on the passions. Paper will, on many occasions, be considered as riches, and that because it may convey the power of acquiring money: and money is not riches, as it is a metal endowed with certain qualities of solidity, weight and fusibility; but only as it has a relation to the pleasures and conveniences of life. Taking then this for granted, which is in itself so evident, we may draw from it one of the strongest arguments I have yet employed to prove the influence of the double relations on pride and humility.

It has been observed in treating of the understanding, that the distinction, which we sometimes make betwixt a *power* and the *exercise* of it, is entirely frivolous, and that neither man nor any other being ought ever to be thought possessed of any ability, unless it be exerted and put in action. But though this be strictly true in a just and *philosophical* way of thinking, it is certain it is not *the philosophy* of our passions; but that many things operate upon them by means of the idea and supposition of power, independent of its actual exercise. We are pleased when we acquire an ability of procuring pleasure, and are displeased when another acquires a power of giving pain. This is evident from experience; but in order to give a just explication of the matter, and account for this satisfaction and uneasiness, we must weigh the following reflections.

It is evident the error of distinguishing power from its exercise proceeds not entirely from the scholastic doctrine of *free-will*, which, indeed, enters very little into common life, and has but small influence on our vulgar and popular ways of thinking. According to that doctrine, motives deprive us not of free-will, nor take away our power of performing or forbearing any action. But according to common notions a man has no power, where very considerable motives lie betwixt him and the satisfaction of his desires, and determine him to forbear what he wishes to perform. I do not think I have fallen into my enemy's power, when I see him pass me in the streets with a sword by his side, while I am unprovided of any weapon. I know that the fear of the civil magistrate is as strong a restraint as any of iron, and that I am in as perfect safety as if he were chained or imprisoned. But when a person acquires such an authority over me, that not only there is no external obstacle to his actions; but also that he may punish or reward me as he pleases, without any dread of punishment in his turn, I then attribute a full power to him, and consider myself as his subject or vassal.

Now if we compare these two cases, that of a person, who has very strong motives of interest or safety to forbear any action, and that of another, who lies under no such obligation, we shall find, according to the philosophy explained in the foregoing book, that the only *known* difference betwixt them lies in this, that in the former case we conclude from *past experience*, that the person never will perform that action, and in the latter, that he possibly or probably will perform it. Nothing is more fluctuating and inconstant on many occasions, than the will of man; nor is there any thing but strong motives, which can give us an absolute certainty in pronouncing concerning any of his future actions. When we see a person free from these motives, we suppose a possibility either of his acting or forbearing; and though in general we may conclude him to be determined by motives and causes, yet this removes not the uncertainty of our judgment concerning these causes, nor the influence of that uncertainty on the passions. Since therefore we ascribe a power of performing an action to every one, who has no very powerful motive to forbear it, and refuse it to such as have; it may justly be concluded, that *power* has always a reference to its *exercise*, either actual or probable, and that we consider a person as endowed with any ability when we find from past experience, that it is probable, or at least possible he may exert it. And indeed, as our passions always regard the real existence of objects, and we always judge of this reality from past instances; nothing can be more likely of itself, without any farther reasoning, than that power consists in the possibility or probability of any action, as discovered by experience and the practice of the world.

Now it is evident, that wherever a person is in such a situation with regard to me, that there is no very powerful motive to deter him from injuring me, and consequently it is *uncertain* whether he will injure me or not, I must be uneasy in such a situation, and cannot consider the possibility or probability of that injury without a sensible concern. The passions are not only affected by such events as are certain and infallible, but also in an inferior degree by such as are possible and contingent. And though perhaps I never really feel any harm, and discover by the event, that, philosophically speaking, the person never had any power of harming me; since he did not exert any; this prevents not my uneasiness from the preceding uncertainty. The agreeable passions may here operate as well as the uneasy, and convey a pleasure when I perceive a good to become either possible or probable by the possibility or probability of another's bestowing it on me, upon the removal of any strong motives, which might formerly have hindered him.

But we may farther observe, that this satisfaction increases, when any good approaches in such a manner that it it in one's *own* power to take or leave it, and there neither is any physical impediment, nor any very strong motive to hinder our enjoyment. As all men desire pleasure, nothing can be more probable, than its existence when there is no external obstacle to the producing it, and men perceive no danger in following their inclinations. In that case their imagination easily anticipates the satisfaction, and conveys the same joy, as if they were persuaded of its real and actual existence.

But this accounts not sufficiently for the satisfaction, which attends riches. A miser receives delight from his money; that is, from the *power* it affords him of procuring all the pleasures and conveniences of life, though he knows he has enjoyed his riches for forty years without ever employing them; and consequently cannot conclude by any species of reasoning, that the real existence of these pleasures is nearer, than if he were entirely deprived of all his possessions. But though he cannot form any such conclusion in a way of reasoning concerning the nearer approach of the pleasure, it is certain he *imagines* it to approach nearer, whenever all external obstacles are removed, along with the more powerful motives of interest and danger, which oppose it. For farther satisfaction on this head I must refer to my account of the will, where I shall* explain that false sensation of liberty, which makes us imagine we can perform any thing, that is not very dangerous or destructive. Whenever any other person is under no strong obligations of interest to forbear any pleasure, we judge from *experience*, that the pleasure will exist, and that he will probably obtain it. But when ourselves are in that situation, we judge from an *illusion of the fancy*, that the pleasure is still closer and more immediate. The will seems to move easily every way, and casts a shadow or image of itself, even to that side, on which it did not settle. By means of this image the enjoyment seems to approach nearer to us, and gives us the same lively satisfaction, as if it were perfectly certain and unavoidable.

* Part 3, Section 2.

It will now be easy to draw this whole reasoning to a point, and to prove, that when riches produce any pride or vanity in their possessors, as they never fail to do, it is only by means of a double relation of impressions and ideas. The very essence of riches consists in the power of procuring the pleasures and conveniences of life. The very essence of this power consists in the probability of its exercise, and in its causing us to anticipate, by a *true* or *false* reasoning, the real existence of the pleasure. This anticipation of pleasure is, in itself, a very considerable pleasure; and as its cause is some possession or property, which we enjoy, and which is thereby related to us, we here clearly see all the parts of the foregoing system most exactly and distinctly drawn out before us. For the same reason, that riches cause pleasure and pride, and poverty excites uneasiness and humility, power must produce the former emotions, and slavery the latter. Power or an authority over others makes us capable of satisfying all our desires; as slavery, by subjecting us to the will of others, exposes us to a thousand wants, and mortifications.

It is here worth observing, that the vanity of power, or shame of slavery, are much augmented by the consideration of the persons, over whom we exercise our authority, or who exercise it over us. For supposing it possible to frame statues of such an admirable mechanism, that they could move and act in obedience to the will; it is evident the possession of them would give pleasure and pride, but not to such a degree, as the same authority, when exerted over sensible and rational creatures, whose condition, being compared to our own, makes it seem more agreeable and honourable. Comparison is in every case a sure method of augmenting our esteem of any thing. A rich man feels the felicity of his condition better by opposing it to that of a beggar. But there is a peculiar advantage in power, by the contrast, which is, in a manner, presented to us, betwixt ourselves and the person we command. The comparison is obvious and natural: the imagination finds it in the very subject: the passage of the thought to its conception is smooth and easy. And that this circumstance has a considerable effect in augmenting its influence, will appear afterwards in examining the nature of *malice* and *envy*.

SECTION ELEVEN

Of the love of fame

But beside these original causes of pride and humility, there is a secondary one in the opinions of others, which has an equal influence on the affections. Our reputation, our character, our name are considerations of vast weight and importance; and even the other causes of pride; virtue, beauty and riches; have little influence, when not seconded by the opinions and sentiments of others. In order to account for this phenomenon it will be necessary to take some compass, and first explain the nature of *sympathy*.

No quality of human nature is more remarkable, both in itself and in its consequences, than that propensity we have to sympathize with others, and to receive by communication their inclinations and sentiments, however different from, or even contrary to our own. This is not only conspicuous in children, who implicitly embrace every opinion proposed to them; but also in men of the greatest judgment and understanding, who find it very difficult to follow their own reason or inclination, in opposition to that of their friends and daily companions. To this principle we ought to ascribe the great uniformity we may observe in the humours and turn of thinking of those of the same nation; and it is much more probable, that this resemblance arises from sympathy, than from any influence of the soil and climate, which, though they continue invariably the same, are not able to preserve the character of a nation the same for a century together. A good-natured man finds himself in an instant of the same humour with his company; and even the proudest and most surly take a tincture from their countrymen and acquaintance. A chearful countenance infuses a sensible complacency and serenity into my mind; as an angry or sorrowful one throws a sudden dump upon me. Hatred, resentment, esteem, love, courage, mirth and melancholy; all these passions I feel more from communication than from my own natural temper and disposition. So remarkable a phenomenon merits our attention, and must be traced up to its first principles.

When any affection is infused by sympathy, it is at first known only by its effects, and by those external signs in the countenance and conversation, which convey an idea of it. This idea is presently converted into an impression, and acquires such a degree of force and vivacity, as to become the very passion itself, and produce an equal emotion, as any original affection. However instantaneous this change of the idea into an impression may be, it proceeds from certain views and reflections, which will not escape the strict scrutiny of a philosopher, though they may the person himself, who makes them.

It is evident, that the idea, or rather impression of ourselves is always intimately present with us, and that our consciousness gives us so lively a conception of our own person, that it is not possible to imagine, that any thing can in this particular go beyond it. Whatever object, therefore, is related to ourselves must be conceived with a little vivacity of conception, according to the foregoing principles; and though this relation should not be so strong as that of causation, it must still have a considerable influence. Resemblance and contiguity are relations not to be neglected; especially when by an inference from cause and effect, and by the observation of external signs, we are informed of the real existence of the object, which is resembling or contiguous.

Now it is obvious, that nature has preserved a great resemblance among all human creatures, and that we never remark any passion or principle in others, of which, in some degree or other, we may not find a parallel in ourselves. The case is the same with the fabric of the mind, as with that of the body. However the parts may differ in shape or size, their structure and composition are in general the same. There is a very remarkable resemblance, which preserves itself amidst all their variety; and this resemblance must very much contribute to make us enter into the sentiments of others; and embrace them with facility and pleasure. Accordingly we find, that where, beside the general resemblance of our natures, there is any peculiar similarity in our manners, or character, or country, or language, it facilitates the sympathy. The stronger the relation is betwixt ourselves and any object, the more easily does the imagination make the transition, and convey to the related idea the vivacity of conception, with which we always form the idea of our own person.

Nor is resemblance the only relation, which has this effect, but receives new force from other relations, that may accompany it. The sentiments of others have little influence, when far removed from us, and require the relation of contiguity, to make them communicate themselves entirely. The relations of blood, being a species of causation, may sometimes contribute to the same effect; as also acquaintance, which operates in the same manner with education and custom; as we shall see more fully* afterwards. All these relations, when united together, convey the impression or consciousness of our own person to the idea of the sentiments or passions of others, and makes us conceive them in the strongest and most lively manner.

It has been remarked in the beginning of this treatise, that all ideas are borrowed from impressions, and that these two kinds of perceptions differ only in the degrees of force and vivacity, with which they strike upon the soul. The component part of ideas and impressions are precisely alike. The manner and order of their appearance may be the same. The different degrees of their force and vivacity are, therefore, the only particulars, that distinguish them: and as this difference may be removed, in some measure, by a relation betwixt the impressions and ideas, it is no wonder an idea of a sentiment or passion, may by this means be so enlivened as to become the very sentiment or passion. The lively idea of any object always approaches its impression; and it is certain we may feel sickness and pain from the mere force of imagination, and make a malady real by often thinking of it. But this is most remarkable in the opinions and affections; and it is there principally that a lively idea is converted into an impression. Our affections depend more upon ourselves, and the internal operations of the mind, than any other impressions; for which reason they arise more naturally from the imagination, and from every lively idea we form of them. This is the nature and cause of sympathy; and it is after this manner we enter so deep into the opinions and affections of others, whenever we discover them.

What is principally remarkable in this whole affair is the strong confirmation these phenomena give to the foregoing system concerning the understanding, and consequently to the present one concerning the passions; since these are analogous to each other. It is indeed evident, that when we sympathize with the passions and sentiments of others, these movements appear at first in *our* mind as mere ideas, and are conceived to belong to another person, as we

* Part 2, Section 4.

conceive any other matter of fact. It is also evident, that the ideas of the affections of others are converted into the very impressions they represent, and that the passions arise in conformity to the images we form of them. All this is an object of the plainest experience, and depends not on any hypothesis of philosophy. That science can only be admitted to explain the phenomena; though at the same time it must be confessed, they are so clear of themselves, that there is but little occasion to employ it. For besides the relation of cause and effect, by which we are convinced of the reality of the passion, with which we sympathize; besides this, I say, we must be assisted by the relations of resemblance and contiguity, in order to feel the sympathy in its full perfection. And since these relations can entirely convert an idea into an impression, and convey the vivacity of the latter into the former, so perfectly as to lose nothing of it in the transition, we may easily conceive how the relation of cause and effect alone, may serve to strengthen and enliven an idea. In sympathy there is an evident conversion of an idea into an impression. This conversion arises from the relation of objects to ourself. Ourself is always intimately present to us. Let us compare all these circumstances, and we shall find, that sympathy is exactly correspondent to the operations of our understanding; and even contains something more surprizing and extraordinary.

It is now time to turn our view from the general consideration of sympathy, to its influence on pride and humility, when these passions arise from praise and blame, from reputation and infamy. We may observe, that no person is ever praised by another for any quality, which would not, if real, produce of itself, a pride in the person possessed of it. The elogiums either turn upon his power, or riches, or family, or virtue; all of which are subjects of vanity, that we have already explained and accounted for. It is certain, then, that if a person considered himself in the same light, in which he appears to his admirer, he would first receive a separate pleasure, and afterwards a pride or self-satisfaction, according to the hypothesis above explained. Now nothing is more natural than for us to embrace the opinions of others in this particular; both from *sympathy*, which renders all their sentiments intimately present to us; and from *reasoning*, which makes us regard their judgment, as a kind of argument for what they affirm. These two principles of authority and sympathy influence almost all our opinions; but must have a peculiar influence, when we judge of our own worth and character. Such judgments are always attended with passion;* and nothing tends more to disturb our understanding, and precipitate us into any opinions, however unreasonable, than their connexion with passion; which diffuses itself over the imagination, and gives an additional force to every related idea. To which we may add, that being conscious of great partiality in our own favour, we are peculiarly pleased with any thing, that confirms the good opinion we have of ourselves, and are easily shocked with whatever opposes it.

All this appears very probable in theory; but in order to bestow a full certainty on this reasoning, we must examine the phenomena of the passions, and see if they agree with it.

Among these phenomena we may esteem it a very favourable one to our present purposes that though fame in general be agreeable, yet we receive a much greater satisfaction from the approbation of those, whom we ourselves esteem and approve of, than of those, whom we hate and despise. In like measure we are principally mortified with the contempt of persons, upon whose judgment we set some value, and are, in a great measure, indifferent about the opinions of the rest of mankind. But if the mind received from any original instinct a desire of fame and aversion to infamy, fame and infamy would influence us without distinction; and every opinion, according as it were favourable or unfavourable, would equally excite that desire or aversion. The judgment of a fool is the judgment of another person, as well as that of a wise man, and is only inferior in its influence on our own judgment.

We are not only better pleased with the approbation of a wise man than with that of a fool, but receive an additional satisfaction from the former, when it is obtained after a long and intimate acquaintance. This is accounted for after the same manner.

The praises of others never give us much pleasure, unless they concur with our own opinion, and extol us for those qualities, in which we chiefly excel. A mere soldier little values the character of eloquence: a gownman of courage: a bishop of humour: or a merchant of learning. Whatever esteem a man may have for any quality, abstractedly considered; when he is conscious he is not possessed of it; the opinions of the whole world will give him little

* Book 1, Part 3, Section 10.

pleasure in that particular, and that because they never will be able to draw his own opinion after them.

Nothing is more usual than for men of good families, but narrow circumstances, to leave their friends and country, and rather seek their livelihood by mean and mechanical employments among strangers, than among those, who are acquainted with their birth and education. We shall be unknown, say they, where we go. No body will suspect from what family we are sprung. We shall be removed from all our friends and acquaintance, and our poverty and meanness will by that means sit more easy upon us. In examining these sentiments, I find they afford many very convincing arguments for my present purpose.

First, We may infer from them, that the uneasiness of being contemned depends on sympathy, and that sympathy depends on the relation of objects to ourselves; since we are most uneasy under the contempt of persons, who are both related to us by blood, and contiguous in place. Hence we seek to diminish this sympathy and uneasiness by separating these relations, and placing ourselves in a contiguity to strangers, and at a distance from relations.

Secondly, We may conclude, that relations are requisite to sympathy, not absolutely considered as relations, but by their influence in converting our ideas of the sentiments of others into the very sentiments, by means of the association betwixt the idea of their persons, and that of our own. For here the relations of kindred and contiguity both subsist; but not being united in the same persons, they contribute in a less degree to the sympathy.

Thirdly, This very circumstance of the diminution of sympathy by the separation of relations is worthy of our attention. Suppose I am placed in a poor condition among strangers, and consequently am but lightly treated; I yet find myself easier in that situation, than when I was every day exposed to the contempt of my kindred and countrymen. Here I feel a double contempt; from my relations, but they are absent; from those about me, but they are strangers. This double contempt is likewise strengthened by the two relations of kindred and contiguity. But as the persons are not the same, who are connected with me by those two relations, this difference of ideas separates the impressions arising from the contempt, and keeps them from running into each other. The contempt of my neighbours has a certain influence; as has also that of my kindred: but these influences are distinct, and never unite; as when the contempt proceeds from persons who are at once both my neighbours and kindred. This phenomenon is analogous to the system of pride and humility above-explained, which may seem so extraordinary to vulgar apprehensions.

Fourthly, A person in these circumstances naturally conceals his birth from those among whom he lives, and is very uneasy, if any one suspects him to be of a family, much superior to his present fortune and way of living. Every thing in this world is judged of by comparison. What is an immense fortune for a private gentleman is beggary for a prince. A peasant would think himself happy in what cannot afford necessaries for a gentleman. When a man has either been acustomed to a more splendid way of living, or thinks himself entitled to it by his birth and quality, every thing below is disagreeable and even shameful; and it is with the greatest industry he conceals his pretensions to a better fortune. Here he himself knows his misfortunes; but as those, with whom he lives. are ignorant of them, he has the disagreeable reflection and comparison suggested only by his own thoughts, and never receives it by a sympathy with others; which must contribute very much to his ease and satisfaction.

If there be any objections to this hypothesis, *that the pleasure, which we receive from praise, arises from a communication of sentiments*, we shall find, upon examination, that these objections, when taken in a proper light, will serve to confirm it. Popular fame may be agreeable even to a man, who despises the vulgar; but it is because their multitude gives them additional weight and authority. Plagiaries are delighted with praises, which they are conscious they do not deserve; but this is a kind of castle-building, where the imagination amuses itself with its own fictions, and strives to render them firm and stable by a sympathy with the sentiments of others. Proud men are most shocked with contempt, though they do not most readily assent to it; but it is because of the opposition betwixt the passion, which is natural so them, and that received by sympathy. A violent lover in like manner is very much displeased when you blame and condemn his love; though it is evident your opposition can have no influence, but by the hold it takes of himself, and by his sympathy with you. If he despises you, or perceives you are in jest, whatever you say has no effect upon him.

SECTION TWELVE

Of the pride and humility of animals

Thus in whatever light we consider this subject, we may still observe, that the causes of pride and humility correspond exactly to our hypothesis, and that nothing can excite either of these passions, unless it be both related to ourselves, and produces a pleasure or pain independent of the passion. We have not only proved, that a tendency to produce pleasure or pain is common to all the causes of pride or humility, but also that it is the only thing, which is common; and consequently is the quality, by which they operate. We have farther proved, that the most considerable causes of these passions are really nothing but the power of producing either agreeable or uneasy sensations; and therefore that all their effects, and amongst the rest, pride and humility, are derived solely from that origin. Such simple and natural principles, founded on such solid proofs, cannot fail to be received by philosophers, unless opposed by some objections, that have escaped me.

It is usual with anatomists to join their observations and experiments on human bodies to those on beasts, and from the agreement of these experiments to derive an additional argument for any particular hypothesis. It is indeed certain, that where the structure of parts in brutes is the same as in men, and the operation of these parts also the same, the causes of that operation cannot be different, and that whatever we discover to be true of the one species, may be concluded without hesitation to be certain of the other. Thus though the mixture of humours and the composition of minute parts may justly be presumed so be somewhat different in men from what it is in mere animals; and therefore any experiment we make upon the one concerning the effects of medicines will not always apply to the other; yet as the structure of the veins and muscles, the fabric and situation of the heart, of the lungs, the stomach, the liver and other parts, are the same or nearly the same in all animals, the very same hypothesis, which in one species explains muscular motion, the progress of the chyle, the circulation of the blood, must be applicable to every one; and according as it agrees or disagrees with the experiments we may make in any species of creatures, we may draw a proof of its truth or falsehood on the whole. Let us, therefore, apply this method of enquiry, which is found so just and useful in reasonings concerning the body, to our present anatomy of the mind, and see what discoveries we can make by it.

In order to this we must first shew the correspondence of *passions* in men and animals, and afterwards compare the *causes*, which produce these passions.

It is plain, that almost in every species of creatures, but especially of the nobler kind, there are many evident marks of pride and humility. The very port and gait of a swan, or turkey, or peacock show the high idea he has entertained of himself, and his contempt of all others. This is the more remarkable, that in the two last species of animals, the pride always attends the beauty, and is discovered in the male only. The vanity and emulation of nightingales in singing have been commonly remarked; as likewise that of horses in swiftness, of hounds in sagacity and smell, of the bull and cock in strength, and of every other animal in his particular excellency. Add to this, that every species of creatures, which approach so often to man, as to familiarize themselves with him, show an evident pride in his approbation, and are pleased with his praises and caresses, independent of every other consideration. Nor are they the caresses of every one without distinction, which give them this vanity, but those principally of the persons they know and love; in the same manner as that passion is excited in mankind. All these are evident proofs, that pride and humility are not merely human passions, but extend themselves over the whole animal creation.

The *causes* of these passions are likewise much the same in beasts as in us, making a just allowance for our superior knowledge and understanding. Thus animals have little or no sense of virtue or vice; they quickly lose sight of the relations of blood; and are incapable of that of right and property: for which reason the causes of their pride and humility must lie solely in the body, and can never be placed either in the mind or external objects. But so far as regards the body, the same qualities cause pride in the animal as in the human kind; and it is on beauty, strength, swiftness or some other useful or agreeable quality that this passion is always founded.

The next question is, whether, since those passions are the same, and arise from the same causes through the whole creation, the *manner*, in which the causes operate, be also the same. According to all rules of analogy, this is justly to be expected; and if we find upon trial, that the explication of these phenomena, which we make use of in one species, will not apply to the rest, we may presume that that explication, however specious, is in reality without foundation.

In order to decide this question, let us consider, that there is evidently the same *relation* of ideas, and derived from the same causes, in the minds of animals as in those of men. A dog, that has hid a bone, often forgets the place; but when brought to it, his thought passes easily to what he formerly concealed, by means of the contiguity, which produces a relation among his ideas. In like manner, when he has been heartily beat in any place, he will tremble on his approach to it, even though he discover no signs of any present danger. The effects of resemblance are not so remarkable; but as that relation makes a considerable ingredient in causation, of which all animals shew so evident a judgment, we may conclude that the three relations of resemblance, contiguity and causation operate in the same manner upon beasts as upon human creatures.

There are also instances of the relation of impressions, sufficient to convince us, that there is an union of certain affections with each other in the inferior species of creatures as well as in the superior, and that their minds are frequently conveyed through a series of connected emotions. A dog, when elevated with joy, runs naturally into love and kindness, whether of his master or of the sex. In like manner, when full of pain and sorrow, he becomes quarrelsome and illnatured; and that passion, which at first was grief, is by the smallest occasion converted into anger.

Thus all the internal principles, that are necessary in us to produce either pride or humility, are common to all creatures; and since the causes, which excite these passions, are likewise the same, we may justly conclude, that these causes operate after the same *manner* through the whole animal creation. My hypothesis is so simple, and supposes so little reflection and judgment, that it is applicable to every sensible creature; which must not only be allowed to be a convincing proof of its veracity, but, I am confident, will be found an objection to every other system.

It is altogether impossible to give any definition of the passions of *love* and *hatred*; and that because they produce merely a simple impression, without any mixture or composition. It would be as unnecessary to attempt any description of them, drawn from their nature, origin, causes and objects; and that both because these are the subjects of our present enquiry, and because these passions of themselves are sufficiently known from our common feeling and experience. This we have already observed concerning pride and humility, and here repeat it concerning love and hatred; and indeed there is so great a resemblance betwixt these two sets of passions, that we shall be obliged to begin with a kind of abridgment of our reasonings concerning the former, in order to explain the latter.

As the immediate *object* of pride and humility is self or that identical person, of whose thoughts, actions, and sensations we are intimately conscious; so the *object* of love and hatred is some other person, of whose thoughts, actions, and sensations we are not conscious. This is sufficiently evident from experience. Our love and hatred are always directed to some sensible being external to us; and when we talk of *self-love*, it is not in a proper sense, nor has the sensation it produces any thing in common with that tender emotion which is excited by a friend or mistress. It is the same case with hatred. We may be mortified by our own faults and follies; but never feel any anger or hatred except from the injuries of others.

But though the object of love and hatred be always some other person, it is plain that the object is not, properly speaking, the *cause* of these passions, or alone sufficient to excite them. For since love and hatred are directly contrary in their sensation, and have the same object in common, if that object were also their cause, it would produce these opposite passions in an equal degree; and as they must, from the very first moment, destroy each other, none of them would ever be able to make its appearance. There must, therefore, be some cause different from the object.

If we consider the causes of love and hatred, we shall find they are very much diversified, and have not many things in common. The virtue, knowledge, wit, good sense, good humour of any person, produce love and esteem; as the opposite qualities, hatred and contempt. The same passions arise from bodily accomplishments, such as beauty, force, swiftness, dexterity; and from their contraries; as likewise from the external advantages and disadvantages of family, possession, clothes, nation and climate. There is not one of these objects, but what by its different qualities may produce love and esteem, or hatred and contempt.

From the view of these causes we may derive a new distinction betwixt the *quality* that operates, and the *subject* on which it is placed. A prince, that is possessed of a stately palace, commands the esteem of the people upon that account; and that *first*, by the beauty of the palace, and *secondly*, by the relation of property, which connects it with him. The removal of either of these destroys the passion; which evidently proves that the cause is a compounded one.

It would be tedious to trace the passions of love and hatred, through all the observations which we have formed concerning pride and humility, and which are equally applicable to both sets of passions. It will be sufficient to *remark* in general, that the object of love and hatred is evidently some thinking person; and that the sensation of the former passion is always agreeable, and of the latter uneasy. We may also *suppose* with some shew of probability, *that the cause of both these passions is always related to a thinking being, and that the cause of the former produces a separate pleasure, and of the latter a separate uneasiness.*

One of these suppositions, *viz*, that the cause of love and hatred must be related to a person or thinking being, in order to produce these passions, is not only probable, but too evident to be contested. Virtue and vice, when considered in the abstract;

beauty and deformity, when placed on inanimate objects; poverty and riches when belonging to a third person, excite no degree of love or hatred, esteem or contempt towards those, who have no relation to them. A person looking out at a window, sees me in the street, and beyond me a beautiful palace, with which I have no concern: I believe none will pretend, that this person will pay me the same respect, as if I were owner of the palace.

It is not so evident at first sight, that a relation of impressions is requisite to these passions, and that because in the transition the one impression is so much confounded with the other, that they become in a manner undistinguishable. But as in pride and humility, we have easily been able to make the separation, and to prove, that every cause of these passions, produces a separate pain or pleasure, I might here observe the same method with the same success, in examining particularly the several causes of love and hatred. But as I hasten to a full and decisive proof of these systems, I delay this examination for a moment: and in the mean time shall endeavour to convert to my present purpose all my reaaonings concerning pride and humility, by an argument that is founded on unquestionable examination.

There are few persons, that are satisfied with their own character, or genius, or fortune, who are nor desirous of shewing themselves to the world, and of acquiring the love and approbation of mankind. Now it is evident, that the very same qualities and circumstances, which are the causes of pride or self-esteem, are also the causes of vanity or the desire of reputation; and that we always put to view those particulars with which in ourselves we are best satisfied. But if love and esteem were not produced by the same qualities as pride, according as these qualities are related to ourselves or others, this method of proceeding would be very absurd, nor could men expect a correspondence in the sentiments of every other person, with those themselves have entertained. It is true, few can form exact systems of the passions, or make reflections on their general nature and resemblances. But without such a progress in philosophy, we are not subject to many mistakes in this particular, but are sufficiently guided by common experience, as well as by a kind of *presensation*; which tells us what will operate on others, by what we feel immediately in ourselves. Since then the same qualities that produce pride or humility, cause love or hatred; all the arguments that have been employed to prove, that the causes of the former passions excite a pain or pleasure independent of the passion, will be applicable with equal evidence to the causes of the latter.

SECTION TWO

Experiments to confirm this system

Upon duly weighing these arguments, no one will make any scruple to assent to that condusion I draw from them, concerning the transition along related impressions and ideas, especially as it is a principle, in itself, so easy and natural. But that we may place this system beyond doubt both with regard to love and hatred, pride and humility, it will be proper to make some new experiments upon all these passions, as well as to recall a few of these observations, which I have formerly touched upon.

In order to make these experiments, let us suppose I am in company with a person, whom I formerly regarded without any sentiments either of friendship or enmity. Here I have the natural and ultimate object of all these four passions placed before me. Myself am the proper object of pride or humility; the other person of love or hatred.

Regard now with attention the nature of these passions, and their situation with respect to each other. It is evident here are four affections, placed, as it were, in a square or regular connexion with, and distance from each other. The passions of pride and humility, as well as thosc of love and hatred, are connected together by the identity of their object, which to the first set of passions is self, to the second some other person. These two lines of communication or connexion form two opposite sides of the square. Again, pride and love are agreeable passions; hatred and humility uneasy. This similitude of sensation betwixt pride and love, and that betwixt humility and hatred form a new connexion, and may be considered as the other two sides of the square. Upon the whole, pride is connected with humility, love with hatred, by their objects or ideas: pride with love, humility with hatred, by their sensations or impressions.

I say then, that nothing can produce any of these passions without bearing it a double relation, *viz*, of ideas to the object of the passion, and of sensation to the passion itself. This we must prove by our experiments.

First Experiment. To proceed with the greater order in these experiments, let us first suppose, that being placed in the situation above-mentioned, *viz*, in company with some other person, there is an object presented, that has no relation either of impressions or ideas to any of these passions. Thus suppose we regard together an ordinary stone, or other common object, belonging to neither of us, and causing of itself no emotion, or independent pain and pleasure: it is evident such an object will produce none of these four passions. Let us try it upon each of them successively. Let us apply it to love, to hatred, to humility, to pride; none of them ever arises in the smallest degree imaginable. Let us change the object, as oft as we please; provided still we choose one, that has neither of these two relations. Let us repeat the experiment in all the dispositions, of which the mind is susceptible. No object, in the vast variety of nature, will, in any disposition, produce any passion without these relations.

Second Experiment. Since an object, that wants both these relations can never produce any passion, let us bestow on it only one of these relations; and see what will follow. Thus suppose, I regard a stone or any common object, that belongs either to me or my companion, and by that means acquires a relation of ideas to the object of the passions: it is plain, that to consider the matter *a priori*, no emotion of any kind can reasonably be expected. For besides, that a relation of ideas operates secretly and calmly on the mind, it bestows an equal impulse towards the opposite passions of pride and humility, love and hatred, according as the object belongs to ourselves or others; which opposition of the passions must destroy both, and leave the mind perfectly free from any affection or emotion. This reasoning *a priori* is confirmed by experience. No trivial or vulgar object, that causes not a pain or pleasure, independent of the passion, will ever, by its property or other relations either to ourselves or others, be able to produce the affections of pride or humility, love or hatred.

Third Experiment. It is evident, therefore, that a relation of ideas is not able alone to give rise to these affections. Let us now remove this relation, and in its stead place a relation of impressions, by presenting an object, which is agreeable or disagreeable, but has no relation either to ourself or companion; and let us observe the consequences. To consider the matter first *a priori*, as in the preceding experiment; we may conclude, that the object will have a small, but an uncertain connexion with these passions. For besides, that this relation is not a cold and imperceptible one, it has not the inconvenience of the relation of ideas, nor directs us with equal force to two contrary passions, which by their opposition destroy each other. But if we consider, on the other hand, that this transition from the sensation to the affection is not forwarded by any principle, that produces a transition of ideas; but, on the contrary, that though the one impression be easily transfused into the other, yet the change of objects is supposed contrary to all the principles, that cause a transition of that kind; we may from thence infer, that nothing will ever be a steady or durable cause of any passion, that is connected with the passion merely by a relation of impressions. What our reason would conclude from analogy, after balancing these arguments, would be, that an object, which produces pleasure or uneasiness, but has no manner of connexion either with ourselves or others, may give such a turn to the disposition, as that may naturally fall into pride or love, humility or hatred, and search for other objects, upon which by a double relation, it can found these affections; but that an object, which has only one of these relations, though the most advantageous one, can never give rise to any constant and established passion.

Most fortunately all this reasoning is found to be exactly conformable to experience, and the phenomena of the passions. Suppose I were travelling with a companion through a country, to which we are both utter strangers; it is evident, that if the prospects be beautiful, the roads agreeable, and the inns commodious, this may put me into good humour both with myself and fellow-traveller. But as we suppose, that this country has no relation either to myself or friend it can never be the immediate cause of pride or love; and therefore if I found not the passion on some other object, that bears either of us a closer relation, my emotions are rather to be considerd as the overflowings of an elevate or humane disposition, than as an established passion. The case is the same where the object produces uneasiness.

Fourth Experiment. Having found, that neither an object without any relation of ideas or impressions, nor an object, that has only one relation, can ever cause pride or humility, love or hatred; reason alone may convince us, without any farther experiment, that whatever has a double relation must necessarily excite these passions; since it is evident they must have some cause. But to leave as little room for doubt as possible, let us renew our experiments, and see whether the event in this case answers our expectation. I choose an object, such as virtue, that causes a separate satisfaction: on this object I bestow a relation to self; and find, that from this disposition of affairs, there immediately arises a passion. But what passion? That very one of pride, to which this object bears a double relation. Its idea is related to that of self, the object of the passion: the sensation it causes resembles the sensation of the passion. That I may be sure I am not mistaken in this experiment, I remove first one relation; then another; and find, that each removal destroys the passion, and leaves the object perfectly indifferent. But I am not content with this. I make a still farther trial; and instead of removing the relation, I only change it for one of a different kind. I suppose the virtue to belong to my companion, not to myself; and observe what follows from this alteration. I immediately perceive the affections to wheel about, and leaving pride, where there is only one relation, *viz*, of impressions, fall to the side of love, where they are attracted by a double relation of impressions and ideas. By repeating the same experiment, in changing anew the relation of ideas, I bring the affections back to pride; and by a new repetition I again place them at love or kindness. Being fully convinced of the influence of this relation, I try the effects of the other; and by changing virtue for vice, convert the pleasant impression, which arises from the former, into the disagreeable one, which proceeds from the latter. The effect still answers expectation. Vice, when placed on another, excites, by means of its double relations, the passion of hatred, instead of love, which for the same reason arises from virtue. To continue the experiment, I change anew the relation of ideas, and suppose the vice to belong to myself. What follows? What is usual. A subsequent change of the passion from hatred to humility. This humility I convert into pride by a new change of the impression; and find after all that I have compleated the round, and have by these changes brought back the passion to that very situation, in which I first found it.

But to make the matter still more certain, I alter the object; and instead of vice and virtue, make the trial upon beauty and deformity, riches and poverty, power and servitude. Each of these objects runs the circle of the passions in the same manner, by a change of their relations: and in whatever order we proceed, whether through pride, love, hatred, humility, or through humility, hatred, love, pride, the experiment is not in the least diversified. Esteem and contempt, indeed, arise on some occasions instead of love and hatred; but these are at the bottom the same passions, only diversified by some causes, which we shall explain afterwards.

Fifth Experiment. To give greater authority to these experiments, let us change the situation of affairs as much as possible, and place the passions and objects in all the different positions, of which they are susceptible. Let us suppose, beside the relations above-mentioned, that the person, along with whom I make all these experiments, is closely connected with me either by blood or friendship. He is, we shall suppose, my son or brother, or is united to me by a long and familiar acquaintance. Let us next suppose, that the cause of the passion acquires a double relation of impressions and ideas to this person; and let us see what the effects are of all these complicated attractions and relations.

Before we consider what they are in fact, let us determine what they ought to be, conformable to my hypothesis. It is plain, that, according as the impression is either pleasant or uneasy, the passion of love or hatred must arise towards the person, who is thus connected to the cause of the impression by these double relations, which I have all along required. The virtue of a brother must make me love him; as his vice or infamy must excite the contrary passion. But to judge only from the situation of affairs, I should not expect, that the affections would rest there, and never transfuse themselves into any other impression. As there is here a person, who by means of a double relation is the object of my passion, the very same reasoning leads me to think the passion will be carried farther. The person has a relation of ideas to myself, according to the supposition; the passion, of which he is the object, by being either agreeable or uneasy, has a relation of impressions to pride or humility. It is evident, then, that one of these passions must arise from the love or hatred.

This is the reasoning I form in conformity to my hypothesis; and am pleased to find upon trial that every thing answers exactly to my expectation. The virtue or vice of a son or brother not only excites love or hatred, but by a new transition, from similar causes, gives rise to pride or humility. Nothing causes greater vanity than any shining quality in our relations; as nothing mortifies us more than their vice or infamy. This exact conformity of experience to our reasoning is a convincing proof of the solidity of that hypothesis, upon which we reason.

Sixth Experiment. This evidence will be still augmented, if we reverse the experiment, and preserving still the same relations, begin only with a different passion. Suppose, that instead of the virtue or vice of a son or brother, which causes first love or hatred, and afterwards pride or humility, we place these good or bad qualities on ourselves, without any immediate connexion with the person, who is related to us: experience shews us, that by this change of situation the whole chain is broke, and that the mind is not conveyed from one passion to another, as in the preceding instance. We never love or hate a son or brother for the virtue or vice we discern in ourselves; though it is evident the same qualities in him give us a very sensible pride or humility. The transition from pride or humility to love or hatred is not so natural as from love or hatred to pride or humility. This may at first sight be esteemed contrary to my hypothesis; since the relations of impressions and ideas are in both cases precisely the same. Pride and humility are impressions related to love and hatred. Myself am related to the person. It should, therefore, be expected, that like causes must produce like effects, and a perfect transition arise from the double relation, as in all other cases. This difficulty we may easily solve by the following reflections.

It is evident, that as we are at all times intimately conscious of ourselves, our sentiments and passions, their ideas must strike upon us with greater vivacity than the ideas of the sentiments and passions of any other person. But every thing, that strikes upon us with vivacity, and appears in a full and strong light, forces itself, in a manner, into our consideration, and becomes present to the mind on the smallest hint and most trivial relation. For the same reason, when it is once present, it engages the attention, and keeps it from wandering to other objects, however strong may be their relation to our first object. The imagination passes easily from obscure to lively ideas, but with difficulty from lively to obscure. In the one case the relation is aided by another principle: in the other case, it is opposed by it.

Now I have observed, that those two faculties of the mind, the imagination and passions, assist each other in their operations when their propensities are similar, and when they act upon the same object. The mind has always a propensity to pass from a passion to any other related to it; and this propensity is forwarded when the object of the one passion is related to that of the other. The two impulses concur with each other, and render the whole transition more smooth and easy. But if it should happen, that while the relation of ideas, strictly speaking, continues the same, its influence, in causing a transition of the imagination, should no longer take place, it is evident its influence on the passions must also cease, as being dependent entirely on that transition. This is the reason why pride or humility is not transfused into love or hatred with the same ease, that the latter passions are changed into the former. If a person be my brother I am his likewise: but though the relations be reciprocal they have very different effects on the imagination. The passage is smooth and open from the consideration of any person related to us to that of ourself, of whom we are every moment conscious. But when the affections are once directed to ourself, the fancy passes not with the same facility from that object to any other person, how closely so ever connected with us. This easy or difficult transition of the imagination operates upon the passions, and facilitates or retards their transition, which is a clear proof, that these two faculties of the passions and imagination are connected together, and that the relations of ideas have an influence upon the affections. Besides innumerable experiments that prove this, we here find, that even when the relation remains; if by any particular circumstance its usual effect upon the fancy in producing an association or transition of ideas, is prevented; its usual effect upon the passions, in conveying us from one to another, is in like manner prevented.

Some may, perhaps, find a contradiction betwixt this phenomenon and that of sympathy, where the mind passes easily from the idea of ourselves to that of any other object related to us. But this difficulty will vanish, if we consider that in sympathy our own person is not the object of any passion, nor is there any thing, that fixes our attention on ourselves; as in the present case, where we are supposed to be actuated with pride or humility. Ourself, independent of the perception of every other object, is in reality nothing: for which reason we must turn our view to external objects; and it is natural for us to consider with most attention such as lie contiguous to us, or resemble us. But when self is the object of a passion, it is not natural to quit the consideration of it, till the passion be exhausted: in which case the double relations of impressions and ideas can no longer operate.

Seventh Experiment. To put this whole reasoning to a farther trial, let us make a new experiment; and as we have already seen the effects of related passions and ideas, let us here suppose an identity of passions along with a relation of ideas; and let us consider the effects of this new situation. It is evident a transition of the passions from the one object to the other is here in all reason to be expected; since the relation of ideas is supposed still to continue, and identity of impressions must produce a stronger connexion, than the most perfect resemblance, that can be imagined. If a double relation, therefore, of impressions and ideas is able to produce a transition from one to the other, much more an identity of impressions with a relation of ideas. Accordingly we find, that when we either love or hate any person, the passions seldom continue within their first bounds; but extend themselves towards all the contiguous objects, and comprehend the friends and relations of him we love or hate. Nothing is more natural than to bear a kindness to one brother on account of our friendship for another, without any farther examination of his character. A quarrel with one person gives us a hatred for the whole family, though entirely innocent of that, which displeases us. Instances of this kind are every where to be met with.

There is only one difficulty in this experiment, which it will be necessary to account for, before we proceed any farther. It is evident, that though all passions pass easily from one object to another related to it, yet this transition is made with greater facility, where the more considerable object is first presented, and the lesser follows it, than where this order is reversed, and the lesser takes the precedence. Thus it is more natural for us to love the son upon account of the father, than the father upon account of the son; the servant for the master, than the master for the servant; the subject for the prince, than the prince for the subject. In like manner we more readily contract a hatred against a whole family, where our first quarrel is with the head of it, than where we are displeased with a son, or servant, or some inferior member. In short, our passions, like other objects, descend with greater facility than they ascend.

That we may comprehend, wherein consists the difficulty of explaining this phenomenon, we must consider, that the very same reason, which determines the imagination to pass from remote to contiguous objects, with more facility than from contiguous to remote, causes it likewise to change with more ease, the less for the greater, than the greater for the less. Whatever has the greatest influence is most taken notice of; and whatever is most taken notice of, presents itself most readily to the imagination. We are more apt to over-look in any subject, what is trivial, than what appears of considerable moment; but especially if the latter takes the precedence, and first engages our attention. Thus if any accident makes us consider the *Satellites* of *Jupiter*, our fancy is naturally determined to form the idea of that planet; but if we first reflect on the principal planet, it is more natural for us to over-look its attendants. The mention of the provinces of any empire conveys our thought to the seat of the empire; but the fancy returns not with the same facility to the consideration of the provinces. The idea of the servant makes us think of the master; that of the subject carries our view to the prince. But the same relation has not an equal influence in conveying us back again. And on this is founded that reproach of *Cornelia* to her sons, that they ought to be ashamed she should be more known by the title of the daughter of *Scipio* than by that of the mother of the *Gracchi*. This was, in other words, exhorting them to render themselves as illustrious and famous as their grandfather, otherwise the imagination of the people, passing from her who was intermediate, and placed in an equal relation to both, would always leave them, and denominate her by what was more considerable and of greater moment. On the same principle is founded that common custom of making wives bear the name of their husbands, rather than husbands that of their wives; as also the ceremony of giving the precedency to those, whom we honour and respect. We might find many other instances to confirm this principle, were it not already sufficiently evident.

Now since the fancy finds the same facility in passing from the lesser to the greater, as from remote to contiguous, why does not this easy transition of ideas assist the transition of passions in the former case, as well as in the latter? The virtues of a friend or brother produce first love, and then pride; because in that case the imagination passes from remote to contiguous, according to its propensity. Our own virtues produce not first pride, and then love to a friend or brother; because the passage in that case would be from contiguous to remote, contrary to its propensity. But the love or hatred of an inferior causes not readily any passion to the superior, though that be the natural propensity of the imagination: while the love or hatred of a superior, causes a passion to the inferior, contrary to its propensity. In short, the same facility of transition operates not in the same manner upon superior and inferior as upon contiguous and remote. These two phenomena appear contradictory, and require some attention to be reconciled.

As the transition of ideas is here made contrary to the natural propensity of the imagination, that faculty must be overpowered by some stronger principle of another kind; and as there is nothing ever present to the mind but impressions and ideas, this principle must necessarily lie in the impressions. Now it has been observed, that impressions or passions are connected only by their resemblance, and that where any two passions place the mind in the same or in similar dispositions, it very naturally passes from the one to the other: as on the contrary, a repugnance in the dispositions produces a difficulty in the transition of the passions. But it is observable, that this repugnance may arise from a difference of degree as well as of kind; nor do we experience a greater difficulty in passing suddenly from a small degree of love to a small degree of hatred, than from a small to a great degree of either of these affections. A man, when calm or only moderately agitated, is so different, in every respect, from himself, when disturbed with a violent passion, that no two persons can be more unlike; nor is it easy to pass from the one extreme to the other, without a considerable interval betwixt them.

The difficulty is not less, if it be not rather greater, in passing from the strong passion to the weak, than in passing from the weak to the strong, provided the one passion upon its appearance destroys the other, and they do not both of them exist at once. But the case is entirely altered, when the passions unite together, and actuate the mind at the same time. A weak passion, when added to a strong, makes not so considerable a change in the disposition, as a strong when added to a weak; for which reason there is a closer connexion betwixt the great degree and the small, than betwixt the small degree and the great.

The degree of any passion depends upon the nature of its object; and an affection directed to a person, who is considerable in our eyes, fills and possesses the mind much more than one, which has for its object a person we esteem of less consequence. Here then the contradiction betwixt the propensities of the imagination and passion displays itself. When we turn our thought to a great and a small object, the imagination finds more facility in passing from the small to the great, than from the great to the small; but the affections find a greater difficulty: and as the affections are a more powerful principle than the imagination, no wonder they prevail over it, and draw the mind to their side. In spite of the difficulty of passing from the idea of great to that of little, a passion directed to the former, produces always a similar passion towards the latter; when the great and little are related together. The idea of the servant conveys our thought most readily to the master; but the hatred or love of the master produces with greater facility anger or good-will to the servant. The strongest passion in this case takes the precedence; and the addition of the weaker making no considerable change on the disposition, the passage is by that means rendered more easy and natural betwixt them.

As in the foregoing experiment we found, that a relation of ideas, which, by any particular circumstance, ceases to produce its usual effect of facilitating the transition of ideas, ceases likewise to operate on the passions; so in the present experiment we find the same property of the impressions. Two different degrees of the same passion are surely related together; but if the smaller be first present, it has little or no tendency to introduce the greater; and that because the addition of the great to the little, produces a more sensible alteration on the temper, than the addition of the little to the great. These phenomena, when duly weighed, will be found convincing proofs of this hypothesis.

And these proofs will be confirmed, if we consider the manner in which the mind here reconciles the contradiction, I have observed betwixt the passions and the imagination. The fancy passes with more facility from the less to the greater, than from the greater to the less: but on the contrary a violent passion produces more easily a feeble, than that does a violent. In this opposition the passion in the end prevails over the imagination; but it is commonly by complying with it, and by seeking another quality, which may counter-balance that principle, from whence the opposition arises. When we love the father or master of a family, we little think of his children or servants. But when these are present with us, or when it lies any ways in our power to serve them, the nearness and contiguity in this case increases their magnitude, or at least removes that opposition, which the fancy makes to the transition of the affections. If the imagination finds a difficulty in passing from greater to less, it finds an equal facility in passing from remote to contiguous, which brings the matter to an equality, and leaves the way open from the one passion to the other.

Eighth Experiment. I have observed that the transition from love or hatred to pride or humility, is more easy than from pride or humility to love or hatred; and that the difficulty, which the imagination finds in passing from contiguous to remote, is the cause why we scarce have any instance of the latter transition of the affections. I must, however, make one exception, *viz*, when the very cause of the pride and humility is placed in some other person. For in that case the imagination is necessitated to consider the person, nor can it possibly confine its view to ourselves. Thus nothing more readily produces kindness and affection to any person, than his approbation of our conduct and character: as on the other hand, nothing inspires us with a stronger hatred, than his blame or contempt. Here it is evident, that the original passion is pride or humility, whose object is self; and that this passion is transfused into love or hatred, whose object is some other person, notwithstanding the rule I have already established, *that the imagination passes with difficulty from contiguous to remote.* But the transition in this case is not made merely on account of the relation betwixt ourselves and the person; but because that very person is the real cause of our first passion, and of consequence is intimately connected with it. It is his approbation that produces pride; and disapprobation, humility. No wonder, then, the imagination returns back again attended with the related passions of love and hatred. This is not a contradiction, but an exception to the rule; and an exception that arises from the same reason with the rule itself.

Such an exception as this is, therefore, rather a confirmation of the rule. And indeed, if we consider all the eight experiments I have explained, we shall find that the same principle appears in all of them, and that it is by means of a transition arising from a double relation of impressions and ideas, pride and humility, love and hatred are produced. An object without a relation,* or with but one,† never produces either of these passions; and it is found‡ that the passion always varies in conformity to the relation. Nay we may observe, that where the relation, by any particular circumstance, has not its usual effect of producing a transition either of ideas or of impressions,§ it ceases to operate upon the passions, and gives rise neither to pride nor love, humility nor hatred. This rule we find still to hold good# even under the appearance of its contrary; and as relation is frequently experienced to have no effect; which upon examination is found to proceed from some particular circumstance, that prevents the transition; so even in instances, where that circumstance, though present, prevents not the transition, it is found to arise from some other circumstance, which counter-balances it. Thus not only the variations resolve themselves into the general principle, but even the variations of these variations.

---

* First Experiment.
† Second and Third Experiments.
‡ Fourth Experiment.
§ Sixth Experiment.
# Seventh and Eighth Experiments.

SECTION THREE
Difficulties solved

After so many and such undeniable proofs drawn from daily experience and observation, it may seem superfluous to enter into a particular examination of all the causes of love and hatred. I shall, therefore, employ the sequel of this part, *First*, In removing some difficulties, concerning particular causes of these passions. *Secondly*, In examining the compound affections, which arise from the mixture of love and hatred with other emotions.

Nothing is more evident, than that any person acquires our kindness, or is exposed to our ill-will, in proportion to the pleasure or uneasiness we receive from him, and that the passions keep pace exactly with the sensations in all their changes and variations. Whoever can find the means either by his services, his beauty, or his flattery, to render himself useful or agreeable to us, is sure of our affections: as on the other hand, whoever harms or displeases us never fails to excite our anger or hatred. When our own nation is at war with any other, we detest them under the character of cruel, perfidious, unjust and violent: but always esteem ourselves and allies equitable, moderate, and merciful. If the general of our enemies be successful, it is with difficulty we allow him the figure and character of a man. He is a sorcerer: he has a communication with daemons; as is reported of *Oliver Cromwell*, and the *Duke of Luxembourg*: he is bloody-minded, and takes a pleasure in death and destruction. But if the success be on our side, our commander has all the opposite good qualities, and is a pattern of virtue, as well as of courage and conduct. His treachery we call policy: his cruelty is an evil inseparable from war. In short, every one of his faults we either endeavour to extenuate, or dignify it with the name of that virtue, which approaches it. It is evident the same method of thinking runs through common life.

There are some, who add another condition, and require not only that the pain and pleasure arise from the person, but likewise that it arise knowingly, and with a particular design and intention. A man, who wounds and harms us by accident, becomes not our enemy upon that account, nor do we think ourselves bound by any ties of gratitude to one, who does us any service after the same manner. By the intention we judge of the actions, and according as that is good or bad, they become causes of love or hatred.

But here we must make a distinction. If that quality in another, which pleases or displeases, be constant and inherent in his person and character, it will cause love or hatred independent of the intention: but otherwise a knowledge and design is requisite, in order to give rise to these passions. One that is disagreeable by his deformity or folly is the object of our aversion, though nothing be more certain, than that he has not the least intention of displeasing us by these qualities. But if the uneasiness proceed not from a quality, but an action, which is produced and annihilated in a moment, it is necessary, in order to produce some relation, and connect this action sufficiently with the person, that it be derived from a particular fore-thought and design. It is not enough, that the action arise from the person, and have him for its immediate cause and author. This relation alone is too feeble and inconstant to be a foundation for these passions. It reaches not the sensible and thinking part, and neither proceeds from any thing *durable* in him, nor leaves any thing behind it; but passes in a moment, and is as if it had never been. On the other hand, an intention shews certain qualities, which remaining after the action is performed, connect it with the person, and facilitate the transition of ideas from one to the other. We can never think of him without reflecting on these qualities; unless repentance and a change of life have produced an alteration in that respect: in which case the passion is likewise altered. This therefore is one reason, why an intention is requisite to excite either love or hatred.

But we must farther consider, that an intention, besides its strengthening the relation of ideas, is often necessary to produce a relation of impressions, and give rise to pleasure and uneasiness. For it is observable, that the principal part of an injury is the contempt and hatred, which it shews in the person, that injures us; and without that, the mere harm gives us a less sensible uneasiness. In like manner, a good office is agreeable, chiefly because it flatters our vanity, and is a proof of the kindness and esteem of the person, who performs it. The removal of the intention, removes the mortification in the one case, and vanity in the other, and must of course cause a remarkable diminution in the passions of love and hatred.

I grant, that these effects of the removal of design, in diminishing the relations of impressions and ideas, are not entire, nor able to remove every degree of these relations. But then I ask, if the removal of design be able entirely to remove the passions of love and hatred? Experience, I am sure, informs us of the contrary, nor is there any thing more certain, than that men often fall into a violent anger for injuries, which they themselves must own to be entirely involuntary and accidental. This emotion, indeed, cannot be of long continuance; but still is sufficient to shew, that there is a natural connexion betwixt uneasiness and anger, and that the relation of impressions will operate upon a very small relation of ideas. But when the violence of the impression is once a little abated, the defect of the relation begins to be better felt; and as the character of a person is no wise interested in such injuries as are casual and involuntary, it seldom happens that on their account, we entertain a lasting enmity.

To illustrate this doctrine by a parallel instance, we may observe, that not only the uneasiness, which proceeds from another by accident, has but little force to excite our passion, but also that which arises from an acknowledged necessity and duty. One that has a real design of harming us, proceeding not from hatred and ill-will, but from justice and equity, draws not upon him our anger, if we be in any degree reasonable; notwithstanding he is both the cause, and the knowing cause of our sufferings. Let us examine a little this phenomenon.

It is evident in the first place, that this circumstance is not decisive; and though it may be able to diminish the passions, it is seldom it can entirely remove them. How few criminals are there, who have no ill-will to the person, that accuses them, or to the judge, that condemns them, even though they be conscious of their own deserts? In like manner our antagonist in a law-suit, and our competitor for any office, are commonly regarded as our enemies; though we must acknowledge, if we would but reflect a moment, that their motive is entirely as justifiable as our own.

Besides we may consider, that when we receive harm from any person, we are apt to imagine him criminal, and it is with extreme difficulty we allow of his justice and innocence. This is a clear proof, that, independent of the opinion of iniquity, any harm or uneasiness has a natural tendency to excite our hatred, and that afterwards we seek for reasons upon which we may justify and establish the passion. Here the idea of injury produces not the passion, but arises from it.

Nor is it any wonder that passion should produce the opinion of injury; since otherwise it must suffer a considerable diminution, which all the passions avoid as much as possible. The removal of injury may remove the anger, without proving that the anger arises only from the injury. The harm and the justice are two contrary objects, of which the one has a tendency to produce hatred, and the other love; and it is according to their different degrees, and our particular turn of thinking, that either of the objects prevails, and excites its proper passion.

SECTION FOUR

Of the love of relations

Having given a reason, why several actions, that cause a real pleasure or uneasiness, excite not any degree, or but a small one, of the passion of love or hatred towards the actors; it will be necessary to shew, wherein consists the pleasure or uneasiness of many objects, which we find by experience to produce these passions.

According to the preceding system there is always required a double relation of impressions and ideas betwixt the cause and effect, in order to produce either love or hatred. But though this be universally true, it is remarkable that the passion of love may be excited by only one *relation* of a different kind, *viz*, betwixt ourselves and the object; or more properly speaking, that this relation is always attended with both the others. Whoever is united to us by any connexion is always sure of a share of our love, proportioned to the connexion, without enquiring into his other qualities. Thus the relation of blood produces the strongest tie the mind is capable of in the love of parents to their children, and a lesser degree of the same affection, as the relation lessens. Nor has consanguinity alone this effect, but any other relation without exception. We love our country-men, our neighbours, those of the same trade, profession, and even name with ourselves. Every one of these relations is esteemed some tie, and gives a title to a share of our affection.

There is another phenomenon, which is parallel to this, *viz*, that *acquaintance*, without any kind of relation, gives rise to love and kindness. When we have contracted a habitude and intimacy with any person; though in frequenting his company we have not been able to discover any very valuable quality, of which he is possessed; yet we cannot forbear preferring him to strangers, of whose superior merit we are fully convinced. These two phenomena of the effects of relation and acquaintance will give mutual light to each other, and may be both explained from the same principle.

Those, who take a pleasure in declaiming against human nature, have observed, that man is altogether insufficient to support himself; and that when you loosen all the holds, which he has of external objects, he immediately drops down into the deepest melancholy and despair. From this, say they, proceeds that continual search after amusement in gaming, in hunting, in business; by which we endeavour to forget ourselves, and excite our spirits from the languid state, into which they fall, when not sustained by some brisk and lively emotion. To this method of thinking I so far agree, that I own the mind to be insufficient, of itself, to its own entertainment, and that it naturally seeks after foreign objects, which may produce a lively sensation, and agitate the spirits. On the appearance of such an object it awakes, as it were, from a dream: the blood flows with a new tide: the heart is elevated: and the whole man acquires a vigour, which he cannot command in his solitary and calm moments. Hence company is naturally so rejoicing, as presenting the liveliest of all objects, *viz*, a rational and thinking Being like ourselves, who communicates to us all the actions of his mind; makes us privy to his inmost sentiments and affections; and lets us see, in the very instant of their production, all the emotions, which are caused by any object. Every lively idea is agreeable, but especially that of a passion, because such an idea becomes a kind of passion, and gives a more sensible agitation to the mind, than any other image or conception.

This being once admitted, all the rest is easy. For as the company of strangers is agreeable to us for *a short time*, by enlivening our thought; so the company of our relations and acquaintance must be peculiarly agreeable, because it has this effect in a greater degree, and is of more *durable* influence. Whatever is related to us is conceived in a lively manner by the easy transition from ourselves to the related object. Custom also, or acquaintance facilitates the entrance, and strengthens the conception of any object. The first case is parallel to our reasonings from cause and effect; the second to education. And as reasoning and education concur only in producing a lively and strong idea of any object; so is this the only particular, which is common to relation and acquaintance. This must, therefore, be the influencing quality, by which they produce all their common effects; and love or kindness being one of these effects, it must be from the force and liveliness of conception, that the passion is derived. Such a conception is peculiarly agreeable, and makes us have an affectionate regard for every thing, that produces it, when the proper object of kindness and goodwill.

It is obvious, that people associate together according to their particular tempers and dispositions, and that men of gay tempers naturally love the gay; as the serious bear an affection to the serious. This not only happens, where they remark this resemblance betwixt themselves and others, but also by the natural course of the disposition, and by a certain sympathy, which always arises betwixt similar characters. Where they remark the resemblance, it operates after the manner of a relation, by producing a connexion of ideas. Where they do not remark it, it operates by some other principle; and if this latter principle be similar to the former, it must be received as a confirmation of the foregoing reasoning.

The idea of ourselves is always intimately present to us, and conveys a sensible degree of vivacity to the idea of any other object, to which we are related. This lively idea changes by degrees into a real impression; these two kinds of perception being in a great measure the same, and differing only in their degrees of force and vivacity. But this change must be produced with the greater ease, that our natural temper gives us a propensity to the same impression, which we observe in others, and makes it arise upon any slight occasion. In that case resemblance converts the idea into an impression, not only by means of the relation, and by transfusing the original vivacity into the related idea; but also by presenting such materials as take fire from the least spark. And as in both cases a love or affection arises from the resemblance, we may learn that a sympathy with others is agreeable only by giving an emotion to the spirits, since an easy sympathy and correspondent emotions are alone common to *relation*, *acquaintance*, and *resemblance*.

The great propensity men have to pride may be considered as another similar phenomenon. It often happens, that after we have lived a considerable time in any city; however at first it might be disagreeable to us; yet as we become familiar with the objects, and contract an acquaintance, though merely with the streets and buildings, the aversion diminishes by degrees, and at last changes into the opposite passion. The mind finds a satisfaction and ease in the view of objects, to which it is accustomed, and naturally prefers them to others, which, though perhaps in themselves more valuable, are less known to it. By the same quality of the mind we are seduced into a good opinion of ourselves, and of all objects, that belong to us. They appear in a stronger light; are more agreeable; and consequently fitter subjects of pride and vanity, than any other.

It may not be amiss, in treating of the affection we bear our acquaintance and relations, to observe some pretty curious phenomena, which attend it. It is easy to remark in common life, that children esteem their relation to their mother to be weakened, in a great measure, by her second marriage, and no longer regard her with the same eye, as if she had continued in her state of widow-hood. Nor does this happen only, when they have felt any inconveniences from her second marriage, or when her husband is much her inferior; but even without any of these considerations, and merely because she has become part of another family. This also takes place with regard to the second marriage of a father; but in a much less degree: and it is certain the ties of blood are not so much loosened in the latter case as by the marriage of a mother. These two phenomena are remarkable in themselves, but much more so when compared.

In order to produce a perfect relation betwixt two objects, it is requisite, not only that the imagination be conveyed from one to the other by resemblance, contiguity or causation, but also that it return back from the second to the first with the same ease and facility. At first sight this may seem a necessary and unavoidable consequence. If one object resemble another, the latter object must necessarily resemble the former. If one object be the cause of another, the second object is effect to its cause. It is the same case with contiguity: and therefore the relation being always reciprocal, it may be thought, that the return of the imagination from the second to the first must also, in every case, be equally natural as its passage from the first to the second. But upon farther examination we shall easily discover our mistake. For supposing the second object, beside its reciprocal relation to the first, to have also a strong relation to a third object; in that case the thought, passing from the first object to the second, returns not back with the same facility, though the relation continues the same; but is readily carried on to the third object, by means of the new relation, which presents itself, and gives a new impulse to the imagination. This new relation, therefore, weakens the tie betwixt the first and second objects. The fancy is by its very nature wavering and inconstant; and considers always two objects as more strongly related together, where it finds the passage equally easy both in going and returning, than where the transition is easy only in one of these motions. The double motion is a kind of a double tie, and binds the objects together in the closest and most intimate manner.

The second marriage of a mother breaks not the relation of child and parent; and that relation suffices to convey my imagination from myself to her with the greatest ease and facility. But after the imagination is arrived at this point of view, it finds its object to be surrounded with so many other relations, which challenge its regard, that it knows not which to prefer, and is at a loss what new object to pitch upon. The ties of interest and duty bind her to another family, and prevent that return of the fancy from her to myself, which is necessary to support the union. The thought has no longer the vibration, requisite to set it perfectly at ease, and indulge its inclination to change. It goes with facility, but returns with difficulty; and by that interruption finds the relation much weakened from what it would be were the passage open and easy on both sides.

Now to give a reason, why this effect follows not in the same degree upon the second marriage of a father: we may reflect on what has been proved already, that though the imagination goes easily from the view of a lesser object to that of a greater, yet it returns not with the same facility from the greater to the less.

When my imagination goes from myself to my father, it passes not so readily from him to his second wife, nor considers him as entering into a different family, but as continuing the head of that family, of which I am myself a part. His superiority prevents the easy transition of the thought from him to his spouse, but keeps the passage still open for a return to myself along the same relation of child and parent. He is not sunk in the new relation he acquires; so that the double motion or vibration of thought is still easy and natural. By this indulgence of the fancy in its inconstancy, the tie of child and parent still preserves its full force and influence.

A mother thinks not her tie to a son weakened, because it is shared with her husband: nor a son his with a parent, because it is shared with a brother. The third object is here related to the first, as well as to the second; so that the imagination goes and comes along all of them with the greatest facility.

SECTION FIVE

Of our esteem for the rich and powerful

Nothing has a greater tendency to give us an esteem for any person, than his power and riches; or a contempt, than his poverty and meanness: and as esteem and contempt are to be considered as species of love and hatred, it will be proper in this place to explain these phenomena.

Here it happens most fortunately, that the greatest difficulty is not to discover a principle capable of producing such an effect, but to choose the chief and predominant among several, that present themselves. The *satisfaction* we take in the riches of others, and the *esteem* we have for the possessors may be ascribed to three different causes. *First*, To the objects they possess; such as houses, gardens, equipages; which, being agreeable in themselves, necessarily produce a sentiment of pleasure in every one; that either considers or surveys them. *Secondly*, To the expectation of advantage from the rich and powerful by our sharing their possessions. *Thirdly*, To sympathy, which makes us partake of the satisfaction of every one, that approaches us. All these principles may concur in producing the present phenomenon. The question is, to which of them we ought principally to ascribe it.

It is certain, that the first principle, *viz*, the reflection on agreeable objects, has a greater influence, than what, at first sight, we may be apt to imagine. We seldom reflect on what is beautiful or ugly, agreeable or disagreeable, without an emotion of pleasure or uneasiness; and though these sensations appear not much in our common indolent way of thinking, it is easy, either in reading or conversation, to discover them. Men of wit always turn the discourse on subjects that are entertaining to the imagination; and poets never present any objects but such as are of the same nature. Mr *Philips* has chosen *Cyder* for the subject of an excellent poem. Beer would not have been so proper, as being neither so agreeable to the taste nor eye. But he would certainly have preferred wine to either of them, could his native country have afforded him so agreeable a liquor. We may learn from thence, that every thing, which is agreeable to the senses, is also in some measure agreeable to the fancy, and conveys to the thought an image of that satisfaction, which it gives by its real application to the bodily organs.

But though these reasons may induce us to comprehend this delicacy of the imagination among the causes of the respect, which we pay the rich and powerful, there are many other reasons, that may keep us from regarding it as the sole or principal. For as the ideas of pleasure can have an influence only by means of their vivacity, which makes them approach impressions, it is most natural those ideas should have that influence, which are favoured by most circumstances, and have a natural tendency to become strong and lively; such as our ideas of the passions and sensations of any human creature. Every human creature resembles ourselves, and by that means has an advantage above any other object, in operating on the imagination.

Besides, if we consider the nature of that faculty, and the great influence which all relations have upon it, we shall easily be persuaded, that however the ideas of the pleasant wines, music, or gardens, which the rich man enjoys, may become lively and agreeable, the fancy will not confine itself to them, but will carry its view to the related objects; and in particular, to the person, who possesses them. And this is the more natural, that the pleasant idea or image produces here a passion towards the person, by means of his relation to the object; so that it is unavoidable but he must enter into the original conception, since he makes the object of the derivative passion: but if he enters into the original conception, and is considered as enjoying these agreeable objects, it is *sympathy*, which is properly the cause of the affection; and the *third* principle is more powerful and universal than the *first*.

Add to this, that riches and power alone, even though unemployed, naturally cause esteem and respect: and consequently these passions arise not from the idea of any beautiful or agreeable objects. It is true; money implies a kind of representation of such objects, by the power it affords of obtaining them; and for that reason may still be esteemed proper to convey those agreeable images, which may give rise to the passion. But as this prospect is very distant, it is more natural for us to take a contiguous object, *viz*, the satisfaction, which this power affords the person, who is possessed of it. And of this we shall be farther satisfied, if we consider, that riches represent the goods of life, only by means of the will, which employs them; and therefore imply in their very nature an idea of the person, and cannot be considered without a kind of sympathy with his sensations and enjoyments.

This we may confirm by a reflection, which to some will, perhaps, appear too subtile and refined. I have already observed, that power, as distinguished from its exercise, has either no meaning at all, or is nothing but a possibility or probability of existence; by which any object approaches to reality, and has a sensible influence on the mind. I have also observed, that this approach, by an illusion of the fancy, appears much greater, when we ourselves are possessed of the power, than when it is enjoyed by another; and that in the former case the objects seem to touch upon the very verge of reality, and convey almost an equal satisfaction, as if actually in our possession. Now I assert, that where we esteem a person upon account of his riches, we must enter into this sentiment of the proprietor, and that without such a sympathy the idea of the agreeable objects, which they give him the power to produce, would have but a feeble influence upon us. An avaricious man is respected for his money, though he scarce is possessed of a *power*; that is, there scarce is a *probability* or even *possibility* of his employing it in the acquisition of the pleasures and conveniences of life. To himself alone this power seems perfect and entire; and therefore we must receive his sentiments by sympathy, before we can have a strong intense idea of these enjoyments, or esteem him upon account of them.

Thus we have found, that the *first* principle, *viz, the agreeable idea of those objects, which riches afford the enjoyment of,* resolves itself in a great measure into the *third*, and becomes a *sympathy* with the person we esteem or love. Let us now examine the *second* principle, *viz, the agreeable expectation of advantage*, and see what force we may justly attribute to it.

It is obvious, that though riches and authority undoubtedly give their owner a power of doing us service, yet this power is not to be considered as on the same footing with that, which they afford him, of pleasing himself, and satisfying his own appetites. Self-love approaches the power and exercise very near each other in the latter case; but in order to produce a similar effect in the former, we must suppose a friendship and good-will to be conjoined with the riches. Without that circumstance it is difficult to conceive on what we can found our hope of advantage from the riches of others, though there is nothing more certain, than that we naturally esteem and respect the rich, even before we discover in them any such favourable disposition towards us.

But I carry this farther, and observe, not only that we respect the rich and powerful, where they shew no inclination to serve us, but also when we lie so much out of the sphere of their activity, that they cannot even be supposed to be endowed with that power. Prisoners of war are always treated with a respect suitable to their condition; and it is certain riches go very far towards fixing the condition of any person. If birth and quality enter for a share, this still affords us an argument of the same kind. For what is it we call a man of birth, but one who is descended from a long succession of rich and powerful ancestors, and who acquires our esteem by his relation to persons whom we esteem? His ancestors, therefore, though dead, are respected, in some measure, on account of their riches, and consequently without any kind of expectation.

But not to go so far as prisoners of war and the dead to find instances of this disinterested esteem for riches, let us observe with a little attention those phenomena that occur to us in common life and conversation. A man, who is himself of a competent fortune, upon coming into a company of strangers, naturally treats them with different degrees of respect and deference, as he is informed of their different fortunes and conditions; though it is impossible he can ever propose, and perhaps would not accept of any advantage from them. A traveller is always admitted into company, and meets with civility, in proportion as his train and equipage speak him a man of great or moderate fortune. In short, the different ranks of men are, in a great measure, regulated by riches, and that with regard to superiors as well as inferiors, strangers as well as acquaintance.

There is, indeed, an answer to these arguments, drawn from the influence of *general rules*. It may be pretended, that being accustomed to expect succour and protection from the rich and powerful, and to esteem them upon that account, we extend the same sentiments to those, who resemble them in their fortune, but from whom we can never hope for any advantage. The general rule still prevails, and by giving a bent to the imagination draws along the passion, in the same manner as if its proper object were real and existent.

But that this principle does not here take place, will easily appear, if we consider, that in order to establish a general rule, and extend it beyond its proper bounds, there is required a certain uniformity in our experience, and a great superiority of those instances, which are conformable to the rule, above the contrary. But here the case is quite otherwise. Of a hundred men of credit and fortune I meet with, there is not, perhaps, one from whom I can expect advantage; so that it is impossible any custom can ever prevail in the present case.

Upon the whole, there remains nothing, which can give us an esteem for power and riches, and a contempt for meanness and poverty, except the principle of *sympathy*, by which we enter into the sentiments of the rich and poor, and partake of their pleasure and uneasiness. Riches give satisfaction to their possessor; and this satisfaction is conveyed to the beholder by the imagination, which produces an idea resembling the original impression in force and vivacity. This agreeable idea or impression is connected with love, which is an agreeable passion. It proceeds from a thinking conscious being, which is the very object of love. From this relation of impressions, and identity of ideas, the passion arises, according to my hypothesis.

The best method of reconciling us to this opinion is to take a general survey of the universe, and observe the force of sympathy through the whole animal creation, and the easy communication of sentiments from one thinking being to another. In all creatures, that prey not upon others, and are not agitated with violent passions, there appears a remarkable desire of company, which associates them together, without any advantages they can ever propose to reap from their union. This is still more conspicuous in man, as being the creature of the universe, who has the most ardent desire of society, and is fitted for it by the most advantages. We can form no wish, which has not a reference to society. A perfect solitude is, perhaps, the greatest punishment we can suffer. Every pleasure languishes when enjoyed a-part from company, and every pain becomes more cruel and intolerable. Whatever other passions we may be actuated by; pride, ambition, avarice, curiosity, revenge or lust; the soul or animating principle of them all is sympathy; nor would they have any force, were we to abstract entirely from the thoughts and sentiments of others. Let all the powers and elements of nature conspire to serve and obey one man: let the sun rise and set at his command: the sea and rivers roll as he pleases, and the earth furnish spontaneously whatever may be useful or agreeable to him: he will still be miserable, till you give him some one person at least, with whom he may share his happiness, and whose esteem and friendship he may enjoy.

This conclusion from a general view of human nature, we may confirm by particular instances, wherein the force of sympathy is very remarkable. Most kinds of beauty are derived from this origin; and though our first object be some senseless inanimate piece of matter, it is seldom we rest there, and carry not our view to its influence on sensible and rational creatures. A man, who shews us any house or building, takes particular care among other things to point out the convenience of the apartments, the advantages of their situation, and the little room lost in the stairs, antichambers and passages; and indeed it is evident, the chief part of the beauty consists in these particulars. The observation of convenience gives pleasure, since convenience is a beauty. But after what manner does it give pleasure? It is certain our own interest is not in the least concerned; and as this is a beauty of interest, not of form, so to speak, it must delight us merely by communication, and by our sympathizing with the proprietor of the lodging. We enter into his interest by the force of imagination, and feel the same satisfaction, that the objects naturally occasion in him.

This observation extends to tables, chairs, scritoires, chimneys, coaches, saddles, ploughs, and indeed to every work of art; it being an universal rule, that their beauty is chiefly derived from their utility, and from their fitness for that purpose, to which they are destined. But this is an advantage, that concerns only the owner, nor is there any thing but sympathy, which can interest the spectator.

It is evident, that nothing renders a field more agreeable than its fertility, and that scarce any advantages of ornament or situation will be able to equal this beauty. It is the same case with particular trees and plants, as with the field on which they grow. I know not but a plain, overgrown with furze and broom, may be, in itself, as beautiful as a hill covered with vines or olive-trees; though it will never appear so to one, who is acquainted with the value of each. But this is a beauty merely of imagination, and has no foundation in what appears to the senses. Fertility and value have a plain reference to use; and that to riches, joy, and plenty; in which though we have no hope of partaking, yet we enter into them by the vivacity of the fancy, and share them, in some measure, with the proprietor.

There is no rule in painting more reasonable than that of balancing the figures, and placing them with the greatest exactness on their proper centers of gravity. A figure, which is not justly balanced, is disagreeable; and that because it conveys the ideas of its fall, of harm, and of pain: which ideas are painful, when by sympathy they acquire any degree of force and vivacity.

Add to this, that the principal part of personal beauty is an air of health and vigour, and such a construction of members as promises strength and activity. This idea of beauty cannot be accounted for but by sympathy.

In general we may remark, that the minds of men are mirrors to one another, not only because they reflect each other's emotions, but also because those rays of passions, sentiments and opinions may be often reverberated, and may decay away by insensible degrees.

Thus the pleasure, which a rich man receives from his possessions, being thrown upon the beholder, causes a pleasure and esteem; which sentiments again, being perceived and sympathized with, increase the pleasure of the possessor; and being once more reflected, become a new foundation for pleasure and esteem in the beholder. There is certainly an original satisfaction in riches derived from that power, which they bestow, of enjoying all the pleasures of life; and as this is their very nature and essence, it must be the first source of all the passions, which arise from them. One of the most considerable of these passions is that of love or esteem in others, which therefore proceeds from a sympathy with the pleasure of the possessor. But the possessor has also a secondary satisfaction in riches arising from the love and esteem he acquires by them, and this satisfaction is nothing but a second reflexion of that original pleasure, which proceeded from himself. This secondary satisfaction or vanity becomes one of the principal recommendations of riches, and is the chief reason, why we either desire them for ourselves, or esteem them in others. Here then is a third rebound of the original pleasure; after which it is difficult to distinguish the images and reflexions, by reason of their faintness and confusion.

SECTION SIX
Of benevolence and anger

Ideas may be compared to the extension and solidity of matter, and impressions, especially reflective ones, to colours, tastes, smells and other sensible qualities. Ideas never admit of a total union, but are endowed with a kind of impenetrability, by which they exclude each other, and are capable of forming a compound by their conjunction, not by their mixture. On the other hand, impressions and passions are susceptible of an entire union; and like colours, may be blended so perfectly together, that each of them may lose itself, and contribute only to vary that uniform impression, which arises from the whole. Some of the most curious phenomena of the human mind are derived from this property of the passions.

In examining those ingredients, which are capable of uniting with love and hatred, I begin to be sensible, in some measure, of a misfortune, that has attended every system of philosophy, with which the world has been yet acquainted. It is commonly found, that in accounting for the operations of nature by any particular hypothesis; among a number of experiments, that quadrate exactly with the principles we would endeavour to establish; there is always some phenomenon, which is more stubborn, and will not so easily bend to our purpose. We need not be surprized, that this should happen in natural philosophy. The essence and composition of external bodies are so obscure, that we must necessarily, in our reasonings, or rather conjectures concerning them, involve ourselves in contradictions and absurdities. But as the perceptions of the mind are perfectly known, and I have used all imaginable caution in forming conclusions concerning them, I have always hoped to keep clear of those contradictions, which have attended every other system. Accordingly the difficulty, which I have at present in my eye, is nowise contrary to my system; but only departs a little from that simplicity, which has been hitherto its principal force and beauty.

The passions of love and hatred are always followed by, or rather conjoined with benevolence and anger. It is this conjunction, which chiefly distinguishes these affections from pride and humility. For pride and humility are pure emotions in the soul, unattended with any desire, and not immediately exciting us to action. But love and hatred are not compleated within themselves, nor rest in that emotion, which they produce, but carry the mind to something farther. Love is always followed by a desire of the happiness of the person beloved, and an aversion to his misery: as hatred produces a desire of the misery and an aversion to the happiness of the person hated. So remarkable a difference betwixt these two sets of passions of pride and humility, love and hatred, which in so many other particulars correspond to each other, merits our attention.

The conjunction of this desire and aversion with love and hatred may be accounted for by two different hypotheses. The first is, that love and hatred have not only a *cause*, which excites them, *viz*, pleasure and pain; and an *object*, to which they are directed, *viz*, a person or thinking being; but likewise an *end*, which they endeavour to attain, *viz*, the happiness or misery of the person beloved or hated; all which views, mixing together, make only one passion. According to this system, love is nothing but the desire of happiness to another person, and hatred that of misery. The desire and aversion constitute the very nature of love and hatred. They are not only inseparable but the same.

But this is evidently contrary to experience. For though it is certain we never love any person without desiring his happiness, nor hate any without wishing his misery, yet these desires arise only upon the ideas of the happiness or misery of our friend or enemy being presented by the imagination, and are not absolutely essential to love and hatred. They are the most obvious and natural sentiments of these affections, but not the only ones. The passions may express themselves in a hundred ways, and may subsist a considerable time, without our reflecting on the happiness or misery of their objects; which clearly proves, that these desires are not the same with love and hatred, nor make any essential part of them.

We may, therefore, infer, that benevolence and anger are passions different from love and hatred, and only conjoined with them, by the original constitution of the mind. As nature has given to the body certain appetites and inclinations, which she increases, diminishes, or changes according to the situation of the fluids or solids; she has proceeded in the same manner with the mind. According as we are possessed with love or hatred, the correspondent desire of the happiness or misery of the person, who is the object of these passions, arises in the mind, and varies with each variation of these opposite passions. This order of things, abstractedly considered, is not necessary. Love and hatred might have been unattended with any such desires, or their particular connexion might have been entirely reversed. If nature had so pleased, love might have had the same effect as hatred, and hatred as love. I see no contradiction in supposing a desire of producing misery annexed to love, and of happiness to hatred. If the sensation of the passion and desire be opposite, nature could have altered the sensation without altering the tendency of the desire, and by that means made them compatible with each other.

SECTION SEVEN

Of compassion

But though the desire of the happiness or misery of others, according to the love or hatred we bear them, be an arbitrary and original instinct implanted in our nature, we find it may be counterfeited on many occasions, and may arise from secondary principles. *Pity* is a concern for, and *malice* a joy in the misery of others, without any friendship or enmity to occasion this concern or joy. We pity even strangers, and such as are perfectly indifferent to us: and if our ill-will to another proceed from any harm or injury, it is not, properly speaking, malice, but revenge. But if we examine these affections of pity and malice we shall find them to be secondary ones, arising from original affections, which are varied by some particular turn of thought and imagination.

It will be easy to explain the passion of *pity*, from the precedent reasoning concerning *sympathy*. We have a lively idea of every thing related to us. All human creatures are related to us by resemblance. Their persons, therefore, their interests, their passions, their pains and pleasures must strike upon us in a lively manner, and produce an emotion similar to the original one; since a lively idea is easily converted into an impression. If this be true in general, it must be more so of affliction and sorrow. These have always a stronger and more lasting influence than any pleasure or enjoyment.

A spectator of a tragedy passes through a long train of grief, terror, indignation, and other affections, which the poet represents in the persons he introduces. As many tragedies end happily, and no excellent one can be composed without some reverses of fortune, the spectator must sympathize with all these changes, and receive the fictitious joy as well as every other passion. Unless, therefore, it be asserted, that every distinct passion is communicated by a distinct original quality, and is not derived from the general principle of sympathy above-explained, it must be allowed, that all of them arise from that principle. To except any one in particular must appear highly unreasonable. As they are all first present in the mind of one person, and afterwards appear in the mind of another; and as the manner of their appearance, first as an idea, then as an impression, is in every case the same, the transition must arise from the same principle. I am at least sure, that this method of reasoning would be considered as certain, either in natural philosophy or common life.

Add to this, that pity depends, in a great measure, on the contiguity, and even sight of the object; which is a proof, that it is derived from the imagination. Not to mention that women and children are most subject to pity, as being most guided by that faculty. The same infirmity, which makes them faint at the sight of a naked sword, though in the hands of their best friend, makes them pity extremely those, whom they find in any grief or affliction. Those philosophers, who derive this passion from I know not what subtile reflections on the instability of fortune, and our being liable to the same miseries we behold, will find this observation contrary to them among a great many others, which it were easy to produce.

There remains only to take notice of a pretty remarkable phenomenon of this passion; which is, that the communicated passion of sympathy sometimes acquires strength from the weakness of its original, and even arises by a transition from affections, which have no existence. Thus when a person obtains any honourable office, or inherits a great fortune, we are always the more rejoiced for his prosperity, the less sense he seems to have of it, and the greater equanimity and indifference he shews in its enjoyment. In like manner a man, who is not dejected by misfortunes, is the more lamented on account of his patience; and if that virtue extends so far as utterly to remove all sense of uneasiness, it still farther increases our compassion. When a person of merit falls into what is vulgarly esteemed a great misfortune, we form a notion of his condition; and carrying our fancy from the cause to the usual effect, first conceive a lively idea of his sorrow, and then feel an impression of it, entirely over-looking that greatness of mind, which elevates him above such emotions, or only considering it so far as to increase our admiration, love and tenderness for him. We find from experience, that such a degree of passion is usually connected with such a misfortune; and though there be an exception in the present case, yet the imagination is affected by the *general rule*, and makes us conceive a lively idea of the passion, or rather feel the passion itself, in the same manner, as if the person were really actuated by it. From the same principles we blush for the conduct of those, who behave themselves foolishly before us; and that though they shew no sense of shame, nor seem in the least conscious of their folly. All this proceeds from sympathy; but it is of a partial kind, and views its objects only on one side, without considering the other, which has a contrary effect, and would entirely destroy that emotion, which arises from the first appearance.

We have also instances, wherein an indifference and insensibility under misfortune increases our concern for the misfortunate, even though the indifference proceed not from any virtue and magnanimity. It is an aggravation of a murder, that it was committed upon persons asleep and in perfect security; as historians readily observe of any infant prince, who is captive in the hands of his enemies, that he is the more worthy of compassion the less sensible he is of his miserable condition. As we ourselves are here acquainted with the wretched situation of the person, it gives us a lively idea and sensation of sorrow, which is the passion that generally attends it; and this idea becomes still more lively, and the sensation more violent by a contrast with that security and indifference, which we observe in the person himself. A contrast of any kind never fails to affect the imagination, especially when presented by the subject; and it is on the imagination that pity entirely depends.*

SECTION EIGHT
Of malice and envy

We must now proceed to account for the passion of *malice*, which imitates the effects of hatred, as pity does those of love; and gives us a joy in the sufferings and miseries of others, without any offence or injury on their part.

So little are men governed by reason in their sentiments and opinions, that they always judge more of objects by comparison than from their intrinsic worth and value. When the mind con-

---

* To prevent all ambiguity, I must observe, that where I oppose the imagination to the memory, I mean in general the faculty that presents our fainter ideas. In all other places, and particularly when it is opposed to the understanding, I understand the same faculty, excluding only our demonstrative and probable reasonings.

siders, or is accustomed to, any degree of perfection, whatever falls short of it, though really esteemable, has notwithstanding the same effect upon the passions; as what is defective and ill. This is an *original* quality of the soul, and similar to what we have every day experience of in our bodies. Let a man heat one hand and cool the other; the same water will, at the same time, seem both hot and cold, according to the disposition of the different organs. A small degree of any quality, succeeding a greater, produces the same sensation, as if less than it really is, and even sometimes as the opposite quality. Any gentle pain, that follows a violent one, seems as nothing, or rather becomes a pleasure; as on the other hand a violent pain, succeeding a gentle one, is doubly grievous and uneasy.

This no one can doubt of with regard to our passions and sensations. But there may arise some difficulty with regard to our ideas and objects. When an object augments or diminishes to the eye or imagination from a comparison with others, the image and idea of the object are still the same, and are equally extended in the *retina*, and in the brain or organ of perception. The eyes refract the rays of light, and the optic nerves convey the images to the brain in the very same manner, whether a great or small object has preceded; nor does even the imagination alter the dimensions of its object on account of a comparison with others. The question then is, how from the same impression and the same idea we can form such different judgments concerning the same object, and at one time admire its bulk, and at another despise its littleness. This variation in our judgments must certainly proceed from a variation in some perception; but as the variation lies not in the immediate impression or idea of the object, it must lie in some other impression, that accompanies it.

In order to explain this matter, I shall just touch upon two principles, one of which shall be more fully explained in the progress of this treatise; the other has been already accounted for. I believe it may safely be established for a general maxim, that no object is presented to the senses, nor image formed in the fancy, but what is accompanied with some emotion or movement of spirits proportioned to it; and however custom may make us insensible of this sensation and cause us to confound it with the object or idea, it will be easy, by careful and exact experiments, to separate and distinguish them. For to instance only in the cases of extension and number; it is evident, that any very bulky object, such as the ocean, an extended plain, a vast chain of mountains, a wide forest: or any very numerous collection of objects, such as an army, a fleet, a crowd, excite in the mind a sensible emotion; and that the admiration, which arises on the appearance of such objects, is one of the most lively pleasures, which human nature is capable of enjoying. Now as this admiration increases or diminishes by the increase or diminution of the objects, we may conclude, according to our foregoing principles,* that it is a compound effect, proceeding from the conjunction of the several effects, which arise from each part of the cause. Every part, then, of extension, and every unit of number has a separate emotion attending it; and though that emotion be not always agreeable, yet by its conjunction with others, and by its agitating the spirits to a just pitch, it contributes to the production of admiration, which is always agreeable. If this be allowed with respect to extension and number, we can make no difficulty with respect to virtue and vice, wit and folly, riches and poverty, happiness and misery, and other objects of that kind, which are always attended with an evident emotion.

The second principle I shall take notice of is that of our adherence to *general rules*; which has such a mighty influence on the actions and understanding, and is able to impose on the very senses. When an object is found by experience to be always accompanied with another; whenever the first object appears, though changed in very material circumstances; we naturally fly to the conception of the second, and form an idea of it in as lively and strong a manner, as if we had inferred its existence by the justest and most authentic conclusion of our understanding. Nothing can undeceive us, not even our senses, which, instead of correcting this false judgment, are often perverted by it, and seem to authorize its errors.

The conclusion I draw from these two principles, joined to the influence of comparison above-mentioned, is very short and decisive. Every object is attended with some emotion proportioned to it; a great object with a great emotion, a small object with a small emotion. A great *object*, therefore, succeeding a small one makes a great *emotion* succeed a small one. Now a great emotion succeeding a small one becomes still greater, and rises beyond

---

* Book 1, Part 3, Section 15.

its ordinary proportion. But as there is a certain degree of an emotion, which commonly attends every magnitude of an object; when the emotion increases, we naturally imagine that the object has likewise increased. The effect conveys our view to its usual cause, a certain degree of emotion to a certain magnitude of the object; nor do we consider, that comparison may change the emotion without changing anything in the object. Those who are acquainted with the metaphysical part of optics and know how we transfer the judgments and conclusions of the understanding to the senses, will easily conceive this whole operation.

But leaving this new discovery of an impression, that secretly attends every idea; we must at least allow of that principle, from whence the discovery arose, *that objects appear greater or less by a comparison with others*. We have so many instances of this, that it is impossible we can dispute its veracity; and it is from this principle I derive the passions of malice and envy.

It is evident we must receive a greater or less satisfaction or uneasiness from reflecting on our own condition and circumstances, in proportion as they appear more or less fortunate or unhappy, in proportion to the degrees of riches, and power, and merit, and reputation, which we think ourselves possessed of. Now as we seldom judge of objects from their intrinsic value, but form our notions of them from a comparison with other objects; it follows, that according as we observe a greater or less share of happiness or misery in others, we must make an estimate of our own, and feel a consequent pain or pleasure. The misery of another gives us a more lively idea of our happiness, and his happiness of our misery. The former, therefore, produces delight; and the latter uneasiness.

Here then is a kind of pity reversed, or contrary sensations arising in the beholder, from those which are felt by the person, whom he considers. In general we may observe, that in all kinds of comparison an object makes us always receive from another, to which it is compared, a sensation contrary to what arises from itself in its direct and immediate survey. A small object makes a great one appear still greater. A great object makes a little one appear less. Deformity of itself produces uneasiness; but makes us receive new pleasure by its contrast with a beautiful object, whose beauty is augmented by it; as on the other hand, beauty, which of itself produces pleasure, makes us receive a new pain by the contrast with any thing ugly, whose deformity it augments. The case, therefore, must be the same with happiness and misery. The direct survey of another's pleasure naturally gives us pleasure, and therefore produces pain when cornpared with our own. His pain, considered in itself, is painful to us, but augments the idea of our own happiness, and gives us pleasure.

Nor will it appear strange, that we may feel a reversed sensation from the happiness and misery of others; since we find the same comparison may give us a kind of malice against ourselves, and make us rejoice for our pains, and grieve for our pleasures. Thus the prospect of past pain is agreeable, when we are satisfied with our present condition; as on the other hand our past pleasures give us uneasiness, when we enjoy nothing at present equal to them. The comparison being the same, as when we reflect on the sentiments of others, must be attended with the same effects.

Nay a person may extend this malice against himself, even to his present fortune, and carry it so far as designedly to seek affliction, and increase his pains and sorrows. This may happen upon two occasions. *First*, Upon the distress and misfortune of a friend, or person dear to him. *Secondly*, Upon the feeling any remorses for a crime, of which he has been guilty. It is from the principle of comparison that both these irregular appetites for evil arise. A person, who indulges himself in any pleasure, while his friend lies under affliction, feels the reflected uneasiness from his friend more sensibly by a comparison with the original pleasure, which he himself enjoys. This contrast, indeed, ought also to enliven the present pleasure. But as grief is here supposed to be the predominant passion, every addition falls to that side, and is swallowed up in it, without operating in the least upon the contrary affection. It is the same case with those penances, which men inflict on themselves for their past sins and failings. When a criminal reflects on the punishment he deserves, the idea of it is magnified by a comparison with his present ease and satisfaction; which forces him, in a manner, to seek uneasiness, in order to avoid so disagreeable a contrast.

This reasoning will account for the origin of *envy* as well as of malice. The only difference betwixt these passions lies in this, that envy is excited by some present enjoyment of another, which by comparison diminishes our idea of our own: whereas malice is the unprovoked desire of producing evil to another, in order to reap a pleasure from the comparison. The enjoyment, which is the object of envy, is commonly superior to our own. A superiority naturally seems to overshade us, and presents a disagreeable comparison. But even in the case of an inferiority, we still desire a greater distance, in order to augment still more the idea of ourself. When this distance diminishes, the comparison is less to our advantage; and consequently gives us less pleasure, and is even disagreeable. Hence arises that species of envy, which men feel, when they perceive their inferiors approaching or overtaking them in the pursuits of glory or happiness. In this envy we may see the effects of comparison twice repeated. A man, who compares himself to his inferior, receives a pleasure from the comparison: and when the inferiority decreases by the elevation of the inferior, what should only have been a decrease of pleasure, becomes a real pain, by a new comparison with its preceding condition.

It is worthy of observation concerning that envy, which arises from a superiority in others, that it is not the great disproportion betwixt ourself and another, which produces it; but on the contrary, our proximity. A common soldier bears no such envy to his general as to his sergeant or corporal; nor does an eminent writer meet with so great jealousy in common hackney scribblers, as in authors, that more nearly approach him. It may, indeed, be thought, that the greater the disproportion is, the greater must be the uneasiness from the comparison. But we may consider on the other hand, that the great disproportion cuts off the relation, and either keeps us from comparing ourselves with what is remote from us, or diminishes the effects of the comparison. Resemblance and proximity always produce a relation of ideas; and where you destroy these ties, however other accidents may bring two ideas together; as they have no bond or connecting quality to join them in the imagination; it is impossible they can remain long united, or have any considerable influence on each other.

I have observed in considering the nature of ambition, that the great feel a double pleasure in authority from the comparison of their own condition with that of their slaves; and that this comparison has a double influence, because it is natural, and presented by the subject. When the fancy, in the comparison of objects, passes not easily from the one object to the other, the action of the mind is, in a great measure, broke, and the fancy, in considering the second object, begins, as it were, upon a new footing. The impression, which attends every object, seems not greater in that case by succeeding a less of the same kind; but these two impressions are distinct, and produce their distinct effects, without any communication together. The want of relation in the ideas breaks the relation of the impressions, and by such a separation prevents their mutual operation and influence.

To confirm this we may observe, that the proximity in the degree of merit is not alone sufficient to give rise to envy, but must be assisted by other relations. A poet is not apt to envy a philosopher, or a poet of a different kind, of a different nation, or of a different age. All these differences prevent or weaken the comparison, and consequently the passion.

This too is the reason, why all objects appear great or little, merely by a comparison with those of the same species. A mountain neither magnifies nor diminishes a horse in our eyes; but when a *Flemish* and a *Welsh* horse are seen together, the one appears greater and the other less, than when viewed apart.

From the same principle we may account for that remark of historians, that any party in a civil war always choose to call in a foreign enemy at any hazard rather than submit to their fellow-citizens. *Guicciardin* applies this remark to the wars in *Italy*, where the relations betwixt the different states are, properly speaking, nothing but of name, language, and contiguity. Yet even these relations, when joined with superiority, by making the comparison more natural, make it likewise more grievous, and cause men to search for some other superiority, which may be attended with no relation, and by that means may have a less sensible influence on the imagination. The mind quickly perceives its several advantages and disadvantages; and finding its situation to be most uneasy, where superiority is conjoined with other relations, seeks its repose as much as possible, by their separation, and by breaking that association of ideas, which renders the comparison so much more natural and efficacious. When it cannot break the association, it feels a stronger desire to remove the superiority; and this is the reason why travellers are commonly so lavish of their praises to the

Chinese and *Persians*, at the same time, that they depreciate those neighbouring nations, which may stand upon a foot of rivalship with their native country.

These examples from history and common experience are rich and curious; but we may find parallel ones in the arts, which are no less remarkable. Should an author compose a treatise, of which one part was serious and profound, another light and humorous, every one would condemn so strange a mixture, and would accuse him of the neglect of all rules of art and criticism. These rules of art are founded on the qualities of human nature; and the quality of human nature, which requires a consistency in every performance is that which renders the mind incapable of passing in a moment from one passion and disposition to a quite different one. Yet this makes us not blame Mr *Prior* for joining his *Alma* and his *Solomon* in the same volume; though that admirable poet has succeeded perfectly well in the gaiety of the one, as well as in the melancholy of the other. Even supposing the reader should peruse these two compositions without any interval, he would feel little or no difficulty in the change of passions: why, but because he considers these performances as entirely different, and by this break in the ideas, breaks the progress of the affections, and hinders the one from influencing or contradicting the other?

An heroic and burlesque design, united in one picture, would be monstrous; though we place two pictures of so opposite a character in the same chamber, and even close by each other, without any scruple or difficulty.

In a word, no ideas can affect each other, either by comparison, or by the passions they separately produce, unless they be united together by some relation, which may cause an easy transition of the ideas, and consequently of the emotions or impressions, attending the ideas; and may preserve the one impression in the passage of the imagination to the object of the other. This principle is very remarkable, because it is analogous to what we have observed both concerning the *understanding* and the *passions*. Suppose two objects to be presented to me, which are not connected by any kind of relation. Suppose that each of these objects separately produces a passion; and that these two passions are in themselves contrary: we find from experience, that the want of relation in the objects or ideas hinders the natural contrariety of the passions, and that the break in the transition of the thought removes the affections from each other, and prevents their opposition. It is the same case with comparison; and from both these phenomena we may safely conclude, that the relation of ideas must forward the transition of impressions; since its absence alone is able to prevent it, and to separate what naturally should have operated upon each other. When the absence of an object or quality removes any usual or natural effect, we may certalnly conclude that its presence contributes to the production of the effect.

SECTION NINE

Of the mixture of benevolence and anger with compassion and malice

Thus we have endeavoured to account for *pity* and *malice*. Both these affections arise from the imagination, according to the light, in which it places its object. When our fancy considers directly the sentiments of others, and enters deep into them, it makes us sensible of all the passions it surveys, but in a particular manner of grief or sorrow. On the contrary, when we compare the sentiments of others to our own, we feel a sensation directly opposite to the original one, *viz.* a joy from the grief of others, and a grief from their joy. But these are only the first found-ations of the affections of pity and malice. Other passions are afterwards confounded with them. There is always a mixture of love or tenderness with pity, and of hatred or anger with malice. But it must be confessed, that this mixture seems at first sight to be contradictory to my system. For as pity is an uneasiness, and malice a joy, arising from the misery of others, pity should naturally, as in all other cases, produce hatred; and malice, love. This contradiction I endeavour to reconcile, after the following manner.

In order to cause a transition of passions, there is required a double relation of impressions and ideas, nor is one relation sufficient to produce this effect. But that we may understand the full force of this double relation, we must consider, that it is not the present sensation alone or momentary pain or pleasure, which determines the character of any passion, but the whole bent or tendency of it from the beginning to the end. One impression may be related to another, not only when their sensations are resembling, as we have all along supposed in the preceding cases; but also when their impulses or directions are similar and correspondent. This cannot take place with regard to pride and humility; because these are only pure sensations, without any direction or tendency to action. We are, therefore, to look for instances of this peculiar relation of impressions only in such affections, as are attended with a certain appetite or desire; such as those of love and hatred.

Benevolence or the appetite, which attends love, is a desire of the happiness of the person beloved, and an aversion to his misery; as anger or the appetite, which attends hatred, is a desire of the misery of the person hated, and an aversion to his happiness. A desire, therefore, of the happiness of another, and aversion to his misery, are similar to benevolence; and a desire of his misery and aversion to his happiness are correspondent to anger. Now pity is a desire of happiness to another, and aversion to his misery; as malice is the contrary appetite. Pity, then, is related to benevolence; and malice to anger: and as benevolence has been already found to be connected with love, by a natural and original quality, and anger with hatred; it is by this chain the passions of pity and malice are connected with love and hatred.

This hypothesis is founded on sufficient experience. A man, who from any motives has entertained a resolution of performing an action, naturally runs into every other view or motive, which may fortify that resolution, and give it authority and influence on the mind. To confirm us in any design, we search for motives drawn from interest, from honour, from duty. What wonder, then, that pity and benevolence, malice, and anger, being the same desires arising from different principles, should so totally mix together as to be undistinguishable? As to the connexion betwixt benevolence and love, anger and hatred, being *original* and primary, it admits of no difficulty.

We may add to this another experiment, *viz*, that benevolence and anger, and consequently love and hatred, arise when our happiness or misery have any dependance on the happiness or misery of another person, without any farther relation. I doubt not but this experiment will appear so singular as to excuse us for stopping a moment to consider it.

Suppose, that two persons of the same trade should seek employment in a town, that is not able to maintain both, it is plain the success of one is perfectly incompatible with that of the other, and that whatever is for the interest of either is contrary to that of his rival, and so *vice versa*. Suppose again, that two merchants, though living in different parts of the world, should enter into co-partnership together, the advantage or loss of one becomes immediately the advantage or loss of his partner, and the same fortune necessarily attends both. Now it is evident, that in the first case, hatred always follows upon the contrariety of interests; as in the second, love arises from their union. Let us consider to what principle we can ascribe these passions.

It is plain they arise not from the double relations of impressions and ideas, if we regard only the present sensation. For taking the first case of rivalship; though the pleasure and advantage of an antagonist necessarily causes my pain and loss, yet to counterbalance this, his pain and loss causes my pleasure and advantage; and supposing him to be unsuccessful, I may by this means receive from him a superior degree of satisfaction. In the same manner the success of a partner rejoices me, but then his misfortunes afflict me in an equal proportion; and it is easy to imagine, that the latter sentiment may in many cases preponderate. But whether the fortune of a rival or partner be good or bad, I always hate the former and love the latter.

This love of a partner cannot proceed from the relation or connexion betwixt us; in the same manner as I love a brother or countryman. A rival has almost as close a relation to me as a partner. For as the pleasure of the latter causes my pleasure, and his pain my pain; so the pleasure of the former causes my pain, and his pain my pleasure. The connexion, then, of cause and effect is the same in both cases; and if in the one case, the cause and effect have a farther relation of resemblance, they have that of contrariety in the other; which, being also a species of resemblance, leaves the matter pretty equal.

The only explication, then, we can give of this phenomenon is derived from that principle of a parallel direction above-mentioned. Our concern for our own interest gives us a pleasure in the pleasure, and a pain in the pain of a partner, after the same manner as by sympathy we feel a sensation correspondent to those, which appear in any person, who is present with us. On the other hand, the same concern for our interest makes us feel a pain in the pleasure, and a pleasure in the pain of a rival; and in short the same contrariety of sentiments as arises from comparison and malice. Since, therefore, a parallel direction of the affections, proceeding from interest, can give rise to benevolence or anger, no wonder the same parallel direction, derived from sympathy and from comparison, should have the same effect.

In general we may observe, that it is impossible to do good to others, from whatever motive, without feeling some touches of kindness and good-will towards them; as the injuries we do, not only cause hatred in the person, who suffers them, but even in ourselves. These phenomena, indeed, may in part be accounted for from other principles.

But here there occurs a considerable objection, which it will be necessary to examine before we proceed any farther. I have endeavoured to prove, that power and riches, or poverty and meanness; which give rise to love or hatred, without producing any original pleasure or uneasiness; operate upon us by means of a secondary sensation derived from a sympathy with that pain or satisfaction, which they produce in the person, who possesses them. From a sympathy with his pleasure there arises love; from that with his uneasiness, hatred. But it is a maxim, which I have just now established, and which is absolutely necessary to the explication of the phenomena of pity and malice, that it is not the present sensation or momentary pain or pleasure, which determines the character of any passion, but the general bent or tendency of it from the beginning to the end. For this reason, pity or a sympathy with pain produces love, and that because it interests us in the fortunes of others, good or bad, and gives us a secondary sensation correspondent to the primary; in which it has the same influence with love and benevolence. Since then this rule holds good in one case, why does it not prevail throughout, and why does sympathy in uneasiness ever produce any passion beside good-will and kindness? Is it becoming a philosopher to alter his method of reasoning, and run from one principle to its contrary, according to the particular phenomenon, which he would explain?

I have mentioned two different causes, from which a transition of passion may arise, *viz*, a double relation of ideas and impressions, and what is similar to it, a conformity in the tendency and direction of any two desires, which arise from different principles. Now I assert, that when a sympathy with uneasiness is weak, it produces hatred or contempt by the former cause; when strong, it produces love or tenderness by the latter. This is the solution of the foregoing difficulty, which seems so urgent; and this is a principle founded on such evident arguments, that we ought to have established it, even though it were not necessary to the explication of any phenomenon.

It is certain, that sympathy is not always limited to the present moment, but that we often feel by communication the pains and pleasures of others, which are not in being, and which we only anticipate by the force of imagination. For supposing I saw a person perfectly unknown to me, who, while asleep in the fields, was in danger of being trod under foot by horses, I should immediately run to his assistance; and in this I should be actuated by the same principle of sympathy, which makes me concerned for the present sorrows of a stranger. The bare mention of this is sufficient. Sympathy being nothing but a lively idea converted into an impression, it is evident, that, in considering the future possible or probable condition of any person, we may enter into it with so vivid a conception as to make it our own concern; and by that means be sensible of pains and pleasures, which neither belong to ourselves, nor at the present instant have any real existence.

But however we may look forward to the future in sympathizing with any person, the extending of our sympathy depends in a great measure upon our sense of his present condition. It is a great effort of imagination, to form such lively ideas even of the present sentiments of others as to feel these very sentiments; but it is impossible we could extend this sympathy to the future, without being aided by some circumstance in the present, which strikes upon us in a lively manner. When the present misery of another has any strong influence upon me, the vivacity of the conception is not confined merely to its immediate object, but diffuses its influence over all the related ideas, and gives me a lively notion of all the circumstances of that person, whether past, present, or future; possible, probable or certain. By means of this lively notion I am interested in them; take part with them; and feel a sympathetic motion in my breast, conformable to whatever I imagine in his. If I diminish the vivacity of the first conception, I diminish that of the related ideas; as pipes can convey no more water than what arises at the fountain. By this diminution I destroy the future prospect, which is necessary to interest me perfectly in the fortune of another. I may feel the present impression, but carry my sympathy no farther, and never transfuse the force of the first conception into my ideas of the related objects. If it be another's misery, which is presented in this feeble manner, I receive it by communication, and am affected with all the passions related to it: but as I am not so much interested as to concern myself in his good fortune, as well as his bad, I never feel the extensive sympathy, nor the passions related to *it*.

Now in order to know what passions are related to these different kinds of sympathy, we must consider, that benevolence is an original pleasure arising from the pleasure of the person beloved, and a pain proceeding from his pain: from which correspondence of impressions there arises a subsequent desire of his pleasure, and aversion to his pain. In order, then, to make a passion run parallel with benevolence, it is requisite we should feel these double impressions, correspondent to those of the person, whom we consider; nor is any one of them alone sufficient for that purpose. When we sympathize only with one impression, and that a painful one, this sympathy is related to anger and to hatred, upon account of the uneasiness it conveys to us. But as the extensive or limited sympathy depends upon the force of the first sympathy; it follows, that the passion of love or hatred depends upon the same principle. A strong impression, when communicated, gives a double tendency of the passions; which is related to benevolence and love by a similarity of direction; however painful the first impression might have been. A weak impression, that is painful, is related to anger and hatred by the resemblance of sensations. Benevolence, therefore, arises from a great degree of misery, or any degree strongly sympathized with: hatred or contempt from a small degree, or one weakly sympathized with; which is the principle I intended to prove and explain.

Nor have we only our reason to trust to for this principle, but also experience. A certain degree of poverty produces contempt; but a degree beyond causes compassion and good-will. We may under-value a peasant or servant; but when the misery of a beggar appears very great, or is painted in very lively colours, we sympathize with him in his afflictions; and feel in our heart evident touches of pity and benevolence. The same object causes contrary passions according to its different degrees. The passions, therefore, must depend upon principles, that operate in such certain degrees, according to my hypothesis. The increase of the sympathy has evidently the same effect as the increase of the misery.

A barren or desolate country always seems ugly and disagreeable, and commonly inspires us with contempt for the inhabitants. This deformity, however, proceeds in a great measure from a sympathy with the inhabitants, as has been already observed; but it is only a weak one, and reaches no farther than the immediate sensation, which is disagreeable. The view of a city in ashes conveys benevolent sentiments; because we there enter so deep into the interests of the miserable inhabitants, as to wish for their prosperity, as well as feel their adversity.

But though the force of the impression generally produces pity and benevolence, it is certain, that by being carried too far it ceases to have that effect. This, perhaps, may be worth our notice. When the uneasiness is either small in itself, or remote from us, it engages not the imagination, nor is able to convey an equal concern for the future and contingent good, as for the present and real evil. Upon its acquiring greater force, we become so interested in the concerns of the person, as to be sensible both of his good and had fortune; and from that compleat sympathy there arises pity and benevolence. But it will easily be imagined, that where the present evil strikes with more than ordinary force, it may entirely engage our attention, and prevent that double sympathy, above-mentioned. Thus we find, that though every one, but especially women, are apt to contract a kindness for criminals, who go to the scaffold, and readily imagine them to be uncommonly handsome and well-shaped; yet one, who is present at the cruel execution of the rack, feels no such tender emotions; but is in a manner overcome with horror, and has no leisure to temper this uneasy sensation by any opposite sympathy.

But the instance, which makes the most clearly for my hypothesis, is that wherein by a change of the objects we separate the double sympathy even from a middling degree of the passion; in which case we find, that pity, instead of producing love and tenderness as usual, always gives rise to the contrary affection. When we observe a person in misfortunes, we are affected with pity and love; but the author of that misfortune becomes the object of our strongest hatred, and is the more detested in proportion to the degree of our compassion. Now for what reason should the same passion of pity produce love to the person, who suffers the misfortune, and hatred to the person, who causes it; unless it be because in the latter case the author bears a relation only to the misfortune; whereas in considering the sufferer we carry our view on every side, and wish for his prosperity, as well as are sensible of his affliction?

I shall just observe, before I leave the present subject, that this phenomenon of the double sympathy, and its tendency to cause love, may contribute to the production of the kindness, which we naturally bear our relations and acquaintance. Custom and relation make us enter deeply into the sentiments of others; and whatever fortune we suppose to attend them, is rendered present to us by the imagination, and operates as if originally our own. We rejoice in their pleasures, and grieve for their sorrows, merely from the force of sympathy. Nothing that concerns them is indifferent to us; and as this correspondence of sentiments is the natural attendant of love, it readily produces that affection.

SECTION TEN
Of respect and contempt

There now remains only to explain the passions of *respect* and *contempt*, along with the *amorous* affection, in order to understand all the passions which have any mixture of love or hatred. Let us begin with respect and contempt.

In considering the qualities and circumstances of others, we may either regard them as they really are in themselves; or may make a comparison betwixt them and our own qualities and circumstances; or may join these two methods of consideration. The good qualities of others, from the first point of view, produce love; from the second, humility; and from the third, respect; which is a mixture of these two passions. Their bad qualities, after the same manner, cause either hatred, or pride, or contempt, according to the light in which we survey them.

That there is a mixture of pride in contempt, and of humility in respect, is, I think, too evident, from their very feeling or appearance, to require any particular proof. That this mixture arises from a tacit comparison of the person contemned or respected with ourselves is no less evident. The same man may cause either respect, love, or contempt by his condition and talents, according as the person, who considers him, from his inferior becomes his equal or superior. In changing the point of view, though the object may remain the same, its proportion to ourselves entirely alters; which is the cause of an alteration in the passions. These passions, therefore, arise from our observing the proportion; that is, from a comparison.

I have already observed, that the mind has a much stronger propensity to pride than to humility, and have endeavoured, from the principles of human nature, to assign a cause for this phenomenon. Whether my reasoning be received or not, the phenomenon is undisputed, and appears in many instances. Among the rest, it is the reason why there is a much greater mixture of pride in contempt, than of humility in respect, and why we are more elevated with the view of one below us, than mortified with the presence of one above us. Contempt or scorn has so strong a tincture of pride, that there scarce is any other passion discernable: whereas in esteem or respect, love makes a more considerable ingredient than humility. The passion of vanity is so prompt, that it rouses at the least call; while humility requires a stronger impulse to make it exert itself.

But here it may reasonably be asked, why this mixture takes place only in some cases, and appears not on every occasion. All those objects, which cause love, when placed on another person, are the causes of pride, when transferred to ourselves; and consequently ought to be causes of humility, as well as love, while they belong to others, and are only compared to those, which we ourselves possess. In like manner every quality, which, by being directly considered, produces hatred, ought always to give rise to pride by comparison, and by a mixture of these passions of hatred and pride ought to excite contempt or scorn. The difficulty then is, why any objects ever cause pure love or hatred, and produce not always the mixed passions of respect and contempt.

I have supposed all along, that the passions of love and pride, and those of humility and hatred are similar in their sensations, and that the two former are always agreeable, and the two latter painful. But though this be universally true, it is observable, that the two agreeable, as well as the two painful passions, have some difference, and even contrarieties, which distinguish them. Nothing invigorates and exalts the mind equally with pride and vanity; though at the same time love or tenderness is rather found to weaken and enfeeble it. The same difference is observable betwixt the uneasy passions. Anger and hatred bestow a new force on all our thoughts and actions; while humility and shame deject and discourage us. Of these qualities of the passions, it will be necessary to form a distinct idea. Let us remember, that pride and hatred invigorate the soul; and love and humility enfeeble it.

From this it follows, that though the conformity betwixt love and pride in the agreeableness of their sensation makes them always be excited by the same objects, yet this other contrariety is the reason, why they are excited in very different degrees. Genius and learning are pleasant and magnificent objects, and by both these circumstances are adapted to pride and vanity; but have a relation to love by their pleasure only. Ignorance and simplicity are *disagreeable* and *mean*, which in the same manner gives them a double connexion with humility, and a single one with hatred. We may, therefore, consider it as certain, that though the same object always produces love and pride, humility and hatred, according to its different situations, yet it seldom produces either the two former or the two latter passions, in the same proportion.

It is here we must seek for a solution of the difficulty above-mentioned, why any object ever excites pure love or hatred, and does not always produce respect or contempt, by a mixture of humility or pride. No quality in another gives rise to humility by comparison, unless it would have produced pride by being placed in ourselves; and *vice versa* no object excites pride by comparison, unless it would have produced humility by the direct survey. This is evident, objects always produce by *comparison* a sensation directly contrary to their *original* one. Suppose, therefore, an object to be presented, which is peculiarly fitted to produce love, but imperfectly to excite pride; this object, belonging to another, gives rise directly to a great degree of love, but to a small one of humility by comparison; and consequently that latter passion is scarce felt in the compound, nor is able to convert the love into respect. This is the case with good nature, good humour, facility, generosity, beauty, and many other qualities. These have a peculiar aptitude to produce love in others; but not so great a tendency to excite pride in ourselves: for which reason the view of them, as belonging to another person, produces pure love, with but a small mixture of humility and respect. It is easy to extend the same reasoning to the opposite passions.

Before we leave this subject, it may not be amiss to account for a pretty curious phenomenon, *viz*, why we commonly keep at a distance such as we contemn, and allow not our inferiors to approach too near even in place and situation. It has already been observed, that almost every kind of idea is attended with some emotion, even the ideas of number and extension, much more those of such objects as are esteemed of consequence in life, and fix our attention. It is not with entire indifference we can survey either a rich man or a poor one, but must feel some faint touches at least, of respect in the former case, and of contempt in the latter. These two passions are contrary to each other; but in order to make this contrariety be felt, the objects must be someway related; otherwise the affections are totally separate and distinct, and never encounter. The relation takes place wherever the persons become contiguous; which is a general reason why we are uneasy at seeing such disproportioned objects, as a rich man and a poor one, a nobleman and a porter, in that situation.

This uneasiness, which is common to every spectator, must be more sensible to the superior; and that because the near approach of the inferior is regarded as a piece of ill-breeding, and shews that he is not sensible of the disproportion, and is no way affected by it. A sense of superiority in another breeds in all men an inclination to keep themselves at a distance from him, and determines them to redouble the marks of respect and reverence, when they are obliged to approach him; and where they do not observe that conduct, it is a proof they are not sensible of his superiority. From hence too it proceeds, that any great *difference* in the degrees of any quality is called a *distance* by a common metaphor, which, however trivial it may appear, is founded on natural principles of the imagination. A great difference inclines us to produce a distance. The ideas of distance and difference are, therefore, connected together. Connected ideas are readily taken for each other; and this is in general the source of the metaphor, as we shall have occasion to observe afterwards.

SECTION ELEVEN

Of the amorous passion, or love between the sexes

Of all the compound passions, which proceed from a mixture of love and hatred with other affections, no one better deserves our attention, than that love, which arises betwixt the sexes, as well on account of its force and violence, as those curious principles of philosophy, for which it affords us an uncontestable argument. It is plain, that this affection, in its most natural state, is derived from the conjunction of three different impressions or passions, *viz.* The pleasing sensation arising from beauty; the bodily appetite for generation; and a generous kindness or good-will. The origin of kindness from beauty may be explained from the foregoing reasoning. The question is how the bodily appetite is excited by it.

The appetite of generation, when confined to a certain degree, is evidently of the pleasant kind, and has a strong connexion with all the agreeable emotions. Joy, mirth, vanity, and kindness are all incentives to this desire; as well as music, dancing, wine, and good cheer. On the other hand, sorrow, melancholy, poverty, humility are destructive of it. From this quality it is easily conceived why it should be connected with the sense of beauty.

But there is another principle that contributes to the same effect. I have observed that the parallel direction of the desires is a real relation, and no less than a resemblance in their sensation, produces a connexion among them. That we may fully comprehend the extent of this relation, we must consider, that any principal desire may be attended with subordinate ones, which are connected with it, and to which if other desires are parallel, they are by that means related to the principal one. Thus hunger may oft be considered as the primary inclination of the soul, and the desire of approaching the meat as the secondary one; since it is absolutely necessary to the satisfying that appetite. If an object, therefore, by any separate qualities, inclines us to approach the meat, it naturally increases our appetite; as on the contrary, whatever inclines us to set our victuals at a distance, is contradictory to hunger, and diminishes our inclination to them. Now it is plain that beauty has the first effect, and deformity the second: which is the reason why the former gives us a keener appetite for our victuals, and the latter is sufficient to disgust us at the most savoury dish that cookery has invented. All this is easily applicable to the appetite for generation.

From these two relations, *viz*, resemblance and a parallel desire, there arises such a connexion betwixt the sense of beauty, the bodily appetite, and benevolence, that they become in a manner inseparable: and we find from experience that it is indifferent which of them advances first; since any of them is almost sure to be attended with the related affections. One, who is inflamed with lust, feels at least a momentary kindness towards the object of it, and at the same time fancies her more beautiful than ordinary; as there are many, who begin with kindness and esteem for the wit and merit of the person, and advance from that to the other passions. But the most common species of love is that which first arises from beauty, and afterwards diffuses itself into kindness and into the bodily appetite. Kindness or esteem, and the appetite to generation, are too remote to unite easily together. The one is, perhaps, the most refined passion of the soul; the other the most gross and vulgar. The love of beauty is placed in a just medium betwixt them, and partakes of both their natures: from whence it proceeds, that it is so singularly fitted to produce both.

This account of love is not peculiar to my system, but is unavoidable on any hypothesis. The three affections, which compose this passion, are evidently distinct, and have each of them its distinct object. It is certain, therefore, that it is only by their relation they produce each other. But the relation of passions is not alone sufficient. It is likewise necessary, there should be a relation of ideas. The beauty of one person never inspires us with love for another. This then is a sensible proof of the double relation of impressions and ideas. From one instance so evident as this we may form a judgment of the rest.

This may also serve in another view to illustrate what I have insisted on concerning the origin of pride and humility, love and hatred. I have observed, that though self be the object of the first set of passions, and some other person of the second, yet these objects cannot alone be the causes of the passions; as having each of them a relation to two contrary affections, which must from the very first moment destroy each other. Here then is the situation of the mind, as I have already described it. It has certain organs naturally fitted to produce a passion; that passion, when produced, naturally turns the view to a certain object. But this not being sufficient to produce the passion, there is required some other emotion, which by a double relation of impressions and ideas may set these principles in action, and bestow on them their first impulse. This situation is still more remarkable with regard to the appetite of generation. Sex is not only the object, but also the cause of the appetite. We not only turn our view to it, when actuated by that appetite; but the reflecting on it suffices to excite the appetite. But as this cause loses its force by too great frequency, it is necessary it should be quickened by some new impulse; and that impulse we find to arise from the *beauty* of the *person*; that is, from a double relation of impressions and ideas. Since this double relation is necessary where an affection has both a distinct cause, and object, how much more so, where it has only a distinct object, without any determinate cause?

SECTION TWELVE

Of the love and hatred of animals

But to pass from the passions of love and hatred, and from their mixtures and compositions, as they appear m man, to the same affections, as they display themselves in brutes; we may observe, not only that love and hatred are common to the whole sensitive creation, but likewise that their causes, as above-explained, are of so simple a nature, that they may easily be supposed to operate on mere animals. There is no force of reflection or penetration required. Every thing is conducted by springs and principles, which are not peculiar to man, or any one species of animals. The conclusion from this is obvious in favour of the foregoing system.

Love in animals, has not for its only object animals of the same species, but extends itself farther, and comprehends almost every sensible and thinking being. A dog naturally loves a man above his own species, and very commonly meets with a return of affection.

As animals are but little susceptible either of the pleasures or pains of the imagination, they can judge of objects only by the sensible good or evil, which they produce, and from *that* must regulate their affections towards them. Accordingly we find, that by benefits or injuries we produce their love or hatred; and that by feeding and cherishing any animal, we quickly acquire his affections; as by beating and abusing him we never fail to draw on us his enmity and ill-will.

Love in beasts is not caused so much by relation, as in our species; and that because their thoughts are not so active as to trace relations, except in very obvious instances. Yet it is easy to remark, that on some occasions it has a considerable influence upon them. Thus acquaintance, which has the same effect as relation, always produces love in animals either to men or to each other. For the same reason any likeness among them is the source of affection. An ox confined to a park with horses, will naturally join their company, if I may so speak, but always leaves it to enjoy that of his own species, where he has the choice of both.

The affection of parents to their young proceeds from a peculiar instinct in animals, as well as in our species.

It is evident, that *sympathy*, or the communication of passions, takes place among animals, no less than among men. Fear, anger, courage, and other affections are frequently communicated from one animal to another, without their knowledge of that cause, which produced the original passion. Grief likewise is received by sympathy; and produces almost all the same consequences, and excites the same emotions as in our species. The howlings and lamentations of a dog produce a sensible concern in his fellows. And it is remarkable, that though almost all animals use in play the same member, and nearly the same action as in fighting; a lion, a tyger, a cat their paws; an ox his horns; a dog his teeth; a horse his heels: yet they most carefully avoid harming their companion, even though they have nothing to fear from his resentment; which is an evident proof of the sense brutes have of each other's pain and pleasure.

Every one has observed how much more dogs are animated when they hunt in a pack, than when they pursue their game apart; and it is evident this can proceed from nothing but from sympathy. It is also well known to hunters, that this effect follows in a greater degree, and even in too great a degree, where two packs, that are strangers to each other, are joined together. We might, perhaps, be at a loss to explain this phenomenon, if we had not experience of a similar in ourselves.

Envy and malice are passions very remarkable in animals. They are perhaps more common than pity; as requiring less effort of thought and imagination.

PART THREE

Of the Will and Direct Passions

SECTION ONE

Of liberty and necessity

We come now to explain the *direct* passions, or the impressions, which arise immediately from good or evil, from pain or pleasure. Of this kind are, *desire and aversion, grief and joy, hope and fear.*

Of all the immediate effects of pain and pleasure, there is none more remarkable than the WILL; and though properly speaking, it be not comprehended among the passions, yet as the full understanding of its nature and properties, is necessary to the explanation of them, we shall here make it the subject of our enquiry. I desire it may be observed, that by the will, I mean nothing but *the internal impression we feel and are conscious of, when we knowingly give rise to any new motion of our body, or new perception of our mind.* This impression, like the preceding ones of pride and humility, love and hatred, it is impossible to define, and needless to describe any farther; for which reason we shall cut off all those definitions and distinctions, with which philosophers are wont to perplex rather than clear up this question; and entering at first upon the subject, shall examine that long disputed question concerning *liberty and necessity*; which occurs so naturally in treating of the will.

It is universally acknowledged, that the operations of external bodies are necessary, and that in the communication of their motion, in their attraction, and mutual cohesion, there are not the least traces of indifference or liberty. Every object is determined by an absolute fate to a certain degree and direction of irs motion, and can no more depart from that precise line, in which it moves, than it can convert itself into an angel, or spirit, or any superior substance. The actions, therefore, of matter are to be regarded as instances of necessary actions; and whatever is in this respect on the same footing with matter, must be acknowledged to be necessary. That we may know whether this be the case with the actions of the mind, we shall begin with examining matter, and considering on what the idea of a necessity in its operations are founded, and why we conclude one body or action to be the infallible cause of another.

It has been observed already, that in no single instance the ultimate connexion of any objects is discoverable, either by our senses or reason, and that we can never penetrate so far into the essence and construction of bodies, as to perceive the principle, on which their mutual influence depends. It is their constant union alone, with which we are acquainted; and it is from the constant union the necessity arises. If objects had not an uniform and regular conjunction with each other, we should never arrive at any idea of cause and effect; and even after all, the necessity, which enters into that idea, is nothing but a determination of the mind to pass from one object to its usual attendant, and infer the existence of one from that of the other. Here then are two particulars, which we are to consider as essential to necessity, *viz*, the constant *union* and the *inference* of the mind; and wherever we discover these we must acknowledge a necessity. As the actions of matter have no necessity, but what is derived from these circumstances, and it is not by any insight into the essence of bodies we discover their connexion, the absence of this insight, while the union and inference remain, will never, in any case, remove the necessity. It is the observation of the union, which produces the inference; for which reason it might be thought sufficient, if we prove a constant union in the actions of the mind, in order to establish the inference, along with the necessity of these actions. But that I may bestow a greater force on my reasoning, I shall examine these particulars apart, and shall first prove from experience that our actions have a constant union with our motives, tempers, and circumstances, before I consider the inferences we draw from it.

To this end a very slight and general view of the common course of human affairs will be sufficient. There is no light, in which we can take them, that does nor confirm this principle.

Whether we consider mankind according to the difference of sexes, ages, governments, conditions, or methods of education; the same uniformity and regular operation of natural principles are discernible. Like causes still produce like effects; in the same manner as in the mutual action of the elements and powers of nature.

There are different trees, which regularly produce fruit, whose relish is different from each other; and this regularity will be admitted as an instance of necessity and causes in external bodies. But are the products of *Guienne* and of *Champagne* more regularly different than the sentiments, actions, and passions of the two sexes, of which the one are distinguished by their force and maturity, the other by their delicacy and softness?

Are the changes of our body from infancy to old age more regular and certain than those of our mind and conduct? And would a man be more ridiculous, who would expect that an infant of four years old will raise a weight of three hundred pound, than one, who from a person of the same age would look for a philosophical reasoning, or a prudent and well-concerted action?

We must certainly allow, that the cohesion of the parts of matter arises from natural and necessary principles, whatever difficulty we may find in explaining them: and for a like reason we must allow, that human society is founded on like principles; and our reason in the latter case, is better than even that in the former; because we not only observe, that men *always* seek society, but can also explain the principles, on which this universal propensity is founded. For is it more certain, that two flat pieces of marble will unite together, than that two young savages of different sexes will copulate? Do the children arise from this copulation more uniformly, than does the parents' care for their safety and preservation? And after they have arrived at years of discretion by the care of their parents, are the inconveniencies attending their separation more certain than their foresight of these inconveniencies and their care of avoiding them by a close union and confederacy?

The skin, pores, muscles, and nerves of a day-labourer are different from those of a man of quality: so are his sentiments, actions and manners. The different stations of life influence the whole fabric, external and internal; and these different stations arise necessarily, because uniformly, from the necessary and uniform principles of human nature. Men cannot live without society, and cannot be associated without government. Government makes a distinction of property, and establishes the different ranks of men. This produces industry, traffic, manufactures, law-suits, war, leagues, alliances, voyages, travels, cities, fleets, ports, and all those other actions and objects, which cause such a diversity, and at the same time maintain such an uniformity in human life.

Should a traveller, returning from a far country, tell us, that he had seen a climate in the fiftieth degree of northern latitude, where all the fruits ripen and come to perfection in the winter, and decay in the summer, after the same manner as in *England* they are produced and decay in the contrary seasons, he would find few so credulous as to believe him. I am apt to think a travellar would meet with as little credit, who should inform us of people exactly of the same character with those in *Plato's Republic* on the one hand, or those in *Hobbes's Leviathan* on the other. There is a general course of nature in human actions, as well as in the operations of the sun and the climate. There are also characters peculiar to different nations and particular persons, as well as common to mankind. The knowledge of these characters is founded on the observation of an uniformity in the actions, that flow from them; and this uniformity forms the very essence of necessity.

I can imagine only one way of eluding this argument, which is by denying that uniformity of human actions, on which it is founded. As long as actions have a constant union and connexion with the situation and temper of the agent, however we may in words refuse to acknowledge the necessity, we really allow the thing. Now some may, perhaps, find a pretext to deny this regular union and connexion. For what is more capricious than human actions? What more inconstant than the desires of man? And what creature departs more widely, not only from right reason, but from his own character and disposition? An hour, a moment is sufficient to make him change from one extreme to another, and overturn what cost the greatest pain and labour to establish. Necessity is regular and certain. Human conduct is irregular and uncertain. The one, therefore, proceeds not from the other.

To this I reply, that in judging of the actions of men we must proceed upon the same maxims, as when we reason concerning

external objects. When any phenomena are constantly and invariably conjoined together, they acquire such a connexion in the
imagination, that it passes from one to the other, without any doubt
or hesitation. But below this there are many inferior degrees of
evidence and probability, nor does one single contrariety of experiment entirely destroy all our reasoning. The mind balances
the contrary experiments, and deducting the inferior from the
superior, proceeds with that degree of assurance or evidence, which
remains. Even when these contrary experiments are entirely equal,
we remove not the notion of causes and necessity; but supposing
that the usual contrariety proceeds from the operation of contrary
and concealed causes, we conclude, that the chance or indifference
lies only in our judgment on account of our imperfect knowledge,
not in the things themselves, which are in every case equally
necessary, though to appearance not equally constant or certain. No
union can be more constant and certain, than that of some actions
with some motives and characters; and if in other cases the union is
uncertain, it is no more than what happens in the operations of
body, nor can we conclude any thing from the one irregularity,
which will not follow equally from the other.

It is commonly allowed that mad-men have no liberty. But
were we to judge by their actions, these have less regularity and
constancy than the actions of wise-men, and consequently are
farther removed from necessity. Our way of thinking in this
particular is, therefore, absolutely inconsistent; but is a natural
consequence of these confused ideas and undefined terms, which
we so commonly make use of in our reasonings, especially on the
present subject.

We must now shew, that as the *union* betwixt motives and actions
has the same constancy, as that in any natural operations, so its
influence on the understanding is also the same, in *determining* us
to infer the existence of one from that of another. If this shall
appear, there is no known circumstance, that enters into the
connexion and production of the actions of matter, that is not to be
found in all the operations of the mind; and consequently we
cannot, without a manifest absurdity, attribute necessity to the one,
and refuse into the other.

There is no philosopher, whose judgment is so riveted to this
fantastical system of liberty, as not to acknowledge the force of

moral evidence, and both in speculation and practice proceed upon it, as upon a reasonable foundation. Now moral evidence is nothing but a conclusion concerning the actions of men, derived from the consideration of their motives, temper and situation. Thus when we see certain characters or figures described upon paper, we infer that the person, who produced them, would affirm such facts, the death of *Caesar*, the success of *Augustus*, the cruelty of *Nero*; and remembering many other concurrent testimonies we conclude, that those facts were once really existent, and that so many men, without any interest, would never conspire to deceive us; especially since they must, in the attempt, expose themselves to the derision of all their contemporaries, when these facts were asserted to be recent and universally known. The same kind of reasoning runs through politics, war, commerce, economy, and indeed mixes itself so entirely in human life, that it is impossible to act or subsist a moment without having recourse to it. A prince, who imposes a tax upon his subjects, expects their compliance. A general, who conducts an army, makes account of a certain degree of courage. A merchant looks for fidelity and skill in his factor or super-cargo. A man, who gives orders for his dinner, doubts not of the obedience of his servants. In short, as nothing more nearly interests us than our own actions and those of others, the greatest part of our reasonings is employed in judgments concerning them. Now I assert, that whoever reasons after this manner, does *ipso facto* believe the actions of the will to arise from necessity, and that he knows not what he means, when he denies it.

All those objects, of which we call the one *cause* and the other *effect*, considered in themselves, are as distinct and separate from each other, as any two things in nature, nor can we ever, by the most accurate survey of them, infer the existence of the one from that of the other. It is only from experience and the observation of their constant union, that we are able to form this inference; and even after all, the inference is nothing but the effects of custom on the imagination. We must not here be content with saying, that the idea of cause and effect arises from objects constantly united; but must affirm, that it is the very same with the idea of those objects, and that the *necessary connexion* is not discovered by a conclusion of the understanding, but is merely a perception of the mind. Wherever, therefore, we observe the same union, and wherever the union operates in the same manner upon the belief and opinion, we have the idea of causes and necessity, though perhaps we may avoid those expressions. Motion in one body in all past instances, that have fallen under our observation, is followed upon impulse by motion in another. It is impossible for the mind to penetrate farther. From this constant union it *forms* the idea of cause and effect, and by its influence *feels* the necessity. As there is the same constancy, and the same influence in what we call moral evidence, I ask no more. What remains can only be a dispute of words.

And indeed, when we consider how aptly *natural* and *moral* evidence cement together, and form only one chain of argument betwixt them, we shall make no scruple to allow, that they are of the same nature, and derived from the same principles. A prisoner, who has neither money nor interest, discovers the impossibility of his escape, as well from the obstinacy of the goaler, as from the walls and bars with which he is surrounded; and in all attempts for his freedom chooses rather to work upon the stone and iron of the one, than upon the inflexible nature of the other. The same prisoner, when conducted to the scaffold, foresees his death as certainly from the constancy and fidelity of his guards as from the operation of the axe or wheel. His mind runs along a certain train of ideas: the refusal of the soldiers to consent to his escape, the action of the executioner; the separation of the head and body; bleeding, convulsive motions, and death. Here is a connected chain of natural causes and voluntary actions; but the mind feels no difference betwixt them in passing from one link to another; nor is less certain of the future event than if it were connected with the present impressions of the memory and senses by a train of causes cemented together by what we are pleased to call a *physical necessity*. The same experienced union has the same effect on the mind, whether the united objects be motives, volitions and actions; or figure and motion. We may change the names of things; but their nature and their operation on the understanding never change.

I dare be positive no one will ever endeavour to refute these reasonings otherwise than by altering my definitions, and assigning a different meaning to the terms of *cause, and effect, and necessity, and liberty, and chance*. According to my definitions, necessity makes an essential part of causation; and consequently liberty, by removing necessity, removes also causes, and is the very same thing with chance. As chance is commonly thought to imply a contradiction, and is at least directly contrary to experience, there are always the same arguments against liberty or free-will. If any one alters the definitions, I cannot pretend to argue with him, until I know the meaning he assigns to these terms.

SECTION TWO

The same subject continued

I believe we may assign the three following reasons for the prevalance of the doctrine of liberty, however absurd it may be in one sense, and unintelligible in any other. First, After we have performed any action; though we confess we were influenced by particular views and motives; it is difficult for us to persuade ourselves we were governed by necessity, and that it was utterly impossible for us to have acted otherwise; the idea of necessity seeming to imply something of force, and violence, and constraint, of which we are not sensible. Few are capable of distinguishing betwixt the liberty of *spontaneity*, as it is called in the schools, and the liberty of *indifference*; betwixt that which is opposed to violence, and that which means a negation of necessity and causes. The first is even the most common sense of the word; and as it is only that species of liberty, which it concerns us to preserve, our thoughts have been principally turned towards it, and have almost universally confounded it with the other.

Secondly, There is a *false sensation or experience* even of the liberty of indifference; which is regarded as an argument for its real existence. The necessity of any action, whether of matter or of the mind, is not properly a quality in the agent, but in any thinking or intelligent being, who may consider the action, and consists in the determination of his thought to infer its existence from some preceding objects: as liberty or chance, on the other hand, is nothing but the want of that determination, and a certain looseness, which we feel in passing or not passing from the idea of one to that of the other. Now we may observe, that though in reflecting on human actions we seldom feel such a looseness or indifference, yet it very commonly happens, that in performing the actions themselves we are sensible of something like it: and as all related or resembling objects are readily taken for each other, this has been employed as a demonstrative or even an intuitive proof of human liberty. We feel that our actions are subject to our will on most occasions, and imagine we feel that the will itself is subject to nothing; because when by a denial of it we are provoked to try, we feel that it moves easily every way, and produces an image of itself even on that side, on which it did not settle. This image or faint motion, we persuade ourselves, could have been compleated into the thing itself; because, should that be denied, we find, upon a second trial, that it can. But these efforts are all in vain; and whatever capricious and irregular actions we may perform; as the desire of showing our liberty is the sole motive of our actions; we can never free ourselves from the bonds of necessity. We may imagine we feel a liberty within ourselves; but a spectator can commonly infer our actions from our motives and character; and even where he cannot, he concludes in general, that he might, were he perfectly acquainted with every circumstance of our situation and temper, and the most secret springs of our complexion and disposition. Now this is the very essence of necessity, according to the foregoing doctrine.

A third reason why the doctrine of liberty has generally been better received in the world, than its antagonist, proceeds from *religion*, which has been very unnecessarily interested in this question. There is no method of reasoning more common, and yet none more blameable, than in philosophical debates to endeavour to refute any hypothesis by a pretext of its dangerous consequences to religion and morality. When any opinion leads us into absurdities, it is certainly false; but it is not certain an opinion is false, because it is of dangerous consequence. Such topics, therefore, ought entirely to be forborne, as serving nothing to the discovery of truth, but only to make the person of an antagonist odious. This I observe in general, without pretending to draw any advantage from it. I submit myself frankly to an examination of this kind, and dare venture to affirm, that the doctrine of necessity, according to my explication of it, is not only innocent, but even advantageous to religion and morality.

I define necessity two ways, conformable to the two definitions of *cause*, of which it makes an essential part. I place it either in the constant union and conjunction of like objects, or in the inference of the mind from the one to the other. Now necessity, in both these senses, has universally, though tacitly, in the schools, in the pulpit, and in common life, been allowed to belong to the will of man, and no one has ever pretended to deny, that we can draw inferences concerning human actions, and that those inferences are founded on the experienced union of like actions with like motives and circumstances. The only particular in which any one can differ from me, is either, that perhaps he will refuse to call this necessity. But as long as the meaning is understood, I hope the word can do no harm. Or that he will maintain there is something else in the operations of matter. Now whether it be so or not is of no consequence to religion, whatever it may be to natural philosophy. I may be mistaken in asserting, that we have no idea of any other connexion in the actions of body, and shall be glad to be farther instructed on that head: but sure I am, I ascribe nothing to the actions of the mind, but what must readily be allowed of. Let no one, therefore, put an invidious construction on my words, by saying simply, that I assert the necessity of human actions, and place them on the same footing with the operations of senseless matter. I do not ascribe to the will that unintelligible necessity, which is supposed to lie in matter. But I ascribe to matter, that intelligible quality, call it necessity or not, which the most rigorous orthodoxy does or must allow to belong to the will. I change, therefore, nothing in the received systems, with regard to the will, but only with regard to material objects.

Nay I shall go farther, and assert, that this kind of necessity is so essential to religion and morality, that without it there must ensue an absolute subversion of both, and that every other supposition is entirely destructive to all laws both *divine* and *human*. It is indeed certain, that as all human laws are founded on rewards and punishments, it is supposed as a fundamental principle, that these motives have an influence on the mind, and both produce the good and prevent the evil actions. We may give to this influence what name we please; but as it is usually conjoined with the action, common sense requires it should be esteemed a cause, and be looked upon as an instance of that necessity, which I would establish.

This reasoning is equally solid, when applied to *divine* laws, so far as the deity is considered as a legislator, and is supposed to inflict punishment and bestow rewards with a design to produce obedience. But I also maintain, that even where he acts not in his magisterial capacity, but is regarded as the avenger of crimes merely on account of their odiousness and deformity, not only it is impossible, without the necessary connexion of cause and effect in human actions, that punishments could be inflicted compatible with justice and moral equity; but also that it could ever enter into the thoughts of any reasonable being to inflict them. The constant and universal object of hatred or anger is a person or creature endowed with thought and consciousness; and when any criminal or injurious actions excite that passion, it is only by their relation to the person or connexion with him. But according to the doctrine of liberty or chance, this connexion is reduced to nothing, nor are men more accountable for those actions, which are designed and premeditated, than for such as are the most casual and accidental. Actions are by their very nature temporary and perishing; and where they proceed not from some cause in the characters and disposition of the person, who performed them, they infix not themselves upon him, and can neither redound to his honour, if good, nor infamy, if evil. The action itself may be blameable; it may be contrary to all the rules of morality and religion: but the person is not responsible for it; and as it proceeded from nothing in him, that is durable or constant, and leaves nothing of that nature behind it, it is impossible he can, upon its account, become the object of punishment or vengeance. According to the hypothesis of liberty, therefore, a man is as pure and untainted, after having committed the most horrid crimes, as at the first moment of his birth, nor is his character any way concerned in his actions; since they are not derived from it, and the wickedness of the one can never be used as a proof of the depravity of the other. It is only upon the principles of necessity, that a person acquires any merit or demerit from his actions, however the common opinion may incline to the contrary.

But so inconsistent are men with themselves, that though they often assert, that necessity utterly destroys all merit and demerit either towards mankind or superior powers, yet they continue still to reason upon these very principles of necessity in all their judgments concerning this matter. Men are not blamed for such evil actions as they perform ignorantly and casually, whatever may be their consequences. Why? but because the causes of these actions are only momentary, and terminate in them alone. Men are less blamed for such evil actions, as they perform hastily and unpremeditately, than for such as proceed from thought and deliberation. For what reason? but because a hasty temper, though a constant cause in the mind, operates only by intervals, and infects not the whole character. Again, repentance wipes off every crime, especially if attended with an evident reformation of life and manners. How is this to be accounted for? but by asserting that actions render a person criminal, merely as they are proofs of criminal passions or principles in the mind; and when by any alteration of these principles they cease to be just proofs, they likewise cease to be criminal. But according to the doctrine of *liberty* or *chance* they never were just proofs, and consequently never were criminal.

Here then I turn to my adversary, and desire him to free his own system from these odious consequences before he charge them upon others. Or if he rather chooses, that this question should be decided by fair arguments before philosophers, than by declamations before the people, let him return to what I have advanced to prove that liberty and chance are synonimous; and concerning the nature of moral evidence and the regularity of human actions. Upon a review of these reasonings, I cannot doubt of an entire victory; and therefore having proved, that all actions of the will have particular causes, I proceed to explain what these causes are, and how they operate.

SECTION THREE

Of the influencing motives of the will

Nothing is more usual in philosophy, and even in common life, than to talk of the combat of passion and reason, to give the preference to reason, and assert that men are only so far virtuous as they conform themselves to its dictates. Every rational creature, it is said, is obliged to regulate his actions by reason; and if any other motive or principle challenge the direction of his conduct, he ought to oppose it, till it be entirely subdued, or at least brought to a conformity with that superior principle. On this method of thinking the greatest part of moral philosophy, ancient and modern, seems to be founded; nor is there an ampler field, as well for metaphysical arguments, as popular declamations, than this supposed pre-eminence of reason above passion. The eternity, invariableness, and divine origin of the former have been displayed to the best advantage: the blindness, unconstancy, and deceitfulness of the latter have been as strongly insisted on. In order to shew the fallacy of all this philosophy, I shall endeavour to prove *first*, that reason alone can never be a motive to any action of the will; and *secondly*, that it can never oppose passion in the direction of the will.

The understanding exerts itself after two different ways, as it judges from demonstration or probability; as it regards the abstract relations of our ideas, or those relations of objects, of which experience only gives us information. I believe it scarce will be asserted, that the first species of reasoning alone is ever the cause of any action. As its proper province is the world of ideas, and as the will always places us in that of realities, demonstration and volition seem, upon that account, to be totally removed from each other. Mathematics, indeed, are useful in all mechanical operations, and arithmetic in almost every art and profession: but it is not of themselves they have any influence: mechanics are the art of regulating the motions of bodies *to some designed end or purpose*; and the reason why we employ arithmetic in fixing the proportions of numbers, is only that we may discover the proportions of their influence and operation. A merchant is desirous of knowing the sum total of his accounts with any person. Why? but that he may learn what sum will have the same *effects* in paying his debt, and going to market, as all the particular articles taken together. Abstract or demonstrative reasoning, therefore, never influences any of our actions, but only as it directs our judgment concerning causes and effects; which leads us to the second operation of the understanding.

It is obvious, that when we have the prospect of pain or pleasure from any object, we feel a consequent emotion of aversion or propensity, and are carried to avoid or embrace what will give us this uneasiness or satisfaction. It is also obvious, that this emotion rests not here, but making us cast our view on every side, comprehends whatever objects are connected with its original one by the relation of cause and effect. Here then reasoning takes place to discover this relation; and according as our reasoning varies, our actions receive a subsequent variation. But it is evident in this case that the impulse arises not from reason, but is only directed by it. It is from the prospect of pain or pleasure that the aversion or propensity arises towards any object: and these emotions extend themselves to the causes and effects of that object, as they are pointed out to us by reason and experience. It can never in the least concern us to know, that such objects are causes, and such others effects, if both the causes and effects be indifferent to us. Where the objects themselves do not affect us, their connexion can never give them any influence; and it is plain, that as reason is nothing but the discovery of this connexion, it cannot be by its means that the objects are able to affect us.

Since reason alone can never produce any action, or give rise to volition, I infer, that the same faculty is as incapable of preventing volition, or of disputing the preference with any passion or emotion. This consequence is necessary. It is impossible reason could have the latter effect of preventing volition, but by giving an impulse in a contrary direction to our passion; and that impulse, had it operated alone, would have been able to produce volition. Nothing can oppose or retard the impulse of passion, but a contrary impulse; and if this contrary impulse ever arises from reason, that latter faculty must have an original influence on the will, and must be able to cause, as well as hinder any act of volition. But if reason has no original influence, it is impossible it can withstand any principle, which has such an efficacy, or ever keep the mind in suspense a moment. Thus it appears, that the principle, which opposes our passion, cannot be the same with reason, and is only called so in an improper sense. We speak not strictly and philosophically when we talk of the combat of passion and of reason. Reason is, and ought only to be the slave of the passions, and can never pretend to any other office than to serve and obey them. As this opinion may appear somewhat extraordinary, it may not be improper to confirm it by some other considerations.

A passion is an original existence, or, if you will, modification of existence, and contains not any representative quality, which renders it a copy of any other existence or modification. When I am angry, I am actually possessed with the passion, and in that emotion have no more a reference to any other object, than when I am thirsty, or sick, or more than five foot high. It is impossible, therefore, that this passion can be opposed by, or be contradictory to truth and reason; since this contradiction consists in the disagreement of ideas, considered as copies, with those objects, which they represent.

What may at first occur on this head, is, that as nothing can be contrary to truth or reason, except what has a reference to it, and as the judgments of our understanding only have this reference, it must follow, that passions can be contrary to reason only so far as they are *accompanied* with some judgment or opinion. According to this principle, which is so obvious and natural, it is only in two senses, that any affection can be called unreasonable. First, When a passion, such as hope or fear, grief or joy, despair or security, is founded on the supposition or the existence of objects, which really do not exist. Secondly, When in exerting any passion in action, we choose means insufficient for the designed end, and deceive ourselves in our judgment of causes and effects. Where a passion is neither founded on false suppositions, nor chooses means insufficient for the end, the understanding can neither justify nor condemn it. It is not contrary to reason to prefer the destruction of the whole world to the scratching of my finger. It is not contrary to reason for me to choose my total ruin, to prevent the least uneasiness of an *Indian* or person wholly unknown to me. It is as little contrary to reason to prefer even my own acknowledged lesser good to my greater, and have a more ardent affection for the former than the latter. A trivial good may, from certain circumstances, produce a desire superior to what arises from the greatest and most valuable enjoyment; nor is there any thing more extraordinary in this, than in mechanics to see one pound weight raise up a hundred by the advantage of its situation. In short, a passion must be accompanied with some false judgment in order to its being unreasonable; and even then it is not the passion, properly speaking, which is unreasonable, but the judgment.

The consequences are evident. Since a passion can never, in any sense, be called unreasonable, but when founded on a false supposition or when it chooses means insufficient for the designed end, it is impossible, that reason and passion can ever oppose each other, or dispute for the government of the will and actions. The moment we perceive the falsehood of any supposition, or the insufficiency of any means our passions yield to our reason without any opposition. I may desire any fruit as of an excellent relish; but whenever you convince me of my mistake, my longing ceases. I may will the performance of certain actions as means of obtaining any desired good; but as my willing of these actions is only secondary, and founded on the supposition, that they are causes of the proposed effect; as soon as I discover the falsehood of that supposition, they must become indifferent to me.

It is natural for one, that does not examine objects with a strict philosophic eye, to imagine, that those actions of the mind are entirely the same, which produce not a different sensation, and are not immediately distinguishable to the feeling and perception. Reason, for instance, exerts itself without producing any sensible emotion; and except in the more sublime disquisitions of philosophy, or in the frivolous subtilties of the school, scarce ever conveys any pleasure or uneasiness. Hence it proceeds, that every action of the mind, which operates with the same calmness and tranquillity, is confounded with reason by all those, who judge of things from the first view and appearance. Now it is certain, there are certain calm desires and tendencies, which, though they be real passions, produce little emotion in the mind, and are more known by their effects than by the immediate feeling or sensation. These desires are of two kinds; either certain instincts originally implanted in our natures, such as benevolence and resentment, the love of life, and kindness to children; or the general appetite to good, and aversion to evil, considered merely as such. When any of these passions are calm, and cause no disorder in the soul, they are very readily taken for the determinations of reason, and are supposed to proceed from the same faculty, with that, which judges of truth and falshood. Their nature and principles have been supposed the same, because their sensations are not evidently different.

Beside these calm passions, which often determine the will, there are certain violent emotions of the same kind, which have likewise a great influence on that faculty. When I receive any injury from another, I often feel a violent passion of resentment, which makes me desire his evil and punishment, independent of all considerations of pleasure and advantage to myself. When I am immediately threatened with any grievous ill, my fears, apprehensions, and aversions rise to a great height, and produce a sensible emotion.

The common error of metaphysicians has lain in ascribing the direction of the will entirely to one of these principles, and supposing the other to have no influence. Men often act knowingly against their interest: for which reason the view of the greatest possible good does not always influence them. Men often counteract a violent passion in prosecution of their interests and designs: it is not therefore the present uneasiness alone, which determines them. In general we may observe, that both these principles operate on the will; and where they are contrary, that either of them prevails, according to the *general* character or *present* disposition of the person. What we call strength of mind, implies the prevalence of the calm passions above the violent; though we may easily observe, there is no man so constantly possessed of this virtue, as never on any occasion to yield to the sollicitations of passion and desire. From these variations of temper proceeds the great difficulty of deciding concerning the actions and resolutions of men, where there is any contrariety of motives and passions.

SECTION FOUR

Of the causes of the violent passions

There is not in philosophy a subject of more nice speculation than this of the different *causes* and *effects* of the calm and violent passions. It is evident passions influence not the will in proportion to their violence, or the disorder they occasion in the temper; but on the contrary, that when a passion has once become a settled principle of action, and is the predominant inclination of the soul, it commonly produces no longer any sensible agitation. As repeated custom and its own force have made every thing yield to it, it directs the actions and conduct without that opposition and emotion, which so naturally attend every momentary gust of passion. We must, therefore, distinguish betwixt a calm and a weak passion; betwixt a violent and a strong one. But notwithstanding this, it is certain, that when we would govern a man, and push him to any action, it will commonly be better policy to work upon the violent than the calm passions, and rather take him by his inclination, than what is vulgarly called his reason. We ought to place the object in such particular situations as are proper to increase the violence of the passion. For we may observe, that all depends upon the situation of the object, and that a variation in this particular will be able to change the calm and the violent passions into each other. Both these kinds of passions pursue good, and avoid evil; and both of them are increased or diminished by the increase or diminution of the good or evil. But herein lies the difference betwixt them: the same good, when near, will cause a violent passion, which, when remote, produces only a calm one. As this subject belongs very properly to the present question concerning the will, we shall here examine it to the bottom, and shall consider some of those circumstances and situations of objects, which render a passion either calm or violent.

It is a remarkable property of human nature, that any emotion, which attends a passion, is easily converted into it, though in their natures they be originally different from, and even contrary to each other. It is true; in order to make a perfect union among passions, there is always required a double relation of impressions and ideas; nor is one relation sufficient for that purpose. But though this be confirmed by undoubted experience, we must understand it with its proper limitations, and must regard the double relation, as requisite only to make one passion produce another. When two passions are already produced by their separate causes, and are both present in the mind, they readily mingle and unite, though they have but one relation, and sometimes without any. The predominant passion swallows up the inferior, and converts it into itself. The spirits, when once excited, easily receive a change in their direction; and it is natural to imagine this change will come from the prevailing affection. The connexion is in many respects closer betwixt any two passions, than betwixt any passion and indifference.

When a person is once heartily in love, the little faults and caprices of his mistress, the jealousies and quarrels, to which that commerce is so subject; however unpleasant and related to anger and hatred; are yet found to give additional force to the prevailing passion. It is a common artifice of politicians, when they would affect any person very much by a matter of fact, of which they intend to inform him, first to excite his curiosity; delay as long as possible the satisfying it; and by that means raise his anxiety and impatience to the utmost, before they give him a full insight into the business. They know that his curiosity will precipitate him into the passion they design to raise, and assist the object in its influence on the mind. A soldier advancing to the battle, is naturally inspired with courage and confidence, when he thinks on his friends and fellow-soldiers; and is struck with fear and terror, when he reflects on the enemy. Whatever new emotion, therefore, proceeds from the former naturally increases the courage; as the same emotion, proceeding from the latter, augments the fear; by the relation of ideas, and the conversion of the inferior emotion into the predominant. Hence it is that in martial discipline, the uniformity and lustre of our habit, the regularity of our figures and motions, with all the pomp and majesty of war, encourage ourselves and allies; while the same objects in the enemy strike terror into us, though agreeable and beautiful in themselves.

Since passions, however independent, are naturally transfused into each other, if they are both present at the same time; it follows, that when good or evil is placed in such a situation, as to cause any particular emotion, beside its direct passion of desire or aversion, that latter passion must acquire new force and violence.

This happens, among other cases, whenever any object excites contrary passions. For it is observable that an opposition of passions commonly causes a new emotion in the spirits, and produces more disorder, than the concurrence of any two affections of equal force. This new emotion is easily converted into the predominant passion, and increases its violence, beyond the pitch it would have arrived at had it met with no opposition. Hence we naturally desire what is forbid, and take a pleasure in performing actions, merely because they are unlawful. The notion of duty, when opposite to the passions, is seldom able to overcome them; and when it fails of that effect, is apt rather to increase them, by producing an opposition in our motives and principles.

The same effect follows whether the opposition arises from internal motives or external obstacles. The passion commonly acquires new force and violence in both cases. The efforts, which the mind makes to surmount the obstacle, excite the spirits and enliven the passion.

Uncertainty has the same influence as opposition. The agitation of the thought; the quick turns it makes from one view to another; the variety of passions, which succeed each other, according to the different views; all these produce an agitation in the mind, and transfuse themselves into the predominant passion.

There is not in my opinion any other natural cause, why security diminishes the passions, than because it removes that uncertainty, which increases them. The mind, when left to itself, immediately languishes; and in order to preserve its ardour, must be every moment supported by a new flow of passion. For the same reason, despair, though contrary to security, has a like influence.

It is certain nothing more powerfully animates any affection, than to conceal some part of its object by throwing it into a kind of shade, which at the same time that it shews enough to pre-possess us in favour of the object, leaves still some work for the imagination. Besides that obscurity is always attended with a kind of uncertainty; the effort, which the fancy makes to compleat the idea, rouses the spirits, and gives an additional force to the passion.

As despair and security, though contrary to each other, produce the same effects; so absence is observed to have contrary effects, and in different circumstances either increases or diminishes our affections. The *Duc de La Rochefoucault* has very well observed, that absence destroys weak passions, but increases strong; as the wind extinguishes a candle, but blows up a fire. Long absence naturally weakens our idea, and diminishes the passion: but where the idea is so strong and lively as to support itself, the uneasiness, arising from absence, increases the passion and gives it new force and violence.

SECTION FIVE

Of the effects of custom

But nothing has a greater effect both to increase and diminish our passions, to convert pleasure into pain, and pain into pleasure, than custom and repetition. Custom has two *original* effects upon the mind, in bestowing a *facility* in the performance of any action or the conception of any object; and afterwards a *tendency or inclination* towards it; and from these we may account for all its other effects, however extraordinary.

When the soul applies itself to the performance of any action, or the conception of any object, to which it is not accustomed, there is a certain unpliableness in the faculties, and a difficulty of the spirit's moving in their new direction. As this difficulty excites the spirits, it is the source of wonder, surprize, and of all the emotions, which arise from novelty; and is in itself very agreeable, like every thing, which enlivens the mind to a moderate degree. But though surprize be agreeable in itself, yet as it puts the spirits in agitation, it not only augments our agreeable affections, but also our painful, according to the foregoing principle, *that every emotion, which precedes or attends a passion, is easily converted into it.* Hence every thing, that is new, is most affecting, and gives us either more pleasure or pain, than what, strictly speaking, naturally belongs to it. When it often returns upon us, the novelty wears off; the passions subside; the hurry of the spirits is over; and we survey the objects with greater tranquillity.

By degrees the repetition produces a facility of the human mind, and an infallible source of pleasure, where the facility goes not beyond a certain degree. And here it is remarkable that the pleasure, which arises from a moderate facility, has not the same tendency with that which arises from novelty, to augment the painful, as well as the agreeable affections. The pleasure of facility does not so much consist in any ferment of the spirits, as in their orderly motion; which will sometimes be so powerful as even to convert pain into pleasure, and give us a relish in time for what at first was most harsh and disagreeable.

But again, as facility converts pain into pleasure, so it often converts pleasure into pain, when it is too great, and renders the actions of the mind so faint and languid, that they are no longer able to interest and support it. And indeed, scarce any other objects become disagreeable through custom; but such as are naturally attended with some emotion or affection, which is destroyed by the too frequent repetition. One can consider the clouds, and heavens, and trees, and stones, however frequently repeated, without ever feeling any aversion. But when the fair sex, or music, or good cheer, or any thing, that naturally ought to be agreeable, becomes indifferent, it easily produces the opposite affection.

But custom not only gives a facility to perform any action, but likewise an inclination and tendency towards it, where it is not entirely disagreeable, and can never be the object of inclination. And this is the reason why custom increases all *active* habits, but diminishes *passive*, according to the observation of a late eminent philosopher. The facility takes off from the force of the passive habits by rendering the motion of the spirits faint and languid. But as in the active, the spirits are sufficiently supported of themselves, the tendency of the mind gives them new force, and bends them more strongly to the action.

SECTION SIX

Of the influence of the imagination on the passions

It is remarkable, that the imagination and affections have close union together, and that nothing, which affects the former, can be entirely indifferent to the latter. Wherever our ideas of good or evil acquire a new vivacity, the passions become more violent; and keep pace with the imagination in all its variations. Whether this proceeds from the principle above-mentioned, *that any attendant emotion is easily converted into the predominant*, I shall not determine. It is sufficient for my present purpose, that we have many instances to confirm this influence of the imagination upon the passions.

Any pleasure, with which we are acquainted, affects us more than any other, which we own to be superior, but of whose nature we are wholly ignorant. Of the one we can form a particular and determinate idea: the other we conceive under the general notion of pleasure; and it is certain, that the more general and universal any of our ideas are, the less influence they have upon the imagination. A general idea, though it be nothing but a particular one considered in a certain view, is commonly more obscure; and that because no particular idea, by which we represent a general one, is ever fixed or determinate, but may easily be changed for other particular ones, which will serve equally in the representation.

There is a noted passage in the history of *Greece*, which may serve for our present purpose. *Themistocles* told the *Athenians*, that he had formed a design, which would be highly useful to the public, but which it was impossible for him to communicate to them without ruining the execution, since its success depended entirely on the secrecy with which it should be conducted. The *Athenians*, instead of granting him full power to act as he thought fitting, ordered him to communicate his design to *Aristides*, in whose prudence they had an entire confidence, and whose opinion they were resolved blindly to submit to. The design of *Themistocles* was secretly to set fire to the fleet of all the *Grecian* commonwealths, which was assembled in a neighbouring port, and which being once destroyed would give the *Athenians* the empire of the sea without any rival. *Aristides* returned to the assembly, and told them, that nothing could be more advantageous than the design of *Themistocles* but at the same time that nothing could be more unjust: upon which the people unanimously rejected the project.

A late celebrated historian* admires this passage of ancient history, as one of the most singular that is any where to be met.

Here, says he, *they are not philosophers, to whom it is easy in their schools to establish the finest maxims and most sublime rules of morality, who decide that interest ought never to prevail above justice. It is a whole people interested in the proposal which is made to them, who consider it as of importance to the public good, and who notwithstanding reject it unanimously, and without hesitation, merely because it is contrary to justice.* For my part I see nothing so extraordinary in this proceeding of the *Athenians*. The same reasons, which render it so easy for philosophers to establish these sublime maxims, tend, in part, to diminish the merit of such a conduct in that people. Philosophers never balance betwixt profit and honesty, because their decisions are general, and neither their passions nor imaginations are interested in the objects. And though in the present case the advantage was immediate to the *Athenians*, yet as it was known only under the general notion of advantage, without being conceived by any particular idea, it must have had a less considerable influence on their imaginations, and have been a less violent temptation, than if they had been acquainted with all its circumstances: otherwise it is difficult to conceive, that a whole people, unjust and violent as men commonly are, should so unanimously have adhered to justice, and rejected any considerable advantage.

Any satisfaction, which we lately enjoyed, and of which the memory is fresh and recent, operates on the will with more violence, than another of which the traces are decayed, and

* Mons. *Rollin.*

almost obliterated. From whence does this proceed, but that the memory in the first case assists the fancy and gives an additional force and vigour to its conceptions? The image of the past pleasure being strong and violent, bestows these qualities on the idea of the future pleasure, which is connected with it by the relation of resemblance.

A pleasure, which is suitable to the way of life, in which we are engaged, excites more our desires and appetites than another, which is foreign to it. This phenomenon may be explained from the same principle.

Nothing is more capable of infusing any passion into the mind, than eloquence, by which objects are represented in their strongest and most lively colours. We may of ourselves acknowledge, that such an object is valuable, and such another odious; but until an orator excites the imagination, and gives force to these ideas, they may have but a feeble influence either on the will or the affections.

But eloquence is not always necessary. The bare opinion of another, especially when inforced with passion, will cause an idea of good or evil to have an influence upon us, which would otherwise have been entirely neglected. This proceeds from the principle of sympathy or communication; and sympathy, as I have already observed, is nothing but the conversion of an idea into an impression by the force of imagination.

It is remarkable, that lively passions commonly attend a lively imagination. In this respect, as well as others, the force of the passion depends as much on the temper of the person, as the nature or situation of the object.

I have already observed, that belief is nothing but a lively idea related to a present impression. This vivacity is a requisite circumstance to the exciting all our passions, the calm as well as the violent; nor has a mere fiction of the imagination any considerable influence upon either of them. It is too weak to take hold of the mind, or be attended with emotion.

SECTION SEVEN
Of contiguity, and distance in space and time

There is an easy reason, why every thing contiguous to us, either in space or time, should be conceived with a peculiar force and vivacity, and excel every other object, in its influence on the imagination. Ourself is intimately present to us, and whatever is related to self must partake of that quality. But where an object is so far removed as to have lost the advantage of this relation, why, as it is farther removed, its idea becomes still fainter and more obscure, would, perhaps, require a more particular examination.

It is obvious, that the imagination can never totally forget the points of space and time, in which we are existent; but receives such frequent advertisements of them from the passions and senses, that however it may turn its attention to foreign and remote objects, it is necessitated every moment to reflect on the present. It is also remarkable, that in the conception of those objects, which we regard as real and existent, we take them in their proper order and situation, and never leap from one object to another, which is distant from it, without running over, at least in a cursory manner, all those objects, which are interposed betwixt them. When we reflect, therefore, on any object distant from ourselves, we are obliged not only to reach it at first by passing through all the intermediate space betwixt ourselves and the object, but also to renew our progress every moment; being every moment recalled to the consideration of ourselves and our present situation. It is easily conceived, that this interruption must weaken the idea by breaking the action of the mind, and hindering the conception from being so intense and continued, as when we reflect on a nearer object. The *fewer* steps we make to arrive at the object, and the *smoother* the road is, this diminution of vivacity is less sensibly felt, but still may be observed more or less in proportion to the degrees of distance and difficulty.

Here then we are to consider two kinds of objects, the contiguous and remote; of which the former, by means of their relation to ourselves, approach an impression in force and vivacity; the latter by reason of the interruption in our manner of conceiving them, appear in a weaker and more imperfect light. This is their effect on the imagination. If my reasoning be just, they must have a proportionable effect on the will and passions. Contiguous objects must have an influence much superior to the distant and remote. Accordingly we find in common life, that men are principally concerned about those objects, which are not much removed either in space or time, enjoying the present, and leaving what is afar off to the care of chance and fortune. Talk to a man of his condition thirty years hence, and he will not regard you. Speak of what is to happen tomorrow, and he will lend you attention. The breaking of a mirror gives us more concern when at home, than the burning of a house, when abroad, and some hundred leagues distant.

But farther; though distance both in space and time has a considerable effect on the imagination, and by that means on the will and passions, yet the consequence of a removal in *space* are much inferior to those of a removal in *time*. Twenty years are certainly but a small distance of time in comparison of what history and even the memory of some may inform them of, and yet I doubt if a thousand leagues, or even the greatest distance of place this globe can admit of, will so remarkably weaken our ideas, and diminish our passions. A *West-India* merchant will tell you, that he is not without concern about what passes in *Jamaica*; though few extend their views so far into futurity, as to dread very remote accidents.

The cause of this phenomenon must evidently lie in the different properties of space and time. Without having recourse to metaphysics, any one may easily observe, that space or extension consists of a number of co-existent parts disposed in a certain order, and capable of being at once present to the sight or feeling. On the contrary, time or succession, though it consists likewise of parts, never presents to us more than one at once; nor is it possible for any two of them ever to be co-existent. These qualities of the objects have a suitable effect on the imagination. The parts of extension being susceptible of an union to the senses, acquire an union in the fancy; and as the appearance of one part excludes not another, the transition or passage of the thought through the contiguous parts is by that means rendered more smooth and easy. On the other hand, the incompatibility of the parts of time in their real existence separates them in the imagination, and makes it more *difficult* for that faculty to trace any long succession or series of events. Every part must appear single and alone, nor can regularly have entrance into the fancy without banishing what is supposed to have been immediately precedent. By this means any distance in time causes a greater interruption in the thought than an equal distance in space, and consequently weakens more considerably the idea, and consequently the passions; which depend in a great measure, on the imagination, according to my system.

There is another phenomenon of a like nature with the foregoing, *viz, the superior effects of the same distance in futurity above that in the past*. This difference with respect to the will is easily accounted for. As none of our actions can alter the past, it is not strange it should never determine the will. But with respect to the passions the question is yet entire, and well worth the examining.

Besides the propensity to a gradual progression through the points of space and time, we have another peculiarity in our method of thinking, which concurs in producing this phenomenon. We always follow the succession of time in placing our ideas, and from the consideration of any object pass more easily to that, which follows immediately after it, than to that which went before it. We may learn this, among other instances, from the order, which is always observed in historical narrations. Nothing but an absolute necessity can oblige an historian to break the order of time, and in his *narration* give the precedence to an event, which was in *reality* posterior to another.

This will easily be applied to the question in hand, if we reflect on what I have before observed, that the present situation of the person is always that of the imagination, and that it is from thence we proceed to the conception of any distant object. When the object is past, the progression of the thought in passing to it from the present is contrary to nature, as proceeding from one point of time to that which is preceding, and from that to another preceding, in opposition to the natural course of the succession. On the other hand, when we turn our thought to a future object, our fancy flows along the stream of time, and arrives at the object by an order, which seems most natural, passing always from one point of time to that which is immediately posterior to it. This *easy* progression of ideas favours the imagination, and makes it conceive its object in a stronger and fuller light, than when we are continually opposed in our passage, and are obliged to overcome the difficulties arising from the natural propensity of the fancy. A small degree of distance in the past has, therefore, a greater effect, in interupting and weakening the conception, than a much greater in the future. From this effect of it on the imagination is derived its influence on the will and passions.

There is another cause, which both contributes to the same effect, and proceeds from the same quality of the fancy, by which we are determined to trace the succession of time by a similar succession of ideas. When from the present instant we consider two points of time equally distant in the future and in the past, it is evident, that, abstractedly considered, their relation to the present is almost equal. For as the future will *sometime* be present, so the past was *once* present. If we could, therefore, remove this quality of the imagination, an equal distance in the past and in the future, would have a similar influence. Nor is this only true, when the fancy remains fixed, and from the present instant surveys the future and the past; but also when it changes its situation, and places us in different periods of time. For as on the one hand, in supposing ourselves existent in a point of time interposed betwixt the present instant and the future object, we find the future object approach to us, and the past retire, and become more distant: so on the other hand, in supposing ourselves existent in a point of time interposed betwixt the present and the past, the past approaches to us, and the future becomes more distant. But from the property of the fancy above-mentioned we rather choose to fix our thought on the point of time interposed betwixt the present and the future, than on that betwixt the present and the past. We advance, rather than retard our existence; and following what seems the natural succession of time, proceed from past to present, and from present to future. By which means we conceive the future as flowing every moment nearer us, and the past as retiring. An equal distance, therefore, in the past and in the future, has not the same effect on the imagination; and that because we consider the one as continually increasing, and the other as continually diminishing. The fancy anticipates the course of things, and surveys the object in that condition, to which it tends, as well as in that, which is regarded as the present.

SECTION EIGHT
The same subject continued

Thus we have accounted for three phenomena, which seem pretty remarkable. Why distance weakens the conception and passion: Why distance in time has a greater effect than that in space: and Why distance in past time has still a greater effect than that in future. We must now consider three phenomena, which seem to be, in a manner, the reverse of these: Why a very great distance increases our esteem and admiration for an object; Why such a distance in time increases it more than that in space: And a distance in past time more than that in future. The curiousness of the subject will, I hope, excuse my dwelling on it for some time.

To begin with the first phenomenon, why a great distance increases our esteem and admiration for an object; it is evident that the mere view and contemplation of any greatness, whether successive or extended, enlarges the soul, and gives it a sensible delight and pleasure. A wide plain, the ocean, eternity, a succession of several ages; all these are entertaining objects, and excel every thing, however beautiful, which accompanies not its beauty with a suitable greatness. Now when any very distant object is presented to the imagination, we naturally reflect on the interposed distance, and by that means, conceiving something great and magnificent, receive the usual satisfaction. But as the fancy passes easily from one idea to another related to it, and transports to the second all the passions excited by the first, the admiration, which is directed to the distance, naturally diffuses itself over the distant object. Accordingly we find, that it is not necessary the object should be actually distant from us, in order to cause our admiration; but that it is sufficient, if, by the natural association of ideas, it conveys our view to any considerable distance. A great traveller, though in the same chamber, will pass for a very extraordinary person; as a *Greek* medal, even in our cabinet, is always esteemed a valuable curiosity. Here the object, by a natural transition, conveys our views to the distance; and the admiration, which arises from that distance, by another natural transition, returns back to the object.

But though every great distance produces an admiration for the distant object, a distance in time has a more considerable effect than that in space. Ancient busts and inscriptions are more valued than *Japan* tables: and not to mention the *Greeks* and *Romans*, it is certain we regard with more veneration the old *Chaldeans* and *Egyptians*, than the modern *Chinese* and *Persians*, and bestow more fruitless pains to clear up the history and chronology of the former, than it would cost us to make a voyage, and be certainly informed of the character, learning and government of the latter. I shall be obliged to make a digression in order to explain this phenomenon.

It is a quality very observable in human nature, that any opposition, which does not entirely discourage and intimidate us, has rather a contrary effect, and inspires us with a more than ordinary grandeur and magnanimity. In collecting our force to overcome the opposition, we invigorate the soul, and give it an elevation with which otherwise it would never have been acquainted. Compliance, by rendering our strength useless, makes us insensible of it: but opposition awakens and employs it.

This is also true in the universe. Opposition not only enlarges the soul; but the soul, when full of courage and magnanimity, in a manner seeks opposition.

> *Spumantemque dari pecora inter inertia votis*
> *Optat aprum, aut fulvum descendere monte leonem.**

Whatever supports and fills the passions is agreeable to us; as on the contrary, what weakens and enfeebles them is uneasy. As opposition has the first effect, and facility the second, no wonder the mind, in certain dispositions, desires the former, and is averse to the latter.

These principles have an effect on the imagination as well as on the passions. To be convinced of this we need only consider the influence of *heights* and *depths* on that faculty. Any great elevation of place communicates a kind of pride or sublimity of imagination, and gives a fancied superiority over those that lie below; and, *vice versa*, a sublime and strong imagination conveys the idea of ascent and elevation. Hence it proceeds, that we associate, in

[* And, among the passive beasts, he wishes, in his prayers, for a slavering boar, or that a tawny lion should come down from the mountain.]

a manner, the idea of whatever is good with that of height, and evil with lowness. Heaven is supposed to be above, and hell below. A noble genius is called an elevate and sublime one. *Atque udam spernit humum fugiente penna.** On the contrary, a vulgar and trivial conception is styled indifferently low or mean. Prosperity is denominated ascent, and adversity descent. Kings and princes are supposed to be placed at the top of human affairs; as peasants and day-labourers are said to be in the lowest stations. These methods of thinking, and of expressing ourselves, are not of so little consequence as they may appear at first sight.

It is evident to common sense, as well as philosophy, that there is no natural nor essential difference betwixt high and low, and that this distinction arises only from the gravitation of matter, which produces a motion from the one to the other. The very same direction, which in this part of the globe is called *ascent*, is denominated *descent* in our antipodes; which can proceed from nothing but the contrary tendency of bodies. Now it is certain, that the tendency of bodies, continually operating upon our senses, must produce, from custom, a like tendency in the fancy, and that when we consider any object situated in an ascent, the idea of its weight gives us a propensity to transport it from the place, in which it is situated, to the place immediately below it, and so on, until we come to the ground, which equally stops the body and our imagination. For a like reason we feel a difficulty in mounting, and pass not without a kind of reluctance from the inferior to that which is situated above it; as if our ideas acquired a kind of gravity from their objects. As a proof of this, do we not find, that the facility, which is so much studied in music and poetry, is called the fall or cadency of the harmony or period; the idea of facility communicating to us that of descent, in the same manner as descent produces a facility?

Since the imagination, therefore, in running from low to high, finds an opposition in its internal qualities and principles, and since the soul, when elevated with joy and courage, in a manner seeks opposition, and throws itself with alacrity into any scene of thought or action, where its courage meets with matter to nourish and employ it; it follows, that everything, which invigorates and enlivens the soul, whether by touching the passions

[* And spurns the dank soil in winged flight.]

or imagination naturally conveys to the fancy this inclination for ascent, and determines it to run against the natural stream of its thoughts and conceptions. This aspiring progress of the imagination suits the present disposition of the mind; and the difficulty, instead of extinguishing its vigour and alacrity, has the contrary affect, of sustaining and increasing it. Virtue, genius, power, and riches are for this reason associated with height and sublimity; as poverty, slavery, and folly are conjoined with descent and lowness. Were the case the same with us as *Milton* represents it to be with the angels, to whom *descent is adverse*, and who *cannot sink without labour and compulsion*, this order of things would be entirely inverted; as appears hence, that the very nature of ascent and descent is derived from the difficulty and propensity, and consequently every one of their effects proceeds from that origin.

All this is easily applied to the present question, why a considerable distance in time produces a greater veneration for the distant objects than a like removal in space. The imagination moves with more difficulty in passing from one portion of time to another, than in a transition through the parts of space; and that because space or extension appears united to our senses, while time or succession is always broken and divided. This difficulty, when joined with a small distance, interrupts and weakens the fancy: but has a contrary effect in a great removal. The mind, elevated by the vastness of its object, is still farther elevated by the difficulty of the conception; and being obliged every moment to renew its efforts in the transition from one part of time to another, feels a more vigorous and sublime disposition, than in a transition through the parts of space, where the ideas flow along with easiness and facility. In this disposition, the imagination, passing, as is usual, from the consideration of the distance to the view of the distant objects, gives us a proportionable veneration for it; and this is the reason why all the relics of antiquity are so precious in our eyes, and appear more valuable than what is brought even from the remotest parts of the world.

The third phenomenon I have remarked will be a full confirmation of this. It is not every removal in time, which has the effect of producing veneration and esteem. We are not apt to imagine our posterity will excel us, or equal our ancestors. This phenomenon is the more remarkable, because any distance in futurity weakens not our ideas so much as an equal removal in the past. Though a removal in the past, when very great, increases our passions beyond a like removal in the future, yet a small removal has a greater influence in diminishing them.

In our common way of thinking we are placed in a kind of middle station betwixt the past and future; and as our imagination finds a kind of difficulty in running along the former, and a facility in following the course of the latter, the difficulty conveys the notion of ascent, and the facility of the contrary. Hence we imagine our ancestors to be, in a manner, mounted above us, and our posterity to lie below us. Our fancy arrives not at the one without effort, but easily reaches the other: which effort weakens the conception, where the distance is small; but enlarges and elevates the imagination, when attended with a suitable object. As on the other hand, the facility assists the fancy in a small removal, but takes off from its force when it contemplates any considerable distance.

It may not be improper, before we leave this subject of the will, to resume, in a few words, all that has been said concerning it, in order to set the whole more distinctly before the eyes of the reader. What we commonly understand by *passion* is a violent and sensible emotion of mind, when any good or evil is presented, or any object, which, by the original formation of our faculties, is fitted to excite an appetite. By *reason* we mean affections of the very same kind with the former; but such as operate more calmly, and cause no disorder in the temper: which tranquillity leads us into a mistake concerning them, and causes us to regard them as conclusions only of our intellectual faculties. Both the *causes* and *effects* of these violent and calm passions are pretty variable, and depend, in a great measure, on the peculiar temper and disposition of every individual. Generally speaking, the violent passions have a more powerful influence on the will; though it is often found, that the calm ones, when corroborated by reflection, and seconded by resolution, are able to control them in their most furious movements. What makes this whole affair more uncertain, is, that a calm passion may easily be changed into a violent one, either by a change of temper, or of the circumstances and situation of the object, as by the borrowing of force from any attendant passion, by custom, or by exciting the imagination. Upon the whole, this struggle of passion and of reason, as it is called, diversifies human life, and makes men so different not only from each other, but also from themselves in different times. Philosophy can only account for a few of the greater and more sensible events of this war; but must leave all the smaller and more delicate revolutions, as dependent on principles too fine and minute for her comprehension.

SECTION NINE

Of the direct passions

It is easy to observe, that the passions, both direct and indirect, are founded on pain and pleasure, and that in order to produce an affection of any kind, it is only requisite to present some good or evil. Upon the removal of pain and pleasure there immediately follows a removal of love and hatred, pride and humility, desire and aversion, and of most of our reflective or secondary impressions.

The impressions, which arise from good and evil most naturally, and with the least preparation are the *direct* passions of desire and aversion, grief and joy, hope and fear, along with volition. The mind by an *original* instinct tends to unite itself with the good, and to avoid the evil, though they be conceived merely in idea, and be considered as to exist in any future period of time.

But supposing that there is an immediate impression of pain or pleasure, and *that* arising from an object related to ourselves or others, this does not prevent the propensity or aversion, with the consequent emotions, but by concurring with certain dormant principles of the human mind, excites the new impressions of pride or humility, love or hatred. That propensity, which unites us to the object, or separates us from it, still continues to operate, but in conjunction with the *indirect* passions, which arise from a double relation of impressions and ideas.

These indirect passions, being always agreeable or uneasy, give in their turn additional force to the direct passions, and increase our desire and aversion to the object. Thus a suit of fine clothes produces pleasure from their beauty; and this pleasure produces the direct passions, or the impressions of volition and desire. Again, when these clothes are considered as belonging to ourself, the double relation conveys to us the sentiment of pride, which is an indirect passion; and the pleasure, which attends that passion, returns back to the direct affections, and gives new force to our desire or volition, joy or hope.

When good is certain or probable, it produces JOY. When evil is in the same situation there arises GRIEF or SORROW.

When either good or evil is uncertain, it gives rise to FEAR or HOPE, according to the degrees of uncertainty on the one side or the other.

DESIRE arises from good considered simply, and AVERSION is derived from evil. The WILL exerts itself, when either the good or the absence of the evil may be attained by any action of the mind or body.

Beside good and evil, or in other words, pain and pleasure, the direct passions frequently arise from a natural impulse or instinct, which is perfectly unaccountable. Of this kind is the desire of punishment to our enemies, and of happiness to our friends; hunger, lust, and a few other bodily appetites. These passions, properly speaking, produce good and evil, and proceed not from them, like the other affections.

None of the direct affections seem to merit our particular attention, except hope and fear, which we shall here endeavour to account for. It is evident that the very same event, which by its certainty would produce grief or joy, gives always rise to fear or hope, when only probable and uncertain. In order, therefore, to understand the reason why this circumstance makes such a considerable difference, we must reflect on what I have already advanced in the preceding book concerning the nature of probability.

Probability arises from an opposition of contrary chances or causes, by which the mind is not allowed to fix on either side, but is incessantly tossed from one to another, and at one moment is determined to consider an object as existent, and at another moment as the contrary. The imagination or understanding, call it which you please, fluctuates betwixt the opposite views; and though perhaps it may be oftener turned to the one side than the other, it is impossible for it, by reason of the opposition of causes or chances, to rest on either. The *pro* and *con* of the question alternately prevail; and the mind, surveying the object in its opposite principles, finds such a contrariety as utterly destroys all certainty and established opinion.

Suppose, then, that the object, concerning whose reality we are doubtful, is an object either of desire or aversion, it is evident that, according as the mind turns itself either to the one side or the other, it must feel a momentary impression of joy or sorrow. An object, whose existence we desire, gives satisfaction, when we reflect on those causes, which produce it; and for the same reason excites grief or uneasiness from the opposite consideration: so that as the understanding, in all probable questions, is divided betwixt the contrary points of view, the affections must in the same manner be divided betwixt opposite emotions.

Now if we consider the human mind, we shall find, that with regard to the passions, it is not the nature of a wind-instrument of music, which in running over all the notes immediately loses the sound after the breath ceases; but rather resembles a string-instrument, where after each stroke the vibrations still retain some sound, which gradually and insensibly decays. The imagination is extreme quick and agile; but the passions are slow and restive: for which reason, when any object is presented, that affords a variety of views to the one, and emotions to the other; though the fancy may change its views with great celerity; each stroke will not produce a clear and distinct note of passion, but the one passion will always be mixed and confounded with the other. According as the probability inclines to good or evil, the passion of joy or sorrow predominates in the composition: because the nature of probability is to cast a superior number of views or chances on one side; or, which is the same thing, a superior number of returns of one passion; or since the dispersed passions are collected into one, a superior degree of that passion. That is, in other words, the grief and joy being intermingled with each other, by means of the contrary views of the imagination, produce by their union the passions of hope and fear.

Upon this head there may be started a very curious question concerning that contrariety of passions, which is our present subject. It is observable, that where the objects of contrary passions are presented at once, beside the increase of the predominant passion (which has been already explained, and commonly arises at their first shock or rencounter) it sometimes happens, that both the passions exist successively, and by short intervals; sometimes, that they destroy each other, and neither of them takes place; and sometimes that both of them remain united in the mind. It may, therefore, be asked, by what theory we can explain these variations, and to what general principle we can reduce them.

When the contrary passions arise from objects entirely different, they take place alternately, the want of relation in the ideas separating the impressions from each other, and preventing their opposition. Thus when a man is afflicted for the loss of a law-suit, and joyful for the birth of a son, the mind running from the agreeable to the calamitous object, with whatever celerity it may perform this motion, can scarcely temper the one affection with the other, and remain betwixt them in a state of indifference.

It more easily attains that calm situation, when the same event is of a mixed nature, and contains something adverse and something prosperous in its different circumstances. For in that case, both the passions, mingling with each other by means of the relation, become mutually destructive, and leave the mind in perfect tranquillity.

But suppose, in the third place, that the object is not a compound of good or evil, but is considered as probable or improbable in any degree; in that case I assert, that the contrary passions will both of them be present at once in the soul, and instead of destroying and tempering each other, will subsist together, and produce a third impression or affection by their union. Contrary passions are not capable of destroying each other, except when their contrary movements exactly rencounter, and are opposite in their direction, as well as in the sensation they produce. This exact rencounter depends upon the relations of those ideas, from which they are derived, and is more or less perfect, according to the degrees of the relation. In the case of probability the contrary chances are so far related, that they determine concerning the existence or non-existence of the same object. But this relation is far from being perfect; since some of the chances lie on the side of existence, and others on that of non-existence; which are objects altogether incompatible. It is impossible by one steady view to survey the opposite chances, and the events dependent on them;

but it is necessary, that the imagination should run alternately from the one to the other. Each view of the imagination produces its peculiar passion, which decays away by degrees, and is followed by a sensible vibration after the stroke. The incompatibility of the views keeps the passions from shocking in a direct line, if that expression may be allowed; and yet their relation is sufficient to mingle their fainter emotions. It is after this manner that hope and fear arise from the different mixture of these opposite passions of grief and joy, and from their imperfect union and conjunction.

Upon the whole, contrary passions succeed each other alternately, when they arise from different objects: they mutually destroy each other, when they proceed from different parts of the same: and they subsist both of them and mingle together, when they are derived from the contrary and incompatible chances or possibilities, on which any one object depends. The influence of the relations of ideas is plainly seen in this whole affair. If the objects of the contrary passions be totally different, the passions are like two opposite liquors in different bottles, which have no influence on each other. If the objects be intimately connected, the passions are like an alcali and an acid, which, being mingled, destroy each other. If the relation be more imperfect, and consists in the contradictory views of the same object, the passions are like oil and vinegar, which, however mingled, never perfectly unite and incorporate.

As the hypothesis concerning hope and fear carries its own evidence along with it, we shall be the more concise in our proofs. A few strong arguments are better than many weak ones.

The passions of fear and hope may arise when the chances are equal on both sides, and no superiority can be discovered in the one above the other. Nay, in this situation the passions are rather the strongest, as the mind has then the least foundation to rest upon, and is tossed with the greatest uncertainty. Throw in a superior degree of probability to the side of grief, you immediately see that passion diffuse itself over the composition, and tincture it into fear. Increase the probability, and by that means the grief, the fear prevails still more and more, till at last it runs insensibly, as the joy continually diminishes, into pure grief. After you have brought it to this situation, diminish the grief, after the same manner that you increased it, by diminishing the probability on that side, and you'll see the passion clear every moment, until it changes insensibly into hope; which again runs, after the same manner, by slow degrees, into joy, as you increase that part of the composition by the increase of the probability. Are not these as plain proofs, that the passions of fear and hope are mixtures of grief and joy, as in optics it is a proof, that a coloured ray of the sun passing through a prism, is a composition of two others, when, as you diminish or increase the quantity of either, you find it prevail proportionably more or less in the composition? I am sure neither natural nor moral philosophy admits of stronger proofs.

Probability is of two kinds, either when the object is really in itself uncertain, and to be determined by chance; or when, though the object be already certain, yet it is uncertain to our judgment, which finds a number of proofs on each side of the question. Both these kinds of probabilities cause fear and hope; which can only proceed from that property, in which they agree, *viz*, the uncertainty and fluctuation they bestow on the imagination by that contrariety of views, which is common to both.

It is a probable good or evil, that commonly produces hope or fear; because probability, being a wavering and unconstant method of surveying an object, causes naturally a like mixture and uncertainty of passion. But we may observe, that wherever from other causes this mixture can be produced, the passions of fear and hope will arise, even though there be no probability; which must be allowed to be a convincing proof of the present hypothesis. We find that an evil, barely conceived as possible, does sometimes produce fear; especially if the evil be very great. A man cannot think of excessive pains and tortures without trembling, if he be in the least danger of suffering them. The smallness of the probability is compensated by the greatness of the evil; and the sensation is equally lively, as if the evil were more probable. One view or glimpse of the former, has the same effect as several of the latter.

But they are not only possible evils, that cause fear, but even some allowed to be impossible; as when we tremble on the brink of a precipice, though we know ourselves to be in perfect security, and have it in our choice whether we will advance a step farther. This proceeds from the immediate presence of the evil, which influences the imagination in the same manner as the certainty of it would do; but being encountered by the reflection on our security, is immediately retracted, and causes the same kind of passion, as when from a contrariety of chances contrary passions are produced.

Evils, that are *certain*, have sometimes the same effect in producing fear, as the possible or impossible. Thus a man in a strong prison well-guarded, without the least means of escape, trembles at the thought of the rack, to which he is sentenced. This happens only when the certain evil is terrible and confounding; in which case the mind continually rejects it with horror, while it continually presses in upon the thought. The evil is there fixed and established, but the mind cannot endure to fix upon it; from which fluctuation and uncertainty there arises a passion of much the same appearance with fear.

But it is not only where good or evil is uncertain, as to its *existence*, but also as to its kind, that fear or hope arises. Let one be told by a person, whose veracity he cannot doubt of, that one of his sons is suddenly killed, it is evident the passion this event would occasion, would not settle into pure grief, till he got certain information, which of his sons he had lost. Here there is an evil certain, but the kind of it uncertain. Consequently the fear we feel on this occasion is without the least mixture of joy, and arises merely from the fluctuation of the fancy betwixt its objects. And though each side of the question produces here the same passion, yet that passion cannot settle, but receives from the imagination a tremulous and unsteady motion, resembling in its cause, as well as in its sensation, the mixture and contention of grief and joy.

From these principles we may account for a phenomenon in the passions, which at first sight seems very extraordinary, *viz*, that surprize is apt to change into fear, and every thing that is unexpected affrights us. The most obvious conclusion from this is, that human nature is in general pusillanimous; since upon the sudden appearance of any object. we immediately conclude it to be an evil, and without waiting till we can examine its nature, whether it be good or bad, are at first affected with fear. This I say is the most obvious conclusion; but upon farther examination we shall find that the phenomenon is otherwise to be accounted for. The suddenness and strangeness of an appearance naturally excite a commotion in the mind, like every thing for which we are not prepared, and to which we are not accustomed. This commotion, again, naturally produces a curiosity or inquisitiveness, which being very violent, from the strong and sudden impulse of the object, becomes uneasy, and resembles in its fluctuation and uncertainty, the sensation of fear or the mixed passions of grief and joy. This image of fear naturally converts into the thing itself, and gives us a real apprehension of evil, as the mind always forms its judgments more from its present disposition than from the nature of its objects.

Thus all kinds of uncertainty have a strong connexion with fear, even though they do not cause any opposition of passions by the opposite views and considerations they present to us. A person, who has left his friend in any malady, will feel more anxiety upon his account, than if he were present, though perhaps he is not only incapable of giving him assistance, but likewise of judging of the event of his sickness. In this case, though the principal object of the passion, *viz*, the life or death of his friend, be to him equally uncertain when present as when absent; yet there are a thousand little circumstances of his friend's situation and condition, the knowledge of which fixes the idea, and prevents that fluctuation and uncertainty so near allied to fear. Uncertainty is, indeed, in one respect as near allied to hope as to fear, since it makes an essential part in the composition of the former passion; but the reason, why it inclines not to that side, is, that uncertainty alone is uneasy, and has a relation of impressions to the uneasy passions.

It is thus our uncertainty concerning any minute circumstance relating to a person increases our apprehensions of his death or misfortune. *Horace* has remarked this phenomenon.

> *Ut assidens implumibus pullus avis*
> *Serpentium allapsus timet,*
> *Magis relictis; non, ut adsit, auxili*
> *Latura plus pesentibus.**

But this principle of the connexion of fear with uncertainty I carry farther, and observe that any doubt produces that passion, even though it presents nothing to us on any side but what is good and desirable. A virgin, on her bridal-night goes to bed full of fears and apprehensions, though she expects nothing but pleasure of the highest kind, and what she has long wished for. The newness and

[* As a bird, watching over her fledgelings, is more afraid of their being attacked by snakes if she were to leave them even though, were she to stay, she would not be any more capable of helping them, when they were with her.]

greatness of the event, the confusion of wishes and joys so embarrass the mind, that it knows not on what passion to fix itself; from whence arises a fluttering or unsettledness of the spirits which being, in some degree, uneasy, very naturally degenerates into fear.

Thus we still find, that whatever causes any fluctuation or mixture of passions, with any degree of uneasiness, always produces fear, or at least a passion so like it, that they are scarcely to be distinguished.

I have here confined myself to the examination of hope and fear in their most simple and natural situation, without considering all the variations they may receive from the mixture of different views and reflections. *Terror, consternation, astonishment, anxiety*, and other passions of that kind, are nothing but different species and degrees of fear. It is easy to imagine how a different situation of the object, or a different turn of thought, may change even the sensation of a passion; and this may in general account for all the particular sub-divisions of the other affections, as well as of fear. Love may shew itself in the shape of *tenderness, friendship, intimacy, esteem, good-will*, and in many other appearances; which at the bottom are the same affections; and arise from the same causes, though with a small variation, which it is not necessary to give any particular account of. It is for this reason I have all along confined myself to the principal passion.

The same care of avoiding prolixity is the reason why I waive the examination of the will and direct passions, as they appear in animals; since nothing is more evident, than that they are of the same nature, and excited by the same causes as in human creatures. I leave this to the reader's own observation; desiring him at the same time to consider the additional force this bestows on the present system.

SECTION TEN
Of curiosity, or the love of truth

But methinks we have been not a little inattentive to run over so many different parts of the human mind, and examine so many passions, without taking once into the consideration that love of truth, which was the first source of all our enquiries. It will therefore be proper, before we leave this subject, to bestow a few reflections on that passion, and shew its origin in human nature. It is an affection of so peculiar a kind, that it would have been impossible to have treated of it under any of those heads, which we have examined, without danger of obscurity and confusion.

Truth is of two kinds, consisting either in the discovery of the proportions of ideas, considered as such, or in the conformity of our ideas of objects to their real existence. It is certain, that the former species of truth, is not desired merely as truth, and that it is not the justness of our conclusions, which alone gives the pleasure. For these conclusions are equally just, when we discover the equality of two bodies by a pair of compasses, as when we learn it by a mathematical demonstration; and though in the one case the proofs be demonstrative, and in the other only sensible, yet generally speaking, the mind acquiesces with equal assurance in the one as in the other. And in an arithmetical operation, where both the truth and the assurance are of the same nature, as in the most profound algebraical problem, the pleasure is very inconsiderable, if rather it does not degenerate into pain: which is an evident proof, that the satisfaction, which we sometimes receive from the discovery of truth, proceeds not from it, merely as such, but only as endowed with certain qualities.

The first and most considerable circumstance requisite to render truth agreeable, is the genius and capacity, which is employed in its invention and discovery. What is easy and obvious is never valued; and even what is *in itself* difficult, if we come to the knowledge of it without difficulty, and without any stretch of thought or judgment, is but little regarded. We love to trace the demonstrations of mathematicians; but should receive small entertainment from a person, who should barely inform us of the proportions of lines and angles, though we reposed the utmost confidence both in his judgment and veracity. In this case it is sufficient to have ears to learn the truth. We never are obliged to fix our attention or exert our genius; which of all other exercises of the mind is the most pleasant and agreeable.

But though the exercise of genius be the principal source of that satisfaction we receive from the sciences, yet I doubt, if it be alone sufficient to give us any considerable enjoyment. The truth we discover must also be of some importance. It is easy to multiply algebraical problems to infinity, nor is there any end in the discovery of the proportions of conic sections; though few mathematicians take any pleasure in these researches, but turn their thoughts to what is more useful and important. Now the question is, after what manner this utility and importance operate upon us? The difficulty on this head arises from hence, that many philosophers have consumed their time, have destroyed their health, and neglected their fortune, in the search of such truths, as they esteemed important and useful to the world, though it appeared from their whole conduct and behaviour, that they were not endowed with any share of public spirit, nor had any concern for the interests of mankind. Were they convinced, that their discoveries were of no consequence, they would entirely lose all relish for their studies, and that though the consequences be entirely indifferent to them; which seems to be a contradiction.

To remove this contradiction, we must consider, that there are certain desires and inclinations, which go no farther than the imagination, and are rather the faint shadows and images of passions, than any real affections. Thus, suppose a man, who takes a survey of the fortifications of any city; considers their strength and advantages, natural or acquired; observes the disposition and contrivance of the bastions, ramparts, mines, and other military works; it is plain, that in proportion as all these are fitted to attain their ends he will receive a suitable pleasure and satisfaction. This pleasure, as it arises from the utility, not the form of the objects, can be no other than a sympathy with the inhabitants, for whose security all this art is employed; though it is possible, that this person, as a stranger or an enemy, may in his heart have no kindness for them, or may even entertain a hatred against them.

It may indeed be objected, that such a remote sympathy is a very slight foundation for a passion, and that so much industry and application, as we frequently observe in philosophers, can never be derived from so inconsiderable an original. But here I return to what I have already remarked, that the pleasure of study consists chiefly in the action of the mind, and the exercise of the genius and understanding in the discovery or comprehension of any truth. If the importance of the truth be requisite to compleat the pleasure, it is not on account of any considerable addition, which of itself it brings to our enjoyment, but only because it is, in some measure, requisite to fix our attention. When we are careless and inattentive, the same action of the understanding has no effect upon us, nor is able to convey any of that satisfaction, which arises from it, when we are in another disposition.

But beside the action of the mind, which is the principal foundation of the pleasure, there is likewise required a degree of success in the attainment of the end, or the discovery of that truth we examine. Upon this head I shall make a general remark, which may be useful on many occasions, *viz*, that where the mind pursues any end with passion; though that passion be not derived originally from the end, but merely from the action and pursuit; yet by the natural course of the affections, we acquire a concern for the end itself, and are uneasy under any disappointment we meet with in the pursuit of it. This proceeds from the relation and parallel direction of the passions above-mentioned.

To illustrate all this by a similar instance, I shall observe, that there cannot be two passions more nearly resembling each other, than those of hunting and philosophy, whatever disproportion may at first sight appear betwixt them. It is evident, that the pleasure of hunting consists in the action of the mind and body; the motion, the attention, the difficulty, and the uncertainty. It is evident likewise, that these actions must be attended with an idea of utility, in order to their having any effect upon us. A man of the greatest fortune, and the farthest removed from avarice, though he takes a pleasure in hunting after partridges and pheasants, feels no satisfaction in shooting crows and magpies; and that because he considers the first as fit for the table, and the other as entirely useless. Here it is certain, that the utility or importance of itself causes no real passion, but is only requisite to support the imagination; and the same person, who over-looks a ten times greater profit in any other subject, is pleased to bring home half a dozen woodcocks or plovers, after having employed several hours in hunting after them. To make the parallel betwixt hunting and philosophy more complete, we may observe, that though in both cases the end of our action may in itself be despised, yet in the heat of the action we acquire such an attention to this end, that we are very uneasy under any disappointments, and are sorry when we either miss our game, or fall into any error in our reasoning.

If we want another parallel to these affections, we may consider the passion of gaming, which affords a pleasure from the same principles as hunting and philosophy. It has been remarked, that the pleasure of gaming arises not from interest alone; since many leave a sure gain for this entertainment: neither is it derived from the game alone; since the same persons have no satisfaction, when they play for nothing: but proceeds from both these causes united, though separately they have no effect. It is here, as in certain chymical preparations, where the mixture of two clear and transparent liquids produces a third, which is opaque and coloured.

The interest, which we have in any game, engages our attention, without which we can have no enjoyment, either in that or in any other action. Our attention being once engaged, the difficulty, variety, and sudden reverses of fortune, still farther interest us; and it is from that concern our satisfaction arises. Human life is so tiresome a scene, and men generally are of such indolent dispositions, that whatever amuses them, though by a passion mixed with pain, does in the main give them a sensible pleasure. And this pleasure is here increased by the nature of the objects, which being sensible, and of a narrow compass, are entered into with facility, and are agreeable to the imagination.

The same theory, that accounts for the love of truth in mathematics and algebra may be extended to morals, politics, natural philosophy, and other studies, where we consider not the other abstract relations of ideas, but their real connexions and existence. But beside the love of knowledge, which displays itself in the sciences, there is a certain curiosity implanted in human nature, which is a passion derived from a quite different principle. Some people have an insatiable desire of knowing the actions and circumstances of their neighbours, though their interest be no way concerned in them, and they must entirely depend on others for their information; in which case there is no room for study or application. Let us search for the reason of this phenomenon.

It has been proved at large, that the influence of belief is at once to enliven and infix any idea in the imagination, and prevent all kind of hesitation and uncertainty about it. Both these circumstances are advantageous. By the vivacity of the idea we interest the fancy, and produce, though in a lesser degree, the same pleasure, which arises from a moderate passion. As the vivacity of the idea gives pleasure, so its certainty prevents uneasiness, by fixing one particular idea in the mind, and keeping it from wavering in the choice of its objects. It is a quality of human nature, which is conspicuous on many occasions, and is common both to the mind and body, that too sudden and violent a change is unpleasant to us, and that however any objects may in themselves be indifferent, yet their alteration gives uneasiness. As it is the nature of doubt to cause a variation in the thought, and transport us suddenly from one idea to another, it must of consequence be the occasion of pain. This pain chiefly takes place, where interest, relation, or the greatness and novelty of any event interests us in it. It is not every matter of fact, of which we have a curiosity to be informed; neither are they such only as we have an interest to know. It is sufficient if the idea strikes on us with such force, and concerns us so nearly, as to give us an uneasiness in its instability and inconstancy. A stranger, when he arrives first at any town, may be entirely indifferent about knowing the history and adventures of the inhabitants; but as he becomes farther acquainted with them, and has lived any considerable time among them, he acquires the same curiosity as the natives. When we are reading the history of a nation, we may have an ardent desire of clearing up any doubt or difficulty, that occurs in it; but become careless in such researches, when the ideas of these events are, in a great measure, obliterated.

ADVERTISEMENT

I think it proper to inform the public, that though this be a third volume of the *Treatise of Human Nature*, yet it is in some measure independent of the other two, and requires not that the reader should enter into all the abstract reasonings contained in them. I am hopeful it may be understood by ordinary readers, with as little attention as is usually given to any books of reasoning. It must only be observed, that I continue to make use of the terms, *impressions* and *ideas*, in the same sense as formerly; and that by impressions I mean our stronger perceptions, such as our sensations, affections and sentiments; and by ideas the fainter perceptions, or the copies of these in the memory and imagination.

BOOK THREE

OF MORALS

PART ONE

Of Virtue and Vice in general

SECTION ONE

Moral distinctions not derived from reason

There is an inconvenience which attends all abstruse reasoning, that it may silence, without convincing an antagonist, and requires the same intense study to make us sensible of its force, that was at first requisite for its invention. When we leave our closet, and engage in the common affairs of life, its conclusions seem to vanish, like the phantoms of the night on the appearance of the morning; and it is difficult for us to retain even that conviction, which we had attained with difficulty. This is still more conspicuous in a long chain of reasoning, where we must preserve to the end the evidence of the first propositions, and where we often lose sight of all the most received maxims, either of philosophy or common life. I am not, however, without hopes, that the present system of philosophy will acquire new force as it advances; and that our reasonings concerning *morals* will corroborate whatever has been said concerning the *understanding* and the *passions*. Morality is a subject that interests us above all others: we fancy the peace of society to be at stake in every decision concerning it; and it is evident, that this concern must make our speculations appear more real and solid, than where the subject is, in a great measure, indifferent to us. What affects us, we conclude can never be a chimera; and as our passion is engaged on the one side or the other, we naturally think that the question lies within human comprehension; which, in other cases of this nature, we are apt to entertain some doubt of. Without this advantage I never should have ventured upon a third volume of such abstruse philosophy, in an age, wherein the greatest part of men seem agreed to convert reading into an amusement, and to reject every thing that requires any considerable degree of attention to be comprehended.

It has been observed, that nothing is ever present to the mind but its perceptions; and that all the actions of seeing, hearing, judging, loving, hating, and thinking, fall under this denomination. The mind can never exert itself in any action, which we may not comprehend under the term of *perception*; and consequently that term is no less applicable to those judgments, by which we distinguish moral good and evil, than to every other operation of the mind. To approve of one character, to condemn another, are only so many different perceptions.

Now as perceptions resolve themselves into two kinds, *viz.* *impressions* and *ideas*, this distinction gives rise to a question, with which we shall open up our present enquiry concerning morals. *Whether it is by means of our* ideas *or* impressions *we distinguish betwixt vice and virtue, and pronounce an action blameable or praiseworthy*? This will immediately cut off all loose discourses and declamations, and reduce us to something precise and exact on the present subject.

Those who affirm that virtue is nothing but a conformity to reason; that there are eternal fitnesses and unfitnesses of things, which are the same to every rational being that considers them; that the immutable measures of right and wrong impose an obligation, not only on human creatures, but also on the Deity himself: all these systems concur in the opinion, that morality, like truth, is discerned merely by ideas, and by their juxta-position and comparison. In order, therefore, to judge of these systems, we need only consider, whether it be possible, from reason alone, to distinguish betwixt moral good and evil, or whether there must concur some other principles to enable us to make that distinction.

If morality had naturally no influence on human passions and actions, it were in vain to take such pains to inculcate it; and nothing would be more fruitless than that multitude of rules and precepts, with which all moralists abound. Philosophy is commonly divided into *speculative* and *practical*; and as morality is always comprehended under the latter division, it is supposed to influence our passions and actions, and to go beyond the calm and indolent judgments of the understanding. And this is confirmed by common experience, which informs us, that men are often governed by their duties, and are detered from some actions by the opinion of injustice, and impelled to others by that of obligation.

Since morals, therefore, have an influence on the actions and affections, it follows, that they cannot be derived from reason; and that because reason alone, as we have already proved, can never have any such influence. Morals excite passions, and produce or prevent actions. Reason of itself is utterly impotent in this particular. The rules of morality therefore, are not conclusions of our reason.

No one, I believe, will deny the justness of this inference; nor is there any other means of evading it, than by denying that principle, on which it is founded. As long as it is allowed, that reason has no influence on our passions and action, it is in vain to pretend, that morality is discovered only by a deduction of reason. An active principle can never be founded on an inactive; and if reason be inactive in itself, it must remain so in all its shapes and appearances, whether it exerts itself in natural or moral subjects, whether it considers the powers of external bodies, or the actions of rational beings.

It would be tedious to repeat all the arguments, by which I have proved,* that reason is perfectly inert, and can never either prevent or produce any action or affection. It will be easy to recollect what has been said upon that subject. I shall only recall on this occasion one of these arguments, which I shall endeavour to render still more conclusive, and more applicable to the present subject.

Reason is the discovery of truth or falsehood. Truth or falsehood consists in an agreement or disagreement either to the *real* relations of ideas, or to *real* existence and matter of fact. Whatever, therefore, is not susceptible of this agreement or disagreement, is incapable of being true or false, and can never be an object of our reason. Now it is evident our passions, volitions, and actions, are not susceptible of any such agreement or disagreement; being original facts and realities, complete in themselves, and implying no reference to

* Book 2, Part 3, Section 3.

other passions, volitions, and actions. It is impossible, therefore, they can be pronounced either true or false, and be either contrary or conformable to reason.

This argument is of double advantage to our present purpose. For it proves *directly*, that actions do not derive their merit from a conformity to reason, nor their blame from a contrariety to it; and it proves the same truth more *indirectly*, by shewing us, that as reason can never immediately prevent or produce any action by contradicting or approving of it, it cannot be the source of moral good and evil, which are found to have that influence. Actions may be laudable or blameable; but they cannot be reasonable: laudable or blameable, therefore, are not the same with reasonable or unreasonable. The merit and demerit of actions frequently contradict, and sometimes control our natural propensities. But reason has no such influence. Moral distinctions, therefore, are not the offspring of reason. Reason is wholly inactive, and can never be the source of so active a principle as conscience, or a sense of morals.

But perhaps it may be said, that though no will or action can be immediately contradictory to reason, yet we may find such a contradiction in some of the attendants of the action, that is, in its causes or effects. The action may cause a judgment, or may be *obliquely* caused by one, when the judgment concurs with a passion; and by an abusive way of speaking, which philosophy will scarce allow of, the same contrariety may, upon that account, be ascribed to the action. How far this truth or falsehood may be the source of morals, it will now be proper to consider.

It has been observed, that reason, in a strict and philosophical sense, can have influence on our conduct only after two ways: either when it excites a passion by informing us of the existence of something which is a proper object of it; or when it discovers the connexion of causes and effects, so as to afford us means of exerting any passion. These are the only kinds of judgment, which can accompany our actions, or can be said to produce them in any manner; and it must be allowed, that these judgments may often be false and erroneous. A person may be affected with passion, by supposing a pain or pleasure to lie in an object, which has no tendency to produce either of these sensations, or which produces the contrary to what is imagined. A person may also take false measures for the attaining his end, and may retard, by his foolish conduct, instead of forwarding the execution of any project. These false judgments may be thought to affect the passions and actions, which are connected with them, and may be said to render them unreasonable, in a figurative and improper way of speaking. But though this be acknowledged, it is easy to observe, that these errors are so far from being the source of all immorality, that they are commonly very innocent, and draw no manner of guilt upon the person who is so unfortunate as to fail into them. They extend not beyond a mistake of *fact*, which moralists have not generally supposed criminal, as being perfectly involuntary. I am more to be lamented than blamed, if I am mistaken with regard to the influence of objects in producing pain or pleasure, or if I know not the proper means of satisfying my desires. No one can ever regard such errors as a defect in my moral character. A fruit, for instance, that is really disagreeable, appears to me at a distance, and through mistake I fancy it to be pleasant and delicious. Here is one error. I choose certain means of reaching this fruit, which are not proper for my end. Here is a second error; nor is there any third one, which can ever possibly enter into our reasonings concerning actions. I ask, therefore, if a man, in this situation, and guilty of these two errors, is to be regarded as vicious and criminal, however unavoidable they might have been? Or if it be possible to imagine, that such errors are the sources of all immorality?

And here it may be proper to observe, that if moral distinctions be derived from the truth or falsehood of those judgments, they must take place wherever we form the judgments; nor will there be any difference, whether the question be concerning an apple or a kingdom, or whether the error be avoidable or unavoidable. For as the very essence of morality is supposed to consist in an agreement or disagreement to reason, the other circumstances are entirely arbitrary, and can never either bestow on any action the character of virtuous or vicious, or deprive it of that character. To which we may add, that this agreement or disagreement, not admitting of degrees, all virtues and vices would of course be equal.

Should it be pretended, that though a mistake of *fact* be not criminal, yet a mistake of *right* often is; and that this may be the source of immorality: I would answer, that it is impossible such a mistake can ever be the original source of immorality, since it supposes a real right and wrong; that is, a real distinction in morals, independent of these judgments. A mistake, therefore, of right may become a species of immorality; but it is only a secondary one, and is founded on some other, antecedent to it.

As to those judgments which are the *effects* of our actions, and which, when false, give occasion to pronounce the actions contrary to truth and reason; we may observe, that our actions never cause any judgment, either true or false, in ourselves, and that it is only on others they have such an influence. It is certain, that an action, on many occasions, may give rise to false conclusions in others; and that a person, who through a window sees any lewd behaviour of mine with my neighbour's wife, may be so simple as to imagine she is certainly my own. In this respect my action resembles somewhat a lie or falsehood; only with this difference, which is material, that I perform not the action with any intention of giving rise to a false judgment in another, but merely to satisfy my lust and passion. It causes, however, a mistake and false judgment by accident; and the falsehood of its effects may be ascribed, by some odd figurative way of speaking, to the action itself. But still I can see no pretext of reason for asserting, that the tendency to cause such an error is the first spring or original source of all immorality.*

* One might think It were entirely superfluous to prove this, if a late author [Wollaston], who has had the good fortune to obtain some reputation, had not seriously affirmed, that such a falsehood is the foundation of all guilt and moral deformity. That we may discover the fallacy of his hypothesis, we need only consider, that a false conclusion is drawn from an action, only by means of an obscurity of natural principles, which makes a cause be secretly interrupted In its operation, by contrary causes, and renders the connexion betwixt two objects uncertain and variable. Now, as a like uncertainty and variety of causes take place, even in natural objects, and produce a like error in our judgment, if that tendency to produce error were the very essence of vice and immorality, it should follow, that even inanimate objects might be vicious and immoral.

It is in vain to urge, that inanimate objects act without liberty and choice. For as liberty and choice are not necessary to make an action produce in us an erroneous conclusion, they can be, in no respect, essential to morality; and I do not readily perceive, upon this system, how they can ever come to be regarded by it. If the tendency to cause error be the origin of immorality, that tendency and immorality would in every case be inseparable.

Add to this, that if I had used the precaution of shutting the windows, while I indulged myself in those liberties with my neighbour's wife, I should have been guilty of no immorality; and that because my action, being perfectly concealed, would have had no tendency to produce any false conclusion.

For the same reason, a thief, who steals in by a ladder at a window, and takes all imaginable care to cause no disturbance, is in no respect criminal. For either he

Thus upon the whole, it is impossible, that the distinction betwixt moral good and evil, can be made by reason; since that distinction has an influence upon our actions, of which reason alone is incapable. Reason and judgment may, indeed, be the mediate cause of an action, by prompting, or by directing a passion: but it is not pretended, that a judgment of this kind, either in its truth or falsehood, is attended with virtue or vice. And as to the judgments, which are caused by our actions, they can still less bestow those moral qualities on the actions, which are their causes.

But to be more particular, and to shew, that those eternal immutable fitnesses and unfitnesses of things cannot be defended by sound philosophy, we may weigh the following considerations.

If the thought and understanding were alone capable of fixing the boundaries of right and wrong, the character of virtuous and vicious either must lie in some relations of objects, or must be a

---

will not be perceived, or if he be, it is impossible he can produce any error, nor will any one, from these circumstances, take him to be other than what he really is.

It is well known, that those who are squint-sighted, do very readily cause mistakes in others, and that we imagine they salute or are talking to one person, while they address themselves to another. Are they therefore, upon that account, immoral?

Besides, we may easily observe, that in all those arguments there is an evident reasoning in a circle. A person who takes possession of *another's* goods, and uses them as his *own*, in a manner declares them to be his own; and this falsehood is the source of the immorality of injustice. But is property, or right, or obligation, intelligible, without an antecedent morality?

A man that is ungrateful to his benefactor, in a manner affirms, that he never received any favours from him. But in what manner? Is it because it is his duty to be grateful? But this supposes, that there is some antecedent rule of duty and morals. Is it because human nature is generally grateful, and makes us conclude, that a man who does any harm never received any favour from the person he harmed? But human nature is not so generally grateful, as to justify such a conclusion. Or if it were, is an exception to a general rule in every case criminal, for no other reason than because it is an exception?

But what may suffice entirely to destroy this whimsical system is, that it leaves us under the same difficulty to give a reason why truth is virtuous and falsehood vicious, as to account for the merit or turpitude of any other action. I shall allow, if you please, that all immorality is derived from this supposed falsehood in action, provided you can give me any plausible reason, why such a falsehood is immoral. If you consider rightly of the matter, you will find yourself in the same difficulty as at the beginning.

This last argument is very conclusive; because, if there be not an evident merit or turpitude annexed to this species of truth or falsehood, It can never have any influence upon our actions. For, who ever thought of forbearing any action, because others might possibly draw false conclusions from it? Or, who ever performed any, that he might give rise to true conclusions?

matter of fact, which is discovered by our reasoning. This consequence is evident. As the operations of human understanding divide themselves into two kinds, the comparing of ideas, and the inferring of matter of fact; were virtue discovered by the understanding; it must be an object of one of these operations, nor is there any third operation of the understanding. which can discover it. There has been an opinion very industriously propagated by certain philosophers, that morality is susceptible of demonstration; and though no one has ever been able to advance a single step in those demonstrations; yet it is taken for granted, that this science may be brought to an equal certainty with geometry or algebra. Upon this supposition vice and virtue must consist in some relations; since it is allowed on all hands, that no matter of fact is capable of being demonstrated. Let us, therefore, begin with examining this hypothesis, and endeavour, if possible, to fix those moral qualities, which have been so long the objects of our fruitless researches. Point out distinctly the relations, which constitute morality or obligation, that we may know wherein they consist, and after what manner we must judge of them.

If you assert, that vice and virtue consist in relations susceptible of certainty and demonstration, you must confine yourself to those *four* relations, which alone admit of that degree of evidence; and in that case you run into absurdities, from which you will never be able to extricate yourself. For as you make the very essence of morality to lie in the relations, and as there is no one of these relations but what is applicable, not only to an irrational, but also to an inanimate object; it follows, that even such objects must be susceptible of merit or demerit. *Resemblance, contrariety, degrees in quality*, and *proportions in quantity and number;* all these relations belong as properly to matter, as to our actions, passions, and volitions. It is unquestionable, therefore, that morality lies not in any of these relations, nor the sense of it in their discovery.*

---

* As a proof, how confused our way of thinking on this subject commonly is, we may observe, that those who assert, that morality is demonstrable, do not say, that morality lies in the relations, and that the relations are distinguishable by reason. They only say, that reason can discover such an action, in such relations, to be virtuous, and such another vicious. It seems they thought it sufficient, if they could bring the word, Relation, into the proposition, without troubling themselves whether it was to the purpose or not. But here, I think, is plain argument. Demonstrative reason discovers only relations. But that reason, according to this hypothesis, discovers also vice and virtue. These moral qualities, therefore, must

Should it be asserted, that the sense of morality consists in the discovery of some relation, distinct from these, and that our enumeration was not complete, when we comprehended all demonstrable relations under four general heads: to this I know not what to reply, till some one be so good as to point out to me this new relation. It is impossible to refute a system, which has never yet been explained. In such a manner of fighting in the dark, a man loses his blows in the air, and often places them where the enemy is not present.

I must, therefore, on this occasion, rest contented with requiring the two following conditions of any one that would undertake to clear up this system. *First*, As moral good and evil belong only to the actions of the mind, and are derived from our situation with regard to external objects, the relations, from which these moral distinctions arise, must lie only betwixt internal actions, and external objects, and must not be applicable either to internal actions, compared among themselves, or to external objects, when placed in opposition to other external objects. For as morality is supposed to attend certain relations, if these relations could belong to internal actions considered singly, it would follow, that we might be guilty of crimes in ourselves, and independent of our situation, with respect to the universe: and in like manner, if these moral relations could be applied to external objects, it would follow, that even inanimate beings would be susceptible of moral beauty and deformity. Now it seems difficult to imagine, that any relation can be discovered betwixt our passions, volitions and actions, compared to external objects, which relation might not belong either to these passions and volitions, or to these external objects, compared among *themselves*.

But it will be still more difficult to fulfil the *second* condition, requisite to justify this system. According to the principles of those who maintain an abstract rational difference betwixt moral good and evil, and a natural fitness and unfitness of things, it is not only supposed, that these relations, being eternal and immutable, are the same, when considered by every rational creature, but their *effects*

---

be relations. When we blame any action, in any situation, the whole complicated object, of action and situation, must form certain relations, wherein the essence of vice consists. This hypothesis is not otherwise intelligible. For what does reason discover, when it pronounces any action vicious? Does it discover a relation or a matter of fact? These questions are decisive, and must not be eluded.

are also supposed to be necessarily the same; and it is concluded they have no less, or rather a greater, influence in directing the will of the deity, than in governing the rational and virtuous of our own species. These two particulars are evidently distinct. It is one thing to know virtue, and another to conform the will to it. In order, therefore, to prove, that the measures of right and wrong are eternal laws, *obligatory* on every rational mind, it is not sufficient to shew the relations upon which they are founded: we must also point out the connexion betwixt the relation and the will; and must prove that this connexion is so necessary, that in every well-disposed mind, it must take place and have its influence; though the difference betwixt these minds be in other respects immense and infinite. Now besides what I have already proved, that even in human nature no relation can ever alone produce any action: besides this, I say, it has been shewn, in treating of the understanding, that there is no connexion of cause and effect, such as this is supposed to be, which is discoverable otherwise than by experience, and of which we can pretend to have any security by the simple consideration of the objects. All beings in the universe, considered in themselves, appear entirely loose and independent of each other. It is only by experience we learn their influence and connexion; and this influence we ought never to extend beyond experience.

Thus it will be impossible to fulfil the *first* condition required to the system of eternal measures of right and wrong; because it is impossible to shew those relations, upon which such a distinction may be founded: and it is as impossible to fulfil the second condition; because we cannot prove *a priori*, that these relations, if they really existed and were perceived, would be universally forcible and obligatory.

But to make these general reflections more clear and convincing, we may illustrate them by some particular instances, wherein this character of moral good or evil is the most universally acknowledged. Of all crimes that human creatures are capable of committing, the most horrid and unnatural is ingratitude, especially when it is committed against parents, and appears in the more flagrant instances of wounds and death. This is acknowledged by all mankind, philosophers as well as the people; the question only arises among philosophers, whether the guilt or moral deformity of this action be discovered by demonstrative reasoning, or be felt by an internal sense, and by means of some sentiment, which the reflecting on such an action naturally occasions. This question will soon be decided against the former opinion, if we can shew the same relations in other objects, without the notion of any guilt or iniquity attending them. Reason or science is nothing but the comparing of ideas, and the discovery of their relations; and if the same relations have different characters, it must evidently follow, that those characters are not discovered merely by reason. To put the affair, therefore, to this trial, let us choose any inanimate object, such as an oak or elm; and let us suppose, that by the dropping of its seed, it produces a sapling below it, which springing up by degrees, at last overtops and destroys the parent tree: I ask, if in this instance there be wanting any relation, which is discoverable in parricide or ingratitude? Is not the one tree the cause of the other's existence; and the latter the cause of the destruction of the former, in the same manner as when a child murders his parent? It is not sufficient to reply, that a choice or will is wanting. For in the case of parricide, a will does not give rise to any *different* relations, but is only the cause from which the action is derived; and consequently produces the *same* relations, that in the oak or elm arise from some other principles. It is a will or choice, that determines a man to kill his parent; and they are the laws of matter and motion, that determine a sapling to destroy the oak, from which it sprung. Here then the same relations have different causes; but still the relations are the same: and as their discovery is not in both cases attended with a notion of immorality, it follows, that that notion does not arise from such a discovery.

But to choose an instance, still more resembling; I would fain ask any one, why incest in the human species is criminal, and why the very same action, and the same relations in animals have not the smallest moral turpitude and deformity? If it be answered, that this action is innocent in animals, because they have not reason sufficient to discover its turpitude; but that man, being endowed with that faculty which ought to restrain him to his duty, the same action instantly becomes criminal to him; should this be said, I would reply, that this is evidently arguing in a circle. For before reason can perceive this turpitude, the turpitude must exist; and consequently is independent of the decisions of our reason, and is their object more properly than their effect. According to this system, then, every animal, that has sense, and appetite, and will; that is, every animal must be susceptible of all the same virtues and vices, for which we ascribe praise and blame to human creatures. All the difference is, that our superior reason may serve to discover the vice or virtue, and by that means may augment the blame or praise: but still this discovery supposes a separate being in these moral distinctions, and a being, which depends only on the will and appetite, and which, both in thought and reality, may be distinguished from the reason. Animals are susceptible of the same relations, with respect to each other, as the human species, and therefore would also be susceptible of the same morality, if the essence of morality consisted in these relations. Their want of a sufficient degree of reason may hinder them from perceiving the duties and obligations of morality, but can never hinder these duties from existing; since they must antecedently exist, in order to their being perceived. Reason must find them, and can never produce them. This argument deserves to be weighed, as being, in my opinion, entirely decisive.

Nor does this reasoning only prove, that morality consists not in any relations, that are the objects of science; but if examined, will prove with equal certainty, that it consists not in any *matter of fact*, which can be discovered by the understanding. This is the *second* part of our argument; and if it can be made evident, we may conclude, that morality is not an object of reason. But can there be any difficulty in proving, that vice and virtue are not matters of fact, whose existence we can infer by reason? Take any action allowed to be vicious: wilful murder, for instance. Examine it in all lights, and see if you can find that matter of fact, or real existence, which you call *vice*. In which-ever way you take it, you find only certain passions, motives, volitions and thoughts. There is no other matter of fact in the case. The vice entirely escapes you, as long as you consider the object. You never can find it, till you turn your reflection into your own breast, and find a sentiment of disapprobation, which arises in you, towards this action. Here is a matter of fact; but it is the object of feeling, not of reason. It lies in yourself, not in the object. So that when you pronounce any action or character to be vicious, you mean nothing, but that from the constitution of your nature you have a feeling or sentiment of blame from the contemplation of it. Vice and virtue, therefore, may be compared to sounds, colours, heat and cold, which, according to modern philosophy, are not qualities in objects, but perceptions in the mind: and this discovery in morals, like that other in physics, is to be regarded as a considerable advancement of the speculative sciences; though, like that too, it has little or no influence on practice. Nothing can be more real, or concern us more, than our own sentiments of pleasure and uneasiness; and if these be favourable to virtue, and unfavourable to vice, no more can be requisite to the regulation of our conduct and behaviour.

I cannot forbear adding to these reasonings an observation, which may, perhaps, be found of some importance. In every system of morality, which I have hitherto met with, I have always remarked, that the author proceeds for some time in the ordinary way of reasoning, and establishes the being of a God, or makes observations concerning human affairs; when of a sudden I am surprized to find, that instead of the usual copulations of propositions, *is*, and *is not*, I meet with no proposition that is not connected with an *ought*, or an *ought not*. This change is imperceptible; but is, however, of the last consequence. For as this *ought*, or *ought not*, expresses some new relation or affirmation, it is necessary that it should be observed and explained; and at the same time that a reason should be given, for what seems altogether inconceivable, how this new relation can be a deduction from others, which are entirely different from it. But as authors do not commonly use this precaution, I shall presume to recommend it to the readers; and am persuaded, that this small attention would subvert all the vulgar systems of morality, and let us see, that the distinction of vice and virtue is not founded merely on the relations of objects, nor is perceived by reason.

SECTION TWO
Moral distinctions derived from a moral sense

Thus the course of the argument leads us to conclude, that since vice and virtue are not discoverable merely by reason, or the comparison of ideas, it must be by means of some impression or sentiment they occasion, that we are able to mark the difference betwixt them. Our decisions concerning moral rectitude and depravity are evidently perceptions; and as all perceptions are either impressions or ideas, the exclusion of the one is a convincing argument for the other. Morality, therefore, is more properly felt than judged of; though this feeling or sentiment is commonly so soft and gentle, that we are apt to confound it with an idea, according to our common custom of taking all things for the same, which have any near resemblance to each other.

The next question is, Of what nature are these impressions, and after what manner do they operate upon us? Here we cannot remain long in suspense, but must pronounce the impression arising from virtue, to be agreeable, and that proceding from vice to be uneasy. Every moment's experience must convince us of this. There is no spectacle so fair and beautiful as a noble and generous action; nor any which gives us more abhorrence than one that is cruel and treacherous. No enjoyment equals the satisfaction we receive from the company of those we love and esteem; as the greatest of all punishments is to be obliged to pass our lives with those we hate or contemn. A very play or romance may afford us instances of this pleasure, which virtue conveys to us; and pain, which arises from vice.

Now since the distinguishing impressions, by which moral good or evil is known, are nothing but *particular* pains or pleasures; it follows, that in all enquiries concerning these moral distinctions, it will be sufficient to shew the principles, which make us feel a satisfaction or uneasiness from the survey of any character, in order to satisfy us why the character is laudable or blameable. An action, or sentiment, or character is virtuous or vicious; why? because its view causes a pleasure or uneasiness of a particular kind. In giving a reason, therefore, for the pleasure or uneasiness, we sufficiently explain the vice or virtue. To have the sense of virtue, is nothing but to *feel* a satisfaction of a particular kind from the contemplation of a character. The very *feeling* constitutes our praise or admiration. We go no farther; nor do we enquire into the cause of the satisfaction. We do not infer a character to be virtuous, because it pleases: but in feeling that it pleases after such a particular manner, we in effect feel that it is virtuous. The case is the same as in our judgments concerning all kinds of beauty, and tastes, and sensations. Our approbation is implied in the immediate pleasure they convey to us.

I have objected to the system, which establishes eternal rational measures of right and wrong, that it is impossible to shew, in the actions of reasonable creatures, any relations, which are not found in external objects; and therefore, if morality always attended these relations, it were possible for inanimate matter to become virtuous or vicious. Now it may, in like manner, be objected to the present system, that if virtue and vice be determined by pleasure and pain, these qualities must, in every case, arise from the sensations; and consequently any object, whether animate or inanimate, rational or irrational, might become morally good or evil, provided it can excite a satisfaction or uneasiness. But though this objection seems to be the very same, it has by no means the same force, in the one case as in the other. For, *first*, it is evident, that under the term *pleasure*, we comprehend sensations, which are very different from each other, and which have only such a distant resemblance, as is requisite to make them be expressed by the same abstract term. A good composition of music and a bottle of good wine equally produce pleasure; and what is more, their goodness is determined merely by the pleasure. But shall we say upon that account, that the wine is harmonious, or the music of a good flavour? In like manner an inanimate object, and the character or sentiments of any person may, both of them, give satisfaction; but as the satisfaction is different, this keeps our sentiments concerning them from being confounded, and makes us ascribe virtue to the one, and not to the other. Nor is every sentiment of pleasure or pain, which arises from characters and actions, of that *peculiar* kind, which makes us praise or condemn. The good qualities of an enemy are hurtful to us; but may still command our esteem and respect. It is only when a character is considered in general, without reference to our particular interest, that it causes such a feeling or sentiment, as denominates it morally good or evil. It is true, those sentiments, from interest and morals, are apt to be confounded, and naturally run into one another. It seldom happens, that we do not think an enemy vicious, and can distinguish betwixt his opposition to our interest and real villainy or baseness. But this hinders not, but that the sentiments are, in themselves, distinct; and a man of temper and judgment may preserve himself from these illusions. In like manner, though it is certain a musical voice is nothing but one that naturally gives a *particular* kind of pleasure; yet it is difficult for a man to be sensible, that the voice of an enemy is agreeable, or to allow it to be musical. But a person of a fine ear, who has the command of himself, can separate these feelings, and give praise to what deserves it.

Secondly, We may call to remembrance the preceding system of the passions, in order to remark a still more considerable difference among our pains and pleasures. Pride and humility, love and hatred are excited, when there is any thing presented to us, that both bears a relation to the object of the passion, and produces a separate sensation related to the sensation of the passion. Now virtue and vice are attended with these circumstances. They must necessarily be placed either in ourselves or others, and excite either pleasure or uneasiness; and therefore must give rise to one of these four passions; which clearly distinguishes them from the pleasure and pain arising from inanimate objects, that often bear no relation to us: and this is, perhaps, the most considerable effect that virtue and vice have upon the human mind.

It may now be asked *in general*, concerning this pain or pleasure, that distinguishes moral good and evil, *From what principles is it derived, and whence does it arise in the human mind*? To this I reply, *first*, that it is absurd to imagine, that in every particular instance, these sentiments are produced by an *original* quality and *primary* constitution. For as the number of our duties is, in a manner, infinite, it is impossible that our original instincts should extend to each of them, and from our very first infancy impress on the human mind all that multitude of precepts, which are contained in the completest system of ethics. Such a method of proceeding is not conformable to the usual maxims, by which nature is conducted, where a few principles produce all that variety we observe in the universe, and every thing is carried on in the easiest and most simple manner. It is necessary, therefore, to abridge these primary impulses, and find some more general principles, upon which all our notions of morals are founded.

But in the *second* place, should it be asked, Whether we ought to search for these principles in *nature*, or whether we must look for them in some other origin? I would reply, that our answer to this question depends upon the definition of the word, Nature, than which there is none more ambiguous and equivocal. If *nature* be opposed to miracles, not only the distinction betwixt vice and virtue is natural, but also every event, which has ever happened in the world, *excepting those miracles, on which our religion is founded*. In saying, then, that the sentiments of vice and virtue are natural in this sense, we make no very extraordinary discovery.

But *nature* may also be opposed to rare and unusual; and in this sense of the word, which is the common one, there may often arise disputes concerning what is natural or unnatural; and one may in general affirm, that we are not possessed of any very precise standard, by which these disputes can be decided. Frequent and rare depend upon the number of examples we have observed; and as this number may gradually increase or diminish, it will be impossible to fix any exact boundaries betwixt them. We may only affirm on this head, that if ever there was any thing, which could be called natural in this sense, the sentiments of morality certainly may; since there never was any nation of the world, nor any single person in any nation, who was utterly deprived of them, and who never, in any instance, shewed the least approbation or dislike of manners. These sentiments are so rooted in our constitution and temper, that without entirely confounding the human mind by disease or madness, it is impossible to extirpate and destroy them.

But *nature* may also be opposed to artifice, as well as to what is rare and unusual; and in this sense it may be disputed, whether the notions of virtue be natural or not. We readily forget, that the designs, and projects, and views of men are principles as necessary in their operation as heat and cold, moist and dry: but taking them to be free and entirely our own, it is usual for us to set them in opposition to the other principles of nature. Should it, therefore, be demanded, whether the sense of virtue be natural or artificial, I am of opinion, that it is impossible for me at present to give any precise answer to this question. Perhaps it will appear afterwards, that our sense of some virtues is artificial, and that of others natural. The discussion of this question will be more proper, when we enter upon an exact detail of each particular vice and virtue.*

---

* In the following discourse *natural* is also opposed sometimes to *civil*, sometimes to *moral*. The opposition will always discover the sense, in which it is taken.

Mean while it may not be amiss to observe from these definitions of *natural* and *unnatural*, that nothing can be more unphilosophical than those systems, which assert, that virtue is the same with what is natural, and vice with what is unnatural. For in the first sense of the word, Nature, as opposed to miracles, both vice and virtue are equally natural; and in the second sense, as opposed to what is unusual, perhaps virtue will be found to be the most unnatural. At least it must be owned, that heroic virtue, being as unusual, is as little natural as the most brutal barbarity. As to the third sense of the word, it is certain, that both vice and virtue are equally artificial, and out of nature. For however it may be disputed, whether the notion of a merit or demerit in certain actions be natural or artificial, it is evident, that the actions themselves are artificial, and are performed with a certain design and intention; otherwise they could never be ranked under any of these denominations. It is impossible, therefore, that the character of natural and unnatural can ever, in any sense, mark the boundaries of vice and virtue.

Thus we are still brought back to our first position, that virtue is distinguished by the pleasure, and vice by the pain, that any action, sentiment or character gives us by the mere view and contemplation. This decision is very commodious; because it reduces us to this simple question, *Why any action or sentiment upon the general view or survey, gives a certain satisfaction or uneasiness,* in order to shew the origin of its moral rectitude or depravity, without looking for any incomprehensible relations and qualities, which never did exist in nature, nor even in our imagination, by any clear and distinct conception. I flatter myself I have executed a great part of my present design by a state of the question, which appears to me so free from ambiguity and obscurity.

I have already hinted, that our sense of every kind of virtue is not natural; but that there are some virtues, that produce pleasure and approbation by means of an artifice or contrivance, which arises from the circumstances and necessity of mankind. Of this kind I assert *justice* to be; and shall endeavour to defend this opinion by a short, and, I hope, convincing argument, before I examine the nature of the artifice, from which the sense of that virtue is derived.

It is evident, that when we praise any actions, we regard only the motives that produced them, and consider the actions as signs or indications of certain principles in the mind and temper. The external performance has no merit. We must look within to find the moral quality. This we cannot do directly; and therefore fix our attention on actions, as on external signs. But these actions are still considered as signs; and the ultimate object of our praise and approbation is the motive, that produced them.

After the same manner, when we require any action, or blame a person for not performing it, we always suppose, that one in that situation should be influenced by the proper motive of that action, and we esteem it vicious in him to be regardless of it. If we find, upon enquiry, that the virtuous motive was still powerful over his breast, though checked in its operation by some circumstances unknown to us, we retract our blame, and have the same esteem for him, as if he had actually performed the action, which we require of him.

It appears, therefore, that all virtuous actions derive their merit only from virtuous motives, and are considered merely as signs of those motives. From this principle I conclude, that the first virtuous motive, which bestows a merit on any action, can never be a regard to the virtue of that action, but must be some other natural motive or principle. To suppose, that the mere regard to the virtue of the action may be the first motive, which produced the action, and rendered it virtuous, is to reason in a circle. Before we can have such a regard, the action must be really virtuous; and this virtue must be derived from some virtuous motive: and consequently the virtuous motive must be different from the regard to the virtue of the action. A virtuous motive is requisite to render an action virtuous. An action must be virtuous, before we can have a regard to its virtue. Some virtuous motive, therefore, must be antecedent to that regard.

Nor is this merely a metaphysical subtilty; but enters into all our reasonings in common life, though perhaps we may not be able to place it in such distinct philosophical terms. We blame a father for neglecting his child. Why? Because it shews a want of natural affection, which is the duty of every parent. Were not natural affection a duty, the care of children could not be a duty; and it were impossible we could have the duty in our eye in the attention we give to our offspring. In this case, therefore, all men suppose a motive to the action distinct from a sense of duty.

Here is a man, that does many benevolent actions; relieves the distressed, comforts the afflicted, and extends his bounty even to the greatest strangers. No character can be more amiable and virtuous. We regard these actions as proofs of the greatest humanity. This humanity bestows a merit on the actions. A regard to this merit is, therefore, a secondary consideration, and derived from the antecedent principle of humanity, which is meritorious and laudable.

In short, it may be established as an undoubted maxim, *that no action can be virtuous, or morally good, unless there be in human nature some motive to produce it, distinct from the sense of its morality.*

But may not the sense of morality or duty produce an action, without any other motive? I answer, It may: but this is no objection to the present doctrine. When any virtuous motive or principle is common in human nature, a person, who feels his heart devoid of that motive, may hate himself upon that account, and may perform the action without the motive, from a certain sense of duty, in order to acquire by practice, that virtuous principle, or at least, to disguise to himself, as much as possible, his want of it. A man that really feels no gratitude in his temper, is still pleased to perform grateful actions, and thinks he has, by that means, fulfilled his duty. Actions are at first only considered as signs of motives: but it is usual, in this case, as in all others, to fix our attention on the signs, and neglect, in some measure, the thing signified. But though, on some occasions, a person may perform an action merely out of regard to its moral obligation, yet still this supposes in human nature some distinct principles, which are capable of producing the action, and whose moral beauty renders the action meritorious.

Now to apply all this to the present case; I suppose a person to have lent me a sum of money, on condition that it be restored in a few days; and also suppose, that after the expiration of the term agreed on, he demands the sum: I ask, *What reason or motive have I to restore the money*? It will, perhaps, be said, that my regard to justice, and abhorrence of villainy and knavery, are sufficient reasons for me, if I have the least grain of honesty, or sense of duty and obligation. And this answer, no doubt, is just and satisfactory to man in his civilized state, and when trained up according to a certain discipline and education. But in his rude and more *natural* condition, if you are pleased to call such a condition natural, this answer would be rejected as perfectly unintelligible and sophistical. For one in that situation would immediately ask you, *Wherein consists this honesty and justice, which you find in restoring a loan, and abstaining from the property of others*? It does not surely lie in the external action. It must, therefore be placed in the motive, from which the external action is derived. This motive can never be a regard to the honesty of the action. For it is a plain fallacy to say, that a virtuous motive is requisite to render an action honest, and at the same time that a regard to the honesty is the motive of the action. We can never have a regard to the virtue of an action, unless the action be antecedently virtuous. No action can be virtuous, but so far as it proceeds from a virtuous motive. A virtuous motive, therefore, must precede the regard to the virtue, and it is impossible, that the virtuous motive and the regard to the virtue can be the same.

It is requisite, then, to find some motive to acts of justice and honesty, distinct from our regard to the honesty; and in this lies the great difficulty. For should we say, that a concern for our private interest or reputation is the legitimate motive to all honest actions; it would follow, that wherever that concern ceases, honesty can no longer have place. But it is certain, that self-love, when it acts at its liberty, instead of engaging us to honest actions, is the source of all injustice and violence; nor can a man ever correct those vices, without correcting and restraining the natural movements of that appetite.

But should it be affirmed, that the reason or motive of such actions is the *regard to publick interest*, to which nothing is more contrary than examples of injustice and dishonesty; should this be said, I would propose the three following considerations, as worthy of our attention. *First*, public interest is not naturally attached to the observation of the rules of justice; but is only connected with it, after an artificial convention for the establishment of these rules, as shall be shewn more at large hereafter. *Secondly*, if we suppose, that the loan was secret, and that it is necessary for the interest of the person, that the money be restored in the same manner (as when the lender would conceal his riches) in that case the example ceases, and the public is no longer interested in the actions of the borrower; though I suppose there is no moralist, who will affirm, that the duty and obligation ceases. *Thirdly*, experience sufficiently proves, that men, in the ordinary conduct of life, look not so far as the public interest, when they pay their creditors, perform their promises, and abstain from theft, and robbery, and injustice of every kind. That is a motive too remote and too sublime to affect the generality of mankind, and operate with any force in actions so contrary to private interest as are frequently those of justice and common honesty.

In general, it may be affirmed, that there is no such passion in human minds, as the love of mankind, merely as such, independent of personal qualities, of services, or of relation to ourself. It is true, there is no human, and indeed no sensible, creature, whose happiness or misery does not, in some measure, affect us when brought near to us, and represented in lively colours: but this proceeds merely from sympathy, and is no proof of such an universal affection to mankind, since this concern extends itself beyond our own species. An affection betwixt the sexes is a passion evidently implanted in human nature; and this passion not only appears in its peculiar symptoms, but also in inflaming every other principle of affection, and raising a stronger love from beauty, wit, kindness, than what would otherwise flow from them. Were there an universal love among all human creatures, it would appear after the same manner. Any degree of a good quality would cause a stronger affection than the same degree of a bad quality would cause hatred; contrary to what we find by experience. Men's tempers are different, and some have a propensity to the tender, and others to the rougher, affections: but in the main, we may affirm, that man in general, or human nature, is nothing but the object both of love and hatred, and requires some other cause, which by a double relation of impressions and ideas, may excite these passions. In vain would we endeavour to elude this hypothesis. There are no phenomena that point out any such kind affection to men, independent of their merit, and every other circumstance. We love company in general; but it is as we love any other amusement. An *Englishman* in *Italy* is a friend: A *European* in *China*; and perhaps a man would be beloved as such, were we to meet him in the moon. But this proceeds only from the relation to ourselves; which in these cases gathers force by being confined to a few persons.

If public benevolence, therefore, or a regard to the interests of mankind, cannot be the original motive to justice, much less can *private benevolence*, or a *regard to the interests of the party concerned*, be this motive. For what if he be my enemy, and has given me just cause to hate him? What if he be a vicious man, and deserves the hatred of all mankind? What if he be a miser, and can make no use of what I would deprive him of? What if he be a profligate debauchee, and would rather receive harm than benefit from large possessions? What if I be in necessity, and have urgent motives to acquire something to my family? In all these cases, the original motive to justice would fail; and consequently the justice itself, and along with it all property, right, and obligation.

A rich man lies under a moral obligation to communicate to those in necessity a share of his superfluities. Were private benevolence the original motive to justice, a man would not be obliged to leave others in the possession of more than he is obliged to give them. At least the difference would be very inconsiderable. Men generally fix their affections more on what they are possessed of, than on what they never enjoyed: for this reason, it would be greater cruelty to dispossess a man of any thing, than not to give it him. But who will assert, that this is the only foundation of justice?

Besides, we must consider, that the chief reason, why men attach themselves so much to their possessions is, that they consider them as their property, and as secured to them inviolably by the laws of society. But this is a secondary consideration, and dependent on the preceding notions of justice and property.

A man's property is supposed to be fenced against every mortal, in every possible case. But private benevolence is, and ought to be, weaker in some persons, than in others: and in many, or indeed in most persons, must absolutely fail. Private benevolence, therefore, is not the original motive of justice.

From all this it follows, that we have no real or universal motive for observing the laws of equity, but the very equity and merit of that observance; and as no action can be equitable or meritorious, where it cannot arise from some separate motive, there is here an evident sophistry and reasoning in a circle. Unless, therefore, we will allow, that nature has established a sophistry, and rendered it necessary and unavoidable, we must allow, that the sense of justice and injustice is not derived from nature, but arises artificially, though necessarily from education, and human conventions.

I shall add, as a corollary to this reasoning, that since no action can be laudable or blameable, without some motives or impelling passions, distinct from the sense of morals, these distinct passions must have a great influence on that sense. It is according to their general force in human nature, that we blame or praise. In judging of the beauty of animal bodies, we always carry in our eye the oeconomy of a certain species; and where the limbs and features observe that proportion, which is common to the species, we pronounce them handsome and beautiful. In like manner we always consider the *natural* and *usual* force of the passions, when we determine concerning vice and virtue; and if the passions depart very much from the common measures on either side, they are always disapproved as vicious. A man naturally loves his children better than his nephews, his nephews better than his cousins, his cousins better than strangers, where every thing else is equal. Hence arise our common measures of duty, in preferring the one to the other. Our sense of duty always follows the common and natural course of our passions.

To avoid giving offence, I must here observe, that when I deny justice to be a natural virtue, I make use of the word, *natural*, only as opposed to *artificial*. In another sense of the word; as no principle of the human mind is more natural than a sense of virtue; so no virtue is more natural than justice. Mankind is an inventive species; and where an invention is obvious and absolutely necessary, it may as properly be said to be natural as any thing that proceeds immediately from original principles, without the intervention of thought or reflection. Though the rules of justice be *artificial*, they are not *arbitrary*. Nor is the expression improper to call them *Laws of Nature*; if by natural we understand what is common to any species, or even if we confine it to mean what is inseparable from the species.

SECTION TWO

Of the origin of justice and property

We now proceed to examine two questions, *viz, concerning the manner, in which the rules of justice are established by the artifice of men*; and *concerning the reasons, which determine us to attribute to the observance or neglect of these rules a moral beauty and deformity*. These questions will appear afterwards to be distinct. We shall begin with the former.

Of all the animals, with which this globe is peopled, there is none towards whom nature seems, at first sight, to have exercised more cruelty than towards man, in the numberless wants and necessities, with which she has loaded him, and in the slender means, which she affords to the relieving these necessities. In other creatures these two particulars generally compensate each other. If we consider the lion as a voracious and carnivorous animal, we shall easily discover him to be very necessitous; but if we turn our eye to his make and temper, his agility, his courage, his arms, and his force, we shall find, that his advantages hold proportion with his wants. The sheep and ox are deprived of all these advantages; but their appetites are moderate, and their food is of easy purchase. In man alone, this unnatural conjunction of infirmity, and of necessity, may be observed in its greatest perfection. Not only the food, which is required for his sustenance, flies his search and approach, or at least requires his labour to be produced, but he must be possessed of clothes and lodging, to defend him against the injuries of the weather; though to consider him only in himself, he is provided neither with arms, nor force, nor other natural abilities, which are in any degree answerable to so many necessities.

It is by society alone he is able to supply his defects, and raise himself up to an equality with his fellow-creatures, and even acquire a superiority above them. By society all his infirmities are compensated; and though in that situation his wants multiply every moment upon him, yet his abilities are still more augmented, and leave him in every respect more satisfied and happy, than it is possible for him, in his savage and solitary condition, ever to become. When every individual person labours a-part, and only for himself, his force is too small to execute any considerable work; his labour being employed in supplying all his different necessities, he never attains a perfection in any particular art; and as his force and success are not at all times equal, the least failure in either of these particulars must be attended with inevitable ruin and misery. Society provides a remedy for these three inconveniences. By the conjunction of forces, our power is augmented: by the partition of employments, our ability increases: and by mutual succour we are less exposed to fortune and accidents. It is by this additional *force*, *ability*, and *security*, that society becomes advantageous.

But in order to form society, it is requisite not only that it be advantageous, but also that men be sensible of these advantages; and it is impossible, in their wild uncultivated state, that by study and reflection alone, they should ever be able to attain this knowledge. Most fortunately, therefore, there is conjoined to those necessities, whose remedies are remote and obscure, another necessity, which having a present and more obvious remedy, may justly be regarded as the first and original principle of human society. This necessity is no other than that natural appetite betwixt the sexes, which unites them together, and preserves their union, till a new tie takes place in their concern for their common offspring. This new concern becomes also a principle of union betwixt the parents and offspring, and forms a more numerous society; where the parents govern by the advantage of their superior strength and wisdom, and at the same time are restrained in the exercise of their authority by that natural affection, which they bear their children. In a little time, custom and habit operating on the tender minds of the children, makes them sensible of the advantages, which they may reap from society, as well as fashions them by degrees for it, by rubbing off those rough corners and untoward affections, which prevent their coalition.

For it must be confessed, that however the circumstances of human nature may render an union necessary, and however those passions of lust and natural affection may seem to render it unavoidable; yet there are other particulars in our *natural temper*, and in our *outward circumstances*, which are very incommodious, and are even contrary to the requisite conjunction. Among the former, we may justly esteem our *selfishness* to be the most considerable. I am sensible, that generally speaking, the representations of this quality have been carried much too far; and that the descriptions, which certain philosophers delight so much to form of mankind in this particular, are as wide of nature as any accounts of monsters, which we meet with in fables and romances. So far from thinking, that men have no affection for any thing beyond themselves, I am of opinion, that though it be rare to meet with one, who loves any single person better than himself; yet it is as rare to meet with one, in whom all the kind affections, taken together, do not overbalance all the selfish. Consult common experience: do you not see, that though the whole expence of the family be generally under the direction of the master of it, yet there are few that do not bestow the largest part of their fortunes on the pleasures of their wives, and the education of their children, reserving the smallest portion for their own proper use and entertainment. This is what we may observe concerning such as have those endearing ties; and may presume, that the case would be the same with others, were they placed in a like situation.

But though this generosity must be acknowledged to the honour of human nature, we may at the same time remark, that so noble an affection, instead of fitting men for large societies, is almost as contrary to them, as the most narrow selfishness. For while each person loves himself better than any other single person, and in his love to others bears the greatest affection to his relations and acquaintance, this must necessarily produce an oppositon of passions, and a consequent opposition of actions; which cannot but be dangerous to the new-established union.

It is however worth while to remark, that this contrariety of passions would be attended with but small danger, did it not concur with a peculiarity in our *outward circumstances*, which affords it an opportunity of exerting itself. There are three different species of goods, which we are possessed of: the internal satisfaction of our minds, the external advantages of our body, and the enjoyment of such possessions as we have acquired by our industry and good fortune. We are perfectly secure in the enjoyment of the first. The second may be ravished from us, but can be of no advantage to him who deprives us of them. The last only are both exposed to the violence of others, and may be transferred without suffering any loss or alteration; while at the same time, there is not a sufficient quantity of them to supply every one's desires and necessities. As the improvement, therefore, of these goods is the chief advantage of society, so the *instability* of their possession, along with their *scarcity*, is the chief impediment.

In vain should we expect to find, in *uncultivated nature*, a remedy to this inconvenience; or hope for any inartificial principle of the human mind, which might control those partial affections, and make us overcome the temptations arising from our circumstances. The idea of justice can never serve to this purpose, or be taken for a natural principle, capable of inspiring men with an equitable conduct towards each other. That virtue, as it is now understood, would never have been dreamed of among rude and savage men. For the notion of injury or injustice implies an immorality or vice committed against some other person: and as every immorality is derived from some defect or unsoundness of the passions, and as this defect must be judged of, in a great measure, from the ordinary course of nature in the constitution of the mind; it will be easy to know, whether we be guilty of any immorality, with regard to others, by considering the natural, and usual force of those several affections, which are directed towards them. Now it appears, that in the original frame of our mind, our strongest attention is confined to ourselves; our next is extended to our relations and acquaintance; and it is only the weakest which reaches to strangers and indifferent persons. This partiality, then, and unequal affection, must not only have an influence on our behaviour and conduct in society, but even on our ideas of vice and virtue; so as to make us regard any remarkable transgression of such a degree of partiality, either by too great an enlargement, or contraction of the affections, as vicious and immoral. This we may observe in our common judgments concerning actions, where we blame a person, who either centers all his affections in his family, or is so regardless of them, as, in any opposition of interest, to give the preference to a stranger, or mere chance acquaintance. From all which it follows, that our natural uncultivated ideas of morality, instead of providing a remedy for the partiality of our affections, do rather conform themselves to that partiality, and give it an additional force and influence.

The remedy, then, is not derived from nature, but from *artifice*; or more properly speaking, nature provides a remedy in the judgment and understanding, for what is irregular and incommodious in the affections. For when men, from their early education in society, have become sensible of the infinite advantages that result from it, and have besides acquired a new affection to company and conversation; and when they have observed, that the principal disturbance in society arises from those goods, which we call external, and from their looseness and easy transition from one person to another; they must seek for a remedy by putting these goods, as far as possible, on the same footing with the fixed and constant advantages of the mind and body. This can be done after no other manner, than by a convention entered into by all the members of the society to bestow stability on the possession of those external goods, and leave every one in the peaceable enjoyment of what he may acquire by his fortune and industry. By this means, every one knows what he may safely possess; and the passions are restrained in their partial and contradictory motions. Nor is such a restraint contrary to these passions; for if so, it could never be entered into, nor maintained; but it is only contrary to their heedless and impetuous movement. Instead of departing from our own interest, or from that of our nearest friends, by abstaining from the possessions of others, we cannot better consult both these interests, than by such a convention; because it is by that means we maintain society, which is so necessary to their well-being and subsistence, as well as to our own.

This convention is not of the nature of a *promise*: for even promises themselves, as we shall see afterwards, arise from human conventions. It is only a general sense of common interest; which sense all the members of the society express to one another, and which induces them to regulate their conduct by certain rules. I observe, that it will be for my interest to leave another in the possession of his goods, *provided* he will act in the same manner with regard to me. He is sensible of a like interest in the regulation of his conduct. When this common sense of interest is mutually expressed, and is known to both, it produces a suitable resolution and behaviour. And this may properly enough be called a convention or agreement betwixt us, though without the interposition of a promise; since the actions of each of us have a reference to those of the other, and are performed upon the supposition, that something is to be performed on the other part. Two men, who pull the oars of a boat, do it by an agreement or convention, though they have never given promises to each other. Nor is the rule concerning the stability of possession the less derived from human conventions, that it arises gradually, and acquires force by a slow progression, and by our repeated experience of the inconveniences of transgressing it. On the contrary, this experience assures us still more, that the sense of interest has become common to all our fellows, and gives us a confidence of the future regularity of their conduct: and it is only on the expectation of this, that our moderation and abstinence are founded. In like manner are languages gradually established by human conventions without any promise. In like manner do gold and silver become the common measures of exchange, and are esteemed sufficient payment for what is of a hundred times their value.

After this convention, concerning abstinence from the possessions of others, is entered into, and every one has acquired a stability in his possessions, there immediately arise the ideas of justice and injustice; as also those of *property*, *right*, and *obligation*. The latter are altogether unintelligible without first understanding the former. Our property is nothing but those goods, whose constant possession is established by the laws of society; that is, by the laws of justice. Those, therefore, who make use of the words *property*, or *right*, or *obligation*, before they have explained the origin of justice, or even make use of them in that explication, are guilty of a very gross fallacy, and can never reason upon any solid foundation. A man's property is some object related to him. This relation is not natural, but moral, and founded on justice. It is very preposterous, therefore, to imagine, that we can have any idea of property, without fully comprehending the nature of justice, and shewing its origin in the artifice and contrivance of man. The origin of justice explains that of property. The same artifice gives rise to both. As our first and most natural sentiment of morals is founded on the nature of our passions, and gives the preference to ourselves and friends, above strangers; it is impossible there can be naturally any such thing as a fixed right or property, while the opposite passions of men impel them in contrary directions, and are not restrained by any convention or agreement.

No one can doubt, that the convention for the distinction of property, and for the stability of possession, is of all circumstances the most necessary to the establishment of human society, and that after the agreement for the fixing and observing of this rule, there remains little or nothing to be done towards settling a perfect harmony and concord. All the other passions, besides this of interest, are either easily restrained, or are not of such pernicious consequence, when indulged. *Vanity* is rather to be esteemed a social passion, and a bond of union among men. *Pity* and *love* are to be considered in the same light. And as to *envy* and *revenge*, though pernicious, they operate only by intervals, and are directed against particular persons, whom we consider as our superiors or enemies. This avidity alone, of acquiring goods and possessions for ourselves and our nearest friends, is insatiable, perpetual, universal, and directly destructive of society. There scarce is any one, who is not actuated by it; and there is no one, who has not reason to fear from it, when it acts without any restraint, and gives way to its first and most natural movements. So that upon the whole, we are to esteem the difficulties in the establishment of society, to be greater or less, according to those we encounter in regulating and restraining this passion.

It is certain, that no affection of the human mind has both a sufficient force, and a proper direction to counterbalance the love of gain, and render men fit members of society, by making them abstain from the possessions of others. Benevolence to strangers is too weak for this purpose; and as to the other passions, they rather inflame this avidity, when we observe, that the larger our possessions are, the more ability we have of gratifying all our appetites. There is no passion, therefore, capable of controlling the interested affection, but the very affection itself, by an alteration of its direction. Now this alteration must necessarily take place upon the least reflection; since it is evident, that the passion is much better satisfied by its restraint, than by its liberty, and that in preserving society, we make much greater advances in the acquiring possessions, than in the solitary and forlorn condition, which must follow upon violence and an universal licence. The question, therefore, concerning the wickedness or goodness of human nature, enters not in the least into that other question concerning the origin of society; nor is there any thing to be considered but the degrees of men's sagacity or folly. For whether the passion of self-interest be esteemed vicious or virtuous, it is all a case; since itself alone restrains it: so that if it be virtuous, men become social by their virtue; if vicious, their vice has the same effect.

Now as it is by establishing the rule for the stability of possession, that this passion restrains itself; if that rule be very abstruse, and of difficult invention; society must be esteemed, in a manner, accidental, and the effect of many ages. But if it be found, that nothing can be more simple and obvious than that rule; that every parent, in order to preserve peace among his children, must establish it; and that these first rudiments of justice must every day be improved, as the society enlarges: if all this appear evident, as it certainly must, we may conclude, that it is utterly impossible for men to remain any considerable time in that savage condition, which precedes society; but that his very first state and situation may justly be esteemed social. This, however, hinders not, but that philosophers may, if they please, extend their reasoning to the supposed *state of nature*; provided they allow it to be a mere philosophical fiction, which never had, and never could have any reality. Human nature being composed of two principal parts, which are requisite in all its actions, the affections and understanding; it is certain, that the blind motions of the former, without the direction of the latter, incapacitate men for society: and it may be allowed us to consider separately the effects, that result from the separate operations of these two component parts of the mind. The same liberty may be permitted to moral, which is allowed to natural philosophers; and it is very usual with the latter to consider any motion as compounded and consisting of two parts separate from each other, though at the same time they acknowledge it to be in itself uncompounded and inseparable.

This *state of nature*, therefore, is to be regarded as a mere fiction, not unlike that of the *golden age*, which poets have invented; only with this difference, that the former is described as full of war, violence and injustice; whereas the latter is pointed out to us, as the most charming and most peaceable condition, that can possibly be imagined. The seasons, in that first age of nature, were so temperate, if we may believe the poets, that there was no necessity for men to provide themselves with clothes and houses as a security against the violence of heat and cold. The rivers flowed with wine and milk: the oaks yielded honey; and nature spontaneously produced her greatest delicacies. Nor were these the chief advantages of that happy age. The storms and tempests were not alone removed from nature; but those more furious tempests were unknown to human breasts, which now cause such uproar, and engender such confusion. Avarice, ambition, cruelty, selfishness, were never heard of: cordial affection, compassion, sympathy, were the only movements, with which the human mind was yet acquainted. Even the distinction of *mine* and *thine* was banished from that happy race of mortals, and carried with them the very notions of property and obligation, justice and injustice.

This, no doubt, is to be regarded as an idle fiction; but yet deserves our attention, because nothing can more evidently shew the origin of those virtues, which are the subjects of our present enquiry. I have already observed, that justice takes its rise from human conventions; and that these are intended as a remedy to some inconveniences, which proceed from the concurrence of certain *qualities* of the human mind with the *situation* of external objects. The qualities of the mind are *selfishness* and *limited generosity*: and the situation of external objects is their *easy change*, joined to their *scarcity* in comparison of the wants and desires of men. But however philosophers may have been bewildered in those speculations, poets have been guided more infallibly, by a certain taste or common instinct, which in most kinds of reasoning goes farther than any of that art and philosophy, with which we have been yet acquainted. They easily perceived, if every man had a tender regard for another, or if nature supplied abundantly all our wants and desires, that the jealousy of interest, which justice supposes, could no longer have place; nor would there be any occasion for those distinctions and limits of property and possession, which at present are in use among mankind. Increase to a sufficient degree the benevolence of men, or the bounty of nature, and you render justice useless, by supplying its place with much nobler virtues, and more valuable blessings. The selfishness of men is animated by the few possessions we have, in proportion to our wants; and it is to restrain this selfishness, that men have been obliged to separate themselves from the community, and to distinguish betwixt their own goods and those of others.

Nor need we have recourse to the fictions of poets to learn this; but beside the reason of the thing, may discover the same truth by common experience and observation. It is easy to remark, that a cordial affection renders all things common among friends; and that married people in particular mutually lose their property, and are unacquainted with the *mine* and *thine*, which are so necessary, and yet cause such disturbance in human society. The same effect arises from any alteration in the circumstances of mankind; as when there is such a plenty of any thing as satisfies all the desires of men: in which case the distinction of property is entirely lost, and every thing remains in common. This we may observe with regard to air and water, though the most valuable of all external objects; and may easily conclude, that if men were supplied with every thing in the same abundance, or if *every one* had the same affection and tender regard for *every one* as for himself; justice and injustice would be equally unknown among mankind.

Here then is a proposition, which, I think, may be regarded as certain, that *it is only from the selfishness and confined generosity of men, along with the scanty provision nature has made for his wants, that justice derives its origin*. If we look backward we shall find, that this proposition bestows an additional force on some of those observations, which we have already made on this subject.

First, we may conclude from it, that a regard to public interest, or a strong extensive benevolence, is not our first and original motive for the observation of the rules of justice; since it is allowed, that if men were endowed with such a benevolence, these rules would never have been dreamt of.

Secondly, we may conclude from the same principle, that the sense of justice is not founded on reason, or on the discovery of certain connexions and relations of ideas, which are eternal, immutable, and universally obligatory. For since it is confessed, that such an alteration as that above-mentioned, in the temper and circumstances of mankind, would entirely alter our duties and obligations, it is necessary upon the common system, *that the sense of virtue is derived from reason*, to shew the change which this must produce in the relations and ideas. But it is evident, that the only cause, why the extensive generosity of man, and the perfect abundance of every thing, would destroy the very idea of justice, is because they render it useless; and that, on the other hand, his confined benevolence, and his necessitous condition, give rise to that virtue, only by making it requisite to the publick interest, and to that of every individual. It was therefore a concern for our own, and the publick interest, which made us establish the laws of justice; and nothing can be more certain, than that it is not any relation of ideas, which gives us this concern, but our impressions and sentiments, without which every thing in nature is perfectly indifferent to us, and can never in the least affect us. The sense of justice, therefore, is not founded on our ideas, but on our impressions.

Thirdly, we may farther confirm the foregoing proposition, *that those impressions, which give rise to this sense of justice, are not natural to the mind of man, but arise from artifice and human conventions.* For since any considerable alteration of temper and circumstances destroys equally justice and injustice; and since such an alteration has an effect only by changing our own and the publick interest; it follows, that the first establishment of the rules of justice depends on these different interests. But if men pursued the publick interest naturally, and with a hearty affection, they would never have dreamed of restraining each other by these rules; and if they pursued their own interest, without any precaution, they would run head-long into every kind of injustice and violence.

These rules, therefore, are artificial, and seek their end in an oblique and indirect manner; nor is the interest, which gives rise to them, of a kind that could be pursued by the natural and inartificial passions of men.

To make this more evident, consider, that though the rules of justice are established merely by interest, their connexion with interest is somewhat singular, and is different from what may be observed on other occasions. A single act of justice is frequently contrary to *public interest*; and were it to stand alone, without being followed by other acts, may, in itself, be very prejudicial to society. When a man of merit, of a beneficent disposition, restores a great fortune to a miser, or a seditious bigot, he has acted justly and laudably, but the public is a real sufferer. Nor is every single act of justice, considered apart, more conducive to private interest, than to public; and it is easily conceived how a man may impoverish himself by a signal instance of integrity, and have reason to wish, that with regard to that single act, the laws of justice were for a moment suspended in the universe. But however single acts of justice may be contrary, either to public or private interest, it is certain, that the whole plan or scheme is highly conducive, or indeed absolutely requisite, both to the support of society, and the well-being of every individual. It is impossible to separate the good from the ill. Property must be stable, and must be fixed by general rules. Though in one instance the public be a sufferer, this momentary ill is amply compensated by the steady prosecution of the rule, and by the peace and order, which it establishes in society. And even every individual person must find himself a gainer, on balancing the account; since, without justice society must immediately dissolve, and every one must fall into that savage and solitary condition, which is infinitely worse than the worst situation that can possibly be supposed in society. When therefore men have had experience enough to observe, that whatever may be the consequence of any single act of justice, performed by a single person, yet the whole system of actions, concurred in by the whole society, is infinitely advantageous to the whole, and to every part; it is not long before justice and property take place. Every member of society is sensible of this interest: every one expresses this sense to his fellows, along with the resolution he has taken of squaring his actions by it, on condition that others will do the same. No more is requisite to induce any one of them to perform an act of justice, who has the first opportunity. This becomes an example to others. And thus justice establishes itself by a kind of convention or agreement; that is, by a sense of interest, supposed to be common to all, and where every single act is performed in expectation that others are to perform the like. Without such a convention, no one would ever have dreamed, that there was such a virtue as justice, or have been induced to conform his actions to it. Taking any single act, my justice may be pernicious in every respect; and it is only upon the supposition that others are to imitate my example, that I can be induced to embrace that virtue; since nothing but this combination can render justice advantageous, or afford me any motives to conform my self to its rules.

We come now to the second question we proposed, *viz. Why we annex the idea of virtue to justice, and of vice to injustice.* This question will not detain us long after the principles, which we have already established. All we can say of it at present will be dispatched in a few words: and for farther satisfaction, the reader must wait till we come to the *third* part of this book. The *natural* obligation to justice, *viz*, interest, has been fully explained; but as to the *moral* obligation, or the sentiment of right and wrong, it will first be requisite to examine the natural virtues, before we can give a full and satisfactory account of it.

After men have found by experience, that their selfishness and confined generosity, acting at their liberty, totally incapacitate them for society; and at the same time have observed, that society is necessary to the satisfaction of those very passions, they are naturally induced to lay themselves under the restraint of such rules, as may render their commerce more safe and commodious. To the imposition then, and observance of these rules, both in general, and in every particular instance, they are at first induced only by a regard to interest; and this motive, on the first formation of society, is sufficiently strong and forcible. But when society has become numerous, and has increased to a tribe or nation, this interest is more remote; nor do men so readily perceive, that disorder and confusion follow upon every breach of these rules, as in a more narrow and contracted society. But though in our own actions we may frequently lose sight of that interest, which we have in maintaining order, and may follow a lesser and more present interest, we never fail to observe the prejudice we receive, either mediately or immediately, from the injustice of others; as not being in that case either blinded by passion, or biased by any contrary temptation. Nay when the injustice is so distant from us, as no way to affect our interest, it still displeases us; because we consider it as prejudicial to human society, and pernicious to every one that approaches the person guilty of it. We partake of their uneasiness by *sympathy*; and as every thing, which gives uneasiness in human actions, upon the general survey, is called Vice, and whatever produces satisfaction, in the same manner, is denominated Virtue; this is the reason why the sense of moral good and evil follows upon justice and injustice. And though this sense, in the present case, be derived only from contemplating the actions of others, yet we fail not to extend it even to our own actions. The *general rule* reaches beyond those instances, from which it arose; while at the same time we naturally *sympathize* with others in the sentiments they entertain of us. *Thus self-interest is the original motive to the* establishment *of justice*: *but a* sympathy *with public interest is the source of the* moral approbation, *which attends that virtue.*

Though this progress of the sentiments be *natural*, and even necessary, it is certain, that it is here forwarded by the artifice of politicians, who, in order to govern men more easily, and preserve peace in human society, have endeavoured to produce an esteem for justice, and an abhorrence of injustice. This, no doubt, must have its effect; but nothing can be more evident, than that the matter has been carried too far by certain writers on morals, who seem to have employed their utmost efforts to extirpate all sense of virtue from among mankind. Any artifice of politicians may assist nature in the producing of those sentiments, which she suggests to us, and may even on some occasions, produce alone an approbation or esteem for any particular action; but it is impossible it should be the sole cause of the distinction we make betwixt vice and virtue. For if nature did not aid us in this particular, it would be in vain for politicians to talk of *honourable* or *dishonourable*, *praiseworthy* or *blameable*. These words would be perfectly unintelligible, and would no more have any idea annexed to them, than if they were of a tongue perfectly unknown to us. The utmost politicians can perform, is, to extend the natural sentiments beyond their original bounds; but still nature must furnish the materials, and give us some notion of moral distinctions.

As publick praise and blame increase our esteem for justice; so private education and instruction contribute to the same effect. For as parents easily observe, that a man is the more useful, both to himself and others, the greater degree of probity and honour he is endowed with; and that those principles have greater force, when custom and education assist interest and reflection: for these reasons they are induced to inculcate on their children, from their earliest infancy, the principles of probity, and teach them to regard the observance of those rules, by which society is maintained, as worthy and honourable, and their violation as base and infamous. By this means the sentiments of honour may take root in their tender minds, and acquire such firmness and solidity, that they may fall little short of those principles, which are the most essential to our natures, and the most deeply radicated in our internal constitution.

What farther contributes to increase their solidity, is the interest of our reputation, after the opinion, *that a merit or demerit attends justice or injustice*, is once firmly established among mankind. There is nothing, which touches us more nearly than our reputation, and nothing on which our reputation more depends than our conduct, with relation to the property of others. For this reason, every one, who has any regard to his character, or who intends to live on good terms with mankind, must fix an inviolable law to himself, never, by any temptation, to be induced to violate those principles, which are essential to a man of probity and honour.

I shall make only one observation before I leave this subject, *viz*, that though I assert, that in the *state of nature*, or that imaginary state, which preceded society, there be neither justice nor injustice, yet I assert not, that it was allowable, in such a state, to violate the property of others. I only maintain, that there was no such thing as property; and consequently could be no such thing as justice or injustice. I shall have occasion to make a similar reflection with regard to *promises*, when I come to treat of them; and I hope this reflection, when duly weighed, will suffice to remove all odium from the foregoing opinions, with regard to justice and injustice.

SECTION THREE

Of the rules which determine property

Though the establishment of the rule, concerning the stability of possession, be not only useful, but even absolutely necessary to human society, it can never serve to any purpose, while it remains in such general terms. Some method must be shewn, by which we may distinguish what particular goods are to be assigned to each particular person, while the rest of mankind are excluded from their possession and enjoyment. Our next business, then, must be to discover the reasons which modify this general rule, and fit it to the common use and practice of the world.

It is obvious, that those reasons are not derived from any utility or advantage, which either the *particular* person or the public may reap from his enjoyment of any *particular* goods, beyond what would result from the possession of them by any other person. It were better, no doubt, that every one were possessed of what is most suitable to him, and proper for his use: but besides, that this relation of fitness may be common to several at once, it is liable to so many controversies, and men are so partial and passionate in judging of these controversies, that such a loose and uncertain rule would be absolutely incompatible with the peace of human society. The convention concerning the stability of possession is entered into, in order to cut off all occasions of discord and contention; and this end would never be attained, were we allowed to apply this rule differently in every particular case, according to every particular utility, which might be discovered in such an application. Justice, in her decisions, never regards the fitness or unfitness of objects to particular persons, but conducts herself by more extensive views. Whether a man be generous, or a miser, he is equally well received by her, and obtains with the same facility a decision in his favours, even for what is entirely useless to him.

It follows, therefore, that the general rule, *that possession must be stable*, is not applied by particular judgments, but by other general rules, which must extend to the whole society, and be inflexible either by spite or favour. To illustrate this, I propose the following instance. I first consider men in their savage and solitary condition; and suppose, that being sensible of the misery of that state, and foreseeing the advantages that would result from society, they seek each other's company, and make an offer of mutual protection and assistance. I also suppose, that they are endowed with such sagacity as immediately to perceive, that the chief impediment to this project of society and partnership lies in the avidity and selfishness of their natural temper; to remedy which, they enter into a convention for the stability of possession, and for mutual restraint and forbearance. I am sensible, that this method of proceeding is not altogether natural; but besides that I here only suppose those reflections to be formed at once, which in fact arise insensibly and by degrees; besides this, I say, it is very possible, that several persons, being by different accidents separated from the societies, to which they formerly belonged, may be obliged to form a new society among themselves; in which case they are entirely in the situation above-mentioned.

It is evident, then, that their first difficulty, in this situation, after the general convention for the establishment of society, and for the constancy of possession, is, how to separate their possessions, and assign to each his particular portion, which he must for the future inalterably enjoy. This difficulty will not detain them long; but it must immediately occur to them, as the most natural expedient, that every one continue to enjoy what he is at present master of, and that property or constant possession be conjoined to the immediate possession. Such is the effect of custom, that it not only reconciles us to any thing we have long enjoyed, but even gives us an affection for it, and makes us prefer it to other objects, which may be more valuable, but are less known to us. What has long lain under our eye, and has often been employed to our advantage, *that* we are always the most unwilling to part with; but can easily live without possessions, which we never have enjoyed, and are not accustomed to. It is evident, therefore, that men would easily acquiesce in this expedient, *that every one continue to enjoy what he is at present possessed of;* and this is the reason, why they would so naturally agree in preferring it.*

* No questions in philosophy are more difficult, than when a number of causes present themselves for the same phenomenon, to determine which is the principal and predominant. There seldom is any very precise argument to fix our choice, and men must be contented to be guided by a kind of taste or fancy, arising from analogy, and a comparison of familiar instances. Thus, in the present case, there are, no doubt, motives of public interest for most of the rules, which determine property; but still I suspect, that these rules are principally fixed by the

But we may observe, that though the rule of the assignment of property to the present possessor be natural, and by that means useful, yet its utility extends not beyond the first formation of society; nor would any thing be more pernicious, than the constant observance of it; by which restitution would be excluded, and every injustice would be authorized and rewarded. We must, therefore, seek for some other circumstance, that may give rise to property after society is once established; and of this kind, I find four most considerable, *viz.* Occupation, Prescription, Accession, and Succession. We shall briefly examine each of these, beginning with *Occupation.*

---

imagination, or the more frivolous properties of our thought and conception. I shall continue to explain these causes, leaving it to the reader's choice, whether he will prefer those derived from publick utility, or those derived from the imagination. We shall begin with the right of the present possessor.

It is a quality, which I have already observed in human nature, that when two objects appear in a close relation to each other, the mind is apt to ascribe to them any additional relation, in order to compleat the union; and this inclination is so strong, as often to make us run into errors (such as that of the conjunction of thought and matter) if we find that they can serve to that purpose. Many of our impressions are incapable of place or local position; and yet those very impressions we suppose to have a local conjunction with the impressions of sight and touch, merely because they are conjoined by causation, and are already united in the imagination. Since, therefore, we can feign a new relation, and even an absurd one, in order to compleat any union, it will easily be imagined, that if there be any relations, which depend on the mind, it will readily conjoin them to any preceding relation, and unite, by a new bond, such objects as have already an union in the fancy. Thus for instance, we never fail, in our arrangement of bodies, to place those which are *resembling* in *contiguity* to each other, or at least in *correspondent* points of view; because we feel a satisfaction in joining the relation of contiguity to that of resemblance, or the resemblance of situation to that of qualities. And this is easily accounted for from the known properties of human nature. When the mind is determined to join certain objects, but undetermined in its choice of the particular objects, it naturally turns its eye to such as are related together. They are already united in the mind: they present themselves at the same time to the conception; and instead of requiring any new reason for their conjunction, it would require a very powerful reason to make us over-look this natural affinity. This we shall have occasion to explain more fully afterwards, when we come to treat of *beauty.* In the mean time, we may content ourselves with observing, that the same love of order and uniformity, which arranges the books in a library, and the chairs in a parlour, contribute to the formation of society, and to the well-being of mankind, by modifying the general rule concerning the stability of possession. And as property forms a relation betwixt a person and an object, it is natural to found it on some preceding relation; and as property is nothing but a constant possession, secured by the laws of society, it is natural to add it to the present possession, which is a relation that resembles it. For this also has its influence. If it be natural to conjoin all sorts of relations, it is more so, to conjoin such relations as are resembling, and are related together.

The possession of all external goods is changeable and uncertain; which is one of the most considerable impediments to the establishment of society, and is the reason why, by universal agreement, express or tacit, men restrain themselves by what we now call the rules of justice and equity. The misery of the condition, which precedes this restraint, is the cause why we submit to that remedy as quickly as possible; and this affords us an easy reason, why we annex the idea of property to the first possession, or to *occupation*. Men are unwilling to leave property in suspense, even for the shortest time, or open the least door to violence and disorder. To which we may add, that the first possession always engages the attention most; and did we neglect it, there would be no colour of reason for assigning property to any succeeding possession.*

There remains nothing, but to determine exactly, what is meant by possession; and this is not so easy as may at first sight be imagined. We are said to be in possession of any thing, not only when we immediately touch it, but also when we are so situated with respect to it, as to have it in our power to use it; and may move, alter, or destroy it, according to our present pleasure or advantage. This relation, then, is a species of cause and effect; and as property is nothing but a stable possession, derived from the rules of justice, or the conventions of men, it is to be considered as the same species of relation. But here we may observe, that as the power of using any object becomes more or less certain, according as the interruptions we may meet with are more or less probable; and as this probability may increase by insensible degrees; it is in many cases impossible to determine when possession begins or ends; nor is there any certain standard, by which we can decide such controversies. A wild boar, that falls into our snares, is deemed to be in our possession, if it be impossible for him to escape. But what do we mean by impossible? How do we separate

---

* Some philosophers account for the right of occupation, by saying, that every one has a property in his own labour; and when he joins that labour to any thing, it gives him the property of the whole: But, 1. There are several kinds of occupation, where we cannot be said to join our labour to the object we acquire: as when we possess a meadow by grazing our cattle upon it. 2. This accounts for the matter by means of *accession*; which is taking a needless circuit. 3. We cannot be said to join our labour to any thing but in a figurative sense. Properly speaking, we only make an alteration on it by our labour. This forms a relation betwixt us and the object; and thence arises the property, according to the preceding principles.

this impossibility from an improbability? And how distinguish that exactly from a probability? Mark the precise limits of the one and the other, and shew the standard, by which we may decide all disputes that may arise, and, as we find by experience, frequently do arise upon this subject.*

* If we seek a solution of these difficulties in reason and public interest, we never shall find satisfaction; and if we look for it in the imagination, it is evident, that the qualities, which operate upon that faculty, run so insensibly and gradually into each other, that it is impossible to give them any precise bounds or termination. The difficulties on this head must increase, when we consider, that our judgment alters very sensibly, according to the subject, and that the same power and proximity will be deemed possession in one case, which is not esteemed such in another. A person, who has hunted a hare to the last degree of weariness, would look upon it as an injustice for another to rush in before him, and seize his prey. But the same person advancing to pluck an apple, that hangs within his reach, has no reason to complain, if another, more alert, passes him, and takes possession. What is the reason of this difference, but that immobility, not being natural to the hare, but the effect of industry, forms in that case a strong relation with the hunter, which is wanting in the other?

Here then it appears, that a certain and infallible power of enjoyment, without touch or some other sensible relation, often produces not property: and I farther observe, that a sensible relation, without any present power, is sometimes sufficient to give a title to any object. The sight of a thing is seldom a considerable relation, and is only regarded as such, when the object is hidden, or very obscure; in which case we find, that the view alone conveys a property; according to that maxim, *that even a whole continent belongs to the nation, which first discovered it.* It is however remarkable that both in the case of discovery and that of possession, the first discoverer and possessor must join to the relation an intention of rendering himself proprietor, otherwise the relation will not have its effect; and that because the connexion in our fancy betwixt the property and the relation is not so great, but that it requires to be helped by such an intention.

From all these circumstances, it is easy to see how perplexed many questions may become concerning the acquisition of property by occupation; and the least effort of thought may present us with instances, which are not susceptible of any reasonable decision. If we prefer examples, which are real, to such as are feigned, we may consider the following one, which is to be met with in almost every writer, that has treated of the laws of nature. Two *Grecian* colonies, leaving their native country, in search of new seats, were informed that a city near them was deserted by its inhabitants. To know the truth of this report, they dispatched at once two messengers, one from each colony; who finding on their approach, that their information was true, begun a race together with an intention to take possession of the city, each of them for his countrymen. One of these messengers, finding that he was not an equal match for the other, launched his spear at the gates of the city, and was so fortunate as to fix it there before the arrival of his companion. This produced a dispute betwixt the two colonies, which of them was the proprietor of the empty city; and this dispute still subsists among philosophers. For my part I find the dispute impossible to be decided, and that because the whole question hangs upon the fancy, which in this case is not possessed of any precise or determinate standard, upon which it can give sentence. To make this evident, let us consider, that if these two persons had

But such disputes may not only arise concerning the real existence of property and possession, but also concerning their extent; and these disputes are often susceptible of no decision, or can be decided by no other faculty than the imagination. A person who lands on the shore of a small island, that is desert and uncultivated, is deemed its possessor from the very first moment, and acquires the property of the whole; because the object is there bounded and circumscribed in the fancy, and at the same time is proportioned to the new possessor. The same person landing on a desert island, as large as *Great Britain*, extends his property no farther than his immediate possession; though a numerous colony are esteemed the proprietors of the whole from the instant of their debarkment.

But it often happens, that the title of first possession becomes obscure through time; and that it is impossible to determine many controversies, which may arise concerning it. In that case long possession or *prescription* naturally takes place, and gives a person a sufficient property in any thing he enjoys. The nature of human society admits not of any great accuracy; nor can we always remount to the first origin of things, in order to determine their present condition. Any considerable space of time sets objects at such a distance, that they seem, in a manner, to lose their reality, and have as little influence on the mind, as if they never had been in being. A man's title, that is clear and certain at present, will seem obscure and doubtful fifty years hence, even though the facts, on which it is founded, should be proved with the greatest evidence and certainty. The same facts have not the same influence after so long an interval of time. And this may be received as a convincing argument for our preceding

---

been simply members of the colonies, and not messengers or deputies, their actions would not have been of any consequence; since in that case their relation to the colonies would have been but feeble and imperfect. Add to this, that nothing determined them to run to the gates rather than the walls, or any other part of the city, but that the gates, being the most obvious and remarkable part, satisfy the fancy best in taking them for the whole; as we find by the poets, who frequently draw their images and metaphors from them. Besides we may consider, that the touch or contact of the one messenger is not properly possession, no more than the piercing the gates with a spear; but only forms a relation; and there is a relation, in the other case, equally obvious, tho' not, perhaps, of equal force. Which of these relations, then, conveys a right and property, or whether any of them be sufficient for that effect, I leave to the decision of such as are wiser than myself.

doctrine with regard to property and justice. Possession during a long tract of time conveys a title to any object. But as it is certain, that, however every thing be produced in time, there is nothing real that is produced by time; it follows, that property being produced by time, is not any thing real in the objects, but is the off-spring of the sentiments, on which alone time is found to have any influence.*

We acquire the property of objects by *accession*, when they are connected in an intimate manner with objects that are already our property, and at the same time are inferior to them. Thus the fruits of our garden, the offspring of our cattle, and the work of our slaves, are all of them esteemed our property, even before possession. Where objects are connected together in the imagination, they are apt to be put on the same footing, and are commonly supposed to be endowed with the same qualities. We readily pass from one to the other, and make no difference in our judgments concerning them; especially if the latter be inferior to the former.†

* Present possession is plainly a relation betwixt a person and an object; but is not sufficient to counter-balance the relation of first possession, unless the former be long and uninterrupted: in which case the relation is increased on the side of the present possession, by the extent of time, and diminished on that of first possession, by the distance, This change in the relation produces a consequent change in the property.

† This source of property can never be explained but from the imaginations; and one may affirm, that the causes are here unmixed. We shall proceed to explain them more particularly, and illustrate them by examples from common life and experience.

It has been observed above, that the mind has a natural propensity to join relations, especially resembling ones, and finds a kind of fitness and uniformity in such an union. From this propensity are derived these laws of nature, *that upon the first formation of society, property always follows the present possession;* and afterwards, *that it arises from first or from long possession.* Now we may easily observe, that relation is not confined merely to one degree; but that from an object, that is related to us, we acquire a relation to every other object, which is related to it, and so on, till the thought loses the chain by too long a progress, However the relation may weaken by each remove, it is not immediately destroyed; but frequently connects two objects by means of an intermediate one, which is related to both. And this principle is of such force as to give rise to the right of *accession,* and causes us to acquire the property not only of such objects as we are immediately possessed of; but also of such as are closely connected with them.

Suppose a *German,* a *Frenchman,* and a *Spaniard* to come into a room, where there are placed upon the table three bottles of wine, *Rhenish, Burgundy* and *Port;* and suppose they should fall a quarrelling about the division of them; a person, who was chosen for umpire would naturally, to shew his impartiality, give every one the product of his own country: and this from a principle, which, in some

The right of *succession* is a very natural one, from the presumed consent of the parent or near relation, and from the general interest of mankind, which requires, that men's possessions should pass to those, who are dearest to them, in order to render them

---

measure, is the source of those laws of nature, that ascribe property to occupation, prescription and accession.

In all these cases, and particularly that of accession, there is first a *natural* union betwixt the idea of the person and that of the object, and afterwards a new and *moral* union produced by that right or property, which we ascribe to the person. But here there occurs a difficulty, which merits our attention, and may afford us an opportunity of putting to trial that singular method of reasoning, which has been employed on the present subject. I have already observed that the imagination passes with greater facility from little to great, than from great to little, and that the transition of ideas is always easier and smoother in the former case than in the latter. Now as the right of accession arises from the easy transition of ideas, by which related objects are connected together, it should naturally be imagined, that the right of accession must increase in strength, in proportion as the transition of ideas is performed with greater facility. It may, therefore, be thought, that when we have acquired the property of any small object, we shall readily consider any great object related to it as an accession, and as belonging to the proprietor of the small one; since the transition is in that case very easy from the small object to the great one, and should connect them together in the closest manner. But in fact the case is always found to be otherwise, The empire of *Great Britain* seems to draw along with it the dominion of the *Orkneys*, the *Hebrides*, the isle of *Man*, and the isle of *Wight*; but the authority over those lesser islands does not naturally imply any title to *Great Britain*. In short, a small object naturally follows a great one as its accession; but a great one is never supposed to belong to the proprietor of a small one related to it, merely on account of that property and relation. Yet in this latter case the transition of ideas is smoother from the proprietor to the small object, which is his property, and from the small object to the great one, than in the former case from the proprietor to the great object, and from the great one to the small. It may therefore be thought, that these phenomena are objections to the foregoing hypothesis, *that the ascribing of property to accession is nothing but an effect of the relations of ideas, and of the smooth transition of the imagination.*

It will be easy to solve this objection, if we consider the agility and unsteadiness of the imagination, with the different views, in which it is continually placing its objects. When we attribute to a person a property in two objects, we do not always pass from the person to one object, and from that to the other related to it. The objects being here to be considered as the property of the person, we are apt to join them together, and place them in the same light. Suppose, therefore, a great and a small object to be related together; if a person be strongly related to the great object, he will likewise be strongly related to both the objects, considered together, because he is related to the most considerable part. On the contrary, if he be only related to the small object, he will not be strongly related to both, considered together, since his relation lies only with the most trivial part, which is not apt to strike us in any great degree, when we consider the whole. And this is the reason, why small objects become accessions to great ones, and not great to small.

more industrious and frugal. Perhaps these causes are seconded by the influence of *relation*, or the association of ideas, by which we are naturally directed to consider the son after the parent's

---

It is the general opinion of philosophers and civilians, that the sea is incapable of becoming the property of any nation; and that because it is impossible to take possession of it, or form any such distinct relation with it, as may be the foundation of property. Where this reason ceases, property immediately takes place. Thus the most strenuous advocates for the liberty of the seas universally allow, that friths and bays naturally belong as an accession to the proprietors of the surrounding continent. These have properly no more bond or union with the land, than the *Pacific* ocean would have; but having an union in the fancy, and being at the same time *inferior*, they are of course regarded as an accession.

The property of rivers, by the laws of most nations, and by the natural turn of our thought, is attributed to the proprietors of their banks, excepting such vast rivers as the *Rhine* or the *Danube*, which seem too large to the imagination to follow as an accession the property of the neighbouring fields. Yet even these rivers are considered as the property of that nation, thro' whose dominions they run; the idea of a nation being of a suitable bulk to correspond with them, and bear them such a relation in the fancy.

The accessions, which are made to lands bordering upon rivers, follow the land, say the civilians, provided it be made by what they call *alluvion*, that is, insensibly and imperceptibly; which are circumstances that mightily assist the imagination in the conjunction. Where there is any considerable portion torn at once from one bank, and joined to another, it becomes not his property, whose land it falls on, till it unite with the land, and till the trees or plants have spread their roots into both. Before that, the imagination does not sufficiently join them.

There are other cases, which somewhat resemble this of accession, but which, at the bottom, are considerably different, and merit our attention. Of this kind is the conjunction of the properties of different persons, after such a manner as not to admit of *separation*. The question is, to whom the united mass must belong.

Where this conjunction is of such a nature as to admit of *division*, but not of *separation*, the decision is natural and easy. The whole mass must be supposed to be common betwixt the proprietors of the several parts, and afterwards must be divided according to the proportions of these parts. But here I cannot forbear taking notice of a remarkable subtilty of the *Roman* law, in distinguishing betwixt *confusion* and *commixtion*. Confusion is an union of two bodies, such as different liquors, where the parts become entirely undistinguishable. Commixtion is the blending of two bodies, such as two bushels of corn, where the parts remain separate in an obvious and visible manner. As in the latter case the imagination discovers not so entire an union as in the former, but is able to trace and preserve a distinct idea of the property of each; this is the reason, why the *civil* law, though it established an entire community in the case of *confusion*, and after that a proportional division, yet in the case of *commixtion*, supposes each of the proprietors to maintain a distinct right; however necessity may at last force them to submit to the same division.

Quod si frumentum Titii frumento tuo mistum fuerit: siquidem ex voluntate vestra, commune est: quia singula corpora, id est, singula grana, quae cujusque propria fuerunt, ex consensu vestro communicata sunt. Quod si casu id mistum fuerit, vel Titius id miscuerit sine tua voluntate, non videtur id commune esse; quia singula corpora in sua substantia durant. Sed nec magis istis casibus commune sit frumentum quam grex intelligitur esse communis, si pecora Titii tuis pecoribus mista fuerint. Sed si ab alterutro vestrum totum id frumentum

decease, and ascribe to him a title to his father's possessions. Those goods must become the property of some body: but of *whom* is the question. Here it is evident the person's children naturally present

---

retineatur, in rem quidem actio pro modo frumenti cujusque competit. Arbitrio autem judicis, ut ipse aestimet quale cujusque frumentum fuerit. Inst. Lib. ii. Tit. i. 28.

Where the properties of two persons are united after such a manner as neither to admit of *division* nor *separation*, as when one builds a house on another's ground, in that case, the whole must belong to one of the proprietors: and here I assert, that it naturally is conceived to belong to the proprietor of the most considerable part. For however the compound object may have a relation to two different persons, and carry our view at once to both of them, yet as the most considerable part principally engages our attention, and by the strict union draws the inferior along it; for this reason, the whole bears a relation to the proprietor of that part, and is regarded as his property. The only difficulty is, what we shall be pleased to call the most considerable part, and most attractive to the imagination.

This quality depends on several different circumstances, which have little connexion with each other. One part of a compound object may become more considerable than another, either because it is more constant and durable; because it is of greater value; because it is more obvious and remarkable; because it is of greater extent; or because its existence is more separate and independent. It will be easy to conceive, that, as these circumstances may be conjoined and opposed in all the different ways, and according to all the different degrees, which can be imagined, there will result many cases, where the reasons on both sides are so equally balanced, that it is impossible for us to give any satisfactory decision. Here then is the proper business of municipal laws, to fix what the principles of human nature have left undetermined.

The superficies yields to the soil, says the civil law: the writing to the paper: the canvas to the picture. These decisions do not well agree together, and are a proof of the contrariety of those principles, from which they are derived.

But of all the questions of this kind the most curious is that, which for so many ages divided the disciples of *Proculus* and *Sabinus*. Suppose a person should make a cup from the metal of another, or a ship from his wood, and suppose the proprietor of the metal or wood should demand his goods, the question is, whether he acquires a title to the cup or ship. *Sabinus* maintained the affirmative, and asserted that the substance or matter is the foundation of all the qualities; that it is incorruptible and immortal, and therefore superior to the form, which is casual and dependent. On the other hand, *Proculus* observed, that the form is the most obvious and remarkable part, and that from it bodies are denominated of this or that particular species. To which he might have added, that the matter or substance is in most bodies so fluctuating and uncertain, that it is utterly impossible to trace it in all its changes. For my part, I know not from what principles such a controversy can be certainly determined. I shall therefore content my self with observing, that the decision of *Trebonian* seems to me pretty ingenious; that the cup belongs to the proprietor of the metal, because it can be brought back to its first form: But that the ship belongs to the author of its form for a contrary reason. But however ingenious this reason may seem, it plainly depends upon the fancy, which by the possibility of such a reduction, finds a closer connexion and relation betwixt a cup and the proprietor of its metal, than betwixt a ship and the proprietor of its wood, where the substance is more fixed and unalterable.

themselves to the mind; and being already. connected to those possessions by means of their deceased parent, we are apt to connect them still farther by the relation of property. Of this there are many parallel instances.*

SECTION FOUR

Of the transference of property by consent

However useful, or even necessary, the stability of possession may be to human society, it is attended with very considerable inconveniences. The relation of fitness or suitableness ought never to enter into consideration, in distributing the properties of mankind; but we must govern ourselves by rules, which are more general in their application, and more free from doubt and uncertainty. Of this kind is *present* possession upon the first establishment of society; and afterwards *occupation, prescription, accession,* and *succession.* As these depend very much on chance, they must frequently prove contradictory both to men's wants and desires; and persons and possessions must often be very ill adjusted. This is a grand inconvenience, which calls for a remedy. To apply one directly, and allow every man to seize by violence what he judges to be fit for him, would destroy society; and therefore the rules of justice seek some medium betwixt a rigid stability, and this changeable and uncertain adjustment. But there is no medium better than that obvious one, that possession and property should always be stable, except when the proprietor consents to bestow them on some other person. This rule can have no ill consequence, in occasioning

---

* In examining the different titles to authority in government, we shall meet with many reasons to convince us, that the right of succession depends, in a great measure on the imagination. Mean while I shall rest contented with observing one example, which belongs to the present subject. Suppose that a person die without children, and that a dispute arises among his relations concerning his inheritance; it is evident, that if his riches be derived partly from his father, partly from his mother, the most natural way of determining such a dispute, is, to divide his possessions, and assign each part to the family, from whence it is derived. Now as the person is supposed to have been once the full and entire proprietor of those goods; I ask, what is it makes us find a certain equity and natural reason in this partition, except it be the imagination? His affection to these families does not depend upon his possessions; for which reason his consent can never be presumed precisely for such a partition. And as to the public interest, it seems not to be in the least concerned on the one side or the other.

wars and dissentions; since the proprietor's consent, who alone is concerned, is taken along in the alienation: and it may serve to many good purposes in adjusting property to persons. Different parts of the earth produce different commodities; and not only so, but different men both are by nature fitted for different employments, and attain to greater perfection in any one, when they confine themselves to it alone. All this requires a mutual exchange and commerce; for which reason the translation of property by consent is founded on a law of nature, as well as its stability without such a consent.

So far is determined by a plain utility and interest. But perhaps it is from more trivial reasons, that *delivery*, or a sensible transference of the object is commonly required by civil laws, and also by the laws of nature, according to most authors, as a requisite circumstance in the translation of property. The property of an object, when taken for something real, without any reference to morality, or the sentiments of the mind, is a quality perfectly insensible, and even inconceivable; nor can we form any distinct notion, either of its stability or translation. This imperfection of our ideas is less sensibly felt with regard to its stability, as it engages less our attention, and is easily passed over by the mind, without any scrupulous examination. But as the translation of property from one person to another is a more remarkable event, the defect of our ideas becomes more sensible on that occasion, and obliges us to turn ourselves on every side in search of some remedy. Now as nothing more enlivens any idea than a present impression, and a relation betwixt that impression and the idea; it is natural for us to seek some false light from this quarter. In order to aid the imagination in conceiving the transference of property, we take the sensible object, and actually transfer its possession to the person, on whom we would bestow the property. The supposed resemblance of the actions, and the presence of this sensible delivery, deceive the mind, and make it fancy, that it conceives the mysterious transition of the property. And that this explication of the matter is just, appears hence, that men have invented a *symbolical* delivery, to satisfy the fancy, where the real one is impracticable. Thus the giving the keys of a granary is understood to be the delivery of the corn contained in it: the giving of stone and earth represents the delivery of a manor. This is a kind of superstitious practice in civil laws, and in the laws of nature, resembling the *Roman catholic* superstitions in religion. As the *Roman catholics* represent the inconceivable mysteries of the *Christian* religion, and render them more present to the mind, by a taper, or habit, or grimace, which is supposed to resemble them; so lawyers and moralists have run into like inventions for the same reason, and have endeavoured by those means to satisfy themselves concerning the transference of property by consent.

SECTION FIVE

Of the obligation of promises

That the rule of morality, which enjoins the performance of promises, is not *natural*, will sufficiently appear from these two propositions, which I proceed to prove, *viz*, *that a promise would not be intelligible, before human conventions had established it*; and *that even if it were intelligible, it would not be attended with any moral obligation*.

I say, *first*, that a promise is not intelligible naturally, nor antecedent to human conventions; and that a man, unacquainted with society, could never enter into any engagements with another, even though they could perceive each other's thoughts by intuition. If promises be natural and intelligible, there must be some act of the mind attending these words, *I promise*; and on this act of the mind must the obligation depend. Let us, therefore, run over all the faculties of the soul, and see which of them is exerted in our promises.

The act of the mind, expressed by a promise, is not a *resolution* to perform any thing: for that alone never imposes any obligation. Nor is it a *desire* of such a performance: for we may bind ourselves without such a desire, or even with an aversion, declared and avowed. Neither is it the *willing* of that action, which we promise to perform: for a promise always regards some future time, and the will has an influence only on present actions. It follows, therefore, that since the act of the mind, which enters into a promise, and produces its obligation, is neither the resolving, desiring, nor willing any particular performance, it must necessarily be the *willing* of that *obligation*, which arises from the promise. Nor is this only a conclusion of philosophy; but is entirely conformable to our common ways of thinking and of expressing ourselves, when we say that we are bound by our own consent, and that the obligation arises from our mere will and pleasure. The only question then is, whether there be not a manifest absurdity in supposing this act of the mind, and such an absurdity as no man could fall into, whose ideas are not confounded with prejudice and the fallacious use of language.

All morality depends upon our sentiments; and when any action, or quality of the mind, pleases us *after a certain manner*, we say it is virtuous; and when the neglect, or nonperformance of it, displeases us *after a like manner*, we say that we lie under an obligation to perform it. A change of the obligation supposes a change of the sentiment; and a creation of a new obligation supposes some new sentiment to arise. But it is certain we can naturally no more change our own sentiments, than the motions of the heavens; nor by a single act of our will, that is, by a promise, render any action agreeable or disagreeable, moral or immoral; which, without that act, would have produced contrary impressions, or have been endowed with different qualities. It would be absurd, therefore, to will any new obligation, that is, any new sentiment of pain or pleasure; nor is it possible, that men could naturally fall into so gross an absurdity. A promise, therefore, is *naturally* something altogether unintelligible, nor is there any act of the mind belonging to it.*

* Were morality discoverable by reason, and not by sentiment, it would be still more evident, that promises could make no alteration upon it. Morality is supposed to consist in relation. Every new imposition of morality, therefore, must arise from some new relation of objects; and consequently the will coud not produce *immediately* any change in morals, but could have that effect only by producing a change upon the objects. But as the moral obligation of a promise is the pure effect of the will, without the least change in any part of the universe; it follows, that promises have no *natural* obligation.

Should it be said, that this act of the will being in effect a new object, produces new relations and new duties; I would answer, that this is a pure sophism, which may be detected by a very moderate share of accuracy and exactness. To will a new obligation, is to will a new relation of objects; and therefore, if this new relation of objects were formed by the volition itself, we should in effect will the volition; which is plainly absurd and impossible. The will has here no object to which it could tend; but must return upon itself *in infinitum*. The new obligation depends upon new relations. The new relations depend upon a new volition. The new volition has for object a new obligation, and consequently new relations, and consequently a new volition; which volition again has in view a new obligation, relation and volition, without any termination. It is impossible, therefore, we could ever will a new obligation; and consequently it is impossible the will could ever accompany a promise, or produce a new obligation of morality.

But, *secondly*, if there was any act of the mind belonging to it, it could not *naturally* produce any obligation. This appears evidently from the foregoing reasoning. A promise creates a new obligation. A new obligation supposes new sentiments to arise. The will never creates new sentiments. There could not naturally, therefore, arise any obligation from a promise, even supposing the mind could fall into the absurdity of willing that obligation.

The same truth may be proved still more evidently by that reasoning, which proved justice in general to be an artificial virtue. No action can be required of us as our duty, unless there be implanted in human nature some actuating passion or motive, capable of producing the action. This motive cannot be the sense of duty. A sense of duty supposes an antecedent obligation: and where an action is not required by any natural passion, it cannot be required by any natural obligation; since it may be omitted without proving any defect or imperfection in the mind and temper, and consequently without any vice. Now it is evident we have no motive leading us to the performance of promises, distinct from a sense of duty. If we thought, that promises had no moral obligation, we never should feel any inclination to observe them. This is not the case with the natural virtues. Though there was no obligation to relieve the miserable, our humanity would lead us to it; and when we omit that duty, the immorality of the omission arises from its being a proof, that we want the natural sentiments of humanity. A father knows it to be his duty to take care of his children: but he has also a natural inclination to it. And if no human creature had that inclination, no one could lie under any such obligation. But as there is naturally no inclination to observe promises, distinct from a sense of their obligation; it follows, that fidelity is no natural virtue, and that promises have no force, antecedent to human conventions.

If any one dissent from this, he must give a regular proof of these two propositions, *viz. that there is a peculiar act of the mind, annexed to promises*; and *that consequent to this act of the mind, there arises an inclination to perform, distinct from a sense of duty*. I presume, that it is impossible to prove either of these two points; and therefore I venture to conclude that promises are human inventions, founded on the necessities and interests of society.

In order to discover these necessities and interests, we must consider the same qualities of human nature, which we have already found to give rise to the preceding laws of society. Men being naturally selfish, or endowed only with a confined generosity, they are not easily induced to perform any action for the interest of strangers, except with a view to some reciprocal advantage, which they had no hope of obtaining but by such a performance. Now as it frequently happens, that these mutual performances cannot be finished at the same instant, it is necessary, that one party be contented to remain in uncertainty, and depend upon the gratitude of the other for a return of kindness. But so much corruption is there among men, that, generally speaking, this becomes but a slender security; and as the benefactor is here supposed to bestow his favours with a view to self-interest, this both takes off from the obligation, and sets an example to selfishness, which is the true mother of ingratitude. Were we, therefore, to follow the natural course of our passions and inclinations, we should perform but few actions for the advantage of others, from disinterested views; because we are naturally very limited in our kindness and affection: and we should perform as few of that kind, out of a regard to interest; because we cannot depend upon their gratitude. Here then is the mutual commerce of good offices in a manner lost among mankind, and every one reduced to his own skill and industry for his well-being and subsistence. The invention of the law of nature, concerning the *stability* of possession, has already rendered men tolerable to each other; that of the *transference* of property and possession by consent has begun to render them mutually advant-ageous: but still these laws of nature, however strictly observed, are not sufficient to render them so serviceable to each other, as by nature they are fitted to become. Though possession be *stable*, men may often reap but small advantage from it, while they are possessed of a greater quantity of any species of goods than they have occasion for, and at the same time suffer by the want of others. The *transference* of property, which is the proper remedy for this incon-venience, cannot remedy it entirely; because it can only take place with regard to such objects as are *present* and *individual*, but not to such as are *absent* or *general*. One cannot transfer the property of a particular house, twenty leagues distant; because the consent cannot be attended with delivery, which is a requisite circumstance. Neither can one transfer the property of ten bushels of corn, or five hogsheads of wine, by the mere expression and consent; because these are only general terms, and have no direct relation to any particular heap of corn, or barrels of wine. Besides, the commerce of mankind is not confined to the barter of commodities, but may extend to services and actions, which we may exchange to our mutual interest and advantage. Your corn is ripe today; mine will be so tomorrow. It is profitable for us both, that I should labour with you today, and that you should aid me tomorrow. I have no kindness for you, and know you have as little for me. I will not, therefore, take any pains upon your account; and should I labour with you upon my own account, in expectation of a return, I know I should be disappointed, and that I should in vain depend upon your gratitude. Here then I leave you to labour alone: you treat me in the same manner. The seasons change; and both of us lose our harvests for want of mutual confidence and security.

All this is the effect of the natural and inherent principles and passions of human nature; and as these passions and principles are inalterable, it may be thought, that our conduct, which depends on them, must be so too, and that it would be in vain, either for moralists or politicians, to tamper with us, or attempt to change the usual course of our actions, with a view to public interest. And indeed, did the success of their designs depend upon their success in correcting the selfishness and ingratitude of men, they would never make any progress, unless aided by omnipotence, which is alone able to new-mould the human mind, and change its character in such fundamental articles. All they can pretend to, is, to give a new direction to those natural passions, and teach us that we can better satisfy our appetites in an oblique and artificial manner, than by their headlong and impetuous motion. Hence I learn to do a service to another, without bearing him any real kindness; because I forsee, that he will return my service, in expectation of another of the same kind, and in order to maintain the same correspondence of good offices with me or with others. And accordingly, after I have served him, and he is in possession of the advantage arising from my action, he is induced to perform his part, as foreseeing the consequences of his refusal.

But though this self-interested commerce of man begins to take place, and to predominate in society, it does not entirely abolish the more generous and noble intercourse of friendship and good offices. I may still do services to such persons as I love, and am more particularly acquainted with, without any prospect of advantage; and they may make me a return in the same manner, without any view but that of recompensing my past services. In order, therefore, to distinguish those two different sorts of commerce, the interested and the disinterested, there is a *certain form of words* invented for the former, by which we bind ourselves to the performance of any action. This form of words constitutes what we call a *promise*, which is the sanction of the interested commerce of mankind. When a man says *he promises any thing*, he in effect expresses a *resolution* of performing it; and along with that, by making use of this *form of words*, subjects himself to the penalty of never being trusted again in case of failure. A resolution is the natural act of the mind, which promises express: but were there no more than a resolution in the case, promises would only declare our former motives, and would not create any new motive or obligation. They are the conventions of men, which create a new motive, when experience has taught us, that human affairs would be conducted much more for mutual advantage, were there certain symbols or signs instituted, by which we might give each other security of our conduct in any particular incident, After these signs are instituted, whoever uses them is immediately bound by his interest to execute his engagements, and must never expect to be trusted any more, if he refuse to perform what he promised.

Nor is that knowledge, which is requisite to make mankind sensible of this interest in the *institution* and *observance* of promises, to be esteemed superior to the capacity of human nature, however savage and uncultivated. There needs but a very little practice of the world, to make us perceive all these consequences and advantages. The shortest experience of society discovers them to every mortal; and when each individual perceives the same sense of interest in all his fellows, he immediately performs his part of any contract, as being assured, that they will not be wanting in theirs. All of them, by concert, enter into a scheme of actions, calculated for common benefit, and agree to be true to their word; nor is there any thing requisite to form this concert or convention, but that every one have a sense of interest in the faithful fulfilling of engagements, and express that sense to other members of the society. This immediately causes that interest to operate upon them; and interest is the *first* obligation to the performance of promises.

Afterwards a sentiment of morals concurs with interest, and becomes a new obligation upon mankind. This sentiment of morality, in the performance of promises, arises from the same principles as that in the abstinence from the property of others. *Public interest, education*, and *the artifices of politicians*, have the same effect in both cases. The difficulties, that occur to us, in supposing a moral obligation to attend promises, we either surmount or elude. For instance; the expression of a resolution is not commonly supposed to be obligatory; and we cannot readily conceive how the making use of a certain form of words should be able to cause any material difference. Here, therefore, we *feign* a new act of the mind, which we call the *willing* an obligation; and on this we suppose the morality to depend. But we have proved already, that there is no such act of the mind, and consequently that promises impose no natural obligation.

To confirm this, we may subjoin some other reflections concerning that will, which is supposed to enter into a promise, and to cause its obligation. It is evident, that the will alone is never supposed to cause the obligation, but must be expressed by words or signs, in order to impose a tie upon any man. The expression being once brought in as subservient to the will, soon becomes the principal part of the promise; nor will a man be less bound by his word, though he secretly give a different direction to his intention, and with-hold himself both from a resolution, and from willing an obligation. But though the expression makes on most occasions the whole of the promise, yet it does not always so; and one, who should make use of any expression, of which he knows not the meaning, and which he uses without any intention of binding himself, would not certainly be bound by it. Nay, though he knows its meaning, yet if he uses it in jest only, and with such signs as shew evidently he has no serious intention of binding himself, he would not lie under any obligation of performance; but it is necessary, that the words be a perfect expression of the will, without any contrary signs. Nay, even this we must not carry so far as to imagine, that one, whom, by our quickness of understanding, we conjecture, from certain signs, to have an intention of deceiving us, is not bound by his expression or verbal promise, if we accept of it; but must limit this conclusion to those cases, where the signs are of a different kind from those of deceit. All these contradictions are easily accounted for, if the obligation of promises be merely a human invention for the convenience of society; but will never be explained, if it be something *real* and *natural*, arising from any action of the mind or body.

I shall farther observe, that since every new promise imposes a new obligation of morality on the person who promises, and since this new obligation arises from his will; it is one of the most mysterious and incomprehensible operations that can possibly be imagined, and may even be compared to *transubstantiation*, or *holy orders*,* where a certain form of words, along with a certain intention, changes entirely the nature of an external object, and even of a human nature. But though these mysteries be so far alike, it is very remarkable, that they differ widely in other particulars, and that this difference may be regarded as a strong proof of the difference of their origins. As the obligation of promises is an invention for the interest of society, it is warped into as many different forms as that interest requires, and even runs into direct contradictions, rather than lose sight of its object. But as those other monstrous doctines are mere priestly inventions, and have no public interest in view, they are less disturbed in their progress by new obstacles; and it must be owned, that, after the first absurdity, they follow more directly the current of reason and good sense. Theologians clearly perceived, that the external form of words, being mere sound, require an intention to make them have any efficacy; and that this intention being once considered as a requisite circumstance, its absence must equally prevent the effect, whether avowed or concealed, whether sincere or deceitful. Accordingly they have commonly determined, that the intention of the priest makes the sacrament, and that when he secretly withdraws his intention, he is highly criminal in himself; but still destroys the baptism, or communion, or holy orders. The terrible consequences of this doctrine were not able to hinder its taking place; as the inconvenience of a similar doctrine, with regard to promises, have prevented that doctrine from establishing itself. Men are always more concerned about the present life than the future; and are

---

* I mean so far, as holy orders are supposed to produce the *indelible character*. In other respects they are only a legal qualification.

apt to think the smallest evil, which regards the former, more important than the greatest, which regards the latter.

We may draw the same conclusion, concerning the origin of promises, from the *force*, which is supposed to invalidate all contracts, and to free us from their obligation. Such a principle is a proof, that promises have no natural obligation, and are mere artificial contrivances for the convenience and advantage of society. If we consider aright of the matter, force is not essentially different from any other motive of hope or fear, which may induce us to engage our word, and lay ourselves under any obligation. A man, dangerously wounded, who promises a competent sum to a surgeon to cure him, would certainly be bound to performance; though the case be not so much different from that of one, who promises a sum to a robber, as to produce so great a difference in our sentiments of morality, if these sentiments were not built entirely on public interest and convenience.

SECTION SIX

Some farther reflections concerning justice and injustice

We have now run over the three fundamental laws of nature, *that of the stability of possession, of its transference by consent,* and *of the performance of promises.* It is on the strict observance of those three laws, that the peace and security of human society entirely depend; nor is there any possibility of establishing a good correspondence among men, where these are neglected. Society is absolutely necessary for the well-being of men; and these are as necessary to the support of society. Whatever restraint they may impose on the passions of men, they are the real offspring of those passions, and are only a more artful and more refined way of satisfying them. Nothing is more vigilant and inventive than our passions; and nothing is more obvious, than the convention for the observance of these rules. Nature has, therefore, trusted this affair entirely to the conduct of men, and has not placed in the mind any peculiar original principles, to determine us to a set of actions, into which the other principles of our frame and constitution were sufficient to lead us. And to convince us the more fully of this truth, we may here stop a moment, and from a review of the preceding reasonings may draw some new arguments, to prove that those laws, however necessary, are entirely artificial, and of human invention; and consequently that justice is an artificial, and not a natural virtue.

I. The first argument I shall make use of is derived from the vulgar definition of justice. Justice is commonly defined to be *a constant and perpetual will of giving every one his due*. In this definition it is supposed, that there are such things as right and property, independent of justice, and antecedent to it; and that they would have subsisted, though men had never dreamt of practising such a virtue. I have already observed, in a cursory manner, the fallacy of this opinion, and shall here continue to open up a little more distinctly my sentiments on that subject.

I shall begin with observing, that this quality, which we shall call *property*, is like many of the imaginary qualities of the *peripatetic* philosophy, and vanishes upon a more accurate inspection into the subject, when considered a-part from our moral sentiments. It is evident property does not consist in any of the sensible qualities of the object. For these may continue invariably the same, while the property changes. Property, therefore, must consist in some relation of the object. But it is not in its relation with regard to other external and inanimate objects. For these may also continue invariably the same, while the property changes. This quality, therefore, consists in the relations of objects to intelligent and rational beings. But it is not the external and corporeal relation, which forms the essence of property. For that relation may be the same betwixt inanimate objects, or with regard to brute creatures; though in those cases it forms no property. It is, therefore, in some internal relation, that the property consists; that is, in some influence, which the external relations of the object have on the mind and actions. Thus the external relation, which we call *occupation* or first possession, is not of itself imagined to be the property of the object, but only to cause its property. Now it is evident, this external relation causes nothing in external objects, and has only an influence on the mind, by giving us a sense of duty in abstaining from that object, and in restoring it to the first possessor. These actions are properly what we call *justice*; and consequently it is on that virtue that the nature of property depends, and not the virtue on the property.

If any one, therefore, would assert, that justice is a natural virtue, and injustice a natural vice, he must assert, that abstracting from the notions of *property*, and *right* and *obligation*, a certain conduct and train of actions, in certain external relations of objects, has naturally a moral beauty or deformity, and causes an original pleasure or uneasiness. Thus the restoring a man's goods to him is considered as virtuous, not because nature has annexed a certain sentiment of pleasure to such a conduct, with regard to the property of others, but because she has annexed that sentiment to such a conduct, with regard to those external objects, of which others have had the first or long possession, or which they have received by the consent of those, who have had first or long possession. If nature has given us no such sentiment, there is not, naturally, nor antecedent to human conventions, any such thing as property. Now, though it seems sufficiently evident, in this dry and accurate consideration of the present subject, that nature has annexed no pleasure or sentiment of approbation to such a conduct; yet that I may leave as little room for doubt as possible, I shall subjoin a few more arguments to confirm my opinion.

First, If nature had given us a pleasure of this kind, it would have been as evident and discernible as on every other occasion; nor should we have found any difficulty to perceive, that the consideration of such actions, in such a situation, gives a certain pleasure and sentiment of approbation. We should not have been obliged to have recourse to notions of property in the definition of justice, and at the same time make use of the notions of justice in the definition of property. This deceitful method of reasoning is a plain proof, that there are contained in the subject some obscurities and difficulties, which we are not able to surmount, and which we desire to evade by this artifice.

Secondly, Those rules, by which properties, rights, and obligations are determined, have in them no marks of a natural origin but many of artifice and contrivance. They are too numerous to have proceeded from nature: they are changeable by human laws: and have all of them a direct and evident tendency to public good, and the support of society. This last circumstance is remarkable upon two accounts. *First*, because, though the cause of the establishment of these laws had been a *regard* for the public good, as much as the public good is their natural tendency, they would still have been artificial, as being purposely contrived and directed to a certain end. *Secondly*, because, if men had been endowed with such a strong regard for public good, they would never have restrained themselves by these rules; so that the laws of justice arise from natural principles in a manner still more oblique and artificial. It is self-love which is their real origin; and as the self-love of one person is naturally contrary to that of another, these several interested passions are obliged to adjust themselves after such a manner as to concur in some system of conduct and behaviour. This system, therefore, comprehending the interest of each individual, is of course advantageous to the public; though it be not intended for that purpose by the inventors.

II. In the second place we may observe, that all kinds of vice and virtue run insensibly into each other, and may approach by such imperceptible degrees as will make it very difficult, if not absolutely impossible, to determine when the one ends, and the other begins; and from this observation we may derive a new argument for the foregoing principle. For whatever may be the case, with regard to all kinds of vice and virtue, it is certain, that rights, and obligations, and property, admit of no such insensible gradation, but that a man either has a full and perfect property, or none at all; and is either entirely obliged to perform any action, or lies under no manner of obligation. However civil laws may talk of a perfect *dominion*, and of an imperfect, it is easy to observe, that this arises from a fiction, which has no foundation in reason, and can never enter into our notions of natural justice and equity. A man that hires a horse, though but for a day, has as full a right to make use of it for that time, as he whom we call its proprietor has to make use of it any other day; and it was evident, that however the use may be bounded in time or degree, the right itself is not susceptible of any such gradation, but is absolute and entire, so far as it extends. Accordingly we may observe, that this right both arises and perishes in an instant; and that a man entirely acquires the property of any object by occupation, or the consent of the proprietor; and loses it by his own consent; without any of that insensible gradation, which is remarkable in other qualities and relations, Since, therefore, this is the case with regard to property, and rights, and obligations, I ask, how it stands with regard to justice and injustice? After whatever manner you answer this question, you run into inextricable difficulties. If you reply, that justice and injustice admit of degree, and run insensibly into each other, you expressly contradict the foregoing position, that obligation and property are not susceptible of such a gradation. These depend entirely upon justice and injustice, and follow them in all their variations. Where the justice is entire, the property is also entire: where the justice is imperfect, the property must also be imperfec: and *vice versa*, if the property admit of no such variations, they must also be incompatible with justice. If you assent, therefore, to this last proposition, and assert, that justice and injustice are not susceptible of degrees, you in effect assert, that they are not *naturally* either vicious or virtuous; since vice and virtue, moral good and evil, and indeed all *natural* qualities, run insensibly into each other, and are, on many occasions, undistinguishable.

And here it may be worth while to observe, that though abstract reasoning, and the general maxims of philosophy and law establish this position, *that property, and right, and obligation admit not of degrees*, yet in our common and negligent way of thinking, we find great difficulty to entertain that opinion, and do even *secretly* embrace the contrary principle. An object must either be in the possession of one person or another. An action must either be performed or not. The necessity there is of choosing one side in these dilemmas, and the impossibility there often is of finding any just medium, oblige us, when we reflect on the matter, to acknowledge, that all property and obligations are entire. But on the other hand, when we consider the origin of property and obligation, and find that they depend on public utility, and sometimes on the propensities of the imagination, which are seldom entire on any side; we are naturally inclined to imagine, that these moral relations admit of an insensible gradation. Hence it is, that in references, where the consent of the parties leave the referees entire masters of the subject, they commonly discover so much equity and justice on both sides, as induces them to strike a medium, and divide the difference betwixt the parties. Civil judges, who have not this liberty, but are obliged to give a decisive sentence on some one side, are often at a loss how to determine, and are necessitated to proceed on the most frivolous reasons in the world. Half rights and obligations, which seem so natural in common life, are perfect absurdities in their tribunal; for which reason they are often obliged to take half arguments for whole ones, in order to terminate the affair one way or other.

III. The third argument of this kind I shall make use of may be explained thus. If we consider the ordinary course of human actions, we shall find, that the mind restrains not itself by any general and universal rules; but acts on most occasions as it is determined by its present motives and inclination. As each action is a particular individual event, it must proceed from particular principles, and from our immediate situation within ourselves, and with respect to the rest of the universe. If on some occasions we extend our motives beyond those very circumstances, which gave rise to them, and form something like *general rules* for our conduct, it is easy to observe, that these rules are not perfectly inflexible, but allow of many exceptions. Since, therefore, this is the ordinary course of human actions, we may conclude, that the laws of justice, being universal and perfectly inflexible, can never be derived from nature, nor be the immediate offspring of any natural motive or inclination. No action can be either morally good or evil, unless there be some natural passion or motive to impel us to it, or deter us from it; and it is evident, that the morality must be susceptible of all the same variations, which are natural to the passion. Here are two persons, who dispute for an estate; of whom one is rich, a fool, and a batchelor; the other poor, a man of sense, and has a numerous family: the first is my enemy; the second my friend. Whether I be actuated in this affair by a view to public or private interest, by friendship or enmity, I must be induced to do my utmost to procure the estate to the latter. Nor would any consideration of the right and property of the persons be able to restrain me, were I actuated only by natural motives, without any combination or convention with others. For as all property depends on morality; and as all morality depends on the ordinary course of our passions and actions; and as these again are only directed by particular motives; it is evident, such a partial conduct must be suitable to the strictest morality, and could never be a violation of property. Were men, therefore, to take the liberty of acting with regard to the laws of society, as they do in every other affair, they would conduct themselves, on most occasions, by particular judgments, and would take into consideration the characters and circumstances of the persons, as well as the general nature of the question. But it is easy to observe, that this would produce an infinite confusion in human society, and that the avidity and partiality of men would quickly bring disorder into the world, if not restrained by some general and inflexible principles. It was, therefore, with a view to this inconvenience, that men have established those principles, and have agreed to restrain themselves by general rules, which are unchangeable by spite and favour, and by particular views of private or public interest. These rules, then, are artificially invented for a certain purpose, and are contrary to the common principles of human nature, which accommodate themselves to circumstances, and have no stated invariable method of operation.

Nor do I perceive how I can easily be mistaken in this matter. I see evidently, that when any man imposes on himself general inflexible rules in his conduct with others, he considers certain objects as their property, which he supposes to be sacred and inviolable. But no proposition can be more evident, than that property is perfectly unintelligible without first supposing justice and injustice; and that these virtues and vices are as unintelligible, unless we have motives, independent of the morality, to impel us to just actions, and deter us from unjust ones. Let those motives, therefore, be what they will, they must accommodate themselves to circumstances, and must admit of all the variations, which human affairs, in their incessant revolutions, are susceptible of. They are consequently a very improper foundation for such rigid inflexible rules as the laws of nature; and it is evident these laws can only be derived from human conventions, when men have perceived the disorders that result from following their natural and variable principles.

Upon the whole, then, we are to consider this distinction betwixt justice and injustice, as having two different foundations, *viz*, that of *self-interest*, when men observe, that it is impossible to live in society without restraining themselves by certain rules; and that of *morality*, when this interest is once observed and men receive a pleasure from the view of such actions as tend to the peace of society, and an uneasiness from such as are contrary to it. It is the voluntary convention and artifice of men, which makes the first interest take place; and therefore those laws of justice are so far to be considered as *artificial*. After that interest is once established and acknowledged, the sense of morality in the observance of these rules follows *naturally*, and of itself; though it is certain, that it is also augmented by a new *artifice*, and that the public instructions of politicians, and the private education of parents, contribute to the giving us a sense of honour and duty in the strict regulation of our actions with regard to the properties of others.

SECTION SEVEN

Of the origin of government

Nothing is more certain, than that men are, in a great measure, governed by interest, and that even when they extend their concern beyond themselves, it is not to any great distance; nor is it usual for them, in common life, to look farther than their nearest friends and acquaintance. It is no less certain, that it is impossible for men to consult their interest in so effectual a manner, as by an universal and inflexible observance of the rules of justice, by which alone they can preserve society, and keep themselves from falling into that wretched and savage condition, which is commonly represented as the *state of nature*. And as this interest, which all men have in the upholding of society, and the observation of the rules of justice, is great, so is it palpable and evident, even to the most rude and uncultivated of human race; and it is almost impossible for any one, who has had experience of society, to be mistaken in this particular. Since, therefore, men are so sincerely attached to their interest, and their interest is so much concerned in the observance of justice, and this interest is so certain and avowed; it may be asked, how any disorder can ever arise in society, and what principle there is in human nature so *powerful* as to overcome so strong a passion, or so *violent* as to obscure so clear a knowledge?

It has been observed, in treating of the passions, that men are mightily governed by the imagination, and proportion their affections more to the light, under which any object appears to them, than to its real and intrinsic value. What strikes upon them with a strong and lively idea commonly prevails above what lies in a more obscure light; and it must be a great superiority of value, that is able to compensate this advantage. Now as every thing, that is contiguous to us, either in space or time, strikes upon us with such an idea, it has a proportional effect on the will and passions, and commonly operates with more force than any object, that lies in a more distant and obscure light. Though we may be fully convinced, that the latter object excels the former, we are not able to regulate our actions by this judgment; but yield to the sollicitations of our passions, which always plead in favour of whatever is near and contiguous.

This is the reason why men so often act in contradiction to their known interest; and in particular why they prefer any trivial advantage, that is present, to the maintenance of order in society, which so much depends on the observance of justice. The consequences of every breach of equity seem to lie very remote, and are not able to counter-balance any immediate advantage, that may be reaped from it. They are, however, never the less real for being remote; and as all men are, in some degree, subject to the same weakness, it necessarily happens, that the violations of equity must become very frequent in society, and the commerce of men, by that means, be rendered very dangerous and uncertain. You have the same propension, that I have, in favour of what is contiguous above what is remote. You are, therefore, naturally carried to commit acts of injustice as well as me. Your example both pushes me forward in this way by imitation, and also affords me a new reason for any breach of equity, by shewing me, that I should be the cully of my integrity, if I alone should impose on myself a severe restraint amidst the licentiousness of others.

This quality, therefore, of human nature, not only is very dangerous to society, but also seems, on a cursory view, to be incapable of any remedy. The remedy can only come from the consent of men; and if men be incapable of themselves to prefer remote to contiguous, they will never consent to any thing, which would oblige them to such a choice, and contradict, in so sensible a manner, their natural principles and propensities. Whoever chooses the means, chooses also the end; and if it be impossible for us to prefer what is remote, it is equally impossible for us to submit to any necessity, which would oblige us to such a method of acting.

But here it is observable, that this infirmity of human nature becomes a remedy to itself, and that we provide against our negligence about remote objects, merely because we are naturally inclined to that negligence. When we consider any objects at a distance, all their minute distinctions vanish, and we always give the preference to whatever is in itself preferable, without considering its situation and circumstances. This gives rise to what in an improper sense we call *reason*, which is a principle, that is often contradictory to those propensities that display themselves upon the approach of the object. In reflecting on any action, which I am to perform a twelve-month hence, I always resolve to prefer the greater good, whether at that time it will be more contiguous or remote; nor does any difference in that particular make a difference in my present intentions and resolutions. My distance from the final determination makes all those minute differences vanish, nor am I affected by any thing, but the general and more discernible qualities of good and evil. But on my nearer approach, those circumstances, which I at first overlooked, begin to appear, and have an influence on my conduct and affections. A new inclination to the present good springs up, and makes it difficult for me to adhere inflexibly to my first purpose and resolution. This natural infirmity I may very much regret, and I may endeavour, by all possible means, to free my self from it. I may have recourse to study and reflection within myself; to the advice of friends; to frequent meditation, and repeated resolution: and having experienced how ineffectual all these are, I may embrace with pleasure any other expedient, by which I may impose a restraint upon myself, and guard against this weakness.

The only difficulty, therefore, is to find out this expedient, by which men cure their natural weakness, and lay themselves under the necessity of observing the laws of justice and equity, notwithstanding their violent propension to prefer contiguous to remote. It is evident such a remedy can never be effectual without correcting this propensity; and as it is impossible to change or correct any thing material in our nature, the utmost we can do is to change our circumstances and situation, and render the observance of the laws of justice our nearest interest, and their violation our most remote. But this being impracticable with respect to all mankind, it can only take place with respect to a few, whom we thus immediately interest in the execution of justice. There are the persons, whom we call civil magistrates, kings and their ministers, our governors and rulers, who being indifferent persons to the greatest part of the state, have no interest, or but a remote one, in any act of injustice; and being satisfied with their present condition, and with their part in society, have an immediate interest in every execution of justice, which is so necessary to the upholding of society. Here then is the origin of civil government and society. Men are not able radically to cure, either in themselves or others, that narrowness of soul, which makes them prefer the present to the remote. They cannot change their natures. All they can do is to change their situation, and render the observance of justice the immediate interest of some particular persons, and its violation their more remote. These persons, then, are not only induced to observe those rules in their own conduct, but also to constrain others to a like regularity, and enforce the dictates of equity through the whole society. And if it be necessary, they may also interest others more immediately in the execution of justice, and create a number of officers, civil and military, to assist them in their government.

But this execution of justice, though the principal, is not the only advantage of government. As violent passion hinders men from seeing distinctly the interest they have in an equitable behaviour towards others; so it hinders them from seeing that equity itself, and gives them a remarkable partiality in their own favours. This inconvenience is corrected in the same manner as that abovementioned. The same persons, who execute the laws of justice, will also decide all controversies concerning them; and being indifferent to the greatest part of the society, will decide them more equitably than every one would in his own case.

By means of these two advantages, in the *execution* and *decision* of justice, men acquire a security against each other's weakness and passion, as well as against their own, and under the shelter of their governors, begin to taste at ease the sweets of society and mutual assistance. But government extends farther its beneficial influence; and not contented to protect men in those conventions they make for their mutual interest, it often obliges them to make such conventions, and forces them to seek their own advantage, by a concurrence in some common end or purpose. There is no quality in human nature, which causes more fatal errors in our conduct, than that which leads us to prefer whatever is present to the distant and remote, and makes us desire objects more according to their situation than their intrinsic value. Two neighbours may agree to drain a meadow, which they possess in common; because it is easy for them to know each other's mind; and each must perceive, that the immediate consequence of his failing in his part, is, the abandoning the whole project. But it is very difficult, and indeed impossible, that a thousand persons should agree in any such action; it being difficult for them to concert so complicated a design, and still more difficult for them to execute it; while each seeks a pretext to free himself of the trouble and expense, and would lay the whole burden on others. Political society easily remedies both these inconveniences. Magistrates find an immediate interest in the interest of any considerable part of their subjects. They need consult no body but themselves to form any scheme for the promoting of that interest. And as the failure of any one piece in the execution is connected, though not immediately, with the failure of the whole, they prevent that failure, because they find no interest in it, either immediate or remote. Thus bridges are built; harbours opened; ramparts raised; canals formed; fleets equipped; and armies disciplined every where, by the care of government, which, though composed of men subject to all human infirmities, becomes, by one of the finest and most subtle inventions imaginable, a composition, which is, in some measure, exempted from all these infirmities.

SECTION EIGHT

Of the source of allegiance

Though government be an invention very advantageous, and even in some circumstances absolutely necessary to mankind; it is not necessary in all circumstances, nor is it impossible for men to preserve society for some time, without having recourse to such an invention. Men, it is true, are always much inclined to prefer present interest to distant and remote; nor is it easy for them to resist the temptation of any advantage, that they may immediately enjoy, in apprehension of an evil that lies at a distance from them: but still this weakness is less conspicuous where the possessions, and the pleasures of life are few, and of little value, as they always are in the infancy of society. An *Indian* is but little tempted to dispossess another of his hut, or to steal his bow, as being already provided of the same advantages; and as to any superior fortune, which may attend one above another in hunting and fishing, it is only casual and temporary, and will have but small tendency to disturb society. And so far am I from thinking with some philosophers, that men are utterly incapable of society without government, that I assert the first rudiments of government to arise from quarrels, not among men of the same society, but among those of different societies. A less degree of riches will suffice to this latter effect, than is requisite for the former. Men fear nothing from public war and violence but the resistance they meet with, which, because they share it in common, seems less terrible; and because it comes from strangers, seems less pernicious in its consequences, than when they are exposed singly against one whose commerce is advantageous to them, and without whose society it is impossible they can subsist. Now foreign war to a society without government necessarily produces civil war. Throw any considerable goods among men, they instantly fall a quarrelling, while each strives to get possession of what pleases him, without regard to the consequences. In a foreign war the most considerable of all goods, life and limbs, are at stake; and as every one shuns dangerous ports, seizes the best arms, seeks excuse for the slightest wounds, the laws, which may be well enough observed while men were calm, can now no longer take place, when they are in such commotion.

This we find verified in the *American* tribes, where men live in concord and amity among themselves without any established government and never pay submission to any of their fellows, except in time of war, when their captain enjoys a shadow of authority, which he loses after their return from the field, and the establishment of peace with the neighbouring tribes. This authority, however, instructs them in the advantages of government, and teaches them to have recourse to it, when either by the pillage of war, by commerce, or by any fortuitous inventions, their riches and possessions have become so considerable as to make them forget, on every emergence, the interest they have in the preservation of peace and justice. Hence we may give a plausible reason, among others, why all governments are at first monarchical, without any mixture and variety; and why republics arise only from the abuses of monarchy and despotic power. Camps are the true mothers of cities; and as war cannot be administered, by reason of the suddenness of every exigency, without some authority in a single person, the same kind of authority naturally takes place in that civil government, which succeeds the military. And this reason I take to be more natural, than the common one derived from patriarchal government, or the authority of a father, which is said first to take place in one family, and to accustom the members of it to the government of a single person. The state of society without government is one of the most natural states of men, and must submit with the conjunction of many families, and long after the first generation. Nothing but an increase of riches and possessions could oblige men to quit it; and so barbarous and uninstructed are all societies on their first formation, that many years must elapse before these can increase to such a degree, as to disturb men in the enjoyment of peace and concord.

But though it be possible for men to maintain a small uncultivated society without government, it is impossible they should maintain a society of any kind without justice, and the observance of those three fundamental laws concerning the stability of possession, its translation by consent, and the performance of promises. These are, therefore, antecedent to government, and are supposed to impose an obligation before the duty of allegiance to civil magistrates has once been thought of. Nay, I shall go farther, and assert, that government, *upon its first establishment*, would naturally be supposed to derive its obligation from those laws of nature, and, in particular, from that concerning the performance of promises. When men have once perceived the necessity of government to maintain peace, and execute justice, they would naturally assemble together, would choose magistrates, determine power, and promise them obedience. As a promise is supposed to be a bond or security already in use, and attended with a moral obligation, it is to be considered as the original sanction of government, and as the source of the first obligation to obedience. This reasoning appears so natural, that it has become the foundation of our fashionable system of politics, and is in a manner the creed of a party amongst us, who pride themselves, with reason, on the soundness of their philosophy, and their liberty of thought. *All men*, say they, *are born free and equal: government and superiority can only be established by consent: the consent of men, in establishing government, imposes on them a new obligation, unknown to the laws of nature. Men, therefore, are bound to obey their magistrates, only because they promise it; and if they had not given their word, either expressly or tacitly, to preserve allegiance, it would never have become a part of their moral duty.* This conclusion, however, when carried so far as to comprehend government in all its ages and situations, is entirely erroneous; and I maintain, that though the duty of allegiance be at first grafted on the obligation of promises, and be for some time supported by that obligation, yet it quickly takes root of itself, and has an original obligation and authority, independent of all contracts. This is a principle of moment, which we must examine with care and attention, before we proceed any farther.

It is reasonable for those philosophers, who assert justice to be a natural virtue, and antecedent to human conventions, to resolve all civil allegiance into the obligation of a promise, and assert that it is our own consent alone, which binds us to any submission to magistracy. For as all government is plainly an invention of men, and the origin of most governments is known in history, it is necessary to mount higher, in order to find the source of our political duties, if we would assert them to have any *natural* obligation of morality. These philosophers, therefore, quickly observe, that society is as ancient as the human species, and those three fundamental laws of nature as ancient as society: so that taking advantage of the antiquity, and obscure origin of these laws, they first deny them to be artificial and voluntary inventions of men, and then seek to engraft on them those other duties, which are more plainly artificial. But being once undeceived in this particular, and having found that *natural*, as well as *civil* justice, derives its origin from human conventions, we shall quickly perceive, how fruitless it is to resolve the one into the other, and seek, in the laws of nature, a stronger foundation for our political duties than interest, and human conventions; while these laws themselves are built on the very same foundation. On which ever side we turn this subject, we shall find, that these two kinds of duty are exactly on the same footing, and have the same source both of their *first invention* and *moral obligation*. They are contrived to remedy like inconveniences, and acquire their moral sanction in the same manner, from their remedying those inconveniences. These are two points, which we shall endeavour to prove as distinctly as possible.

We have already shewn, that men *invented* the three fundamental laws of nature, when they observed the necessity of society to their mutual subsistance, and found, that it was impossible to maintain any correspondence together, without some restraint on their natural appetites. The same self-love, therefore, which renders men so incommodious to each other, taking a new and more convenient direction, produces the rules of justice, and is the *first* motive of their observance. But when men have observed, that though the rules of justice be sufficient to maintain any society, yet it is impossible for them, of themselves, to observe those rules, in large and polished societies; they establish government, as a new invention to attain their ends, and preserve the old, or procure new advantages, by a more strict execution of justice. So far, therefore, our *civil* duties are connected with our *natural*, that the former are invented chiefly for the sake of the latter; and that the principal object of government is to constrain men to observe the laws of nature. In this respect, however, that law of nature, concerning the performance of promises, is only comprized along with the rest; and its exact observance is to be considered as an effect of the institution of government, and not the obedience to government as an effect of the obligation of a promise. Though the object of our civil duties be the enforcing of our natural, yet the first* motive of the invention, as well as performance of both, is nothing but self-interest: and since there is a separate interest in the obedience to government, from that in the performance of promises, we must also allow of a separate obligation. To obey the civil magistrate is requisite to preserve order and concord in society. To perform promises is requisite to beget mutual trust and confidence in the common offices of life. The ends, as well as the means, are perfectly distinct; nor is the one subordinate to the other.

To make this more evident, let us consider, that men will often bind themselves by promises to the performance of what it

---

* First in time, not in dignity or force.

would have been their interest to perform, independent of these promises; as when they would give others a fuller security, by super-adding a new obligation of interest to that which they formerly lay under. The interest in the performance of promises, besides its moral obligation, is general, avowed, and of the last consequence in life. Other interests may be more particular and doubtful; and we are apt to entertain a greater suspicion, that men may indulge their humour, or passion, in acting contrary to them. Here, therefore, promises come naturally in play, and are often required for fuller satisfaction and security. But supposing those other interests to be as general and avowed as the interest in the performance of a promise, they will be regarded as on the same footing, and men will begin to repose the same confidence in them. Now this is exactly the case with regard to our civil duties, or obedience to the magistrate; without which no government could subsist, nor any peace or order be maintained in large societies, where there are so many possessions on the one hand, and so many wants, real or imaginary, on the other. Our civil duties, therefore, must soon detach themselves from our promises, and acquire a separate force and influence. The interest in both is of the very same kind: it is general, avowed, and prevails in all times and places. There is, then, no pretext of reason for founding the one upon the other; while each of them has a foundation peculiar to itself. We might as well resolve the obligation to abstain from the possessions of others, into the obligation of a promise, as that of allegiance. The interests are not more distinct in the one case than the other. A regard to property is not more necessary to natural society, than obedience is to civil society or government; nor is the former society more necessary to the being of mankind, than the latter to their well-being and happiness. In short, if the performance of promises be advantageous, so is obedience to government: if the former interest be general, so is the latter: if the one interest be obvious and avowed, so is the other. And as these two rules are founded on like obligations of interest, each of them must have a peculiar authority, independent of the other.

But it is not only the *natural* obligations of interest, which are distinct in promises and allegiance; but also the *moral* obligations of honour and conscience: nor does the merit or demerit of the one depend in the least upon that of the other. And indeed, if we consider the close connexion there is betwixt the natural and moral obligations, we shall find this conclusion to be entirely unavoidable. Our interest is always engaged on the side of obedience to magistracy; and there is nothing but a great present advantage, that can lead us to rebellion, by making us over-look the remote interest, which we have in the preserving of peace and order in society. But though a present interest may thus blind us with regard to our own actions, it takes not place with regard to those of others; nor hinders them from appearing in their true colours, as highly prejudicial to public interest, and to our own in particular. This naturally gives us an uneasiness, in considering such seditious and disloyal actions, and makes us attach to them the idea of vice and moral deformity. It is the same principle, which causes us to disapprove of all kinds of private injustice, and in particular of the breach of promises. We blame all treachery and breach of faith; because we consider, that the freedom and extent of human commerce depend entirely on a fidelity with regard to promises. We blame all disloyalty to magistrates; because we perceive, that the execution of justice, in the stability of possession, its translation by consent, and the performance of promises, is impossible, without submission to government. As there are here two interests entirely distinct from each other, they must give rise to two moral obligations, equally separate and independent. Though there was no such thing as a promise in the world, government would still be necessary in all large and civilized societies; and if promises had only their own proper obligation, without the separate sanction of government, they would have but little efficacy in such societies. This separates the boundaries of our public and private duties, and shews that the latter are more dependent on the former, than the former on the latter. *Education*, and *the artifice of politicians*, concur to bestow a farther morality on loyalty, and to brand all rebellion with a greater degree of guilt and infamy. Nor is it a wonder, that politicians should be very industrious in inculcating such notions, where their interest is so particularly concerned.

Lest those arguments should not appear entirely conclusive (as I think they are) I shall have recourse to authority, and shall prove, from the universal consent of mankind, that the obligation of submission to government is not derived from any promise of the subjects. Nor need any one wonder, that though I have all along endeavoured to establish my system on pure reason, and have scarce ever cited the judgment even of philosophers or historians on any article, I should now appeal to popular authority, and oppose the sentiments of the rabble to any philosophical reasoning. For it must be observed, that the opinions of men, in this case, carry with them a peculiar authority, and are, in a great measure, infallible. The distinction of moral good and evil is founded on the pleasure or pain, which results from the view of any sentiment, or character; and as that pleasure or pain cannot be unknown to the person who feels it, it follows,* that there is just so much vice or virtue in any character, as every one places in it, and that it is impossible in this particular we can ever be mistaken. And though our judgments concerning the *origin* of any vice or virtue, be not so certain as those concerning their *degrees*; yet, since the question in this case regards not any philosophical origin of an obligation, but a plain matter of fact, it is not easily conceived how we can fall into an error. A man, who acknowledges himself to be bound to another, for a certain sum, must certainly know whether it be by his own bond, or that of his father; whether it be of his mere good-will, or for money lent him; and under what conditions, and for what purposes he has bound himself. In like manner, it being certain, that there is a moral obligation to submit to government, because every one thinks so; it must be as certain, that this obligation arises not from a promise; since no one, whose judgment has not been led astray by too strict adherence to a system of philosophy, has ever yet dreamt of ascribing it to that origin. Neither magistrates nor subjects have formed this idea of our civil duties.

We find, that magistrates are so far from deriving their authority, and the obligation to obedience in their subjects, from the foundation of a promise or original contract, that they conceal, as far as possible, from their people, especially from the vulgar, that they have their origin from thence. Were this the sanction of

---

* This proposition must hold strictly true, with regard to every quality, that is determined merely by sentiment. In what sense we can talk either of a *right* or a *wrong* taste in morals, eloquence, or beauty, shall be considerd afterwards. In the mean time, it may be observed, that there is such an uniformity in the *general* sentiments of mankind, as to render such questions of but small importance.

government, our rulers would never receive it tacitly, which is the utmost that can be pretended; since what is given tacitly and insensibly can never have such influence on mankind, as what is performed expressly and openly. A tacit promise is, where the will is signified by other more diffuse signs than those of speech; but a will there must certainly be in the case, and that can never escape the person's notice, who exerted it, however silent or tacit. But were you to ask the far greatest part of the nation, whether they had ever consented to the authority of their rulers, or promised to obey them, they would be inclined to think very strangely of you; and would certainly reply, that the affair depended not on their consent, but that they were born to such an obedience. In consequence of this opinion, we frequently see them imagine such persons to be their natural rulers, as are at that time deprived of all power and authority, and whom no man, however foolish, would voluntarily choose; and this merely because they are in that line, which ruled before, and in that degree of it, which used to succeed; though perhaps in so distant a period, that scarce any man alive could ever have given any promise of obedience. Has a government, then, no authority over such as these, because they never consented to it, and would esteem the very attempt of such a free choice a piece of arrogance and impiety? We find by experience, that it punishes them very freely for what it calls treason and rebellion, which, it seems, according to this system, reduces itself to common injustice. If you say, that by dwelling in its dominions, they in effect consented to the established government; I answer, that this can only be, where they think the affair depends on their choice, which few or none, beside those philosophers, have ever yet imagined. It never was pleaded as an excuse for a rebel, that the first act he performed, after he came to years of discretion, was to levy war against the sovereign of the state; and that while he was a child he could not bind himself by his own consent, and having become a man, showed plainly, by the first act he performed, that he had no design to impose on himself any obligation to obedience. We find, on the contrary, that civil laws punish this crime at the same age as any other, which is criminal, of itself, without our consent; that is, when the person is come to the full use of reason: whereas to this crime they ought in justice to allow some intermediate time, in which a tacit consent at least might be supposed. To which we may add, that a man living under an absolute government, would owe it no allegiance; since, by its very nature, it depends not on consent. But as that is as *natural* and *common* a government as any, it must certainly occasion some obligation; and it is plain from experience, that men, who are subjected to it, do always think so. This is a clear proof, that we do not commonly esteem our allegiance to be derived from our consent or promise; and a farther proof is, that when our promise is upon any account expressly engaged, we always distinguish exactly betwixt the two obligations, and believe the one to add more force to the other, than in a repetition of the same promise. Where no promise is given, a man looks not on his faith as broken in private matters, upon account of rebellion; but keeps those two duties of honour and allegiance perfectly distinct and separate. As the uniting of them was thought by these philosophers a very subtile invention, this is a convincing proof, that it is not a true one; since no man can either give a promise, or be restrained by its sanction and obligation unknown to himself.

SECTION NINE
Of the measures of allegiance

Those political writers, who have had recourse to a promise, or original contract, as the source of our allegiance to government, intended to establish a principle, which is perfectly just and reasonable; though the reasoning, upon which they endeavoured to establish it, was fallacious and sophistical. They would prove, that our submission to government admits of exceptions, and that an egregious tyranny in the rulers is sufficient to free the subjects from all ties of allegiance. Since men enter into society, say they, and submit themselves to government, by their free and voluntary consent, they must have in view certain advantages, which they propose to reap from it, and for which they are contented to resign their native liberty. There is, therefore, something mutual engaged on the part of the magistrate, *viz*, protection and security; and it is only by the hopes he affords of these advantages, that he can ever persuade men to submit to him. But when instead of protection and security, they meet with tyranny and oppression, they are freed from their promises (as happens in all conditional contracts), and return to that state of liberty, which preceded the institution of government. Men would never be so foolish as to enter into such engagements as should turn entirely to the advantage of others, without any view of bettering their own condition. Whoever proposes to draw any profit from our submission, must engage himself, either expressly or tacitly, to make us reap some advantage from his authority; nor ought he to expect, that without the performance of his part we will ever continue in obedience.

I repeat it: this conclusion is just, though the principles be erroneous; and I flatter myself, that I can establish the same conclusion on more reasonable principles. I shall not take such a compass, in establishing our political duties, as to assert, that men perceive the advantages of government; that they institute government with a view to those advantages; that this institution requires a promise of obedience; which imposes a moral obligation to a certain degree, but being conditional, ceases to be binding, whenever the other contracting party performs not his part of the engagement. I perceive, that a promise itself arises entirely from human conventions, and is invented with a view to a certain interest. I seek, therefore, some such interest more immediately connected with government, and which may be at once the original motive to its institution, and the source of our obedience to it. This interest I find to consist in the security and protection, which we enjoy in political society, and which we can never attain, when perfectly free and independent. As interest, therefore, is the immediate sanction of government, the one can have no longer being than the other; and whenever the civil magistrate carries his oppression so far as to render his authority perfectly intolerable, we are no longer bound to submit to it. The cause ceases; the effect must cease also.

So far the conclusion is immediate and direct, concerning the *natural* obligation which we have to allegiance. As to the *moral* obligation, we may observe, that the maxim would here be false, that *when the cause ceases, the effect must cease also.* For there is a principle of human nature, which we have frequently taken notice of, that men are mightily addicted to *general rules*, and that we often carry our maxims beyond those reasons, which first induced us to establish them. Where cases are similar in many circumstances, we are apt to put them on the same footing, without considering, that they differ in the most material circumstances, and that the resemblance is more apparent than real. It may, therefore, be thought, that in the case of allegiance our moral obligation of duty will not cease, even though the natural obligation of interest, which is its cause, has ceased; and that men may be bound by *conscience* to submit to a tyrannical government against their own and the public interest. And indeed, to the force of this argument I so far submit, as to acknowledge, that general rules commonly extend beyond the principles, on which they are founded; and that we seldom make any exception to them, unless that exception have the qualities of a general rule, and be founded on very numerous and common instances. Now this I assert to be entirely the present case. When men submit to the authority of others, it is to procure themselves some security against the wickedness and injustice of men, who are perpetually carried, by their unruly passions, and by their present and immediate interest, to the violation of all the laws of society. But as this imperfection is inherent in human nature, we know that it must attend men in all their states and conditions; and that these, whom we choose for rulers, do not immediately become of a superior nature to the rest of mankind, upon account of their superior power and authority. What we expect from them depends not on a change of their nature but of their situation, when they acquire a more immediate interest in the preservation of order and the execution of justice. But besides that this interest is only more immediate in the execution of justice among their subjects; besides this, I say, we may often expect, from the irregularity of human nature, that they will neglect even this immediate interest, and be transported by their passions into all the excesses of cruelty and ambition. Our general knowledge of human nature, our observation of the past history of mankind, our experience of present times; all these causes must induce us to open the door to exceptions, and must make us conclude, that we may resist the more violent effects of supreme power, without any crime or injustice.

Accordingly we may observe, that this is both the general practice and principle of mankind, and that no nation, that could find any remedy, ever yet suffered the cruel ravages of a tyrant, or were blamed for their resistance. Those who took up arms against *Dionysius* or *Nero*, or *Philip the second*, have the favour of every reader in the perusal of their history: and nothing but the most violent perversion of common sense can ever lead us to condemn them. It is certain, therefore, that in all our notions of morals we never entertain such an absurdity as that of passive obedience, but make allowances for resistance in the more flagrant instances of tyranny and oppression. The general opinion of mankind has some authority in all cases; but in this of morals it is perfectly infallible. Nor is it less infallible, because men cannot distinctly explain the principles, on which it is founded. Few persons can carry on this train of reasoning: 'Government is a mere human invention for the interest of society. Where the tyranny of the governor removes this interest, it also removes the natural obligation to obedience. The moral obligation is founded on the natural, and therefore must cease where *that* ceases; especially where the subject is such as makes us foresee very many occasions wherein the natural obligation may cease, and causes us to form a kind of general rule for the regulation of our conduct in such occurrences.' But though this train of reasoning be too subtile for the vulgar, it is certain, that all men have an implicit notion of it, and are sensible, that they owe obedience to government merely on account of the public interest; and at the same time, that human nature is so subject to frailties and passions, as may easily pervert this institution, and change their governors into tyrants and public enemies. If the sense of common interest were not our original motive to obedience, I would fain ask, what other principle is there in human nature capable of subduing the natural ambition of men, and forcing them to such a submission? Imitation and custom are not sufficient. For the question still recurs, what motive first produces those instances of submission, which we imitate, and that train of actions, which produces the custom? There evidently is no other principle than public interest; and if interest first produces obedience to government, the obligation to obedience must cease, whenever the interest ceases, in any great degree, and in a considerable number of instances.

SECTION TEN
Of the objects of allegiance

But though, on some occasions, it may be justifiable, both in sound politics and morality, to resist supreme power, it is certain, that in the ordinary course of human affairs nothing can be more pernicious and criminal; and that besides the convulsions, which always attend revolutions, such a practice tends directly to the subversion of all government, and the causing an universal anarchy and confusion among mankind. As numerous and civilized societies cannot subsist without government, so government is entirely useless without an exact obedience. We ought always to weigh the advantages, which we reap from authority, against the disadvantages; and by this means we shall become more scrupulous of putting in practice the doctrine of resistance. The common rule requires submission; and it is only in cases of grievous tyranny and oppression, that the exception can take place.

Since then such a blind submission is commonly due to magistracy, the next question is, *to whom it is due, and whom we are to regard as our lawful magistrates?* In order to answer this question, let us recollect what we have already established concerning the origin of government and political society. When men have once experienced the impossibility of preserving any steady order in society, while every one is his own master, and violates or observes the laws of society, according to his present interest or pleasure, they naturally run into the invention of government, and put it out of their own power, as far as possible, to transgress the laws of society. Government, therefore, arises from the same voluntary conversation of men; and it is evident, that the same convention, which establishes government, will also determine the persons who are to govern, and will remove all doubt and ambiguity in this particular. And the voluntary consent of men must here have the greater efficacy, that the authority of the magistrate does *at first* stand upon the foundation of a promise of the subjects, by which they bind themselves to obedience; as in every other contract or engagement. The same promise, then, which binds them to obedience, ties them down to a particular person, and makes him the object of their allegiance.

But when government has been established on this footing for some considerable time, and the separate interest, which we have in submission, has produced a separate sentiment of morality, the case is entirely altered, and a promise is no longer able to determine the particular magistrate since it is no longer considered as the foundation of government. We naturally suppose ourselves born to submission; and imagine, that such particular persons have a right to command, as we on our part are bound to obey. These notions of right and obligation are derived from nothing but the *advantage* we reap from government, which gives us a repugnance to practise resistance ourselves, and makes us displeased with any instance of it in others. But here it is remarkable, that in this new state of affairs, the original sanction of government, which is *interest*, is not admitted to determine the persons, whom we are to obey, as the original sanction did at first, when affairs were on the footing of a *promise*. A *promise* fixes and determines the persons, without any uncertainty: but it is evident, that if men were to regulate their conduct in this particular, by the view of a peculiar *interest*, either public or private, they would involve themselves in endless confusion, and would render all government, in a great measure, ineffectual. The private interest of every one is different; and though the public interest in itself be always one and the same, yet it becomes the source of as great dissensions, by reason of the different opinions of particular persons concerning it. The same interest, therefore, which causes us to submit to magistracy, makes us renounce itself in the choice of our magistrates, and binds us down to a certain form of government, and to particular persons, without allowing us to aspire to the utmost perfection in either. The case is here the same as in that law of nature concerning the stability of possession. It is highly advantageous, and even absolutely necessary to society, that possession should be stable; and this leads us to the establishment of such a rule: but we find, that were we to follow the same advantage, in assigning particular possessions to particular persons, we should disappoint our end, and perpetuate the confusion, which that rule is intended to prevent. We must, therefore, proceed by general rules, and regulate ourselves by general interests, in modifying the law of nature concerning the stability of possession. Nor need we fear, that our attachment to this law will diminish upon account of the seeming frivolousness of those interests, by which it is determined. The impulse of the mind is derived from a very strong interest; and those other more minute interests serve only to direct the motion, without adding any thing to it, or diminishing from it. It is the same case with government. Nothing is more advantageous to society than such an invention; and this interest is sufficient to make us embrace it with ardour and alacrity; though we are obliged afterwards to regulate and direct our devotion to government by several considerations, which are not of the same importance, and to choose our magistrates without having in view any particular advantage from the choice.

The *first* of those principles I shall take notice of, as a foundation of the right of magistracy, is that which gives authority to all the most established governments of the world without exception: I mean, *long possession* in any one form of government, or succession of princes. It is certain, that if we remount to the first origin of every nation, we shall find, that there scarce is any race of kings, or form of a commonwealth, that is not primarily founded on usurpation and rebellion, and whose title is not at first worse than doubtful and uncertain. Time alone gives solidity to their right; and operating gradually on the minds of men, reconciles them to any authority, and makes it seem just and reasonable. Nothing causes any sentiment to have a greater influence upon us than custom, or turns our imagination more strongly to any object. When we have been long accustomed to obey any set of men, that general instinct or tendency, which we have to suppose a moral obligation attending loyalty, takes easily this direction, and chooses that set of men for its objects. It is interest which gives the general instinct; but it is custom which gives the particular direction.

And here it is observable, that the same length of time has a different influence on our sentiments of morality, according to its different influence on the mind. We naturally judge of every thing by comparison; and since in considering the fate of kingdoms and republics, we embrace a long extent of time, a small duration has not in this case a like influence on our sentiments, as when we consider any other object. One thinks he acquires a right to a horse, or a suit of clothes, in a very short time; but a century is scarce sufficient to establish any new government, or remove all scruples in the minds of the subjects concerning it. Add to this, that a shorter period of time will suffice to give a prince a title to any additional power he may usurp, than will serve to fix his right, where the whole is an usurpation. The kings of *France* have not been possessed of absolute power for above two reigns; and yet nothing will appear more extravagant to *Frenchmen* than to talk of their liberties. If we consider what has been said concerning *accession*, we shall easily account for this phenomenon.

When there is no form of government established by *long* possession, the *present* possession is sufficient to supply its place, and may be regarded as the *second* source of all public authority. Right to authority is nothing but the constant possession of authority, maintained by the laws of society and the interests of mankind; and nothing can be more natural than to join this constant possession to the present one, according to the principles above-mentioned. If the same principles did not take place with regard to the property of private persons, it was because these principles were counter-balanced by very strong considerations of interest; when we observed, that all restitution would by that means be prevented, and every violence be authorized and protected. And though the same motives may seem to have force, with regard to public authority, yet they are opposed by a contrary interest; which consists in the preservation of peace, and the avoiding of all changes, which, however they may be easily produced in private affairs, are unavoidably attended with blood-shed and confusion, where the public is interested.

Any one, who finding the impossibility of accounting for the right of the present possessor, by any received system of ethics, should resolve to deny absolutely that right, and assert, that it is not authorized by morality, would be justly thought to maintain a very extravagant paradox, and to shock the common sense and judgment of mankind. No maxim is more conformable, both to prudence and morals, than to submit quietly to the government, which we find established in the country where we happen to live, without enquiring too curiously into its origin and first establishment. Few governments will bear being examined so rigorously. How many kingdoms are there at present in the world, and how many more do we find in history, whose governors have no better foundation for their authority than that of present possession? To confine ourselves to the *Roman* and *Grecian* empire;

is it not evident, that the long succession of emperors, from the dissolution of the *Roman* liberty, to the final extinction of that empire by the *Turks*, could not so much as pretend to any other title to the empire? The election of the senate was a mere form, which always followed the choice of the legions; and these were almost always divided in the different provinces, and nothing but the sword was able to terminate the difference. It was by the sword, therefore, that every emperor acquired, as well as defended his right; and we must either say, that all the known world, for so many ages, had no government, and owed no allegiance to any one, or must allow, that the right of the stronger, in public affairs, is to be received as legitimate, and authorized by morality, when not opposed by any other title.

The right of *conquest* may be considered as a *third* source of the title of sovereigns. This right resembles very much that of present possession; but has rather a superior force, being seconded by the notions of glory and honour, which we ascribe to *conquerors*, instead of the sentiments of hatred and detestation, which attend *usurpers*. Men naturally favour those they love; and therefore are more apt to ascribe a right to successful violence, betwixt one sovereign and another, than to the successful rebellion of a subject against his sovereign.*

When neither long possession, nor present possession, nor conquest take place, as when the first sovereign, who founded any monarchy, dies; in that case, the right of *succession* naturally prevails in their stead, and men are commonly induced to place the son of their late monarch on the throne, and suppose him to inherit his father's authority. The presumed consent of the father, the imitation of the succession to private families, the interest, which the state has in choosing the person, who is most powerful, and has the most numerous followers; all these reasons lead men to prefer the son of their late monarch to any other person.†

* It is not here asserted, that present possession or conquest are sufficient to give a title against long possession and positive laws but only that they have some force, and will be able to call the balance where the titles are otherwise equal, and will even be sufficient sometimes to sanctify the weaker title. What degree of force they have is difficult to determine. I believe all moderate men will allow, that they have great force in all disputes concerning the rights of princes.

† To prevent mistakes I must observe, that this case of succession is not the same with that of hereditary monarchies, where custom has fixed the right of succession. These depend upon the principle of long possession above explained.

These reasons have some weight; but I am persuaded, that to one, who considers impartially of the matter, it will appear, that there concur some principles of the imagination, along with those views of interest. The royal authority seems to be connected with the young prince even in his father's life-time, by the natural transition of the thought; and still more after his death: so that nothing is more natural than to complete this union by a new relation, and by putting him actually in possession of what seems so naturally to belong to him.

To confirm this we may weigh the following phenomena, which are pretty curious in their kind. In elective monarchies the right of succession has no place by the laws and settled custom; and yet its influence is so natural, that it is impossible entirely to exclude it from the imagination, and render the subjects indifferent to the son of their deceased monarch. Hence in some governments of this kind, the choice commonly falls on one or other of the royal family; and in some governments they are all excluded. Those contrary phenomena proceed from the same principle. Where the royal family is excluded, it is from a refinement in politics, which makes people sensible of their propensity to choose a sovereign in that family, and gives them a jealousy of their liberty, lest their new monarch, aided by this propensity, should establish his family, and destroy the freedom of elections for the future.

The history of *Artaxerxes*, and the younger *Cyrus*, may furnish us with some reflections to the same purpose. *Cyrus* pretended a right to the throne above his elder brother, because he was born after his father's accession. I do not pretend, that this reason was valid. I would only infer from it, that he would never have made use of such a pretext, were it not for the qualities of the imagination above-mentioned, by which we are naturally inclined to unite by a new relation whatever objects we find already united. *Artaxerxes* had an advantage above his brother, as being the eldest son, and the first in succession: but *Cyrus* was more closely related to the royal authority, as being begot after his father was invested with it.

Should it here be pretended, that the view of convenience may be the source of all the right of succession, and that men gladly take advantage of any rule, by which they can fix the successor of their late sovereign, and prevent that anarchy and confusion, which attends all new elections; to this I would answer, that I readily allow, that this motive may contribute something to the effect; but at the same time I assert, that without another principle, it is impossible such a motive should take place. The interest of a nation requires, that the succession to the crown should be fixed one way or other; but it is the same thing to its interest in what way it be fixed: so that if the relation of blood had not an effect independent of public interest, it would never have been regarded, without a positive law; and it would have been impossible, that so many positive laws of different nations could ever have concurred precisely in the same views and intentions.

This leads us to consider the *fifth* source of authority, *viz. positive laws*; when the legislature establishes a certain form of government and succession of princes. At first sight it may be thought, that this must resolve into some of the preceding titles of authority. The legislative power, whence the positive law is derived, must either be established by original contract, long possession, present possession, conquest, or succession; and consequently the positive law must derive its force from some of those principles. But here it is remarkable, that though a positive law can only derive its force from these principles, yet it acquires not all the force of the principle from whence it is derived, but loses considerably in the transition; as it is natural to imagine. For instance; a government is established for many centuries on a certain system of laws, forms, and methods of succession. The legislative power, established by this long succession, changes all on a sudden the whole system of government, and introduces a new constitution in its stead. I believe few of the subjects will think themselves bound to comply with this alteration, unless it have an evident tendency to the public good: but men think themselves still at liberty to return to the ancient government. Hence the notion of *fundamental laws*; which are supposed to be inalterable by the will of the sovereign: and of this nature the *Salic* law is understood to be in *France*. How far these fundamental laws extend is not determined in any government; nor is it possible it ever should. There is such an indefensible gradation from the most material laws to the most trivial, and from the most ancient laws to the most modem, that it will be impossible to set bounds to the legislative power, and determine how far it may innovate in the principles of government. That is the work more of imagination and passion than of reason.

Whoever considers the history of the several nations of the world; their revolutions, conquests, increase, and diminution; the manner in which their particular governments are established, and the successive right transmitted from one person to another, will soon learn to treat very lightly all disputes concerning the rights of princes, and will be convinced, that a strict adherence to any general rules, and the rigid loyalty to particular persons and families, on which some people set so high a value, are virtues that hold less of reason, than of bigotry and superstition. In this particular, the study of history confirms the reasonings of true philosophy; which, shewing us the original qualities of human nature, teaches us to regard the controversies in politics as incapable of any decision in most cases, and as entirely subordinate to the interests of peace and liberty. Where the public good does not evidently demand a change; it is certain, that the concurrence of all those titles, *original contract, long possession, present possession, succession,* and *positive laws,* forms the strongest title to sovereignty, and is justly regarded as sacred and inviolable. But when these titles are mingled and opposed in different degrees, they often occasion perplexity; and are less capable of solution from the arguments of lawyers and philosophers, than from the swords of the soldiery. Who shall tell me, for instance, whether *Germanicus,* or *Drusus,* ought to have succeeded *Tiberius,* had he died while they were both alive, without naming any of them for his successor? Ought the right of adoption to be received as equivalent to that of blood in a nation, where it had the same effect in private families, and had already, in two instances, taken place in the public? Ought *Germanicus* to be esteemed the eldest son, because he was born before *Drusus;* or the younger, because he was adopted after the birth of his brother? Ought the right of the elder to be regarded in a nation, where the eldest brother had no advantage in the succession to private families? Ought the *Roman* empire at that time to be esteemed hereditary, because of two examples; or ought it, even so early, to be regarded as belonging to the stronger, or the present possessor, as being founded on so recent an usurpation? Upon whatever principles we may pretend to answer these and such like questions, I am afraid we shall never be able to satisfy an impartial enquirer, who adopts no party in political controversies, and will be satisfied with nothing but sound reason and philosophy.

But here an *English* reader will be apt to enquire concerning that famous *revolution*, which has had such a happy influence on our constitution, and has been attended with such mighty consequences. We have already remarked, that in the case of enormous tyranny and oppression, it is lawful to take arms even against supreme power; and that as government is a mere human invention for mutual advantage and security, it no longer imposes any obligation, either natural or moral, when once it ceases to have that tendency. But though this *general* principle be authorized by common sense, and the practice of all ages, it is certainly impossible for the laws, or even for philosophy, to establish any *particular* rules, by which we may know when resistance is lawful; and decide all controversies, which may arise on that subject. This may not only happen with regard to supreme power; but it is possible, even in some constitutions, where the legislative authority is not lodged in one person, that there may be a magistrate so eminent and powerful, as to oblige the laws to keep silence in this particular. Nor would this silence be an effect only of their *respect*, but also of their *prudence*; since it is certain, that in the vast variety of circumstances, which occur in all governments, an exercise of power, in so great a magistrate, may at one time be beneficial to the public, which at another time would be pernicious and tyrannical. But notwithstanding this silence of the laws in limited monarchies, it is certain, that the people still retain the right of resistance; since it is impossible, even in the most despotic governments, to deprive them of it. The same necessity of self-preservation, and the same motive of public good, give them the same liberty in the one case as in the other. And we may farther observe, that in such mixed governments, the cases, wherein resistance is lawful, must occur much oftener, and greater indulgence be given to the subjects to defend themselves by force of arms, than in arbitrary governments. Not only where the chief magistrate enters into measures, in themselves, extremely pernicious to the public, but even when he would encroach on the other parts of the constitution, and extend his power beyond the legal bounds, it is allowable to resist and dethrone him; though such resistance and violence may, in the general tenor of the laws, be deemed unlawful and rebellious. For besides that nothing is more essential to public interest, than the preservation of public liberty; it is evident, that if such a mixed government be once supposed to be established, every part or member of the constitution must have a right of self-defence, and of maintaining its ancient bounds against the encroachment of every other authority. As matter would have been created in vain, were it deprived of a power of resistance, without which no part of it could preserve a distinct existence, and the whole might be crowded up into a single point: so it is a gross absurdity to suppose, in any government, a right without a remedy, or allow, that the supreme power is shared with the people, without allowing, that it is lawful for them to defend their share against every invader. Those, therefore, who would seem to respect our free government, and yet deny the right of resistance, have renounced all pretensions to common sense, and do not merit a serious answer.

It does not belong to my present purpose to shew, that these general principles are applicable to the late *revolution*; and that all the rights and privileges, which ought to be sacred to a free nation, were at that time threatened with the utmost danger. I am better pleased to leave this controverted subject, if it really admits of controversy; and to indulge myself in some philosophical reflections, which naturally arise from that important event.

First, We may observe, that should the *lords* and *commons* in our constitution, without any reason from public interest, either depose the king in being, or after his death exclude the prince, who, by laws and settled custom, ought to succeed, no one would esteem their proceedings legal, or think themselves bound to comply with them. But should the king, by his unjust practices, or his attempts for a tyrannical and despotic power, justly forfeit his legal, it then not only becomes morally lawful and suitable to the nature of political society to dethrone him; but what is more, we are apt likewise to think, that the remaining members of the constitution acquire a right of excluding his next heir, and of choosing whom they please for his successor. This is founded on a very singular quality of our thought and imagination. When a king forfeits his authority, his heir ought naturally to remain in the same situation, as if the king were removed by death; unless by mixing himself in the tyranny, he forfeit it for himself. But though this may seem reasonable, we easily comply with the contrary opinion. The deposition of a king, in such a government as ours, is certainly an act beyond all common authority, and an illegal assuming a power for public good, which, in the ordinary course of government, can belong to no member of the constitution. When the public good is so great and so evident as to justify the action, the commendable use of this licence causes us naturally to attribute to the *parliament* a right of using farther licences; and the ancient bounds of the laws being once transgressed with approbation, we are not apt to be so strict in confining ourselves precisely within their limits. The mind naturally runs on with any train of action, which it has begun; nor do we commonly make any scruple concerning our duty, after the first action of any kind, which we perform. Thus at the *revolution*, no one who thought the deposition of the father justifiable, esteemed themselves to be confined to his infant son; though had that unhappy monarch died innocent at that time, and had his son, by any accident, been conveyed beyond seas, there is no doubt but a regency would have been appointed till he should come to age, and could be restored to his dominions. As the slightest properties of the imagination have an effect on the judgments of the people, it shews the wisdom of the laws and of the parliament to take advantage of such properties, and to choose the magistrates either in or out of a line, according as the vulgar will most naturally attribute authority and right to them.

Secondly, Though the accession of the *Prince of Orange* to the throne might at first give occasion to many disputes, and his title be contested, it ought not now to appear doubtful, but must have acquired a sufficient authority from those three princes, who have succeeded him upon the same title. Nothing is more usual, though nothing may, at first sight, appear more unreasonable, than this way of thinking. Princes often seem to acquire a right from their successors, as well as from their ancestors; and a king, who during his life-time might justly be deemed an usurper, will be regarded by posterity as a lawful prince, because he has had the good fortune to settle his family on the throne, and entirely change the ancient form of government. *Julius Caesar* is regarded as the first *Roman* emperor; while *Sylla* and *Marius*, whose titles were really the same as his, are treated as tyrants and usurpers. Time and custom give authority to all forms of government, and all successions of princes; and that power, which at first was founded only on injustice and violence, becomes in time legal and obligatory. Nor does the mind rest there; but returning back upon its footsteps, transfers to their predecessors and ancestors that right, which it naturally ascribes to the posterity, as being related together, and united in the imagination. The present king of *France* makes *Hugh Capet* a more lawful prince than *Cromwell*; as the established liberty of the *Dutch* is no inconsiderable apology for their obstinate resistance to *Philip* the second.

SECTION ELEVEN
Of the laws of nations

When civil government has been established over the greatest part of mankind, and different societies have been formed contiguous to each other, there arises a new set of duties among the neighbouring states, suitable to the nature of that commerce, which they carry on with each other. Political writers tell us, that in every kind of intercourse, a body politic is to be considered as one person; and indeed this assertion is so far just, that different nations, as well as private persons, require mutual assistance; at the same time that their selfishness and ambition are perpetual sources of war and discord. But though nations in this particular resemble individuals, yet as they are very different in other respects, no wonder they regulate themselves by different maxims, and give rise to a new set of rules, which we call *the laws of nations*. Under this head we may comprize the sacredness of the persons of ambassadors, the declaration of war, the abstaining from poisoned arms, with other duties of that kind, which are evidently calculated for the commerce, that is peculiar to different societies.

But though these rules be super-added to the laws of nature, the former do not entirely abolish the latter; and one may safely affirm, that the three fundamental rules of justice, the stability of possession, its transference by consent, and the performance of promises, are duties of princes, as well as of subjects. The same interest produces the same effect in both cases. Where possession has no stability, there must be perpetual war. Where property is not transferred by consent, there can be no commerce. Where promises are not observed, there can be no leagues nor alliances. The advantages, therefore, of peace, commerce, and mutual succour, make us extend to different kingdoms the same notions of justice, which take place among individuals.

There is a maxim very current in the world, which few politicians are willing to avow, but which has been authorized by the practice of all ages, *that there is a system of morals calculated for princes, much more free than that which ought to govern private persons.* It is evident this is not to be understood of the lesser extent of public duties and obligations; nor will any one be so extravagant as to assert, that the most solemn treaties ought to have no force among princes. For as princes do actually form treaties among themselves, they must propose some advantage from the execution of them; and the prospect of such advantage for the future must engage them to perform their part, and must establish that law of nature. The meaning, therefore, of this political maxim is, that though the morality of princes has the same extent, yet it has not the same *force* as that of private persons, and may lawfully be trangressed from a more trivial motive. However shocking such a proposition may appear to certain philosophers, it will be easy to defend it upon those principles, by which we have accounted for the origin of justice and equity.

When men have found by experience, that it is impossible to subsist without society, and that it is impossible to maintain society, while they give free course to their appetites; so urgent an interest quickly restrains their actions, and imposes an obligation to observe those rules, which we call *the laws of justice.* This obligation of interest rests not here; but by the necessary course of the passions and sentiments, gives rise to the moral obligation of duty; while we approve of such actions as tend to the peace of society, and disapprove of such as tend to its disturbance. The same *natural* obligation of interest takes place among independent kingdoms, and gives rise to the same *morality*; so that no one of ever so corrupt morals will approve of a prince, who voluntarily, and of his own accord, breaks his word, or violates any treaty. But here we may observe, that though the intercourse of different states be advantageous, and even sometimes necessary, yet it is not so necessary nor advantageous as that among individuals, without which it is utterly impossible for human nature ever to subsist. Since, therefore, the *natural* obligation to justice, among different states, is not so strong as among individuals, the *moral* obligation, which arises from it, must partake of its weakness; and we must necessarily give a greater indulgence to a prince or minister, who deceives another; than to a private gentleman, who breaks his word of honour.

Should it be asked, *what proportion these two species of morality bear to each other?* I would answer, that this is a question, to which we can never give any precise answer; nor is it possible to reduce to numbers the proportion, which we ought to fix betwixt them. One may safely affirm, that this proportion finds itself, without any art or study of men; as we may observe on many other occasions. The practice of the world goes farther in teaching us the degrees of our duty, than the most subtile philosophy, which was ever yet invented. And this may serve as a convincing proof, that all men have an implicit notion of the foundation of those moral rules concerning natural and civil justice, and are sensible, that they arise merely from human conventions, and from the interest, which we have in the preservation of peace and order. For otherwise the diminution of the interest would never produce a relaxation of the morality, and reconcile us more easily to any transgression of justice among princes and republics, than in the private commerce of one subject with another.

SECTION TWELVE
Of chastity and modesty

If any difficulty attend this system concerning the laws of nature and nations, it will be with regard to the universal approbation or blame, which follows their observance or transgression, and which some may not think sufficiently explained from the general interests of society. To remove, as far as possible, all scruples of this kind, I shall here consider another set of duties, *viz*, the *modesty* and *chastity* which belong to the fair sex: and I doubt not but these virtues will be found to be still more conspicuous instances of the operation of those principles, which I have insisted on.

There are some philosophers, who attack the female virtues with great vehemence, and fancy they have gone very far in detecting popular errors, when they can show, that there is no foundation in nature for all that exterior modesty, which we require in the expressions, and dress, and behaviour of the fair sex. I believe I may spare myself the trouble of insisting on so obvious a subject, and may proceed, without farther preparation, to examine after what manner such notions arise from education, from the voluntary conventions of men, and from the interest of society.

Whoever considers the length and feebleness of human infancy, with the concern which both sexes naturally have for their off-spring, will easily perceive, that there must be an union of male and female for the education of the young, and that this union must be of considerable duration. But in order to induce the men to impose on themselves this restraint, and undergo cheerfully all the fatigues and expenses, to which it subjects them, they must believe, that the children are their own, and that their natural instinct is not directed to a wrong object, when they give a loose to love and tenderness. Now if we examine the structure of the human body, we shall find, that this security is very difficult to be attained on our part; and that since, in the copulation of the sexes, the principle of generation goes from the man to the woman, an error may easily take place on the side of the former, though it be utterly impossible with regard to the latter. From this trivial and anatomical observation is derived that vast difference betwixt the education and duties of the two sexes.

Were a philosopher to examine the matter *a priori*, he would reason after the following manner. Men are induced to labour for the maintenance and education of their children, by the persuasion that they are really their own; and therefore it is reasonable, and even necessary, to give them some security in this particular. This security cannot consist entirely in the imposing of severe punishments on any transgressions of conjugal fidelity on the part of the wife; since these public punishments cannot be inflicted without legal proof, which it is difficult to meet with in this subject. What restraint, therefore, shall we impose on women, in order to counter-balance so strong a temptation as they have to infidelity? There seems to be no restraint possible, but in the punishment of bad fame or reputation; a punishment, which has a mighty influence on the human mind, and at the same time is inflicted by the world upon surmizes, and conjectures, and proofs, that would never be received in any court of judicature. In order, therefore, to impose a due restraint on the female sex, we must attach a peculiar degree of shame to their infidelity, above what arises merely from its injustice, and must bestow proportionable praises on their chastity.

But though this be a very strong motive to fidelity, our philosopher would quickly discover, that it would not alone be sufficient to that purpose. All human creatures, especially of the female sex, are apt to over-look remote motives in favour of any present temptation: the temptation is here the strongest imaginable: its approaches are insensible and seducing: and a woman easily finds, or flatters herself she shall find, certain means of securing her reputation, and preventing all the pernicious consequences of her pleasures. It is necessary, therefore, that, beside the infamy attending such licences, there should be some preceding backwardness or dread, which may prevent their first approaches, and may give the female sex a repugnance to all expressions, and postures, and liberties, that have an immediate relation to that enjoyment.

Such would be the reasonings of our speculative philosopher: But I am persuaded, that if he had not a perfect knowledge of human nature, he would be apt to regard them as mere chimerical speculations, and would consider the infamy attending infidelity, and backwardness to all its approaches, as principles that were rather to be wished than hoped for in the world. For what means, would he say, of persuading mankind, that the transgressions of conjugal duty are more infamous than any other kind of injustice, when it is evident they are more excusable, upon account of the greatness of the temptation? And what possibility of giving a backwardness to the approaches of a pleasure, to which nature has inspired so strong a propensity; and a propensity that it is absolutely necessary in the end to comply with, for the support of the species?

But speculative reasonings, which cost so much pains to philosophers, are often formed by the world naturally, and without reflection: as difficulties, which seem unsurmountable in theory, are easily got over in practice. Those, who have an interest in the fidelity of women, naturally disapprove of their infidelity, and all the approaches to it. Those, who have no interest, are carried along with the stream. Education takes possession of the ductile minds of the fair sex in their infancy. And when a general rule of this kind is once established, men are apt to extend it beyond those principles, from which it first arose. Thus batchelors, however debauched, cannot choose but be shocked with any instance of lewdness or impudence in women. And though all these maxims have a plain reference to generation, yet women past child-bearing have no more privilege in this respect, than those who are in the flower of their youth and beauty. Men have undoubtedly an implicit notion, that all those ideas of modesty and decency have a regard to generation; since they impose not the same laws, *with the same force*, on the male sex, where that reason takes not place. The exception is there obvious and extensive, and founded on a remarkable difference, which produces a clear separation and disjunction of ideas. But as the case is not the same with regard to the different ages of women, for this reason, though men know, that these notions are founded on the public interest, yet the general rule carries us beyond the original principle, and makes us extend the notions of modesty over the whole sex, from their earliest infancy to their extremest old-age and infirmity.

Courage, which is the point of honour among men, derives its merit, in a great measure, from artifice, as well as the chastity of women; though it has also some foundation in nature, as we shall see afterwards.

As to the obligations which the male sex lie under, with regard to chastity, we may observe, that according to the general notions of the world, they bear nearly the same proportion to the obligations of women, as the obligations of the law of nations do to those of the law of nature. It is contrary to the interest of civil society, that men should have an *entire* liberty of indulging their appetites in venereal enjoyment: but as this interest is weaker than in the case of the female sex, the moral obligation, arising from it, must be proportionably weaker. And to prove this we need only appeal to the practice and sentiments of all nations and ages.

We come now to the examination of such virtues and vices as are entirely natural, and have no dependance on the artifice and contrivance of men. The examination of these will conclude this system of morals.

The chief spring or actuating principle of the human mind is pleasure or pain; and when these sensations are removed, both from our thought and feeling, we are, in a great measure, incapable of passion or action, of desire or volition. The most immediate effects of pleasure and pain are the propense and averse motions of the mind; which are diversified into volition, into desire and aversion, grief and joy, hope and fear, according as the pleasure or pain changes its situation, and becomes probable or improbable, certain or uncertain, or is considered as out of our power for the present moment. But when along with this, the objects, that cause pleasure or pain, acquire a relation to ourselves or others; they still continue to excite desire and aversion, grief and joy: but cause, at the same time, the indirect passions of pride or humility, love or hatred, which in this case have a double relation of impressions and ideas to the pain or pleasure.

We have already observed, that moral distinctions depend entirely on certain peculiar sentiments of pain and pleasure, and that whatever mental quality in ourselves or others gives us a satisfaction, by the survey or reflection, is of course virtuous; as every thing of this nature, that gives uneasiness, is vicious. Now since every quality in ourselves or others, which gives pleasure, always causes pride or love; as every one, that produces uneasiness, excites humility or hatred: it follows, that these two particulars are to be considered as equivalent, with regard to our mental qualities, *virtue* and the power of producing love or pride, *vice* and the power of producing humility or hatred. In every case, therefore, we must judge of the one by the other; and may pronounce any *quality* of the mind virtuous, which causes love or pride; and any one vicious, which causes hatred or humility.

If any *action* be either virtuous or vicious, it is only as a sign of some quality or character. It must depend upon durable principles of the mind, which extend over the whole conduct, and enter into the personal character. Actions themselves, not proceeding from any constant principle, have no influence on love or hatred, pride or humility; and consequently are never considered in morality.

This reflection is self-evident, and deserves to be attended to, as being of the utmost importance in the present subject. We are never to consider any single action in our enquiries concerning the origin of morals; but only the quality or character from which the action proceeded. These alone are *durable* enough to affect our sentiments concerning the person. Actions are, indeed, better indications of a character than words, or even wishes and sentiments; but it is only so far as they are such indications, that they are attended with love or hatred, praise or blame.

To discover the true origin of morals, and of that love or hatred, which arises from mental qualities, we must take the matter pretty deep, and compare some principles, which have been already examined and explained.

We may begin with considering a-new the nature and force of *sympathy*. The minds of all men are similar in their feelings and operations; nor can any one be actuated by any affection, of which all others are not, in some degree, susceptible. As in strings equally wound up, the motion of one communicates itself to the rest; so all the affections readily pass from one person to another, and beget correspondent movements in every human creature. When I see the *effects* of passion in the voice and gesture of any person, my mind immediately passes from these effects to their causes, and forms such a lively idea of the passion, as is presently converted into the passion itself. In like manner, when I perceive the *causes* of any emotion, my mind is conveyed to the effects, and is actuated with a like emotion. Were I present at any of the more terrible operations of surgery, it is certain, that even before it begun, the preparation of the instruments, the laying of the bandages in order, the heating of the irons, with all the signs of anxiety and concern in the patient and assistants, would have a great effect upon my mind, and excite the strongest sentiments of pity and terror. No passion of another discovers itself immediately to the mind. We are only sensible of its causes or effects. From *these* we infer the passion: and consequently *these* give rise to our sympathy.

Our sense of beauty depends very much on this principle; and where any object has a tendency to produce pleasure in its possessor, it is always regarded as beautiful; as every object, that has a tendency to produce pain, is disagreeable and deformed. Thus the conveniency of a house, the fertility of a field, the strength of a horse, the capacity, security, and swift-sailing of a vessel, form the principal beauty of these several objects. Here the object, which is denominated beautiful, pleases only by its tendency to produce a certain effect. That effect is the pleasure or advantage of some other person. Now the pleasure of a stranger, for whom we have no friendship, pleases us only by sympathy. To this principle, therefore, is owing the beauty, which we find in every thing that is useful. How considerable a part this is of beauty can easily appear upon reflection. Wherever an object has a tendency to produce pleasure in the possessor, or in other words, is the proper *cause* of pleasure, it is sure to please the spectator, by a delicate sympathy with the possessor. Most of the works of art are esteemed beautiful, in proportion to their fitness for the use of man, and even many of the productions of nature derive their beauty from that source. Handsome and beautiful, on most occasions, is nor an absolute but a relative quality, and pleases us by nothing but its tendency to produce an end that is agreeable.*

The same principle produces, in many instances, our sentiments of morals, as well as those of beauty. No virtue is more esteemed

---

* Decentior equus cujus astricta sunt ilia; sed idem velocior. Pulcher aspectu sit athleta, cujus lacertos exercitatio expressit; idem certamini paratior. Nunquam vero species ab utilitate dividitur. Sed hoc quidem discernere, modici judicii est. Quinct. lib. 8. (A horse with narrow flanks looks more comely; it also moves faster. An athlete whose muscles have been developed by training presents a handsome appearance; he is also better prepared for the contest. Attractive appearance is always found in conjunction with efficient functioning. Yet it takes but a modeast degree of judgment to perceive this.)

than justice, and no vice more detested than injustice; nor are there any qualities, which go farther to the fixing the character, either as amiable or odious. Now justice is a moral virtue, merely because it has that tendency to the good of mankind; and, indeed, is nothing but an artificial invention to that purpose. The same may be said of allegiance, of the laws of nations, of modesty, and of good-manners. All these are mere human contrivances for the interest of society. And since there is a very strong sentiment of morals, which in all nations, and all ages, has attended them, we must allow, that the reflecting on the tendency of characters and mental qualities, is sufficient to give us the sentiments of approbation and blame. Now as the means to an end can only be agreeable, where the end is agreeable; and as the good of society, where our own interest is not concerned, or that of our friends, pleases only by sympathy: it follows, that sympathy is the source of the esteem, which we pay to all the artificial virtues.

Thus it appears, *that* sympathy is a very powerful principle in human nature, *that* it has a great influence on our taste of beauty, and *that* it produces our sentiment of morals in all the artificial virtues. From thence we may presume, that it also gives rise to many of the other virtues; and that qualities acquire our approbation, because of their tendency to the good of mankind. This presumption must become a certainty, when we find that most of those qualities, which we *naturally* approve of, have actually that tendency, and render a man a proper member of society: while the qualities, which we *naturally* disapprove of, have a contrary tendency, and render any intercourse with the person dangerous or disagreeable. For having found, that such tendencies have force enough to produce the strongest sentiment of morals, we can never reasonably, in these cases, look for any other cause of approbation or blame; it being an inviolable maxim in philosophy, that where any particular cause is sufficient for an effect, we ought to rest satisfied with it, and ought not to multiply causes without necessity. We have happily attained experiments in the artificial virtues, where the tendency of qualities to the good of society, is the sole cause of our approbation, without any suspicion of the concurrence of another principle. From thence we learn the force of that principle. And where that principle may take place, and the quality approved of is really beneficial to society, a true philosopher will never require any other principle to account for the strongest approbation and esteem.

That many of the natural virtues have this tendency to the good of society, no one can doubt of. Meekness, beneficence, charity, generosity, clemency, moderation, equity bear the greatest figure among the moral qualities, and are commonly denominated the social virtues, to mark their tendency to the good of society. This goes so far, that some philosophers have represented all moral distinctions as the effect of artifice and education, when skilful politicians endeavoured to restrain the turbulent passions of men, and make them operate to the public good, by the notions of honour and shame. This system, however, is nor consistent with experience. For, *first*, there are other virtues and vices beside those which have this tendency to the public advantage and loss. *Secondly*, had not men a natural sentiment of approbation and blame, it could never be excited by politicians; nor would the words *laudable* and *praise-worthy*, *blameable* and *odious* be any more intelligible, than if they were a language perfectly unknown to us, as we have already observed. But though this system be erroneous, it may teach us, that moral distinctions arise, in a great measure, from the tendency of qualities and characters to the interests of society, and that it is our concern for that interest, which makes us approve or disapprove of them. Now we have no such extensive concern for society but from sympathy; and consequently it is that principle, which takes us so far out of ourselves, as to give us the same pleasure or uneasiness in the characters of others, as if they had a tendency to our own advantage or loss.

The only difference betwixt the natural virtues and justice lies in this, that the good, which results from the former, arises from every single act, and is the object of some natural passion: whereas a single act of justice, considered in itself, may often be contrary to the public good; and it is only the concurrence of mankind, in a general scheme or system of action, which is advantageous. When I relieve persons in distress, my natural humanity is my motive; and so far as my succour extends, so far have I promoted the happiness of my fellow-creatures. But if we examine all the questions, that come before any tribunal of justice, we shall find, that, considering each case apart, it would as often be an instance of humanity to decide contrary to the laws of justice as conformable to them. Judges take from a poor man to give to a rich; they bestow on the dissolute the labour of the industrious; and put into the hands of the vicious the means of harming both themselves and others. The whole scheme, however, of law and justice is advantageous to the society; and it was with a view to this advantage, that men, by their voluntary conventions, established it. After it is once established by these conventions, it is *naturally* attended with a strong sentiment of morals; which can proceed from nothing but our sympathy with the interests of society. We need no other explication of that esteem, which attends such of the natural virtues, as have a tendency to the public good.

I must farther add, that there are several circumstances, which render this hypothesis much more probable with regard to the natural than the artificial virtues. It is certain that the imagination is more affected by what is particular, than by what is general; and that the sentiments are always moved with difficulty, where their objects are, in any degree, loose and undetermined: now every particular act of justice is not beneficial to society, but the whole scheme or system: and it may not, perhaps, be any individual person for whom we are concerned, who receives benefit from justice, but the whole society alike. On the contrary, every particular act of generosity, or relief of the industrious and indigent, is beneficial; and is beneficial to a particular person, who is not undeserving of it. It is more natural, therefore, to think, that the tendencies of the latter virtue will affect our sentiments, and command our approbation, than those of the former; and therefore, since we find, that the approbation of the former arises from their tendencies, we may ascribe, with better reason, the same cause to the approbation of the latter. In any number of similar effects, if a cause can be discovered for one, we ought to extend that cause to all the other effects, which can be accounted for by it: but much more, if these other effects be attended with peculiar circumstances, which facilitate the operation of that cause.

Before I proceed farther, I must observe two remarkable circumstances in this affair, which may seem objections to the present system. The first may be thus explained. When any quality, or character, has a tendency to the good of mankind, we are pleased with it, and approve of it; because it presents the lively idea of pleasure; which idea affects us by sympathy, and is itself a kind of pleasure. But as this sympathy is very variable, it may be thought that our sentiments of morals must admit of all the same variations. We sympathize more with persons contiguous to us, than with persons remote from us: with our acquaintance, than with strangers: with our countrymen, than with foreigners. But notwithstanding this variation of our sympathy, we give the same approbation to the same moral qualities in *China* as in *England*. They appear equally virtuous, and recommend themselves equally to the esteem of a judicious spectator. The sympathy varies without a variation in our esteem. Our esteem, therefore, proceeds not from sympathy.

To this I answer: The approbation of moral qualities most certainly is not derived from reason, or any comparison of ideas; but proceeds entirely from a moral taste, and from certain sentiments of pleasure or disgust, which arise upon the contemplation and view of particular qualities or characters. Now it is evident, that those sentiments, whence-ever they are derived, must vary according to the distance or contiguity of the objects; nor can I feel the same lively pleasure from the virtues of a person, who lived in *Greece* two thousand years ago, that I feel from the virtues of a familiar friend and acquaintance. Yet I do not say, that I esteem the one more than the other: and therefore, if the variation of the sentiment, without a variation of the esteem, be an objection, it must have equal force against every other system, as against that of sympathy. But to consider the case a-right, it has no force at all; and it is the easiest matter in the world to account for it. Our situation, with regard both to persons and things, is in continual fluctuation; and a man, that lies at a distance from us, may, in a little time, become a familiar acquaintance. Besides, every particular man has a peculiar position with regard to others; and it is impossible we could ever converse together on any reasonable terms, were each of us to consider characters and persons, only as they appear from his peculiar point of view. In order, therefore, to prevent those continual *contradictions*, and arrive at a more *stable* judgment of things, we fix on some *steady* and *general* points of view; and always, in our thoughts, place ourselves in them, whatever may be our present situation. In like manner, external beauty is determined merely by pleasure; and it is evident, a beautiful countenance cannot give so much pleasure, when seen at the distance of twenty paces, as when it is brought nearer us. We say not, however, that it appears to us less beautiful: because we know what effect it will have in such a position, and by that reflection we correct its momentary appearance.

In general, all sentiments of blame or praise are variable, according to our situation of nearness or remoteness, with regard to the person blamed or praised, and according to the present disposition of our mind. But these variations we regard not in our general decision, but still apply the terms expressive of our liking or dislike, in the same manner, as if we remained in one point of view. Experience soon teaches us this method of correcting our sentiments, or at least, of correcting our language, where the sentiments are more stubborn and inalterable. Our servant, if diligent and faithful, may excite stronger sentiments of love and kindness than *Marcus Brutus*, as represented in history; but we say not upon that account, that the former character is more laudable than the latter. We know, that were we to approach equally near to that renowned patriot, he would command a much higher degree of affection and admiration. Such corrections are common with regard to all the senses; and indeed it were impossible we could ever make use of language, or communicate our sentiments to one another, did we not correct the momentary appearances of things, and overlook our present situation.

It is therefore from the influence of characters and qualities, upon those who have an intercourse with any person, that we blame or praise him. We consider not whether the persons, affected by the qualities, be our acquaintance or strangers, countrymen or foreigners. Nay, we over-look our own interest in those general judgments; and blame not a man for opposing us in any of our pretensions, when his own interest is particularly concerned. We make allowance for a certain degree of selfishness in men; because we know it to be inseparable from human nature, and inherent in our frame and constitution. By this reflection we correct those sentiments of blame, which so naturally arise upon any opposition.

But however the general principle of our blame or praise may be corrected by those other principles, it is certain, they are not altogether efficacious, nor do our passions often correspond entirely to the present theory. It is seldom men heartily love what lies at a distance from them, and what no way redounds to their particular benefit; as it is no less rare to meet with persons, who can pardon another any opposition he makes to their interest, however justifiable that opposition may be by the general rules of morality. Here we are contented with saying, that reason requires such an impartial conduct, but that it is seldom we can bring ourselves to it, and that our passions do not readily follow the determination of our judgment. This language will be easily understood, if we consider what we formerly said concerning that *reason*, which is able to oppose our passion; and which we have found to be nothing but a general calm determination of the passions, founded on some distant view or reflection. When we form our judgments of persons, merely from the tendency of their characters to our own benefit, or to that of our friends, we find so many contradictions to our sentiments in society and conversation, and such an uncertainty from the incessant changes of our situation, that we seek some other standard of merit and demerit, which may not admit of so great variation. Being thus loosened from our first station, we cannot afterwards fix ourselves so commodiously by any means as by a sympathy with those, who have any commerce with the person we consider. This is far from being as lively as when our own interest is concerned, or that of our particular friends; nor has it such an influence on our love and hatred: but being equally conformable to our calm and general principles, it is said to have an equal authority over our reason, and to command our judgment and opinion. We blame equally a bad action, which we read of in history, with one performed in our neighbourhood the other day: the meaning of which is, that we know from reflection, that the former action would excite as strong sentiments of disapprobation as the latter, were it placed in the same position.

I now proceed to the *second* remarkable circumstance, which I proposed to take notice of. Where a person is possessed of a character, that in its natural tendency is beneficial to society, we esteem him virtuous, and are delighted with the view of his character, even though particular accidents prevent its operation, and incapacitate him from being serviceable to his friends and country. Virtue in rags is still virtue; and the love, which it procures, attends a man into a dungeon or desert, where the virtue can no longer be exerted in action, and is lost to all the world.

Now this may be esteemed an objection to the present system. Sympathy interests us in the good of mankind; and if sympathy were the source of our esteem for virtue, that sentiment of approbation could only take place, where the virtue actually attained its end, and was beneficial to mankind. Where it fails of its end, it is only an imperfect means; and therefore can never acquire any merit from that end. The goodness of an end can bestow a merit on such means alone as are complete, and actually produce the end.

To this we may reply, that where any object, in all its parts, is fitted to attain any agreeable end, it naturally gives us pleasure, and is esteemed beautiful, even though some external circumstances be wanting to render it altogether effectual. It is sufficient if every thing be complete in the object itself. A house, that is contrived with great judgment for all the commodities of life, pleases us upon that account; though perhaps we are sensible, that no-one will ever dwell in it. A fertile soil, and a happy climate, delight us by a reflection on the happiness which they would afford the inhabitants, though at present the country be desert and uninhabited. A man, whose limbs and shape promise strength and activity, is esteemed handsome, though condemned to perpetual imprisonment. The imagination has a set of passions belonging to it, upon which our sentiments of beauty much depend. These passions are moved by degrees of liveliness and strength, which are inferior to *belief*, and independent of the real existence of their objects. Where a character is, in every respect, fitted to be beneficial to society, the imagination passes easily from the cause to the effect, without considering that there are some circumstances wanting to render the cause a complete one. *General rules* create a species of probability, which sometimes influences the judgment, and always the imagination.

It is true, when the cause is complete, and a good disposition is attended with good fortune, which renders it really beneficial to society, it gives a stronger pleasure to the spectator, and is attended with a more lively sympathy. We are more affected by it; and yet we do not say that it is more virtuous, or that we esteem it more. We know, that an alteration of fortune may render the benevolent disposition entirely impotent; and therefore we separate, as much as possible, the fortune from the disposition. The case is the same, as when we correct the different sentiments of virtue, which proceed from its different distances from ourselves. The passions do not always follow our corrections; but these corrections serve sufficiently to regulate our abstract notions, and are alone regarded, when we pronounce in general concerning the degrees of vice and virtue.

It is observed by critics, that all words or sentences, which are difficult to the pronunciation, are disagreeable to the ear. There is no difference, whether a man hear them pronounced, or read them silently to himself. When I run over a book with my eye, I Imagine I hear it all; and also, by the force of imagination, enter into the uneasiness, which the delivery of it would give the speaker. The uneasiness is not real; but as such a composition of words has a natural tendency to produce it, this is sufficient to affect the mind with a painful sentiment, and render the discourse harsh and disagreeable. It is a similar case, where any real quality is, by accidental circumstances, rendered impotent, and is deprived of its natural influence on society.

Upon these principles we may easily remove any contradiction, which may appear to be betwixt the *extensive sympathy*, on which our sentiments of virtue depend, and that *limited generosity* which I have frequently observed to be natural to men, and which justice and property suppose, according to the precedent reasoning. My sympathy with another may give me the sentiment of pain and disapprobation, when any object is presented, that has a tendency to give him uneasiness; though I may not be willing to sacrifice any thing of my own interest, or cross any of my passions, for his satisfaction. A house may displease me by being ill-contrived for the convenience of the owner; and yet I may refuse to give a shilling towards the rebuilding of it. Sentiments must touch the heart, to make them control our passions: but they need not extend beyond the imagination, to make them influence our taste. When a building seems clumsy and tottering to the eye, it is ugly and disagreeable; though we be fully assured of the solidity of the workmanship. It is a kind of fear, which causes this sentiment of disapprobation; but the passion is not the same with that which we feel, when obliged to stand under a wall, that we really think tottering and insecure. The *seeming tendencies* of objects affect the mind: and the emotions they excite are of a like species with those, which proceed from the *real consequences* of objects, but their feeling is different. Nay, these emotions are so different in their feeling, that they may often be contrary, without destroying each other; as when the fortifications of a city belonging to an enemy are esteemed beautiful upon account of their strength, though we could wish that they were entirely destroyed. The imagination adheres to the general views of things, and distinguishes the feelings they produce, from those which arise from our particular and momentary situation.

If we examine the panegyrics that are commonly made of great men, we shall find, that most of the qualities, which are attributed to them, may be divided into two kinds, *viz.* such as make them perform their part in society; and such as render them serviceable to themselves, and enable them to promote their own interest. Their *prudence, temperance, frugality, industry, assiduity, enterprize, dexterity,* are celebrated, as well as their *generosity* and *humanity*. If we ever give an indulgence to any quality, that disables a man from making a figure in life, it is to that of *indolence,* which is not supposed to deprive one of his parts and capacity, but only suspends their exercise; and that without any inconvenience to the person himself, since it is, in some measure, from his own choice. Yet indolence is always allowed to be a fault, and a very great one, if extreme: nor do a man's friends ever acknowledge him to be subject to it, but in order to save his character in more material articles. He could make a figure, say they, if he pleased to give application: his understanding is sound, his conception quick, and his memory tenacious; but he hates business, and is indifferent about his fortune. And this a man sometimes may make even a subject of vanity; though with the air of confessing a fault: because he may think, that his incapacity for business implies much more noble qualities; such as a philosophical spirit, a fine taste, a delicate wit, or a relish for pleasure and society. But take any other case: suppose a quality, that without being an indication of any other good qualities, incapacitates a man *always* for business, and is destructive to his interest; such as a blundering understanding, and a wrong judgment of every thing in life; inconstancy and irresolution; or a want of address in the management of men and business: these are all allowed to be imperfections in a character; and many men would rather acknowledge the greatest crimes, than have it suspected, that they are, in any degree, subject to them.

It is very happy, in our philosophical researches, when we find the same phenomenon diversified by a variety of circumstances; and by discovering what is common among them, can the better assure ourselves of the truth of any hypothesis we may make use of to explain it. Were nothing esteemed virtue but what were beneficial to society, I am persuaded, that the foregoing explication of the moral sense ought still to be received, and that upon sufficient evidence: but this evidence must grow upon us, when we find other kinds of virtue, which will not admit of any explication except from that hypothesis. Here is a man, who is not remarkably defective in his social qualities; but what principally recommends him is his dexterity in business, by which he has extricated himself from the greatest difficulties, and conducted the most delicate affairs with a singular address and prudence. I find an esteem for him immediately to arise in me: his company is a satisfaction to me; and before I have any farther acquaintance with him, I would rather do him a service than another, whose character is in every other respect equal, but is deficient in that particular. In this case, the qualities that please me are all considered as useful to the person, and as having a tendency to promote his interest and satisfaction. They are only regarded as means to an end, and please me in proportion to their fitness for that end. The end, therefore, must be agreeable to me. But what makes the end agreeable? The person is a stranger: I am no way interested in him, nor lie under any obligation to him: his happiness concerns not me, farther than the happiness of every human, and indeed of every sensible creature: that is, it affects me only by sympathy. From that principle, whenever I discover his happiness and good, whether in its causes or effects, I enter so deeply into it, that it gives me a sensible emotion. The appearance of qualities, that have a tendency to promote it, have an agreeable effect upon my imagination, and command my love and esteem.

This theory may serve to explain, why the same qualities, in all cases, produce both pride and love, humility and hatred; and the same man is always virtuous or vicious, accomplished or despicable to others, who is so to himself. A person, in whom we discover any passion or habit, which originally is only incommodious to himself, becomes always disagreeable to us, merely on its account; as on the other hand, one whose character is only dangerous and disagreeable to others, can never be satisfied with himself, as long as he is sensible of that disadvantage. Nor is this observable only with regard to characters and manners, but may be remarked even in the most minute circumstances. A violent cough in another gives us uneasiness; though in itself it does not in the least affect us. A man will be mortified, if you tell him he has a stinking breath; though it is evidently no annoyance to himself. Our fancy easily changes its situation; and either surveying ourselves as we appear to others, or considering others as they feel themselves, we enter, by that means, into sentiments, which no way belong to us, and in which nothing but sympathy is able to interest us. And this sympathy we sometimes carry so far, as even to be displeased with a quality commodious to us, merely because it displeases others, and makes us disagreeable in their eyes; though perhaps we never can have any interest in rendering ourselves agreeable to them.

There have been many systems of morality advanced by philosophers in all ages; but if they are strictly examined, they may be reduced to two, which alone merit our attention. Moral good and evil are certainly distinguished by our *sentiments*, not by *reason*: but these sentiments may arise either from the mere species or appearance of characters and passions, or from reflections on their tendency to the happiness of mankind, and of particular persons. My opinion is, that both these causes are intermixed in our judgments of morals; after the same manner as they are in our decisions concerning most kinds of external beauty: though I am also of opinion, that reflections on the tendencies of actions have by far the greatest influence, and determine all the great lines of our duty. There are, however, instances, in cases of less moment, wherein this immediate taste or sentiment produces our approbation. Wit, and a certain easy and disengaged behaviour, are qualities *immediately agreeable* to others, and command their love and esteem. Some of these qualities produce satisfaction in others by particular *original* principles of human nature, which cannot be accounted for: others may be resolved into principles, which are more general. This will best appear upon a particular enquiry.

As some qualities acquire their merit from their being *immediately agreeable* to others, without any tendency to public interest;

so some are denominated virtuous from their being *immediately agreeable* to the person himself, who possesses them. Each of the passions and operations of the mind has a particular feeling, which must be either agreeable or disagreeable. The first is virtuous, the second vicious. This particular feeling constitutes the very nature of the passion; and therefore needs not be accounted for.

But however directly the distinction of vice and virtue may seem to flow from the immediate pleasure or uneasiness, which particular qualities cause to ourselves or others; it is easy to observe, that it has also a considerable dependence on the principle of *sympathy* so often insisted on. We approve of a person, who is possessed of qualities *immediately agreeable* to those, with whom he has any commerce; though perhaps we ourselves never reaped any pleasure from them. We also approve of one, who is possessed of qualities, that are *immediately agreeable* to himself; though they be of no service to any mortal. To account for this we must have recourse to the foregoing principles.

Thus, to take a general review of the present hypothesis: every quality of the mind is denominated virtuous, which gives pleasure by the mere survey; as every quality, which produces pain, is called vicious. This pleasure and this pain may arise from four different sources. For we reap a pleasure from the view of a character, which is naturally fitted to be useful to others, or to the person himself, or which is agreeable to others, or to the person himself. One may, perhaps, be surprized. that amidst all these interests and pleasures, we should forget our own, which touch us so nearly on every other occasion. But we shall easily satisfy ourselves on this head, when we consider, that every particular person's pleasure and interest being different, it is impossible men could ever agree in their sentiments and judgments, unless they chose some common point of view, from which they might survey their object, and which might cause it to appear the same to all of them. Now in judging of characters, the only interest or pleasure, which appears the same to every spectator, is that of the person himself, whose character is examined; or that of persons, who have a connexion with him. And though such interests and pleasures touch us more faintly than our own, yet being more constant and universal, they counter-balance the latter even in practice, and are alone admitted in speculation as the standard of virtue and morality. They alone produce that particular feeling or sentiment, on which moral distinctions depend.

As to the good or ill desert of virtue or vice, it is an evident consequence of the sentiments of pleasure or uneasiness. These sentiments produce love or hatred; and love or hatred, by the original constitution of human passion, is attended with benevolence or anger; that is, with a desire of making happy the person we love, and miserable the person we hate. We have treated of this more fully on another occasion.

SECTION TWO
Of greatness of mind

It may now be proper to illustrate this general system of morals, by applying it to particular instances of virtue and vice, and shewing how their merit or demerit arises from the four sources here explained. We shall begin with examining the passions of *pride* and *humility*, and shall consider the vice or virtue that lies in their excesses or just proportion. An excessive pride or overweaning conceit of ourselves is always esteemed vicious, and is universally hated; as modesty, or a just sense of our weakness, is esteemed virtuous, and procures the good-will of every-one. Of the four sources of moral distinctions, this is to be ascribed to the *third*; *viz*, the immediate agreeableness and disagreeableness of a quality to others, without any reflections on the tendency of that quality.

In order to prove this, we must have recourse to two principles, which are very conspicuous in human nature. The *first* of these is the *sympathy*, and communication of sentiments and passions above-mentioned. So close and intimate is the correspondence of human souls, that no sooner any person approaches me, than he diffuses on me all his opinions, and draws along my judgment in a greater or lesser degree. And though, on many occasions, my sympathy with him goes not so far as entirely to change my sentiments, and way of thinking; yet it seldom is so weak as not to disturb the easy course of my thought, and give an authority to that opinion, which is recommended to me by his assent and approbation. Nor is it any way material upon what subject he and I employ our thoughts. Whether we judge of an indifferent person, or of my own character, my sympathy gives equal force to his decision: and even his sentiments of his own merit make me consider him in the same light, in which he regards himself.

This principle of sympathy is of so powerful and insinuating a nature, that it enters into most of our sentiments and passions, and often takes place under the appearance of its contrary. For it is remarkable, that when a person opposes me in any thing, which I am strongly bent upon, and rouses up my passion by contradiction, I have always a degree of sympathy with him, nor does my commotion proceed from any other origin. We may here observe an evident conflict or rencounter of opposite principles and passions. On the one side there is that passion or sentiment, which is natural to me; and it is observable, that the stronger this passion is, the greater is the commotion. There must also be some passion or sentiment on the other side; and this passion can proceed from nothing but sympathy. The sentiments of others can never affect us, but by becoming, in some measure, our own; in which case they operate upon us, by opposing and increasing our passions, in the very same manner, as if they had been originally derived from our own temper and disposition. While they remain concealed in the minds of others, they can never have an influence upon us: and even when they are known, if they went no farther than the imagination, or conception; that faculty is so accustomed to objects of every different kind, that a mere idea, though contrary to our sentiments and inclinations, would never alone be able to affect us.

The *second* principle I shall take notice of is that of *comparison*, or the variation of our judgments concerning objects, according to the proportion they bear to those with which we compare them. We judge more of objects by comparison, than by their intrinsic worth and value; and regard every thing as mean, when set in opposition to what is superior of the same kind. But no comparison is more obvious than that with ourselves; and hence it is that on all occasions it takes place, and mixes with most of our passions. This kind of comparison is directly contrary to sympathy in its operation, as we have observed in treating of *compassion* and *malice.** In all kinds of comparison an object makes us always receive from another, to which it is compared, a sensation contrary to what arises from*

* Book 2, Part 2, Section 8.

itself in its direct and immediate survey. The direct survey of another's pleasure naturally gives us pleasure; and therefore produces pain, when compared with our own. His pain, considered in itself, is painful; but augments the idea of our own happiness, and gives us pleasure.

Since then those principles of sympathy, and a comparison with ourselves, are directly contrary, it may be worth while to consider, what general rules can be formed, beside the particular temper of the person, for the prevalence of the one or the other. Suppose I am now in safety at land, and would willingly reap some pleasure from this consideration: I must think on the miserable condition of those who are at sea in a storm, and must endeavour to render this idea as strong and lively as possible, in order to make me more sensible of my own happiness. But whatever pains I may take, the comparison will never have an equal efficacy, as if I were really on the shore,* and saw a ship at a distance tossed by a tempest, and in danger every moment of perishing on a rock or sand-bank. But suppose this idea to become still more lively. Suppose the ship to be driven so near me, that I can perceive distinctly the horror, painted on the countenance of the seamen and passengers, hear their lamentable cries, see the dearest friends give their last adieu, or embrace with a resolution to perish in each others arms: no man has so savage a heart as to reap any pleasure from such a spectacle, or withstand the motions of the tenderest compassion and sympathy. It is evident, therefore, there is a medium in this case; and that if the idea be too faint, it has no influence by comparison; and on the other hand, if it be too strong, it operates on us entirely by sympathy, which is the contrary to comparison. Sympathy being the conversion of an idea into an impression, demands a greater force and vivacity in the idea than is requisite to comparison.

All this is easily applied to the present subject. We sink very much in our own eyes, when in the presence of a great man, or

---

*   Suave mari magno turbantibus aequora ventis
      E terra magnum alterius spectare laborem;
      Non quia vexari quenquam est jucunda voluptas,
      Sed quibus ipse malis careas quia cernere suave est.   LUCRETIUS
[There is something pleasant in watching, from dry land, the great difficulties another man is undergoing out on the high sea, with the winds lashing the waters. This is not because one derives delight from any man's distress, but because it is pleasurable to perceive from what troubles one is oneself free.]

one of a superior genius; and this humility makes a considerable ingredient in that *respect*, which we pay our superiors, according to our foregoing reasonings* on that passion. Sometimes even envy and hatred arise from the comparison; but in the greatest part of men, it rests at respect and esteem. As sympathy has such a powerful influence on the human mind, it causes pride to have, in some measure, the same effect as merit; and by making us enter into those elevated sentiments, which the proud man entertains of himself, presents that comparison, which is so mortifying and disagreeable. Our judgment does not entirely accompany him in the flattering conceit, in which he pleases himself; but still is so shaken as to receive the idea it presents, and to give it an influence above the loose conceptions of the imagination. A man who, in an idle humour, would form a notion of a person of a merit very much superior to his own, would not be mortified by that fiction: but when a man, whom we are really persuaded to be of inferior merit, is presented to us; if we observe in him any extraordinary degree of pride and self-conceit; the firm persuasion he has of his own merit, takes hold of the imagination, and diminishes us in our own eyes, in the same manner, as if he were really possessed of all the good qualities which he so liberally attributes to himself. Our idea is here precisely in that medium, which is requisite to make it operate on us by comparison. Were it accompanied with belief, and did the person appear to have the same merit, which he assumes to himself, it would have a contrary effect, and would operate on us by sympathy. The influence of that principle would then be superior to that of comparison, contrary to what happens where the person's merit seems below his pretensions.

The necessary consequence of these principles is, that pride, or an over-weaning conceit of ourselves, must be vicious; since it causes uneasiness in all men, and presents them every moment with a disagreeable comparison. It is a trite observation in philosophy, and even in common life and conversation, that it is our own pride, which makes us so much displeased with the pride of other people; and that vanity becomes insupportable to us merely because we are vain. The gay naturally associate themselves with the gay, and the amorous with the amorous: but the proud never can endure the proud, and rather seek the company of those who

* Book 2, Part 2, Section 10.

are of an opposite disposition. As we are, all of us, proud in some degree, pride is universally blamed and condemned by all mankind; as having a natural tendency to cause uneasiness in others by means of comparison. And this effect must follow the more naturally, that those, who have an ill-grounded conceit of themselves, are for ever making those comparisons, nor have they any other method of supporting their vanity. A man of sense and merit is pleased with himself, independent of all foreign considerations: but a fool must always find some person, that is more foolish, in order to keep himself in good humour with his own parts and understanding.

But though an over-weaning conceit of our own merit be vicious and disagreeable, nothing can be more laudable, than to have a value for ourselves, where we really have qualities that are valuable. The utility and advantage of any quality to ourselves is a source of virtue, as well as its agreeableness to others; and it is certain, that nothing is more useful to us in the conduct of life, than a due degree of pride, which makes us sensible of our own merit, and gives us a confidence and assurance in all our projects and enterprizes. Whatever capacity any one may be endowed with, it is entirely useless to him, if he be not acquainted with it, and form not designs suitable to it. It is requisite on all occasions to know our own force; and were it allowable to err on either side, it would be more advantageous to over-rate our merit, than to form ideas of it, below its just standard. Fortune commonly favours the bold and enterprizing; and nothing inspires us with more boldness than a good opinion of ourselves.

Add to this, that though pride, or self-applause, be sometimes disagreeable to others, it is always agreeable to ourselves; as on the other hand, modesty, though it gives pleasure to every one, who observes it, produces often uneasiness in the person endowed with it. Now it has been observed, that our own sensations determine the vice and virtue of any quality, as well as those sensations, which it may excite in others.

Thus self-satisfaction and vanity may not only be allowable, but requisite in a character. It is, however, certain, that good-breeding and decency require that we should avoid all signs and expressions, which tend directly to show that passion. We have, all of us, a wonderful partiality for ourselves, and were we always to give vent to our sentiments in this particular, we should mutually cause the greatest indignation in each other, not only by the immediate presence of so disagreeable a subject of comparison, but also by the contrariety of our judgments. In like manner, therefore, as we establish the *laws of nature*, in order to secure property in society, and prevent the opposition of self-interest; we establish the *rules of good-breeding*, in order to prevent the opposition of men's pride, and render conversation agreeable and inoffensive. Nothing is more disagreeable than a man's over-weaning conceit of himself: every one almost has a strong propensity to this vice: no one can well distinguish *in himself* betwixt the vice and virtue, or be certain, that his esteem of his own merit is well-founded: for these reasons, all direct expressions of this passion are condemned; nor do we make any exception to this rule in favour of men of sense and merit. They are not allowed to do themselves justice openly, in words, no more than other people; and even if they show a reserve and secret doubt in doing themselves justice in their own thoughts, they will be more applauded. That impertinent, and almost universal propensity of men, to over-value themselves, has given us such a *prejudice* against self-applause, that we are apt to condemn it, by a *general rule*, wherever we meet with it; and it is with some difficulty we give a privilege to men of sense, even in their most secret thoughts. At least, it must be owned, that some disguise in this particular is absolutely requisite; and that if we harbour pride in our breasts, we must carry a fair outside, and have the appearance of modesty and mutual deference in all our conduct and behaviour. We must, on every occasion, be ready to prefer others to ourselves; to treat them with a kind of deference, even though they be our equals; to seem always the lowest and least in the company, where we are not very much distinguished above them: and if we observe these rules in our conduct, men will have more indulgence for our secret sentiments, when we discover them in an oblique manner.

I believe no one, who has any practice of the world, and can penetrate into the inward sentiments of men, will assert, that the humility, which good-breeding and decency require of us, goes beyond the outside, or that a thorough sincerity in this particular is esteemed a real part of our duty. On the contrary, we may observe, that a genuine and hearty pride, or self-esteem, if well concealed and well founded, is essential to the character of a man of honour, and that there is no quality of the mind, which is more indispensibly requisite to procure the esteem and approbation of mankind. There are certain deferences and mutual submissions, which custom requires of the different ranks of men towards each other; and whoever exceeds in this particular, if through interest, is accused of meanness; if through ignorance, of simplicity. It is necessary, therefore, to know our rank and station in the world, whether it be fixed by our birth, fortune, employments, talents or reputation. It is necessary to feel the sentiment and passion of pride in conformity to it, and to regulate our actions accordingly. And should it be said, that prudence may suffice to regulate our actions in this particular, without any real pride, I would observe, that here the object of prudence is to conform our actions to the general usage and custom; and, that it is impossible those tacit airs of superiority should ever have been established and authorized by custom, unless men were generally proud, and unless that passion were generally approved, when well-grounded.

If we pass from common life and conversation to history, this reasoning acquires new force, when we observe, that all those great actions and sentiments, which have become the admiration of mankind, are founded on nothing but pride and self-esteem. '*Go*,' says *Alexander* the Great to his soldiers, when they refused to follow him to the *Indies*, '*go tell your countrymen, that you left Alexander completing the conquest of the world.*' This passage was always particularly admired by the prince of *Condé*, as we learn from *St Evremond*. '*Alexander*,' said that prince, '*abandoned by his soldiers, among barbarians, not yet fully subdued, felt in himself such a dignity of right and of empire, that he could not believe it possible any one could refuse to obey him. Whether in Europe or in Asia, among Greeks or Persians, all was indifferent to him: wherever he found men, he fancied he found subjects.*'

In general we may observe, that whatever we call *heroic virtue*, and admire under the character of greatness and elevation of mind, is either nothing but a steady and wellestablished pride and self-esteem, or partakes largely of that passion. Courage, intrepidity, ambition, love of glory, magnanimity, and all the other shining virtues of that kind, have plainly a strong mixture of self-esteem in them, and derive a great part of their merit from that origin. Accordingly we find, that many religious declaimers decry those virtues as purely pagan and natural, and represent to us the excellency of the *Christian* religion, which places humility in the rank of virtues, and corrects the judgment of the world, and even of philosophers, who so generally admire all the efforts of pride and ambition. Whether this virtue of humility has been rightly understood, I shall not pretend to determine. I am content with the concession, that the world naturally esteems a well-regulated pride, which secretly animates our conduct, without breaking out into such indecent expressions of vanity, as many offend the vanity of others.

The merit of pride or self-esteem is derived from two circumstances, *viz*, its utility and its agreeableness to ourselves; by which it capacitates us for business, and, at the same time, gives us an immediate satisfaction. When it goes beyond its just bounds, it loses the first advantage, and even becomes prejudicial; which is the reason why we condemn an extravagant pride and ambition, however regulated by the decorums of good-breeding and politeness. But as such a passion is still agreeable, and conveys an elevated and sublime sensation to the person, who is actuated by it, the sympathy with that satisfaction diminishes considerably the blame, which naturally attends its dangerous influence on his conduct and behaviour. Accordingly we may observe, that an excessive courage and magnanimity, especially when it displays itself under the frowns of fortune, contributes, in a great measure, to the character of a hero, and will render a person the admiration of posterity; at the same time, that it ruins his affairs, and leads him into dangers and difficulties, with which otherwise he would never have been acquainted.

Heroism, or military glory, is much admired by the generality of mankind. They consider it as the most sublime kind of merit. Men of cool reflection are not so sanguine in their praises of it. The infinite confusions and disorder, which it has caused in the world, diminish much of its merit in their eyes. When they would oppose the popular notions on this head, they always paint out the evils, which this supposed virtue has produced in human society; the subversion of empires, the devastation of provinces, the sack of cities. As long as these are present to us, we are more inclined to hate than admire the ambition of heroes. But when we fix our view on the person himself, who is the author of all this mischief, there is something so dazzling in his character, the mere contemplation of it so elevates the mind, that we cannot refuse it our admiration. The pain, which we receive from its tendency to the prejudice of society, is over-powered by a stronger and more immediate sympathy.

Thus our explication of the merit or demerit, which attends the degrees of pride or self-esteem, may serve as a strong argument for the preceding hypothesis, by shewing the effects of those principles above explained in all the variations of our judgments concerning that passion. Nor will this reasoning be advantageous to us only by shewing, that the distinction of vice and virtue arises from the *four* principles of the *advantage* and of the *pleasure* of the *person himself,* and of *others*: but may also afford us a strong proof of some under-parts of that hypothesis.

No one, who duly considers of this matter, will make any scruple of allowing, that any piece of ill-breeding, or any expression of pride and haughtiness, is displeasing to us, merely because it shocks our own pride, and leads us by sympathy into a comparison, which causes the disagreeable passion of humility. Now as an insolence of this kind is blamed even in a person who has always been civil to ourselves in particular; nay, in one, whose name is only known to us in history; it follows, that our disapprobation proceeds from a sympathy with others, and from the reflection, that such a character is highly displeasing and odious to every one, who converses or has any intercourse with the person possessed of it. We sympathize with those people in their uneasiness; and as their uneasiness proceeds in part from a sympathy with the person who insults them, we may here observe a double rebound of the sympathy; which is a principle very similar to what we have observed on another occasion.*

* Book 2, Part 2, Section 5.

SECTION THREE

Of goodness and benevolence

Having thus explained the origin of that praise and approbation, which attends every thing we call *great* in human affections; we now proceed to give an account of their *goodness*, and shew whence its merit is derived.

When experience has once given us a competent knowledge of human affairs, and has taught us the proportion they bear to human passion, we perceive, that the generosity of men is very limited, and that it seldom extends beyond their friends and family, or, at most, beyond their native country. Being thus acquainted with the nature of man, we expect not any impossibilities from him; but confine our view to that narrow circle, in which any person moves, in order to form a judgment of his moral character. When the natural tendency of his passions leads him to be serviceable and useful within his sphere, we approve of his character, and love his person, by a sympathy with the sentiments of those, who have a more particular connexion with him. We are quickly obliged to forget our own interest in our judgments of this kind, by reason of the perpetual contradictions, we meet with in society and conversation, from persons that are not placed in the same situation, and have not the same interest with ourselves. The only point of view, in which our sentiments concur with those of others, is, when we consider the tendency of any passion to the advantage or harm of those, who have any immediate connexion or intercourse with the person possessed of it. And though this advantage or harm be often very remote from ourselves, yet sometimes it is very near us, and interests us strongly by sympathy. This concern we readily extend to other cases, that are resembling; and when these are very remote, our sympathy is proportionably weaker, and our praise or blame fainter and more doubtful. The case is here the same as in our judgments concerning external bodies. All objects seem to diminish by their distance: but though the appearance of objects to our senses be the original standard, by which we judge of them, yet we do not say, that they actually diminish by the distance; but correcting the appearance by reflection, arrive at a more constant and established judgment concerning them. In like manner, though sympathy be much fainter than our concern for ourselves, and a sympathy with persons remote from us much fainter than that with persons near and contiguous; yet we neglect all these differences in our calm judgments concerning the characters of men. Besides, that we ourselves often change our situation in this particular, we every day meet with persons, who are in a different situation from ourselves, and who could never converse with us on any reasonable terms, were we to remain constantly in that situation and point of view, which is peculiar to us. The intercourse of sentiments, therefore, in society and conversation, makes us form some general inalterable standard, by which we may approve or disapprove of characters and manners. And though the *heart* does not always take part with those general notions, or regulate its love and hatred by them, yet are they sufficient for discourse, and serve all our purposes in company, in the pulpit, on the theatre, and in the schools.

From these principles we may easily account for that merit, which is commonly ascribed to *generosity*, *humanity*, *compassion*, *gratitude*, *friendship*, *fidelity*, *zeal*, *disinterestedness*, *liberality*, and all those other qualities, which form the character of good and benevolent. A propensity to the tender passions makes a man agreeable and useful in all the parts of life; and gives a just direction to all his other qualities, which otherwise may become prejudicial to society. Courage and ambition, when not regulated by benevolence, are fit only to make a tyrant and public robber. It is the same case with judgment and capacity, and all the qualities of that kind. They are indifferent in themselves to the interests of society, and have a tendency to the good or ill of mankind, according as they are directed by these other passions.

As love is *immediately agreeable* to the person, who is actuated by it, and hatred *immediately disagreeable*; this may also be a considerable reason, why we praise all the passions that partake of the former, and blame all those that have any considerable share of the latter. It is certain we are infinitely touched with a tender sentiment, as well as with a great one. The tears naturally start in our eyes at the conception of it; nor can we forbear giving a loose to the same tenderness towards the person who exerts it. All this seems to me a proof, that our approbation has, in those cases, an origin different from the prospect of utility and advantage, either to ourselves or others. To which we may add, that men naturally, without reflection, approve of that character, which is most like their own. The man of a mild disposition and tender affections, in forming a notion of the most perfect virtue, mixes in it more of benevolence and humanity, than the man of courage and enterprize, who naturally looks upon a certain elevation of mind as the most accomplished character. This must evidently proceed from an *immediate* sympathy, which men have with characters similar to their own. They enter with more warmth into such sentiments, and feel more sensibly the pleasure, which arises from them.

It is remarkable, that nothing touches a man of humanity more than any instance of extraordinary delicacy in love or friendship, where a person is attentive to the smallest concerns of his friend, and is willing to sacrifice to them the most considerable interest of his own. Such delicacies have little influence on society; because they make us regard the greatest trifles: but they are the more engaging, the more minute the concern is, and are a proof of the highest merit in any one, who is capable of them. The passions are so contagious, that they pass with the greatest facility from one person to another, and produce correspondent movements in all human breasts. Where friendship appears in very signal instances, my heart catches the same passion, and is warmed by those warm sentiments, that display themselves before me. Such agreeable movements must give me an affection to every one that excites them. This is the case with every thing that is agreeable in any person. The transition from pleasure to love is easy: but the transition must here be still more easy; since the agreeable sentiment, which is excited by sympathy, is love itself; and there is nothing required but to change the object.

Hence the peculiar merit of benevolence in all its shapes and appearances. Hence even its weaknesses are virtuous and amiable; and a person, whose grief upon the loss of a friend were excessive, would be esteemed upon that account. His tenderness bestows a merit, as it does a pleasure, on his melancholy.

We are not, however, to imagine, that all the angry passions are vicious, though they are disagreeable. There is a certain indulgence due to human nature in this respect. Anger and hatred are passions inherent in our very frame and constitutions. The want of them, on some occasions, may even be a proof of weakness and imbecillity. And where they appear only in a low degree, we not only excuse them because they are natural; but even bestow our applauses on them, because they are inferior to what appears in the greatest part of mankind.

Where these angry passions rise up to cruelty, they form the most detested of all vices. All the pity and concern which we have for the miserable sufferers by this vice, turns against the person guilty of it, and produces a stronger hatred than we are sensible of on any other occasion.

Even when the vice of inhumanity rises not to this extreme degree, our sentiments concerning it are very much influenced by reflections on the harm that results from it. And we may observe in general, that if we can find any quality in a person, which renders him incommodious to those, who live and converse with him, we always allow it to be a fault or blemish, without any farther examination. On the other hand, when we enumerate the good qualities of any person, we always mention those parts of his character, which render him a safe companion, an easy friend, a gentle master, an agreeable husband, or an indulgent father. We consider him with all his relations in society; and love or hate him, according as he affects those, who have any immediate intercourse with him. And it is a most certain rule, that if there be no relation of life, in which I could not wish to stand to a particular person, his character must so far be allowed to be perfect. If he be as little wanting to himself as to others, his character is entirely perfect. This is the ultimate test of merit and virtue.

SECTION FOUR
Of natural abilities

No distinction is more usual in all systems of ethics, than that betwixt *natural abilities* and *moral virtues*; where the former are placed on the same footing with bodily endowments, and are supposed to have no merit or moral worth annexed to them. Whoever considers the matter accurately, will find, that a dispute upon this head would be merely a dispute of words, and that though these qualities are not altogether of the same kind, yet they agree in the most material circumstances. They are both of them equally mental qualities: and both of them equally produce pleasure; and have of course an equal tendency to procure the love and esteem of mankind. There are few, who are not as jealous of their character, with regard to sense and knowledge, as to honour and courage; and much more than with regard to temperance and sobriety. Men are even afraid of passing for goodnatured; lest *that* should be taken for want of understanding: and often boast of more debauches than they have been really engaged in, to give themselves airs of fire and spirit. In short, the figure a man makes in the world, the reception he meets with in company, the esteem paid him by his acquaintance; all these advantages depend almost as much upon his good sense and judgment, as upon any other part of his character. Let a man have the best intentions in the world, and be the farthest from all injustice and violence, he will never be able to make himself be much regarded without a moderate share, at least, of parts and understanding. Since then natural abilities, though perhaps inferior, yet are on the same footing, both as to their causes and effects, with those qualities which we call moral virtues, why should we make any distinction betwixt them?

Though we refuse to natural abilities the title of virtues, we must allow, that they procure the love and esteem of mankind; that they give a new lustre to the other virtues; and that a man possessed of them is much more entitled to our good-will and services, than one entirely void of them. It may, indeed, be pretended that the sentiment of approbation, which those qualities produce, besides its being *inferior*, is also somewhat *different* from that, which attends the other virtues. But this, in my opinion, is not a sufficient reason for excluding them from the catalogue of virtues. Each of the virtues, even benevolence, justice, gratitude, integrity, excites a different sentiment or feeling in the spectator. The characters of *Caesar* and *Cato*, as drawn by *Sallust*, are both of them virtuous, in the strictest sense of the word; but in a different way: nor are the sentiments entirely the same, which arise from them. The one produces love; the other esteem: the one is amiable; the other awful: we could wish to meet with the one character in a friend; the other character we would be ambitious of in ourselves. In like manner, the approbation which attends natural abilities, may be somewhat different to the feeling from that, which arises from the other virtues, without making them entirely of a different species. And indeed we may observe, that the natural abilities, no more than the other virtues, produce not, all of them, the same kind of approbation. Good sense and genius beget esteem: wit and humour excite love.[*]

Those, who represent the distinction betwixt natural abilities and moral virtues as very material, may say, that the former are entirely involuntary, and have therefore no merit attending them, as having no dependance on liberty and free-will. But to this I answer, *first*, that many of those qualities, which all moralists, especially the ancients, comprehend under the title of moral virtues, are equally involuntary and necessary, with the qualities of the judgment and imagination. Of this nature are constancy, fortitude, magnanimity; and, in short, all the qualities which form the *great* man. I might say the same, in some degree, of the others; it being almost impossible for the mind to change its character in any considerable article, or cure itself of a passionate or splenetic temper, when they are natural to it. The greater degree there is of these blameable qualities, the more vicious they become, and yet they are the less voluntary. *Secondly*, I would have anyone give me a reason, why virtue and vice may not be involuntary, as well as beauty and deformity. These moral distinctions arise from the natural distinctions of pain and pleasure; and when we receive those feelings from the general consideration of any quality or character, we denominate it vicious or virtuous. Now I believe no one will assert, that a quality can never produce pleasure or pain to the person who considers it, unless it be perfectly voluntary in the person who possesses it. *Thirdly*, As to free-will, we have shewn that it has no place with regard to the actions, no more than the qualities of men. It is not a just consequence, that what is voluntary is free. Our actions are more voluntary than our judgments; but we have not more liberty in the one than in the other.

But though this distinction betwixt voluntary and involuntary be not sufficient to justify the distinction betwixt natural abilities and moral virtues, yet the former distinction will afford us a plausible

---

[*] Love and esteem are at the bottom the same passions, and arise from like causes. The qualities, that produce both, are agreeable, and give pleasure. But where this pleasure is severe and serious; or where its object is great, and makes a strong impression; or where it produces any degree of humility and awe: in all these cases, the passion, which arises from the pleasure, is more properly denominated esteem than love. Benevolence attends both: but is connected with love in a more eminent degree.

reason, why moralists have invented the latter. Men have observed, that though natural abilities and moral qualities be in the main on the same footing, there is, however, this difference betwixt them, that the former are almost invariable by any art or industry; while the latter, or at least, the actions, that proceed from them, may be changed by the motives of rewards and punishments, praise and blame. Hence legislators, and divines, and moralists, have principally applied themselves to the regulating these voluntary actions, and have endeavoured to produce additional motives, for being virtuous in that particular. They knew, that to punish a man for folly, or exhort him to be prudent and sagacious, would have but little effect; though the same punishments and exhortations, with regard to justice and injustice, might have a considerable influence. But as men, in common life and conversation, do not carry those ends in view, but naturally praise or blame whatever pleases or displeases them, they do not seem much to regard this distinction, but consider prudence under the character of virtue as well as benevolence, and penetration as well as justice. Nay, we find, that all moralists, whose judgment is not perverted by a strict adherence to a system, enter into the same way of thinking; and that the ancient moralists in particular made no scruple of placing prudence at the head of the cardinal virtues. There is a sentiment of esteem and approbation, which may be excited, in some degree, by any faculty of the mind, in its perfect state and condition; and to account for this sentiment is the business of *Philosophers*. It belongs to *Grammarians* to examine what qualities are entitled to the denomination of *virtue*; nor will they find, upon trial, that this is so easy a task, as at first sight they may be apt to imagine.

The principal reason why natural abilities are esteemed, is because of their tendency to be useful to the person, who is possessed of them. It is impossible to execute any design with success, where it is not conducted with prudence and discretion; nor will the goodness of our intentions alone suffice to procure us a happy issue to our enterprizes. Men are superior to beasts principally by the superiority of their reason; and they are the degrees of the same faculty, which set such an infinite difference betwixt one man and another. All the advantages of art are owing to human reason; and where fortune is not very capricious, the most considerable part of these advantages must fall to the share of the prudent and sagacious.

When it is asked, whether a quick or a slow apprehension be most valuable? whether one, that at first view penetrates into a subject, but can perform nothing upon study; or a contrary character, which must work out every thing by dint of application? whether a clear head, or a copious invention? whether a profound genius, or a sure judgment? in short, what character, or peculiar understanding, is more excellent than another? it is evident we can answer none of these questions, without considering which of those qualities capacitates a man best for the world, and carries him farthest in any of his undertakings.

There are many other qualities of the mind, whose merit is derived from the same origin. *Industry, perseverance, patience, activity, vigilance, application, constancy,* with other virtues of that kind, which it will be easy to recollect, are esteemed valuable upon no other account, than their advantage in the conduct of life. It is the same case with *temperance, frugality, economy, resolution*: as on the other hand, *prodigality, luxury, irresolution, uncertainty,* are vicious, merely because they draw ruin upon us, and incapacitate us for business and action.

As wisdom and good-sense are valued, because they are *useful* to the person possessed of them; so wit and eloquence are valued, because they are *immediately agreeable* to others. On the other hand, *good humour* is loved and esteemed, because it is *immediately agreeable* to the person himself. It is evident, that the conversation of a man of wit is very satisfactory; as a cheerful good-humoured companion diffuses a joy over the whole company, from a sympathy with his gaiety. These qualities, therefore, being agreeable, they naturally beget love and esteem, and answer to all the characters of virtue.

It is difficult to tell, on many occasions, what it is that renders *one man's conversation so agreeable and entertaining, and another's* so insipid and distasteful. As conversation is a transcript of the mind as well as books, the same qualities, which render the one valuable, must give us an esteem for the other. This we shall consider afterwards. In the mean time it may be affirmed in general, that all the merit a man may derive from his conversation (which, no doubt, may be very considerable) arises from nothing but the pleasure it conveys to those who are present.

In this view, *cleanliness* is also to be regarded as a virtue; since it naturally renders us agreeable to others, and is a very considerable source of love and affection. No one will deny, that a negligence in this particular is a fault; and as faults are nothing but smaller vices, and this fault can have no other origin than the uneasy sensation, which it excites in others, we may in this instance, seemingly so trivial, dearly discover the origin of the moral distinction of vice and virtue in other instances.

Besides all those qualities, which render a person lovely or valuable, there is also a certain *je-ne-scai-quoi* of agreeable and handsome, that concurs to the same effect. In this case, as well as in that of wit and eloquence, we must have recourse to a certain sense, which acts without reflection, and regards not the tendencies of qualities and characters. Some moralists account for all the sentiments of virtue by this sense. Their hypothesis is very plausible. Nothing but a particular enquiry can give the preference to any other hypothesis. When we find, that almost all the virtues have such particular tendencies; and also find, that these tendencies are sufficient alone to give a strong sentiment of approbation: we cannot doubt, after this, that qualities are approved of, in proportion to the advantage, which results from them.

The *decorum* or *indecorum* of a quality, with regard to the age, or character, or station, contributes also to its praise or blame. This decorum depends, in a great measure, upon experience. It is usual to see men lose their levity, as they advance in years. Such a degree of gravity, therefore, and such years, are connected together in our thoughts. When we observe them separated in any person's character, this imposes a kind of violence on our imagination, and is disagreeable.

That faculty of the soul, which, of all others, is of the least consequence to the character, and has the least virtue or vice in its several degrees, at the same time, that it admits of a great variety of degrees, is the *memory*. Unless it rise up to that stupendous height as to surprize us, or sink so low as, in some measure, to affect the judgment, we commonly take no notice of its variations, nor ever mention them to the praise or disparise of any person. It is so far from being a virtue to have a good memory, that men generally affect to complain of a bad one; and endeavouring to persuade the world, that what they say is entirely of their own invention, sacrifice it to the praise of genius and judgment. Yet to consider the matter abstractedly, it would be difficult to give a reason, why the faculty of recalling past ideas with truth and clearness, should not have as much merit in it, as the faculty of placing our present ideas, in such an order, as to form true propositions and opinions. The reason of the difference certainly must be, that the memory is exerted without any sensation of pleasure or pain; and in all its middling degrees serves almost equally well in business and affairs. But the least variations in the judgment are sensibly felt in their consequences; while at the same time that faculty is never exerted in any eminent degree, without an extraordinary delight and satisfaction. The sympathy with this utility and pleasure bestows a merit on the understanding; and the absence of it makes us consider the memory as a faculty very indifferent to blame or praise.

Before I leave this subject of _natural abilities_, I must observe, that, perhaps, one source of the esteem and affection, which attends them, is derived from the _importance_ and _weight_, which they bestow on the person possessed of them. He becomes of greater consequence in life. His resolutions and actions affect a greater number of his fellow-creatures. Both his friendship and enmity are of moment. And it is easy to observe, that whoever is elevated, after this manner, above the rest of mankind, must excite in us the sentiments of esteem and approbation. Whatever is important engages our attention, fixes our thought, and is contemplated with satisfaction. The histories of kingdoms are more interesting than domestic stories: the histories of great empires more than those of small cities and principalities: and the histories of wars and revolutions more than those of peace and order. We sympathize with the persons that suffer, in all the various sentiments which belong to their fortunes. The mind is occupied by the multitude of the objects, and by the strong passions, that display themselves. And this occupation or agitation of the mind is commonly agreeable and amusing. The same theory accounts for the esteem and regard we pay to men of extraordinary parts and abilities. The good and ill of multitudes are connected with their actions. Whatever they undertake is important, and challenges our attention. Nothing is to be over-looked and despised, that regards them. And where any person can excite these sentiments, he soon acquires our esteem; unless other circumstances of his character render him odious and disagreeable.

SECTION FIVE

Some farther reflections concerning the natural virtues

It has been observed, in treating of the passions, that pride and humility, love and hatred, are excited by any advantages or disadvantages of the *mind, body*, or *fortune*; and that these advantages or disadvantages have that effect by producing a separate impression of pain or pleasure. The pain or pleasure, which arises from the general survey or view of any action or quality of the mind, constitutes its vice or virtue, and gives rise to our approbation or blame, which is nothing but a fainter and more imperceptible love or hatred. We have assigned four different sources of this pain and pleasure; and in order to justify more fully that hypothesis, it may here be proper to observe, that the advantages or disadvantages of the *body* and of *fortune*, produce a pain or pleasure from the very same principles. The tendency of any object to be *useful* to the person possessed of it, or to others; to convey *pleasure* to him or to others; all these circumstances convey an immediate pleasure to the person, who considers the object, and command his love and approbation.

To begin with the advantages of the *body*; we may observe a phenomenon, which might appear somewhat trivial and ludicrous, if any thing could be trivial, which fortified a conclusion of such importance, or ludicrous, which was employed in a philosophical reasoning. It is a general remark, that those we call good *women's men*, who have either signalized themselves by their amorous exploits, or whose make of body promises any extraordinary vigour of that kind, are well received by the fair sex, and naturally engage the affections even of those, whose virtue prevents any design of ever giving employment to those talents. Here it is evident, that the ability of such a person to give enjoyment, is the real source of that love and esteem he meets with among the females; at the same time that the women, who love and esteem him, have no prospect of receiving that enjoyment themselves, and can only be affected by means of their sympathy with one, that has a commerce of love with him. This instance is singular, and merits our attention.

Another source of the pleasure we receive from considering bodily advantages, is their utility to the person himself, who is possessed of them. It is certain, that a considerable part of the beauty of men, as well as of other animals, consists in such a conformation of members, as we find by experience to be attended with strength and agility, and to capacitate the creature for any action or exercise. Broad shoulders, a lank belly, firm joints, taper legs; all these are beautiful in our species because they are signs of force and vigour, which being advantages we naturally sympathize with, they convey to the beholder a share of that satisfaction they produce in the possessor.

So far as to the *utility*, which may attend any quality of the body. As to the immediate *pleasure*, it is certain, that an air of health, as well as of strength and agility, makes a considerable part of beauty; and that a sickly air in another is always disagreeable, upon account of that idea of pain and uneasiness, which it conveys to us. On the other hand, we are pleased with the regularity of our own features, though it be neither useful to ourselves nor others; and it is necessary at a distance, to make it convey to us any satisfaction. We commonly consider ourselves as we appear in the eyes of others, and sympathize with the advantageous sentiments they entertain with regard to us.

How far the advantages of *fortune* produce esteem and approbation from the same principles, we may satisfy ourselves by reflecting on our precedent reasoning on that subject. We have observed, that our approbation of those, who are possessed of the advantages of fortune, may be ascribed to three different causes. *First*, To that immediate pleasure, which a rich man gives us, by the view of the beautiful clothes, equipage, gardens, or houses, which he possesses. *Secondly*, To the advantage, which we hope to reap from him by his generosity and liberality. *Thirdly*, To the pleasure and advantage, which he himself reaps from his possessions, and which produce an agreeable sympathy in us. Whether we ascribe our esteem of the rich and great to one or all of these causes, we may clearly see the traces of those principles, which give rise to the sense of vice and virtue. I believe most people, at first sight, will be inclined to ascribe our esteem of the rich to self-interest, and the prospect of advantage. But as it is certain, that our esteem or deference extends beyond any prospect of advantage to ourselves, it is evident, that that sentiment must proceed from a sympathy with those, who are dependent on the person we esteem and respect, and who have an immediate connexion with him. We consider him as a person capable of contributing to the happiness or enjoyment of his fellow-creatures, whose sentiments, with regard to him, we naturally embrace. And this consideration will serve to justify my hypothesis in preferring the *third* principle to the other two, and ascribing our esteem of the rich to a sympathy with the pleasure and advantage, which they themselves receive from their possessions. For as even the other two principles cannot operate to a due extent, or account for all the phenomena, without having recourse to a sympathy of one kind or other; it is much more natural to choose that sympathy, which is immediate and direct, than that which is remote and indirect. To which we may add, that where the riches or power are very great, and render the person considerable and important in the world, the esteem attending them, may, in part, be ascribed to another source, distinct from these three, *viz.* their interesting the mind by a prospect of the multitude, and importance of their consequences: though, in order to account for the operation of this principle, we must also have recourse to *sympathy*; as we have observed in the preceding section.

It may not be amiss, on this occasion, to remark the flexibility of our sentiments, and the several changes they so readily receive from the objects, with which they are conjoined. All the sentiments of approbation, which attend any particular species of objects, have a great resemblance to each other, though derived from different sources; and, on the other hand, those sentiments, when directed to different objects, are different to the feeling, though derived from the same source. Thus the beauty of all visible objects causes a pleasure pretty much the same, though it be sometimes derived from the mere *species* and appearance of the objects; sometimes from sympathy, and an idea of their utility. In like manner, whenever we survey the actions and characters of men, without any particular interest in them, the pleasure, or pain, which arises from the survey (with some minute differences) is, in the main, of the same kind, though perhaps there be a great diversity in the causes, from which it is derived. On the other hand, a convenient house, and a virtuous character, cause not the same feeling of approbation; even though the source of our approbation be the same, and flow from sympathy and an idea of their utility. There is something very inexplicable in this variation of our feelings; but it is what we have experience of with regard to all our passions and sentiments.

SECTION SIX

Conclusion of this book

Thus upon the whole I am hopeful, that nothing is wanting to an accurate proof of this system of ethics. We are certain, that sympathy is a very powerful principle in human nature. We are also certain, that it has a great influence on our sense of beauty, when we regard external objects, as well as when we judge of morals. We find, that it has force sufficient to give us the strongest sentiments of approbation, when it operates alone, without the concurrence of any other principle; as in the cases of justice, allegiance, chastity, and good-manners. We may observe, that all the circumstances requisite for its operation are found in most of the virtues; which have, for the most part, a tendency to the good of society, or to that of the person possessed of them. If we compare all these circumstances, we shall not doubt, that sympathy is the chief source of moral distinctions; especially when we reflect, that no objection can be raised against this hypothesis in one case, which will not extend to all cases. Justice is certainly approved of for no other reason, than because it has a tendency to the public good: and the public good is indifferent to us, except so far as sympathy interests us in it. We may presume the like with regard to all the other virtues, which have a like tendency to the public good. They must derive all their merit from our sympathy with those, who reap any advantage from them: as the virtues, which have a tendency to the good of the person possessed of them, derive their merit from our sympathy with him.

Most people will readily allow, that the useful qualities of the mind are virtuous, because of their utility. This way of thinking is so natural, and occurs on so many occasions, that few will make any scruple of admitting it. Now this being once admitted, the force of sympathy must necessarily be acknowledged. Virtue is considered as means to an end. Means to an end are only valued so far as the end is valued. But the happiness of strangers affects us by sympathy alone. To that principle, therefore, we are to ascribe the sentiment of approbation, which arises from the survey of all those virtues, that are useful to society, or to the person possessed of them. These form the most considerable part of morality.

*　　*　　*

Were it proper in such a subject to bribe the reader's assent, or employ any thing but solid argument, we are here abundantly supplied with topics to engage the affections. All lovers of virtue (and such we all are in speculation, however we may degenerate in practice) must certainly be pleased to see moral distinctions derived from so noble a source, which gives us a just notion both of the *generosity* and *capacity* of human nature. It requires but very little knowledge of human affairs to perceive, that a sense of morals is a principle inherent in the soul, and one of the most powerful that enters into the composition. But this sense must certainly acquire new force, when reflecting on itself, it approves of those principles, from whence it is derived, and finds nothing but what is great and good in its rise and origin. Those who resolve the sense of morals into original instincts of the human mind, may defend the cause of virtue with sufficient authority; but want the advantage, which those possess, who account for that sense by an extensive sympathy with mankind. According to their system, not only virtue must be approved of, but also the sense of virtue: and not only that sense, but also the principles, from whence it is derived. So that nothing is presented on any side, but what is laudable and good.

This observation may be extended to justice, and the other virtues of that kind. Though justice be artificial, the sense of its morality is natural. It is the combination of men, in a system of conduct, which renders any act of justice beneficial to society. But when once it has that tendency, we *naturally* approve of it; and if we did not so, it is impossible any combination or convention could ever produce that sentiment.

Most of the inventions of men are subject to change. They depend upon humour and caprice. They have a vogue for a time, and then sink into oblivion. It may, perhaps, be apprehended, that if justice were allowed to be a human invention, it must be placed on the same footing. But the cases are widely different. The interest, on which justice is founded, is the greatest imaginable, and extends to all times and places. It cannot possibly be served by any other invention. It is obvious, and discovers itself on the very first formation of society. All these causes render the rules of justice steadfast and immutable; at least, as immutable as human nature. And if they were founded on original instincts, could they have any greater stability?

The same system may help us to form a just notion of the *happiness*, as well as of the *dignity* of virtue, and may interest every principle of our nature in the embracing and cherishing that noble quality. Who indeed does not feel an accession of alacrity in his pursuits of knowledge and ability of every kind, when he considers, that besides the advantage, which immediately result from these acquisitions, they also give him a new lustre in the eyes of mankind, and are universally attended with esteem and approbation? And who can think any advantages of fortune a sufficient compensation for the least breach of the *social* virtues, when he considers, that not only his character with regard to others, but also his peace and inward satisfaction entirely depend upon his strict observance of them; and that a mind will never be able to bear its own survey, that has been wanting in its part to mankind and society? But I forbear insisting on this subject. Such reflections require a work a-part, very different from the genius of the present. The anatomist ought never to emulate the painter; nor in his accurate dissections and portraitures of the smaller parts of the human body, pretend to give his figures any graceful and engaging attitude or expression. There is even something hideous, or at least minute in the views of things, which he presents; and it is necessary the objects should be set more at a distance, and be more covered up from sight, to make them engaging to the eye and imagination. An anatomist, however, is admirably fitted to give advice to a painter; and it is even impracticable to excel in the latter art, without the assistance of the former. We must have an exact knowledge of the parts, their situation and connexion, before we can design with any elegance or correctness. And thus the most abstract speculations concerning human nature, however cold and unentertaining, become subservient to *practical morality*; and may render this latter science more correct in its precepts, and more persuasive in its exhortations.

APPENDIX

There is nothing I would more willingly lay hold of, than an opportunity of confessing my errors; and should esteem such a return to truth and reason to be more honourable than the most unerring judgment. A man, who is free from mistakes, can pretend to no praises, except from the justness of his understanding: but a man, who corrects his mistakes, shews at once the justness of his understanding, and the candour and ingenuity of his temper. I have not yet been so fortunate as to discover any very considerable mistakes in the reasonings delivered in the preceding volumes, except on one article: but I have found by experience, that some of my expressions have not been so well chosen, as to guard against all mistakes in the readers; and it is chiefly to remedy this defect, I have subjoined the following appendix.

We can never be induced to believe any matter of fact, except where its cause, or its effect, is present to us; but what the nature is of that belief, which arises from the relation of cause and effect, few have had the curiosity to ask themselves. In my opinion, this dilemma is inevitable. Either the belief is some new idea, such as that of *reality* or *existence*, which we join to the simple conception of an object, or it is merely a peculiar *feeling* or *sentiment*. That it is not a new idea, annexed to the simple conception, may be evinced from these two arguments. *First*, We have no abstract idea of existence, distinguishable and separable from the idea of particular objects. It is impossible, therefore, that this idea of existence can be annexed to the idea of any object, or form the difference betwixt a simple conception and belief. *Secondly*, The mind has the command over all its ideas, and can separate, unite, mix, and vary them, as it pleases; so that if belief consisted merely in a new idea, annexed to the conception, it would be in a man's power to believe what he pleased. We may, therefore, conclude, that belief consists merely in a certain feeling or sentiment; in something, that depends not on the will, but must arise from certain determinate causes and principles, of which we are not masters. When we are convinced of any matter of fact, we do nothing but conceive it, along with a certain feeling, different from what attends the mere *reveries* of the imagination. And when we express our incredulity concerning any fact, we mean, that the arguments for the fact produce not that feeling. Did not the belief consist in a sentiment different from our mere conception, whatever objects were presented by the wildest imagination, would be on an equal footing with the most established truths founded on history and experience. There is nothing but the feeling, or sentiment, to distinguish the one from the other.

This, therefore, being regarded as an undoubted truth, *that belief is nothing but a peculiar feeling, different from the simple conception*, the next question, that naturally occurs, is, *what is the nature of this feeling, or sentiment, and whether it be analogous to any other sentiment of the human mind?* This question is important. For if it be not analogous to any other sentiment, we must despair of explaining its causes, and must consider it as an original principle of the human mind. If it be analogous, we may hope to explain its causes from analogy, and trace it up to more general principles. Now that there is a greater firmness and solidity in the conceptions, which are the objects of conviction and assurance, than in the loose and indolent reveries of a castle-builder, every one will readily own. They strike upon us with more force; they are more present to us; the mind has a firmer hold of them, and is more actuated and moved by them. It acquiesces in them; and, in a manner, fixes and reposes itself on them. In short, they approach nearer to the impressions, which are immediately present to us; and are therefore analogous to many other operations of the mind.

There is not, in my opinion, any possibility of evading this conclusion, but by asserting, that belief, beside the simple conception, consists in some impression or feeling, distinguishable from the conception. It does not modify the conception, and render it more present and intense: it is only annexed to it, after the same manner that *will* and *desire* are annexed to particular conceptions of good and pleasure. But the following considerations will, I hope, be sufficient to remove this hypothesis. *First*, It is directly contrary to experience, and our immediate consciousness. All men have ever allowed reasoning to be merely an operation of our thoughts or ideas; and however those ideas may be varied to the feeling, there is nothing ever enters into our *conclusions* but ideas, or our fainter conceptions. For instance; I hear at present a person's voice, whom I am acquainted with; and this sound comes from the next room. This impression of my senses immediately conveys my thoughts to the person, along with all the surrounding objects. I paint them out to myself as existent at present, with the same qualities and relations, that I formerly knew them possessed of. These ideas take faster hold of my mind, than the ideas of an enchanted castle. They are different to the feeling; but there is no distinct or separate impression attending them. It is the same case when I recollect the several incidents of a journey, or the events of any history. Every particular fact is there the object of belief. Its idea is modified differently from the loose reveries of a castle-builder: but no distinct impression attends every distinct idea, or conception of matter of fact. This is the subject of plain experience. If ever this experience can be disputed on any occasion, it is when the mind has been agitated with doubts and difficulties; and afterwards, upon taking the object in a new point of view, or being presented with a new argument, fixes and reposes itself in one settled conclusion and belief. In this case there is a feeling distinct and separate from the conception. The passage from doubt and agitation to tranquillity and repose, conveys a satisfaction and pleasure to the mind. But take any other case. Suppose I see the legs and thighs of a person in motion, while some interposed object conceals the rest of his body. Here it is certain, the imagination spreads out the whole figure. I give him a head and shoulders, and breast and neck. These members I conceive and believe him to be possessed of. Nothing can be more evident, than that this whole operation is performed by the thought or imagination alone. The transition is immediate. The ideas presently strike us. Their customary connexion with the present impression, varies them and modifies them in a certain manner, but produces no act of the mind, distinct from this peculiarity of conception. Let any one examine his own mind, and he will evidently find this to be the truth.

Secondly, Whatever may be the case, with regard to this distinct impression, it must be allowed, that the mind has a firmer hold, or more steady conception of what it takes to be matter of fact, than of fictions. Why then look any farther, or multiply suppositions without necessity?

Thirdly, We can explain the *causes* of the firm conception, but not those of any separate impression. And not only so, but the causes of the firm conception exhaust the whole subject, and nothing is left to produce any other effect. An inference concerning a matter of fact is nothing but the idea of an object, that is frequently conjoined, or is associated with a present impression. This is the whole of it. Every part is requisite to explain, from analogy, the more steady conception; and nothing remains capable of producing any distinct impression.

Fourthly, The *effects* of belief, in influencing the passions and imagination, can all be explained from the firm conception; and there is no occasion to have recourse to any other principle. These arguments, with many others, enumerated in the foregoing volumes, sufficiently prove, that belief only modifies the idea or conception; and renders it different to the feeling, without producing any distinct impression.

Thus upon a general view of the subject, there appear to be two questions of importance, which we may venture to recommend to the consideration of philosophers, *Whether there be any thing to distinguish belief from the simple conception beside the feeling of sentiment?* And, *Whether this feeling be any thing but a firmer conception, or a faster hold, that we take of the object?*

If, upon impartial enquiry, the same conclusion, that I have formed, be assented to by philosophers, the next business is to examine the analogy, which there is betwixt belief, and other acts of the mind, and find the cause of the firmness and strength of conception: and this I do not esteem a difficult task. The transition from a present impression, always enlivens and strengthens any idea. When any object is presented, the idea of its usual attendant immediately strikes us, as something real and solid. It is *felt*, rather than conceived, and approaches the impression, from which it is derived, in its force and influence. This I have proved at large. I cannot add any new arguments; though perhaps my reasoning on this whole question, concerning cause and effect, would have been more convincing, had the following passages been inserted in the places, which I have marked for them. I have added a few illustrations on other points, where I thought it necessary.

To be inserted in Book 1, Part 3, Section 5, after the words 'fainter and more obscure', beginning a new paragraph.

It frequently happens, that when two men have been engaged in any scene of action, the one shall remember it much better than the other, and shall have all the difficulty in the world to make his companion recollect it. He runs over several circumstances in vain; mentions the time, the place, the company, what was said, what was done on all sides; till at last he hits on some lucky circumstance, that revives the whole, and gives his friend a perfect memory of every thing. Here the person that forgets receives at first all the ideas from the discourse of the other, with the same circumstances of time and place; though he considers them as mere fictions of the imagination. But as soon as the circumstance is mentioned, that touches the memory, the very same ideas now appear in a new light, and have, in a manner, a different feeling from what they had before. Without any other alteration, beside that of the feeling, they become immediately ideas of the memory, and are assented to.

Since, therefore, the imagination can represent all the same objects that the memory can offer to us, and since those faculties are only distinguished by the different *feeling* of the ideas they present, it may be proper to consider what is the nature of that feeling. And here I believe every one will readily agree with me, that the ideas of the memory are more *strong* and *lively* than those of the fancy.

To be inserted in Book 1, Part 3, Section 7, after the words 'according to the foregoing definition', beginning a new paragraph.

This operation of the mind, which forms the belief of any matter of fact, seems hitherto to have been one of the greatest mysteries of philosophy; though no one has so much as suspected, that there was any difficulty in explaining it. For my part I must own, that I find a considerable difficulty in the case; and that even when I think I understand the subject perfectly, I am at a loss for terms to express my meaning. I conclude, by an induction which seems to me very evident, that an opinion or belief is nothing but an idea, that is different from a fiction, not in the nature or the order of its parts, but in the *manner* of its being conceived. But when I would explain this *manner*, I scarce find any word that fully answers the case, but am obliged to have recourse to every one's feeling, in order to give him a perfect notion of this operation of the mind. An idea assented to *feels* different from a fictitious idea, that the fancy alone presents to us: and this different feeling I endeavour to explain by calling it a superior *force*, or *vivacity*, or *solidity*, or *firmness*, or *steadiness*. This variety of terms, which may seem so unphilosophical, is intended only to express that act of the mind, which renders realities more present to us than fictions, causes them to weigh more in the thought, and gives them a superior influence on the passions and imagination. Provided we agree about the thing, it is needless to dispute about the terms. The imagination has the command over all its ideas, and can join, and mix, and vary them in all the ways possible. It may conceive objects with all the circumstances of place and time. It may set them, in a manner, before our eyes in their true colours, just as they might have existed. But as it is impossible, that that faculty can ever, of itself, reach belief, it is evident, that belief consists not in the nature and order of our ideas, but in the manner of their conception, and in their feeling to the mind. I confess, that it is impossible to explain perfectly this feeling or manner of conception. We may make use of words, that express something near it. But its true and proper name is *belief*, which is a term that every one sufficiently understands in common life. And in philosophy we can go no farther, than assert, that it is something *felt* by the mind, which distinguishes the ideas of the judgment from the fictions of the imagination. It gives them more force and influence; makes them appear of greater importance; infixes them in the mind; and renders them the governing principles of all our actions.

A note to Book 1, Part 3, Section 8, after the words 'immediate impression'

Naturane nobis, inquit, datum dicam, an errore quodam, ut, cum ea loca videamus, in quibus memoria dignos viros acceperimus multum esse versatos, magis moveamur, quam siquando eorum ipsorum aut jacta audiamus, aut scriptum aliquod legamus? Velut ego nunc moveor. Venit enim mihi Platonis in mentem: quem accipimus primum hic disputare solitum: cujus etiam illi hortuli propinqui non memoriam solum mihi afferunt, sed ipsum videntur in conspectu meo hic ponere. Hic Speusippus, hic Xenocrates, hic ejus auditor Polemo; cujus ipsa illa sessio fuit, quam videamus. Equidem etiam curiam nostram, hostiliam dico, non hanc

novam, quae mihi minor esse videtur post quam est major, solebam
intuens Scipionem, Catonem, Laelium, nostrum vero in primis avum
cogitare. Tanta vis admonitionis inest in locis, ut non sine causa ex his
memoriae ducta sit disciplina. Cicero de Finibus, lib. 5.

'Should I,' he said, 'attribute to instinct or to some kind of illusion
the fact that when we see those places in which we are told
notable men spent much of their time, we are more powerfully
affected than when we hear of the exploits of the men themselves
or read something written? This is just what is happening to me
now; for I am reminded of Plato who, we are told, was the first to
make a practice of holding discussions here. Those gardens of his
nearby do not merely put me in mind of him; they seem to set the
man himself before my very eyes. Speusippus was here; so was
Xenocrates; so was his pupil, Polemo, and that very seat which we
may view was his.

'Then again, when I looked at our Senate-house (I mean the old
building of Hostilius, not this new one; when it was enlarged, it
diminished in my estimation), I used to think of Scipio, Cato,
Laelius and in particular of my own grandfather.

'Such is the power of places to evoke associations; so it is with
good reason that they are used as a basis for memory training.'

To be inserted in Book 1, Part 3, Section 10, after the words 'impressions
of the senses', beginning a new paragraph.

We may observe the same effect of poetry in a lesser degree; and
this is common both to poetry and madness, that the vivacity they
bestow on the ideas is not derived from the particular situations or
connexions of the objects of these ideas, but from the present
temper and disposition of the person. But how great soever the
pitch may be, to which this vivacity rises, it is evident, that in
poetry it never has the same *feeling* with that which arises in the
mind, when we reason, though even upon the lowest species of
probability. The mind can easily distinguish betwixt the one and
the other; and whatever emotion the poetical enthusiasm may
give to the spirits, it is still the mere phantom of belief or persuasion. The case is the same with the idea, as with the passion it
occasions. There is no passion of the human mind but what may
arise from poetry; though at the same time the *feelings* of the

passions are very different when excited by poetical fictions, from what they are when they arise from belief and reality. A passion, which is disagreeable in real life, may afford the highest entertainment in a tragedy, or epic poem. In the latter case, it lies not with that weight upon us: it feels less firm and solid: and has no other than the agreeable effect of exciting the spirits, and rousing the attention. The difference in the passions is a clear proof of a like difference in those ideas, from which the passions are derived. Where the vivacity arises from a customary conjunction with a present impression; though the imagination may not, in appearance, be so much moved; yet there is always something more forcible and real in its actions, than in the fervors of poetry and eloquence. The force of our mental actions in this case, no more than in any other, is not to be measured by the apparent agitation of the mind. A poetical description may have a more sensible effect on the fancy, than an historical narration. It may collect more of those circumstances, that form a complete image or picture. It may seem to set the object before us in more lively colours. But still the ideas it presents are different to the *feeling* from those, which arise from the memory and the judgment. There is something weak and imperfect amidst all that seeming vehemence of thought and sentiment, which attends the fictions of poetry.

We shall afterwards have occasion to remark both the resemblance and differences betwixt a poetical enthusiasm, and a serious conviction. In the mean time I cannot forbear observing, that the great difference in their feeling proceeds in some measure from reflection and *general rules*. We observe, that the vigour of conception, which fictions receive from poetry and eloquence, is a circumstance merely accidental, of which every idea is equally susceptible; and that such fictions are connected with nothing that is real. This observation makes us only lend ourselves, so to speak, to the fiction: but causes the idea to feel very different from the eternal established persuasions founded on memory and custom. They are somewhat of the same kind: but the one is much inferior to the other, both in its causes and effects.

A like reflection on *general rules* keeps us from augmenting our belief upon every increase of the force and vivacity of our ideas. Where an opinion admits of no doubt, or opposite probability, we attribute to it a full conviction: though the want of resemblance, or contiguity, may render its force inferior to that of other opinions. It is thus the understanding corrects the appearances of the senses, and makes us imagine, that an object at twenty foot distance seems even to the eye as large as one of the same dimensions at ten.

To be inserted in Book 1, Part 3, Section 14, after the words 'any idea of power', beginning a new paragraph.

Some have asserted, that we feel an energy, or power, in our own mind; and that having in this manner acquired the idea of power, we transfer that quality to matter, where we are not able immediately to discover it. The motions of our body, and the thoughts and sentiments of our mind, (say they) obey the will; nor do we seek any farther to acquire a just notion of force or power. But to convince us how fallacious this reasoning is, we need only consider, that the will being here considered as a cause, has no more a discoverable connexion with its effects, than any material cause has with its proper effect. So far from perceiving the connexion betwixt an act of volition, and a motion of the body; it is allowed that no effect is more inexplicable from the powers and essence of thought and matter. Nor is the empire of the will over our mind more intelligible. The effect is there distinguishable and separable from the cause, and could not be foreseen without the experience of their constant conjunction. We have command over our mind to a certain degree, but beyond *that*, lose all empire over it: and it is evidently impossible to fix any precise bounds to our authority, where we consult not experience. In short, the actions of the mind are, in this respect, the same with those of matter. We perceive only their constant conjunction; nor can we ever reason beyond it. No internal impression has an apparent energy, more than external objects have. Since, therefore, matter is confessed by philosophers to operate by an unknown force, we should in vain hope to attain an idea of force by consulting our own minds.*

*   *   *

---

* The same imperfection attends our ideas of the Deity; but this can have no effect either on religion or morals. The order of the universe proves an omnipotent mind; that is, a mind whose will is *constantly attended* with the obedience of every creature and being. Nothing more is requisite to give a foundation to all the articles of religion, nor is it necessary we should form a distinct idea of the force and energy of the supreme Being.

I had entertained some hopes, that however deficient our theory of the intellectual world might be, it would be free from those contradictions, and absurdities, which seem to attend every explication, that human reason can give of the material world. But upon a more strict review of the section concerning *personal identity*, I find myself involved in such a labyrinth, that, I must confess, I neither know how to correct my former opinions, nor how to render them consistent. If this be not a good *general* reason for scepticism, it is at least a sufficient one (if I were not already abundantly supplied) for me to entertain a diffidence and modesty in all my decisions. I shall propose the arguments on both sides, beginning with those that induced me to deny the strict and proper identity and simplicity of a self or thinking being.

When we talk of *self* or *substance*, we must have an idea annexed to these terms, otherwise they are altogether unintelligible. Every idea is derived from preceding impressions; and we have no impression of self or substance, as something simple and individual. We have, therefore, no idea of them in that sense.

Whatever is distinct, is distinguishable; and whatever is distinguishable, is separable by the thought or imagination. All perceptions are distinct. They are, therefore, distinguishable, and separable, and may be conceived as separately existent, and may exist separately, without any contradiction or absurdity.

When I view this table and that chimney, nothing is present to me but particular perceptions, which are of a like nature with all the other perceptions. This is the doctrine of philosophers. But this table, which is present to me, and the chimney, may and do exist separately. This is the doctrine of the vulgar, and implies no contradiction. There is no contradiction, therefore, in extending the same doctrine to all the perceptions.

In general, the following reasoning seems satisfactory. All ideas are borrowed from preceding perceptions. Our ideas of objects, therefore, are derived from that source. Consequently no proposition can be intelligible or consistent with regard to objects, which is not so with regard to perceptions. But it is intelligible and consistent to say, that objects exist distinct and independent, without any common *simple* substance or subject of inhesion. This proposition, therefore, can never be absurd with regard to perceptions.

When I turn my reflection on *myself*, I never can perceive this *self* without some one or more perceptions; nor can I ever perceive any thing but the perceptions. It is the composition of these, therefore, which forms the self.

We can conceive a thinking being to have either many or few perceptions. Suppose the mind to be reduced even below the life of an oyster. Suppose it to have only one perception, as of thirst or hunger. Consider it in that situation. Do you conceive any thing but merely that perception? Have you any notion of *self* or *substance*? If not, the addition of other perceptions can never give you that notion.

The annihilation, which some people suppose to follow upon death, and which entirely destroys this self, is nothing but an extinction of all particular perceptions; love and hatred, pain and pleasure, thought and sensation. These therefore must be the same with self; since the one cannot survive the other.

Is *self* the same with *substance*? If it be, how can that question have place, concerning the subsistence of self, under a change of substance? If they be distinct, what is the difference betwixt them? For my part, I have a notion of neither, when conceived distinct from particular perceptions.

Philosophers begin to be reconciled to the principle, *that we have no idea of external substance, distinct from the ideas of particular qualities.* This must pave the way for a like principle with regard to the mind, *that we have no notion of it, distinct from the particular perceptions.*

So far I seem to be attended with sufficient evidence. But having thus loosened all our particular perceptions, when I proceed to explain the principle of connexion, which binds them together, and makes us attribute to them a real simplicity and identity; I am sensible, that my account is very defective, and that nothing but the seeming evidence of the precedent reasonings could have induced me to receive it. If perceptions are distinct existences, they form a whole only by being connected together. But no connexions among distinct existences are ever discoverable by human understanding. We only *feel* a connexion or determination of the thought, to pass from one object to another. It follows, therefore, that the thought alone finds personal identity, when reflecting on the train of past perceptions, that compose a mind, the ideas of them are felt to be connected together, and naturally introduce each other. However extraordinary this conclusion may seem, it need not surprize us. Most philosophers seem inclined to think, that personal identity *arises* from consciousness; and consciousness is nothing but a reflected thought or perception. The present philosophy, therefore, has so far a promising aspect. But all my hopes vanish, when I come to explain the principles, that unite our successive perceptions in our thought or consciousness. I cannot discover any theory, which gives me satisfaction on this head.

In short there are two principles, which I cannot render consistent; nor is it in my power to renounce either of them, *viz, that all our distinct perceptions are distinct existences*, and *that the mind never perceives any real connexion among distinct existences*. Did our perceptions either inhere in something simple and individual, or did the mind perceive some real connexion among them, there would be no difficulty in the case. For my part, I must plead the privilege of a sceptic, and confess, that this difficulty is too hard for my understanding. I pretend not, however, to pronounce it absolutely insuperable. Others, perhaps, or myself, upon more mature reflections, may discover some hypothesis, that will reconcile those contradictions.

I shall also take this opportunity of confessing two other errors of less importance, which more mature reflection has discovered to me in my reasoning. The first may be found in [Book 1, Part 2, Section 5], where I say, that the distance betwixt two bodies is known, among other things, by the angles, which the rays of light flowing from the bodies make with each other. It is certain, that these angles are not known to the mind, and consequently can never discover the distance. The second error may be found in [Book 1, Part 3, Section 7], where I say, that two ideas of the same object can only be different by their different degrees of force and vivacity. I believe there are other differences among ideas, which cannot properly be comprehended under these terms. Had I said, that two ideas of the same object can only be different by their different feeling, I should have been nearer the truth.

There are two errors of the press, which affect the sense, and therefore the reader is desired to correct them.

[*corrections made in this edition*]

A note to Book 1, Part 1, Section 7, after the words 'When we have found a resemblance'.

It is evident, that even different simple ideas may have a similarity or resemblance to each other; nor is it necessary, that the point or circumstance of resemblance should be distinct or separable from that in which they differ. *Blue* and *green* are different simple ideas, but are more resembling than *blue* and *scarlet*; though their perfect simplicity excludes all possibility of separation or distinction. It is the same case with particular sounds, and tastes and smells. These admit of infinite resemblances upon the general appearance and comparison, without having any common circumstance the same. And of this we may be certain, even from the very abstract terms *simple idea*. They comprehend all simple ideas under them. These resemble each other in their simplicity. And yet from their very nature, which excludes all composition, this circumstance, in which they resemble, is not distinguishable nor separable from the rest. It is the same case with all the degrees in any quality. They are all resembling and yet the quality, in any individual, is not distinct from the degree.

To be inserted in Book 1, Part 2, Section 4, after the words 'solution of the present difficulty', beginning a new paragraph.

There are many philosophers, who refuse to assign any standard of *equality*, but assert, that it is sufficient to present two objects, that are equal, in order to give us a just notion of this proportion. All definitions, say they, are fruitless, without the perception of such objects; and where we perceive such objects, we no longer stand in need of any definition. To this reasoning, I entirely agree; and assert, that the only useful notion of equality, or inequality, is derived from the whole united appearance and the comparison of particular objects. For it is evident, etc.

To be inserted in Book 1, Part 2, Section 5, after the words 'either practicable or imaginable', beginning a new paragraph.

To whatever side mathematicians turn, this dilemma still meets them. If they judge of equality, or any other proportion, by the accurate and exact standard, *viz.* the enumeration of the minute indivisible parts, they both employ a standard, which is useless in practice, and actually establish the indivisibility of extension, which they endeavour to explode. Or if they employ, as is usual, the inaccurate standard, derived from a comparison of objects, upon their general appearance, corrected by measuring and juxtaposition; their first principles, though certain and infallible, are too coarse to afford any such subtle inferences as they commonly draw from them. The first principles are founded on the imagination and senses: the conclusion, therefore, can never go beyond, much less contradict these faculties.

A note to Book 1, Part 2, Section 5, after the words 'our perceptions, or impressions and ideas'.

As long as we confine our speculations to *the appearances* of objects to our senses, without entering into disquisitions concerning their real nature and operations, we are safe from all difficulties, and can never be embarrassed by any question. Thus, if it be asked, if the invisible and intangible distance, interposed betwixt two objects, be something or nothing: it is easy to answer, that it is *something*, *viz.* a property of the objects, which affect the *senses* after such a particular manner. If it be asked whether two objects, having such a distance betwixt them, touch or not: it may be answered, that this depends upon the definition of the word, *touch*. If objects be said to touch, when there is nothing *sensible* interposed betwixt them, these objects touch: if objects be said to touch, when their *images* strike contiguous parts of the eye, and when the hand *feels* both objects successively, without any interposed motion, these objects do not touch. The appearances of objects to our senses are all consistent; and no difficulties can ever arise, but from the obscurity of the terms we make use of.

If we carry our enquiry beyond the appearances of objects to the senses, I am afraid, that most of our conclusions will be full of scepticism and uncertainty. Thus if it be asked, whether or not the invisible and intangible distance be always full of *body*, or of something that by an improvement of our organs might become visible or tangible, I must acknowledge, that I find no very decisive arguments on either side; though I am inclined to the contrary opinion, as being more suitable to vulgar and popular notions. If the *Newtonian* philosophy be rightly understood, it will be found to mean no more. A vacuum is asserted: that is, bodies are said to be placed after such a manner, is to receive bodies betwixt them, without impulsion or penetration. The real nature of this position of bodies is unknown. We are only acquainted with its effects on the senses, and its power of receiving body. Nothing is more suitable to that philosophy, than a modest scepticism to a certain degree, and a fair confession of ignorance in subjects, that exceed all human capacity.

FINIS

AN ABSTRACT
of a book lately published
ENTITLED
*A Treatise of Human
Nature, &c.*

PREFACE

My expectations in this small performance may seem somewhat extraordinary, when I declare that my intentions are to render a larger work more intelligible to ordinary capacities, by abridging it. It is however certain, that those who are not accustomed to abstract reasoning, are apt to lose the thread of argument, where it is drawn out to a great length, and each part fortified with all the arguments, guarded against all the objections, and illustrated with all the views, which occur to a writer in the diligent survey of his subject. Such Readers will more readily apprehend a chain of reasoning, that is more single and concise, where the chief propositions are only linked one to another, illustrated by some simple examples, and confirmed by a few of the more forcible arguments. The parts lying nearer together can better be compared, and the connexion be more easily traced from the first principles to the last conclusion.

The work, of which I here present the Reader with an abstract, has been complained of as obscure and difficult to be comprehended, and I am apt to think, that this proceeded as much from the length as from the abstractedness of the argument. If I have remedied this inconvenience in any degree, I have attained my end. The book seemed to me to have such an air of singularity, and novelty as claimed the attention of the public; especially if it be found, as the Author seems to insinuate, that were his philosophy received, we must alter from the foundation the greatest part of the sciences. Such bold attempts are always advantageous in the republic of letters, because they shake off the yoke of authority, accustom men to think for themselves, give new hints, which men of genius may carry further, and by the very opposition, illustrate points, wherein no one before suspected any difficulty.

The Author must be contented to wait with patience for some time before the learned world can agree in their sentiments of his performance. It is his misfortune, that he cannot make an appeal to the people, who in all matters of common reason and eloquence are found so infallible a tribunal. He must be judged by the FEW, *whose verdict is more apt to be corrupted by partiality and prejudice, especially as no one is a proper judge in these subjects, who has not often thought of them; and such are apt to form to themselves systems of their own, which they resolve not to relinquish. I hope the Author will excuse me for intermeddling in this affair, since my aim is only to increase his auditory, by removing some difficulties, which have kept many from apprehending his meaning.*

I have chosen one simple argument, which I have carefully traced from the beginning to the end. This is the only point I have taken care to finish. The rest is only hints of particular passages, which seemed to me curious and remarkable.

ABSTRACT

This book seems to be written upon the same plan with several other works that have had a great vogue of late years in *England*. The philosophical spirit, which has been so much improved all over *Europe* within these last fourscore years, has been carried to as great a length in this kingdom as in any other. Our writers seem even to have started a new kind of philosophy, which promises more, both to the entertainment and advantage of mankind, than any other with which the world has been yet acquainted. Most of the philosophers of antiquity who treated of human nature have shown more of a delicacy of sentiment, a just sense of morals, or a greatness of soul, than a depth of reasoning and reflection. They content themselves with representing the common sense of mankind in the strongest lights, and with the best turn of thought and expression, without following out steadily a chain of propositions, or forming the several truths into a regular science. But it is at least worth while to try if the science of *man* will not admit of the same accuracy, which several parts of natural philosophy are found susceptible of. There seems to be all the reason in the world to imagine that it may he carried to the greatest degree of exactness. If, in examining several phenomena, we find that they resolve themselves into one common principle, and can trace this principle into another, we shall at last arrive at those few simple principles on which all the rest depend. And though we can never arrive at the ultimate principles, it is a satisfaction to go as far as our faculties will allow us.

This seems to have been the aim of our late philosophers, and, among the rest, of this author. He proposes to anatomize human nature in a regular manner, and promises to draw no conclusions but where he is authorized by experience. He talks with contempt of hypotheses; and insinuates that such of our countrymen as have banished them from moral philosophy, have done a more signal service to the world than *my Lord Bacon*, whom he considers as the father of experimental physics. He mentions, on this occasion, *Mr Locke, my Lord Shaftesbury, Dr Mandeville, Mr Hutcheson, Dr Butler,* who, though they differ in many points among themselves, seem all to agree in founding their accurate disquisitions of human nature entirely upon experience.

Beside the satisfaction of being acquainted with what most nearly concerns us, it may be safely affirmed that almost all the sciences are comprehended in the science of human nature, and are dependent on it. *The sole end of* logic *is to explain the principles and operations of our reasoning faculty, and the nature of our ideas*; morals and criticism *regard our tastes and sentiments; and* politics *consider men as united in society, and dependent on each other.* This treatise, therefore, of human nature seems intended for a system of the sciences. The author has finished what regards logic, and has laid the foundation of the other parts in his account of the passions.

The celebrated *Monsieur Leibnitz* has observed it to be a defect in the common systems of logic that they are very copious when they explain the operations of the understanding in the forming of demonstrations, but are too concise when they treat of probabilities, and those other measures of evidence on which life and action entirely depend, and which are our guides even in most of our philosophical speculations. In this censure he comprehends *The Essay on Human Understanding, Le Recherche de la Vérité,* and *L'Art de Penser.* The author of the *Treatise of Human Nature* seems to have been sensible of this defect in these philosophers, and has endeavoured, as much as he can, to supply it. As his book contains a great number of speculations very new and remarkable, it will be impossible to give the reader a just notion of the whole. We shall, therefore, chiefly confine ourselves to his explication of our reasonings from cause and effect. If we can make this intelligible to the reader, it may serve as a specimen of the whole.

Our author begins with some definitions. He calls a *perception* whatever can be present to the mind, whether we employ our senses, or are actuated with passion, or exercise our thought and reflection. He divides our perceptions into two kinds, *viz. impressions* and *ideas.* When we feel a passion or emotion of any kind, or have the images of external objects conveyed by our senses, the perception of the mind is what he calls an *impression*, which is a word that he employs in a new sense. When we reflect on a passion or an object which is not present, this perception is an *idea*. *Impressions*, therefore, are our lively and strong perceptions; *ideas* are the fainter and weaker. This distinction is evident; as evident as that betwixt feeling and thinking.

The first proposition he advances is that all our ideas, or weak perceptions, are derived from our impressions, or strong perceptions, and that we can never think of anything which we have not seen without us, or felt in our own minds. This proposition seems to be equivalent to that which *Mr Locke* has taken such pains to establish, *viz. that no ideas are innate*. Only it may be observed, as an inaccuracy of that famous philosopher, that he comprehends all our perceptions under the term of idea, in which sense it is false that we have no innate ideas. For it is evident our stronger perceptions or impressions are innate, and that natural affection, love of virtue, resentment, and all the other passions, arise immediately from nature. I am persuaded whoever would take the question in this light, would be easily able to reconcile all parties. *Father Malebranche* would find himself at a loss to point out any thought of the mind which did not represent something antecedently felt by it, either internally, or by means of the external senses, and must allow that however

we may compound, and mix, and augment, and diminish our ideas, they are all derived from these sources. *Mr Locke*, on the other hand, would readily acknowledge that all our passions are a kind of natural instincts, derived from nothing but the original constitution of the human mind.

Our author thinks, 'that no discovery could have been made more happily for deciding all controversies concerning ideas than this, that impressions always take the precedency of them, and that every idea with which the imagination is furnished first makes its appearance in a correspondent impression. These latter perceptions are all so clear and evident that they admit of no controversy; though many of our ideas are so obscure that it is almost impossible, even for the mind which forms them, to tell exactly their nature and composition.' Accordingly, wherever any idea is ambiguous, he has always recourse to the impression, which must render it clear and precise. And when he suspects that any philosophical term has no idea annexed to it (as is too common) he always asks *from what impression that ptretended idea is derived*? And if no impression can he produced, he concludes that the term is altogether insignificant. It is after this manner he examines our idea of *substance* and *essence*; and it were to be wished that this rigorous method were more practised in all philosophical debates.

It is evident that all reasonings concerning *matter of fact* are founded on the relation of cause and effect, and that we can never infer the existence of one object from another, unless they be connected together, either mediately or immediately. In order, therefore, to understand these reasonings, we must be perfectly acquainted with the idea of a cause; and in order to that, must look about us to find something that is the cause of another.

9. Here is a billiard-ball lying on the table, and another ball moving towards it with rapidity. They strike; and the ball which was formerly at rest now acquires a motion. This is as perfect an instance of the relation of cause and effect as any which we know, either by sensation or reflection. Let us therefore examine it. It is evident that the two balls touched one another before the motion was communicated, and that there was no interval betwixt the shock and the motion. *Contiguity* in time and place is therefore a requisite circumstance to the operation of all causes. It is evident, likewise, that the motion which was the cause is prior to the motion which was the effect. *Priority* in time is therefore another requisite circumstance in every cause. But this is not all. Let us try any other balls of the same kind in a like situation, and we shall always find that the impulse of the one produces motion in the other. Here, therefore, is a *third* circumstance, *viz*. that of a *constant conjunction* betwixt the cause and effect. Every object like the cause produces always some object like the effect. Beyond these three circumstances of contiguity, priority, and constant conjunction, I can discover nothing in this cause. The first ball is in motion; touches the second; immediately the second is in motion: and when I try the experiment with the same or like balls, in the same or like circumstances, I find that upon the motion and touch of the one ball, motion always follows in the other. In whatever shape I turn this matter, and however I examine it, I can find nothing farther.

This is the case when both the cause and effect are present to the senses. Let us now see upon what our inference is founded, when we conclude from the one that the other has existed or will exist. Suppose I see a ball moving in a straight line towards another, I immediately conclude that they will shock and that the second will be in motion. This is the inference from cause to effect, and of this nature are all our reasonings in the conduct of life: on this is founded all our belief in history; and from hence is derived all philosophy, excepting only geometry and arithmetic. If we can explain the inference from the shock of two balls, we shall be able to account for this operation of the mind in all instances.

Were a man, such as *Adam*, created in the full vigour of understanding, without experience, he would never be able to infer motion in the second ball from the motion and impulse of the first. It is not anything that reason sees in the cause which makes us *infer* the effect. Such an inference, were it possible, would amount to a demonstration, as being founded merely on the comparison of ideas. But no inference from cause to effect amounts to a demonstration, of which there is this evident proof. The mind can always *conceive* any effect to follow from any cause, and indeed any event to follow upon another: whatever we *conceive* is possible, at least in a metaphysical sense; but wherever a demonstration takes place, the contrary is impossible, and implies a contradiction. There is no demonstration, therefore, for any conjunction of cause and effect. And this is a principle which is generally allowed by philosophers.

It would have been necessary, therefore, for *Adam* (if he was not inspired) to have had *experience* of the effect which followed upon the impulse of these two balls. He must have seen, in several instances, that when the one ball struck upon the other, the second always acquired motion. If he had seen a sufficient number of instances of this kind, whenever he saw the one ball moving towards the other, he would always conclude without hesitation that the second would acquire motion. His understanding would anticipate his sight and form a conclusion suitable to his past experience.

It follows, then, that all reasonings concerning cause and effect are founded on experience, and that all reasonings from experience are founded on the supposition that the course of nature will continue uniformly the same. We conclude that like causes, in like circumstances, will always produce like effects. It may now be worth while to consider what determines us to form a conclusion of such infinite consequence.

It is evident that *Adam*, with all his science, would never have been able to *demonstrate* that the course of nature must continue uniformly the same, and that the future must be conformable to the past. What is possible can never be demonstrated to be false; and it is possible the course of nature may change, since we can conceive such a change. Nay, I will go farther, and assert that he could not so much as prove by any probable arguments that the future must be conformable to the past. All *probable* arguments are built on the supposition that there is this conformity betwixt the future and the past, and therefore can never prove it. This conformity is a *matter of fact*, and, if it must be proved, will admit of no proof but from experience. But our experience in the past can be a proof of nothing for the future, but upon a supposition that there is a resemblance betwixt them. This, therefore, is a point which can admit of no proof at all, and which we take for granted without any proof.

We are determined by CUSTOM alone to suppose the future conformable to the past. When I see a billiard ball moving towards another, my mind is immediately carried by habit to the usual effect, and anticipates my sight by conceiving the second ball in motion. There is nothing in these objects, abstractly considered, and independent of experience, which leads me to form any such conclusion; and even after I have had experience of many repeated effects of this kind, there is no argument which determines me to suppose that the effect will be conformable to past experience. The powers by which bodies operate are entirely unknown. We perceive only their sensible qualities: and what *reason* have we to think that the same powers will always be conjoined with the same sensible qualities?

It is not, therefore, reason which is the guide of life, but custom. That alone determines the mind, in all instances, to suppose the future conformable to the past. However easy this step may seem, reason would never, to all eternity, be able to make it.

This is a very curious discovery, but leads us to others that are still more curious. *When I see a billiard-ball moving towards another, my mind is immediately carried by habit to the usual effect, and anticipates my sight by conceiving the second ball in motion.* But is this all? Do I nothing but CONCEIVE the motion of the second ball? No, surely. I also BELEIVE that it will move. What then is this *belief?* And how does it differ from the simple conception of anything? Here is a new question unthought of by philosophers.

When a demonstration convinces me of any proposition, it not only makes me conceive the proposition, but also makes me sensible that it is impossible to conceive anything contrary. What is demonstratively false implies a contradiction; and what implies a contradiction cannot be conceived. But with regard to any matter of fact, however strong the proof may be from experience, I can always conceive the contrary, though I cannot always believe it. The belief, therefore, makes some difference betwixt the conception to which we assent, and that to which we do not assent.

To account for this, there are only two hypotheses. It may be said that belief joins some new idea to those which we may conceive without assenting to them. But this hypothesis is false. For *first*, no such idea can be produced. When we simply conceive an object, we conceive it in all its parts. We conceive it as it might exist, though we do not believe it to exist. Our belief of it would discover no new qualities. We may paint out the entire object in imagination without believing it. We may set it, in a manner, before our eyes, with every circumstance of time and place. It is the very object conceived as it might exist; and when we believe it, we can do no more.

Secondly, the mind has a faculty of joining all ideas together, which involve not a contradiction; and therefore, if belief consisted in some idea, which we add to the simple conception, it would be in a man's power, by adding this idea to it, to believe anything which he can conceive.

Since, therefore, belief implies a conception, and yet is something more; and since it adds no new idea to the conception; it follows that it is a different MANNER of conceiving an object; *something* that is distinguishable to the feeling, and depends not upon our will, as all our ideas do. My mind runs by habit from the visible object of one ball moving towards another, to the usual effect of motion in the second ball. It not only conceives that motion, but *feels* something different in the conception of it from a mere reverie of the imagination. The presence of this visible object, and the constant conjunction of that particular effect, render the idea different to the *feeling* from those loose ideas which come into the mind without any introduction. This conclusion seems a little surprising; but we are led into it by a chain of propositions which admit of no doubt. To ease the reader's memory I shall briefly resume them. No matter of fact can be proved but from its cause or its effect. Nothing can be known to be the cause of another but by experience. We can give no reason for extending to the future our experience in the past, but are entirely determined by custom when we conceive an effect to follow from its usual cause. But we also believe an effect to follow, as well as conceive it. This belief joins no new idea to the conception. It only varies the manner of conceiving, and makes a difference to the feeling or sentiment. Belief, therefore, in all matters of fact arises only from custom, and is an idea conceived in a peculiar manner.

Our author proceeds to explain the manner or feeling, which renders belief different from a loose conception. He seems sensible that it is impossible by words to describe this feeling, which everyone must be conscious of in his own breast. He calls it sometimes a *stronger* conception, sometimes a more *lively*, a more *vivid*, a *firmer*, or a more *intense* conception. And, indeed, whatever name we may give to this feeling which constitutes belief, our author thinks it evident that it has a more forcible effect on the mind than fiction and mere conception. This he proves by its influence on the passions and on the imagination, which are only moved by truth, or what is taken for such. Poetry, with all its art, can never cause a passion like one in real life. It fails in the original conception of its objects, which never *feel* in the same manner as those which command our belief and opinion.

Our author, presuming that he had sufficiently proved that the ideas we assent to are different to the feeling from the other ideas, and that this feeling is more firm and lively than our common conception, endeavours in the next place to explain the cause of this lively feeling by an analogy with other acts of the mind. His reasoning seems to be curious; but could scarce be rendered intelligible, or at least probable to the reader, without a long detail, which would exceed the compass I have prescribed to myself.

*   *   *

I have likewise omitted many arguments which he adduces to prove that belief consists merely in a peculiar feeling or sentiment. I shall only mention one; our past experience is not always uniform. Sometimes one effect follows from a cause, sometimes another: in which case we always believe that that will exist which is most common. I see a billiard ball moving towards another. I cannot distinguish whether it moves upon its axis, or was struck so as to skim along the table. In the first case, I know it will not stop after the shock. In the second it may stop. The first is most common, and therefore I lay my account with that effect. But I also conceive the other effect, and conceive it as possible, and as connected with the cause. Were not the one conception different in the feeling or sentiment from the other, there would be no difference betwixt them.

We have confined ourselves in this whole reasoning to the relation of cause and effect, as discovered in the motions and operations of matter. But the same reasoning extends to the operations of the mind. Whether we consider the influence of the will in moving our body, or in governing our thought, it may safely be affirmed that we could never foretell the effect, merely from the consideration of the cause, without experience. And even after we have experience of these effects, it is custom alone, not reason, which determines us to make it the standard of our future judgments. When the cause is presented, the mind, from habit, immediately passes to the conception and belief of the usual effect. This belief is something different from the conception. It does not, however, join any new idea to it. It only makes it be felt differently, and renders it stronger and more lively.

Having dispatched this material point concerning the nature of the inference from cause and effect, our author returns upon his footsteps, and examines anew the idea of that relation. In the considering of motion communicated from one ball to another, we could find nothing but contiguity, priority in the cause, and constant conjunction. But, beside these circumstances, it is commonly supposed that there is a necessary connexion betwixt the cause and effect, and that the cause possesses something, which we call a *power*, or *force*, or *energy*. The question is, what idea is annexed to these terms? If all our ideas or thoughts be derived from our impressions, this *power* must either discover itself to our senses, or to our internal feeling. But so little does any power discover itself to the senses in the operations of matter, that the *Cartesians* have made no scruple to assert that matter is utterly deprived of energy, and that all its operations are performed merely by the energy of the supreme Being. But the question still recurs, *What idea have we of energy or power even in the supreme Being?* All our idea of a Deity (according to those who deny innate ideas) is nothing but a composition of those ideas which we acquire from reflecting on the operations of our minds. Now our own minds afford us no more notion of energy than matter does. When we consider our will or volition *a priori*, abstracting from experience, we should never be able to infer any effect from it. And when we take the assistance of experience, it only shows us objects contiguous, successive, and constantly conjoined. Upon the whole, then, either we have no idea at all of force and energy, and these words are altogether insignificant, or they can mean nothing but that determination of the thought, acquired by habit, to pass from the cause to its usual effect. But whoever would thoroughly understand this must consult the author himself. It is sufficient if I can make the learned world apprehend that there is some difficulty in the case, and that whoever solves the difficulty must say something very new and extraordinary; as new as the difficulty itself.

By all that has been said the reader will easily perceive that the philosophy contained in this book is very sceptical, and tends to give us a notion of the imperfections and narrow limits of human understanding. Almost all reasoning is there reduced to experience; and the belief, which attends experience, is explained to be nothing but a peculiar sentiment, or lively conception produced by habit. Nor is this all; when we believe anything of *external* existence, or suppose an object to exist a moment after it is no longer perceived, this belief is nothing but a sentiment of the same kind. Our author insists upon several other sceptical topics; and upon the whole concludes that we assent to our faculties, and employ our reason, only because we cannot help it. Philosophy would render us entirely *Pyrrhonian*, were not nature too strong for it.

I shall conclude the logics of this author with an account of two opinions, which seem to be peculiar to himself, as indeed are most of his opinions. He asserts that the soul, as far as we can conceive it, is nothing but a system or train of different perceptions, those of heat and cold, love and anger, thoughts and sensations, all united together, but without any perfect simplicity or identity. *Des Cartes* maintained that thought was the essence of the mind; not this thought or that thought, but thought in general. This seems to be absolutely unintelligible, since everything that exists is particular; and, therefore, it must be our several particular perceptions that compose the mind. I say, *compose* the mind, not *belong* to it. The mind is not a substance, in which the perceptions inhere. That notion is as unintelligible as the *Cartesian*, that thought or perception in general is the essence of the mind. We have no idea of substance of any kind, since we have no idea but what is derived from some impression, and we have no impression of any substance either material or spiritual. We know nothing but particular qualities and perceptions. As our idea of any body, a peach, for instance, is only that of a particular taste, colour, figure, size, consistence, etc. So our idea of any mind is only that of particular perceptions, without the notion of anything we call substance, either simple or compound.

The second principle, which I proposed to take notice of, is with regard to Geometry. Having denied the infinite divisibility of extension, our author finds himself obliged to refute those mathematical arguments which have been adduced for it; and these indeed are the only ones of any weight. This he does by denying Geometry to be a science exact enough to admit of conclusions so subtle as those which regard infinite divisibility. His arguments may be thus explained. All Geometry is founded on the notions of equality and inequality, and, therefore, according as we have or have not an exact standard of that relation, the science itself will or will not admit of great exactness. Now there is an exact standard of equality, if we suppose that quantity is composed of indivisible points. Two lines are equal when the numbers of the points that compose them are equal, and when there is a point in one corresponding to a point in the other. But though this standard be exact, it is useless; since we can never compute the number of points in any line. It is besides founded on the supposition of finite divisibility, and therefore can never afford any conclusion against it. If we reject this standard of equality, we have none that has any pretensions to exactness. I find two that are commonly made use of. Two lines above a yard, for instance, are said to be equal when they contain any inferior quantity, as an inch, an equal number of times. But this runs in a circle. For the quantity we call an inch in the one is supposed to be *equal* to what we call an inch in the other: and the question still is, by what standard we proceed when we judge them to be equal; or, in other words, what we mean when we say they are equal. If we take still inferior quantities, we go on *in infinitum*. This therefore is no standard of equality. The greatest part of philosophers, when asked what they mean by equality, say that the word admits of no definition, and that it is sufficient to place before us two equal bodies, such as two diameters of a circle, to make us understand that term. Now this is taking the *general appearance* of the objects for the standard of that proportion, and renders our imagination and senses the ultimate judges of it. But such a standard admits of no exactness, and can never afford any conclusion contrary to the imagination and senses. Whether this question be just or not must he left to the learned world to judge. It were certainly to be wished that some expedient were fallen upon to reconcile philosophy and common sense, which, with regard to the question of infinite divisibility, have waged most cruel wars with each other.

We must now proceed to give some account of the second volume of this work, which treats of the PASSIONS. It is of more easy comprehension than the first, but contains opinions that are together as new and extraordinary. The author begins with *pride* and *humility*. He observes that the objects which excite these passions are very numerous, and seemingly very different from each other. Pride or self-esteem may arise from the qualities of the mind; wit, good-scnse, learning, courage, integrity: from those of the body; beauty, strength, agility, good mien, address in dancing, riding, fencing: from external advantages; country, family, children, relations, riches, houses, gardens, horses, dogs, clothes. He afterwards proceeds to find out that common circumstance in which all these objects agree, and which causes them to operate on the passions. His theory likewise extends to love and hatred, and other affections. As these questions, though curious, could not be rendered intelligible without a long discourse, we shall here omit them.

31. It may perhaps be more acceptable to the reader to be informed of what our author says concerning *free-will*. He has

laid the foundation of his doctrine in what he said concerning cause and effect, as above explained. 'It is universally acknowledged, that the operations of external bodies are necessary, and that in the communication of their motion, in their attraction and mutual cohesion, there are not the least traces of indifference or liberty.' . . . 'Whatever, therefore, is in this respect on the same footing with matter, must be acknowledged to be necessary. That we may know whether this be the case with the actions of the mind, we may examine matter, and consider on what the idea of a necessity in its operations are founded, and why we conclude one body or action to be the infallible cause of another.

'It has been observed already, that in no single instance the ultimate connexion of any object is discoverable either by our senses or reason, and that we can never penetrate so far into the essence and construction of bodies, as to perceive the principle on which their mutual influence is founded. It is their constant union alone with which we are acquainted; and it is from the constant union the necessity arises, when the mind is determined to pass from one object to its usual attendant, and infer the existence of one from that of the other. Here then are two particulars, which we are to regard as essential to *necessity*, *viz.* the constant *union* and the *inference* of the mind, and wherever we discover these we must acknowledge a necessity.' Now nothing is more evident than the constant union of particular actions with particular motives. If all actions be not constantly united with their proper motives, this uncertainty is no more than what may be observed every day in the actions of matter, where, by reason of the mixture and uncertainty of causes, the effect is often variable and uncertain. Thirty grains of opium will kill any man that is not accustomed to it, though thirty grains of rhubarb will not always purge him. In like manner, the fear of death will always make a man go twenty paces out of his road, though it will not always make him do a bad action.

And as there is often a constant conjunction of the actions of the will with their motives, so the inference from the one to the other is often as certain as any reasoning concerning bodies; and there is always an inference proportioned to the constancy of the conjunction. On this is founded our belief in witnesses, our credit in history, and indeed all kinds of moral evidence, and almost the whole conduct of life.

Our author pretends, that this reasoning puts the whole controversy in a new light, by giving a new definition of necessity. And indeed the most zealous advocates for free-will must allow this union and inference with regard to human actions. They will only deny that this makes the whole of necessity. But then they must show that we have an idea of something else in the actions of matter; which, according to the foregoing reasoning, is impossible.

Through this whole book, there are great pretensions to new discoveries in philosophy; but if anything can entitle the author to so glorious a name as that of an *inventor*, it is the use he makes of the principle of the association of ideas, which enters into most of his philosophy. Our imagination has a great authority over our ideas; and there are no ideas that are different from each other which it cannot separate, and join, and compose into all the varieties of fiction. But notwithstanding the empire of the imagination, there is a secret tie or union among particular ideas, which causes the mind to conjoin them more frequently together, and makes the one, upon its appearance, introduce the other. Hence arises what we call the *apropos* of discourse; hence the connexion of writing; and hence that thread, or chain of thought, which a man naturally supports even in the loosest *reverie*. These principles of association are reduced to three, *viz. Resemblance*; a picture naturally makes us think of the man it was drawn for: *Contiguity*; when *St Denis* is mentioned, the idea of Paris naturally occurs: *Causation*; when we think of the son, we are apt to carry our attention to the father. It will be easy to conceive of what vast consequence these principles must be in the science of human nature, if we consider that, so far as regards the mind, these are the only links that bind the parts of the universe together, or connect us with any person or object exterior to ourselves. For as it is by means of thought only that anything operates upon our passions, and as these are the only ties of our thoughts, they are really to us the cement of the universe, and all the operations of the mind must, in a great measure, depend on them.

FINIS

ADVERTISEMENT

Most of the principles, and reasonings, contained in this volume,* were published in a work in three volumes, called *A Treatise of Human Nature*: a work which the Author had projected before he left College, and which he wrote and published not long after. But not finding it successful, he was sensible of his error in going to the press too early, and he cast the whole anew in the following pieces, where some negligences in his former reasoning and more in the expression, are, he hopes, corrected. Yet several writers who have honoured the Author's Philosophy with answers, have taken care to direct all their batteries against that juvenile work, which the author never acknowledged, and have affected to triumph in any advantages, which, they imagined, they had obtained over it: a practice very contrary to all rules of candour and fair-dealing, and a strong instance of those polemical artifices which a bigoted zeal thinks itself authorized to employ. Henceforth, the Author desires, that the following Pieces may alone be regarded as containing his philosophical sentiments and principles.

[* Volume 2 of the posthumous edition of Hume's works published in 1777 and containing, besides the present Enquiry, *A Dissertation on the Passions*, and *An Enquiry concerning Human Understanding*.]

AN ENQUIRY CONCERNING
HUMAN UNDERSTANDING

Of the different species of philosophy

1. Moral philosophy, or the science of human nature, may be treated after two different manners; each of which has its peculiar merit, and may contribute to the entertainment, instruction, and reformation of mankind. The one considers man chiefly as born for action; and as influenced in his measures by taste and sentiment; pursuing one object, and avoiding another, according to the value which these objects seem to possess, and according to the light in which they present themselves. As virtue, of all objects, is allowed to be the most valuable, this species of philosophers paint her in the most amiable colours; borrowing all helps from poetry and eloquence, and treating their subject in an easy and obvious manner, and such as is best fitted to please the imagination, and engage the affections. They select the most striking observations and instances from common life; place opposite characters in a proper contrast; and alluring us into the paths of virtue by the views of glory and happiness, direct our steps in these paths by the soundest precepts and most illustrious examples. They make us *feel* the difference between vice and virtue; they excite and regulate our sentiments; and so they can but bend our hearts to the love of probity and true honour, they think, that they have fully attained the end of all their labours.

2. The other species of philosophers consider man in the light of a reasonable rather than an active being, and endeavour to form his understanding more than cultivate his manners. They regard human nature as a subject of speculation; and with a narrow scrutiny examine it, in order to find those principles, which regulate our understanding, excite our sentiments, and make us approve or blame any particular object, action, or behaviour. They think it a reproach to all literature, that philosophy should not yet have fixed, beyond controversy, the foundation of morals,

reasoning, and criticism; and should for ever talk of truth and falsehood, vice and virtue, beauty and deformity, without being able to determine the source of these distinctions. While they attempt this arduous task, they are deterred by no difficulties; but proceeding from particular instances to general principles, they still push on their enquiries to principles more general, and rest not satisfied till they arrive at those original principles, by which, in every science, all human curiosity must be bounded. Though their speculations seem abstract, and even unintelligible to common readers, they aim at the approbation of the learned and the wise; and think themselves sufficiently compensated for the labour of their whole lives, if they can discover some hidden truths, which may contribute to the instruction of posterity.

3. It is certain that the easy and obvious philosophy will always, with the generality of mankind, have the preference above the accurate and abstruse; and by many will be recommended, not only as more agreeable, but more useful than the other. It enters more into common life; moulds the heart and affections; and, by touching those principles which actuate men, reforms their conduct, and brings them nearer to that model of perfection which it describes. On the contrary, the abstruse philosophy, being founded on a turn of mind, which cannot enter into business and action, vanishes when the philosopher leaves the shade, and comes into open day; nor can its principles easily retain any influence over our conduct and behaviour. The feelings of our heart, the agitation of our passions, the vehemence of our affections, dissipate all its conclusions, and reduce the profound philosopher to a mere plebeian.

4. This also must be confessed, that the most durable, as well as justest fame, has been acquired by the easy philosophy, and that abstract reasoners seem hitherto to have enjoyed only a momentary reputation, from the caprice or ignorance of their own age, but have not been able to support their renown with more equitable posterity. It is easy for a profound philosopher to commit a mistake in his subtile reasonings; and one mistake is the necessary parent of another, while he pushes on his consequences, and is not deterred from embracing any conclusion, by its unusual appearance, or its contradiction to popular opinion. But a philosopher, who purposes only to represent the common sense of mankind in more beautiful and more engaging colours, if by accident he falls into error, goes

no farther; but renewing his appeal to common sense, and the natural sentiments of the mind, returns into the right path, and secures himself from any dangerous illusions. The fame of Cicero flourishes at present; but that of Aristotle is utterly decayed. La Bruyère passes the seas, and still maintains his reputation: but the glory of Malebranche is confined to his own nation, and to his own age. And Addison, perhaps, will be read with pleasure, when Locke shall be entirely forgotten.

The mere philosopher is a character, which is commonly but little acceptable in the world, as being supposed to contribute nothing either to the advantage or pleasure of society; while he lives remote from communication with mankind, and is wrapped up in principles and notions equally remote from their comprehension. On the other hand, the mere ignorant is still more despised; nor is any thing deemed a surer sign of an illiberal genius in an age and nation where the sciences flourish, than to be entirely destitute of all relish for those noble entertainments. The most perfect character is supposed to lie between those extremes; retaining an equal ability and taste for books, company, and business; preserving in conversation that discernment and delicacy which arise from polite letters; and in business, that probity and accuracy which are the natural result of a just philosophy. In order to diffuse and cultivate so accomplished a character, nothing can be more useful than compositions of the easy style and manner, which draw not too much from life, require no deep application or retreat to be comprehended, and send back the student among mankind full of noble sentiments and wise precepts, applicable to every exigence of human life. By means of such compositions, virtue becomes amiable, science agreeable, company instructive, and retirement entertaining.

Man is a reasonable being; and as such, receives from science his proper food and nourishment: but so narrow are the bounds of human understanding, that little satisfaction can be hoped for in this particular, either from the extent of security or his acquisitions. Man is a sociable, no less than a reasonable being: but neither can he always enjoy company agreeable and amusing, or preserve the proper relish for them. Man is also an active being; and from that disposition, as well as from the various necessities of human life, must submit to business and occupation: but the mind requires some relaxation, and cannot always support its bent to care and industry. It seems, then, that nature has pointed out a mixed kind of life as most suitable to the human race, and secretly admonished them to allow none of these biases to *draw* too much, so as to incapacitate them for other occupations and entertainments. Indulge your passion for science, says she, but let your science be human, and such as may have a direct reference to action and society. Abstruse thought and profound researches I prohibit, and will severely punish, by the pensive melancholy which they introduce, by the endless uncertainty in which they involve you, and by the cold reception which your pretended discoveries shall meet with, when communicated. Be a philosopher; but, amidst all your philosophy, be still a man.

5. Were the generality of mankind contented to prefer the easy philosophy to the abstract and profound, without throwing any blame or contempt on the latter, it might not be improper, perhaps, to comply with this general opinion, and allow every man to enjoy, without opposition, his own taste and sentiment. But as the matter is often carried farther, even to the absolute rejecting of all profound reasonings, or what is commonly called *metaphysics*, we shall now proceed to consider what can reasonably be pleaded in their behalf.

We may begin with observing, that one considerable advantage, which results from the accurate and abstract philosophy, is, its subserviency to the easy and humane; which, without the former, can never attain a sufficient degree of exactness in its sentiments, precepts, or reasonings. All polite letters are nothing but pictures of human life in various attitudes and situations; and inspire us with different sentiments, of praise or blame, admiration or ridicule, according to the qualities of the object, which they set before us. An artist must be better qualified to succeed in this undertaking, who, besides a delicate taste and a quick apprehension, possesses an accurate knowledge of the internal fabric, the operations of the understanding, the workings of the passions, and the various species of sentiment which discriminate vice and virtue. How painful soever this inward search or enquiry may appear, it becomes, in some measure, requisite to those, who would describe with success the obvious and outward appearances of life and manners. The anatomist presents to the eye the most hideous and disagreeable objects; but his science is useful to the painter in delineating even a Venus or an Helen. While the latter employs all the richest colours of his art, and gives his figures the most graceful and engaging airs; he must still carry his attention to the inward structure of the human body, the position of the muscles, the fabric of the bones, and the use and figure of every part or organ. Accuracy is, in every case, advantageous to beauty, and just reasoning to delicate sentiment. In vain would we exalt the one by depreciating the other.

Besides, we may observe, in every art or profession, even those which most concern life or action, that a spirit of accuracy, however acquired, carries all of them nearer their perfection, and renders them more subservient to the interests of society. And though a philosopher may live remote from business, the genius of philosophy, if carefully cultivated by several, must gradually diffuse itself throughout the whole society, and bestow a similar correctness on every art and calling. The politician will acquire greater foresight and subtility, in the subdividing and balancing of power; the lawyer more method and finer principles in his reasonings; and the general more regularity in his discipline, and more caution in his plans and operations. The stability of modern governments above the ancient, and the accuracy of modern philosophy, have improved, and probably will still improve, by similar gradations.

6. Were there no advantage to be reaped from these studies, beyond the gratification of an innocent curiosity, yet ought not even this to be despised; as being one accession to those few safe and harmless pleasures, which are bestowed on human race. The sweetest and most inoffensive path of life leads through the avenues of science and learning; and whoever can either remove any obstructions in this way, or open up any new prospect, ought so far to be esteemed a benefactor to mankind. And though these researches may appear painful and fatiguing, it is with some minds as with some bodies, which being endowed with vigorous and florid health, require severe exercise, and reap a pleasure from what, to the generality of mankind, may seem burdensome and laborious. Obscurity, indeed, is painful to the mind as well as to the eye; but to bring light from obscurity, by whatever labour, must needs be delightful and rejoicing.

But this obscurity in the profound and abstract philosophy, is objected to, not only as painful and fatiguing, but as the inevitable source of uncertainty and error. Here indeed lies the justest and most plausible objection against a considerable part of metaphysics, that they are not properly a science; but arise either from the fruitless efforts of human vanity, which would penetrate into subjects utterly inaccessible to the understanding, or from the craft of popular superstitions, which, being unable to defend themselves on fair ground, raise these entangling brambles to cover and protect their weakness. Chased from the open country, these robbers fly into the forest, and lie in wait to break in upon every unguarded avenue of the mind, and overwhelm it with religious fears and prejudices. The stoutest antagonist, if he remit his watch a moment, is oppressed. And many, through cowardice and folly, open the gates to the enemies, and willingly receive them with reverence and submission, as their legal sovereigns.

7. But is this a sufficient reason, why philosophers should desist from such researches, and leave superstition still in possession of her retreat? Is it not proper to draw an opposite conclusion, and perceive the necessity of carrying the war into the most secret recesses of the enemy? In vain do we hope, that men, from frequent disappointment, will at last abandon such airy sciences, and discover the proper province of human reason. For, besides, that many persons find too sensible an interest in perpetually recalling such topics; besides this, I say, the motive of blind despair can never reasonably have place in the sciences; since, however unsuccessful former attempts may have proved, there is still room to hope, that the industry, good fortune, or improved sagacity of succeeding generations may reach discoveries unknown to former ages. Each adventurous genius will still leap at the arduous prize, and find himself stimulated, rather than discouraged, by the failures of his predecessors; while he hopes that the glory of achieving so hard an adventure is reserved for him alone. The only method of freeing learning, at once, from these abstruse questions, is to enquire seriously into the nature of human understanding, and show, from an exact analysis of its powers and capacity, that it is by no means fitted for such remote and abstruse subjects. We must submit to this fatigue, in order to live at ease ever after: and must cultivate true metaphysics with some care, in order

to destroy the false and adulterate. Indolence, which, to some persons, affords a safeguard against this deceitful philosophy, is, with others, overbalanced by curiosity; and despair, which, at some moments, prevails, may give place afterwards to sanguine hopes and expectations. Accurate and just reasoning is the only catholic remedy, fitted for all persons and all dispositions; and is alone able to subvert that abstruse philosophy and metaphysical jargon, which, being mixed up with popular superstition, renders it in a manner impenetrable to careless reasoners, and gives it the air of science and wisdom.

8. Besides this advantage of rejecting, after deliberate enquiry, the most uncertain and disagreeable part of learning, there are many positive advantages, which result from an accurate scrutiny into the powers and faculties of human nature. It is remarkable concerning the operations of the mind, that, though most intimately present to us, yet, whenever they become the object of reflexion, they seem involved in obscurity; nor can the eye readily find those lines and boundaries, which discriminate and distinguish them. The objects are too fine to remain long in the same aspect or situation; and must be apprehended in an instant, by a superior penetration, derived from nature, and improved by habit and reflexion. It becomes, therefore, no inconsiderable part of science barely to know the different operations of the mind, to separate them from each other, to class them under their proper heads, and to correct all that seeming disorder, in which they lie involved, when made the object of reflexion and enquiry. This talk of ordering and distinguishing, which has no merit, when performed with regard to external bodies, the objects of our senses, rises in its value, when directed towards the operations of the mind, in proportion to the difficulty and labour, which we meet with in performing it. And if we can go no farther than this mental geography, or delineation of the distinct parts and powers of the mind, it is at least a satisfaction to go so far; and the more obvious this science may appear (and it is by no means obvious) the more contemptible still must the ignorance of it be esteemed, in all pretenders to learning and philosophy.

Nor can there remain any suspicion, that this science is uncertain and chimerical; unless we should entertain such a scepticism as is entirely subversive of all speculation, and even action. It cannot be doubted, that the mind is endowed with several powers and faculties, that these powers are distinct from each other, that what is really distinct to the immediate perception may be distinguished by reflexion; and consequently, that there is a truth and falsehood in all propositions on this subject, and a truth and falsehood, which lie not beyond the compass of human understanding. There are many obvious distinctions of this kind, such as those between the will and understanding, the imagination and passions, which fall within the comprehension of every human creature; and the finer and more philosophical distinctions are no less real and certain, though more difficult to be comprehended. Some instances, especially late ones, of success in these enquiries, may give us a juster notion of the certainty and solidity of this branch of learning. And shall we esteem it worthy the labour of a philosopher to give us a true system of the planets, and adjust the position and order of those remote bodies; while we affect to overlook those, who, with so much success, delineate the parts of the mind, in which we are so intimately concerned?

9. But may we not hope, that philosophy, if cultivated with care, and encouraged by the attention of the public, may carry its researches still farther, and discover, at least in some degree, the secret springs and principles, by which the human mind is actuated in its operations? Astronomers had long contented themselves with proving, from the phenomena, the true motions, order, and magnitude of the heavenly bodies: till a philosopher, at last, arose, who seems, from the happiest reasoning, to have also determined the laws and forces, by which the revolutions of the planets are governed and directed. The like has been performed with regard to other parts of nature. And there is no reason to despair of equal success in our enquiries concerning the mental powers and economy, if prosecuted with equal capacity and caution. It is probable, that one operation and principle of the mind depends on another; which, again, may be resolved into one more general and universal: and how far these researches may possibly be carried, it will be difficult for us, before, or even after, a careful trial, exactly to determine. This is certain, that attempts of this kind are every day made even by those who philosophize

the most negligently: And nothing can be more requisite than to enter upon the enterprize with thorough care and attention; that, if it lie within the compass of human understanding, it may at last be happily achieved; if not, it may, however, be rejected with some confidence and security. This last conclusion, surely, is not desirable; nor ought it to be embraced too rashly. For how much must we diminish from the beauty and value of this species of philosophy, upon such a supposition? Moralists have hitherto been accustomed, when they considered the vast multitude and diversity of those actions that excite our approbation or dislike, to search for some common principle, on which this variety of sentiments might depend. And though they have sometimes carried the matter too far, by their passion for some one general principle; it must, however, be confessed, that they are excusable in expecting to find some general principles, into which all the vices and virtues were justly to be resolved. The like has been the endeavour of critics, logicians, and even politicians: nor have their attempts been wholly unsuccessful; though perhaps longer time, greater accuracy, and more ardent application may bring these sciences still nearer their perfection. To throw up at once all pretensions of this kind may justly be deemed more rash, precipitate, and dogmatical, than even the boldest and most affirmative philosophy, that has ever attempted to impose its crude dictates and principles on mankind.

10. What though these reasonings concerning human nature seem abstract, and of difficult comprehension? This affords no presumption of their falsehood. On the contrary, it seems impossible, that what has hitherto escaped so many wise and profound philosophers can be very obvious and easy. And whatever pains these researches may cost us, we may think ourselves sufficiently rewarded, not only in point of profit but of pleasure, if, by that means, we can make any addition to our stock of knowledge, in subjects of such unspeakable importance.

But as, after all, the abstractedness of these speculations is no recommendation, but rather a disadvantage to them, and as this difficulty may perhaps be surmounted by care and art, and the avoiding of all unnecessary detail, we have, in the following enquiry, attempted to throw some light upon subjects, from which uncertainty has hitherto deterred the wise, and obscurity the ignorant. Happy, if we can unite the boundaries of the different species of philosophy, by reconciling profound enquiry with clearness, and truth with novelty! And still more happy, if, reasoning in this easy manner, we can undermine the foundations of an abstruse philosophy, which seems to have hitherto served only as a shelter to superstition, and a cover to absurdity and error!

SECTION TWO
Of the origin of ideas

11. Every one will readily allow, that there is a considerable difference between the perceptions of the mind, when a man feels the pain of excessive heat, or the pleasure of moderate warmth, and when he afterwards recalls to his memory this sensation, or anticipates it by his imagination. These faculties may mimic or copy the perceptions of the senses; but they never can entirely reach the force and vivacity of the original sentiment. The utmost we say of them, even when they operate with greatest vigour, is, that they represent their object in so lively a manner, that we could *almost* say we feel or see it. But, except the mind be disordered by disease or madness, they never can arrive at such a pitch of vivacity, as to render these perceptions altogether undistinguishable. All the colours of poetry, however splendid, can never paint natural objects in such a manner as to make the description be taken for a real landscape. The most lively thought is still inferior to the dullest sensation.

We may observe a like distinction to run through all the other perceptions of the mind. A man in a fit of anger, is actuated in a very different manner from one who only thinks of that emotion. If you tell me, that any person is in love, I easily understand your meaning, and form a just conception of his situation; but never can mistake that conception for the real disorders and agitations of the passion. When we reflect on our past sentiments and affections, our thought is a faithful mirror, and copies its objects truly; but the colours which it employs are faint and dull, in comparison of those in which our original perceptions were clothed. It requires no nice discernment or metaphysical head to mark the distinction between them.

12. Here therefore we may divide all the perceptions of the mind into two classes or species, which are distinguished by their

different degrees of force and vivacity. The less forcible and lively are commonly denominated *Thoughts* or *Ideas*. The other species want a name in our language, and in most others; I suppose, because it was not requisite for any but philosophical purposes, to rank them under a general term or appellation. Let us, therefore, use a little freedom, and call them *Impressions*; employing that word in a sense somewhat different from the usual. By the term *impression*, then, I mean all our more lively perceptions, when we hear, or see, or feel, or love, or hate, or desire, or will. And impressions are distinguished from ideas, which are the less lively perceptions, of which we are conscious, when we reflect on any of those sensations or movements above mentioned.

13. Nothing, at first view, may seem more unbounded than the thought of man, which not only escapes all human power and authority, but is not even restrained within the limits of nature and reality. To form monsters, and join incongruous shapes and appearances, costs the imagination no more trouble than to conceive the most natural and familiar objects. And while the body is confined to one planet, along which it creeps with pain and difficulty; the thought can in an instant transport us into the most distant regions of the universe; or even beyond the universe, into the unbounded chaos, where nature is supposed to lie in total confusion. What never was seen, or heard of, may yet be conceived; nor is any thing beyond the power of thought, except what implies an absolute contradiction.

But though our thought seems to possess this unbounded liberty, we shall find, upon a nearer examination, that it is really confined within very narrow limits, and that all this creative power of the mind amounts to no more than the faculty of compounding, transposing, augmenting, or diminishing the materials afforded us by the senses and experience. When we think of a golden mountain, we only join two consistent ideas, *gold*, and *mountain*, with which we were formerly acquainted. A virtuous horse we can conceive; because, from our own feeling, we can conceive virtue; and this we may unite to the figure and shape of a horse, which is an animal familiar to us. In short, all the materials of thinking are derived either from our outward or inward sentiment: the mixture and composition of these belongs alone to the mind and will. Or, to express myself in philosophical language, all our ideas or more feeble perceptions are copies of our impressions or more lively ones.

14. To prove this, the two following arguments will, I hope, be sufficient. First, when we analyze our thoughts or ideas, however compounded or sublime, we always find that they resolve themselves into such simple ideas as were copied from a precedent feeling or sentiment. Even those ideas, which, at first view, seem the most wide of this origin, are found, upon a nearer scrutiny, to be derived from it. The idea of God, as meaning an infinitely intelligent, wise, and good Being, arises from reflecting on the operations of our own mind, and augmenting, without limit, those qualities of goodness and wisdom. We may prosecute this enquiry to what length we please; where we shall always find, that every idea which we examine is copied from a similar impression. Those who would assert that this position is not universally true nor without exception, have only one, and that an easy method of refuting it; by producing that idea, which, in their opinion, is not derived from this source. It will then be incumbent on us, if we would maintain our doctrine, to produce the impression, or lively perception, which corresponds to it.

15. Secondly. If it happen, from a defect of the organ, that a man is not susceptible of any species of sensation, we always find that he is as little susceptible of the correspondent ideas. A blind man can form no notion of colours; a deaf man of sounds. Restore either of them that sense in which he is deficient; by opening this new inlet for his sensations, you also open an inlet for the ideas; and he finds no difficulty in conceiving these objects. The case is the same, if the object, proper for exciting any sensation, has never been applied to the organ. A Laplander or Negro has no notion of the relish of wine. And though there are few or no instances of a like deficiency in the mind, where a person has never felt or is wholly incapable of a sentiment or passion that belongs to his species; yet we find the same observation to take place in a less degree. A man of mild manners can form no idea of inveterate revenge or cruelty; nor can a selfish heart easily conceive the heights of friendship and generosity. It is readily allowed, that other beings may possess many senses of which we can have no conception; because the ideas of them have never been introduced to us in the only manner

by which an idea can have access to the mind, to wit, by the actual feeling and sensation.

16. There is, however, one contradictory phenomenon, which may prove that it is not absolutely impossible for ideas to arise, independent of their correspondent impressions. I believe it will readily be allowed, that the several distinct ideas of colour, which enter by the eye, or those of sound, which are conveyed by the ear, are really different from each other; though, at the same time, resembling. Now if this be true of different colours, it must be no less so of the different shades of the same colour; and each shade produces a distinct idea, independent of the rest. For if this should be denied, it is possible, by the continual gradation of shades, to run a colour insensibly into what is most remote from it; and if you will not allow any of the means to be different, you cannot, without absurdity, deny the extremes to be the same. Suppose, therefore, a person to have enjoyed his sight for thirty years, and to have become perfectly acquainted with colours of all kinds except one particular shade of blue, for instance, which it never has been his fortune to meet with. Let all the different shades of that colour, except that single one, be placed before him, descending gradually from the deepest to the lightest; it is plain that he will perceive a blank, where that shade is wanting, and will be sensible that there is a greater distance in that place between the contiguous colours than in any other. Now I ask, whether it be possible for him, from his own imagination, to supply this deficiency, and raise up to himself the idea of that particular shade, though it had never been conveyed to him by his senses? I believe there are few but will be of opinion that he can: and this may serve as a proof that the simple ideas are not always, in every instance, derived from the correspondent impressions; though this instance is so singular, that it is scarcely worth our observing, and does not merit that for it alone we should alter our general maxim.

17. Here, therefore, is a proposition, which not only seems, in itself, simple and intelligible; but, if a proper use were made of it, might render every dispute equally intelligible, and banish all that jargon, which has so long taken possession of metaphysical reasonings, and drawn disgrace upon them. All ideas, especially abstract ones, are naturally faint and obscure: the mind has but a slender hold of them: they are apt to be confounded with other

resembling ideas; and when we have often employed any term, though without a distinct meaning, we are apt to imagine it has a determinate idea annexed to it. On the contrary, all impressions, that is, all sensations, either outward or inward, are strong and vivid: the limits between them are more exactly determined: nor is it easy to fall into any error or mistake with regard to them. When we entertain, therefore, any suspicion that a philosophical term is employed without any meaning or idea (as is but too frequent), we need but enquire, *from what impression is that supposed idea derived*? And if it be impossible to assign any, this will serve to confirm our suspicion. By bringing ideas into so clear a light we may reasonably hope to remove all dispute, which may arise, concerning their nature and reality.*

---

* It is probable that no more was meant by those, who denied innate ideas, than that all ideas were copies of our impressions; though it must be confessed, that the terms, which they employed, were not chosen with such caution, nor so exactly defined, as to prevent all mistakes about their doctrine. For what is meant by *innate*? If innate be equivalent to natural, then all the perceptions and ideas of the mind must be allowed to be innate or natural, in whatever sense we take the latter word, whether in opposition to what is uncommon, artificial, or miraculous. If by innate be meant, contemporary to our birth, the dispute seems to be frivolous; nor is it worth while to enquire at what time thinking begins, whether before, at, or after our birth. Again, the word *idea*, seems to be commonly taken in a very loose sense, by Locke and others; as standing for any of our perceptions, our sensations and passions, as well as thoughts. Now in this sense, I should desire to know, what can be meant by asserting, that self-love, or resentment of injuries, or the passion between the sexes is not innate?

But admitting these terms, *impressions* and *ideas*, in the sense above explained, and understanding by *innate*, what is original or copied from no precedent perception, then may we assert that all our impressions are innate, and our ideas not innate.

To be ingenuous, I must own it to be my opinion, that Locke was betrayed into this question by the schoolmen, who, making use of undefined terms, draw out their disputes to a tedious length, without ever touching the point in question. A like ambiguity and circumlocution seem to run through that philosopher's reasonings on this as well as most other subjects.

SECTION THREE
Of the association of ideas

18. It is evident that there is a principle of connexion between the different thoughts or ideas of the mind, and that, in their appearance to the memory or imagination, they introduce each other with a certain degree of method and regularity. In our more serious thinking or discourse this is so observable that any particular thought, which breaks in upon the regular tract or chain of ideas, is immediately remarked and rejected. And even in our wildest and most wandering reveries, nay in our very dreams, we shall find, if we reflect, that the imagination ran not altogether at adventures, but that there was still a connexion upheld among the different ideas, which succeeded each other. Were the loosest and freest conversation to be transcribed, there would immediately be observed something which connected it in all its transitions. Or where this is wanting, the person who broke the thread of discourse might still inform you, that there had secretly revolved in his mind a succession of thought, which had gradually led him from the subject of conversation. Among different languages, even where we cannot suspect the least connexion or communication, it is found, that the words, expressive of ideas, the most compounded, do yet nearly correspond to each other: a certain proof that the simple ideas, comprehended in the compound ones, were bound together by some universal principle, which had an equal influence on all mankind.

19. Though it be too obvious to escape observation, that different ideas are connected together; I do not find that any philosopher has attempted to enumerate or class all the principles of association; a subject, however, that seems worthy of curiosity. To me, there appear to be only three principles of connexion among ideas, namely, *Resemblance*, *Contiguity* in time or place, and *Cause or Effect*.

That these principles serve to connect ideas will not, I believe, be much doubted. A picture naturally leads our thoughts to the original:* the mention of one apartment in a building naturally introduces an enquiry or discourse concerning the others:† and if we think of a wound, we can scarcely forbear reflecting on the pain which follows it.‡ But that this enumeration is complete, and that there are no other principles of association except these, may be difficult to prove to the satisfaction of the reader, or even to a man's own satisfaction. All we can do, in such cases, is to run over several instances, and examine carefully the principle which binds the different thoughts to each other, never stopping till we render the principle as general as possible.§ The more instances we examine, and the more care we employ, the more assurance shall we acquire, that the enumeration, which we form from the whole, is complete and entire.

* Resemblance.
† Contiguity.
‡ Cause and effect.
§ For instance, Contrast or Contrariety is also a connexion among Ideas: but it may, perhaps, be considered as a mixture of *Causation* and *Resemblance*. Where two objects are contrary, the one destroys the other; that is, the cause of its annihilation, and the idea of the annihilation of an object, implies the idea of its former existence.

Sceptical doubts concerning the operations of the understanding

20. All the objects of human reason or enquiry may naturally be divided into two kinds, to wit, *Relations of Ideas*, and *Matters of Fact*. Of the first kind are the sciences of Geometry, Algebra, and Arithmetic; and in short, every affirmation which is either intuitively or demonstratively certain. *That the square of the hypothenuse is equal to the square of the two sides*, is a proposition which expresses a relation between these figures. *That three times five is equal to the half of thirty*, expresses a relation between these numbers. Propositions of this kind are discoverable by the mere operation of thought, without dependence on what is anywhere existent in the universe. Though there never were a circle or triangle in nature, the truths demonstrated by Euclid would for ever retain their certainty and evidence.

21. Matters of fact, which are the second objects of human reason, are not ascertained in the same manner; nor is our evidence of their truth, however great, of a like nature with the foregoing. The contrary of every matter of fact is still possible; because it can never imply a contradiction, and is conceived by the mind with the same facility and distinctness, as if ever so conformable to reality. *That the sun will not rise tomorrow* is no less intelligible a proposition, and implies no more contradiction than the affirmation, *that it will rise*. We should in vain, therefore, attempt to demonstrate its falsehood. Were it demonstratively false, it would imply a contradiction, and could never be distinctly conceived by the mind.

It may, therefore, be a subject worthy of curiosity, to enquire what is the nature of that evidence which assures us of any real existence and matter of fact, beyond the present testimony of our senses, or the records of our memory. This part of philosophy, it is observable, has been little cultivated, either by the ancients or moderns; and therefore our doubts and errors, in the prosecution of so important an enquiry, may be the more excusable; while we march through such difficult paths without any guide or direction. They may even prove useful, by exciting curiosity, and destroying that implicit faith and security, which is the bane of all reasoning and free enquiry. The discovery of defects in the common philosophy, if any such there be, will not, I presume, be a discouragement, but rather an incitement, as is usual, to attempt something more full and satisfactory than has yet been proposed to the public.

22. All reasonings concerning matter of fact seem to be founded on the relation of *Cause and Effect*. By means of that relation alone we can go beyond the evidence of our memory and senses. If you were to ask a man, why he believes any matter of fact, which is absent; for instance, that his friend is in the country, or in France; he would give you a reason; and this reason would be some other fact; as a letter received from him, or the knowledge of his former resolutions and promises. A man finding a watch or any other machine in a desert island, would conclude that there had once been men in that island. All our reasonings concerning fact are of the same nature. And here it is constantly supposed that there is a connexion between the present fact and that which is inferred from it. Were there nothing to bind them together, the inference would be entirely precarious. The hearing of an articulate voice and rational discourse in the dark assures us of the presence of some person. Why? because these are the effects of the human make and fabric, and closely connected with it. If we anatomize all the other reasonings of this nature, we shall find that they are founded on the relation of cause and effect, and that this relation is either near or remote, direct or collateral. Heat and light are collateral effects of fire, and the one effect may justly be inferred from the other.

23. If we would satisfy ourselves, therefore, concerning the nature of that evidence, which assures us of matters of fact, we must enquire how we arrive at the knowledge of cause and effect.

I shall venture to affirm, as a general proposition, which admits of no exception, that the knowledge of this relation is not, in any instance, attained by reasonings *a priori*; but arises entirely from experience, when we find that any particular objects are constantly conjoined with each other. Let an object be presented to a man of ever so strong natural reason and abilities; if that object be entirely new to him, he will not be able, by the most accurate examination of its sensible qualities, to discover any of its causes or effects. Adam, though his rational faculties be supposed, at the very first, entirely perfect, could not have inferred from the fluidity and transparency of water that it would suffocate him, or from the light and warmth of fire that it would consume him. No object ever discovers, by the qualities which appear to the senses, either the causes which produced it, or the effects which will arise from it; nor can our reason, unassisted by experience, ever draw any inference concerning real existence and matter of fact.

24. This proposition, *that causes and effects are discoverable, not by reason but by experience*, will readily be admitted with regard to such objects, as we remember to have once been altogether unknown to us; since we must be conscious of the utter inability, which we then lay under, of foretelling what would arise from them. Present two smooth pieces of marble to a man who has no tincture of natural philosophy; he will never discover that they will adhere together in such a manner as to require great force to separate them in a direct line, while they make so small a resistance to a lateral pressure. Such events, as bear little analogy to the common course of nature, are also readily confessed to be known only by experience; nor does any man imagine that the explosion of gunpowder, or the attraction of a loadstone, could ever be discovered by arguments *a priori*. In like manner, when an effect is supposed to depend upon an intricate machinery or secret structure of parts, we make no difficulty in attributing all our knowledge of it to experience. Who will assert that he can give the ultimate reason, why milk or bread is proper nourishment for a man, not for a lion or a tiger?

But the same truth may not appear, at first sight, to have the same evidence with regard to events, which have become familiar to us from our first appearance in the world, which bear a close analogy to the whole course of nature, and which are supposed to depend on the simple qualities of objects, without any secret structure of parts. We are apt to imagine that we could discover these effects by the mere operation of our reason, without experience. We fancy, that were we brought on a sudden into this world, we could at first have inferred that one Billiard-ball would communicate motion to another upon impulse; and that we needed not to have waited for the event, in order to pronounce with certainty concerning it. Such is the influence of custom, that, where it is strongest, it not only covers our natural ignorance, but even conceals itself, and seems not to take place, merely because it is found in the highest degree.

25. But to convince us that all the laws of nature, and all the operations of bodies without exception, are known only by experience, the following reflections may, perhaps, suffice. Were any object presented to us, and were we required to pronounce concerning the effect, which will result from it, without consulting past observation; after what manner, I beseech you, must the mind proceed in this operation? It must invent or imagine some event, which it ascribes to the object as its effect; and it is plain that this invention must be entirely arbitrary. The mind can never possibly find the effect in the supposed cause, by the most accurate scrutiny and examination. For the effect is totally different from the cause, and consequently can never be discovered in it. Motion in the second Billiard-ball is a quite distinct event from motion in the first; nor is there anything in the one to suggest the smallest hint of the other. A stone or piece of metal raised into the air, and left without any support, immediately falls: but to consider the matter *a priori*, is there anything we discover in this situation which can beget the idea of a downward, rather than an upward, or any other motion, in the stone or metal?

And as the first imagination or invention of a particular effect, in all natural operations, is arbitrary, where we consult not experience; so must we also esteem the supposed tie or connexion between the cause and effect, which binds them together, and renders it impossible that any other effect could result from the operation of that cause. When I see, for instance, a Billiard-ball moving in a straight line towards another; even suppose motion in the second ball should by accident be suggested to me, as the result of their contact or impulse; may I not conceive, that a hundred different events might as well follow from that cause? May not both these balls remain at absolute rest? May not the first ball return in a straight line, or leap off from the second in any line or direction? All these suppositions are consistent and conceivable. Why then should we give the preference to one, which is no more consistent or conceivable than the rest? All our reasonings *a priori* will never be able to show us any foundation for this preference.

In a word, then, every effect is a distinct event from its cause. It could not, therefore, be discovered in the cause, and the first invention or conception of it, *a priori*, must be entirely arbitrary. And even after it is suggested, the conjunction of it with the cause must appear equally arbitrary; since there are always many other effects, which, to reason, must seem fully as consistent and natural. In vain, therefore, should we pretend to determine any single event, or infer any cause or effect, without the assistance of observation and experience.

26. Hence we may discover the reason why no philosopher, who is rational and modest, has ever pretended to assign the ultimate cause of any natural operation, or to show distinctly the action of that power, which produces any single effect in the universe. It is confessed, that the utmost effort of human reason is to reduce the principles, productive of natural phenomena, to a greater simplicity, and to resolve the many particular effects into a few general causes, by means of reasonings from analogy, experience, and observation. But as to the causes of these general causes, we should in vain attempt their discovery; nor shall we ever be able to satisfy ourselves, by any particular explication of them. These ultimate springs and principles are totally shut up from human curiosity and enquiry. Elasticity, gravity, cohesion of parts, communication of motion by impulse; these are probably the ultimate causes and principles which we shall ever discover in nature; and we may esteem ourselves sufficiently happy, if, by accurate enquiry and reasoning, we can trace up the particular phenomena to, or near to, these general principles. The most perfect philosophy of the natural kind only staves off our ignorance a little longer: as perhaps the most perfect philosophy of the moral or metaphysical kind serves only to discover larger portions of it. Thus the observation of human blindness and weakness is the result of all philosophy, and meets us at every turn, in spite of our endeavours to elude or avoid it.

27. Nor is geometry, when taken into the assistance of natural philosophy, ever able to remedy this defect, or lead us into the knowledge of ultimate causes, by all that accuracy of reasoning for which it is so justly celebrated. Every part of mixed mathematics proceeds upon the supposition that certain laws are established by nature in her operations; and abstract reasonings are employed, either to assist experience in the discovery of these laws, or to determine their influence in particular instances, where it depends upon any precise degree of distance and quantity. Thus, it is a law of motion, discovered by experience, that the moment or force of any body in motion is in the compound ratio or proportion of its solid contents and its velocity; and consequently, that a small force may remove the greatest obstacle or raise the greatest weight, if, by any contrivance or machinery, we can increase the velocity of that force, so as to make it an overmatch for its antagonist. Geometry assists us in the application of this law, by giving us the just dimensions of all the parts and figures which can enter into any species of machine; but still the discovery of the law itself is owing merely to experience, and all the abstract reasonings in the world could never lead us one step towards the knowledge of it. When we reason *a priori*, and consider merely any object or cause, as it appears to the mind, independent of all observation, it never could suggest to us the notion of any distinct object, such as its effect; much less, show us the inseparable and inviolable connexion between them. A man must be very sagacious who could discover by reasoning that crystal is the effect of heat, and ice of cold, without being previously acquainted with the operation of these qualities.

Part 2

28. But we have not yet attained any tolerable satisfaction with regard to the question first proposed. Each solution still gives rise to a new question as difficult as the foregoing, and leads us on to farther enquiries. When it is asked, *What is the nature of all our reasonings concerning matter of fact?* the proper answer seems to be, that they are founded on the relation of cause and effect. When again it is asked, *What is the foundation of all our reasonings and conclusions concerning that relation?* it may be replied in one word, Experience. But if we still carry on our sifting humour, and ask,

What is the foundation of all conclusions from experience? this implies a new question, which may be of more difficult solution and explication. Philosophers, that give themselves airs of superior wisdom and sufficiency, have a hard task when they encounter persons of inquisitive dispositions, who push them from every corner to which they retreat, and who are sure at last to bring them to some dangerous dilemma. The best expedient to prevent this confusion, is to be modest in our pretensions; and even to discover the difficulty ourselves before it is objected to us. By this means, we may make a kind of merit of our very ignorance.

I shall content myself, in this section, with an easy task, and shall pretend only to give a negative answer to the question here proposed. I say then, that, even after we have experience of the operations of cause and effect, our conclusions from that experience are *not* founded on reasoning, or any process of the understanding. This answer we must endeavour both to explain and to defend.

29. It must certainly be allowed, that nature has kept us at a great distance from all her secrets, and has afforded us only the knowledge of a few superficial qualities of objects; while she conceals from us those powers and principles on which the influence of those objects entirely depends. Our senses inform us of the colour, weight, and consistence of bread; but neither sense nor reason can ever inform us of those qualities which fit it for the nourishment and support of a human body. Sight or feeling conveys an idea of the actual motion of bodies; but as to that wonderful force or power, which would carry on a moving body for ever in a continued change of place, and which bodies never lose but by communicating it to others; of this we cannot form the most distant conception. But notwithstanding this ignorance of natural powers* and principles, we always presume, when we see like sensible qualities, that they have like secret powers, and expect that effects, similar to those which we have experienced, will follow from them. If a body of like colour and consistence with that bread, which we have formerly eat[en], be presented to us, we make no scruple of repeating the experiment, and foresee, with certainty, like nourishment and support. Now this is a process of the mind or thought, of which I would willingly know the

---

* The word, Power, is here used in a loose and popular sense. The more accurate explication of it would give additional evidence to this argument. See Section 7.

foundation. It is allowed on all hands that there is no known connexion between the sensible qualities and the secret powers; and consequently, that the mind is not led to form such a conclusion concerning their constant and regular conjunction, by anything which it knows of their nature. As to past *Experience*, it can be allowed to give *direct* and *certain* information of those precise objects only, and that precise period of time, which fell under its cognizance: but why this experience should be extended to future times, and to other objects, which for aught we know, may be only in appearance similar; this is the main question on which I would insist. The bread, which I formerly ate, nourished me; that is, a body of such sensible qualities was, at that time, endued with such secret powers: but does it follow, that other bread must also nourish me at another time, and that like sensible qualities must always be attended with like secret powers? The consequence seems nowise necessary. At least, it must be acknowledged that there is here a consequence drawn by the mind; that there is a certain step taken; a process of thought, and an inference, which wants to be explained. These two propositions are far from being the same, *I have found that such an object has always been attended with such an effect*, and *I foresee, that other objects, which are, in appearance, similar, will be attended with similar effects*. I shall allow, if you please, that the one proposition may justly be inferred from the other: I know, in fact, that it always is inferred. But if you insist that the inference is made by a chain of reasoning, I desire you to produce that reasoning. The connexion between these propositions is not intuitive. There is required a medium, which may enable the mind to draw such an inference, if indeed it be drawn by reasoning and argument. What that medium is, I must confess, passes my comprehension; and it is incumbent on those to produce it, who assert that it really exists, and is the origin of all our conclusions concerning matter of fact.

30. This negative argument must certainly, in process of time, become altogether convincing, if many penetrating and able philosophers shall turn their enquiries this way and no one be ever able to discover any connecting proposition or intermediate step, which supports the understanding in this conclusion. But as the question is yet new, every reader may not trust so far to his own penetration, as to conclude, because an argument escapes

his enquiry, that therefore it does not really exist. For this reason it may be requisite to venture upon a more difficult task; and enumerating all the branches of human knowledge, endeavour to show that none of them can afford such an argument.

All reasonings may be divided into two kinds, namely, demonstrative reasoning, or that concerning relations of ideas, and moral reasoning, or that concerning matter of fact and existence. That there are no demonstrative arguments in the case seems evident; since it implies no contradiction that the course of nature may change, and that an object, seemingly like those which we have experienced, may be attended with different or contrary effects. May I not clearly and distinctly conceive that a body, falling from the clouds, and which, in all other respects, resembles snow, has yet the taste of salt or feeling of fire? Is there any more intelligible proposition than to affirm, that all the trees will flourish in December and January, and decay in May and June? Now whatever is intelligible, and can be distinctly conceived, implies no contradiction, and can never be proved false by any demonstrative argument or abstract reasoning *a priori*.

If we be, therefore, engaged by arguments to put trust in past experience, and make it the standard of our future judgement, these arguments must be probable only, or such as regard matter of fact and real existence, according to the division above mentioned. But that there is no argument of this kind, must appear, if our explication of that species of reasoning be admitted as solid and satisfactory. We have said that all arguments concerning existence are founded on the relation of cause and effect; that our knowledge of that relation is derived entirely from experience; and that all our experimental conclusions proceed upon the supposition that the future will be conformable to the past. To endeavour, therefore, the proof of this last supposition by probable arguments, or arguments regarding existence, must be evidently going in a circle, and taking that for granted, which is the very point in question.

31. In reality, all arguments from experience are founded on the similarity which we discover among natural objects, and by which we are induced to expect effects similar to those which we have found to follow from such objects. And though none but a fool or madman will ever pretend to dispute the authority of experience, or to reject that great guide of human life, it may surely be allowed

a philosopher to have so much curiosity at least as to examine the principle of human nature, which gives this mighty authority to experience, and makes us draw advantage from that similarity which nature has placed among different objects. From causes which appear *similar* we expect similar effects. This is the sum of all our experimental conclusions. Now it seems evident that, if this conclusion were formed by reason, it would be as perfect at first, and upon one instance, as after ever so long a course of experience. But the case is far otherwise. Nothing so like as eggs; yet no one, on account of this appearing similarity, expects the same taste and relish in all of them. It is only after a long course of uniform experiments in any kind, that we attain a firm reliance and security with regard to a particular event. Now where is that process of reasoning which, from one instance, draws a conclusion, so different from that which it infers from a hundred instances that are nowise different from that single one? This question I propose as much for the sake of information, as with an intention of raising difficulties. I cannot find, I cannot imagine any such reasoning. But I keep my mind still open to instruction, if any one will vouchsafe to bestow it on me.

32. Should it be said that, from a number of uniform experiments, we *infer* a connexion between the sensible qualities and the secret powers; this, I must confess, seems the same difficulty, couched in different terms. The question still recurs, on what process of argument this *inference* is founded? Where is the medium, the interposing ideas, which join propositions so very wide of each other? It is confessed that the colour, consistence, and other sensible qualities of bread appear not, of themselves, to have any connexion with the secret powers of nourishment and support. For otherwise we could infer these secret powers from the first appearance of these sensible qualities, without the aid of experience; contrary to the sentiment of all philosophers, and contrary to plain matter of fact. Here, then, is our natural state of ignorance with regard to the powers and influence of all objects. How is this remedied by experience? It only shows us a number of uniform effects, resulting from certain objects, and teaches us that those particular objects, at that particular time, were endowed with such powers and forces. When a new object, endowed with similar sensible qualities, is produced, we expect similar powers and forces, and look for a like

effect. From a body of like colour and consistence with bread we expect like nourishment and support. But this surely is a step or progress of the mind, which wants to be explained. When a man says, *I have found, in all past instances, such sensible qualities conjoined with such secret powers*: and when he says, *Similar sensible qualities will always be conjoined with similar secret powers*, he is not guilty of a tautology, nor are these propositions in any respect the same. You say that the one proposition is an inference from the other. But you must confess that the inference is not intuitive; neither is it demonstrative. Of what nature is it, then? To say it is experimental, is begging the question. For all inferences from experience suppose, as their foundation, that the future will resemble the past, and that similar powers will be conjoined with similar sensible qualities. If there be any suspicion that the course of nature may change, and that the past may be no rule for the future, all experience becomes useless, and can give rise to no inference or conclusion. It is impossible, therefore, that any arguments from experience can prove this resemblance of the past to the future; since all these arguments are founded on the supposition of that resemblance. Let the course of things be allowed hitherto ever so regular; that alone, without some new argument or inference, proves not that, for the future, it will continue so. In vain do you pretend to have learned the nature of bodies from your past experience. Their secret nature, and consequently all their effects and influence, may change, without any change in their sensible qualities. This happens sometimes, and with regard to some objects: why may it not happen always, and with regard to all objects? What logic, what process of argument secures you against this supposition? My practice, you say, refutes my doubts. But you mistake the purport of my question. As an agent, I am quite satisfied in the point; but as a philosopher, who has some share of curiosity, I will not say scepticism, I want to learn the foundation of this inference. No reading, no enquiry has yet been able to remove my difficulty, or give me satisfaction in a matter of such importance. Can I do better than propose the difficulty to the public, even though, perhaps, I have small hopes of obtaining a solution? We shall at least, by this means, be sensible of our ignorance, if we do not augment our knowledge.

33. I must confess that a man is guilty of unpardonable arrogance who concludes, because an argument has escaped his own

investigation, that therefore it does not really exist. I must also confess that, though all the learned, for several ages, should have employed themselves in fruitless search upon any subject, it may still, perhaps, be rash to conclude positively that the subject must, therefore, pass all human comprehension. Even though we examine all the sources of our knowledge, and conclude them unfit for such a subject, there may still remain a suspicion, that the enumeration is not complete, or the examination not accurate. But with regard to the present subject, there are some considerations which seem to remove all this accusation of arrogance or suspicion of mistake.

It is certain that the most ignorant and stupid peasants – nay infants, nay even brute beasts – improve by experience, and learn the qualities of natural objects, by observing the effects which result from them. When a child has felt the sensation of pain from touching the flame of a candle, he will be careful not to put his hand near any candle; but will expect a similar effect from a cause which is similar in its sensible qualities and appearance. If you assert, therefore, that the understanding of the child is led into this conclusion by any process of argument or ratiocination, I may justly require you to produce that argument; nor have you any pretence to refuse so equitable a demand. You cannot say that the argument is abstruse, and may possibly escape your enquiry; since you confess that it is obvious to the capacity of a mere infant. If you hesitate, therefore, a moment, or if, after reflection, you produce any intricate or profound argument, you, in a manner, give up the question, and confess that it is not reasoning which engages us to suppose the past resembling the future, and to expect similar effects from causes which are, to appearance, similar. This is the proposition which I intended to enforce in the present section. If I be right, I pretend not to have made any mighty discovery. And if I be wrong, I must acknowledge myself to be indeed a very backward scholar; since I cannot now discover an argument which, it seems, was perfectly familiar to me long before I was out of my cradle.

SECTION FIVE
Sceptical solution of these doubts

Part 1

34. The passion for philosophy, like that for religion, seems liable to this inconvenience, that, though it aims at the correction of our manners, and extirpation of our vices, it may only serve, by imprudent management, to foster a predominant inclination, and push the mind, with more determined resolution, towards that side which already *draws* too much, by the bias and propensity of the natural temper. It is certain that, while we aspire to the magnanimous firmness of the philosophic sage, and endeavour to confine our pleasures altogether within our own minds, we may, at last, render our philosophy like that of Epictetus, and other *Stoics*, only a more refined system of selfishness, and reason ourselves out of all virtue as well as social enjoyment. While we study with attention the vanity of human life, and turn all our thoughts towards the empty and transitory nature of riches and honours, we are, perhaps, all the while flattering our natural indolence, which, hating the bustle of the world, and drudgery of business, seeks a pretence of reason to give itself a full and uncontrolled indulgence. There is, however, one species of philosophy which seems little liable to this inconvenience, and that because it strikes in with no disorderly passion of the human mind, nor can mingle itself with any natural affection or propensity; and that is the Academic or Sceptical philosophy. The academics always talk of doubt and suspense of judgement, of danger in hasty determinations, of confining to very narrow bounds the enquiries of the understanding, and of renouncing all speculations which lie not within the limits of common life and practice. Nothing, therefore, can be more contrary than such a philosophy to the supine indolence of the mind, its rash arrogance, its lofty pretensions, and

its superstitious credulity. Every passion is mortified by it, except the love of truth; and that passion never is, nor can be, carried to too high a degree. It is surprising, therefore, that this philosophy, which, in almost every instance, must be harmless and innocent, should be the subject of so much groundless reproach and obloquy. But, perhaps, the very circumstance which renders it so innocent is what chiefly exposes it to the public hatred and resentment. By flattering no irregular passion, it gains few partizans: by opposing so many vices and follies, it raises to itself abundance of enemies, who stigmatize it as libertine, profane, and irreligious.

Nor need we fear that this philosophy, while it endeavours to limit our enquiries to common life, should ever undermine the reasonings of common life, and carry its doubts so far as to destroy all action, as well as speculation. Nature will always maintain her rights, and prevail in the end over any abstract reasoning whatsoever. Though we should conclude, for instance, as in the foregoing section, that, in all reasonings from experience, there is a step taken by the mind which is not supported by any argument or process of the understanding; there is no danger that these reasonings, on which almost all knowledge depends, will ever be affected by such a discovery. If the mind be not engaged by argument to make this step, it must be induced by some other principle of equal weight and authority; and that principle will preserve its influence as long as human nature remains the same. What that principle is may well be worth the pains of enquiry.

35. Suppose a person, though endowed with the strongest faculties of reason and reflection, to be brought on a sudden into this world; he would, indeed, immediately observe a continual succession of objects, and one event following another; but he would not be able to discover anything farther. He would not, at first, by any reasoning, be able to reach the idea of cause and effect; since the particular powers, by which all natural operations are performed, never appear to the senses; nor is it reasonable to conclude, merely because one event, in one instance, precedes another, that therefore the one is the cause, the other the effect. Their conjunction may be arbitrary and casual. There may be no reason to infer the existence of one from the appearance of the other. And in a word, such a person, without more experience,

could never employ his conjecture or reasoning concerning any matter of fact, or be assured of anything beyond what was immediately present to his memory and senses.

Suppose, again, that he has acquired more experience, and has lived so long in the world as to have observed familiar objects or events to be constantly conjoined together; what is the consequence of this experience? He immediately infers the existence of one object from the appearance of the other. Yet he has not, by all his experience, acquired any idea or knowledge of the secret power by which the one object produces the other; nor is it, by any process of reasoning, he is engaged to draw this inference. But still he finds himself determined to draw it: and though he should be convinced that his understanding has no part in the operation, he would nevertheless continue in the same course of thinking. There is some other principle which determines him to form such a conclusion.

36. This principle is Custom or Habit. For wherever the repetition of any particular act or operation produces a propensity to renew the same act or operation, without being impelled by any reasoning or process of the understanding, we always say, that this propensity is the effect of *Custom*. By employing that word, we pretend not to have given the ultimate reason of such a propensity. We only point out a principle of human nature, which is universally acknowledged, and which is well known by its effects. Perhaps we can push our enquiries no farther, or pretend to give the cause of this cause; but must rest contented with it as the ultimate principle, which we can assign, of all our conclusions from experience. It is sufficient satisfaction, that we can go so far, without repining at the narrowness of our faculties because they will carry us no farther. And it is certain we here advance a very intelligible proposition at least, if not a true one, when we assert that, after the constant conjunction of two objects – heat and flame, for instance, weight and solidity – we are determined by custom alone to expect the one from the appearance of the other. This hypothesis seems even the only one which explains the difficulty, why we draw, from a thousand instances, an inference which we are not able to draw from one instance, that is, in no respect, different from them. Reason is incapable of any such variation. The conclusions which it draws from considering one

circle are the same which it would form upon surveying all the circles in the universe. But no man, having seen only one body move after being impelled by another, could infer that every other body will move after a like impulse. All inferences from experience, therefore, are effects of custom, not of reasoning.*

* Nothing is more useful than for writers, even, on *moral*, *political*, or *physical* subjects, to distinguish between *reason* and *experience*, and to suppose, that these species of argumentation are entirely different from each other. The former are taken for the mere result of our intellectual faculties, which, by considering *a priori* the nature of things, and examining the effects, that must follow from their operation, establish particular principles of science and philosophy. The latter are supposed to be derived entirely from sense and observation, by which we learn what has actually resulted from the operation of particular objects, and are thence able to infer, what will, for the future, result from them. Thus, for instance, the limitations and restraints of civil government, and a legal constitution, may be defended, either from *reason*, which reflecting on the great frailty and corruption of human nature, teaches, that no man can safely be trusted with unlimited authority; or from *experience* and history, which inform us of the enormous abuses, that ambition, in every age and country, has been found to make of so imprudent a confidence.

The same distinction between reason and experience is maintained in all our deliberations concerning the conduct of life; while the experienced statesman, general, physician, or merchant is trusted and followed; and the unpractised novice, with whatever natural talents endowed, neglected and despised. Though it be allowed, that reason may form very plausible conjectures with regard to the consequences of such a particular conduct in such particular circumstances; it is still supposed imperfect, without the assistance of experience, which is alone able to give stability and certainty to the maxims, derived from study and reflection.

But notwithstanding that this distinction be thus universally received, both in the active and speculative scenes of life, I shall not scruple to pronounce, that it is, at bottom, erroneous, at least, superficial.

If we examine those arguments, which, in any of the sciences above mentioned, are supposed to be the mere effects of reasoning and reflection, they will be found to terminate, at last, in some general principle or conclusion, for which we can assign no reason but observation and experience. The only difference between them and those maxims, which are vulgarly esteemed the result of pure experience, is, that the former cannot be established without some process of thought, and some reflection on what we have observed, in order to distinguish its circumstances, and trace its consequences: whereas in the latter, the experienced event is exactly and fully familiar to that which we infer as the result of any particular situation. The history of a TIBERIUS or a NERO makes us dread a like tyranny, were our monarchs freed from the restraints of laws and senates: but the observation of any fraud or cruelty in private life is sufficient, with the aid of a little thought, to give us the same apprehension; while it serves as an instance of the general corruption of human nature, and shows us the danger which we must incur by reposing an entire confidence in mankind. In both cases, it is experience which is ultimately the foundation of our inference and conclusion.

There is no man so young and unexperienced, as not to have formed, from observation, many general and just maxims concerning human affairs and the

Custom, then, is the great guide of human life. It is that principle alone which renders our experience useful to us, and makes us expect, for the future, a similar train of events with those which have appeared in the past.

Without the influence of custom, we should be entirely ignorant of every matter of fact beyond what is immediately present to the memory and senses. We should never know how to adjust means to ends, or to employ our natural powers in the production of any effect. There would be an end at once of all action, as well as of the chief part of speculation.

37. But here it may be proper to remark, that though our conclusions from experience carry us beyond our memory and senses, and assure us of matters of fact which happened in the most distant places and most remote ages, yet some fact must always be present to the senses or memory, from which we may first proceed in drawing these conclusions. A man, who should find in a desert country the remains of pompous buildings, would conclude that the country had, in ancient times, been cultivated by civilized inhabitants; but did nothing of this nature occur to him, he could never form such an inference. We learn the events of former ages from history; but then we must peruse the volumes in which this instruction is contained, and thence carry up our inferences from one testimony to another, till we arrive at the eyewitnesses and spectators of these distant events. In a word, if we proceed not upon some fact, present to the memory or senses, our reasonings would be merely hypothetical; and however the particular links might be connected with each other, the whole chain of inferences would have nothing to support it, nor could we ever, by its means, arrive at the knowledge of any real existence. If I ask why

---

conduct of life; but it must be confessed, that, when a man comes to put these in practice, he will be extremely liable to error, till time and farther experience both enlarge these maxims, and teach him their proper use and application. In every situation or incident, there are many particular and seemingly minute circumstances, which the man of greatest talent is, at first, apt to overlook, though on them the justness of his conclusions, and consequently the prudence of his conduct, entirely depend. Not to mention, that, to a young beginner, the general observations and maxims occur not always on the proper occasions, nor can be immediately applied with due calmness and distinction. The truth is, an unexperienced reasoner could be no reasoner at all, were he absolutely unexperienced; and when we assign that character to any one, we mean it only in a comparative sense, and suppose him possessed of experience, in a smaller and more imperfect degree.

you believe any particular matter of fact, which you relate, you must tell me some reason; and this reason will be some other fact, connected with it. But as you cannot proceed after this manner, *in infinitum*, you must at last terminate in some fact, which is present to your memory or senses; or must allow that your belief is entirely without foundation.

38. What, then, is the conclusion of the whole matter? A simple one; though, it must be confessed, pretty remote from the common theories of philosophy. All belief of matter of fact or real existence is derived merely from some object, present to the memory or senses, and a customary conjunction between that and some other object. Or in other words; having found, in many instances, that any two kinds of objects – flame and heat, snow and cold – have always been conjoined together; if flame or snow be presented anew to the senses, the mind is carried by custom to expect heat or cold, and to *believe* that such a quality does exist, and will discover itself upon a nearer approach. This belief is the necessary result of placing the mind in such circumstances. It is an operation of the soul, when we are so situated, as unavoidable as to feel the passion of love, when we receive benefits; or hatred, when we meet with injuries. All these operations are a species of natural instincts, which no reasoning or process of the thought and understanding is able either to produce or to prevent.

At this point, it would be very allowable for us to stop our philosophical researches. In most questions we can never make a single step farther; and in all questions we must terminate here at last, after our most restless and curious enquiries. But still our curiosity will be pardonable, perhaps commendable, if it carry us on to still farther researches, and make us examine more accurately the nature of this *belief*, and of the *customary conjunction*, whence it is derived. By this means we may meet with some explications and analogies that will give satisfaction; at least to such as love the abstract sciences, and can be entertained with speculations, which, however accurate, may still retain a degree of doubt and uncertainty. As to readers of a different taste; the remaining part of this section is not calculated for them, and the following enquiries may well be understood, though it be neglected.

Part 2

39. Nothing is more free than the imagination of man; and though it cannot exceed that original stock of ideas furnished by the internal and external senses, it has unlimited power of mixing, compounding, separating, and dividing these ideas, in all the varieties of fiction and vision. It can feign a train of events, with all the appearance of reality, ascribe to them a particular time and place, conceive them as existent, and paint them out to itself with every circumstance, that belongs to any historical fact, which it believes with the greatest certainty. Wherein, therefore, consists the difference between such a fiction and belief? It lies not merely in any peculiar idea, which is annexed to such a conception as commands our assent, and which is wanting to every known fiction. For as the mind has authority over all its ideas, it could voluntarily annex this particular idea to any fiction, and consequently be able to believe whatever it pleases; contrary to what we find by daily experience. We can, in our conception, join the head of a man to the body of a horse; but it is not in our power to believe that such an animal has ever really existed.

It follows, therefore, that the difference between *fiction* and *belief* lies in some sentiment or feeling, which is annexed to the latter, not to the former, and which depends not on the will, nor can be commanded at pleasure. It must be excited by nature, like all other sentiments; and must arise from the particular situation, in which the mind is placed at any particular juncture. Whenever any object is presented to the memory or senses, it immediately, by the force of custom, carries the imagination to conceive that object, which is usually conjoined to it; and this conception is attended with a feeling or sentiment, different from the loose reveries of the fancy. In this consists the whole nature of belief. For as there is no matter of fact which we believe so firmly that we cannot conceive the contrary, there would be no difference between the conception assented to and that which is rejected, were it not for some sentiment which distinguishes the one from the other. If I see a billiard-ball moving towards another, on a smooth table, I can easily conceive it to stop upon contact. This conception implies no contradiction; but still it feels very differently from that conception by which I represent to myself the impulse and the communication of motion from one ball to another.

40. Were we to attempt a *definition* of this sentiment, we should, perhaps, find it a very difficult, if not an impossible task; in the same manner as if we should endeavour to define the feeling of cold or passion of anger, to a creature who never had any experience of these sentiments. Belief is the true and proper name of this feeling; and no one is ever at a loss to know the meaning of that term; because every man is every moment conscious of the sentiment represented by it. It may not, however, be improper to attempt a *description* of this sentiment; in hopes we may, by that means, arrive at some analogies, which may afford a more perfect explication of it. I say, then, that belief is nothing but a more vivid, lively, forcible, firm, steady conception of an object, than what the imagination alone is ever able to attain. This variety of terms, which may seem so unphilosophical, is intended only to express that act of the mind, which renders realities, or what is taken for such, more present to us than fictions, causes them to weigh more in the thought, and gives them a superior influence on the passions and imagination. Provided we agree about the thing, it is needless to dispute about the terms. The imagination has the command over all its ideas, and can join and mix and vary them, in all the ways possible. It may conceive fictitious objects with all the circumstances of place and time. It may set them, in a manner, before our eyes, in their true colours, just as they might have existed. But as it is impossible that this faculty of imagination can ever, of itself, reach belief, it is evident that belief consists not in the peculiar nature or order of ideas, but in the *manner* of their conception, and in their *feeling* to the mind. I confess, that it is impossible perfectly to explain this feeling or manner of conception. We may make use of words which express something near it. But its true and proper name, as we observed before, is *belief*; which is a term that every one sufficiently understands in common life. And in philosophy, we can go no farther than assert, that *belief* is something felt by the mind, which distinguishes the ideas of the judgement from the fictions of the imagination. It gives them more weight and influence; makes them appear of greater importance; enforces them in the mind; and renders them the governing

principle of our actions. I hear at present, for instance, a person's voice, with whom I am acquainted; and the sound comes as from the next room. This impression of my senses immediately conveys my thought to the person, together with all the surrounding objects. I paint them out to myself as existing at present, with the same qualities and relations, of which I formerly knew them possessed. These ideas take faster hold of my mind than ideas of an enchanted castle. They are very different to the feeling, and have a much greater influence of every kind, either to give pleasure or pain, joy or sorrow.

Let us, then, take in the whole compass of this doctrine, and allow, that the sentiment of belief is nothing but a conception more intense and steady than what attends the mere fictions of the imagination, and that this *manner* of conception arises from a customary conjunction of the object with something present to the memory or senses: I believe that it will not be difficult, upon these suppositions, to find other operations of the mind analogous to it, and to trace up these phenomena to principles still more general.

41. We have already observed that nature has established connexions among particular ideas, and that no sooner one idea occurs to our thoughts than it introduces its correlative, and carries our attention towards it, by a gentle and insensible movement. These principles of connexion or association we have reduced to three, namely, *Resemblance, Contiguity* and *Causation*; which are the only bonds that unite our thoughts together, and beget that regular train of reflection or discourse, which, in a greater or less degree, takes place among all mankind. Now here arises a question, on which the solution of the present difficulty will depend. Does it happen, in all these relations, that, when one of the objects is presented to the senses or memory, the mind is not only carried to the conception of the correlative, but reaches a steadier and stronger conception of it than what otherwise it would have been able to attain? This seems to be the case with that belief which arises from the relation of cause and effect. And if the case be the same with the other relations or principles of associations, this may be established as a general law, which takes place in all the operations of the mind.

We may, therefore, observe, as the first experiment to our present purpose, that, upon the appearance of the picture of an absent friend, our idea of him is evidently enlivened by the *resemblance*, and that every passion, which that idea occasions, whether of joy or sorrow, acquires new force and vigour. In producing this effect, there concur both a relation and a present impression. Where the picture bears him no resemblance, at least was not intended for him, it never so much as conveys our thought to him: and where it is absent, as well as the person, though the mind may pass from the thought of the one to that of the other, it feels its idea to be rather weakened than enlivened by that transition. We take a pleasure in viewing the picture of a friend, when it is set before us; but when it is removed, rather choose to consider him directly than by reflection in an image, which is equally distant and obscure.

The ceremonies of the Roman Catholic religion may be considered as instances of the same nature. The devotees of that superstition usually plead in excuse for the mummeries, with which they are upbraided, that they feel the good effect of those external motions, and postures, and actions, in enlivening their devotion and quickening their fervour, which otherwise would decay, if directed entirely to distant and immaterial objects. We shadow out the objects of our faith, say they, in sensible types and images, and render them more present to us by the immediate presence of these types, than it is possible for us to do merely by an intellectual view and contemplation. Sensible objects have always a greater influence on the fancy than any other; and this influence they readily convey to those ideas to which they are related, and which they resemble. I shall only infer from these practices, and this reasoning, that the effect of resemblance in enlivening the ideas is very common; and as in every case a resemblance and a present impression must concur, we are abundantly supplied with experiments to prove the reality of the foregoing principle.

42. We may add force to these experiments by others of a different kind, in considering the effects of *contiguity* as well as of *resemblance*. It is certain that distance diminishes the force of every idea, and that, upon our approach to any object; though it does not discover itself to our senses; it operates upon the mind with an influence, which imitates an immediate impression. The thinking on any object readily transports the mind to what is contiguous; but it is only the actual presence of an object, that transports it

with a superior vivacity. When I am a few miles from home, whatever relates to it touches me more nearly than when I am two hundred leagues distant; though even at that distance the reflecting on any thing in the neighbourhood of my friends or family naturally produces an idea of them. But as in this latter case, both the objects of the mind are ideas; notwithstanding there is an easy transition between them; that transition alone is not able to give a superior vivacity to any of the ideas, for want of some immediate impression.*

43. No one can doubt but causation has the same influence as the other two relations of resemblance and contiguity. Superstitious people are fond of the reliques of saints and holy men, for the same reason, that they seek after types or images, in order to enliven their devotion, and give them a more intimate and strong conception of those exemplary lives, which they desire to imitate. Now it is evident, that one of the best reliques, which a devotee could procure, would be the handywork of a saint; and if his clothes and furniture are ever to be considered in this light, it is because they were once at his disposal, and were moved and affected by him; in which respect they are to be considered as imperfect effects, and as connected with him by a shorter chain of consequences than any of those, by which we learn the reality of his existence.

Suppose, that the son of a friend, who had been long dead or absent, were presented to us; it is evident, that this object would instantly revive its correlative idea, and recall to our thoughts all past intimacies and familiarities, in more lively colours than they would otherwise have appeared to us. This is another phenomenon, which seems to prove the principle above mentioned.

---

* 'Naturane nobis, inquit, datum dicam, an errore quodam, ut, cum ea loca videamus, in quibus memoria dignos viros acceperimus multum esse versatos, magis moveamur, quam siquando eorum ipsorum aut facta audiamus aut scriptum aliquod legamus? Velut ego nunc moveor. Venit enim mihi Plato in mentem, quem accepimus primum hic disputare solitum: cuius etiam illi hortuli propinqui non memoriam solum mihi afferunt, sed ipsum videntur in conspectu meo hic ponere. Hic Speusippus, hic Xenocrates, hic eius auditor Polemo; cuius ipsa illa sessio fuit, quam videmus. Equidem etiam curiam nostram, Hostiliam dico, non hanc novam, quae mihi minor esse videtur postquam est maior, solebam intuens, Scipionem, Catonem, Laelium, nostrum vero in primis avum cogitare. Tanta vis admonitionis est in locis; ut non sine causa ex his memoriae deducta sit disciplina.' Cicero *de Finibus*. Lib. v

44. We may observe, that, in these phenomena, the belief of the correlative object is always presupposed; without which the relation could have no effect. The influence of the picture supposes, that we *believe* our friend to have once existed. Contiguity to home can never excite our ideas of home, unless we *believe* that it really exists. Now I assert, that this belief, where it reaches beyond the memory or senses, is of a similar nature, and arises from similar causes, with the transition of thought and vivacity of conception here explained. When I throw a piece of dry wood into a fire, my mind is immediately carried to conceive, that it augments, not extinguishes the flame. This transition of thought from the cause to the effect proceeds not from reason. It derives its origin altogether from custom and experience. And as it first begins from an object, present to the senses, it renders the idea or conception of flame more strong and lively than any loose, floating reverie of the imagination. That idea arises immediately. The thought moves instantly towards it, and conveys to it all that force of conception, which is derived from the impression present to the senses. When a sword is levelled at my breast, does not the idea of wound and pain strike me more strongly, than when a glass of wine is presented to me, even though by accident this idea should occur after the appearance of the latter object? But what is there in this whole matter to cause such a strong conception, except only a present object and a customary transition to the idea of another object, which we have been accustomed to conjoin with the former? This is the whole operation of the mind, in all our conclusions concerning matter of fact and existence; and it is a satisfaction to find some analogies, by which it may be explained. The transition from a present object does in all cases give strength and solidity to the related idea.

Here, then, is a kind of pre-established harmony between the course of nature and the succession of our ideas; and though the powers and forces, by which the former is governed, be wholly unknown to us; yet our thoughts and conceptions have still, we find, gone on in the same train with the other works of nature. Custom is that principle, by which this correspondence has been effected; so necessary to the subsistence of our species, and the regulation of our conduct, in every circumstance and occurrence of human life. Had not the presence of an object instantly excited the idea of those objects, commonly conjoined with it, all our knowledge must have been limited to the narrow sphere of our memory and senses; and we should never have been able to adjust means to ends, or employ our natural powers, either to the producing of good, or avoiding of evil. Those, who delight in the discovery and contemplation of *final causes*, have here ample subject to employ their wonder and admiration.

45. I shall add, for a further confirmation of the foregoing theory, that, as this operation of the mind, by which we infer like effects from like causes, and *vice versa*, is so essential to the subsistence of all human creatures, it is not probable, that it could be trusted to the fallacious deductions of our reason, which is slow in its operations; appears not, in any degree, during the first years of infancy; and at best is, in every age and period of human life, extremely liable to error and mistake. It is more conformable to the ordinary wisdom of nature to secure so necessary an act of the mind, by some instinct or mechanical tendency, which may be infallible in its operations, may discover itself at the first appearance of life and thought, and may be independent of all the laboured deductions of the understanding. As nature has taught us the use of our limbs, without giving us the knowledge of the muscles and nerves, by which they are actuated; so has she implanted in us an instinct, which carries forward the thought in a correspondent course to that which she has established among external objects; though we are ignorant of those powers and forces, on which this regular course and succession of objects totally depends.

SECTION SIX
*Of probability**

46. Though there be no such thing as *Chance* in the world; our ignorance of the real cause of any event has the same influence on the understanding, and begets a like species of belief or opinion.

There is certainly a probability, which arises from a superiority of chances on any side; and according as this superiority increases, and surpasses the opposite chances, the probability receives a proportionable increase, and begets still a higher degree of belief or assent to that side, in which we discover the superiority. If a die were marked with one figure or number of spots on four sides, and with another figure or number of spots on the two remaining sides, it would be more probable, that the former would turn up than the latter; though, if it had a thousand sides marked in the same manner, and only one side different, the probability would be much higher, and our belief or expectation of the event more steady and secure. This process of the thought or reasoning may seem trivial and obvious; but to those who consider it more narrowly, it may, perhaps, afford matter for curious speculation.

It seems evident, that, when the mind looks forward to discover the event, which may result from the throw of such a die, it considers the turning up of each particular side as alike probable; and this is the very nature of chance, to render all the particular events, comprehended in it, entirely equal. But finding a greater number of sides concur in the one event than in the other, the mind is carried more frequently to that event, and meets it oftener, in revolving the various possibilities or chances, on which the ultimate result depends. This concurrence of several views in one

* Mr Locke divides all arguments into demonstrative and probable. In this view, we must say, that it is only probable all men must die, or that the sun will rise to-morrow. But to conform our language more to common use, we ought to divide arguments into *demonstrations*, *proofs*, and *probabilities*. By proofs meaning such arguments from experience as leave no room for doubt or opposition.

particular event begets immediately, by an inexplicable contrivance of nature, the sentiment of belief, and gives that event the advantage over its antagonist, which is supported by a smaller number of views, and recurs less frequently to the mind. If we allow, that belief is nothing but a firmer and stronger conception of an object than what attends the mere fictions of the imagination, this operation may, perhaps, in some measure, be accounted for. The concurrence of these several views or glimpses imprints the idea more strongly on the imagination; gives it superior force and vigour; renders its influence on the passions and affections more sensible; and in a word, begets that reliance or security, which constitutes the nature of belief and opinion.

47. The case is the same with the probability of causes, as with that of chance. There are some causes, which are entirely uniform and constant in producing a particular effect; and no instance has ever yet been found of any failure or irregularity in their operation. Fire has always burned, and water suffocated every human creature: the production of motion by impulse and gravity is an universal law, which has hitherto admitted of no exception. But there are other causes, which have been found more irregular and uncertain; nor has rhubarb always proved a purge, or opium a soporific to every one, who has taken these medicines. It is true, when any cause fails of producing its usual effect, philosophers ascribe not this to any irregularity in nature; but suppose, that some secret causes, in the particular structure of parts, have prevented the operation. Our reasonings, however, and conclusions concerning the event are the same as if this principle had no place. Being determined by custom to transfer the past to the future, in all our inferences; where the past has been entirely regular and uniform, we expect the event with the greatest assurance, and leave no room for any contrary supposition. But where different effects have been found to follow from causes, which are to *appearance* exactly similar, all these various effects must occur to the mind in transferring the past to the future, and enter into our consideration, when we determine the probability of the event. Though we give the preference to that which has been found most usual, and believe that this effect will exist, we must not overlook the other effects, but must assign to each of them a particular weight and authority, in proportion as we have found it

to be more or less frequent. It is more probable, in almost every country of Europe, that there will be frost sometime in January, than that the weather will continue open throughout that whole month; though this probability varies according to the different climates, and approaches to a certainty in the more northern kingdoms. Here then it seems evident, that, when we transfer the past to the future, in order to determine the effect, which will result from any cause, we transfer all the different events, in the same proportion as they have appeared in the past, and conceive one to have existed a hundred times, for instance, another ten times, and another once. As a great number of views do here concur in one event, they fortify and confirm it to the imagination, beget that sentiment which we call *belief*, and give its object the preference above the contrary event, which is not supported by an equal number of experiments, and recurs not so frequently to the thought in transferring the past to the future. Let any one try to account for this operation of the mind upon any of the received systems of philosophy, and he will be sensible of the difficulty. For my part, I shall think it sufficient, if the present hints excite the curiosity of philosophers, and make them sensible how defective all common theories are in treating of such curious and such sublime subjects.

SECTION SEVEN
Of the idea of necessary connexion

Part I

48. The great advantage of the mathematical sciences above the moral consists in this, that the ideas of the former, being sensible, are always clear and determinate, the smallest distinction between them is immediately perceptible, and the same terms are still expressive of the same ideas, without ambiguity or variation. An oval is never mistaken for a circle, nor an hyperbola for an ellipsis. The isosceles and scalenum are distinguished by boundaries more exact than vice and virtue, right and wrong. If any term be defined in geometry, the mind readily, of itself, substitutes, on all occasions, the definition for the term defined: or even when no definition is employed, the object itself may be presented to the senses, and by that means be steadily and clearly apprehended. But the finer sentiments of the mind, the operations of the understanding, the various agitations of the passions, though really in themselves distinct, easily escape us, when surveyed by reflection; nor is it in our power to recall the original object, as often as we have occasion to contemplate it. Ambiguity, by this means, is gradually introduced into our reasonings: Similar objects are readily taken to be the same: and the conclusion becomes at last very wide of the premises.

One may safely, however, affirm, that, if we consider these sciences in a proper light, their advantages and disadvantages nearly compensate each other, and reduce both of them to a state of equality. If the mind, with greater facility, retains the ideas of geometry clear and determinate, it must carry on a much longer and more intricate chain of reasoning, and compare ideas much wider of each other, in order to reach the abstruser truths of that science. And if moral ideas are apt, without extreme care, to fall into obscurity and confusion, the inferences are always much shorter in these disquisitions, and the intermediate steps, which lead to the conclusion, much fewer than in the sciences which treat of quantity and number. In reality, there is scarcely a proposition in Euclid so simple, as not to consist of more parts, than are to be found in any moral reasoning which runs not into chimera and conceit. Where we trace the principles of the human mind through a few steps, we may be very well satisfied with our progress; considering how soon nature throws a bar to all our enquiries concerning causes, and reduces us to an acknowledgment of our ignorance. The chief obstacle, therefore, to our improvement in the moral or metaphysical sciences is the obscurity of the ideas, and ambiguity of the terms. The principal difficulty in the mathematics is the length of inferences and compass of thought, requisite to the forming of any conclusion. And, perhaps, our progress in natural philosophy is chiefly retarded by the want of proper experiments and phenomena, which are often discovered by chance, and cannot always be found, when requisite, even by the most diligent and prudent enquiry. As moral philosophy seems hitherto to have received less improvement than either geometry or physics, we may conclude, that, if there be any difference in this respect among these sciences, the difficulties, which obstruct the progress of the former, require superior care and capacity to be surmounted.

49. There are no ideas, which occur in metaphysics, more obscure and uncertain, than those of *power, force, energy* or *necessary connexion*, of which it is every moment necessary for us to treat in all our disquisitions. We shall, therefore, endeavour, in this section, to fix, if possible, the precise meaning of these terms, and thereby remove some part of that obscurity, which is so much complained of in this species of philosophy.

It seems a proposition, which will not admit of much dispute, that all our ideas are nothing but copies of our impressions, or, in other words, that it is impossible for us to *think* of any thing, which we have not antecedently *felt*, either by our external or internal senses. I have endeavoured* to explain and prove this proposition, and have expressed my hopes, that, by a proper

* Section 2.

application of it, men may reach a greater clearness and precision in philosophical reasonings, than what they have hitherto been able to attain. Complex ideas may, perhaps, be well known by definition, which is nothing but an enumeration of those parts or simple ideas, that compose them. But when we have pushed up definitions to the most simple ideas, and find still some ambiguity and obscurity; what resource are we then possessed of? By what invention can we throw light upon these ideas, and render them altogether precise and determinate to our intellectual view? Produce the impressions or original sentiments, from which the ideas are copied. These impressions are all strong and sensible. They admit not of ambiguity. They are not only placed in a full light themselves, but may throw light on their correspondent ideas, which lie in obscurity. And by this means, we may, perhaps, attain a new microscope or species of optics, by which, in the moral sciences, the most minute, and most simple ideas may be so enlarged as to fall readily under our apprehension, and be equally known with the grossest and most sensible ideas, that can be the object of our enquiry.

50. To be fully acquainted, therefore, with the idea of power or necessary connexion, let us examine its impression; and in order to find the impression with greater certainty, let us search for it in all the sources, from which it may possibly be derived.

When we look about us towards external objects, and consider the operation of causes, we are never able, in a single instance, to discover any power or necessary connexion; any quality, which binds the effect to the cause, and renders the one an infallible consequence of the other. We only find, that the one does actually, in fact, follow the other. The impulse of one billiard-ball is attended with motion in the second. This is the whole that appears to the *outward* senses. The mind feels no sentiment or *inward* impression from this succession of objects: consequently, there is not, in any single, particular instance of cause and effect, any thing which can suggest the idea of power or necessary connexion.

From the first appearance of an object, we never can conjecture what effect will result from it. But were the power or energy of any cause discoverable by the mind, we could foresee the effect, even without experience; and might, at first, pronounce with certainty concerning it, by mere dint of thought and reasoning.

In reality, there is no part of matter, that does ever, by its sensible qualities, discover any power or energy, or give us ground to imagine, that it could produce any thing, or be followed by any other object, which we could denominate its effect. Solidity, extension, motion; these qualities are all complete in themselves, and never point out any other event which may result from them. The scenes of the universe are continually shifting, and one object follows another in an uninterrupted succession; but the power or force, which actuates the whole machine, is entirely concealed from us, and never discovers itself in any of the sensible qualities of body. We know, that, in fact, heat is a constant attendant of flame; but what is the connexion between them, we have no room so much as to conjecture or imagine. It is impossible, therefore, that the idea of power can be derived from the contemplation of bodies, in single instances of their operation; because no bodies ever discover any power, which can be the original of this idea.*

51. Since, therefore, external objects as they appear to the senses, give us no idea of power or necessary connexion, by their operation in particular instances, let us see, whether this idea be derived from reflection on the operations of our own minds, and be copied from any internal impression. It may be said, that we are every moment conscious of internal power; while we feel that, by the simple command of our will, we can move the organs of our body, or direct the faculties of our mind. An act of volition produces motion in our limbs, or raises a new idea in our imagination. This influence of the will we know by consciousness. Hence we acquire the idea of power or energy; and are certain, that we ourselves and all other intelligent beings are possessed of power. This idea, then, is an idea of reflection, since it arises from reflecting on the operations of our own mind, and on the command which is exercised by will, both over the organs of the body and faculties of the soul.

52. We shall proceed to examine this pretension; and first with regard to the influence of volition over the organs of the body.

* Mr Locke, in his chapter of power, says that, finding from experience, that there are several new productions in nature, and concluding that there must somewhere be a power capable of producing them, we arrive at last by this reasoning at the idea of power. But no reasoning can ever give us a new, original, simple idea; as this philosopher himself confesses. This, therefore, can never be the origin of that idea.

This influence, we may observe, is a fact, which, like all other natural events, can be known only by experience, and can never be foreseen from any apparent energy or power in the cause, which connects it with the effect, and renders the one an infallible consequence of the other. The motion of our body follows upon the command of our will. Of this we are every moment conscious. But the means, by which this is effected; the energy, by which the will performs so extraordinary an operation; of this we are so far from being immediately conscious, that it must for ever escape our most diligent enquiry.

For *first*; Is there any principle in all nature more mysterious than the union of soul with body; by which a supposed spiritual substance acquires such an influence over a material one, that the most refined thought is able to actuate the grossest matter? Were we empowered, by a secret wish, to remove mountains, or control the planets in their orbit; this extensive authority would not be more extraordinary, nor more beyond our comprehension. But if by consciousness we perceived any power or energy in the will, we must know this power; we must know its connexion with the effect; we must know the secret union of soul and body, and the nature of both these substances; by which the one is able to operate, in so many instances, upon the other.

Secondly, We are not able to move all the organs of the body with a like authority; though we cannot assign any reason besides experience, for so remarkable a difference between one and the other. Why has the will an influence over the tongue and fingers, not over the heart or liver? This question would never embarrass us, were we conscious of a power in the former case, not in the latter. We should then perceive, independent of experience, why the authority of will over the organs of the body is circumscribed within such particular limits. Being in that case fully acquainted with the power or force, by which it operates, we should also know, why its influence reaches precisely to such boundaries, and no farther.

A man, suddenly struck with palsy in the leg or arm, or who had newly lost those members, frequently endeavours, at first, to move them, and employ them in their usual offices. Here he is as much conscious of power to command such limbs, as a man in perfect health is conscious of power to actuate any member which remains in its natural state and condition. But consciousness never deceives. Consequently, neither in the one case nor in the other, are we ever conscious of any power. We learn the influence of our will from experience alone. And experience only teaches us, how one event constantly follows another; without instructing us in the secret connexion, which binds them together, and renders them inseparable.

Thirdly, We learn from anatomy, that the immediate object of power in voluntary motion, is not the member itself which is moved, but certain muscles, and nerves, and animal spirits, and, perhaps, something still more minute and more unknown, through which the motion is successively propagated, ere it reach the member itself whose motion is the immediate object of volition. Can there be a more certain proof, that the power, by which this whole operation is performed, so far from being directly and fully known by an inward sentiment or consciousness, is, to the last degree, mysterious and unintelligible? Here the mind wills a certain event: immediately another event, unknown to ourselves, and totally different from the one intended, is produced: this event produces another, equally unknown: till at last, through a long succession, the desired event is produced. But if the original power were felt, it must be known: were it known, its effect also must be known; since all power is relative to its effect. And *vice versa*, if the effect be not known, the power cannot be known nor felt. How indeed can we be conscious of a power to move our limbs, when we have no such power; but only that to move certain animal spirits, which, though they produce at last the motion of our limbs, yet operate in such a manner as is wholly beyond our comprehension?

We may, therefore, conclude from the whole, I hope, without any temerity, though with assurance; that our idea of power is not copied from any sentiment or consciousness of power within ourselves, when we give rise to animal motion, or apply our limbs to their proper use and office. That their motion follows the command of the will is a matter of common experience, like other natural events: but the power or energy by which this is effected, like that in other natural events, is unknown and inconceivable.*

* It may be pretended, that the resistance which we meet with in bodies, obliging us frequently to exert our force, and call up all our power, this gives us the idea of force and power. It is this *nisus*, or strong endeavour, of which we are conscious, that is the original impression from which this idea is copied.

53. Shall we then assert, that we are conscious of a power or energy in our own minds, when, by an act or command of our will, we raise up a new idea, fix the mind to the contemplation of it, turn it on all sides, and at last dismiss it for some other idea, when we think that we have surveyed it with sufficient accuracy? I believe the same arguments will prove, that even this command of the will gives us no real idea of force or energy.

First, It must be allowed, that, when we know a power, we know that very circumstance in the cause, by which it is enabled to produce the effect: for these are supposed to be synonymous. We must, therefore, know both the cause and effect, and the relation between them. But do we pretend to be acquainted with the nature of the human soul and the nature of an idea, or the aptitude of the one to produce the other? This is a real creation; a production of something out of nothing: which implies a power so great, that it may seem, at first sight, beyond the reach of any being, less than infinite. At least it must be owned, that such a power is not felt, nor known, nor even conceivable by the mind. We only feel the event, namely, the existence of an idea, consequent to a command of the will: but the manner, in which this operation is performed, the power by which it is produced, is entirely beyond our comprehension.

Secondly, The command of the mind over itself is limited, as well as its command over the body; and these limits are not known by reason, or any acquaintance with the nature of cause and effect, but only by experience and observation, as in all other natural events and in the operation of external objects. Our authority over our sentiments and passions is much weaker than that over our ideas; and even the latter authority is circumscribed within very narrow boundaries. Will any one pretend to assign the ultimate

---

But, first, we attribute power to a vast number of objects, where we never can suppose this resistance or exertion of force to take place; to the Supreme Being, who never meets with any resistance; to the mind in its command over its ideas and limbs, in common thinking and motion, where the effect follows immediately upon the will, without any exertion or summoning up of force; to inanimate matter, which is not capable of this sentiment. *Secondly*, This sentiment of an endeavour to overcome resistance has no known connexion with any event: what follows it, we know by experience; but could not know it *a priori*. It must, however, be confessed, that the animal *nisus* which we experience, though it can afford no accurate precise idea of power, enters very much into that vulgar, inaccurate idea, which is formed of it.

reason of these boundaries, or show why the power is deficient in one case, not in another?

Thirdly, This self-command is very different at different times. A man in health possesses more of it than one languishing with sickness. We are more master of our thoughts in the morning than in the evening: fasting, than after a full meal. Can we give any reason for these variations, except experience? Where then is the power, of which we pretend to be conscious? Is there not here, either in a spiritual or material substance, or both, some secret mechanism or structure of parts, upon which the effect depends, and which, being entirely unknown to us, renders the power or energy of the will equally unknown and incomprehensible?

Volition is surely an act of the mind, with which we are sufficiently acquainted. Reflect upon it. Consider it on all sides. Do you find anything in it like this creative power, by which it raises from nothing a new idea, and with a kind of *Fiat*, imitates the omnipotence of its Maker, if I may be allowed so to speak, who called forth into existence all the various scenes of nature? So far from being conscious of this energy in the will, it requires as certain experience as that of which we are possessed, to convince us that such extraordinary effects do ever result from a simple act of volition.

54. The generality of mankind never find any difficulty in accounting for the more common and familiar operations of nature – such as the descent of heavy bodies, the growth of plants, the generation of animals, or the nourishment of bodies by food: but suppose that, in all these cases, they perceive the very force or energy of the cause, by which it is connected with its effect, and is for ever infallible in its operation. They acquire, by long habit, such a turn of mind, that, upon the appearance of the cause, they immediately expect with assurance its usual attendant, and hardly conceive it possible that any other event could result from it. It is only on the discovery of extraordinary phenomena, such as earthquakes, pestilence, and prodigies of any kind, that they find themselves at a loss to assign a proper cause, and to explain the manner in which the effect is produced by it. It is usual for men, in such difficulties, to have recourse to some invisible intelligent principle* as the immediate cause of that event which surprises

* θεὸς ἀπὸ μηχανῆς.

them, and which, they think, cannot be accounted for from the common powers of nature. But philosophers, who carry their scrutiny a little farther, immediately perceive that, even in the most familiar events, the energy of the cause is as unintelligible as in the most unusual, and that we only learn by experience the frequent *Conjunction* of objects, without being ever able to comprehend anything like *Connexion* between them.

55. Here, then, many philosophers think themselves obliged by reason to have recourse, on all occasions, to the same principle, which the vulgar never appeal to but in cases that appear miraculous and supernatural. They acknowledge mind and intelligence to be, not only the ultimate and original cause of all things, but the immediate and sole cause of every event which appears in nature. They pretend that those objects which are commonly denominated *causes*, are in reality nothing but *occasions*; and that the true and direct principle of every effect is not any power or force in nature, but a volition of the Supreme Being, who wills that such particular objects should for ever be conjoined with each other. Instead of saying that one billiard-ball moves another by a force which it has derived from the author of nature, it is the Deity himself, they say, who, by a particular volition, moves the second ball, being determined to this operation by the impulse of the first ball, in consequence of those general laws which he has laid down to himself in the government of the universe. But philosophers advancing still in their inquiries, discover that, as we are totally ignorant of the power on which depends the mutual operation of bodies, we are no less ignorant of that power on which depends the operation of mind on body, or of body on mind; nor are we able, either from our senses or consciousness, to assign the ultimate principle in one case more than in the other. The same ignorance, therefore, reduces them to the same conclusion. They assert that the Deity is the immediate cause of the union between soul and body; and that they are not the organs of sense, which, being agitated by external objects, produce sensations in the mind; but that it is a particular volition of our omnipotent Maker, which excites such a sensation, in consequence of such a motion in the organ. In like manner, it is not any energy in the will that produces local motion in our members: it is God himself, who is pleased to second our will, in itself impotent, and to command

that motion which we erroneously attribute to our own power and efficacy. Nor do philosophers stop at this conclusion. They sometimes extend the same inference to the mind itself, in its internal operations. Our mental vision or conception of ideas is nothing but a revelation made to us by our Maker. When we voluntarily turn our thoughts to any object, and raise up its image in the fancy, it is not the will which creates that idea: it is the universal Creator, who discovers it to the mind, and renders it present to us.

56. Thus, according to these philosophers, every thing is full of God. Not content with the principle, that nothing exists but by his will, that nothing possesses any power but by his concession, they rob nature, and all created beings, of every power, in order to render their dependence on the Deity still more sensible and immediate. They consider not that, by this theory, they diminish, instead of magnifying, the grandeur of those attributes, which they affect so much to celebrate. It argues surely more power in the Deity to delegate a certain degree of power to inferior creatures than to produce every thing by his own immediate volition. It argues more wisdom to contrive at first the fabric of the world with such perfect foresight that, of itself, and by its proper operation, it may serve all the purposes of providence, than if the great Creator were obliged every moment to adjust its parts, and animate by his breath all the wheels of that stupendous machine.

But if we would have a more philosophical confutation of this theory, perhaps the two following reflections may suffice.

57. *First*, it seems to me that this theory of the universal energy and operation of the Supreme Being is too bold ever to carry conviction with it to a man, sufficiently apprized of the weakness of human reason, and the narrow limits to which it is confined in all its operations. Though the chain of arguments which conduct to it were ever so logical, there must arise a strong suspicion, if not an absolute assurance, that it has carried us quite beyond the reach of our faculties, when it leads to conclusions so extraordinary, and so remote from common life and experience. We are got into fairy land, long ere we have reached the last steps of our theory; and *there* we have no reason to trust our common methods of argument, or to think that our usual analogies and probabilities have any authority. Our line is too short to fathom such immense

abysses. And however we may flatter ourselves that we are guided, in every step which we take, by a kind of verisimilitude and experience, we may be assured that this fancied experience has no authority when we thus apply it to subjects that lie entirely out of the sphere of experience. But on this we shall have occasion to touch afterwards.*

Secondly, I cannot perceive any force in the arguments on which this theory is founded. We are ignorant, it is true, of the manner in which bodies operate on each other: their force or energy is entirely incomprehensible: but are we not equally ignorant of the manner or force by which a mind, even the supreme mind, operates either on itself or on body? Whence, I beseech you, do we acquire any idea of it? We have no sentiment or consciousness of this power in ourselves. We have no idea of the Supreme Being but what we learn from reflection on our own faculties. Were our ignorance, therefore, a good reason for rejecting any thing, we should be led into that principle of denying all energy in the Supreme Being as much as in the grossest matter. We surely comprehend as little the operations of one as of the other. Is it more difficult to conceive that motion may arise from impulse than that it may arise from volition? All we know is our profound ignorance in both cases.†

---

* Section 12.

† I need not examine at length the *vis inertiae* which is so much talked of in the new philosophy, and which is ascribed to matter. We find by experience, that a body at rest or in motion continues for ever in its present state, till put from it by some new cause; and that a body impelled takes as much motion from the impelling body as it acquires itself. These are facts. When we call this a *vis inertiae*, we only mark these facts, without pretending to have any idea of the inert power; in the same manner as, when we talk of gravity, we mean certain effects, without comprehending that active power. It was never the meaning of Sir ISAAC NEWTON to rob second causes of all force or energy; though some of his followers have endeavoured to establish that theory upon his authority. On the contrary, that great philosopher had recourse to an etherial active fluid to explain his universal attraction; though he was so cautious and modest as to allow, that it was a mere hypothesis, not to be insisted on, without more experiments. I must confess, that there is something in the fate of opinions a little extraordinary. DES CARTES insinuated that doctrine of the universal and sole efficacy of the Deity, without insisting on it. MALEBRANCHE and other CARTESIANS made it the foundation of all their philosophy. It had, however, no authority in England. LOCKE, CLARKE, and CUDWORTH, never so much as take notice of it, but suppose all along, that matter has a real, though subordinate and derived power. By what means has it become so prevalent among our modern metaphysicians?

Part 2

58. But to hasten to a conclusion of this argument, which is already drawn out to too great a length: we have sought in vain for an idea of power or necessary connexion in all the sources from which we could suppose it to be derived. It appears that, in single instances of the operation of bodies, we never can, by our utmost scrutiny, discover any thing but one event following another, without being able to comprehend any force or power by which the cause operates, or any connexion between it and its supposed effect. The same difficulty occurs in contemplating the operations of mind on body – where we observe the motion of the latter to follow upon the volition of the former, but are not able to observe or conceive the tie which binds together the motion and volition, or the energy by which the mind produces this effect. The authority of the will over its own faculties and ideas is not a whit more comprehensible: so that, upon the whole, there appears not, throughout all nature, any one instance of connexion which is conceivable by us. All events seem entirely loose and separate. One event follows another; but we never can observe any tie between them. They seem *conjoined*, but never *connected*. And as we can have no idea of any thing which never appeared to our outward sense or inward sentiment, the necessary conclusion *seems* to be that we have no idea of connexion or power at all, and that these words are absolutely without any meaning, when employed either in philosophical reasonings or common life.

59. But there still remains one method of avoiding this conclusion, and one source which we have not yet examined. When any natural object or event is presented, it is impossible for us, by any sagacity or penetration, to discover, or even conjecture, without experience, what event will result from it, or to carry our foresight beyond that object which is immediately present to the memory and senses. Even after one instance or experiment where we have observed a particular event to follow upon another, we are not entitled to form a general rule, or foretell what will happen in like cases; it being justly esteemed an unpardonable temerity to judge of the whole course of nature from one single experiment, however accurate or certain. But when one particular species of

event has always, in all instances, been conjoined with another, we make no longer any scruple of foretelling one upon the appearance of the other, and of employing that reasoning, which can alone assure us of any matter of fact or existence. We then call the one object, *Cause*; the other, *Effect*. We suppose that there is some connexion between them; some power in the one, by which it infallibly produces the other, and operates with the greatest certainty and strongest necessity.

It appears, then, that this idea of a necessary connexion among events arises from a number of similar instances which occur of the constant conjunction of these events; nor can that idea ever be suggested by any one of these instances, surveyed in all possible lights and positions. But there is nothing in a number of instances, different from every single instance, which is supposed to be exactly similar; except only, that after a repetition of similar instances, the mind is carried by habit, upon the appearance of one event, to expect its usual attendant, and to believe that it will exist. This connexion, therefore, which we *feel* in the mind, this customary transition of the imagination from one object to its usual attendant, is the sentiment or impression from which we form the idea of power or necessary connexion. Nothing farther is in the case. Contemplate the subject on all sides; you will never find any other origin of that idea. This is the sole difference between one instance, from which we can never receive the idea of connexion, and a number of similar instances, by which it is suggested. The first time a man saw the communication of motion by impulse, as by the shock of two billiard balls, he could not pronounce that the one event was *connected*: but only that it was *conjoined* with the other. After he has observed several instances of this nature, he then pronounces them to be *connected*. What alteration has happened to give rise to this new idea of *connexion*? Nothing but that he now *feels* these events to be connected in his imagination, and can readily foretell the existence of one from the appearance of the other. When we say, therefore, that one object is connected with another, we mean only that they have acquired a connexion in our thought, and give rise to this inference, by which they become proofs of each other's existence: a conclusion which is somewhat extraordinary, but which seems founded on sufficient evidence. Nor will its evidence be weakened by any general diffidence of the understanding, or sceptical suspicion concerning every conclusion which is new and extraordinary. No conclusions can be more agreeable to scepticism than such as make discoveries concerning the weakness and narrow limits of human reason and capacity.

60. And what stronger instance can be produced of the surprising ignorance and weakness of the understanding than the present? For surely, if there be any relation among objects which it imports to us to know perfectly, it is that of cause and effect. On this are founded all our reasonings concerning matter of fact or existence. By means of it alone we attain any assurance concerning objects which are removed from the present testimony of our memory and senses. The only immediate utility of all sciences, is to teach us, how to control and regulate future events by their causes. Our thoughts and enquiries are, therefore, every moment, employed about this relation: yet so imperfect are the ideas which we form concerning it, that it is impossible to give any just definition of cause, except what is drawn from something extraneous and foreign to it. Similar objects are always conjoined with similar. Of this we have experience. Suitably to this experience, therefore, we may define a cause to be *an object, followed by another, and where all the objects similar to the first are followed by objects similar to the second.* Or in other words *where, if the first object had not been, the second never had existed.* The appearance of a cause always conveys the mind, by a customary transition, to the idea of the effect. Of this also we have experience. We may, therefore, suitably to this experience, form another definition of cause, and call it, *an object followed by another, and whose appearance always conveys the thought to that other.* But though both these definitions be drawn from circumstances foreign to the cause, we cannot remedy this inconvenience, or attain any more perfect definition, which may point out that circumstance in the cause, which gives it a connexion with its effect. We have no idea of this connexion, nor even any distinct notion what it is we desire to know, when we endeavour at a conception of it. We say, for instance, that the vibration of this string is the cause of this particular sound. But what do we mean by that affirmation? We either mean *that this vibration is followed by this sound, and that all similar vibrations have been followed by similar sounds*: or, *that this*

vibration is followed by this sound, and that upon the appearance of one the mind anticipates the senses, and forms immediately an idea of the other. We may consider the relation of cause and effect in either of these two lights; but beyond these, we have no idea of it.*

61. To recapitulate, therefore, the reasonings of this section: every idea is copied from some preceding impression or sentiment; and where we cannot find any impression, we may be certain that there is no idea. In all single instances of the operation of bodies or minds, there is nothing that produces any impression, nor consequently can suggest any idea, of power or necessary connexion. But when many uniform instances appear, and the same object is always followed by the same event; we then begin to entertain the notion of cause and connexion. We then *feel* a new sentiment or impression, to wit, a customary connexion in the thought or imagination between one object and its usual attendant; and this sentiment is the original of that idea which we seek for. For as this idea arises from a number of similar

---

* According to these explications and definitions, the idea of *power* is relative as much as that of *cause*; and both have a reference to an effect, or some other event constantly conjoined with the former. When we consider the *unknown* circumstance of an object, by which the degree or quantity of its effect is fixed and determined, we call that its power: And accordingly, it is allowed by all philosophers, that the effect is the measure of the power. But if they had any idea of power, as it is in itself, why could not they measure it in itself? The dispute whether the force of a body in motion be as its velocity, or the square of its velocity; this dispute, I say, need not be decided by comparing its effects in equal or unequal times; but by a direct mensuration and comparison.

As to the frequent use of the words, Force, Power, Energy, &c. which every where occur in common conversation, as well as in philosophy; that is no proof, that we are acquainted, in any instance, with the connecting principle between cause and effect, or can account ultimately for the production of one thing to another. These words, as commonly used, have very loose meanings annexed to them; and their ideas are very uncertain and confused. No animal can put external bodies in motion without the sentiment of a *nisus* or endeavour; and every animal has a sentiment or feeling from the stroke or blow of an external object, that is in motion. These sensations, which are merely animal, and from which we can *a priori* draw no inference, we are apt to transfer to inanimate objects, and to suppose, that they have some such feelings, whenever they transfer or receive motion. With regard to energies, which are exerted, without our annexing to them any idea of communicated motion, we consider only the constant experienced conjunction of the events; and as we *feel* a customary connexion between the ideas, we transfer that feeling to the objects; as nothing is more usual than to apply to external bodies every internal sensation, which they occasion.

instances, and not from any single instance, it must arise from that circumstance, in which the number of instances differ from every individual instance. But this customary connexion or transition of the imagination is the only circumstance in which they differ. In every other particular they are alike. The first instance which we saw of motion communicated by the shock of two billiard balls (to return to this obvious illustration) is exactly similar to any instance that may, at present, occur to us; except only, that we could not, at first, *infer* one event from the other; which we are enabled to do at present, after so long a course of uniform experience. I know not whether the reader will readily apprehend this reasoning. I am afraid that, should I multiply words about it, or throw it into a greater variety of lights, it would only become more obscure and intricate. In all abstract reasonings there is one point of view which, if we can happily hit, we shall go farther towards illustrating the subject than by all the eloquence and copious expression in the world. This point of view we should endeavour to reach, and reserve the flowers of rhetoric for subjects which are more adapted to them.

Of liberty and necessity

Part I

62. It might reasonably be expected in questions which have been canvassed and disputed with great eagerness, since the first origin of science and philosophy, that the meaning of all the terms, at least, should have been agreed upon among the disputants; and our enquiries, in the course of two thousand years, been able to pass from words to the true and real subject of the controversy. For how easy may it seem to give exact definitions of the terms employed in reasoning, and make these definitions, not the mere sound of words, the object of future scrutiny and examination? But if we consider the matter more narrowly, we shall be apt to draw a quite opposite conclusion. From this circumstance alone, that a controversy has been long kept on foot, and remains still undecided, we may presume that there is some ambiguity in the expression, and that the disputants affix different ideas to the terms employed in the controversy. For as the faculties of the mind are supposed to be naturally alike in every individual; otherwise nothing could be more fruitless than to reason or dispute together; it were impossible, if men affix the same ideas to their terms, that they could so long form different opinions of the same subject; especially when they communicate their views, and each party turn themselves on all sides, in search of arguments which may give them the victory over their antagonists. It is true, if men attempt the discussion of questions which lie entirely beyond the reach of human capacity, such as those concerning the origin of worlds, or the economy of the intellectual system or region of spirits, they may long beat the air in their fruitless contests, and never arrive at any determinate conclusion. But if the question regard any subject of common life and experience, nothing, one

would think, could preserve the dispute so long undecided but some ambiguous expressions, which keep the antagonists still at a distance, and hinder them from grappling with each other.

63. This has been the case in the long disputed question concerning liberty and necessity; and to so remarkable a degree that, if I be not much mistaken, we shall find, that all mankind, both learned and ignorant, have always been of the same opinion with regard to this subject, and that a few intelligible definitions would immediately have put an end to the whole controversy. I own that this dispute has been so much canvassed on all hands, and has led philosophers into such a labyrinth of obscure sophistry, that it is no wonder, if a sensible reader indulge his ease so far as to turn a deaf ear to the proposal of such a question, from which he can expect neither instruction or entertainment. But the state of the argument here proposed may, perhaps, serve to renew his attention; as it has more novelty, promises at least some decision of the controversy, and will not much disturb his ease by any intricate or obscure reasoning.

I hope, therefore, to make it appear that all men have ever agreed in the doctrine both of necessity and of liberty, according to any reasonable sense, which can be put on these terms; and that the whole controversy has hitherto turned merely upon words. We shall begin with examining the doctrine of necessity.

64. It is universally allowed that matter, in all its operations, is actuated by a necessary force, and that every natural effect is so precisely determined by the energy of its cause that no other effect, in such particular circumstances, could possibly have resulted from it. The degree and direction of every motion is, by the laws of nature, prescribed with such exactness that a living creature may as soon arise from the shock of two bodies as motion in any other degree or direction than what is actually produced by it. Would we, therefore, form a just and precise idea of *necessity*, we must consider whence that idea arises when we apply it to the operation of bodies.

It seems evident that, if all the scenes of nature were continually shifted in such a manner that no two events bore any resemblance to each other, but every object was entirely new, without any similitude to whatever had been seen before, we should never, in that case, have attained the least idea of necessity, or of a connexion among these objects. We might say, upon such a supposition, that one object or event has followed another; not that one was produced by the other. The relation of cause and effect must be utterly unknown to mankind. Inference and reasoning concerning the operations of nature would, from that moment, be at an end; and the memory and senses remain the only canals, by which the knowledge of any real existence could possibly have access to the mind. Our idea, therefore, of necessity and causation arises entirely from the uniformity observable in the operations of nature, where similar objects are constantly conjoined together, and the mind is determined by custom to infer the one from the appearance of the other. These two circumstances form the whole of that necessity, which we ascribe to matter. Beyond the constant *conjunction* of similar objects, and the consequent *inference* from one to the other, we have no notion of any necessity or connexion.

If it appear, therefore, that all mankind have ever allowed, without any doubt or hesitation, that these two circumstances take place in the voluntary actions of men, and in the operations of mind; it must follow, that all mankind have ever agreed in the doctrine of necessity, and that they have hitherto disputed, merely for not understanding each other.

65. As to the first circumstance, the constant and regular conjunction of similar events, we may possibly satisfy ourselves by the following considerations. It is universally acknowledged that there is a great uniformity among the actions of men, in all nations and ages, and that human nature remains still the same, in its principles and operations. The same motives always produce the same actions. The same events follow from the same causes. Ambition, avarice, self-love, vanity, friendship, generosity, public spirit: these passions, mixed in various degrees, and distributed through society, have been, from the beginning of the world, and still are, the source of all the actions and enterprises, which have ever been observed among mankind. Would you know the sentiments, inclinations, and course of life of the Greeks and Romans? Study well the temper and actions of the French and English: you cannot be much mistaken in transferring to the former *most* of the observations which you have made with regard to the latter. Mankind are so much the same, in all times and places, that history informs us of nothing new or strange in this particular. Its chief use is only to discover the constant and universal principles of human

nature, by showing men in all varieties of circumstances and situations, and furnishing us with materials from which we may form our observations and become acquainted with the regular springs of human action and behaviour. These records of wars, intrigues, factions, and revolutions, are so many collections of experiments, by which the politician or moral philosopher fixes the principles of his science, in the same manner as the physician or natural philosopher becomes acquainted with the nature of plants, minerals, and other external objects, by the experiments which he forms concerning them. Nor are the earth, water, and other elements, examined by Aristotle, and Hippocrates, more like to those which at present lie under our observation than the men described by Polybius and Tacitus are to those who now govern the world.

Should a traveller, returning from a far country, bring us an account of men, wholly different from any with whom we were ever acquainted; men, who were entirely divested of avarice, ambition, or revenge; who knew no pleasure but friendship, generosity, and public spirit; we should immediately, from these circumstances, detect the falsehood, and prove him a liar, with the same certainty as if he had stuffed his narration with stories of centaurs and dragons, miracles and prodigies. And if we would explode any forgery in history, we cannot make use of a more convincing argument, than to prove, that the actions ascribed to any person are directly contrary to the course of nature, and that no human motives, in such circumstances, could ever induce him to such a conduct. The veracity of Quintus Curtius is as much to be suspected, when he describes the supernatural courage of Alexander, by which he was hurried on singly to attack multitudes, as when he describes his supernatural force and activity, by which he was able to resist them. So readily and universally do we acknowledge a uniformity in human motives and actions as well as in the operations of body.

Hence likewise the benefit of that experience, acquired by long life and a variety of business and company, in order to instruct us in the principles of human nature, and regulate our future conduct, as well as speculation. By means of this guide, we mount up to the knowledge of men's inclinations and motives, from their actions, expressions, and even gestures; and again descend to the interpretation of their actions from our knowledge of their motives and inclinations. The general observations treasured up by a course of experience, give us the clue of human nature, and teach us to unravel all its intricacies. Pretexts and appearances no longer deceive us. Public declarations pass for the specious colouring of a cause. And though virtue and honour be allowed their proper weight and authority, that perfect disinterestedness, so often pretended to, is never expected in multitudes and parties; seldom in their leaders; and scarcely even in individuals of any rank or station. But were there no uniformity in human actions, and were every experiment which we could form of this kind irregular and anomalous, it were impossible to collect any general observations concerning mankind; and no experience, however accurately digested by reflection, would ever serve to any purpose. Why is the aged husbandman more skilful in his calling than the young beginner but because there is a certain uniformity in the operation of the sun, rain, and earth towards the production of vegetables; and experience teaches the old practitioner the rules by which this operation is governed and directed.

66. We must not, however, expect that this uniformity of human actions should be carried to such a length as that all men, in the same circumstances, will always act precisely in the same manner, without making any allowance for the diversity of characters, prejudices, and opinions. Such a uniformity in every particular, is found in no part of nature. On the contrary, from observing the variety of conduct in different men, we are enabled to form a greater variety of maxims, which still suppose a degree of uniformity and regularity.

Are the manners of men different in different ages and countries? We learn thence the great force of custom and education, which mould the human mind from its infancy and form it into a fixed and established character. Is the behaviour and conduct of the one sex very unlike that of the other? Is it thence we become acquainted with the different characters which nature has impressed upon the sexes, and which she preserves with constancy and regularity? Are the actions of the same person much diversified in the different periods of his life, from infancy to old age? This affords room for many general observations concerning the gradual change of our sentiments and inclinations, and the different maxims which prevail in the different ages of human creatures. Even the characters, which are peculiar to each individual, have a uniformity in their influence; otherwise our acquaintance with the persons and our observation of their conduct could never teach us their dispositions, or serve to direct our behaviour with regard to them.

67. I grant it possible to find some actions, which seem to have no regular connexion with any known motives, and are exceptions to all the measures of conduct which have ever been established for the government of men. But if we would willingly know what judgement should be formed of such irregular and extraordinary actions, we may consider the sentiments commonly entertained with regard to those irregular events which appear in the course of nature, and the operations of external objects. All causes are not conjoined to their usual effects with like uniformity. An artificer, who handles only dead matter, may be disappointed of his aim, as well as the politician, who directs the conduct of sensible and intelligent agents.

The vulgar, who take things according to their first appearance, attribute the uncertainty of events to such an uncertainty in the causes as makes the latter often fail of their usual influence; though they meet with no impediment in their operation. But philosophers, observing that, almost in every part of nature, there is contained a vast variety of springs and principles, which are hid, by reason of their minuteness or remoteness, find, that it is at least possible the contrariety of events may not proceed from any contingency in the cause, but from the secret operation of contrary causes. This possibility is converted into certainty by farther observation, when they remark that, upon an exact scrutiny, a contrariety of effects always betrays a contrariety of causes, and proceeds from their mutual opposition. A peasant can give no better reason for the stopping of any clock or watch than to say that it does not commonly go right: but an artist easily perceives that the same force in the spring or pendulum has always the same influence on the wheels; but fails of its usual effect, perhaps by reason of a grain of dust, which puts a stop to the whole movement. From the observation of several parallel instances, philosophers form a maxim that the connexion between all causes and effects is equally necessary, and that its seeming uncertainty in some instances proceeds from the secret opposition of contrary causes.

Thus, for instance, in the human body, when the usual symptoms of health or sickness disappoint our expectation; when medicines operate not with their wonted powers; when irregular events follow from any particular cause; the philosopher and physician are not surprised at the matter, nor are ever tempted to deny, in general, the necessity and uniformity of those principles by which the animal economy is conducted. They know that a human body is a mighty complicated machine: that many secret powers lurk in it, which are altogether beyond our comprehension: that to us it must often appear very uncertain in its operations: and that therefore the irregular events, which outwardly discover themselves, can be no proof that the laws of nature are not observed with the greatest regularity in its internal operations and government.

68. The philosopher, if he be consistent, must apply the same reasoning to the actions and volitions of intelligent agents. The most irregular and unexpected resolutions of men may frequently be accounted for by those who know every particular circumstance of their character and situation. A person of an obliging disposition gives a peevish answer: But he has the toothache, or has not dined. A stupid fellow discovers an uncommon alacrity in his carriage: but he has met with a sudden piece of good fortune. Or even when an action, as sometimes happens, cannot be particularly accounted for, cither by the person himself or by others; we know, in general, that the characters of men are, to a certain degree, inconstant and irregular. This is, in a manner, the constant character of human nature; though it be applicable, in a more particular manner, to some persons who have no fixed rule for their conduct, but proceed in a continued course of caprice and inconstancy. The internal principles and motives may operate in a uniform manner, notwithstanding these seeming irregularities; in the same manner as the winds, rain, clouds, and other variations of the weather are supposed to be governed by steady principles; though not easily discoverable by human sagacity and enquiry.

69. Thus it appears, not only that the conjunction between motives and voluntary actions is as regular and uniform as that between the cause and effect in any part of nature; but also that this regular conjunction has been universally acknowledged among mankind, and has never been the subject of dispute, either in

philosophy or common life. Now, as it is from past experience that we draw all inferences concerning the future, and as we conclude that objects will always be conjoined together which we find to have always been conjoined; it may seem superfluous to prove that this experienced uniformity in human actions is a source whence we draw *inferences* concerning them. But in order to throw the argument into a greater variety of lights we shall also insist, though briefly, on this latter topic.

The mutual dependence of men is so great in all societies that scarce any human action is entirely complete in itself, or is performed without some reference to the actions of others, which are requisite to make it answer fully the intention of the agent. The poorest artificer, who labours alone, expects at least the protection of the magistrate, to ensure him the enjoyment of the fruits of his labour. He also expects that, when he carries his goods to market, and offers them at a reasonable price, he shall find purchasers, and shall be able, by the money he acquires, to engage others to supply him with those commodities which are requisite for his subsistence. In proportion as men extend their dealings, and render their intercourse with others more complicated, they always comprehend, in their schemes of life, a greater variety of voluntary actions, which they expect, from the proper motives, to cooperate with their own. In all these conclusions they take their measures from past experience, in the same manner as in their reasonings concerning external objects; and firmly believe that men, as well as all the elements, are to continue, in their operations, the same that they have ever found them. A manufacturer reckons upon the labour of his servants for the execution of any work as much as upon the tools which he employs, and would be equally surprised were his expectations disappointed. In short, this experimental inference and reasoning concerning the actions of others enters so much into human life that no man, while awake, is ever a moment without employing it. Have we not reason, therefore, to affirm that all mankind have always agreed in the doctrine of necessity according to the foregoing definition and explication of it?

70. Nor have philosophers ever entertained a different opinion from the people in this particular. For, not to mention that almost every action of their life supposes that opinion, there are even few

of the speculative parts of learning to which it is not essential. What would become of *history*, had we not a dependence on the veracity of the historian according to the experience which we have had of mankind? How could *politics* be a science, if laws and forms of goverment had not a uniform influence upon society? Where would be the foundation of *morals*, if particular characters had no certain or determinate power to produce particular sentiments, and if these sentiments had no constant operation on actions? And with what pretence could we employ our *criticism* upon any poet or polite author, if we could not pronounce the conduct and sentiments of his actors either natural or unnatural to such characters, and in such circumstances? It seems almost impossible, therefore, to engage either in science or action of any kind without acknowledging the doctrine of necessity, and this *inference* from motive to voluntary actions, from characters to conduct.

And indeed, when we consider how aptly *natural* and *moral* evidence link together, and form only one chain of argument, we shall make no scruple to allow that they are of the same nature, and derived from the same principles. A prisoner who has neither money nor interest, discovers the impossibility of his escape, as well when he considers the obstinacy of the gaoler, as the walls and bars with which he is surrounded; and, in all attempts for his freedom, chooses rather to work upon the stone and iron of the one, than upon the inflexible nature of the other. The same prisoner, when conducted to the scaffold, foresees his death as certainly from the constancy and fidelity of his guards, as from the operation of the axe or wheel. His mind runs along a certain train of ideas: the refusal of the soldiers to consent to his escape; the action of the executioner; the separation of the head and body; bleeding, convulsive motions, and death. Here is a connected chain of natural causes and voluntary actions; but the mind feels no difference between them in passing from one link to another: nor is less certain of the future event than if it were connected with the objects present to the memory or senses, by a train of causes, cemented together by what we are pleased to call a *physical* necessity. The same experienced union has the same effect on the mind, whether the united objects be motives, volition, and actions; or figure and motion. We may change the name of things; but their nature and their operation on the understanding never change.

Were a man, whom I know to be honest and opulent, and with whom I live in intimate friendship, to come into my house, where I am surrounded with my servants, I rest assured that he is not to stab me before he leaves it in order to rob me of my silver standish; and I no more suspect this event than the falling of the house itself, which is new, and solidly built and founded. – *But he may have been seized with a sudden and unknown frenzy.* – So may a sudden earthquake arise, and shake and tumble my house about my ears. I shall therefore change the suppositions. I shall say that I know with certainty that he is not to put his hand into the fire and hold it there till it be consumed: and this event, I think I can foretell with the same assurance, as that, if he throw himself out at the window, and meet with no obstruction, he will not remain a moment suspended in the air. No suspicion of an unknown frenzy can give the least possibility to the former event, which is so contrary to all the known principles of human nature. A man who at noon leaves his purse full of gold on the pavement at Charing-Cross, may as well expect that it will fly away like a feather, as that he will find it untouched an hour after. Above one half of human reasonings contain inferences of a similar nature, attended with more or less degrees of certainty proportioned to our experience of the usual conduct of mankind in such particular situations.

71. I have frequently considered, what could possibly be the reason why all mankind, though they have ever, without hesitation, acknowledged the doctrine of necessity in their whole practice and reasoning, have yet discovered such a reluctance to acknowledge it in words, and have rather shown a propensity, in all ages, to profess the contrary opinion. The matter, I think, may be accounted for after the following manner. If we examine the operations of body, and the production of effects from their causes, we shall find that all our faculties can never carry us farther in our knowledge of this relation than barely to observe that particular objects are *constantly conjoined* together, and that the mind is carried, by a *customary transition*, from the appearance of one to the belief of the other. But though this conclusion concerning human ignorance be the result of the strictest scrutiny of this subject, men still entertain a strong propensity to believe that they penetrate farther into the powers of nature, and perceive something like a necessary connexion between the cause and the

effect. When again they turn their reflections towards the operations of their own minds, and *feel* no such connexion of the motive and the action; they are thence apt to suppose, that there is a difference between the effects which result from material force, and those which arise from thought and intelligence. But being once convinced that we know nothing farther of causation of any kind than merely the *constant conjunction* of objects, and the consequent *inference* of the mind from one to another, and finding that these two circumstances are universally allowed to have place in voluntary actions; we may be more easily led to own the same necessity common to all causes. And though this reasoning may contradict the systems of many philosophers, in ascribing necessity to the determinations of the will, we shall find, upon reflection, that they dissent from it in words only, not in their real sentiment. Necessity, according to the sense in which it is here taken, has never yet been rejected, nor can ever, I think, be rejected by any philosopher. It may only, perhaps, be pretended that the mind can perceive, in the operations of matter, some farther connexion between the cause and effect; and connexion that has not place in voluntary actions of intelligent beings. Now whether it be so or not, can only appear upon examination; and it is incumbent on these philosophers to make good their assertion, by defining or describing that necessity, and pointing it out to us in the operations of material causes.

72. It would seem, indeed, that men begin at the wrong end of this question concerning liberty and necessity, when they enter upon it by examining the faculties of the soul, the influence of the understanding, and the operations of the will. Let them first discuss a more simple question, namely, the operations of body and of brute unintelligent matter; and try whether they can there form any idea of causation and necessity, except that of a constant conjunction of objects, and subsequent inference of the mind from one to another. If these circumstances form, in reality, the whole of that necessity, which we conceive in matter, and if these circumstances be also universally acknowledged to take place in the operations of the mind, the dispute is at an end; at least, must be owned to be thenceforth merely verbal. But as long as we will rashly suppose, that we have some farther idea of necessity and causation in the operations of external objects; at the same time,

that we can find nothing farther in the voluntary actions of the mind; there is no possibility of bringing the question to any determinate issue, while we proceed upon so erroneous a supposition. The only method of undeceiving us is to mount up higher; to examine the narrow extent of science when applied to material causes; and to convince ourselves that all we know of them is the constant conjunction and inference above mentioned. We may, perhaps, find that it is with difficulty we are induced to fix such narrow limits to human understanding: But we can afterwards find no difficulty when we come to apply this doctrine to the actions of the will. For as it is evident that these have a regular conjunction with motives and circumstances and characters, and as we always draw inferences from one to the other, we must be obliged to acknowledge in words that necessity, which we have already avowed, in every deliberation of our lives, and in every step of our conduct and behaviour.*

73. But to proceed in this reconciling project with regard to the question of liberty and necessity; the most contentious question of metaphysics, the most contentious science; it will not require many words to prove, that all mankind have ever agreed in the doctrine of liberty as well as in that of necessity, and that the whole dispute, in this respect also, has been hitherto merely verbal. For what is meant by liberty, when applied to voluntary

---

* The prevalence of the doctrine of liberty may be accounted for, from another cause, *viz.* a false sensation or seeming experience which we have, or may have, of liberty or indifference, in many of our actions. The necessity of any action, whether of matter or of mind, is not, properly speaking, a quality in the agent, but in any thinking or intelligent being, who may consider the action; and it consists chiefly in the determination of his thoughts to infer the existence of that action from some preceding objects; as liberty, when opposed to necessity, is nothing but the want of that determination, and a certain looseness or indifference, which we feel, in passing, or not passing, from the idea of one object to that of any succeeding one. Now we may observe, that, though, in *reflecting* on human actions, we seldom feel such a looseness, or indifference, but are commonly able to infer them with considerable certainty from their motives, and from the dispositions of the agent; yet it frequently happens, that, in *performing* the actions themselves, we are sensible of something like it: and as all resembling objects are readily taken for each other, this has been employed as a demonstrative and even intuitive proof of human liberty. We feel, that our actions are subject to our will, on most occasions; and imagine we feel, that the will itself is subject to nothing, because, when by a denial of it we are provoked to try, we feel, that it moves easily every way, and produces an image of itself (or a *Velleïty*, as it is called in the schools) even on that side, on which it did not settle. This image, or faint motion, we persuade ourselves, could, at that time,

actions? We cannot surely mean that actions have so little connexion with motives, inclinations, and circumstances, that one does not follow with a certain degree of uniformity from the other, and that one affords no inference by which we can conclude the existence of the other. For these are plain and acknowledged matters of fact. By liberty, then, we can only mean *a power of acting or not acting, according to the determinations of the will*; that is, if we choose to remain at rest, we may; if we choose to move, we also may. Now this hypothetical liberty is universally allowed to belong to every one who is not a prisoner and in chains. Here, then, is no subject of dispute.

74. Whatever definition we may give of liberty, we should be careful to observe two requisite circumstances; *first*, that it be consistent with plain matter of fact; *secondly*, that it be consistent with itself. If we observe these circumstances, and render our definition intelligible, I am persuaded that all mankind will be found of one opinion with regard to it.

It is universally allowed that nothing exists without a cause of its existence, and that chance, when strictly examined, is a mere negative word, and means not any real power which has anywhere a being in nature. But it is pretended that some causes are necessary, some not necessary. Here then is the advantage of definitions. Let any one *define* a cause, without comprehending, as a part of the definition, a *necessary connexion* with its effect; and let him show distinctly the origin of the idea, expressed by the definition; and I shall readily give up the whole controversy. But if the foregoing explication of the matter be received, this must be absolutely impracticable. Had not objects a regular conjunction with each other, we should never have entertained any notion of cause and effect; and this regular conjunction produces that inference of the understanding, which is the only

---

have been completed into the thing itself; because, should that be denied, we find, upon a second trial, that, at present, it can. We consider not, that the fantastical desire of shewing liberty, is here the motive of our actions. And it seems certain, that, however we may imagine we feel a liberty within ourselves, a spectator can commonly infer our actions from our motives and character; and even where he cannot, he concludes in general, that he might, were he perfectly acquainted with every circumstance of our situation and temper, and the most secret springs of our complexion and disposition. Now this is the very essence of necessity, according to the foregoing doctrine.

connexion, that we can have any comprehension of. Whoever attempts a definition of cause, exclusive of these circumstances, will be obliged either to employ unintelligible terms or such as are synonymous to the term which he endeavours to define.*
And if the definition above mentioned be admitted; liberty, when opposed to necessity, not to constraint, is the same thing with chance; which is universally allowed to have no existence.

Part 2

75. There is no method of reasoning more common, and yet none more blameable, than, in philosophical disputes, to endeavour the refutation of any hypothesis, by a pretence of its dangerous consequences to religion and morality. When any opinion leads to absurdities, it is certainly false; but it is not certain that an opinion is false, because it is of dangerous consequence. Such topics, therefore, ought entirely to be forborne; as serving nothing to the discovery of truth, but only to make the person of an antagonist odious. This I observe in general, without pretending to draw any advantage from it. I frankly submit to an examination of this kind, and shall venture to affirm that the doctrines, both of necessity and of liberty, as above explained, are not only consistent with morality, but are absolutely essential to its support.

Necessity may be defined two ways, conformably to the two definitions of *cause*, of which it makes an essential part. It consists either in the constant conjunction of like objects, or in the inference of the understanding from one object to another. Now necessity, in both these senses (which, indeed, are at bottom the same) has universally, though tacitly, in the schools, in the pulpit, and in common life, been allowed to belong to the will of man; and no one has ever pretended to deny that we can draw inferences concerning human actions, and that those inferences are founded on the experienced union of like actions, with like

* Thus, if a cause be defined, *that which produces any thing*; it is easy to observe, that *producing* is synonymous to *causing*. In like manner, if a cause be defined, *that by which any thing exists*; this is liable to the same objection. For what is meant by these words, *by which*? Had it been said, that a cause is *that* after which *any thing constantly exists*; we should have understood the terms. For this is, indeed, all we know of the matter. And this constancy forms the very essence of necessity, nor have we any other idea of it.

motives, inclinations, and circumstances. The only particular in which any one can differ, is, that either, perhaps, he will refuse to give the name of necessity to this property of human actions: but as long as the meaning is understood, I hope the word can do no harm: or that he will maintain it possible to discover something farther in the operations of matter. But this, it must be acknowledged, can be of no consequence to morality or religion, whatever it may be to natural philosophy or metaphysics. We may here be mistaken in asserting that there is no idea of any other necessity or connexion in the actions of body: but surely we ascribe nothing to the actions of the mind, but what everyone does, and must readily allow of. We change no circumstance in the received orthodox system with regard to the will, but only in that with regard to material objects and causes. Nothing, therefore, can be more innocent, at least, than this doctrine.

76. All laws being founded on rewards and punishments, it is supposed as a fundamental principle, that these motives have a regular and uniform influence on the mind, and both produce the good and prevent the evil actions. We may give to this influence what name we please; but, as it is usually conjoined with the action, it must be esteemed a *cause*, and be looked upon as an instance of that necessity, which we would here establish.

The only proper object of hatred or vengeance is a person or creature, endowed with thought and consciousness; and when any criminal or injurious actions excite that passion, it is only by their relation to the person, or connexion with him. Actions are, by their very nature, temporary and perishing; and where they proceed not from some *cause* in the character and disposition of the person who performed them, they can neither redound to his honour, if good; nor infamy, if evil. The actions themselves may be blameable; they may be contrary to all the rules of morality and religion: but the person is not answerable for them; and as they proceeded from nothing in him that is durable and constant, and leave nothing of that nature behind them, it is impossible he can, upon their account, become the object of punishment or vengeance. According to the principle, therefore, which denies necessity, and consequently causes, a man is as pure and untainted, after having committed the most horrid crime, as at the first moment of his birth, nor is his character anywise concerned in his actions, since they are not derived from it, and the wickedness of the one can never be used as a proof of the depravity of the other.

Men are not blamed for such actions as they perform ignorantly and casually, whatever may be the consequences. Why? but because the principles of these actions are only momentary, and terminate in them alone. Men are less blamed for such actions as they perform hastily and unpremeditately than for such as proceed from deliberation. For what reason? but because a hasty temper, though a constant cause or principle in the mind, operates only by intervals, and infects not the whole character. Again, repentance wipes off every crime, if attended with a reformation of life and manners. How is this to be accounted for? but by asserting that actions render a person criminal merely as they are proofs of criminal principles in the mind; and when, by an alteration of these principles, they cease to be just proofs, they likewise cease to be criminal. But, except upon the doctrine of necessity, they never were just proofs, and consequently never were criminal.

77. It will be equally easy to prove, and from the same arguments, that *liberty*, according to that definition above mentioned, in which all men agree, is also essential to morality, and that no human actions, where it is wanting, are susceptible of any moral qualities, or can be the objects either of approbation or dislike. For as actions are objects of our moral sentiment, so far only as they are indications of the internal character, passions, and affections; it is impossible that they can give rise either to praise or blame, where they proceed not from these principles, but are derived altogether from external violence.

78. I pretend not to have obviated or removed all objections to this theory, with regard to necessity and liberty. I can foresee other objections, derived from topics which have not here been treated of. It may be said, for instance, that, if voluntary actions be subjected to the same laws of necessity with the operations of matter, there is a continued chain of necessary causes, pre-ordained and pre-determined, reaching from the original cause of all to every single volition of every human creature. No contingency anywhere in the universe; no indifference; no liberty. While we act, we are, at the same time, acted upon. The ultimate Author of all our volitions is the Creator of the world, who first bestowed motion on this immense machine, and placed all beings in that particular position,

whence every subsequent event, by an inevitable necessity, must result. Human actions, therefore, either can have no moral turpitude at all, as proceeding from so good a cause; or if they have any turpitude, they must involve our Creator in the same guilt, while he is acknowledged to be their ultimate cause and author. For as a man, who fired a mine, is answerable for all the consequences whether the train he employed be long or short; so wherever a continued chain of necessary causes is fixed, that Being, either finite or infinite, who produces the first, is likewise the author of all the rest, and must both bear the blame and acquire the praise which belong to them. Our clear and unalterable ideas of morality establish this rule, upon unquestionable reasons, when we examine the consequences of any human action; and these reasons must still have greater force when applied to the volitions and intentions of a Being infinitely wise and powerful. Ignorance or impotence may be pleaded for so limited a creature as man; but those imperfections have no place in our Creator. He foresaw, he ordained, he intended all those actions of men, which we so rashly pronounce criminal. And we must therefore conclude, either that they are not criminal, or that the Deity, not man, is accountable for them. But as either of these positions is absurd and impious, it follows, that the doctrine from which they are deduced cannot possibly be true, as being liable to all the same objections. An absurd consequence, if necessary, proves the original doctrine to be absurd; in the same manner as criminal actions render criminal the original cause, if the connexion between them be necessary and evitable.

This objection consists of two parts, which we shall examine separately; *First*, that, if human actions can be traced up, by a necessary chain, to the Deity, they can never be criminal; on account of the infinite perfection of that Being from whom they are derived, and who can intend nothing but what is altogether good and laudable. Or, *Secondly*, if they be criminal, we must retract the attribute of perfection, which we ascribe to the Deity, and must acknowledge him to be the ultimate author of guilt and moral turpitude in all his creatures.

79. The answer to the first objection seems obvious and convincing. There are many philosophers who, after an exact scrutiny of all the phenomena of nature, conclude, that the whole, considered as one system, is, in every period of its existence, ordered with

perfect benevolence; and that the utmost possible happiness will, in the end, result to all created beings, without any mixture of positive or absolute ill or misery. Every physical ill, say they, makes an essential part of this benevolent system, and could not possibly be removed, even by the Deity himself, considered as a wise agent, without giving entrance to greater ill, or excluding greater good, which will result from it. From this theory, some philosophers, and the ancient *Stoics* among the rest, derived a topic of consolation under all afflictions, while they taught their pupils that those ills under which they laboured were, in reality, goods to the universe; and that to an enlarged view, which could comprehend the whole system of nature, every event became an object of joy and exult-ation. But though this topic be specious and sublime, it was soon found in practice weak and ineffectual. You would surely more irritate than appease a man lying under the racking pains of the gout by preaching up to him the rectitude of those general laws, which produced the malignant humours in his body, and led them through the proper canals, to the sinews and nerves, where they now excite such acute torments. These enlarged views may, for a moment, please the imagination of a speculative man, who is placed in ease and security; but neither can they dwell with constancy on his mind, even though undisturbed by the emotions of pain or passion; much less can they maintain their ground when attacked by such powerful antagonists. The affections take a narrower and more natural survey of their object; and by an economy, more suitable to the infirmity of human minds, regard alone the beings around us, and are actuated by such events as appear good or ill to the private system.

80. The case is the same with *moral* as with *physical* ill. It cannot reasonably be supposed, that those remote considerations, which are found of so little efficacy with regard to one, will have a more powerful influence with regard to the other. The mind of man is so formed by nature that, upon the appearance of certain characters, dispositions, and actions, it immediately feels the sentiment of approbation or blame; nor are there any emotions more essential to its frame and constitution. The characters which engage our approbation are chiefly such as contribute to the peace and security of human society; as the characters which excite blame are chiefly such as tend to public detriment and disturbance: whence it may

reasonably be presumed, that the moral sentiments arise, either mediately or immediately, from a reflection of these opposite interests. What though philosophical meditations establish a different opinion or conjecture; that everything is right with regard to the whole, and that the qualities, which disturb society, are, in the main, as beneficial, and are as suitable to the primary intention of nature as those which more directly promote its happiness and welfare? Are such remote and uncertain speculations able to counterbalance the sentiments which arise from the natural and immediate view of the objects? A man who is robbed of a considerable sum; does he find his vexation for the loss anywise diminished by these sublime reflections? Why then should his moral resentment against the crime be supposed incompatible with them? Or why should not the acknowledgment of a real distinction between vice and virtue be reconcileable to all speculative systems of philosophy, as well as that of a real distinction between personal beauty and deformity? Both these distinctions are founded in the natural sentiments of the human mind: And these sentiments are not to be controlled or altered by any philosophical theory or speculation whatsoever.

81. The *second* objection admits not of so easy and satisfactory an answer; nor is it possible to explain distinctly, how the Deity can be the mediate cause of all the actions of men, without being the author of sin and moral turpitude. These are mysteries, which mere natural and unassisted reason is very unfit to handle; and whatever system she embraces, she must find herself involved in inextricable difficulties, and even contradictions, at every step which she takes with regard to such subjects. To reconcile the indifference and contingency of human actions with prescience; or to defend absolute decrees, and yet free the Deity from being the author of sin, has been found hitherto to exceed all the power of philosophy. Happy, if she be thence sensible of her temerity, when she pries into these sublime mysteries; and leaving a scene so full of obscurities and perplexities, return, with suitable modesty, to her true and proper province, the examination of common life; where she will find difficulties enough to employ her enquiries, without launching into so boundless an ocean of doubt, uncertainty, and contradiction!

Of the reason of animals

82. All our reasonings concerning matter of fact are founded on a species of Analogy, which leads us to expect from any cause the same events, which we have observed to result from similar causes. Where the causes are entirely similar, the analogy is perfect, and the inference, drawn from it, is regarded as certain and conclusive: nor does any man ever entertain a doubt, where he sees a piece of iron, that it will have weight and cohesion of parts; as in all other instances, which have ever fallen under his observation. But where the objects have not so exact a similarity, the analogy is less perfect, and the inference is less conclusive; though still it has some force, in proportion to the degree of similarity and resemblance. The anatomical observations, formed upon one animal, are, by this species of reasoning, extended to all animals; and it is certain, that when the circulation of the blood, for instance, is clearly proved to have place in one creature, as a frog, or fish, it forms a strong presumption, that the same principle has place in all. These analogical observations may be carried farther, even to this science, of which we are now treating; and any theory, by which we explain the operations of the understanding, or the origin and connexion of the passions in man, will acquire additional authority, if we find, that the same theory is requisite to explain the same phenomena in all other animals. We shall make trial of this, with regard to the hypothesis, by which we have, in the foregoing discourse, endeavoured to account for all experimental reasonings; and it is hoped, that this new point of view will serve to confirm all our former observations.

83. *First*, It seems evident, that animals as well as men learn many things from experience, and infer, that the same events will always follow from the same causes. By this principle they become acquainted with the more obvious properties of external objects,

and gradually, from their birth, treasure up a knowledge of the nature of fire, water, earth, stones, heights, depths, &c., and of the effects which result from their operation. The ignorance and inexperience of the young are here plainly distinguishable from the cunning and sagacity of the old, who have learned, by long observation, to avoid what hurt them, and to pursue what gave ease or pleasure. A horse, that has been accustomed to the field, becomes acquainted with the proper height which he can leap, and will never attempt what exceeds his force and ability. An old greyhound will trust the more fatiguing part of the chase to the younger, and will place himself so as to meet the hare in her doubles; nor are the conjectures, which he forms on this occasion, founded in any thing but his observation and experience.

This is still more evident from the effects of discipline and education on animals, who, by the proper application of rewards and punishments, may be taught any course of action, and most contrary to their natural instincts and propensities. Is it not experience, which renders a dog apprehensive of pain, when you menace him, or lift up the whip to beat him? Is it not even experience, which makes him answer to his name, and infer, from such an arbitrary sound, that you mean him rather than any of his fellows, and intend to call him, when you pronounce it in a certain manner, and with a certain tone and accent?

In all these cases, we may observe, that the animal infers some fact beyond what immediately strikes his senses; and that this inference is altogether founded on past experience, while the creature expects from the present object the same consequences, which it has always found in its observation to result from similar objects.

84. *Secondly*, It is impossible, that this inference of the animal can be founded on any process of argument or reasoning, by which he concludes, that like events must follow like objects, and that the course of nature will always be regular in its operations. For if there be in reality any arguments of this nature, they surely lie too abstruse for the observation of such imperfect understandings; since it may well employ the utmost care and attention of a philosophic genius to discover and observe them. Animals, therefore, are not guided in these inferences by reasoning: neither are children: neither are the generality of mankind, in their ordinary actions and conclusions: neither are philosophers themselves,

who, in all the active parts of life, are, in the main, the same with the vulgar, and are governed by the same maxims. Nature must have provided some other principle, of more ready, and more general use and application; nor can an operation of such immense consequence in life, as that of inferring effects from causes, be trusted to the uncertain process of reasoning and argumentation. Were this doubtful with regard to men, it seems to admit of no question with regard to the brute creation; and the conclusion being once firmly established in the one, we have a strong presumption, from all the rules of analogy, that it ought to be universally admitted, without any exception or reserve. It is custom alone, which engages animals, from every object, that strikes their senses, to infer its usual attendant, and carries their imagination, from the appearance of the one, to conceive the other, in that particular manner, which we denominate *belief*. No other explication can be given of this operation, in all the higher, as well as lower classes of sensitive beings, which fall under our notice and observation.*

---

* Since all reasonings concerning facts or causes is derived merely from custom, it may be asked how it happens, that men so much surpass animals in reasoning, and one man so much surpasses another? Has not the same custom the same influence on all?

We shall here endeavour briefly to explain the great difference in human understandings: after which the reason of the difference between men and animals will easily be comprehended.

1. When we have lived any time, and have been accustomed to the uniformity of nature, we acquire a general habit, by which we always transfer the known to the unknown, and conceive the latter to resemble the former. By means of this general habitual principle, we regard even one experiment as the foundation of reasoning, and expect a similar event with some degree of certainty, where the experiment has been made accurately, and free from all foreign circumstances. It is therefore considered as a matter of great importance to observe the consequences of things; and as one man may very much surpass another in attention and memory and observation, this will make a very great difference in their reasoning.

2. Where there is a complication of causes to produce any effect, one mind may be much larger than another, and better able to comprehend the whole system of objects, and to infer justly their consequences.

3. One man is able to carry on a chain of consequences to a greater length than another.

4. Few men can think long without running into a confusion of ideas, and mistaking one for another; and there are various degrees of this infirmity.

5. The circumstance, on which the effect depends, is frequently involved in other circumstances, which are foreign and extrinsic. The separation of it often requires great attention, accuracy, and subtilty.

85. But though animals learn many parts of their knowledge from observation, there are also many parts of it, which they derive from the original hand of nature; which much exceed the share of capacity they possess on ordinary occasions; and in which they improve, little or nothing, by the longest practice and experience. These we denominate Instincts, and are so apt to admire as something very extraordinary, and inexplicable by all the disquisitions of human understanding. But our wonder will, perhaps, cease or diminish, when we consider, that the experimental reasoning itself, which we possess in common with beasts, and on which the whole conduct of life depends, is nothing but a species of instinct or mechanical power, that acts in us unknown to ourselves; and in its chief operations, is not directed by any such relations or comparisons of ideas, as are the proper objects of our intellectual faculties. Though the instinct be different, yet still it is an instinct, which teaches a man to avoid the fire; as much as that, which teaches a bird, with such exactness, the art of incubation, and the whole economy and order of its nursery.

---

6. The forming of general maxims from particular observation is a very nice operation; and nothing is more usual, from haste or a narrowness of mind, which sees not on all sides, than to commit mistakes in this particular.

7. When we reason from analogies, the man, who has the greater experience or the greater promptitude of suggesting analogies, will be the better reasoner.

8. Biases from prejudice, education, passion, party, &c. hang more upon one mind than another.

9. After we have acquired a confidence in human testimony, books and conversation enlarge much more the sphere of one man's experience and thought than those of another.

It would be easy to discover many other circumstances that make a difference in the understandings of men.

Part I

86. There is, in Dr Tillotson's writings, an argument against the *real presence*, which is as concise, and elegant, and strong as any argument can possibly be supposed against a doctrine, so little worthy of a serious refutation. It is acknowledged on all hands, says that learned prelate, that the authority, either of the scripture or of tradition, is founded merely in the testimony of the apostles, who were eye-witnesses to those miracles of our Saviour, by which he proved his divine mission. Our evidence, then, for the truth of the *Christian* religion is less than the evidence for the truth of our senses; because, even in the first authors of our religion, it was no greater; and it is evident it must diminish in passing from them to their disciples; nor can any one rest such confidence in their testimony, as in the immediate object of his senses. But a weaker evidence can never destroy a stronger; and therefore, were the doctrine of the real presence ever so clearly revealed in scripture, it were directly contrary to the rules of just reasoning to give our assent to it. It contradicts sense, though both the scripture and tradition, on which it is supposed to be built, carry not such evidence with them as sense; when they are considered merely as external evidences, and are not brought home to every one's breast, by the immediate operation of the Holy Spirit.

Nothing is so convenient as a decisive argument of this kind, which must at least *silence* the most arrogant bigotry and super-stition, and free us from their impertinent solicitations. I flatter myself, that I have discovered an argument of a like nature, which, if just, will, with the wise and learned, be an everlasting check to all kinds of superstitious delusion, and consequently, will be useful as long as the world endures. For so long, I presume, will the accounts of miracles and prodigies be found in all history, sacred and profane.

87. Though experience be our only guide in reasoning concerning matters of fact; it must be acknowledged, that this guide is not altogether infallible, but in some cases is apt to lead us into errors. One, who in our climate, should expect better weather in any week of June than in one of December, would reason justly, and conformably to experience; but it is certain, that he may happen, in the event, to find himself mistaken. However, we may observe, that, in such a case, he would have no cause to complain of experience; because it commonly informs us beforehand of the uncertainty, by that contrariety of events, which we may learn from a diligent observation. All effects follow not with like certainty from their supposed causes. Some events are found, in all countries and all ages, to have been constantly conjoined together: others are found to have been more variable, and sometimes to disappoint our expectations; so that, in our reasonings concerning matter of fact, there are all imaginable degrees of assurance, from the highest certainty to the lowest species of moral evidence.

A wise man, therefore, proportions his belief to the evidence. In such conclusions as are founded on an infallible experience, he expects the event with the last degree of assurance, and regards his past experience as a full *proof* of the future existence of that event. In other cases, he proceeds with more caution: He weighs the opposite experiments: he considers which side is supported by the greater number of experiments: to that side he inclines, with doubt and hesitation; and when at last he fixes his judgement, the evidence exceeds not what we properly call *probability*. All probability, then, supposes an opposition of experiments and observations, where the one side is found to overbalance the other, and to produce a degree of evidence, proportioned to the superiority. A hundred instances or experiments on one side, and fifty on another, afford a doubtful expectation of any event; though a hundred uniform experiments, with only one that is contradictory, reasonably beget a pretty strong degree of assurance. In all cases, we must balance the opposite experiments, where they are opposite, and deduct the smaller number from the greater, in order to know the exact force of the superior evidence.

88. To apply these principles to a particular instance; we may observe, that there is no species of reasoning more common, more useful, and even necessary to human life, than that which is derived from the testimony of men, and the reports of eye-witnesses and spectators. This species of reasoning, perhaps, one may deny to be founded on the relation of cause and effect. I shall not dispute about a word. It will be sufficient to observe that our assurance in any argument of this kind is derived from no other principle than our observation of the veracity of human testimony, and of the usual conformity of facts to the reports of witnesses. It being a general maxim, that no objects have any discoverable connexion together, and that all the inferences, which we can draw from one to another, are founded merely on our experience of their constant and regular conjunction; it is evident, that we ought not to make an exception to this maxim in favour of human testimony, whose connexion with any event seems, in itself, as little necessary as any other. Were not the memory tenacious to a certain degree, had not men commonly an inclination to truth and a principle of probity; were they not sensible to shame, when detected in a falsehood: Were not these, I say, discovered by *experience* to be qualities, inherent in human nature, we should never repose the least confidence in human testimony. A man delirious, or noted for falsehood and villany, has no manner of authority with us.

And as the evidence, derived from witnesses and human testimony, is founded on past experience, so it varies with the experience, and is regarded either as a *proof* or a *probability*, according as the conjunction between any particular kind of report and any kind of object has been found to be constant or variable. There are a number of circumstances to be taken into consideration in all judgements of this kind; and the ultimate standard, by which we determine all disputes, that may arise concerning them, is always derived from experience and observation. Where this experience is not entirely uniform on any side, it is attended with an unavoidable contrariety in our judgements, and with the same opposition and mutual destruction of argument as in every other kind of evidence. We frequently hesitate concerning the reports of others. We balance the opposite circumstances, which cause any doubt or uncertainty; and when we discover a superiority on any side, we incline to it; but still with a diminution of assurance, in proportion to the force of its antagonist.

89. This contrariety of evidence, in the present case, may be derived from several different causes; from the opposition of contrary testimony; from the character or number of the witnesses; from the manner of their delivering their testimony; or from the union of all these circumstances. We entertain a suspicion concerning any matter of fact, when the witnesses contradict each other; when they are but few, or of a doubtful character; when they have an interest in what they affirm; when they deliver their testimony with hesitation, or on the contrary, with too violent asseverations. There are many other particulars of the same kind, which may diminish or destroy the force of any argument, derived from human testimony.

Suppose, for instance, that the fact, which the testimony endeavours to establish, partakes of the extraordinary and the marvellous; in that case, the evidence, resulting from the testimony, admits of a diminution, greater or less, in proportion as the fact is more or less unusual. The reason why we place any credit in witnesses and historians, is not derived from any *connexion*, which we perceive *a priori*, between testimony and reality, but because we are accustomed to find a conformity between them. But when the fact attested is such a one as has seldom fallen under our observation, here is a contest of two opposite experiences; of which the one destroys the other, as far as its force goes, and the superior can only operate on the mind by the force, which remains. The very same principle of experience, which gives us a certain degree of assurance in the testimony of witnesses, gives us also, in this case, another degree of assurance against the fact, which they endeavour to establish; from which contradiction there necessarily arises a counterpoise, and mutual destruction of belief and authority.

I should not believe such a story were it told me by Cato, was a proverbial saying in Rome, even during the lifetime of that philosophical patriot.* The incredibility of a fact, it was allowed, might invalidate so great an authority.

The Indian prince, who refused to believe the first relations concerning the effects of frost, reasoned justly; and it naturally required very strong testimony to engage his assent to facts, that

---

* Plutarch, in *Vita Catonis*.

arose from a state of nature, with which he was unacquainted, and which bore so little analogy to those events, of which he had had constant and uniform experience. Though they were not contrary to his experience, they were not conformable to it.*

90. But in order to increase the probability against the testimony of witnesses, let us suppose, that the fact, which they affirm, instead of being only marvellous, is really miraculous; and suppose also, that the testimony considered apart and in itself, amounts to an entire proof; in that case, there is proof against proof, of which the strongest must prevail, but still with a diminution of its force, in proportion to that of its antagonist.

A miracle is a violation of the laws of nature; and as a firm and unalterable experience has established these laws, the proof against a miracle, from the very nature of the fact, is as entire as any argument from experience can possibly be imagined. Why is it more than probable, that all men must die; that lead cannot, of itself, remain suspended in the air; that fire consumes wood, and is extinguished by water; unless it be, that these events are found agreeable to the laws of nature, and there is required a violation of these laws, or in other words, a miracle to prevent them? Nothing is esteemed a miracle, if it ever happen in the common course of nature. It is no miracle that a man, seemingly in good health, should die on a sudden: because such a kind of death, though more unusual than any other, has yet been frequently observed to happen. But it is a miracle, that a dead man should come to life; because that has never been observed in any age or

---

* No Indian, it is evident, could have experience that water did not freeze in cold climates. This is placing nature in a situation quite unknown to him; and it is impossible for him to tell *a priori* what will result from it. It is making a new experiment, the consequence of which is always uncertain. One may sometimes conjecture from analogy what will follow; but still this is but conjecture. And it must be confessed, that, in the present case of freezing, the event follows contrary to the rules of analogy, and is such as a rational Indian would not look for. The operations of cold upon water are not gradual, according to the degrees of cold; but whenever it comes to the freezing point, the water passes in a moment, from the utmost liquidity to perfect hardness. Such an event, therefore, may be denominated *extraordinary*, and requires a pretty strong testimony, to render it credible to people in a warm climate: but still it is not *miraculous*, nor contrary to uniform experience of the course of nature in cases where all the circumstances are the same. The inhabitants of Sumatra have always seen water fluid in their own climate, and the freezing of their rivers ought to be deemed a prodigy: but they never saw water in Muscovy during the winter; and therefore they cannot reasonably be positive what would there be the consequence.

country. There must, therefore, be a uniform experience against every miraculous event, otherwise the event would not merit that appellation. And as a uniform experience amounts to a proof, there is here a direct and full *proof*, from the nature of the fact, against the existence of any miracle; nor can such a proof be destroyed, or the miracle rendered credible, but by an opposite proof, which is superior.*

91. The plain consequence is (and it is a general maxim worthy of our attention), 'That no testimony is sufficient to establish a miracle, unless the testimony be of such a kind, that its falsehood would be more miraculous, than the fact, which it endeavours to establish; and even in that case there is a mutual destruction of arguments, and the superior only gives us an assurance suitable to that degree of force, which remains, after deducting the inferior.' When anyone tells me, that he saw a dead man restored to life, I immediately consider with myself, whether it be more probable, that this person should either deceive or be deceived, or that the fact, which he relates, should really have happened. I weigh the one miracle against the other; and according to the superiority, which I discover, I pronounce my decision, and always reject the greater miracle. If the falsehood of his testimony would be more miraculous, than the event which he relates; then, and not till then, can he pretend to command my belief or opinion.

---

* Sometimes an event may not, *in itself*, seem to be contrary to the laws of nature, and yet, if it were real, it might, by reason of some circumstances, be denominated a miracle; because, in *fact*, it is contrary to these laws. Thus if a person, claiming a divine authority, should command a sick person to be well, a healthful man to fall down dead, the clouds to pour rain, the winds to blow, in short, should order many natural events, which immediately follow upon his command; these might justly be esteemed miracles, because they are really, in this case, contrary to the laws of nature. For if any suspicion remain, that the event and command concurred by accident, there is no miracle and no transgression of the laws of nature. If this suspicion be removed, there is evidently a miracle, and a transgression of these laws; because nothing can be more contrary to nature than that the voice or command of a man should have such an influence. A miracle may be accurately defined, *a transgression of a law of nature by a particular volition of the Deity, or by the interposition of some invisible agent.* A miracle may either be discoverable by men or not. This alters not its nature and essence. The raising of a house or ship into the air is a visible miracle. The raising of a feather, when the wind wants ever so little of a force requisite for that purpose, is as real a miracle, though not so sensible with regard to us.

Part 2

92. In the foregoing reasoning we have supposed, that the testimony, upon which a miracle is founded, may possibly amount to an entire proof, and that the falsehood of that testimony would be a real prodigy: but it is easy to shew, that we have been a great deal too liberal in our concession, and that there never was a miraculous event established on so full an evidence.

For *first*, there is not to be found, in all history, any miracle attested by a sufficient number of men, of such unquestioned good-sense, education, and learning, as to secure us against all delusion in themselves; of such undoubted integrity, as to place them beyond all suspicion of any design to deceive others; of such credit and reputation in the eyes of mankind, as to have a great deal to lose in case of their being detected in any falsehood; and at the same time, attesting facts performed in such a public manner and in so celebrated a part of the world, as to render the detection unavoidable: all which circumstances are requisite to give us a full assurance in the testimony of men.

93. *Secondly*. We may observe in human nature a principle which, if strictly examined, will be found to diminish extremely the assurance, which we might, from human testimony, have, in any kind of prodigy. The maxim, by which we commonly conduct ourselves in our reasonings, is, that the objects, of which we have no experience, resemble those, of which we have; that what we have found to be most usual is always most probable; and that where there is an opposition of arguments, we ought to give the preference to such as are founded on the greatest number of past observations. But though, in proceeding by this rule, we readily reject any fact which is unusual and incredible in an ordinary degree; yet in advancing farther, the mind observes not always the same rule; but when anything is affirmed utterly absurd and miraculous, it rather the more readily admits of such a fact, upon account of that very circumstance, which ought to destroy all its authority. The passion of *surprise* and *wonder*, arising from miracles, being an agreeable emotion, gives a sensible tendency towards the belief of those events, from which it is derived. And this goes so far, that even those who cannot enjoy this pleasure immediately, nor can believe those miraculous events, of which they are informed, yet love to

partake of the satisfaction at second-hand or by rebound, and place a pride and delight in exciting the admiration of others.

With what greediness are the miraculous accounts of travellers received, their descriptions of sea and land monsters, their relations of wonderful adventures, strange men, and uncouth manners? But if the spirit of religion join itself to the love of wonder, there is an end of common sense; and human testimony, in these circumstances, loses all pretensions to authority. A religionist may be an enthusiast, and imagine he sees what has no reality: he may know his narrative to be false, and yet persevere in it, with the best intentions in the world, for the sake of promoting so holy a cause: or even where this delusion has not place, vanity, excited by so strong a temptation, operates on him more powerfully than on the rest of mankind in any other circumstances; and self-interest with equal force. His auditors may not have, and commonly have not, sufficient judgement to canvass his evidence: what judgement they have, they renounce by principle, in these sublime and mysterious subjects: or if they were ever so willing to employ it, passion and a heated imagination disturb the regularity of its operations. Their credulity increases his impudence: and his impudence overpowers their credulity.

Eloquence, when at its highest pitch, leaves little room for reason or reflection; but addressing itself entirely to the fancy or the affections, captivates the willing hearers, and subdues their understanding. Happily, this pitch it seldom attains. But what a Tully or a Demosthenes could scarcely effect over a Roman or Athenian audience, every *Capuchin*, every itinerant or stationary teacher can perform over the generality of mankind, and in a higher degree, by touching such gross and vulgar passions.

The many instances of forged miracles, and prophecies, and supernatural events, which, in all ages, have either been detected by contrary evidence, or which detect themselves by their absurdity, prove sufficiently the strong propensity of mankind to the extraordinary and the marvellous, and ought reasonably to beget a suspicion against all relations of this kind. This is our natural way of thinking, even with regard to the most common and most credible events. For instance: there is no kind of report which rises so easily, and spreads so quickly, especially in country places and provincial towns, as those concerning marriages; insomuch that two young persons of equal condition never see each other twice, but the whole neighbourhood immediately join them together. The pleasure of telling a piece of news so interesting, of propagating it, and of being the first reporters of it, spreads the intelligence. And this is so well known, that no man of sense gives attention to these reports, till he find them confirmed by some greater evidence. Do not the same passions, and others still stronger, incline the generality of mankind to believe and report, with the greatest vehemence and assurance, all religious miracles?

94. *Thirdly*. It forms a strong presumption against all supernatural and miraculous relations, that they are observed chiefly to abound among ignorant and barbarous nations; or if a civilized people has ever given admission to any of them, that people will be found to have received them from ignorant and barbarous ancestors, who transmitted them with that inviolable sanction and authority, which always attend received opinions. When we peruse the first histories of all nations, we are apt to imagine ourselves transported into some new world; where the whole frame of nature is disjointed, and every element performs its operations in a different manner, from what it does at present. Battles, revolutions, pestilence, famine and death, are never the effect of those natural causes, which we experience. Prodigies, omens, oracles, judgements, quite obscure the few natural events, that are intermingled with them. But as the former grow thinner every page, in proportion as we advance nearer the enlightened ages, we soon learn, that there is nothing mysterious or supernatural in the case, but that all proceeds from the usual propensity of mankind towards the marvellous, and that, though this inclination may at intervals receive a check from sense and learning, it can never be thoroughly extirpated from human nature.

It is strange, a judicious reader is apt to say, upon the perusal of these wonderful historians, *that such prodigious events never happen in our days*. But it is nothing strange, I hope, that men should lie in all ages. You must surely have seen instances enough of that frailty. You have yourself heard many such marvellous relations started, which, being treated with scorn by all the wise and judicious, have at last been abandoned even by the vulgar. Be assured, that those renowned lies, which have spread and flourished to such a monstrous height, arose from like beginnings; but being sown in a more proper soil, shot up at last into prodigies almost equal to those which they relate.

It was a wise policy in that false prophet, Alexander, who though now forgotten, was once so famous, to lay the first scene of his impostures in Paphlagonia, where, as Lucian tells us, the people were extremely ignorant and stupid, and ready to swallow even the grossest delusion. People at a distance, who are weak enough to think the matter at all worth enquiry, have no opportunity of receiving better information. The stories come magnified to them by a hundred circumstances. Fools are industrious in propagating the imposture; while the wise and learned are contented, in general, to deride its absurdity, without informing themselves of the particular facts, by which it may be distinctly refuted. And thus the impostor above mentioned was enabled to proceed, from his ignorant Paphlagonians, to the enlisting of votaries, even among the Grecian philosophers, and men of the most eminent rank and distinction in Rome: nay, could engage the attention of that sage emperor Marcus Aurelius; so far as to make him trust the success of a military expedition to his delusive prophecies.

The advantages are so great, of starting an imposture among an ignorant people, that, even though the delusion should be too gross to impose on the generality of them (*which, though seldom, is sometimes the case*) it has a much better chance for succeeding in remote countries, than if the first scene had been laid in a city renowned for arts and knowledge. The most ignorant and barbarous of these barbarians carry the report abroad. None of their countrymen have a large correspondence, or sufficient credit and authority to contradict and beat down the delusion. Men's inclination to the marvellous has full opportunity to display itself. And thus a story, which is universally exploded in the place where it was first started, shall pass for certain at a thousand miles distance. But had Alexander fixed his residence at Athens, the philosophers of that renowned mart of learning had immediately spread, throughout the whole Roman empire, their sense of the matter; which, being supported by so great authority, and displayed by all the force of reason and eloquence, had entirely opened the eyes of mankind. It is true; Lucian, passing by chance through Paphlagonia, had an opportunity of performing this good office. But, though much to be wished, it does not always happen, that every Alexander meets with a Lucian, ready to expose and detect his impostures.

95. I may add as a *fourth* reason, which diminishes the authority of prodigies, that there is no testimony for any, even those which have not been expressly detected, that is not opposed by an infinite number of witnesses; so that not only the miracle destroys the credit of testimony, but the testimony destroys itself. To make this the better understood, let us consider, that, in matters of religion, whatever is different is contrary; and that it is impossible the religions of ancient Rome, of Turkey, of Siam, and of China should, all of them, be established on any solid foundation. Every miracle, therefore, pretended to have been wrought in any of these religions (and all of them abound in miracles), as its direct scope is to establish the particular system to which it is attributed; so has it the same force, though more indirectly, to overthrow every other system. In destroying a rival system, it likewise destroys the credit of those miracles, on which that system was established; so that all the prodigies of different religions are to be regarded as contrary facts, and the evidences of these prodigies, whether weak or strong, as opposite to each other. According to this method of reasoning, when we believe any miracle of Mahomet or his successors, we have for our warrant the testimony of a few barbarous Arabians: and on the other hand, we are to regard the authority of Titus Livius, Plutarch, Tacitus, and, in short, of all the authors and witnesses, Grecian, Chinese, and Roman Catholic, who have related any miracle in their particular religion; I say, we are to regard their testimony in the same light as if they had mentioned that Mahometan miracle, and had in express terms contradicted it, with the same certainty as they have for the miracle they relate. This argument may appear over subtile and refined; but is not in reality different from the reasoning of a judge, who supposes, that the credit of two witnesses, maintaining a crime against any one, is destroyed by the testimony of two others, who affirm him to have been two hundred leagues distant, at the same instant when the crime is said to have been committed.

96. One of the best attested miracles in all profane history, is that which Tacitus reports of Vespasian, who cured a blind man in Alexandria, by means of his spittle, and a lame man by the mere touch of his foot; in obedience to a vision of the god Serapis, who

had enjoined them to have recourse to the Emperor, for these miraculous cures. The story may be seen in that fine historian;* where every circumstance seems to add weight to the testimony, and might be displayed at large with all the force of argument and eloquence, if any one were now concerned to enforce the evidence of that exploded and idolatrous superstition. The gravity, solidity, age, and probity of so great an emperor, who, through the whole course of his life, conversed in a familiar manner with his friends and courtiers, and never affected those extraordinary airs of divinity assumed by Alexander and Demetrius: the historian, a cotemporary writer, noted for candour and veracity, and withal, the greatest and most penetrating genius, perhaps, of all antiquity; and so free from any tendency to credulity, that he even lies under the contrary imputation, of atheism and profaneness: the persons, from whose authority he related the miracle, of established character for judgement and veracity, as we may well presume; eye-witnesses of the fact, and confirming their testimony, after the Flavian family was despoiled of the empire, and could no longer give any reward, as the price of a lie. *Utrumque, qui interfuere, nunc quoque memorant, postquam nullum mendacio pretium.* To which if we add the public nature of the facts, as related, it will appear, that no evidence can well be supposed stronger for so gross and so palpable a falsehood.

There is also a memorable story related by Cardinal de Retz, which may well deserve our consideration. When that intriguing politician fled into Spain, to avoid the persecution of his enemies, he passed through Saragossa, the capital of Arragon, where he was shewn, in the cathedral, a man, who had served seven years as a door-keeper, and was well known to every body in town, that had ever paid his devotions at that church. He had been seen, for so long a time, wanting a leg; but recovered that limb by the rubbing of holy oil upon the stump; and the cardinal assures us that he saw him with two legs. This miracle was vouched by all the canons of the church; and the whole company in town were appealed to for a confirmation of the fact; whom the cardinal found, by their zealous devotion, to be thorough believers of the miracle. Here the relater was also cotemporary to the supposed prodigy, of an incredulous and libertine character, as well as of great genius; the miracle of so

---

* *Hist.* lib. iv. cap. 81. Suetonius gives nearly the same account in *Vita Vesp.*

singular a nature as could scarcely admit of a counterfeit, and the witnesses very numerous, and all of them, in a manner, spectators of the fact, to which they gave their testimony. And what adds mightily to the force of the evidence, and may double our surprise on this occasion, is, that the cardinal himself, who relates the story, seems not to give any credit to it, and consequently cannot be suspected of any concurrence in the holy fraud. He considered justly, that it was not requisite, in order to reject a fact of this nature, to be able accurately to disprove the testimony, and to trace its falsehood, through all the circumstances of knavery and credulity which produced it. He knew, that, as this was commonly altogether impossible at any small distance of time and place; so was it extremely difficult, even where one was immediately present, by reason of the bigotry, ignorance, cunning, and roguery of a great part of mankind. He therefore concluded, like a just reasoner, that such an evidence carried falsehood upon the very face of it, and that a miracle, supported by any human testimony, was more properly a subject of derision than of argument.

There surely never was a greater number of miracles ascribed to one person, than those, which were lately said to have been wrought in France upon the tomb of Abbé Paris, the famous Jansenist, with whose sanctity the people were so long deluded. The curing of the sick, giving hearing to the deaf, and sight to the blind, were every where talked of as the usual effects of that holy sepulchre. But what is more extraordinary; many of the miracles were immediately proved upon the spot, before judges of unquestioned integrity, attested by witnesses of credit and distinction, in a learned age, and on the most eminent theatre that is now in the world. Nor is this all: a relation of them was published and dispersed every where; nor were the *Jesuits*, though a learned body, supported by the civil magistrate, and determined enemies to those opinions, in whose favour the miracles were said to have been wrought, ever able distinctly to refute or detect them.* Where shall we find such a

---

* This book was writ by Mons. Montgeron, counsellor or judge of the parliament of Paris, a man of figure and character, who was also a martyr to the cause, and is now said to be somewhere in a dungeon on account of his book.

There is another book in three volumes (called *Recueil des Miracles de l'Abbé Paris*) giving an account of many of these miracles, and accompanied with prefatory discourses, which are very well written. There runs, however, through the whole of these a ridiculous comparison between the miracles of our Saviour

number of circumstances, agreeing to the corroboration of one fact? And what have we to oppose to such a cloud of witnesses, but the absolute impossibility or miraculous nature of the events, which they relate? And this surely, in the eyes of all reasonable people, will alone be regarded as a sufficient refutation.

---

and those of the Abbé; wherein it is asserted, that the evidence for the latter is equal to that for the former: as if the testimony of men could ever be put in the balance with that of God himself, who conducted the pen of the inspired writers. If these writers, indeed, were to be considered merely as human testimony, the French author is very moderate in his comparison; since he might, with some appearance of reason, pretend, that the Jansenist miracles much surpass the other in evidence and authority. The following circumstances are drawn from authentic papers, inserted in the above-mentioned book.

Many of the miracles of Abbé Paris were proved immediately by witnesses before the officiality or bishop's court at Paris, under the eye of cardinal Noailles, whose character for integrity and capacity was never contested even by his enemies.

His successor in the archbishopric was an enemy to the Jansenists, and for that reason promoted to the see by the court. Yet 22 rectors or *curés* of Paris, with infinite earnestness, press him to examine those miracles, which they assert to be known to the whole world, and undisputably certain: but he wisely forbore.

The Molinist party had tried to discredit these miracles in one instance, that of Mademoiselle le Franc. But, besides that their proceedings were in many respects the most irregular in the world, particularly in citing only a few of the Jansenist witnesses, whom they tampered with: besides this, I say, they soon found themselves overwhelmed by a cloud of new witnesses, one hundred and twenty in number, most of them persons of credit and substance in Paris, who gave oath for the miracle. This was accompanied with a solemn and earnest appeal to the parliament. But the parliament were forbidden by authority to meddle in the affair. It was at last observed, that where men are heated by zeal and enthusiasm, there is no degree of human testimony so strong as may not be procured for the greatest absurdity: and those who will be so silly as to examine the affair by that medium, and seek particular flaws in the testimony, are almost sure to be confounded. It must be a miserable imposture, indeed, that does not prevail in that contest.

All who have been in France about that time have heard of the reputation of Mons. Héraut, the *lieutenant de Police*, whose vigilance, penetration, activity, and extensive intelligence have been much talked of. This magistrate, who by the nature of his office is almost absolute, was vested with full powers, on purpose to suppress or discredit these miracles; and he frequently seized immediately, and examined the witnesses and subjects of them: But never could reach any thing satisfactory against them.

In the case of Mademoiselle Thibaut he sent the famous De Sylva to examine her; whose evidence is very curious. The physician declares, that it was impossible she could have been so ill as was proved by witnesses; because it was impossible she could, in so short a time, have recovered so perfectly as he found her. He reasoned, like a man of sense, from natural causes; but the opposite party told him, that the whole was a miracle, and that his evidence was the very best proof of it.

97. Is the consequence just, because some human testimony has the utmost force and authority in some cases, when it relates the battle of Philippi or Pharsalia for instance; that therefore all kinds of testimony must, in all cases, have equal force and authority? Suppose that the Caesarean and Pompeian factions had, each of them, claimed the victory in these battles, and that

---

The Molinists were in a sad dilemma. They durst not assert the absolute insufficiency of human evidence, to prove a miracle. They were obliged to say, that these miracles were wrought by witchcraft and the devil. But they were told, that this was the resource of the Jews of old.

No Jansenist was ever embarrassed to account for the cessation of the miracles, when the church-yard was shut up by the king's edict. It was the touch of the tomb, which produced these extraordinary effects; and when no one could approach the tomb, no effects could be expected. God, indeed, could have thrown down the walls in a moment; but he is master of his own graces and works, and it belongs not to us to account for them. He did not throw down the walls of every city like those of Jericho, on the sounding of the rams' horns, nor break up the prison of every apostle, like that of St Paul.

No less a man, than the Duc de Châtillon, a duke and peer of France, of the highest rank and family, gives evidence of a miraculous cure, performed upon a servant of his, who had lived several years in his house with a visible and palpable infirmity.

I shall conclude with observing, that no clergy are more celebrated for strictness of life and manners than the secular clergy of France, particularly the rectors or *curés* of Paris, who bear testimony to these impostures.

The learning, genius, and probity of the gentlemen, and the austerity of the nuns of Port-Royal, have been much celebrated all over Europe. Yet they all give evidence for a miracle, wrought on the niece of the famous Pascal, whose sanctity of life, as well as extraordinary capacity, is well known. The famous Racine gives an account of this miracle in his famous history of Port-Royal, and fortifies it with all the proofs, which a multitude of nuns, priests, physicians, and men of the world, all of them of undoubted credit, could bestow upon it. Several men of letters, particularly the bishop of Tournay, thought this miracle so certain, as to employ it in the refutation of atheists and free-thinkers. The queen-regent of France, who was extremely prejudiced against the Port-Royal, sent her own physician to examine the miracle, who returned an absolute convert. In short, the supernatural cure was so uncontestable, that it saved, for a time, that famous monastery from the ruin with which it was threatened by the Jesuits. Had it been a cheat, it had certainly been detected by such sagacious and powerful antagonists, and must have hastened the ruin of the contrivers. Our divines, who can build up a formidable castle from such despicable materials; what a prodigious fabric could they have reared from these and many other circumstances, which I have not mentioned! How often would the great names of Pascal, Racine, Arnaud, Nicole, have resounded in our ears? But if they be wise, they had better adopt the miracle, as being more worth, a thousand times, than all the rest of the collection. Besides, it may serve very much to their purpose. For that miracle was really performed by the touch of an authentic holy prickle of the holy thorn, which composed the holy crown, which, &c.

the historians of each party had uniformly ascribed the advantage to their own side; how could mankind, at this distance, have been able to determine between them? The contrariety is equally strong between the miracles related by Herodotus or Plutarch, and those delivered by Mariana, Bede, or any monkish historian.

The wise lend a very academic faith to every report which favours the passion of the reporter; whether it magnifies his country, his family, or himself, or in any other way strikes in with his natural inclinations and propensities. But what greater temptation than to appear a missionary, a prophet, an ambassador from heaven? Who would not encounter many dangers and difficulties, in order to attain so sublime a character? Or if, by the help of vanity and a heated imagination, a man has first made a convert of himself, and entered seriously into the delusion; who ever scruples to make use of pious frauds, in support of so holy and meritorious a cause?

The smallest spark may here kindle into the greatest flame; because the materials are always prepared for it. The *avidum genus auricularum,** the gazing populace, receive greedily, without examination, whatever sooths superstition, and promotes wonder.

How many stories of this nature have, in all ages, been detected and exploded in their infancy? How many more have been celebrated for a time, and have afterwards sunk into neglect and oblivion? Where such reports, therefore, fly about, the solution of the phenomenon is obvious; and we judge in conformity to regular experience and observation, when we account for it by the known and natural principles of credulity and delusion. And shall we, rather than have a recourse to so natural a solution, allow of a miraculous violation of the most established laws of nature?

I need not mention the difficulty of detecting a falsehood in any private or even public history, at the place, where it is said to happen; much more when the scene is removed to ever so small a distance. Even a court of judicature, with all the authority, accuracy, and judgement, which they can employ, find themselves often at a loss to distinguish between truth and falsehood in the most recent actions. But the matter never comes to any issue, if trusted to the common method of altercations and debate and flying rumours; especially when men's passions have taken part on either side.

* Lucret.

In the infancy of new religions, the wise and learned commonly esteem the matter too inconsiderable to deserve their attention or regard. And when afterwards they would willingly detect the cheat, in order to undeceive the deluded multitude, the season is now past, and the records and witnesses, which might clear up the matter, have perished beyond recovery.

No means of detection remain, but those which must be drawn from the very testimony itself of the reporters: and these, though always sufficient with the judicious and knowing, are commonly too fine to fall under the comprehension of the vulgar.

98. Upon the whole, then, it appears, that no testimony for any kind of miracle has ever amounted to a probability, much less to a proof; and that, even supposing it amounted to a proof, it would be opposed by another proof; derived from the very nature of the fact, which it would endeavour to establish. It is experience only, which gives authority to human testimony; and it is the same experience, which assures us of the laws of nature. When, therefore, these two kinds of experience are contrary, we have nothing to do but substract the one from the other, and embrace an opinion, either on one side or the other, with that assurance which arises from the remainder. But according to the principle here explained, this substraction, with regard to all popular religions, amounts to an entire annihilation; and therefore we may establish it as a maxim, that no human testimony can have such force as to prove a miracle, and make it a just foundation for any such system of religion.

99. I beg the limitations here made may be remarked, when I say, that a miracle can never be proved, so as to be the foundation of a system of religion. For I own, that otherwise, there may possibly be miracles, or violations of the usual course of nature, of such a kind as to admit of proof from human testimony; though, perhaps, it will be impossible to find any such in all the records of history. Thus, suppose, all authors, in all languages, agree, that, from the first of January 1600, there was a total darkness over the whole earth for eight days: suppose that the tradition of this extraordinary event is still strong and lively among the people: that all travellers, who return from foreign countries, bring us accounts of the same tradition, without the least variation or contradiction: it is evident, that our present philosophers, instead of doubting the fact, ought to receive it as certain, and ought to search for the

causes whence it might be derived. The decay, corruption, and dissolution of nature, is an event rendered probable by so many analogies, that any phenomenon, which seems to have a tendency towards that catastrophe, comes within the reach of human testimony, if that testimony be very extensive and uniform.

But suppose, that all the historians who treat of England, should agree, that, on the first of January 1600, Queen Elizabeth died; that both before and after her death she was seen by her physicians and the whole court, as is usual with persons of her rank; that her successor was acknowledged and proclaimed by the parliament; and that, after being interred a month, she again appeared, resumed the throne, and governed England for three years: I must confess that I should be surprised at the concurrence of so many odd circumstances, but should not have the least inclination to believe so miraculous an event. I should not doubt of her pretended death, and of those other public circumstances that followed it: I should only assert it to have been pretended, and that it neither was, nor possibly could be real. You would in vain object to me the difficulty, and almost impossibility of deceiving the world in an affair of such consequence; the wisdom and solid judgement of that renowned queen; with the little or no advantage which she could reap from so poor an artifice: all this might astonish me; but I would still reply, that the knavery and folly of men are such common phenomena, that I should rather believe the most extraordinary events to arise from their concurrence, than admit of so signal a violation of the laws of nature.

But should this miracle be ascribed to any new system of religion; men, in all ages, have been so much imposed on by ridiculous stories of that kind, that this very circumstance would be a full proof of a cheat, and sufficient, with all men of sense, not only to make them reject the fact, but even reject it without farther examination. Though the Being to whom the miracle is ascribed, be, in this case, Almighty, it does not, upon that account, become a whit more probable; since it is impossible for us to know the attributes or actions of such a Being, otherwise than from the experience which we have of his productions, in the usual course of nature. This still reduces us to past observation, and obliges us to compare the instances of the violation of truth in the testimony of men, with those of the violation of the laws of nature by miracles, in order to judge which of them is most likely and probable. As the violations of truth are more common in the testimony concerning religious miracles, than in that concerning any other matter of fact; this must diminish very much the authority of the former testimony, and make us form a general resolution, never to lend any attention to it, with whatever specious pretence it may be covered.

Lord Bacon seems to have embraced the same principles of reasoning. 'We ought,' says he, 'to make a collection or particular history of all monsters and prodigious births or productions, and in a word of every thing new, rare, and extraordinary in nature. But this must be done with the most severe scrutiny, lest we depart from truth. Above all, every relation must be considered as suspicious, which depends in any degree upon religion, as the prodigies of Livy: and no less so, every thing that is to be found in the writers of natural magic or alchimy, or such authors, who seem, all of them, to have an unconquerable appetite for falsehood and fable.'*

100. I am the better pleased with the method of reasoning here delivered, as I think it may serve to confound those dangerous friends or disguised enemies to the *Christian Religion*, who have undertaken to defend it by the principles of human reason. Our most holy religion is founded on *Faith*, not on reason; and it is a sure method of exposing it to put it to such a trial as it is, by no means, fitted to endure. To make this more evident, let us examine those miracles, related in scripture; and not to lose ourselves in too wide a field, let us confine ourselves to such as we find in the *Pentateuch*, which we shall examine, according to the principles of these pretended Christians, not as the word or testimony of God himself, but as the production of a mere human writer and historian. Here then we are first to consider a book, presented to us by a barbarous and ignorant people, written in an age when they were still more barbarous, and in all probability long after the facts which it relates, corroborated by no concurring testimony, and resembling those fabulous accounts, which every nation gives of its origin. Upon reading this book, we find it full of prodigies and miracles. It gives an account of a state of the world and of human nature entirely different from the present: of our fall from

---

* *Nov. Org.* lib. ii. aph. 29.

that state: of the age of man, extended to near a thousand years: of the destruction of the world by a deluge: of the arbitrary choice of one people, as the favourites of heaven; and that people the countrymen of the author: of their deliverance from bondage by prodigies the most astonishing imaginable: I desire any one to lay his hand upon his heart, and after a serious consideration declare, whether he thinks that the falsehood of such a book, supported by such a testimony, would be more extraordinary and miraculous than all the miracles it relates; which is, however, necessary to make it be received, according to the measures of probability above established.

101. What we have said of miracles may be applied, without any variation, to prophecies; and indeed, all prophecies are real miracles, and as such only, can be admitted as proofs of any revelation. If it did not exceed the capacity of human nature to foretell future events, it would be absurd to employ any prophecy as an argument for a divine mission or authority from heaven. So that, upon the whole, we may conclude, that the *Christian Religion* not only was at first attended with miracles, but even at this day cannot be believed by any reasonable person without one. Mere reason is insufficient to convince us of its veracity: and whoever is moved by *Faith* to assent to it, is conscious of a continued miracle in his own person, which subverts all the principles of his understanding, and gives him a determination to believe what is most contrary to custom and experience.

Of a particular providence and of a future state

102. I was lately engaged in conversation with a friend who loves sceptical paradoxes; where, though he advanced many principles, of which I can by no means approve, yet as they seem to be curious, and to bear some relation to the chain of reasoning carried on throughout this enquiry, I shall here copy them from my memory as accurately as I can, in order to submit them to the judgement of the reader.

Our conversation began with my admiring the singular good fortune of philosophy, which, as it requires entire liberty above all other privileges, and chiefly flourishes from the free opposition of sentiments and argumentation, received its first birth in an age and country of freedom and toleration, and was never cramped, even in its most extravagant principles, by any creeds, concessions, or penal statutes. For, except the banishment of Protagoras, and the death of Socrates, which last event proceeded partly from other motives, there are scarcely any instances to be met with, in ancient history, of this bigoted jealousy, with which the present age is so much infested. Epicurus lived at Athens to an advanced age, in peace and tranquillity: Epicureans* were even admitted to receive the sacerdotal character, and to officiate at the altar, in the most sacred rites of the established religion: and the public encouragement† of pensions and salaries was afforded equally, by the wisest of all the Roman emperors,‡ to the professors of every sect of philosophy. How requisite such kind of treatment was to philosophy, in her early youth, will easily be conceived, if we reflect, that, even at present, when she may be supposed more hardy and robust, she bears with much difficulty the inclemency of the

---

* Luciani, συμπ. ἢ Λαπίθαι.
† Luciani, εὐνοῦχος.
‡ Luciani and Dio.

seasons, and those harsh winds of calumny and persecution, which blow upon her.

You admire, says my friend, as the singular good fortune of philosophy, what seems to result from the natural course of things, and to be unavoidable in every age and nation. This pertinacious bigotry, of which you complain, as so fatal to philosophy, is really her offspring, who, after allying with superstition, separates himself entirely from the interest of his parent, and becomes her most inveterate enemy and persecutor. Speculative dogmas of religion, the present occasions of such furious dispute, could not possibly be conceived or admitted in the early ages of the world; when mankind, being wholly illiterate, formed an idea of religion more suitable to their weak apprehension, and composed their sacred tenets of such tales chiefly as were the objects of traditional belief, more than of argument or disputation. After the first alarm, therefore, was over, which arose from the new paradoxes and principles of the philosophers; these teachers seem ever after, during the ages of antiquity, to have lived in great harmony with the established superstition, and to have made a fair partition of mankind between them; the former claiming all the learned and wise, the latter possessing all the vulgar and illiterate.

103. It seems then, say I, that you leave politics entirely out of the question, and never suppose, that a wise magistrate can justly be jealous of certain tenets of philosophy, such as those of Epicurus, which, denying a divine existence, and consequently a providence and a future state, seem to loosen, in a great measure, the ties of morality, and may be supposed, for that reason, pernicious to the peace of civil society.

I know, replied he, that in fact these persecutions never, in any age, proceeded from calm reason, or from experience of the pernicious consequences of philosophy; but arose entirely from passion and prejudice. But what if I should advance farther, and assert, that if Epicurus had been accused before the people, by any of the *sycophants* or informers of those days, he could easily have defended his cause, and proved his principles of philosophy to be as salutary as those of his adversaries, who endeavoured, with such zeal, to expose him to the public hatred and jealousy?

I wish, said I, you would try your eloquence upon so extraordinary a topic, and make a speech for Epicurus, which might satisfy, not the mob of Athens, if you will allow that ancient and polite city to have contained any mob, but the more philosophical part of his audience, such as might be supposed capable of comprehending his arguments.

The matter would not be difficult, upon such conditions, replied he. And if you please, I shall suppose myself Epicurus for a moment, and make you stand for the Athenian people, and shall deliver you such an harangue as will fill all the urn with white beans, and leave not a black one to gratify the malice of my adversaries.

Very well: pray proceed upon these suppositions.

104. I come hither, O ye Athenians, to justify in your assembly what I maintained in my school, and I find myself impeached by furious antagonists, instead of reasoning with calm and dispassionate enquirers. Your deliberations, which of right should be directed to questions of public good, and the interest of the commonwealth, are diverted to the disquisitions of speculative philosophy; and these magnificent, but perhaps fruitless enquiries, take place of your more familiar but more useful occupations. But so far as in me lies, I will prevent this abuse. We shall not here dispute concerning the origin and government of worlds. We shall only enquire how far such questions concern the public interest. And if I can persuade you, that they are entirely indifferent to the peace of society and security of government, I hope that you will presently send us back to our schools, there to examine, at leisure, the question the most sublime, but at the same time, the most speculative of all philosophy.

The religious philosophers, not satisfied with the tradition of your forefathers, and doctrine of your priests (in which I willingly acquiesce), indulge a rash curiosity, in trying how far they can establish religion upon the principles of reason; and they thereby excite, instead of satisfying, the doubts, which naturally arise from a diligent and scrutinous enquiry. They paint, in the most magnificent colours, the order, beauty, and wise arrangement of the universe; and then ask, if such a glorious display of intelligence could proceed from the fortuitous concourse of atoms, or if chance could produce what the greatest genius can never sufficiently admire. I shall not examine the justness of this argument. I shall allow it to be as solid as my antagonists and accusers can desire. It is sufficient, if I can prove, from this very reasoning, that the question

is entirely speculative, and that, when, in my philosophical disquisitions, I deny a providence and a future state, I undermine not the
foundations of society, but advance principles, which they themselves, upon their own topics, if they argue consistently, must allow
to be solid and satisfactory.

105. You then, who are my accusers, have acknowledged, that
the chief or sole argument for a divine existence (which I never
questioned) is derived from the order of nature; where there
appear such marks of intelligence and design, that you think it
extravagant to assign for its cause, either chance, or the blind and
unguided force of matter. You allow, that this is an argument
drawn from effects to causes. From the order of the work, you
infer, that there must have been project and forethought in the
workman. If you cannot make out this point, you allow, that your
conclusion fails; and you pretend not to establish the conclusion in
a greater latitude than the phenomena of nature will justify. These
are your concessions. I desire you to mark the consequences.

When we infer any particular cause from an effect, we must
proportion the one to the other, and can never be allowed to
ascribe to the cause any qualities, but what are exactly sufficient to
produce the effect. A body of ten ounces raised in any scale may
serve as a proof, that the counterbalancing weight exceeds ten
ounces; but can never afford a reason that it exceeds a hundred. If
the cause, assigned for any effect, be not sufficient to produce it,
we must either reject that cause, or add to it such qualities as will
give it a just proportion to the effect. But if we ascribe to it farther
qualities, or affirm it capable of producing other effects, we can
only indulge the licence of conjecture, and arbitrarily suppose the
existence of qualities and energics, without reason or authority.

The same rule holds, whether the cause assigned be brute
unconscious matter, or a rational intelligent being. If the cause be
known only by the effect, we never ought to ascribe to it any
qualities, beyond what are precisely requisite to produce the
effect: nor can we, by any rules of just reasoning, return back from
the cause, and infer other effects from it, beyond those by which
alone it is known to us. No one, merely from the sight of one of
Zeuxis's pictures, could know, that he was also a statuary or
architect, and was an artist no less skilful in stone and marble than
in colours. The talents and taste, displayed in the particular work

before us; these we may safely conclude the workman to be possessed of. The cause must be proportioned to the effect; and if we exactly and precisely proportion it, we shall never find in it any qualities, that point farther, or afford an inference concerning any other design or performance. Such qualities must be somewhat beyond what is merely requisite for producing the effect, which we examine.

106. Allowing, therefore, the gods to be the authors of the existence or order of the universe; it follows, that they possess that precise degree of power, intelligence, and benevolence, which appears in their workmanship; but nothing farther can ever be proved, except we call in the assistance of exaggeration and flattery to supply the defects of argument and reasoning. So far as the traces of any attributes, at present, appear, so far may we conclude these attributes to exist. The supposition of farther attributes is mere hypothesis; much more the supposition, that, in distant regions of space or periods of time, there has been, or will be, a more magnificent display of these attributes, and a scheme of administration more suitable to such imaginary virtues. We can never be allowed to mount up from the universe, the effect, to Jupiter, the cause; and then descend downwards, to infer any new effect from that cause; as if the present effects alone were not entirely worthy of the glorious attributes, which we ascribe to that deity. The knowledge of the cause being derived solely from the effect, they must be exactly adjusted to each other; and the one can never refer to anything farther, or be the foundation of any new inference and conclusion.

You find certain phenomena in nature. You seek a cause or author. You imagine that you have found him. You afterwards become so enamoured of this offspring of your brain, that you imagine it impossible, but he must produce something greater and more perfect than the present scene of things, which is so full of ill and disorder. You forget, that this superlative intelligence and benevolence are entirely imaginary, or, at least, without any foundation in reason; and that you have no ground to ascribe to him any qualities, but what you see he has actually exerted and displayed in his productions. Let your gods, therefore, O philosophers, be suited to the present appearances of nature: and presume not to alter these appearances by arbitrary suppositions, in order to suit them to the attributes, which you so fondly ascribe to your deities.

107. When priests and poets, supported by your authority, O Athenians, talk of a golden or silver age, which preceded the present state of vice and misery, I hear them with attention and with reverence. But when philosophers, who pretend to neglect authority, and to cultivate reason, hold the same discourse, I pay them not, I own, the same obsequious submission and pious deference. I ask; who carried them into the celestial regions, who admitted them into the councils of the gods, who opened to them the book of fate, that they thus rashly affirm, that their deities have executed, or will execute, any purpose beyond what has actually appeared? If they tell me, that they have mounted on the steps or by the gradual ascent of reason, and by drawing inferences from effects to causes, I still insist, that they have aided the ascent of reason by the wings of imagination; otherwise they could not thus change their manner of inference, and argue from causes to effects; presuming, that a more perfect production than the present world would be more suitable to such perfect beings as the gods, and forgetting that they have no reason to ascribe to these celestial beings any perfection or any attribute, but what can be found in the present world.

Hence all the fruitless industry to account for the ill appearances of nature, and save the honour of the gods; while we must acknowledge the reality of that evil and disorder, with which the world so much abounds. The obstinate and intractable qualities of matter, we are told, or the observance of general laws, or some such reason, is the sole cause, which controlled the power and benevolence of Jupiter, and obliged him to create mankind and every sensible creature so imperfect and so unhappy. These attributes then, are, it seems, beforehand, taken for granted, in their greatest latitude. And upon that supposition, I own that such conjectures may, perhaps, be admitted as plausible solutions of the ill phenomena. But still I ask; Why take these attributes for granted, or why ascribe to the cause any qualities but what actually appear in the effect? Why torture your brain to justify the course of nature upon suppositions, which, for aught you know, may be entirely imaginary, and of which there are to be found no traces in the course of nature?

The religious hypothesis, therefore, must be considered only as a particular method of accounting for the visible phenomena of the universe: but no just reasoner will ever presume to infer from it any single fact, and alter or add to the phenomena, in any single particular. If you think, that the appearances of things prove such causes, it is allowable for you to draw an inference concerning the existence of these causes. In such complicated and sublime subjects, every one should be indulged in the liberty of conjecture and argument. But here you ought to rest. If you come backward, and arguing from your inferred causes, conclude, that any other fact has existed, or will exist, in the course of nature, which may serve as a fuller display of particular attributes; I must admonish you, that you have departed from the method of reasoning, attached to the present subject, and have certainly added something to the attributes of the cause, beyond what appears in the effect; otherwise you could never, with tolerable sense or propriety, add anything to the effect, in order to render it more worthy of the cause.

108. Where, then, is the odiousness of that doctrine, which I teach in my school, or rather, which I examine in my gardens? Or what do you find in this whole question, wherein the security of good morals, or the peace and order of society, is in the least concerned?

I deny a providence, you say, and supreme governor of the world, who guides the course of events, and punishes the vicious with infamy and disappointment, and rewards the virtuous with honour and success, in all their undertakings. But surely, I deny not the course itself of events, which lies open to every one's inquiry and examination. I acknowledge, that, in the present order of things, virtue is attended with more peace of mind than vice, and meets with a more favourable reception from the world. I am sensible, that, according to the past experience of mankind, friendship is the chief joy of human life, and moderation the only source of tranquillity and happiness. I never balance between the virtuous and the vicious course of life; but am sensible, that, to a well-disposed mind, every advantage is on the side of the former. And what can you say more, allowing all your suppositions and reasonings? You tell me, indeed, that this disposition of things proceeds from intelligence and design. But whatever it proceeds from, the disposition itself, on which depends our happiness or misery, and consequently our conduct and deportment in life is still the same. It is still open for me, as well as you, to regulate my behaviour, by my experience of past events. And if you affirm, that, while a divine providence is allowed, and a supreme distributive justice in the universe, I ought to expect some more particular reward of the good, and punishment of the bad, beyond the ordinary course of events; I here find the same fallacy, which I have before endeavoured to detect. You persist in imagining, that, if we grant that divine existence, for which you so earnestly contend, you may safely infer consequences from it, and add something to the experienced order of nature, by arguing from the attributes which you ascribe to your gods. You seem not to remember, that all your reasonings on this subject can only be drawn from effects to causes; and that every argument, deducted from causes to effects, must of necessity be a gross sophism; since it is impossible for you to know anything of the cause, but what you have antecedently, not inferred, but discovered to the full, in the effect.

109. But what must a philosopher think of those vain reasoners, who, instead of regarding the present scene of things as the sole object of their contemplation, so far reverse the whole course of nature, as to render this life merely a passage to something farther; a porch, which leads to a greater, and vastly different building; a prologue, which serves only to introduce the piece, and give it more grace and propriety? Whence, do you think, can such philosophers derive their idea of the gods? From their own conceit and imagination surely. For if they derived it from the present phenomena, it would never point to anything farther, but must be exactly adjusted to them. That the divinity may *possibly* be endowed with attributes, which we have never seen exerted; may be governed by principles of action, which we cannot discover to be satisfied: all this will freely be allowed. But still this is mere *possibility* and hypothesis. We never can have reason to *infer* any attributes, or any principles of action in him, but so far as we know them to have been exerted and satisfied.

Are there any marks of a distributive justice in the world? If you answer in the affirmative, I conclude, that, since justice here exerts itself, it is satisfied. If you reply in the negative, I conclude, that you have then no reason to ascribe justice, in our sense of it, to the gods. If you hold a medium between affirmation and negation, by saying, that the justice of the gods, at present, exerts itself in part, but not in its full extent; I answer, that you have no reason to give it any particular extent, but only so far as you see it, *at present*, exert itself.

110. Thus I bring the dispute, O Athenians, to a short issue with my antagonists. The course of nature lies open to my contemplation as well as to theirs. The experienced train of events is the great standard, by which we all regulate our conduct. Nothing else can be appealed to in the field, or in the senate. Nothing else ought ever to be heard of in the school, or in the closet. In vain would our limited understanding break through those boundaries, which are too narrow for our fond imagination. While we argue from the course of nature, and infer a particular intelligent cause, which first bestowed, and still preserves order in the universe, we embrace a principle, which is both uncertain and useless. It is uncertain; because the subject lies entirely beyond the reach of human experience. It is useless; because our knowledge of this cause being derived entirely from the course of nature, we can never, according to the rules of just reasoning, return back from the cause with any new inference, or making additions to the common and experienced course of nature, establish any new principles of conduct and behaviour.

111. I observe (said I, finding he had finished his harangue) that you neglect not the artifice of the demagogues of old; and as you were pleased to make me stand for the people, you insinuate yourself into my favour by embracing those principles, to which, you know, I have always expressed a particular attachment. But allowing you to make experience (as indeed I think you ought) the only standard of our judgement concerning this, and all other questions of fact; I doubt not but, from the very same experience, to which you appeal, it may be possible to refute this reasoning, which you have put into the mouth of Epicurus. If you saw, for instance, a half-finished building, surrounded with heaps of brick and stone and mortar, and all the instruments of masonry; could you not *infer* from the effect, that it was a work of design and contrivance? And could you not return again, from this inferred cause, to infer new additions to the effect, and conclude, that the

building would soon be finished, and receive all the further improvements, which art could bestow upon it? If you saw upon the sea-shore the print of one human foot, you would conclude, that a man had passed that way, and that he had also left the traces of the other foot, though effaced by the rolling of the sands or inundation of the waters. Why then do you refuse to admit the same method of reasoning with regard to the order of nature? Consider the world and the present life only as an imperfect building, from which you can infer a superior intelligence; and arguing from that superior intelligence, which can leave nothing imperfect; why may you not infer a more finished scheme or plan, which will receive its completion in some distant point of space or time? Are not these methods of reasoning exactly similar? And under what pretence can you embrace the one, while you reject the other?

112. The infinite difference of the subjects, replied he, is a sufficient foundation for this difference in my conclusions. In works of *human* art and contrivance, it is allowable to advance from the effect to the cause, and returning back from the cause, to form new inferences concerning the effect, and examine the alterations, which it has probably undergone, or may still undergo. But what is the foundation of this method of reasoning? Plainly this; that man is a being, whom we know by experience, whose motives and designs we are acquainted with, and whose projects and inclinations have a certain connexion and coherence, according to the laws which nature has established for the government of such a creature. When, therefore, we find, that any work has proceeded from the skill and industry of man; as we are otherwise acquainted with the nature of the animal, we can draw a hundred inferences concerning what may be expected from him; and these inferences will all be founded in experience and observation. But did we know man only from the single work or production which we examine, it were impossible for us to argue in this manner; because our knowledge of all the qualities, which we ascribe to him, being in that case derived from the production, it is impossible they could point to anything farther, or be the foundation of any new inference. The print of a foot in the sand can only prove, when considered alone, that there was some figure adapted to it, by which it was produced: but the print of a human foot proves

likewise, from our other experience, that there was probably another foot, which also left its impression, though effaced by time or other accidents. Here we mount from the effect to the cause; and descending again from the cause, infer alterations in the effect; but this is not a continuation of the same simple chain of reasoning. We comprehend in this case a hundred other experiences and observations, concerning the *usual* figure and members of that species of animal, without which this method of argument must be considered as fallacious and sophistical.

113. The case is not the same with our reasonings from the works of nature. The Deity is known to us only by his productions, and is a single being in the universe, not comprehended under any species or genus, from whose experienced attributes or qualities, we can, by analogy, infer any attribute or quality in him. As the universe shews wisdom and goodness, we infer wisdom and goodness. As it shews a particular degree of these perfections, we infer a particular degree of them, precisely adapted to the effect which we examine. But farther attributes or farther degrees of the same attributes, we can never be authorised to infer or suppose, by any rules of just reasoning. Now, without some such licence of supposition, it is impossible for us to argue from the cause, or infer any alteration in the effect, beyond what has immediately fallen under our observation. Greater good produced by this Being must still prove a greater degree of goodness: a more impartial distribution of rewards and punishments must proceed from a greater regard to justice and equity. Every supposed addition to the works of nature makes an addition to the attributes of the Author of nature; and consequently, being entirely unsupported by any reason or argument, can never be admitted but as mere conjecture and hypothesis.*

---

* In general, it may, I think, be established as a maxim, that where any cause is known only by its particular effects, it must be impossible to infer any new effects from that cause; since the qualities, which are requisite to produce these new effects along with the former, must either be different, or superior, or of more extensive operation, than those which simply produced the effect, whence alone the cause is supposed to be known to us. We can never, therefore, have any reason to suppose the existence of these qualities. To say, that the new effects proceed only from a continuation of the same energy, which is already known from the first effects, will not remove the difficulty. For even granting this to be the case (which can seldom be supposed), the very continuation and exertion of a like energy (for it is impossible it can be absolutely the same), I say, this

The great source of our mistake in this subject, and of the unbounded licence of conjecture, which we indulge, is, that we tacitly consider ourselves, as in the place of the Supreme Being, and conclude, that he will, on every occasion, observe the same conduct, which we ourselves, in his situation, would have embraced as reasonable and eligible. But, besides that the ordinary course of nature may convince us, that almost everything is regulated by principles and maxims very different from ours; besides this, I say, it must evidently appear contrary to all rules of analogy to reason, from the intentions and projects of men, to those of a Being so different, and so much superior. In human nature, there is a certain experienced coherence of designs and inclinations; so that when, from any fact, we have discovered one intention of any man, it may often be reasonable, from experience, to infer another, and draw a long chain of conclusions concerning his past or future conduct. But this method of reasoning can never have place with regard to a Being, so remote and incomprehensible, who bears much less analogy to any other being in the universe than the sun to a waxen taper, and who discovers himself only by some faint traces or outlines, beyond which we have no authority to ascribe to him any attribute or perfection. What we imagine to be a superior perfection, may really be a defect. Or were it ever so much a perfection, the ascribing of it to the Supreme Being, where it appears not to have been really exerted, to the full, in his works, savours more of flattery and panegyric, than of just reasoning and sound philosophy. All the philosophy, therefore, in the world, and all the religion, which is nothing but a species of philosophy, will never be able to carry us beyond the usual course of experience, or give us measures of conduct and behaviour different from those which are furnished by reflections on common life. No new fact can ever be inferred from the religious hypothesis; no event foreseen or foretold; no reward or punishment expected or dreaded, beyond what is already known by practice and observation. So that my apology for Epicurus will still appear solid and satisfactory; nor have the political

---

exertion of a like energy, in a different period of space and time, is a very arbitrary supposition, and what there cannot possibly be any traces of in the effects, from which all our knowledge of the cause is originally derived. Let the *inferred* cause be exactly proportioned (as it should be) to the known effect; and it is impossible that it can possess any qualities, from which new or different effects can be *inferred*.

interests of society any connexion with the philosophical disputes concerning metaphysics and religion.

114. There is still one circumstance, replied I, which you seem to have overlooked. Though I should allow your premises, I must deny your conclusion. You conclude, that religious doctrines and reasonings *can* have no influence on life, because they *ought* to have no influence; never considering, that men reason not in the same manner you do, but draw many consequences from the belief of a divine Existence, and suppose that the Deity will inflict punishments on vice, and bestow rewards on virtue, beyond what appear in the ordinary course of nature. Whether this reasoning of theirs be just or not, is no matter. Its influence on their life and conduct must still be the same. And, those, who attempt to disabuse them of such prejudices, may, for aught I know, be good reasoners, but I cannot allow them to be good citizens and politicians; since they free men from one restraint upon their passions, and make the infringement of the laws of society, in one respect, more easy and secure.

After all, I may, perhaps, agree to your general conclusion in favour of liberty, though upon different premises from those, on which you endeavour to found it. I think, that the state ought to tolerate every principle of philosophy; nor is there an instance, that any government has suffered in its political interests by such indulgence. There is no enthusiasm among philosophers; their doctrines are not very alluring to the people; and no restraint can be put upon their reasonings, but what must be of dangerous consequence to the sciences, and even to the state, by paving the way for persecution and oppression in points, where the generality of mankind are more deeply interested and concerned.

115. But there occurs to me (continued I) with regard to your main topic, a difficulty, which I shall just propose to you without insisting on it; lest it lead into reasonings of too nice and delicate a nature. In a word, I much doubt whether it be possible for a cause to be known only by its effect (as you have all along supposed) or to be of so singular and particular a nature as to have no parallel and no similarity with any other cause or object, that has ever fallen under our observation. It is only when two *species* of objects are found to be constantly conjoined, that we can infer the one from the other; and were an effect presented, which was

entirely singular, and could not be comprehended under any known *species*, I do not see, that we could form any conjecture or inference at all concerning its cause. If experience and observation and analogy be, indeed, the only guides which we can reasonably follow in inferences of this nature; both the effect and cause must bear a similarity and resemblance to other effects and causes, which we know, and which we have found, in many instances, to be conjoined with each other. I leave it to your own reflection to pursue the consequences of this principle. I shall just observe, that, as the antagonists of Epicurus always suppose the universe, an effect quite singular and unparalleled, to be the proof of a Deity, a cause no less singular and unparalleled; your reasonings, upon that supposition, seem, at least, to merit our attention. There is, I own, some difficulty, how we can ever return from the cause to the effect, and, reasoning from our ideas of the former, infer any alteration on the latter, or any addition to it.

Of the academical or sceptical philosophy

Part 1

116. There is not a greater number of philosophical reasonings, displayed upon any subject, than those, which prove the existence of a Deity, and refute the fallacies of *Atheists*; and yet the most religious philosophers still dispute whether any man can be so blinded as to be a speculative atheist. How shall we reconcile these contradictions? The knights-errant, who wandered about to clear the world of dragons and giants, never entertained the least doubt with regard to the existence of these monsters.

The *Sceptic* is another enemy of religion, who naturally provokes the indignation of all divines and graver philosophers; though it is certain, that no man ever met with any such absurd creature, or conversed with a man, who had no opinion or principle concerning any subject, either of action or speculation. This begets a very natural question; What is meant by a sceptic? And how far it is possible to push these philosophical principles of doubt and uncertainty?

There is a species of scepticism, *antecedent* to all study and philosophy, which is much inculcated by Des Cartes and others, as a sovereign preservative against error and precipitate judgement. It recommends an universal doubt, not only of all our former opinions and principles, but also of our very faculties; of whose veracity, say they, we must assure ourselves, by a chain of reasoning, deduced from some original principle, which cannot possibly be fallacious or deceitful. But neither is there any such original principle, which has a prerogative above others, that are self-evident and convincing: or if there were, could we advance a step beyond it, but by the use of those very faculties, of which we are supposed to be already diffident. The Cartesian doubt, therefore, were it ever possible to be attained by any human creature (as it plainly is not) would be entirely incurable; and no reasoning could ever bring us to a state of assurance and conviction upon any subject.

It must, however, be confessed, that this species of scepticism, when more moderate, may be understood in a very reasonable sense, and is a necessary preparative to the study of philosophy, by preserving a proper impartiality in our judgements, and weaning our mind from all those prejudices, which we may have imbibed from education or rash opinion. To begin with clear and self-evident principles, to advance by timorous and sure steps, to review frequently our conclusions, and examine accurately all their consequences; though by these means we shall make both a slow and a short progress in our systems; are the only methods, by which we can ever hope to reach truth, and attain a proper stability and certainty in our determinations.

117. There is another species of scepticism, *consequent* to science and enquiry, when men are supposed to have discovered, either the absolute fallaciousness of their mental faculties, or their unfitness to reach any fixed determination in all those curious subjects of speculation, about which they are commonly employed. Even our very senses are brought into dispute, by a certain species of philosophers; and the maxims of common life are subjected to the same doubt as the most profound principles or conclusions of metaphysics and theology. As these paradoxical tenets (if they may be called tenets) are to be met with in some philosophers, and the refutation of them in several, they naturally excite our curiosity, and make us enquire into the arguments, on which they may be founded.

I need not insist upon the more trite topics, employed by the sceptics in all ages, against the evidence of *sense*; such as those which are derived from the imperfection and fallaciousness of our organs, on numberless occasions; the crooked appearance of an oar in water; the various aspects of objects, according to their different distances; the double images which arise from the pressing one eye; with many other appearances of a like nature. These sceptical topics, indeed, are only sufficient to prove, that the senses alone are not implicitly to be depended on; but that we must correct their evidence by reason, and by considerations, derived from the nature of the medium, the distance of the object, and the disposition of the organ, in order to render them, within their sphere, the proper *criteria* of truth and falsehood. There are other more profound arguments against the senses, which admit not of so easy a solution.

118. It seems evident, that men are carried, by a natural instinct or prepossession, to repose faith in their senses; and that, without any reasoning, or even almost before the use of reason, we always suppose an external universe, which depends not on our perception, but would exist, though we and every sensible creature were absent or annihilated. Even the animal creation are governed by a like opinion, and preserve this belief of external objects, in all their thoughts, designs, and actions.

It seems also evident, that, when men follow this blind and powerful instinct of nature, they always suppose the very images, presented by the senses, to be the external objects, and never entertain any suspicion, that the one are nothing but representations of the other. This very table, which we see white, and which we feel hard, is believed to exist, independent of our perception, and to be something external to our mind, which perceives it. Our presence bestows not being on it: our absence does not annihilate it. It preserves its existence uniform and entire, independent of the situation of intelligent beings, who perceive or contemplate it.

But this universal and primary opinion of all men is soon destroyed by the slightest philosophy, which teaches us, that nothing can ever be present to the mind but an image or perception, and that the senses are only the inlets, through which these images are conveyed, without being able to produce any immediate intercourse between the mind and the object. The table, which we see, seems to diminish, as we remove farther from it: but the real table, which exists independent of us, suffers no alteration: it was, therefore, nothing but its image, which was present to the mind. These are the obvious dictates of reason; and no man, who reflects, ever doubted, that the existences, which we consider, when we say, *this house* and *that tree*, are nothing but perceptions in the mind, and fleeting copies or representations of other existences, which remain uniform and independent.

119. So far, then, are we necessitated by reasoning to contradict or depart from the primary instincts of nature, and to embrace a new system with regard to the evidence of our senses. But here philosophy finds herself extremely embarrassed, when she would justify this new system, and obviate the cavils and objections of the sceptics. She can no longer plead the infallible and irresistible instinct of nature: for that led us to a quite different system, which is acknowledged fallible and even erroneous. And to justify this pretended philosophical system, by a chain of clear and convincing argument, or even any appearance of argument, exceeds the power of all human capacity.

By what argument can it be proved, that the perceptions of the mind must be caused by external objects, entirely different from them, though resembling them (if that be possible) and could not arise either from the energy of the mind itself, or from the suggestion of some invisible and unknown spirit, or from some other cause still more unknown to us? It is acknowledged, that, in fact, many of these perceptions arise not from anything external, as in dreams, madness, and other diseases. And nothing can be more inexplicable than the manner, in which body should so operate upon mind as ever to convey an image of itself to a substance, supposed of so different, and even contrary a nature.

It is a question of fact, whether the perceptions of the senses be produced by external objects, resembling them: how shall this question be determined? By experience surely; as all other questions of a like nature. But here experience is, and must be entirely silent. The mind has never anything present to it but the perceptions, and cannot possibly reach any experience of their connexion with objects. The supposition of such a connexion is, therefore, without any foundation in reasoning.

120. To have recourse to the veracity of the supreme Being, in order to prove the veracity of our senses, is surely making a very unexpected circuit. If his veracity were at all concerned in this matter, our senses would be entirely infallible; because it is not possible that he can ever deceive. Not to mention, that, if the external world be once called in question, we shall be at a loss to find arguments, by which we may prove the existence of that Being or any of his attributes.

121. This is a topic, therefore, in which the profounder and more philosophical sceptics will always triumph, when they endeavour to introduce an universal doubt into all subjects of human knowledge and enquiry. Do you follow the instincts and propensities of nature, may they say, in assenting to the veracity of sense? But these lead you to believe that the very perception or sensible image is the external object. Do you disclaim this principle, in order to embrace a more rational opinion, that the perceptions are only representations of something external? You here depart from your natural propensities and more obvious sentiments; and yet are not able to satisfy your reason, which can never find any convincing argument from experience to prove, that the perceptions are connected with any external objects.

122. There is another sceptical topic of a like nature, derived from the most profound philosophy; which might merit · our attention, were it requisite to dive so deep, in order to discover arguments and reasonings, which can so little serve to any serious purpose. It is universally allowed by modern enquirers, that all the sensible qualities of objects, such as hard, soft, hot, cold, white, black, &c. are merely secondary, and exist not in the objects themselves, but are perceptions of the mind, without any external archetype or model, which they represent. If this be allowed, with regard to secondary qualities, it must also follow, with regard to the supposed primary qualities of extension and solidity; nor can the latter be any more entitled to that denomination than the former. The idea of extension is entirely acquired from the senses of sight and feeling; and if all the qualities, perceived by the senses, be in the mind, not in the object, the same conclusion must reach the idea of extension, which is wholly dependent on the sensible ideas or the ideas of secondary qualities. Nothing can save us from this conclusion, but the asserting, that the ideas of those primary qualities are attained by *Abstraction*, an opinion, which, if we examine it accurately, we shall find to be unintelligible, and even absurd. An extension, that is neither tangible nor visible, cannot possibly be conceived: and a tangible or visible extension, which is neither hard nor soft, black nor white, is equally beyond the reach of human conception. Let any man try to conceive a triangle in general, which is neither *Isosceles* nor *Scalenum*, nor has any

particular length or proportion of sides; and he will soon perceive the absurdity of all the scholastic notions with regard to abstraction and general ideas.*

123. Thus the first philosophical objection to the evidence of sense or to the opinion of external existence consists in this, that such an opinion, if rested on natural instinct, is contrary to reason, and if referred to reason, is contrary to natural instinct, and at the same time carries no rational evidence with it, to convince an impartial enquirer. The second objection goes farther, and represents this opinion as contrary to reason: at least, if it be a principle of reason, that all sensible qualities are in the mind, not in the object. Bereave matter of all its intelligible qualities, both primary and secondary, you in a manner annihilate it, and leave only a certain unknown, inexplicable *something*, as the cause of our perceptions; a notion so imperfect, that no sceptic will think it worth while to contend against it.

Part 2

124. It may seem a very extravagant attempt of the sceptics to destroy *reason* by argument and ratiocination; yet is this the grand scope of all their enquiries and disputes. They endeavour to find objections, both to our abstract reasonings, and to those which regard matter of fact and existence.

The chief objection against all *abstract* reasonings is derived from the ideas of space and time; ideas, which, in common life and to a careless view, are very clear and intelligible, but when they pass through the scrutiny of the profound sciences (and they are the chief object of these sciences) afford principles, which seem full of absurdity and contradiction. No priestly *dogmas*, invented on purpose to tame and subdue the rebellious reason of mankind, ever shocked common sense more than the doctrine of the infinite

---

* This argument is drawn from Dr Berkeley; and indeed most of the writings of that very ingenious author form the best lessons of scepticism, which are to be found either among the ancient or modern philosopher, Bayle not excepted. He professes, however, in his title-page (and undoubtedly with great truth) to have composed his book against the sceptics as well as against the atheists and free-thinkers. But that all his arguments, though otherwise intended, are, in reality, merely sceptical, appears from this, *that they admit of no answer and produce no conviction.* Their only effect is to cause that momentary amazement and irresolution and confusion, which is the result of scepticism.

divisibility of extension, with its consequences; as they are pompously displayed by all geometricians and metaphysicians, with a kind of triumph and exultation. A real quantity, infinitely less than any finite quantity, containing quantities infinitely less than itself, and so on *in infinitum*; this is an edifice so bold and prodigious, that it is too weighty for any pretended demonstration to support, because it shocks the clearest and most natural principles of human reason.* But what renders the matter more extraordinary, is, that these seemingly absurd opinions are supported by a chain of reasoning, the clearest and most natural; nor is it possible for us to allow the premises without admitting the consequences. Nothing can be more convincing and satisfactory than all the conclusions concerning the properties of circles and triangles; and yet, when these are once received, how can we deny, that the angle of contact between a circle and its tangent is infinitely less than any rectilineal angle, that as you may increase the diameter of the circle *in infinitum*, this angle of contact becomes still less, even *in infinitum*, and that the angle of contact between other curves and their tangents may be infinitely less than those between any circle and its tangent, and so on, *in infinitum*? The demonstration of these principles seems as unexceptionable as that which proves the three angles of a triangle to be equal to two right ones, though the latter opinion be natural and easy, and the former big with contradiction and absurdity. Reason here seems to be thrown into a kind of amazement and suspense, which, without the suggestions of any sceptic, gives her a diffidence of herself, and of the ground on which she treads. She sees a full light, which illuminates certain places; but that light borders upon the most profound darkness. And between these she is so dazzled and confounded, that she scarcely can pronounce with certainty and assurance concerning any one object.

125. The absurdity of these bold determinations of the abstract sciences seems to become, if possible, still more palpable with

* Whatever disputes there may be about mathematical points, we must allow that there are physical points; that is, parts of extension, which cannot be divided or lessened, either by the eye or imagination. These images, then, which are present to the fancy or senses, are absolutely indivisible, and consequently must be allowed by mathematicians to be infinitely less than any real part of extension; and yet nothing appears more certain to reason, than that an infinite number of them composes an infinite extension. How much more an infinite number of those infinitely small parts of extension, which are still supposed infinitely divisible.

regard to time than extension. An infinite number of real parts of time, passing in succession, and exhausted one after another, appears so evident a contradiction, that no man, one should think, whose judgement is not corrupted, instead of being improved, by the sciences, would ever be able to admit of it.

Yet still reason must remain restless, and unquiet, even with regard to that scepticism, to which she is driven by these seeming absurdities and contradictions. How any clear, distinct idea can contain circumstances, contradictory to itself, or to any other clear, distinct idea, is absolutely incomprehensible; and is, perhaps, as absurd as any proposition, which can be formed. So that nothing can be more sceptical, or more full of doubt and hesitation, than this scepticism itself, which arises from some of the paradoxical conclusions of geometry or the science of quantity.*

126. The sceptical objections to *moral* evidence, or to the reasonings concerning matter of fact, are either *popular* or *philosophical.* The popular objections are derived from the natural weakness of human understanding; the contradictory opinions, which have been entertained in different ages and nations; the variations of our judgement in sickness and health, youth and old age, prosperity and adversity; the perpetual contradiction of each particular man's opinions and sentiments; with many other topics of that kind. It is needless to insist farther on this head. These objections are but weak. For as, in common life, we reason every moment concerning fact and existence, and cannot possibly subsist, without continually employing this species of argument, any popular

---

* It seems to me not impossible to avoid these absurdities and contradictions, if it be admitted, that there is no such thing as abstract or general ideas, properly speaking; but that all general ideas are, in reality, particular ones, attached to a general term, which recalls, upon occasion, other particular ones, that resemble, in certain circumstances, the idea, present to the mind. Thus when the term Horse is pronounced, we immediately figure to ourselves the idea of a black or a white animal, of a particular size or figure: but as that term is also usually applied to animals of other colours, figures and sizes, these ideas, though not actually present to the imagination, are easily recalled; and our reasoning and conclusion proceed in the same way, as if they were actually present. If this be admitted (as seems reasonable) it follows that all the ideas of quantity, upon which mathematicians reason, are nothing but particular, and such as are suggested by the senses and imagination, and consequently, cannot be infinitely divisible. It is sufficient to have dropped this hint at present, without prosecuting it any farther. It certainly concerns all lovers of science not to expose themselves to the ridicule and contempt of the ignorant by their conclusions; and this seems the readiest solution of these difficulties.

objections, derived from thence, must be insufficient to destroy that evidence. The great subverter of *Pyrrhonism* or the excessive principles of scepticism is action, and employment, and the occupations of common life. These principles may flourish and triumph in the schools; where it is, indeed, difficult, if not impossible, to refute them. But as soon as they leave the shade, and by the presence of the real objects, which actuate our passions and sentiments, are put in opposition to the more powerful principles of our nature, they vanish like smoke, and leave the most determined sceptic in the same condition as other mortals.

127. The sceptic, therefore, had better keep within his proper sphere, and display those *philosophical* objections, which arise from more profound researches. Here he seems to have ample matter of triumph; while he justly insists, that all our evidence for any matter of fact, which lies beyond the testimony of sense or memory, is derived entirely from the relation of cause and effect; that we have no other idea of this relation than that of two objects, which have been frequently *conjoined* together; that we have no argument to convince us, that objects, which have, in our experience, been frequently conjoined, will likewise, in other instances, be conjoined in the same manner; and that nothing leads us to this inference but custom or a certain instinct of our nature; which it is indeed difficult to resist, but which, like other instincts, may be fallacious and deceitful. While the sceptic insists upon these topics, he shows his force, or rather, indeed, his own and our weakness; and seems, for the time at least, to destroy all assurance and conviction. These arguments might be displayed at greater length, if any durable good or benefit to society could ever be expected to result from them.

128. For here is the chief and most confounding objection to *excessive* scepticism, that no durable good can ever result from it; while it remains in its full force and vigour. We need only ask such a sceptic, *What his meaning is? And what he proposes by all these curious researches?* He is immediately at a loss, and knows not what to answer. A Copernican or Ptolemaic, who supports each his different system of astronomy, may hope to produce a conviction, which will remain constant and durable, with his audience. A Stoic or Epicurean displays principles, which may not be durable, but which have an effect on conduct and behaviour. But a Pyrrhonian

cannot expect, that his philosophy will have any constant influence on the mind: or if it had, that its influence would be beneficial to society. On the contrary, he must acknowledge, if he will acknowledge anything, that all human life must perish, were his principles universally and steadily to prevail. All discourse, all action would immediately cease; and men remain in a total lethargy, till the necessities of nature, unsatisfied, put an end to their miserable existence. It is true; so fatal an event is very little to be dreaded. Nature is always too strong for principle. And though a Pyrrhonian may throw himself or others into a momentary amazement and confusion by his profound reasonings; the first and most trivial event in life will put to flight all his doubts and scruples, and leave him the same, in every point of action and speculation, with the philosophers of every other sect, or with those who never concerned themselves in any philosophical researches. When he awakes from his dream, he will be the first to join in the laugh against himself, and to confess, that all his objections are mere amusement, and can have no other tendency than to show the whimsical condition of mankind, who must act and reason and believe; though they are not able, by their most diligent enquiry, to satisfy themselves concerning the foundation of these operations, or to remove the objections, which may be raised against them.

Part 3

129. There is, indeed, a more *mitigated* scepticism or *academical* philosophy, which may be both durable and useful, and which may, in part, be the result of this Pyrrhonism, or *excessive* scepticism, when its undistinguished doubts are, in some measure, corrected by common sense and reflection. The greater part of mankind are naturally apt to be affirmative and dogmatical in their opinions; and while they see objects only on one side, and have no idea of any counterpoising argument, they throw themselves precipitately into the principles, to which they are inclined; nor have they any indulgence for those who entertain opposite sentiments. To hesitate or balance perplexes their understanding, checks their passion, and suspends their action. They are, therefore, impatient till they escape from a state, which to them is so uneasy: and they think, that they could never remove themselves far enough from

it, by the violence of their affirmations and obstinacy of their belief. But could such dogmatical reasoners become sensible of the strange infirmities of human understanding, even in its most perfect state, and when most accurate and cautious in its determinations; such a reflection would naturally inspire them with more modesty and reserve, and diminish their fond opinion of themselves, and their prejudice against antagonists. The illiterate may reflect on the disposition of the learned, who, amidst all the advantages of study and reflection, are commonly still diffident in their determinations: and if any of the learned be inclined, from their natural temper, to haughtiness and obstinacy, a small tincture of Pyrrhonism might abate their pride, by showing them, that the few advantages, which they may have attained over their fellows, are but inconsiderable, if compared with the universal perplexity and confusion, which is inherent in human nature. In general, there is a degree of doubt, and caution, and modesty, which, in all kinds of scrutiny and decision, ought for ever to accompany a just reasoner.

130. Another species of *mitigated* scepticism which may be of advantage to mankind, and which may be the natural result of the Pyrrhonian doubts and scruples, is the limitation of our enquiries to such subjects as are best adapted to the narrow capacity of human understanding. The *imagination* of man is naturally sublime, delighted with whatever is remote and extraordinary, and running, without control, into the most distant parts of space and time in order to avoid the objects, which custom has rendered too familiar to it. A correct *Judgement* observes a contrary method, and avoiding all distant and high enquiries, confines itself to common life, and to such subjects as fall under daily practice and experience; leaving the more sublime topics to the embellishment of poets and orators, or to the arts of priests and politicians. To bring us to so salutary a determination, nothing can be more serviceable, than to be once thoroughly convinced of the force of the Pyrrhonian doubt, and of the impossibility, that anything, but the strong power of natural instinct, could free us from it. Those who have a propensity to philosophy, will still continue their researches; because they reflect, that, besides the immediate pleasure, attending such an occupation, philosophical decisions are nothing but the reflections of common life, methodized and corrected. But they will never be tempted to go beyond common life, so long as they consider the imperfection

of those faculties which they employ, their narrow reach, and their inaccurate operations. While we cannot give a satisfactory reason, why we believe, after a thousand experiments, that a stone will fall, or fire burn; can we ever satisfy ourselves concerning any determination, which we may form, with regard to the origin of worlds, and the situation of nature, from and to eternity?

This narrow limitation, indeed, of our enquiries, is, in every respect, so reasonable, that it suffices to make the slightest examination into the natural powers of the human mind and to compare them with their objects, in order to recommend it to us. We shall then find what are the proper subjects of science and enquiry.

131. It seems to me, that the only objects of the abstract sciences or of demonstration are quantity and number, and that all attempts to extend this more perfect species of knowledge beyond these bounds are mere sophistry and illusion. As the component parts of quantity and number are entirely similar, their relations become intricate and involved; and nothing can be more curious, as well as useful, than to trace, by a variety of mediums, their equality or inequality, through their different appearances. But as all other ideas are clearly distinct and different from each other, we can never advance farther, by our utmost scrutiny, than to observe this diversity, and, by an obvious reflection, pronounce one thing not to be another. Or if there be any difficulty in these decisions, it proceeds entirely from the undeterminate meaning of words, which is corrected by juster definitions. That *the square of the hypothenuse is equal to the squares of the other two sides*, cannot be known, let the terms be ever so exactly defined, without a train of reasoning and enquiry. But to convince us of this proposition, *that where there is no property, there can be no injustice*, it is only necessary to define the terms, and explain injustice to be a violation of property. This proposition is, indeed, nothing but a more imperfect definition. It is the same case with all those pretended syllogistical reasonings, which may be found in every other branch of learning, except the sciences of quantity and number; and these may safely, I think, be pronounced the only proper objects of knowledge and demonstration.

132. All other enquiries of men regard only matter of fact and existence; and these are evidently incapable of demonstration.

Whatever *is* may *not be*. No negation of a fact can involve a contradiction. The non-existence of any being, without exception, is as clear and distinct an idea as its existence. The proposition, which affirms it not to be, however false, is no less conceivable and intelligible, than that which affirms it to be. The case is different with the sciences, properly so called. Every proposition, which is not true, is there confused and unintelligible. That the cube root of 64 is equal to the half of 10, is a false proposition, and can never be distinctly conceived. But that Caesar, or the angel Gabriel, or any being never existed, may be a false proposition, but still is perfectly conceivable, and implies no contradiction.

The existence, therefore, of any being can only be proved by arguments from its cause or its effect; and these arguments are founded entirely on experience. If we reason *a priori*, anything may appear able to produce anything. The falling of a pebble may, for aught we know, extinguish the sun; or the wish of a man control the planets in their orbits. It is only experience, which teaches us the nature and bounds of cause and effect, and enables us to infer the existence of one object from that of another.* Such is the foundation of moral reasoning, which forms the greater part of human knowledge, and is the source of all human action and behaviour.

Moral reasonings are either concerning particular or general facts. All deliberations in life regard the former; as also all disquisitions in history, chronology, geography, and astronomy.

The sciences, which treat of general facts, are politics, natural philosophy, physic, chemistry, &c. where the qualities, causes and effects of a whole species of objects are enquired into.

Divinity or Theology, as it proves the existence of a Deity, and the immortality of souls, is composed partly of reasonings concerning particular, partly concerning general facts. It has a foundation in *reason*, so far as it is supported by experience. But its best and most solid foundation is *faith* and divine revelation.

Morals and criticism are not so properly objects of the understanding as of taste and sentiment. Beauty, whether moral or

---

* That impious maxim of the ancient philosophy, *Ex nihilo, nihil fit*, by which the creation of matter was excluded, ceases to be a maxim, according to this philosophy. Not only the will of the supreme Being may create matter; but, for aught we know *a priori*, the will of any other being might create it, or any other cause, that the most whimsical imagination can assign.

natural, is felt, more properly than perceived. Or if we reason concerning it, and endeavour to fix its standard, we regard a new fact, to wit, the general tastes of mankind, or some such fact, which may be the object of reasoning and enquiry.

When we run over libraries, persuaded of these principles, what havoc must we make? If we take in our hand any volume; of divinity or school metaphysics, for instance; let us ask, *Does it contain any abstract reasoning concerning quantity or number?* No. *Does it contain any experimental reasoning concerning matter of fact and existence?* No. Commit it then to the flames: for it can contain nothing but sophistry and illusion.

AN ENQUIRY CONCERNING
THE PRINCIPLES OF MORALS

SECTION ONE
Of the general principles of morals

133. Disputes with men, pertinaciously obstinate in their principles, are, of all others, the most irksome; except, perhaps, those with persons, entirely disingenuous, who really do not believe the opinions they defend, but engage in the controversy, from affectation, from a spirit of opposition, or from a desire of showing wit and ingenuity, superior to the rest of mankind. The same blind adherence to their own arguments is to be expected in both; the same contempt of their antagonists; and the same passionate vehemence, in enforcing sophistry and falsehood. And as reasoning is not the source, whence either disputant derives his tenets; it is in vain to expect, that any logic, which speaks not to the affections, will ever engage him to embrace sounder principles.

Those who have denied the reality of moral distinctions, may be ranked among the disingenuous disputants; nor is it conceivable, that any human creature could ever seriously believe, that all characters and actions were alike entitled to the affection and regard of everyone. The difference, which nature has placed between one man and another, is so wide, and this difference is still so much farther widened, by education, example, and habit, that, where the opposite extremes come at once under our apprehension, there is no scepticism so scrupulous, and scarce any assurance so determined, as absolutely to deny all distinction between them. Let a man's insensibility be ever so great, he must often be touched with the images of Right and Wrong; and let his prejudices be ever so obstinate, he must observe, that others are susceptible of like impressions. The only way, therefore, of converting an antagonist of this kind, is to leave him to himself. For, finding that nobody keeps up the controversy with him, it is probable he will, at last, of himself, from mere weariness, come over to the side of common sense and reason.

134. There has been a controversy started of late, much better worth examination, concerning the general foundation of Morals; whether they be derived from Reason, or from Sentiment; whether we attain the knowledge of them by a chain of argument and induction, or by an immediate feeling and finer internal sense; whether, like all sound judgement of truth and falsehood, they should be the same to every rational intelligent being; or whether, like the perception of beauty and deformity, they be founded entirely on the particular fabric and constitution of the human species.

The ancient philosophers, though they often affirm, that virtue is nothing but conformity to reason, yet, in general, seem to consider morals as deriving their existence from taste and sentiment. On the other hand, our modern enquirers, though they also talk much of the beauty of virtue, and deformity of vice, yet have commonly endeavoured to account for these distinctions by metaphysical reasonings, and by deductions from the most abstract principles of the understanding. Such confusion reigned in these subjects, that an opposition of the greatest consequence could prevail between one system and another, and even in the parts of almost each individual system; and yet nobody, till very lately, was ever sensible of it. The elegant Lord Shaftesbury, who first gave occasion to remark this distinction, and who, in general, adhered to the principles of the ancients, is not, himself, entirely free from the same confusion.

135. It must be acknowledged, that both sides of the question are susceptible of specious arguments. Moral distinctions, it may be said, are discernible by pure *reason*: else, whence the many disputes that reign in common life, as well as in philosophy, with regard to this subject: the long chain of proofs often produced on both sides; the examples cited, the authorities appealed to, the analogies employed, the fallacies detected, the inferences drawn, and the several conclusions adjusted to their proper principles. Truth is disputable; not taste: what exists in the nature of things is the standard of our judgement; what each man feels within himself is the standard of sentiment. Propositions in geometry may be proved, systems in physics may be controverted; but the harmony of verse, the tenderness of passion, the brilliancy of wit, must give immediate pleasure. No man reasons concerning another's beauty; but frequently concerning the justice or injustice of his actions. In every criminal trial

the first object of the prisoner is to disprove the facts alleged, and deny the actions imputed to him: the second to prove, that, even if these actions were real, they might be justified, as innocent and lawful. It is confessedly by deductions of the understanding, that the first point is ascertained: how can we suppose that a different faculty of the mind is employed in fixing the other?

136. On the other hand, those who would resolve all moral determinations into *sentiment*, may endeavour to show, that it is impossible for reason ever to draw conclusions of this nature. To virtue, say they, it belongs to be *amiable*, and vice *odious*. This forms their very nature or essence. But can reason or argumentation distribute these different epithets to any subjects, and pronounce beforehand, that this must produce love, and that hatred? Or what other reason can we ever assign for these affections, but the original fabric and formation of the human mind, which is naturally adapted to receive them?

The end of all moral speculations is to teach us our duty; and, by proper representations of the deformity of vice and beauty of virtue, beget correspondent habits, and engage us to avoid the one, and embrace the other. But is this ever to be expected from inferences and conclusions of the understanding, which of themselves have no hold of the affections nor set in motion the active powers of men? They discover truths: but where the truths which they discover are indifferent, and beget no desire or aversion, they can have no influence on conduct and behaviour. What is honourable, what is fair, what is becoming, what is noble, what is generous, takes possession of the heart, and animates us to embrace and maintain it. What is intelligible, what is evident, what is probable, what is true, procures only the cool assent of the understanding; and gratifying a speculative curiosity, puts an end to our researches.

Extinguish all the warm feelings and prepossessions in favour of virtue, and all disgust or aversion to vice: render men totally indifferent towards these distinctions; and morality is no longer a practical study, nor has any tendency to regulate our lives and actions.

137. These arguments on each side (and many more might be produced) are so plausible, that I am apt to suspect, they may, the one as well as the other, be solid and satisfactory, and that *reason* and *sentiment* concur in almost all moral determinations

and conclusions. The final sentence, it is probable, which pronounces characters and actions amiable or odious, praise-worthy or blameable; that which stamps on them the mark of honour or infamy, approbation or censure; that which renders morality an active principle and constitutes virtue our happiness, and vice our misery; it is probable, I say, that this final sentence depends on some internal sense or feeling, which nature has made universal in the whole species. For what else can have an influence of this nature? But in order to pave the way for such a sentiment, and give a proper discernment of its object, it is often necessary, we find, that much reasoning should precede, that nice distinctions be made, just conclusions drawn, distant comparisons formed, complicated relations examined, and general facts fixed and ascertained. Some species of beauty, especially the natural kinds, on their first appearance, command our affection and approbation; and where they fail of this effect, it is impossible for any reasoning to redress their influence, or adapt them better to our taste and sentiment. But in many orders of beauty, particularly those of the finer arts, it is requisite to employ much reasoning, in order to feel the proper sentiment; and a false relish may frequently be corrected by argument and reflection. There are just grounds to conclude, that moral beauty partakes much of this latter species, and demands the assistance of our intellectual faculties, in order to give it a suitable influence on the human mind.

138. But though this question, concerning the general principles of morals, be curious and important, it is needless for us, at present, to employ farther care in our researches concerning it. For if we can be so happy, in the course of this enquiry, as to discover the true origin of morals, it will then easily appear how far either sentiment or reason enters into all determinations of this nature.* In order to attain this purpose, we shall endeavour to follow a very simple method: we shall analyse that complication of mental qualities, which form what, in common life, we call Personal Merit: we shall consider every attribute of the mind, which renders a man an object either of esteem and affection, or of hatred and contempt; every habit or sentiment or faculty, which, if ascribed to any person, implies either praise or blame, and may enter into any panegyric or satire of his character and

* see Appendix 1.

manners. The quick sensibility, which, on this head, is so universal among mankind, gives a philosopher sufficient assurance, that he can never be considerably mistaken in framing the catalogue, or incur any danger of misplacing the objects of his contemplation: he needs only enter into his own breast for a moment, and consider whether or not he should desire to have this or that quality ascribed to him, and whether such or such an imputation would proceed from a friend or an enemy. The very nature of language guides us almost infallibly in forming a judgement of this nature; and as every tongue possesses one set of words which are taken in a good sense, and another in the opposite, the least acquaintance with the idiom suffices, without any reasoning, to direct us in collecting and arranging the estimable or blameable qualities of men. The only object of reasoning is to discover the circumstances on both sides, which are common to these qualities; to observe that particular in which the estimable qualities agree on the one hand, and the blameable on the other; and thence to reach the foundation of ethics, and find those universal principles, from which all censure or approbation is ultimately derived. As this is a question of fact, not of abstract science, we can only expect success, by following the experimental method, and deducing general maxims from a comparison of particular instances. The other scientific method, where a general abstract principle is first established, and is afterwards branched out into a variety of infer-ences and conclusions, may be more perfect in itself, but suits less the imperfection of human nature, and is a common source of illusion and mistake in this as well as in other subjects. Men are now cured of their passion for hypotheses and systems in natural philosophy, and will hearken to no arguments but those which are derived from experience. It is full time they should attempt a like reformation in all moral disquisitions; and reject every system of ethics, however subtle or ingenious, which is not founded on fact and observation.

We shall begin our enquiry on this head by the consideration of the social virtues, Benevolence and Justice. The explication of them will probably give us an opening by which the others may be accounted for.

SECTION TWO
Of benevolence

Part 1

139. It may be esteemed, perhaps, a superfluous task to prove, that the benevolent or softer affections are estimable; and wherever they appear, engage the approbation and good-will of mankind. The epithets *sociable, good-natured, humane, merciful, grateful, friendly, generous, beneficent*, or their equivalents, are known in all languages, and universally express the highest merit, which *human nature* is capable of attaining. Where these amiable qualities are attended with birth and power and eminent abilities, and display themselves in the good government or useful instruction of mankind, they seem even to raise the possessors of them above the rank of *human nature*, and make them approach in some measure to the divine. Exalted capacity, undaunted courage, prosperous success; these may only expose a hero or politician to the envy and ill-will of the public: but as soon as the praises are added of humane and beneficent; when instances are displayed of lenity, tenderness or friendship; envy itself is silent, or joins the general voice of approb-ation and applause.

When Pericles, the great Athenian statesman and general, was on his death-bed, his surrounding friends, deeming him now insensible, began to indulge their sorrow for their expiring patron, by enumerating his great qualities and successes, his conquests and victories, the unusual length of his administration, and his nine trophies erected over the enemies of the republic. *You forget*, cries the dying hero, who had heard all, *You forget the most eminent of my praises, while you dwell so much on those vulgar advantages, in which fortune had a principal share. You have not observed that no citizen has ever yet worn mourning on my account.**

---

* Plut. in *Pericles*.

In men of more ordinary talents and capacity, the social virtues become, if possible, still more essentially requisite; there being nothing eminent, in that case, to compensate for the want of them, or preserve the person from our severest hatred, as well as contempt. A high ambition, an elevated courage, is apt, says Cicero, in less perfect characters, to degenerate into a turbulent ferocity. The more social and softer virtues are there chiefly to be regarded. These are always good and amiable.*

The principal advantage, which Juvenal discovers in the extensive capacity of the human species, is that it renders our benevolence also more extensive, and gives us larger opportunities of spreading our kindly influence than what are indulged to the inferior creation.† It must, indeed, be confessed, that by doing good only, can a man truly enjoy the advantages of being eminent. His exalted station, of itself but the more exposes him to danger and tempest. His sole prerogative is to afford shelter to inferiors, who repose themselves under his cover and protection.

140. But I forget, that it is not my present business to recommend generosity and benevolence, or to paint, in their true colours, all the genuine charms of the social virtues. These, indeed, sufficiently engage every heart, on the first apprehension of them; and it is difficult to abstain from some sally of panegyric, as often as they occur in discourse or reasoning. But our object here being more the speculative, than the practical part of morals, it will suffice to remark, (what will readily, I believe, be allowed) that no qualities are more entitled to the general good-will and approbation of mankind than beneficence and humanity, friendship and gratitude, natural affection and public spirit, or whatever proceeds from a tender sympathy with others, and a generous concern for our kind and species. These wherever they appear seem to transfuse themselves, in a manner, into each beholder, and to call forth, in their own behalf, the same favourable and affectionate sentiments, which they exert on all around.

* Cic. *de Officiis*, lib. i.
† Sat. xv. 139 and seq.

Part 2

141. We may observe that, in displaying the praises of any humane, beneficent man, there is one circumstance which never fails to be amply insisted on, namely, the happiness and satisfaction, derived to society from his intercourse and good offices. To his parents, we are apt to say, he endears himself by his pious attachment and duteous care still more than by the connexions of nature. His children never feel his authority, but when employed for their advantage. With him, the ties of love are consolidated by beneficence and friendship. The ties of friendship approach, in a fond observance of each obliging office, to those of love and inclination. His domestics and dependants have in him a sure resource; and no longer dread the power of fortune, but so far as she exercises it over him. From him the hungry receive food, the naked clothing, the ignorant and slothful skill and industry. Like the sun, an inferior minister of providence he cheers, invigorates, and sustains the surrounding world.

If confined to private life, the sphere of his activity is narrower; but his influence is all benign and gentle. If exalted into a higher station, mankind and posterity reap the fruit of his labours.

As these topics of praise never fail to be employed, and with success, where we would inspire esteem for any one; may it not thence be concluded, that the utility, resulting from the social virtues, forms, at least, a *part* of their merit, and is one source of that approbation and regard so universally paid to them?

142. When we recommend even an animal or a plant as *useful* and *beneficial*, we give it an applause and recommendation suited to its nature. As, on the other hand, reflection on the baneful influence of any of these inferior beings always inspires us with the sentiment of aversion. The eye is pleased with the prospect of corn-fields and loaded vine-yards; horses grazing, and flocks pasturing: but flies the view of briars and brambles, affording shelter to wolves and serpents.

A machine, a piece of furniture, a vestment, a house well contrived for use and conveniency, is so far beautiful, and is contemplated with pleasure and approbation. An experienced eye is here sensible to many excellencies, which escape persons ignorant and uninstructed.

Can anything stronger be said in praise of a profession, such as merchandize or manufacture, than to observe the advantages which it procures to society; and is not a monk and inquisitor enraged when we treat his order as useless or pernicious to mankind?

The historian exults in displaying the benefit arising from his labours. The writer of romance alleviates or denies the bad consequences ascribed to his manner of composition.

In general, what praise is implied in the simple epithet *useful*! What reproach in the contrary!

Your Gods, says Cicero,* in opposition to the Epicureans, cannot justly claim any worship or adoration, with whatever imaginary perfections you may suppose them endowed. They are totally useless and inactive. Even the Egyptians, whom you so much ridicule, never consecrated any animal but on account of its utility.

The sceptics assert,† though absurdly, that the origin of all religious worship was derived from the utility of inanimate objects, as the sun and moon, to the support and well-being of mankind. This is also the common reason assigned by historians, for the deification of eminent heroes and legislators.‡

To plant a tree, to cultivate a field, to beget children; meritorious acts, according to the religion of Zoroaster.

143. In all determinations of morality, this circumstance of public utility is ever principally in view; and wherever disputes arise, either in philosophy or common life, concerning the bounds of duty, the question cannot, by any means, be decided with greater certainty, than by ascertaining, on any side, the true interests of mankind. If any false opinion, embraced from appearances, has been found to prevail; as soon as farther experience and sounder reasoning have given us juster notions of human affairs, we retract our first sentiment, and adjust anew the boundaries of moral good and evil.

Giving alms to common beggars is naturally praised; because it seems to carry relief to the distressed and indigent: but when we observe the encouragement thence arising to idleness and

* *De Natura Deorum* lib. i.
† Sextus Empiricus *adversus Math*. lib. viii.
‡ Diodorus Siculus passim.

debauchery, we regard that species of charity rather as a weakness than a virtue.

Tyrannicide, or the assassination of usurpers and oppressive princes, was highly extolled in ancient times; because it both freed mankind from many of these monsters, and seemed to keep the others in awe, whom the sword or poinard could not reach. But history and experience having since convinced us, that this practice increases the jealousy and cruelty of princes, a Timoleon and a Brutus, though treated with indulgence on account of the prejudices of their times, are now considered as very improper models for imitation.

Liberality in princes is regarded as a mark of beneficence, but when it occurs, that the homely bread of the honest and industrious is often thereby converted into delicious cates for the idle and the prodigal, we soon retract our heedless praises. The regrets of a prince, for having lost a day, were noble and generous: but had he intended to have spent it in acts of generosity to his greedy courtiers, it was better lost than misemployed after that manner.

Luxury, or a refinement on the pleasures and conveniences of life, had long been supposed the source of every corruption in government, and the immediate cause of faction, sedition, civil wars, and the total loss of liberty. It was, therefore, universally regarded as a vice, and was an object of declamation to all satirists, and severe moralists. Those, who prove, or attempt to prove, that such refinements rather tend to the increase of industry, civility, and arts regulate anew our *moral* as well as *political* sentiments, and represent, as laudable or innocent, what had formerly been regarded as pernicious and blameable.

144. Upon the whole, then, it seems undeniable, *that* nothing can bestow more merit on any human creature than the sentiment of benevolence in an eminent degree; and *that* a *part*, at least, of its merit arises from its tendency to promote the interests of our species, and bestow happiness on human society. We carry our view into the salutary consequences of such a character and disposition; and whatever has so benign an influence, and forwards so desirable an end, is beheld with complacency and pleasure. The social virtues are never regarded without their beneficial tendencies, nor viewed as barren and unfruitful. The

happiness of mankind, the order of society, the harmony of families, the mutual support of friends, are always considered as the result of their gentle dominion over the breasts of men.

How considerable a *part* of their merit we ought to ascribe to their utility, will better appear from future disquisitions;* as well as the reason, why this circumstance has such a command over our esteem and approbation.†

* Sections 3 and 4.
† Section 5.

SECTION THREE
Of justice

Part 1

145. That Justice is useful to society, and consequently that *part* of its merit, at least, must arise from that consideration, it would be a superfluous undertaking to prove. That public utility is the *sole* origin of justice, and that reflections on the beneficial consequences of this virtue are the *sole* foundation of its merit; this proposition, being more curious and important, will better deserve our examination and enquiry.

Let us suppose that nature has bestowed on the human race such profuse *abundance* of all *external* conveniencies, that, without any uncertainty in the event, without any care or industry on our part, every individual finds himself fully provided with whatever his most voracious appetites can want, or luxurious imagination wish or desire. His natural beauty, we shall suppose, surpasses all acquired ornaments: the perpetual clemency of the seasons renders useless all clothes or covering: the raw herbage affords him the most delicious fare; the clear fountain, the richest beverage. No laborious occupation required: no tillage: no navigation. Music, poetry, and contemplation form his sole business: conversation, mirth, and friendship his sole amusement.

It seems evident that, in such a happy state, every other social virtue would flourish, and receive tenfold increase; but the cautious, jealous virtue of justice would never once have been dreamed of. For what purpose make a partition of goods, where every one has already more than enough? Why give rise to property, where there cannot possibly be any injury? Why call this object *mine*, when upon the seizing of it by another, I need but stretch out my hand to possess myself to what is equally valuable? Justice, in that case, being totally useless, would be an idle ceremonial, and could never possibly have place in the catalogue of virtues.

We see, even in the present necessitous condition of mankind, that, wherever any benefit is bestowed by nature in an unlimited abundance, we leave it always in common among the whole human race, and make no subdivisions of right and property. Water and air, though the most necessary of all objects, are not challenged as the property of individuals; nor can any man commit injustice by the most lavish use and enjoyment of these blessings. In fertile extensive countries, with few inhabitants, land is regarded on the same footing. And no topic is so much insisted on by those, who defend the liberty of the seas, as the unexhausted use of them in navigation. Were the advantages, procured by navigation, as inexhaustible, these reasoners had never had any adversaries to refute; nor had any claims ever been advanced of a separate, exclusive dominion over the ocean.

It may happen, in some countries, at some periods, that there be established a property in water, none in land;* if the latter be in greater abundance than can be used by the inhabitants, and the former be found, with difficulty, and in very small quantities.

146. Again; suppose, that, though the necessities of human race continue the same as at present, yet the mind is so enlarged, and so replete with friendship and generosity, that every man has the utmost tenderness for every man, and feels no more concern for his own interest than for that of his fellows; it seems evident, that the use of justice would, in this case, be suspended by such an extensive benevolence, nor would the divisions and barriers of property and obligation have ever been thought of. Why should I bind another, by a deed or promise, to do me any good office, when I know that he is already prompted, by the strongest inclination, to seek my happiness, and would, of himself, perform the desired service; except the hurt, he thereby receives, be greater than the benefit accruing to me? In which case, he knows, that, from my innate humanity and friendship, I should be the first to oppose myself to his imprudent generosity. Why raise landmarks between my neighbour's field and mine, when my heart has made no division between our interests; but shares all his joys and sorrows with the same force and vivacity as if

* Genesis, chaps. xiii. and xxi.

originally my own? Every man, upon this supposition, being a second self to another, would trust all his interests to the discretion of every man; without jealousy, without partition, without distinction. And the whole human race would form only one family; where all would lie in common, and be used freely, without regard to property; but cautiously too, with as entire regard to the necessities of each individual, as if our own interests were most intimately concerned.

In the present disposition of the human heart, it would, perhaps, be difficult to find complete instances of such enlarged affections; but still we may observe, that the case of families approaches towards it; and the stronger the mutual benevolence is among the individuals, the nearer it approaches; till all distinction of property be, in a great measure, lost and confounded among them. Between married persons, the cement of friendship is by the laws supposed so strong as to abolish all division of possessions; and has often, in reality, the force ascribed to it. And it is observable, that, during the ardour of new enthusiasms, when every principle is inflamed into extravagance, the community of goods has frequently been attempted; and nothing but experience of its inconveniencies, from the returning or disguised selfishness of men, could make the imprudent fanatics adopt anew the ideas of justice and of separate property. So true is it, that this virtue derives its existence entirely from its necessary *use* to the intercourse and social state of mankind.

147. To make this truth more evident, let us reverse the foregoing suppositions; and carrying everything to the opposite extreme, consider what would be the effect of these new situations. Suppose a society to fall into such want of all common necessaries, that the utmost frugality and industry cannot preserve the greater number from perishing, and the whole from extreme misery; it will readily, I believe, be admitted, that the strict laws of justice are suspended, in such a pressing emergence, and give place to the stronger motives of necessity and self-preservation. Is it any crime, after a shipwreck, to seize whatever means or instrument of safety one can lay hold of, without regard to former limitations of property? Or if a city besieged were perishing with hunger; can we imagine, that men will see any means of preservation before them, and lose their lives, from a scrupulous

regard to what, in other situations, would be the rules of equity and justice? The use and tendency of that virtue is to procure happiness and security, by preserving order in society: but where the society is ready to perish from extreme necessity, no greater evil can be dreaded from violence and injustice; and every man may now provide for himself by all the means, which prudence can dictate, or humanity permit. The public, even in less urgent necessities, opens granaries, without the consent of proprietors; as justly supposing, that the authority of magistracy may, consistent with equity, extend so far: but were any number of men to assemble, without the tie of laws or civil jurisdiction; would an equal partition of bread in a famine, though effected by power and even violence, be regarded as criminal or injurious?

148. Suppose likewise, that it should be a virtuous man's fate to fall into the society of ruffians, remote from the protection of laws and government; what conduct must he embrace in that melancholy situation? He sees such a desperate rapaciousness prevail; such a disregard to equity, such contempt of order, such stupid blindness to future consequences, as must immediately have the most tragical conclusion, and must terminate in destruction to the greater number, and in a total dissolution of society to the rest. He, meanwhile, can have no other expedient than to arm himself, to whomever the sword he seizes, or the buckler, may belong: to make provision of all means of defence and security: and his particular regard to justice being no longer of use to his own safety or that of others, he must consult the dictates of self-preservation alone, without concern for those who no longer merit his care and attention.

When any man, even in political society, renders himself by his crimes, obnoxious to the public, he is punished by the laws in his goods and person; that is, the ordinary rules of justice are, with regard to him, suspended for a moment, and it becomes equitable to inflict on him, for the *benefit* of society, what otherwise he could not suffer without wrong or injury.

The rage and violence of public war; what is it but a suspension of justice among the warring parties, who perceive, that this virtue is now no longer of any *use* or advantage to them? The laws of war, which then succeed to those of equity and justice, are rules calculated for the *advantage* and *utility* of that particular state, in which men are now placed. And were a civilized nation engaged with barbarians, who observed no rules even of war, the former must also suspend their observance of them, where they no longer serve to any purpose; and must render every action or recounter as bloody and pernicious as possible to the first aggressors.

149. Thus, the rules of equity or justice depend entirely on the particular state and condition in which men are placed, and owe their origin and existence to that utility, which results to the public from their strict and regular observance. Reverse, in any considerable circumstance, the condition of men: produce extreme abundance or extreme necessity: implant in the human breast perfect moderation and humanity, or perfect rapaciousness and malice: by rendering justice totally *useless*, you thereby totally destroy its essence, and suspend its obligation upon mankind.

The common situation of society is a medium amidst all these extremes. We are naturally partial to ourselves, and to our friends; but are capable of learning the advantage resulting from a more equitable conduct. Few enjoyments are given us from the open and liberal hand of nature; but by art, labour, and industry, we can extract them in great abundance. Hence the ideas of property become necessary in all civil society: hence justice derives its usefulness to the public: and hence alone arises its merit and moral obligation.

150. These conclusions are so natural and obvious, that they have not escaped even the poets, in their descriptions of the felicity attending the golden age or the reign of Saturn. The seasons, in that first period of nature, were so temperate, if we credit these agreeable fictions, that there was no necessity for men to provide themselves with clothes and houses, as a security against the violence of heat and cold: the rivers flowed with wine and milk: the oaks yielded honey; and nature spontaneously produced her greatest delicacies. Nor were these the chief advantages of that happy age. Tempests were not alone removed from nature; but those more furious tempests were unknown to human breasts, which now cause such uproar, and engender such confusion. Avarice, ambition, cruelty, selfishness, were never heard of: cordial affection, compassion, sympathy, were the only movements with which the mind was yet acquainted. Even the punctilious distinction of *mine* and *thine* was banished from among the happy race

of mortals, and carried with it the very notion of property and obligation, justice and injustice.

151. This *poetical* fiction of the *golden age* , is in some respects, of a piece with the *philosophical* fiction of the *state of nature*; only that the former is represented as the most charming and most peaceable condition, which can possibly be imagined; whereas the latter is painted out as a state of mutual war and violence, attended with the most extreme necessity. On the first origin of mankind, we are told, their ignorance and savage nature were so prevalent, that they could give no mutual trust, but must each depend upon himself and his own force or cunning for protection and security. No law was heard of: no rule of justice known: no distinction of property regarded: power was the only measure of right; and a perpetual war of all against all was the result of men's untamed selfishness and barbarity.*

Whether such a condition of human nature could ever exist, or if it did, could continue so long as to merit the appellation of a *state*, may justly be doubted. Men are necessarily born in a family-society, at least; and are trained up by their parents to some rule of conduct and behaviour. But this must be admitted, that, if such a state of mutual war and violence was ever real, the suspension of all laws of justice, from their absolute inutility, is a necessary and infallible consequence.

152. The more we vary our views of human life, and the newer and more unusual the lights are in which we survey it, the more

---

* This fiction of a state of nature, as a state of war, was not first started by Mr Hobbes, as is commonly imagined. Plato endeavours to refute an hypothesis very like it in the second, third, and fourth books de republica. Cicero, on the contrary, supposes it certain and universally acknowledged in the following passage. 'Quis enim vestrum, judices, ignorat, ita naturam rerum tulisse, ut quodam tempore homines, nondum neque naturali neque civili jure descripto, fusi per agros ac dispersi vagarentur tantumque haberent quantum manu ac viribus, per caedem ac vulnera, aut eripere aut retinere potuissent? Qui igitur primi virtute & consilio praestanti extiterunt, ii perspecto genere humanae docilitatis atque ingenii, dissipatos unum in locum congregarunt, eosque ex feritate illa ad justitiam ac mansuetudinem transduxerunt. Tum res ad communem utilitatem, quas publicas appellamus, tum conventicula hominum, quae postea civitates nominatae sunt, tum domicilia conjuncta, quas urbes dicamus, invento & divino & humano jure moenibus sepserunt. Atque inter hanc vitam, perpolitam humanitate, & illam immanem, nihil tam interest quam JUS atque VIS. Horum utro uti nolimus, altero est utendum. Vim volumus extingui. Jus valeat necesse est, id est, judicia, quibus omne jus continetur. Judicia displicent, aut nulla sunt? Vis dominetur necesse est? Haec vident omnes.' Pro Sest. sec. 42.

shall we be convinced, that the origin here assigned for the virtue of justice is real and satisfactory.

Were there a species of creatures intermingled with men, which, though rational, were possessed of such inferior strength, both of body and mind, that they were incapable of all resistance, and could never, upon the highest provocation, make us feel the effects of their resentment; the necessary consequence, I think, is that we should be bound by the laws of humanity to give gentle usage to these creatures, but should not, properly speaking, lie under any restraint of justice with regard to them, nor could they possess any right or property, exclusive of such arbitrary lords. Our intercourse with them could not be called society, which supposes a degree of equality; but absolute command on the one side, and servile obedience on the other. Whatever we covet, they must instantly resign: our permission is the only tenure, by which they hold their possessions: our compassion and kindness the only check, by which they curb our lawless will: and as no inconvenience ever results from the exercise of a power, so firmly established in nature, the restraints of justice and property, being totally *useless*, would never have place in so unequal a confederacy.

This is plainly the situation of men, with regard to animals; and how far these may be said to possess reason, I leave it to others to determine. The great superiority of civilized Europeans above barbarous Indians, tempted us to imagine ourselves on the same footing with regard to them, and made us throw off all restraints of justice, and even of humanity, in our treatment of them. In many nations, the female sex are reduced to like slavery, and are rendered incapable of all property, in opposition to their lordly masters. But though the males, when united, have in all countries bodily force sufficient to maintain this severe tyranny, yet such are the insinuation, address, and charms of their fair companions, that women are commonly able to break the confederacy, and share with the other sex in all the rights and privileges of society.

153. Were the human species so framed by nature as that each individual possessed within himself every faculty, requisite both for his own preservation and for the propagation of his kind: were all society and intercourse cut off between man and man,

by the primary intention of the supreme Creator: it seems evident, that so solitary a being would be as much incapable of justice, as of social discourse and conversation. Where mutual regards and forbearance serve to no manner of purpose, they would never direct the conduct of any reasonable man. The headlong course of the passions would be checked by no reflection on future consequences. And as each man is here supposed to love himself alone, and to depend only on himself and his own activity for safety and happiness, he would, on every occasion, to the utmost of his power, challenge the preference above every other being, to none of which he is bound by any ties, either of nature or of interest.

But suppose the conjunction of the sexes to be established in nature, a family immediately arises; and particular rules being found requisite for its subsistence, these are immediately embraced; though without comprehending the rest of mankind within their prescriptions. Suppose that several families unite together into one society, which is totally disjoined from all others, the rules, which preserve peace and order, enlarge themselves to the utmost extent of that society; but becoming then entirely useless, lose their force when carried one step farther. But again suppose, that several distinct societies maintain a kind of intercourse for mutual convenience and advantage, the boundaries of justice still grow larger, in proportion to the largeness of men's views, and the force of their mutual connexions. History, experience, reason sufficiently instruct us in this natural progress of human sentiments, and in the gradual enlargement of our regards to justice, in proportion as we become acquainted with the extensive utility of that virtue.

Part 2

154. If we examine the *particular* laws, by which justice is directed, and property determined; we shall still be presented with the same conclusion. The good of mankind is the only object of all these laws and regulations. Not only is it requisite, for the peace and interest of society, that men's possessions should be separated; but the rules, which we follow, in making the separation, are such as can best be contrived to serve farther the interests of society.

We shall suppose that a creature, possessed of reason, but un-acquainted with human nature, deliberates with himself what rules of justice or property would best promote public interest, and establish peace and security among mankind. His most obvious thought would be, to assign the largest possessions to the most extensive virtue, and give every one the power of doing good, proportioned to his inclination. In a perfect theocracy, where a being, infinitely intelligent, governs by particular volitions, this rule would certainly have place, and might serve to the wisest purposes: but were mankind to execute such a law; so great is the uncertainty of merit, both from its natural obscurity, and from the self-conceit of each individual, that no determinate rule of conduct would ever result from it; and the total dissolution of society must be the immediate consequence. Fanatics may suppose, *that dominion is founded on grace*, and *that saints alone inherit the earth*; but the civil magistrate very justly puts these sublime theorists on the same footing with common robbers, and teaches them by the severest discipline, that a rule, which, in speculation, may seem the most advantageous to society, may yet be found, in practice, totally pernicious and destructive.

That there were *religious* fanatics of this kind in England, during the civil wars, we learn from history; though it is probable, that the obvious *tendency* of these principles excited such horror in mankind, as soon obliged the dangerous enthusiasts to renounce, or at least conceal their tenets. Perhaps the *levellers*, who claimed an equal distribution of property, were a kind of *political* fanatics, which arose from the religious species, and more openly avowed their pretensions; as carrying a more plausible appearance, of being practicable in themselves, as well as useful to human society.

155. It must, indeed, be confessed, that nature is so liberal to mankind, that, were all her presents equally divided among the species, and improved by art and industry, every individual would enjoy all the necessaries, and even most of the comforts of life; nor would ever be liable to any ills but such as might accidentally arise from the sickly frame and constitution of his body. It must also be confessed, that, wherever we depart from this equality, we rob the poor of more satisfaction than we add to the rich, and that the slight gratification of a frivolous vanity, in one individual, frequently costs more than bread to many families, and even

provinces. It may appear withal, that the rule of equality, as it would be highly *useful*, is not altogether *impracticable*; but has taken place, at least in an imperfect degree, in some republics; particularly that of Sparta; where it was attended, it is said, with the most beneficial consequences. Not to mention that the Agrarian laws, so frequently claimed in Rome, and carried into execution in many Greek cities, proceeded, all of them, from a general idea of the utility of this principle.

But historians, and even common sense, may inform us, that, however specious these ideas of *perfect* equality may seem, they are really, at bottom, *impracticable*; and were they not so, would be extremely *pernicious* to human society. Render possessions ever so equal, men's different degrees of art, care, and industry will immediately break that equality. Or if you check these virtues, you reduce society to the most extreme indigence; and instead of preventing want and beggary in a few, render it unavoidable to the whole community. The most rigorous inquisition too is requisite to watch every inequality on its first appearance; and the most severe jurisdiction, to punish and redress it. But besides, that so much authority must soon degenerate into tyranny, and be exerted with great partialities; who can possibly be possessed of it, in such a situation as is here supposed? Perfect equality of possessions, destroying all subordination, weakens extremely the authority of magistracy, and must reduce all power nearly to a level, as well as property.

156. We may conclude, therefore, that, in order to establish laws for the regulation of property, we must be acquainted with the nature and situation of man; must reject appearances, which may be false, though specious; and must search for those rules, which are, on the whole, most *useful* and *beneficial*. Vulgar sense and slight experience are sufficient for this purpose; where men give not way to too selfish avidity, or too extensive enthusiasm.

Who sees not, for instance, that whatever is produced or improved by a man's art or industry ought, for ever, to be secured to him, in order to give encouragement to such *useful* habits and accomplishments? That the property ought also to descend to children and relations, for the same *useful* purpose? That it may be alienated by consent, in order to beget that commerce and intercourse, which is so *beneficial* to human society? And that all contracts and promises ought carefully to be fulfilled, in order to secure mutual trust and confidence, by which the general *interest* of mankind is so much promoted?

Examine the writers on the laws of nature; and you will always find, that, whatever principles they set out with, they are sure to terminate here at last, and to assign, as the ultimate reason for every rule which they establish, the convenience and necessities of mankind. A concession thus extorted, in opposition to systems, has more authority than if it had been made in prosecution of them.

What other reason, indeed, could writers ever give, why this must be *mine* and that *yours*; since uninstructed nature surely never made any such distinction? The objects which receive those appellations are, of themselves, foreign to us; they are totally disjoined and separated from us; and nothing but the general interests of society can form the connexion.

157. Sometimes the interests of society may require a rule of justice in a particular case; but may not determine any particular rule, among several, which are all equally beneficial. In that case, the slightest *analogies* are laid hold of, in order to prevent that indifference and ambiguity, which would be the source of perpetual dissension. Thus possession alone, and first possession, is supposed to convey property, where no body else has any preceding claim and pretension. Many of the reasonings of lawyers are of this analogical nature, and depend on very slight connexions of the imagination.

Does any one scruple, in extraordinary cases, to violate all regard to the private property of individuals, and sacrifice to public interest a distinction which had been established for the sake of that interest? The safety of the people is the supreme law: all other particular laws are subordinate to it, and dependent on it: and if, in the *common* course of things, they be followed and regarded; it is only because the public safety and interest *commonly* demand so equal and impartial an administration.

Sometimes both *utility* and *analogy* fail, and leave the laws of justice in total uncertainty. Thus, it is highly requisite, that prescription or long possession should convey property; but what number of days or months or years should be sufficient for that purpose, it is impossible for reason alone to determine. *Civil laws* here supply the place of the natural *code*, and assign different terms for prescription, according to the different *utilities*, proposed by the legislator. Bills of exchange and promissory notes, by the laws of most countries, prescribe sooner than bonds, and mortgages, and contracts of a more formal nature.

158. In general we may observe that all questions of property are subordinate to the authority of civil laws, which extend, restrain, modify, and alter the rules of natural justice, according to the particular *convenience* of each community. The laws have, or ought to have, a constant reference to the constitution of government, the manners, the climate, the religion, the commerce, the situation of each society. A late author of genius, as well as learning, has prosecuted this subject at large, and has established, from these principles, a system of political knowledge, which abounds in ingenious and brilliant thoughts, and is not wanting in solidity.*

What is a man's property? Anything which it is lawful for him, and for him alone, to use. *But what rule have we, by which we can*

---

* The author of *L'Esprit des Lois*. This illustrious writer, however, sets out with a different theory, and supposes all right to be founded on certain *rapports* or relations; which is a system, that, in my opinion, never will be reconciled with true philosophy. Father Malebranche, as far as I can learn, was the first that started this abstract theory of morals, which was afterwards adopted by Cudworth, Clarke, and others; and as it excludes all sentiment, and pretends to found everything on reason, it has not wanted followers in this philosophic age. See Section 1, Appendix 1. With regard to justice, the virtue here treated of, the inference against this theory seems short and conclusive. Property is allowed to be dependent on civil laws; civil laws are allowed to have no other object, but the interest of society: this therefore must be allowed to be the sole foundation of property and justice. Not to mention, that our obligation itself to obey the magistrate and his laws is founded on nothing but the interests of society.

If the ideas of justice, sometimes, do not follow the dispositions of civil law; we shall find, that these cases, instead of objections, are confirmations of the theory delivered above. Where a civil law is so perverse as to cross all the interests of society, it loses all its authority, and men judge by the ideas of natural justice, which are conformable to those interests. Sometimes also civil laws, for useful purposes, require a ceremony or form to any deed; and where that is wanting, their decrees run contrary to the usual tenor of justice; but one who takes advantage of such chicanes, is not commonly regarded as an honest man. Thus, the interests of society require, that contracts be fulfilled; and there is not a more material article either of natural or civil justice: but the omission of a trifling circumstance will often, by law, invalidate a contract, *in foro humano*, but not *in foro conscientiae*, as divines express themselves. In these cases, the magistrate is supposed only to withdraw his power of enforcing the right, not to have altered the right. Where his intention extends to the right, and is conformable to the interests of society; it never fails to alter the right; a clear proof of the origin of justice and of property, as assigned above.

distinguish these objects? Here we must have recourse to statutes, customs, precedents, analogies, and a hundred other circumstances; some of which are constant and inflexible, some variable and arbitrary. But the ultimate point, in which they all professedly terminate, is the interest and happiness of human society. Where this enters not into consideration, nothing can appear more whimsical, unnatural, and even superstitious, than all or most of the laws of justice and of property.

Those who ridicule vulgar superstitions, and expose the folly of particular regards to meats, days, places, postures, apparel, have an easy task; while they consider all the qualities and relations of the objects, and discover no adequate cause for that affection or antipathy, veneration or horror, which have so mighty an influence over a considerable part of mankind. A Syrian would have starved rather than taste pigeon; an Egyptian would not have approached bacon: but if these species of food be examined by the senses of sight, smell, or taste, or scrutinized by the sciences of chemistry, medicine, or physics, no difference is ever found between them and any other species, nor can that precise circumstance be pitched on, which may afford a just foundation for the religious passion. A fowl on Thursday is lawful food; on Friday abominable: eggs in this house and in this diocese, are permitted during Lent; a hundred paces farther, to eat them is a damnable sin. This earth or building, yesterday was profane; to-day, by the muttering of certain words, it has become holy and sacred. Such reflections as these, in the mouth of a philosopher, one may safely say, are too obvious to have any influence; because they must always, to every man, occur at first sight; and where they prevail not, of themselves, they are surely obstructed by education, prejudice, and passion, not by ignorance or mistake.

159. It may appear to a careless view, or rather a too abstracted reflection, that there enters a like superstition into all the sentiments of justice; and that, if a man expose its object, or what we call property, to the same scrutiny of sense and science, he will not, by the most accurate enquiry, find any foundation for the difference made by moral sentiment. I may lawfully nourish myself from this tree; but the fruit of another of the same species, ten paces off, it is criminal for me to touch. Had I worn this apparel an hour ago, I had merited the severest punishment; but a man, by

pronouncing a few magical syllables, has now rendered it fit for my use and service. Were this house placed in the neighbouring territory, it had been immoral for me to dwell in it; but being built on this side the river, it is subject to a different municipal law, and by its becoming mine I incur no blame or censure. The same species of reasoning it may be thought, which so successfully exposes superstition, is also applicable to justice; nor is it possible, in the one case more than in the other, to point out, in the object, that precise quality or circumstance, which is the foundation of the sentiment.

But there is this material difference between *superstition* and *justice*, that the former is frivolous, useless, and burdensome; the latter is absolutely requisite to the well-being of mankind and existence of society. When we abstract from this circumstance (for it is too apparent ever to be overlooked) it must be confessed, that all regards to right and property, seem entirely without foundation, as much as the grossest and most vulgar superstition. Were the interests of society nowise concerned, it is as unintelligible why another's articulating certain sounds implying consent, should change the nature of my actions with regard to a particular object, as why the reciting of a liturgy by a priest, in a certain habit and posture, should dedicate a heap of brick and timber, and render it, thenceforth and for ever, sacred.*

---

* It is evident, that the will or consent alone never transfers property, nor causes the obligation of a promise (for the same reasoning extends to both), but the will must be expressed by words or signs, in order to impose a tie upon any man. The expression being once brought in as subservient to the will, soon becomes the principal part of the promise; nor will a man be less bound by his word, though he secretly give a different direction to his intention, and withhold the assent of his mind. But though the expression makes, on most occasions, the whole of the promise, yet it does not always so; and one who should make use of any expression, of which he knows not the meaning, and which he uses without any sense of the consequences, would not certainly be bound by it. Nay, though he know its meaning, yet if he use it in jest only, and with such signs as evidently show, that he has no serious intention of binding himself, he would not lie under any obligation of performance; but it is necessary, that the words be a perfect expression of the will, without any contrary signs. Nay, even this we must not carry so far as to imagine, that one, whom, by our quickness of understanding, we conjecture, from certain signs, to have an intention of deceiving us, is not bound by his expression or verbal promise, if we accept of it; but must limit this conclusion to those cases where the signs are of a different nature from those of deceit. All these contradictions are easily accounted for, if justice arise entirely from its usefulness to society; but will never be explained on any other hypothesis.

These reflections are far from weakening the obligations of justice, or diminishing anything from the most sacred attention to property. On the contrary, such sentiments must acquire new force from the present reasoning. For what stronger foundation can be desired or conceived for any duty, than to observe, that human society, or even human nature, could not subsist without the establishment of it; and will still arrive at greater degrees of happiness and perfection, the more inviolable the regard is, which is paid to that duty?

160. The dilemma seems obvious: as justice evidently tends to promote public utility and to support civil society, the sentiment of justice is either derived from our reflecting on that tendency, or like hunger, thirst, and other appetites, resentment, love of life, attachment to offspring, and other passions, arises from a simple original instinct in the human breast, which nature has implanted for like salutary purposes. If the latter be the case, it follows, that property, which is the object of justice, is also distinguished by a

---

It is remarkable that the moral decisions of the *Jesuits* and other relaxed casuists, were commonly formed in prosecution of some such subtilties of reasoning as are here pointed out, and proceed as much from the habit of scholastic refinement as from any corruption of the heart, if we may follow the authority of Mons. Bayle. See his Dictionary, article LOYOLA. And why has the indignation of mankind risen so high against these casuists; but because every one perceived, that human society could not subsist were such practices authorized, and that morals must always be handled with a view to public interest, more than philosophical regularity? If the secret direction of the intention, said every man of sense, could invalidate a contract; where is our security? And yet a metaphysical schoolman might think, that, where an intention was supposed to be requisite, if that intention really had not place, no consequence ought to follow, and no obligation be imposed. The casuistical subtilties may not be greater than the subtilties of lawyers, hinted at above; but as the former are *pernicious*, and the latter *innocent* and even *necessary*, this is the reason of the very different reception they meet with from the world.

It is a doctrine of the Church of Rome, that the priest, by a secret direction of his intention, can invalidate any sacrament. This position is derived from a strict and regular prosecution of the obvious truth, that empty words alone, without any meaning or intention in the speaker, can never be attended with any effect. If the same conclusion be not admitted in reasonings concerning civil contracts, where the affair is allowed to be of so much less consequence than the eternal salvation of thousands, it proceeds entirely from men's sense of the danger and inconvenience of the doctrine in the former case: And we may thence observe, that however positive, arrogant, and dogmatical any superstition may appear, it never can convey any thorough persuasion of the reality of its objects, or put them, in any degree, on a balance with the common incidents of life, which we learn from daily observation and experimental reasoning.

simple original instinct, and is not ascertained by any argument or reflection. But who is there that ever heard of such an instinct? Or is this a subject in which new discoveries can be made? We may as well expect to discover, in the body, new senses, which had before escaped the observation of all mankind.

161. But farther, though it seems a very simple proposition to say, that nature, by an instinctive sentiment, distinguishes property, yet in reality we shall find, that there are required for that purpose ten thousand different instincts, and these employed about objects of the greatest intricacy and nicest discernment. For when a definition of *property* is required, that relation is found to resolve itself into any possession acquired by occupation, by industry, by prescription, by inheritance, by contract, &c. Can we think that nature, by an original instinct, instructs us in all these methods of acquisition?

These words too, inheritance and contract, stand for ideas infinitely complicated; and to define them exactly, a hundred volumes of laws, and a thousand volumes of commentators, have not been found sufficient. Does nature, whose instincts in men are all simple, embrace such complicated and artificial objects, and create a rational creature, without trusting anything to the operation of his reason?

But even though all this were admitted, it would not be satisfactory. Positive laws can certainly transfer property. It is by another original instinct, that we recognize the authority of kings and senates, and mark all the boundaries of their jurisdiction? Judges too, even though their sentence be erroneous and illegal, must be allowed, for the sake of peace and order, to have decisive authority, and ultimately to determine property. Have we original innate ideas of praetors and chancellors and juries? Who sees not, that all these institutions arise merely from the necessities of human society?

All birds of the same species in every age and country, build their nests alike: in this we see the force of instinct. Men, in different times and places, frame their houses differently: Here we perceive the influence of reason and custom. A like inference may be drawn from comparing the instinct of generation and the institution of property.

How great soever the variety of municipal laws, it must be confessed, that their chief outlines pretty regularly concur; because the purposes, to which they tend, are everywhere exactly similar. In like manner, all houses have a roof and walls, windows and chimneys; though diversified in their shape, figure, and materials. The purposes of the latter, directed to the conveniencies of human life, discover not more plainly their origin from reason and reflection, than do those of the former, which point all to a like end.

I need not mention the variations, which all the rules of property receive from the finer turns and connexions of the imagination, and from the subtilties and abstractions of law-topics and reasonings. There is no possibility of reconciling this observation to the notion of original instincts.

162. What alone will beget a doubt concerning the theory, on which I insist, is the influence of education and acquired habits, by which we are so accustomed to blame injustice, that we are not, in every instance, conscious of any immediate reflection on the pernicious consequences of it. The views the most familiar to us are apt, for that very reason, to escape us; and what we have very frequently performed from certain motives, we are apt likewise to continue mechanically, without recalling, on every occasion, the reflections, which first determined us. The convenience, or rather necessity, which leads to justice is so universal, and everywhere points so much to the same rules, that the habit takes place in all societies; and it is not without some scrutiny, that we are able to ascertain its true origin. The matter, however, is not so obscure, but that even in common life we have every moment recourse to the principle of public utility, and ask, *What must become of the world, if such practices prevail? How could society subsist under such disorders?* Were the distinction or separation of possessions entirely useless, can any one conceive, that it ever should have obtained in society?

163. Thus we seem, upon the whole, to have attained a knowledge of the force of that principle here insisted on, and can determine what degree of esteem or moral approbation may result from reflections on public interest and utility. The necessity of justice to the support of society is the sole foundation of that virtue; and since no moral excellence is more highly esteemed, we may conclude that this circumstance of usefulness has, in general, the strongest energy, and most entire command

over our sentiments. It must, therefore, be the source of a considerable part of the merit ascribed to humanity, benevolence, friendship, public spirit, and other social virtues of that stamp; as it is the sole source of the moral approbation paid to fidelity, justice, veracity, integrity, and those other estimable and useful qualities and principles. It is entirely agreeable to the rules of philosophy, and even of common reason; where any principle has been found to have a great force and energy in one instance, to ascribe to it a like energy in all similar instances. This indeed is Newton's chief rule of philosophizing.*

* *Principia*, lib. iii.

Of political society

164. Had every man sufficient *sagacity* to perceive, at all times, the strong interest which binds him to the observance of justice and equity, and *strength of mind* sufficient to persevere in a steady adherence to a general and a distant interest, in opposition to the allurements of present pleasure and advantage; there had never, in that case, been any such thing as government or political society, but each man, following his natural liberty, had lived in entire peace and harmony with all others. What need of positive law where natural justice is, of itself, a sufficient restraint? Why create magistrates, where there never arises any disorder or iniquity? Why abridge our native freedom, when, in every instance, the utmost exertion of it is found innocent and beneficial? It is evident, that, if government were totally useless, it never could have place, and that the sole foundation of the duty of allegiance is the *advantage*, which it procures to society, by preserving peace and order among mankind.

165. When a number of political societies are erected, and maintain a great intercourse together, a new set of rules are immediately discovered to be *useful* in that particular situation; and accordingly take place under the title of Laws of Nations. Of this kind are, the sacredness of the person of ambassadors, abstaining from poisoned arms, quarter in war, with others of that kind, which are plainly calculated for the *advantage* of states and kingdoms in their intercourse with each other.

The rules of justice, such as prevail among individuals, are not entirely suspended among political societies. All princes pretend a regard to the rights of other princes; and some, no doubt, without hypocrisy. Alliances and treaties are every day made between independent states, which would only be so much waste of parchment, if they were not found by experience to have *some* influence and authority. But here is the difference between kingdoms and individuals. Human nature cannot by any means subsist, without the association of individuals; and that association never could have place, were no regard paid to the laws of equity and justice. Disorder, confusion, the war of all against all, are the necessary consequences of such a licentious conduct. But nations can subsist without intercourse. They may even subsist, in some degree, under a general war. The observance of justice, though useful among them, is not guarded by so strong a necessity as among individuals; and the *moral obligation* holds proportion with the *usefulness*. All politicians will allow, and most philosophers, that reasons of state may, in particular emergencies, dispense with the rules of justice, and invalidate any treaty or alliance, where the strict observance of it would be prejudicial, in a considerable degree, to either of the contracting parties. But nothing less than the most extreme necessity, it is confessed, can justify individuals in a breach of promise, or an invasion of the properties of others.

In a confederated commonwealth, such as the Achaean republic of old, or the Swiss Cantons and United Provinces in modern times; as the league has here a peculiar *utility*, the conditions of union have a peculiar sacredness and authority, and a violation of them would be regarded as no less, or even as more criminal, than any private injury or injustice.

166. The long and helpless infancy of man requires the combination of parents for the subsistence of their young; and that combination requires the virtue of chastity or fidelity to the marriage bed. Without such a *utility*, it will readily be owned, that such a virtue would never have been thought of.*

An infidelity of this nature is much more *pernicious* in *women* than in *men*. Hence the laws of chastity are much stricter over the one sex than over the other.

---

* The only solution, which Plato gives to all the objections that might be raised against the community of women, established in his imaginary commonwealth, is, κάλλιστα γὰρ δὴ τοῦτο καὶ λέγεται καὶ λελέξεται, ὅτι τὸ μὲν ὠφέλιμον καλόν, τὸ δὲ βλαβερὸν αἰσχρόν. *Scite enim istud et dicitur et dicetur, Id quod utile sit honestum esse, quod autem inutile sit turpe esse.* [*De Rep.* lib v p. 457 ex edit Ser]. And this maxim will admit of no doubt, where public utility is concerned, which is Plato's meaning. And indeed to what other purpose do all the ideas of chastity and modesty serve? *Nisi utile est quod facimus, frustra est gloria*, says Phaedrus. καλὸν τῶν βλαβερῶν οὐδέν, says Plutarch, *de vitioso pudore. Nihil eorum quae damnosa sunt, pulchrum est.* The same was the opinion of the Stoics. φασὶν οὖν οἱ Στωικοὶ ἀγαθὸν εἶναι ὠφέλειαν ἢ οὐχ ἑτέραν ὠφελείας, ὠφελείαν μὲν λέγοντες τὴν ἀρετὴν καὶ τὴν σπουδαίαν πρᾶξιν; from Sext. Emp lib iii cap 20.

167. These rules have all a reference to generation; and yet women past child-bearing are no more supposed to be exempted from them than those in the flower of their youth and beauty. *General rules* are often extended beyond the principle whence they first arise; and this in all matters of taste and sentiment. It is a vulgar story at Paris, that, during the rage of the Mississippi, a hump-backed fellow went every day into the Rue de Quincempoix, where the stock-jobbers met in great crowds, and was well paid for allowing them to make use of his hump as a desk, in order to sign their contracts upon it. Would the fortune, which he raised by this expedient, make him a handsome fellow; though it be confessed, that personal beauty arises very much from ideas of utility? The imagination is influenced by associations of ideas; which, though they arise at first from the judgement, are not easily altered by every particular exception that occurs to us. To which we may add, in the present case of chastity, that the example of the old would be pernicious to the young; and that women, continually foreseeing that a certain time would bring them the liberty of indulgence, would naturally advance that period, and think more lightly of this whole duty, so requisite to society.

168. Those who live in the same family have such frequent opportunities of licence of this kind, that nothing could prevent purity of manners, were marriage allowed, among the nearest relations, or any intercourse of love between them ratified by law and custom. Incest, therefore, being *pernicious* in a superior degree, has also a superior turpitude and moral deformity annexed to it.

What is the reason, why, by the Athenian laws, one might marry a half-sister by the father, but not by the mother? Plainly this: The manners of the Athenians were so reserved, that a man was never permitted to approach the women's apartment, even in the same family, unless where he visited his own mother. His step-mother and her children were as much shut up from him as the woman of any other family, and there was as little danger of any criminal correspondence between them. Uncles and nieces, for a like reason, might marry at Athens; but neither these, nor half-brothers and sisters, could contract that alliance at Rome, where the intercourse was more open between the sexes. Public utility is the cause of all these variations.

169. To repeat, to a man's prejudice, anything that escaped him in private conversation, or to make any such use of his private letters, is highly blamed. The free and social intercourse of minds must be extremely checked, where no such rules of fidelity are established.

Even in repeating stories, whence we can foresee no ill consequences to result, the giving of one's author is regarded as a piece of indiscretion, if not of immorality. These stories, in passing from hand to hand, and receiving all the usual variations, frequently come about to the persons concerned, and produce animosities and quarrels among people, whose intentions are the most innocent and inoffensive.

To pry into secrets, to open or even read the letters of others, to play the spy upon their words and looks and actions; what habits more inconvenient in society? What habits, of consequence, more blameable?

This principle is also the foundation of most of the laws of good manners; a kind of lesser morality, calculated for the ease of company and conversation. Too much or too little ceremony are both blamed, and everything, which promotes ease, without an indecent familiarity, is useful and laudable.

170. Constancy in friendships, attachments, and familiarities, is commendable, and is requisite to support trust and good correspondence in society. But in places of general, though casual concourse, where the pursuit of health and pleasure brings people promiscuously together, public conveniency has dispensed with this maxim; and custom there promotes an unreserved conversation for the time, by indulging the privilege of dropping afterwards every indifferent acquaintance, without breach of civility or good manners.

Even in societies, which are established on principles the most immoral, and the most destructive to the interests of the general society, there are required certain rules, which a species of false honour, as well as private interest, engages the members to observe. Robbers and pirates, it has often been remarked, could not maintain their pernicious confederacy, did they not establish a new distributive justice among themselves, and recall those laws of equity, which they have violated with the rest of mankind.

I hate a drinking companion, says the Greek proverb, who never forgets. The follies of the last debauch should be buried in eternal oblivion, in order to give full scope to the follies of the next.

171. Among nations, where an immoral gallantry, if covered with a thin veil of mystery, is, in some degree, authorized by custom, there immediately arise a set of rules, calculated for the conveniency of that attachment. The famous court or parliament of love in Provence formerly decided all difficult cases of this nature.

In societies for play, there are laws required for the conduct of the game; and these laws are different in each game. The foundation, I own, of such societies is frivolous; and the laws are, in a great measure, though not altogether, capricious and arbitrary. So far is there a material difference between them and the rules of justice, fidelity, and loyalty. The general societies of men are absolutely requisite for the subsistence of the species; and the public conveniency, which regulates morals, is inviolably established in the nature of man, and of the world, in which he lives. The comparison, therefore, in these respects, is very imperfect. We may only learn from it the necessity of rules, wherever men have any intercourse with each other.

They cannot even pass each other on the road without rules. Waggoners, coachmen, and postilions have principles, by which they give the way; and these are chiefly founded on mutual ease and convenience. Sometimes also they are arbitrary, at least dependent on a kind of capricious analogy like many of the reasonings of lawyers.*

To carry the matter farther, we may observe, that it is impossible for men so much as to murder each other without statutes, and maxims, and an idea of justice and honour. War has its laws as well as peace; and even that sportive kind of war, carried on among wrestlers, boxers, cudgel-players, gladiators, is regulated by fixed principles. Common interest and utility beget infallibly a standard of right and wrong among the parties concerned.

---

* That the lighter machine yield to the heavier, and, in machines of the same kind, that the empty yield to the loaded; this rule is founded on convenience. That those who are going to the capital take place of those who are coming from it; this seems to be founded on some idea of dignity of the great city, and of the preference of the future to the past. From like reasons, among foot-walkers, the right-hand entitles a man to the wall, and prevents jostling, which peaceable people find very disagreeable and inconvenient.

Why utility pleases

Part 1

172. It seems so natural a thought to ascribe to their utility the praise, which we bestow on the social virtues, that one would expect to meet with this principle everywhere in moral writers, as the chief foundation of their reasoning and enquiry. In common life, we may observe, that the circumstance of utility is always appealed to; nor is it supposed, that a greater eulogy can be given to any man, than to display his usefulness to the public, and enumerate the services, which he has performed to mankind and society. What praise, even of an inanimate form, if the regularity and elegance of its parts destroy not its fitness for any useful purpose! And how satisfactory an apology for any disproportion or seeming deformity, if we can show the necessity of that particular construction for the use intended! A ship appears more beautiful to an artist, or one moderately skilled in navigation, where its prow is wide and swelling beyond its poop, than if it were framed with a precise geometrical regularity, in contradiction to all the laws of mechanics. A building, whose doors and windows were exact squares, would hurt the eye by that very proportion; as ill adapted to the figure of a human creature, for whose service the fabric was intended. What wonder then, that a man, whose habits and conduct are hurtful to society, and dangerous or pernicious to every one who has an intercourse with him, should, on that account, be an object of disapprobation, and communicate to every spectator the strongest sentiment of disgust and hatred.*

---

* We ought not to imagine, because an inanimate object may be useful as well as a man, that therefore it ought also, according to this system, to merit he appellation of *virtuous*. The sentiments, excited by utility, are, in the two cases, very different; and the one is mixed with affection, esteem, approbation, &c.,

But perhaps the difficulty of accounting for these effects of usefulness, or its contrary, has kept philosophers from admitting them into their systems of ethics, and has induced them rather to employ any other principle, in explaining the origin of moral good and evil. But it is no just reason for rejecting any principle, confirmed by experience, that we cannot give a satisfactory account of its origin, nor are able to resolve it into other more general principles. And if we would employ a little thought on the present subject, we need be at no loss to account for the influence of utility, and to deduce it from principles, the most known and avowed in human nature.

173. From the apparent usefulness of the social virtues, it has readily been inferred by sceptics, both ancient and modern, that all moral distinctions arise from education, and were, at first, invented, and afterwards encouraged, by the art of politicians, in order to render men tractable, and subdue their natural ferocity and selfishness, which incapacitated them for society. This principle, indeed, of precept and education, must so far be owned to have a powerful influence, that it may frequently increase or diminish, beyond their natural standard, the sentiments of approbation or dislike; and may even, in particular instances, create, without any natural principle, a new sentiment of this kind; as is evident in all superstitious practices and observances: But that *all* moral affection or dislike arises from this origin, will never surely be allowed by any judicious enquirer. Had nature made no such distinction, founded on the original constitution of the mind, the words, *honourable* and *shameful*, *lovely* and *odious*, *noble* and *despicable*, had never had place in any language;

---

and not the other. In like manner, an inanimate object may have good colour and proportions as well as a human figure. But can we ever be in love with the former? There are a numerous set of passions and sentiments, of which thinking rational beings are, by the original constitution of nature, the only proper objects: and though the very same qualities be transferred to an insensible, inanimate being, they will not excite the same sentiments. The beneficial qualities of herbs and minerals are, indeed, sometimes called their *virtues*; but this is an effect of the caprice of language, which out not to be regarded in reasoning. For though there be a species of approbation attending even inanimate objects, when beneficial, yet this sentiment is so weak, and so different from that which is directed to beneficent magistrates or statesman; that they ought not to be ranked under the same class or appellation.

A very small variation of the object, even where the same qualities are preserved, will destroy a sentiment. Thus, the same beauty, transferred to a different sex, excites no amorous passion, where nature is not extremely perverted.

nor could politicians, had they invented these terms, ever have been able to render them intelligible, or make them convey any idea to the audience. So that nothing can be more superficial than this paradox of the sceptics; and it were well, if, in the abstruser studies of logic and metaphysics, we could as easily obviate the cavils of that sect, as in the practical and more intelligible sciences of politics and morals.

The social virtues must, therefore, be allowed to have a natural beauty and amiableness, which, at first, antecedent to all precept or education, recommends them to the esteem of uninstructed mankind, and engages their affections. And as the public utility of these virtues is the chief circumstance, whence they derive their merit, it follows, that the end, which they have a tendency to promote, must be some way agreeable to us, and take hold of some natural affection. It must please, either from considerations of self-interest, or from more generous motives and regards.

174. It has often been asserted, that, as every man has a strong connexion with society, and perceives the impossibility of his solitary subsistence, he becomes, on that account, favourable to all those habits or principles, which promote order in society, and ensure to him the quiet possession of so inestimable a blessing, As much as we value our own happiness and welfare, as much must we applaud the practice of justice and humanity, by which alone the social confederacy can be maintained, and every man reap the fruits of mutual protection and assistance.

This deduction of morals from self-love, or a regard to private interest, is an obvious thought, and has not arisen wholly from the wanton sallies and sportive assaults of the sceptics. To mention no others, Polybius, one of the gravest and most judicious, as well as most moral writers of antiquity, has assigned this selfish origin to all our sentiments of virtue.* But though the solid practical sense of that author, and his aversion to all vain

---

* Undutifulness to parents is disapproved of by mankind, προορωμένους τὸ μέλλον, καὶ συλλογιζομένους ὅτι τὸ παραπλήσιον ἑκάστοις αὐτῶν συγκυρήσει. Ingratitude for a like reason he seems there to mix a more generous regard) συναγανακτοῦντας μὲν τῷ πέλας, ἀναφέροντας δ’ ἐπ’ αὐτοὺς τὸ παραπλήσιον, ἐξ ὧν ὑπογίγνεταί τις ἔννοια παρ’ ἑκάστῳ τῆς τοῦ καθήκοντος δυνάμεως καὶ θεωρίας. lib. vi cap. 4. (ed. Gronovius.) Perhaps the historian only meant, that our sympathy and humanity was more enlivened, by our considering the similarity of our case with that of the person suffering; which is a just sentiment.

subtilties, render his authority on the present subject very considerable; yet is not this an affair to be decided by authority, and the voice of nature and experience seems plainly to oppose the selfish theory.

175. We frequently bestow praise on virtuous actions, performed in very distant ages and remote countries; where the utmost subtilty of imagination would not discover any appearance of self-interest, or find any connexion of our present happiness and security with events so widely separated from us.

A generous, a brave, a noble deed, performed by an adversary, commands our approbation; while in its consequences it may be acknowledged prejudicial to our particular interest.

Where private advantage concurs with general affection for virtue, we readily perceive and avow the mixture of these distinct sentiments, which have a very different feeling and influence on the mind. We praise, perhaps, with more alacrity, where the generous humane action contributes to our particular interest: but the topics of praise, which we insist on, are very wide of this circumstance. And we may attempt to bring over others to our sentiments, without endeavouring to convince them, that they reap any advantage from the actions which we recommend to their approbation and applause.

Frame the model of a praiseworthy character, consisting of all the most amiable moral virtues: give instances, in which these display themselves after an eminent and extraordinary manner: You readily engage the esteem and approbation of all your audience, who never so much as enquire in what age and country the person lived, who possessed these noble qualities: a circumstance, however, of all others, the most material to self-love, or a concern for our own individual happiness. Once on a time, a statesman, in the shock and contest of parties, prevailed so far as to procure, by his eloquence, the banishment of an able adversary; whom he secretly followed, offering him money for his support during his exile, and soothing him with topics of consolation in his misfortunes. *Alas!* cries the banished statesman, *with what regret must I leave my friends in this city, where even enemies are so generous!* Virtue, though in an enemy, here pleased him: and we also give it the just tribute of praise and approbation; nor do we retract these sentiments, when we hear, that the action passed

at Athens, about two thousand years ago, and that the persons'
names were Eschines and Demosthenes.

What is that to me? There are few occasions, when this question
is not pertinent: and had it that universal, infallible influence
supposed, it would turn into ridicule every composition, and
almost every conversation, which contain any praise or censure of
men and manners.

176. It is but a weak subterfuge, when pressed by these facts
and arguments, to say, that we transport ourselves, by the force
of imagination, into distant ages and countries, and consider the
advantage, which we should have reaped from these characters,
had we been contemporaries, and had any commerce with the
persons. It is not conceivable, how a *real* sentiment or passion
can ever arise from a known *imaginary* interest; especially when
our *real* interest is still kept in view, and is often acknowledged
to be entirely distinct from the imaginary, and even sometimes
opposite to it.

A man, brought to the brink of a precipice, cannot look down
without trembling; and the sentiment of *imaginary* danger actuates
him, in opposition to the opinion and belief of *real* safety. But the
imagination is here assisted by the presence of a striking object;
and yet prevails not, except it be also aided by novelty, and the
unusual appearance of the object. Custom soon reconciles us
to heights and precipices, and wears off these false and delusive
terrors. The reverse is observable in the estimates which we form
of characters and manners; and the more we habituate ourselves to
an accurate scrutiny of morals, the more delicate feeling do we
acquire of the most minute distinctions between vice and virtue.
Such frequent occasion, indeed, have we, in common life, to
pronounce all kinds of moral determinations, that no object of this
kind can be new or unusual to us; nor could any *false* views or
prepossessions maintain their ground against an experience, so
common and familiar. Experience being chiefly what forms the
associations of ideas, it is impossible that any association could
establish and support itself, in direct opposition to that principle.

177. Usefulness is agreeable, and engages our approbation. This
is a matter of fact, confirmed by daily observation. But, *useful?* for
what? For somebody's interest, surely. Whose interest then? Not
our own only: for our approbation frequently extends farther. It

must, therefore, be the interest of those, who are served by the character or action approved of; and these we may conclude, however remote, are not totally indifferent to us. By opening up this principle, we shall discover one great source of moral distinctions.

Part 2

178. Self-love is a principle in human nature of such extensive energy, and the interest of each individual is, in general, so closely connected with that of the community, that those philosophers were excusable, who fancied that all our concern for the public might be resolved into a concern for our own happiness and preservation. They saw every moment, instances of approbation or blame, satisfaction or displeasure towards characters and actions; they denominated the objects of these sentiments, *virtues*, or *vices*; they observed, that the former had a tendency to increase the happiness, and the latter the misery of mankind; they asked, whether it were possible that we could have any general concern for society, or any disinterested resentment of the welfare or injury of others; they found it simpler to consider all these sentiments as modifications of self-love; and they discovered a pretence, at least, for this unity of principle, in that close union of interest, which is so observable between the public and each individual.

But notwithstanding this frequent confusion of interests, it is easy to attain what natural philosophers, after Lord Bacon, have affected to call the *experimentum crucis*, or that experiment which points out the right way in any doubt or ambiguity. We have found instances, in which private interest was separate from public; in which it was even contrary: and yet we observed the moral sentiment to continue, notwithstanding this disjunction of interests. And wherever these distinct interests sensibly concurred, we always found a sensible increase of the sentiment, and a more warm affection to virtue, and detestation of vice, or what we properly call, *gratitude* and *revenge*. Compelled by these instances, we must renounce the theory, which accounts for every moral sentiment by the principle of self-love. We must adopt a more public affection, and allow, that the interests of society are not, even on their own account, entirely indifferent to us. Usefulness is only a tendency to a certain end; and it is a contradiction in terms, that anything pleases as means to an end, where the end itself no wise affects us. If usefulness, therefore, be a source of moral sentiment, and if this usefulness be not always considered with a reference to self; it follows, that everything, which contributes to the happiness of society, recommends itself directly to our approbation and good-will. Here is a principle, which accounts, in great part, for the origin of morality: and what need we seek for abstruse and remote systems, when there occurs one so obvious and natural?*

179. Have we any difficulty to comprehend the force of hum-anity and benevolence? Or to conceive, that the very aspect of happiness, joy, prosperity, gives pleasure; that of pain, suffering, sorrow, communicates uneasiness? The human countenance, says Horace,† borrows smiles or tears from the human countenance. Reduce a person to solitude, and he loses all enjoyment, except either of the sensual or speculative kind; and that because the movements of his heart are not forwarded by correspondent move-ments in his fellow-creatures. The signs of sorrow and mourning, though arbitrary, affect us with melancholy; but the natural symp-toms, tears and cries and groans, never fail to infuse compassion and uneasiness. And if the effects of misery touch us in so lively a manner; can we be supposed altogether insensible or indifferent towards its causes; when a malicious or treacherous character and behaviour are presented to us?

We enter, I shall suppose, into a convenient, warm, well-contrived apartment: We necessarily receive a pleasure from its very survey; because it presents us with the pleasing ideas of ease, satis-faction, and enjoyment. The hospitable, good-humoured, humane landlord appears. This circumstance surely must embellish the

---

* It is needless to push our researches so far as to ask, why we have humanity or a fellow-feeling with others. It is sufficient, that this is experienced to be a principle in human nature. We must stop somewhere in our examination of causes; and there are, in every science, some general principles, beyond which we cannot hope to find any principle more general. No man is absolutely indifferent to the happiness and misery of others. The first has a natural tendency to give pleasure; the second, pain. This every one may find in himself. It is not probable, that these principles can be resolved into principles more simple and universal, whatever attempts may have been made to that purpose. But if it were possible, it belongs not to the present subject; and we may here safely consider these principles as original; happy, if we can render all the consequences sufficiently plain and perspicuous!

†   Uti ridentibus arrident, ita flentibus adflent
            Humani vultus,   – Hor.

whole; nor can we easily forbear reflecting, with pleasure, on the satisfaction which results to every one from his intercourse and good-offices.

His whole family, by the freedom, ease, confidence, and calm enjoyment, diffused over their countenances, sufficiently express their happiness. I have a pleasing sympathy in the prospect of so much joy, and can never consider the source of it, without the most agreeable emotions.

He tells me, that an oppressive and powerful neighbour had attempted to dispossess him of his inheritance, and had long disturbed all his innocent and social pleasures. I feel an immediate indignation arise in me against such violence and injury.

But it is no wonder, he adds, that a private wrong should proceed from a man, who had enslaved provinces, depopulated cities, and made the field and scaffold stream with human blood. I am struck with horror at the prospect of so much misery, and am actuated by the strongest antipathy against its author.

180. In general, it is certain, that, wherever we go, whatever we reflect on or converse about, everything still presents us with the view of human happiness or misery, and excites in our breast a sympathetic movement of pleasure or uneasiness. In our serious occupations, in our careless amusements, this principle still exerts its active energy.

A man who enters the theatre, is immediately struck with the view of so great a multitude, participating of one common amusement; and experiences, from their very aspect, a superior sensibility or disposition of being affected with every sentiment, which he shares with his fellow-creatures.

He observes the actors to be animated by the appearance of a full audience, and raised to a degree of enthusiasm, which they cannot command in any solitary or calm moment.

Every movement of the theatre, by a skilful poet, is communicated, as it were by magic, to the spectators; who weep, tremble, resent, rejoice, and are inflamed with all the variety of passions, which actuate the several personages of the drama.

Where any event crosses our wishes, and interrupts the happiness of the favourite characters, we feel a sensible anxiety and concern. But where their sufferings proceed from the treachery, cruelty, or tyranny of an enemy, our breasts are affected with the liveliest resentment against the author of these calamities. It is here esteemed contrary to the rules of art to represent anything cool and indifferent. A distant friend, or a confidant, who has no immediate interest in the catastrophe, ought, if possible, to be avoided by the poet; as communicating a like indifference to the audience, and checking the progress of the passions.

Few species of poetry are more entertaining than *pastoral*; and every one is sensible, that the chief source of its pleasure arises from those images of a gentle and tender tranquillity, which it represents in its personages, and of which it communicates a like sentiment to the reader. Sannazarius, who transferred the scene to the sea-shore, though he presented the most magnificent object in nature, is confessed to have erred in his choice. The idea of toil, labour, and danger, suffered by the fishermen, is painful; by an unavoidable sympathy, which attends every conception of human happiness or misery.

When I was twenty, says a French poet, Ovid was my favourite: Now I am forty, I declare for Horace. We enter, to be sure, more readily into sentiments, which resemble those we feel every day: but no passion, when well represented, can be entirely indifferent to us; because there is none, of which every man has not, within him, at least the seeds and first principles. It is the business of poetry to bring every affection near to us by lively imagery and representation, and make it look like truth and reality: a certain proof, that, wherever that reality is found, our minds are disposed to be strongly affected by it.

181. Any recent event or piece of news, by which the fate of states, provinces, or many individuals is affected, is extremely interesting even to those whose welfare is not immediately engaged. Such intelligence is propagated with celerity, heard with avidity, and enquired into with attention and concern. The interest of society appears, on this occasion, to be in some degree the interest of each individual. The imagination is sure to be affected; though the passions excited may not always be so strong and steady as to have great influence on the conduct and behaviour.

The perusal of a history seems a calm entertainment; but would be no entertainment at all, did not our hearts beat with correspondent movements to those which are described by the historian.

Thucydides and Guicciardin support with difficulty our attention; while the former describes the trivial encounters of the small cities of Greece, and the latter the harmless wars of Pisa. The few persons interested and the small interest fill not the imagination, and engage not the affections. The deep distress of the numerous Athenian army before Syracuse; the danger which so nearly threatens Venice; these excite compassion; these move terror and anxiety.

The indifferent, uninteresting style of Suetonius, equally with the masterly pencil of Tacitus, may convince us of the cruel depravity of Nero or Tiberius: but what a difference of sentiment! while the former coldly relates the facts; and the latter sets before our eyes the venerable figures of a Soranus and a Thrasea, intrepid in their fate, and only moved by the melting sorrows of their friends and kindred. What sympathy then touches every human heart! What indignation against the tyrant, whose causeless fear or unprovoked malice gave rise to such detestable barbarity!

182. If we bring these subjects nearer: if we remove all suspicion of fiction and deceit: what powerful concern is excited, and how much superior, in many instances, to the narrow attachments of self-love and private interest! Popular sedition, party zeal, a devoted obedience to factious leaders; these are some of the most visible, though less laudable effects of this social sympathy in human nature.

The frivolousness of the subject too, we may observe, is not able to detach us entirely from what carries an image of human sentiment and affection.

When a person stutters, and pronounces with difficulty, we even sympathize with this trivial uneasiness, and suffer for him. And it is a rule in criticism, that every combination of syllables or letters, which gives pain to the organs of speech in the recital, appears also from a species of sympathy harsh and disagreeable to the ear. Nay, when we run over a book with our eye, we are sensible of such unharmonious composition; because we still imagine, that a person recites it to us, and suffers from the pronunciation of these jarring sounds. So delicate is our sympathy!

Easy and unconstrained postures and motions are always beautiful: an air of health and vigour is agreeable: clothes which warm, without burthening the body; which cover, without imprisoning the limbs, are well-fashioned. In every judgement of beauty, the feelings of the person affected enter into consideration, and communicate to the spectator similar touches of pain or pleasure.* What wonder, then, if we can pronounce no judgement concerning the character and conduct of men, without considering the tendencies of their actions, and the happiness or misery which thence arises to society? What association of ideas would ever operate, were that principle here totally unactive.†

183. If any man from a cold insensibility, or narrow selfishness of temper, is unaffected with the images of human happiness or misery, he must be equally indifferent to the images of vice and virtue: as, on the other hand, it is always found, that a warm concern for the interests of our species is attended with a delicate feeling of all moral distinctions; a strong resentment of injury done to men; a lively approbation of their welfare. In this particular, though great superiority is observable of one man above another; yet none are so entirely indifferent to the interest of their fellow-creatures, as to perceive no distinctions of moral good and evil, in consequence of the different tendencies of actions and principles. How, indeed, can we suppose it possible in any one, who wears a human heart, that if there be subjected to his censure, one character or system of conduct, which is beneficial, and another which is pernicious to his species or community, he will not so much as give a cool preference to the former, or ascribe to it the smallest merit or

* 'Decentior equus cujus astricta suntilia; sed idem velocior. Pulcher aspectu sit athleta, cujus lacertos execitatio expressit; idem certamini paratior. Nunquam enim *species* ab *utilitate* dividitur. Sed hoc quidem discernere modici judicii est.'—Quintilian, *Inst.* lib. viii. cap. 3.

† In proportion to the station which a man possesses, according to the relations in which he is placed; we always expect from him a greater or less degree of good, and when disappointed, blame his inutility; and much more do we blame him, if any ill or prejudice arise from his conduct and behaviour. When the interests of one country interfere with those of another, we estimate the merits of a statesman by the good or ill, which results to his own country from his measures and councils, without regard to the prejudice which he brings on its enemies and rivals. His fellow-citizens are the objects, which lie nearest the eye, while we determine his character. And as nature has implanted in every one a superior affection to his own country, we never expect any regard to distant nations, where a competition arises. Not to mention, that, while every man consults the good of his own community, we are sensible, that the general interest of mankind is better promoted, than any loose indeterminate views to the good of a species, whence no beneficial action could ever result, for want of a duly limited object, on which they could exert themselves.

regard? Let us suppose such a person ever so selfish; let private interest have engrossed ever so much his attention; yet in instances, where that is not concerned, he must unavoidably feel *some* propensity to the good of mankind, and make it an object of choice, if everything else be equal. Would any man, who is walking along, tread as willingly on another's gouty toes, whom he has no quarrel with, as on the hard flint and pavement? There is here surely a difference in the case. We surely take into consideration the happiness and misery of others, in weighing the several motives of action, and incline to the former, where no private regards draw us to seek our own promotion or advantage by the injury of our fellow-creatures. And if the principles of humanity are capable, in many instances, of influencing our actions, they must, at all times, have *some* authority over our sentiments, and give us a general approbation of what is useful to society, and blame of what is dangerous or pernicious. The degrees of these sentiments may be the subject of controversy; but the reality of their existence, one should think, must be admitted in every theory or system.

184. A creature, absolutely malicious and spiteful, were there any such in nature, must be worse than indifferent to the images of vice and virtue. All his sentiments must be inverted, and directly opposite to those, which prevail in the human species. Whatever contributes to the good of mankind, as it crosses the constant bent of his wishes and desires, must produce uneasiness and disapprobation; and on the contrary, whatever is the source of disorder and misery in society, must, for the same reason, be regarded with pleasure and complacency. Timon, who probably from his affected spleen more than an inveterate malice, was denominated the man-hater, embraced Alcibiades with great fondness. *Go on, my boy*! cried he, *acquire the confidence of the people: you will one day, I foresee, be the cause of great calamities to them.** Could we admit the two principles of the Manicheans, it is an infallible consequence, that their sentiments of human actions, as well as of everything else, must be totally opposite, and that every instance of justice and humanity, from its necessary tendency, must please the one deity and displease the other. All mankind so far resemble the good principle, that, where interest or revenge or envy perverts not our disposition, we are always inclined, from our natural philanthropy,

---

* Plutarch in *Vita Alc.*

to give the preference to the happiness of society, and consequently to virtue above its opposite. Absolute, unprovoked, disinterested malice has never perhaps place in any human breast; or if it had, must there pervert all the sentiments of morals, as well as the feelings of humanity. If the cruelty of Nero be allowed entirely voluntary, and not rather the effect of constant fear and resentment; it is evident that Tigellinus, preferably to Seneca or Burrhus, must have possessed his steady and uniform approbation.

185. A statesman or patriot, who serves our own country in our own time, has always a more passionate regard paid to him, than one whose beneficial influence operated on distant ages or remote nations; where the good, resulting from his generous humanity, being less connected with us, seems more obscure, and affects us with a less lively sympathy. We may own the merit to be equally great, though our sentiments are not raised to an equal height, in both cases. The judgement here corrects the inequalities of our internal emotions and perceptions; in like manner, as it preserves us from error, in the several variations of images, presented to our external senses. The same object, at a double distance, really throws on the eye a picture of but half the bulk; yet we imagine that it appears of the same size in both situations; because we know that on our approach to it, its image would expand on the eye, and that the difference consists not in the object itself, but in our position with regard to it. And, indeed, without such a correction of appearances, both in internal and external sentiment, men could never think or talk steadily on any subject; while their fluctuating situations produce a continual variation on objects, and throw them into such different and contrary lights and positions.*

* For a like reason, the tendencies of actions and characters, not their real accidental consequences, are alone regarded in our moral determinations or general judgements; though in our real feeling or sentiment, we cannot help paying greater regard to one whose station, joined to virtue, renders him really useful to society, than to one, who exerts the social virtues only in good intentions and benevolent affections. Separating the character from the fortune, by an easy and necessary effort of thought, we pronounce these persons alike, and give them the same general praise. The judgement corrects or endeavours to correct the appearance: but is not able entirely to prevail over sentiment.

Why is this peach-tree said to be better than that other; but because it produces more or better fruit? And would not the same praise be given it, though snails or vermin had destroyed the peaches, before they came to full maturity? In morals too, is not *the tree known by the fruit*? And cannot we easily distinguish between nature and accident, in the one case as well as in the other?

186. The more we converse with mankind, and the greater social intercourse we maintain, the more shall we be familiarized to these general preferences and distinctions, without which our conversation and discourse could scarcely be rendered intelligible to each other. Every man's interest is peculiar to himself, and the aversions and desires, which result from it, cannot be supposed to affect others in a like degree. General language, therefore, being formed for general use, must be moulded on some more general views, and must affix the epithets of praise or blame, in conformity to sentiments, which arise from the general interests of the community. And if these sentiments, in most men, be not so strong as those, which have a reference to private good; yet still they must make some distinction, even in persons the most depraved and selfish; and must attach the notion of good to a beneficent conduct, and of evil to the contrary. Sympathy, we shall allow, is much fainter than our concern for ourselves, and sympathy with persons remote from us much fainter than that with persons near and contiguous; but for this very reason it is necessary for us, in our calm judgements and discourse concerning the characters of men, to neglect all these differences, and render our sentiments more public and social. Besides, that we ourselves often change our situation in this particular, we every day meet with persons who are in a situation different from us, and who could never converse with us were we to remain constantly in that position and point of view, which is peculiar to ourselves. The intercourse of sentiments, therefore, in society and conversation, makes us form some general unalterable standard, by which we may approve or disapprove of characters and manners. And though the heart takes not part entirely with those general notions, nor regulates all its love and hatred by the universal abstract differences of vice and virtue, without regard to self, or the persons with whom we are more intimately connected; yet have these moral differences a considerable influence, and being sufficient, at least for discourse, serve all our purposes in company, in the pulpit, on the theatre, and in the schools.*

---

* It is wisely ordained by nature, that private connexions should commonly prevail over univeral views and considerations; otherwise our affections and actions would be dissipated and lost, for want of a proper limited object. Thus a small benefit done to ourselves, or our near friends, excites more lively sentiments of love and approbation than a great benefit done to a distant commonwealth: but still we know here, as in all the senses, to correct these inequalities by reflection, and retain a general standard of vice and virtue, founded chiefly on a general usefulness.

187. Thus, in whatever light we take this subject, the merit, ascribed to the social virtues, appears still uniform, and arises chiefly from that regard, which the natural sentiment of benevolence engages us to pay to the interests of mankind and society. If we consider the principles of the human make, such as they appear to daily experience and observation, we must, *a priori*, conclude it impossible for such a creature as man to be totally indifferent to the well or ill-being of his fellow-creatures, and not readily, of himself, to pronounce, where nothing gives him any particular bias, that what promotes their happiness is good, what tends to their misery is evil, without any farther regard or consideration. Here then are the faint rudiments, at least, or outlines, of a *general* distinction between actions; and in proportion as the humanity of the person is supposed to increase, his connexion with those who are injured or benefited, and his lively conception of their misery or happiness; his consequent censure or approbation acquires proportionable vigour. There is no necessity, that a generous action, barely mentioned in an old history or remote gazette, should communicate any strong feelings of applause and admiration. Virtue, placed at such a distance, is like a fixed star, which, though to the eye of reason it may appear as luminous as the sun in his meridian, is so infinitely removed as to affect the senses, neither with light nor heat. Bring this virtue nearer, by our acquaintance or connexion with the persons, or even by an eloquent recital of the case; our hearts are immediately caught, our sympathy enlivened, and our cool approbation converted into the warmest sentiments of friendship and regard. These seem necessary and infallible consequences of the general principles of human nature, as discovered in common life and practice.

188. Again; reverse these views and reasonings: consider the matter *a posteriori*; and weighing the consequences, enquire if the merit of social virtue be not, in a great measure, derived from the feelings of humanity, with which it affects the spectators. It appears to be matter of fact, that the circumstance of *utility*, in all subjects, is a source of praise and approbation: that it is constantly appealed to in all moral decisions concerning the merit and demerit of actions: that it is the *sole* source of that high regard paid to justice, fidelity, honour, allegiance, and chastity: that it is inseparable from all the other social virtues, humanity, generosity, charity, affability, lenity, mercy, and moderation: and, in a

word, that it is a foundation of the chief part of morals, which has a reference to mankind and our fellow-creatures.

189. It appears also, that, in our general approbation of characters and manners, the useful tendency of the social virtues moves us not by any regards to self-interest, but has an influence much more universal and extensive. It appears that a tendency to public good, and to the promoting of peace, harmony, and order in society, does always, by affecting the benevolent principles of our frame, engage us on the side of the social virtues. And it appears, as an additional confirmation, that these principles of humanity and sympathy enter so deeply into all our sentiments, and have so powerful an influence, as may enable them to excite the strongest censure and applause. The present theory is the simple result of all these inferences, each of which seems founded on uniform experience and observation.

190. Were it doubtful, whether there were any such principle in our nature as humanity or a concern for others, yet when we see, in numberless instances, that whatever has a tendency to promote the interests of society, is so highly approved of, we ought thence to learn the force of the benevolent principle; since it is impossible for anything to please as means to an end, where the end is totally indifferent. On the other hand, were it doubtful, whether there were, implanted in our nature, any general principle of moral blame and approbation, yet when we see, in numberless instances, the influence of humanity, we ought thence to conclude, that it is impossible, but that everything which promotes the interest of society must communicate pleasure, and what is pernicious give uneasiness. But when these different reflections and observations concur in establishing the same conclusion, must they not bestow an undisputed evidence upon it?

It is however hoped, that the progress of this argument will bring a farther confirmation of the present theory, by showing the rise of other sentiments of esteem and regard from the same or like principles.

SECTION SIX
Of qualities useful to ourselves

Part I

191. It seems evident, that where a quality or habit is subjected to our examination, if it appear in any respect prejudicial to the person possessed of it, or such as incapacitates him for business and action, it is instantly blamed, and ranked among his faults and imperfections. Indolence, negligence, want of order and method, obstinacy, fickleness, rashness, credulity; these qualities were never esteemed by any one indifferent to a character; much less, extolled as accomplishments or virtues. The prejudice, resulting from them, immediately strikes our eye, and gives us the sentiment of pain and disapprobation.

No quality, it is allowed, is absolutely either blameable or praiseworthy. It is all according to its degree. A due medium, say the Peripatetics, is the characteristic of virtue. But this medium is chiefly determined by utility. A proper celerity, for instance, and dispatch in business, is commendable. When defective, no progress is ever made in the execution of any purpose: when excessive, it engages us in precipitate and ill-concerted measures and enterprises: by such reasonings, we fix the proper and commendable mediocrity in all moral and prudential disquisitions; and never lose view of the advantages, which result from any character or habit.

Now as these advantages are enjoyed by the person possessed of the character, it can never be *self-love* which renders the prospect of them agreeable to us, the spectators, and prompts our esteem and approbation. No force of imagination can convert us into another person, and make us fancy, that we, being that person, reap benefit from those valuable qualities, which belong to him. Or if it did, no celerity of imagination could immediately transport us back, into ourselves, and make us love and esteem the person, as different from us. Views and sentiments, so opposite to known truth and to each other, could never have place, at the same time, in the same person. All suspicion, therefore, of selfish regards, is here totally excluded. It is a quite different principle, which actuates our bosom, and interests us in the felicity of the person whom we contemplate. Where his natural talents and acquired abilities give us the prospect of elevation, advancement, a figure in life, prosperous success, a steady command over fortune, and the execution of great or advantageous undertakings; we are struck with such agreeable images, and feel a complacency and regard immediately arise towards him. The ideas of happiness, joy, triumph, prosperity, are connected with every circumstance of his character, and diffuse over our minds a pleasing sentiment of sympathy and humanity.*

192. Let us suppose a person originally framed so as to have no manner of concern for his fellow-creatures, but to regard the happiness and misery of all sensible beings with greater indifference than even two contiguous shades of the same colour. Let us suppose, if the prosperity of nations were laid on the one hand, and their ruin on the other, and he were desired to choose; that he would stand like the schoolman's ass, irresolute and undetermined, between equal motives; or rather, like the same ass between two pieces of wood or marble, without any inclination or propensity to either side. The consequence, I believe, must be allowed just, that such a person, being absolutely unconcerned, either for the public good of a community or the private utility of others, would look on every quality, however pernicious, or however beneficial, to

---

* One may venture to affirm, that there is no human nature, to whom the appearance of happiness (where envy or revenge has no place) does not give pleasure, that of misery, uneasiness. This seems inseparable from our make and constitution. But they are only more generous minds, that are thence prompted to seek zealously the good of others, and to have a real passion for their welfare. With men of narrow and ungenerous spirits, this sympathy goes not beyond a slight feeling of the imagination, which serves only to excite sentiments of complacency or censure, and makes them apply to the object either honorable or dishonorable appellations. A griping miser, for instance, praises extremely *industry* and *frugality* even in others, and sets them, in his estimation, above all the other virtues. He knows the good that results from them, and feels that species of happiness with a more lively sympathy, than any other you could represent to him; though perhaps he would not part with a shilling to make the fortune of the industrious man, whom he praises so highly.

society, or to its possessor, with the same indifference as on the most common and uninteresting object.

But if, instead of this fancied monster, we suppose a *man* to form a judgement or determination in the case, there is to him a plain foundation of preference, where everything else is equal; and however cool his choice may be, if his heart be selfish, or if the persons interested be remote from him; there must still be a choice or distinction between what is useful, and what is pernicious. Now this distinction is the same in all its parts, with the *moral distinction*, whose foundation has been so often, and so much in vain, enquired after. The same endowments of the mind, in every circumstance, are agreeable to the sentiment of morals and to that of humanity; the same temper is susceptible of high degrees of the one sentiment and of the other; and the same alteration in the objects, by their nearer approach or by connexions, enlivens the one and the other. By all the rules of philosophy, therefore, we must conclude, that these sentiments are originally the same; since, in each particular, even the most minute, they are governed by the same laws, and are moved by the same objects.

Why do philosophers infer, with the greatest certainty, that the moon is kept in its orbit by the same force of gravity, that makes bodies fall near the surface of the earth, but because these effects are, upon computation, found similar and equal? And must not this argument bring as strong conviction, in moral as in natural disquisitions?

193. To prove, by any long detail, that all the qualities, useful to the possessor, are approved of, and the contrary censured, would be superfluous. The least reflection on what is every day experienced in life, will be sufficient. We shall only mention a few instances, in order to remove, if possible, all doubt and hesitation.

The quality, the most necessary for the execution of any useful enterprise, is discretion; by which we carry on a safe intercourse with others, give due attention to our own and to their character, weigh each circumstance of the business which we undertake, and employ the surest and safest means for the attainment of any end or purpose. To a Cromwell, perhaps, or a de Retz, discretion may appear an alderman-like virtue, as Dr Swift calls it; and being incompatible with those vast designs, to which their courage and ambition prompted them, it might really, in them, be a fault or imperfection. But in the conduct of ordinary life, no virtue is more requisite, not only to obtain success, but to avoid the most fatal miscarriages and disappointments. The greatest parts without it, as observed by an elegant writer, may be fatal to their owner; as Polyphemus, deprived of his eye, was only the more exposed, on account of his enormous strength and stature.

The best character, indeed, were it not rather too perfect for human nature, is that which is not swayed by temper of any kind; but alternately employs enterprise and caution, as each is *useful* to the particular purpose intended. Such is the excellence which St Evremond ascribes to Mareschal Turenne, who displayed every campaign, as he grew older, more temerity in his military enterprises; and being now, from long experience, perfectly acquainted with every incident in war, he advanced with greater firmness and security, in a road so well known to him. Fabius, says Machiavel, was cautious; Scipio enterprising: and both succeeded, because the situation of the Roman affairs, during the command of each, was peculiarly adapted to his genius; but both would have failed, had these situations been reversed. He is happy, whose circumstances suit his temper; but he is more excellent, who can suit his temper to any circumstances.

194. What need is there to display the praises of industry, and to extol its advantages, in the acquisition of power and riches, or in raising what we call a *fortune* in the world? The tortoise, according to the fable, by his perseverance, gained the race of the hare, though possessed of much superior swiftness. A man's time, when well husbanded, is like a cultivated field, of which a few acres produce more of what is useful to life, than extensive provinces, even of the richest soil, when over-run with weeds and brambles.

But all prospect of success in life, or even of tolerable subsistence, must fail, where a reasonable frugality is wanting. The heap, instead of increasing, diminishes daily, and leaves its possessor so much more unhappy, as, not having been able to confine his expenses to a large revenue, he will still less be able to live contentedly on a small one. The souls of men, according to Plato,[*] inflamed with impure appetites, and losing the body, which alone afforded means of satisfaction, hover about the earth, and haunt the places, where their bodies are deposited; possessed with a

---

[*] *Phaedo.*

longing desire to recover the lost organs of sensation. So may we see worthless prodigals, having consumed their fortune in wild debauches, thrusting themselves into every plentiful table, and every party of pleasure, hated even by the vicious, and despised even by fools.

The one extreme of frugality is *avarice*, which, as it both deprives a man of all use of his riches, and checks hospitality and every social enjoyment, is justly censured on a double account. *Prodigality*, the other extreme, is commonly more hurtful to a man himself; and each of these extremes is blamed above the other, according to the temper of the person who censures, and according to his greater or less sensibility to pleasure, either social or sensual.

195. Qualities often derive their merit from complicated sources. *Honesty, fidelity, truth*, are praised for their immediate tendency to promote the interests of society; but after those virtues are once established upon this foundation, they are also considered as advantageous to the person himself, and as the source of that trust and confidence, which can alone give a man any consideration in life. One becomes contemptible, no less than odious, when he forgets the duty, which, in this particular, he owes to himself as well as to society.

Perhaps, this consideration is one *chief* source of the high blame, which is thrown on any instance of failure among women in point of *chastity*. The greatest regard, which can be acquired by that sex, is derived from their fidelity; and a woman becomes cheap and vulgar, loses her rank, and is exposed to every insult, who is deficient in this particular. The smallest failure is here sufficient to blast her character. A female has so many opportunities of secretly indulging these appetites, that nothing can give us security but her absolute modesty and reserve; and where a breach is once made, it can scarcely ever be fully repaired. If a man behave with cowardice on one occasion, a contrary conduct reinstates him in his character. But by what action can a woman, whose behaviour has once been dissolute, be able to assure us, that she has formed better resolutions, and has self-command enough to carry them into execution?

196. All men, it is allowed, are equally desirous of happiness; but few are successful in the pursuit: one considerable cause is the want of strength of mind, which might enable them to resist the

temptation of present ease or pleasure, and carry them forward in the search of more distant profit and enjoyment. Our affections, on a general prospect of their objects, form certain rules of conduct, and certain measures of preference of one above another: and these decisions, though really the result of our calm passions and propensities, (for what else can pronounce any object eligible or the contrary?) are yet said, by a natural abuse of terms, to be the determinations of pure *reason* and reflection. But when some of these objects approach nearer to us, or acquire the advantages of favourable lights and positions, which catch the heart or imagination; our general resolutions are frequently confounded, a small enjoyment preferred, and lasting shame and sorrow entailed upon us. And however poets may employ their wit and eloquence, in celebrating present pleasure, and rejecting all distant views to fame, health, or fortune; it is obvious, that this practice is the source of all dissoluteness and disorder, repentance and misery. A man of a strong and determined temper adheres tenaciously to his general resolutions, and is neither seduced by the allurements of pleasure, nor terrified by the menaces of pain; but keeps still in view those distant pursuits, by which he, at once, ensures his happiness and his honour.

197. Self-satisfaction, at least in some degree, is an advantage, which equally attends the fool and the wise man: but it is the only one; nor is there any other circumstance in the conduct of life, where they are upon an equal footing. Business, books, conversation; for all of these, a fool is totally incapacitated, and except condemned by his station to the coarsest drudgery, remains a *useless* burthen upon the earth. Accordingly, it is found, that men are extremely jealous of their character in this particular; and many instances are seen of profligacy and treachery, the most avowed and unreserved; none of bearing patiently the imputation of ignorance and stupidity. Dicaearchus, the Macedonian general, who, as Polybius tells us,* openly erected one altar to impiety, another to injustice, in order to bid defiance to mankind; even he, I am well assured, would have started at the epithet of *fool*, and have meditated revenge for so injurious an appellation. Except the affection of parents, the strongest and most indissoluble bond in nature, no connexion has strength sufficient to support the

* Lib. xvi, cap. 35.

disgust arising from this character. Love itself, which can subsist under treachery, ingratitude, malice, and infidelity, is immediately extinguished by it, when perceived and acknowledged; nor are deformity and old age more fatal to the dominion of that passion. So dreadful are the ideas of an utter incapacity for any purpose or undertaking, and of continued error and misconduct in life!

198. When it is asked, whether a quick or a slow apprehension be most valuable? Whether one, that, at first view, penetrates far into a subject, but can perform nothing upon study; or a contrary character, which must work out everything by dint of application? Whether a clear head or a copious invention? Whether a profound genius or a sure judgement? In short, what character, or peculiar turn of understanding, is more excellent than another? It is evident, that we can answer none of these questions, without considering which of those qualities capacitates a man best for the world, and carries him farthest in any undertaking.

If refined sense and exalted sense be not so *useful* as common sense, their rarity, their novelty, and the nobleness of their objects make some compensation, and render them the admiration of mankind: as gold, though less serviceable than iron, acquires from its scarcity a value which is much superior.

The defects of judgement can be supplied by no art or invention; but those of memory frequently may, both in business and in study, by method and industry, and by diligence in committing everything to writing; and we scarcely ever hear a short memory given as a reason for a man's failure in any undertaking. But in ancient times, when no man could make a figure without the talent of speaking, and when the audience were too delicate to bear such crude, undigested harangues as our extemporary orators offer to public assemblies; the faculty of memory was then of the utmost consequence, and was accordingly much more valued than at present. Scarce any great genius is mentioned in antiquity, who is not celebrated for this talent; and Cicero enumerates it among the other sublime qualities of Caesar himself.*

199. Particular customs and manners alter the usefulness of qualities: they also alter their merit. Particular situations and

---

* Fuit in illo ingenium, ratio, memoria, literae, cura, cogitatio, diligentia &c. *Philipp.* 2.

accidents have, in some degree, the same influence. He will always be more esteemed, who possesses those talents and accomplishments, which suit his station and profession, than he whom fortune has misplaced in the part which she has assigned him. The private or selfish virtues are, in this respect, more arbitrary than the public and social. In other respects they are, perhaps, less liable to doubt and controversy.

In this kingdom, such continued ostentation, of late years, has prevailed among men in *active* life with regard to *public spirit*, and among those in *speculative* with regard to *benevolence*; and so many false pretensions to each have been, no doubt, detected, that men of the world are apt, without any bad intention, to discover a sullen incredulity on the head of those moral endowments, and even sometimes absolutely to deny their existence and reality. In like manner I find, that, of old, the perpetual cant of the *Stoics* and *Cynics* concerning *virtue*, their magnificent professions and slender performances, bred a disgust in mankind; and Lucian, who, though licentious with regard to pleasure, is yet in other respects a very moral writer, cannot sometimes talk of virtue, so much boasted, without betraying symptoms of spleen and irony.* But surely this peevish delicacy, whence-ever it arises, can never be carried so far as to make us deny the existence of every species of merit, and all distinction of manners and behaviour. Besides *discretion, caution, enterprise, industry, assiduity, frugality, economy, good-sense, prudence, discernment*; besides these endowments, I say, whose very names force an avowal of their merit, there are many others, to which the most determined scepticism cannot for a moment refuse the tribute of praise and approbation. *Temperance, sobriety, patience, constancy, perseverance, forethought, considerateness, secrecy, order, insinuation, address, presence of mind, quickness of conception, facility of expression*; these, and a thousand more of the same kind, no man will ever deny to be excellencies and perfections. As their merit consists in their tendency to serve the person, possessed of them, without any magnificent claim to public and social desert, we are the less jealous of their pretensions, and readily admit them into the catalogue of

---

* Ἀρετήν τινα, καὶ ἀσώματα, καὶ λήρους μεγάλῃ τῇ φωνῇ ξυνειρόντων. Luc. *Timon* 9. Again, καὶ συναγαγόντες (οἵ φιλόσοφοι) εὐεξαπάτητα μειράκια τήν τε πολυθρύλητον ἀρετὴν τραγῳδοῦσι. *Icaro-men.* In another place, ἤ ποῦ γάρ ἐστιν ἡ πολυθρύλητος ἀρετή, καὶ φύσις, καὶ εἱμαρμένη, καὶ τύχη, ἀνυπόστατα καὶ κενὰ πραγμάτων ὀνόματα; *Deor. Concil.* 13.

laudable qualities. We are not sensible that, by this concession, we have paved the way for all the other moral excellencies, and cannot consistently hesitate any longer, with regard to disinterested benevolence, patriotism, and humanity.

It seems, indeed, certain, that first appearances are here, as usual, extremely deceitful, and that it is more difficult, in a speculative way, to resolve into self-love the merit which we ascribe to the selfish virtues above mentioned, than that even of the social virtues, justice and beneficence. For this latter purpose, we need but say, that whatever conduct promotes the good of the community is loved, praised, and esteemed by the community, on account of that utility and interest, of which every one partakes; and though this affection and regard be, in reality, gratitude, not self-love, yet a distinction, even of this obvious nature, may not readily be made by superficial reasoners; and there is room, at least, to support the cavil and dispute for a moment. But as qualities, which tend only to the utility of their possessor, without any reference to us, or to the community, are yet esteemed and valued; by what theory or system can we account for this sentiment from self-love, or deduce it from that favourite origin? There seems here a necessity for confessing that the happiness and misery of others are not spectacles entirely indifferent to us; but that the view of the former, whether in its causes or effects, like sunshine or the prospect of well-cultivated plains (to carry our pretensions no higher), communicates a secret joy and satisfaction; the appearance of the latter, like a lowering cloud or barren landscape, throws a melancholy damp over the imagination. And this concession being once made, the difficulty is over; and a natural unforced interpretation of the phenomena of human life will afterwards, we may hope, prevail among all speculative enquirers.

Part 2

200. It may not be improper, in this place, to examine the influence of bodily endowments, and of the goods of fortune, over our sentiments of regard and esteem, and to consider whether these phenomena fortify or weaken the present theory. It will naturally be expected, that the beauty of the body, as is supposed by all ancient moralists, will be similar, in some respects, to that of the

mind; and that every kind of esteem, which is paid to a man, will have something similar in its origin, whether it arise from his mental endowments, or from the situation of his exterior circumstances.

It is evident, that one considerable source of *beauty* in all animals is the advantage which they reap from the particular structure of their limbs and members, suitably to the particular manner of life, to which they are by nature destined. The just proportions of a horse, described by Xenophon and Virgil, are the same that are received at this day by our modern jockeys; because the foundation of them is the same, namely, experience of what is detrimental or useful in the animal.

Broad shoulders, a lank belly, firm joints, taper legs; all these are beautiful in our species, because signs of force and vigour. Ideas of utility and its contrary, though they do not entirely determine what is handsome or deformed, are evidently the source of a considerable part of approbation or dislike.

In ancient times, bodily strength and dexterity, being of greater *use* and importance in war, was also much more esteemed and valued, than at present. Not to insist on Homer and the poets, we may observe, that historians scruple not to mention *force of body* among the other accomplishments even of Epaminondas, whom they acknowledge to be the greatest hero, statesman, and general of all the Greeks.* A like praise is given to Pompey, one of the greatest of the Romans.† This instance is similar to what we observed above with regard to memory.

What derision and contempt, with both sexes, attend *impotence*; while the unhappy object is regarded as one deprived of so capital a pleasure in life, and at the same time, as disabled from communicating it to others. *Barrenness* in women, being also a species of *inutility*, is a reproach, but not in the same degree: of which the reason is very obvious, according to the present theory.

There is no rule in painting or statuary more indispensible than that of balancing the figures, and placing them with the greatest

* Diodorus Siculus, lib. xv. It may not be improper to give the character of Epaminondas, as drawn by the historian, in order to show the idea of perfect merit, which prevailed in those ages. In other illustrious men, says he, you will observe, that each possessed some one shining quality, which was the foundation of his fame: in Epaminondas all the *virtues* are found united; force of body, eloquence of expression, vigour of mind, contempt of riches, gentleness of disposition, and *what is chiefly to be regarded*, courage and conduct of war.

† *Cum alacribus, saltu; cum velocibus, cursu; cum validis recte certabat.* Sallust apud Veget.

exactness on their proper centre of gravity. A figure, which is not justly balanced, is ugly; because it conveys the disagreeable ideas of fall, harm, and pain.*

201. A disposition or turn of mind, which qualifies a man to rise in the world and advance his fortune, is entitled to esteem and regard, as has already been explained. It may, therefore, naturally be supposed, that the actual possession of riches and authority will have a considerable influence over these sentiments.

Let us examine any hypothesis by which we can account for the regard paid to the rich and powerful; we shall find none satisfactory, but that which derives it from the enjoyment communicated to the spectator by the images of prosperity, happiness, ease, plenty, authority, and the gratification of every appetite. Self-love, for instance, which some affect so much to consider as the source of every sentiment, is plainly insufficient for this purpose. Where no good-will or friendship appears, it is difficult to conceive on what we can found our hope of advantage from the riches of others; though we naturally respect the rich, even before they discover any such favourable disposition towards us.

We are affected with the same sentiments, when we lie so much out of the sphere of their activity, that they cannot even be supposed to possess the power of serving us. A prisoner of war, in all civilized nations, is treated with a regard suited to his condition; and riches, it is evident, go far towards fixing the condition of any person. If birth and quality enter for a share, this still affords us an argument to our present purpose. For what is it we call a man of birth, but one who is descended from a long succession of rich and powerful ancestors, and who acquires our esteem by his connexion with persons whom we esteem? His ancestors, therefore, though dead, are respected, in some

---

* All men are equally liable to pain and disease and sickness; and may again recover health and ease. These circumstances, as they make no distinction between one man and another, are no source of pride or humility, regard or contempt. But comparing our own species to superior ones, it is a very mortifying consideration, that we should all be so liable to diseases and infirmities; and divines accordingly employ this topic, in order to depress self-conceit and vanity. They would have more success, if the common bent of our thoughts were not perpetually turned to compare ourselves with others. The infirmities of old age are mortifying; because a comparison with the young may take place. The king's evil is industriously concealed, because it affects others, and is often transmitted to posterity. The case is nearly the same with such diseases as convey any nauseous or frightful images; the epilepsy, for instance, ulcers, sores, scabs, &c.

measure, on account of their riches; and consequently, without any kind of expectation.

But not to go so far as prisoners of war or the dead, to find instances of this disinterested regard for riches; we may only observe, with a little attention, those phenomena which occur in common life and conversation. A man, who is himself, we shall suppose, of a competent fortune, and of no profession, being introduced to a company of strangers, naturally treats them with different degrees of respect, as he is informed of their different fortunes and conditions; though it is impossible that he can so suddenly propose, and perhaps he would not accept of, any pecuniary advantage from them. A traveller is always admitted into company, and meets with civility, in proportion as his train and equipage speak him a man of great or moderate fortune. In short, the different ranks of men are, in a great measure, regulated by riches; and that with regard to superiors as well as inferiors, strangers as well as acquaintance.

202. What remains, therefore, but to conclude, that, as riches are desired for ourselves only as the means of gratifying our appetites, either at present or in some imaginary future period, they beget esteem in others merely from their having that influence. This indeed is their very nature or essence: they have a direct reference to the commodities, conveniences, and pleasures of life. The bill of a banker, who is broke, or gold in a desert island, would otherwise be full as valuable. When we approach a man who is, as we say, at his ease, we are presented with the pleasing ideas of plenty, satisfaction, cleanliness, warmth; a cheerful house, elegant furniture, ready service, and whatever is desirable in meat, drink, or apparel. On the contrary, when a poor man appears, the disagreeable images of want, penury, hard labour, dirty furniture, coarse or ragged clothes, nauseous meat and distasteful liquor, immediately strike our fancy. What else do we mean by saying that one is rich, the other poor? And as regard or contempt is the natural consequence of those different situations in life, it is easily seen what additional light and evidence this throws on our preceding theory, with regard to all moral distinctions.*

* There is something extraordinary, and seemingly unaccountable in the operation of our passions, when we consider the fortune and situation of others. Very often another's advancement and prosperity produces envy, which has a strong mixture of hatred, and arises chiefly from the comparison of ourselves with the

A man who has cured himself of all ridiculous prepossessions, and is fully, sincerely, and steadily convinced, from experience as well as philosophy, that the difference of fortune makes less difference in happiness than is vulgarly imagined; such a one does not measure out degrees of esteem according to the rent-rolls of his acquaintance. He may, indeed, externally pay a superior deference to the great lord above the vassal; because riches are the most convenient, being the most fixed and determinate, source of distinction. But his internal sentiments are more regulated by the personal characters of men, than by the accidental and capricious favours of fortune.

In most countries of Europe, family, that is, hereditary riches, marked with titles and symbols from the sovereign, is the chief source of distinction. In England, more regard is paid to present opulence and plenty. Each practice has its advantages and disadvantages. Where birth is respected, unactive, spiritless minds remain in haughty indolence, and dream of nothing but pedigrees and genealogies: the generous and ambitious seek honour and authority, and reputation and favour. Where riches are the chief idol, corruption, venality, rapine prevail: arts, manufactures, commerce, agriculture flourish. The former prejudice, being favourable to military virtue, is more suited to monarchies. The latter, being the chief spur to industry, agrees better with a republican government. And we accordingly find that each of these forms of government, by varying the utility of those customs, has commonly a proportionable effect on the sentiments of mankind.

---

person. At the very same time, or at least in very short intervals, we may feel the passion of respect, which is a species of affection or good-will, with a mixture of humility. On the other hand, the misfortunes of our fellows often cause pity, which has in it a strong mixture of good-will. This sentiment of pity is nearly allied to contempt, which is a species of dislike, with a mixture of pride. I only point out these phenomena, as a subject of speculation to such as are curious with regard to moral enquiries. It is sufficient for the present purpose to observe in general, that power and riches commonly cause respect, poverty and meanness contempt, though particular views and incidents may sometimes raise the passions of envy and of pity.

Of qualities immediately agreeable to ourselves

203. Whoever has passed an evening with serious melancholy people, and has observed how suddenly the conversation was animated, and what sprightliness diffused itself over the countenance, discourse, and behaviour of every one, on the accession of a good-humoured, lively companion; such a one will easily allow that cheerfulness carries great merit with it, and naturally conciliates the good-will of mankind. No quality, indeed, more readily communicates itself to all around; because no one has a greater propensity to display itself, in jovial talk and pleasant entertainment. The flame spreads through the whole circle; and the most sullen and morose are often caught by it. That the melancholy hate the merry, even though Horace says it, I have some difficulty to allow; because I have always observed that, where the jollity is moderate and decent, serious people are so much the more delighted, as it dissipates the gloom with which they are commonly oppressed, and gives them an unusual enjoyment.

From this influence of cheerfulness, both to communicate itself and to engage approbation, we may perceive that there is another set of mental qualities, which, without any utility or any tendency to farther good, either of the community or of the possessor, diffuse a satisfaction on the beholders, and procure friendship and regard. Their immediate sensation, to the person possessed of them, is agreeable. Others enter into the same humour, and catch the sentiment, by a contagion or natural sympathy; and as we cannot forbear loving whatever pleases, a kindly emotion arises towards the person who communicates so much satisfaction. He is a more animating spectacle; his presence diffuses over us more serene complacency and enjoyment; our imagination, entering into his feelings and disposition, is affected in a more agreeable manner than if a melancholy, dejected, sullen, anxious temper were presented to us. Hence the affection and probation which attend the former: the aversion and disgust with which we regard the latter.*

Few men would envy the character which Caesar gives of Cassius.

> He loves no play,
> As thou do'st, Anthony: he hears no music:
> Seldom he smiles; and smiles in such a sort,
> As if he mock'd himself, and scorn'd his spirit
> That could be mov'd to smile at any thing.

Not only such men, as Caesar adds, are commonly *dangerous*, but also, having little enjoyment within themselves, they can never become agreeable to others, or contribute to social entertainment. In all polite nations and ages, a relish for pleasure, if accompanied with temperance and decency, is esteemed a considerable merit, even in the greatest men; and becomes still more requisite in those of inferior rank and character. It is an agreeable representation, which a French writer gives of the situation of his own mind in this particular, *Virtue I love*, says he, *without austerity: pleasure without effeminacy: and life, without fearing its end.*[†]

204. Who is not struck with any signal instance of greatness of mind or dignity of character; with elevation of sentiment, disdain of slavery, and with that noble pride and spirit, which arises from conscious virtue? The sublime, says Longinus, is often nothing but the echo or image of magnanimity; and where this quality appears in any one, even though a syllable be not uttered, it excites our applause and admiration; as may be observed of the famous silence of Ajax in the *Odyssey*, which expresses more noble disdain and resolute indignation than any language can convey.[‡]

---

* There is no man, who, on particular occasions, is not affected with all the disagreeable passions, fear, anger, dejection, grief, melancholy, anxiety, &c. But these, so far as they are natural, and universal, make no difference between one man and another, and can never be the object of blame. It is only when the disposition gives a *propensity* to any of these disagreeable passions, that they disfigure the character, and by giving uneasiness, convey the sentiment of disapprobation to the spectator.

†   J'aime la vertu, sans rudesse;
          J'aime le plaisir, sans molesse;
          J'aime la vie, et n'en crains point la fin.' – *St Evremond*

‡ Cap. 9.

Were I Alexander, said Parmenio, *I would accept of these offers made by Darius. So would I too,* replied Alexander, *were I Parmenio.* This saying is admirable, says Longinus, from a like principle.*

Go! cries the same hero to his soldiers, when they refused to follow him to the Indies, *Go tell your countrymen, that you left Alexander completing the conquest of the world.* 'Alexander,' said the Prince of Condé, who always admired this passage, 'abandoned by his soldiers, among barbarians, not yet fully subdued, felt in himself such a dignity and right of empire, that he could not believe it possible that any one would refuse to obey him. Whether in Europe or in Asia, among Greeks or Persians, all was indifferent to him: wherever he found men, he fancied he should find subjects.'

The confidant of Medea in the tragedy recommends caution and submission; and enumerating all the distresses of that unfortunate heroine, asks her, what she has to support her against her numerous and implacable enemies. *Myself,* replies she; *Myself I say, and it is enough.* Boileau justly recommends this passage as an instance of true sublime.†

When Phocion, the modest, the gentle Phocion, was led to execution, he turned to one of his fellow-sufferers, who was lamenting his own hard fate, *Is it not glory enough for you,* says he, *that you die with Phocion?*‡

Place in opposition the picture which Tacitus draws of Vitellius, fallen from empire, prolonging his ignominy from a wretched love of life, delivered over to the merciless rabble; tossed, buffeted, and kicked about; constrained, by their holding a poinard under his chin, to raise his head, and expose himself to every contumely. What abject infamy! What low humiliation! Yet even here, says the historian, he discovered some symptoms of a mind not wholly degenerate. To a tribune, who insulted him, he replied, *I am still your emperor.*§

* Idem.
† Réflexion 10 sur Longin.
‡ Plutarch in *Phoc.*
§ Tacit. *Hist.* lib. iii. The author entering upon the narration, says, *Laniata veste, foedum spectaculum ducebatur, multis increpantibus, nullo inlacrimante: deformitas exitus misericordiam abstulerat.* To enter thoroughly into this method of thinking, we must make allowance for the ancient maxims, that no one ought to prolong his life after it became dishonourable; but, as he had always a right to dispose of it, it then became a duty to part with it.

We never excuse the absolute want of spirit and dignity of character, or a proper sense of what is due to one's self, in society and the common intercourse of life. This vice constitutes what we properly call *meanness*; when a man can submit to the basest slavery, in order to gain his ends; fawn upon those who abuse him; and degrade himself by intimacies and familiarities with undeserving inferiors. A certain degree of generous pride or self-value is so requisite, that the absence of it in the mind displeases, after the same manner as the want of a nose, eye, or any of the most material feature of the face or member of the body.*

205. The utility of courage, both to the public and to the person possessed of it, is an obvious foundation of merit. But to any one who duly considers of the matter, it will appear that this quality has a peculiar lustre, which it derives wholly from itself, and from that noble elevation inseparable from it. Its figure, drawn by painters and by poets, displays, in each feature, a sublimity and daring confidence; which catches the eye, engages the affections, and diffuses, by sympathy, a like sublimity of sentiment over every spectator.

Under what shining colours does Demosthenes† represent Philip; where the orator apologizes for his own administration, and justifies that pertinacious love of liberty, with which he had inspired the Athenians. 'I beheld Philip,' says he, 'he with whom was your contest, resolutely, while in pursuit of empire and dominion, exposing himself to every wound; his eye gored, his neck wrested, his arm, his thigh pierced, what ever part of his body fortune should seize on, that cheerfully relinquishing; provided that, with what remained, he might live in honour and renown. And shall it be said that he, born in Pella, a place heretofore mean and ignoble, should be inspired with so high an ambition and thirst of fame: while you, Athenians, &c.' These praises excite the most lively

---

* The absence of virtue may often be a vice; and that of the highest kind; as in the instance of ingratitude, as well as meanness. Where we expect a beauty, the disappointment gives an uneasy sensation, and produces a real deformity. An abjectness of character, likewise, is disgustful and contemptible in another view. Where a man has no sense of value in himself, we are not likely to have any higher esteem of him. And if the same person, who crouches to his superiors, is insolent to his inferiors (as often happens), this contrariety of behaviour, instead of correcting the former vice, aggravates it extremely by the addition of a vice still more odious. See Section 8.

† *De Corona.*

admiration; but the views presented by the orator, carry us not, we see, beyond the hero himself, nor ever regard the future advantageous consequences of his valour.

The martial temper of the Romans, inflamed by continual wars, had raised their esteem of courage so high, that, in their language, it was called *virtue*, by way of excellence and of distinction from all other moral qualities. *The Suevi*, in the opinion of Tacitus,* *dressed their hair with a laudable intent: not for the purpose of loving or being loved; they adorned themselves only for their enemies, and in order to appear more terrible.* A sentiment of the historian, which would sound a little oddly in other nations and other ages.

The Scythians, according to Herodotus,† after scalping their enemies, dressed the skin like leather, and used it as a towel; and whoever had the most of those towels was most esteemed among them. So much had martial bravery, in that nation, as well as in many others, destroyed the sentiments of humanity; a virtue surely much more useful and engaging.

It is indeed observable, that, among all uncultivated nations, who have not as yet had full experience of the advantages attending beneficence, justice, and the social virtues, courage is the predominant excellence; what is most celebrated by poets, recommended by parents and instructors, and admired by the public in general. The ethics of Homer are, in this particular, very different from those of Fénelon, his elegant imitator; and such as were well suited to an age, when one hero, as remarked by Thucydides,‡ could ask another, without offence, whether he were a robber or not. Such also very lately was the system of ethics which prevailed in many barbarous parts of Ireland; if we may credit Spencer, in his judicious account of the state of that kingdom.§

206. Of the same class of virtues with courage is that undisturbed philosophical tranquillity, superior to pain, sorrow, anxiety, and each assault of adverse fortune. Conscious of his own virtue, say the

---

* *De moribus Germ.*

† Lib. iv.

‡ Lib. i.

§ It is a common use, says he, amongst their gentlemen's sons, that, as soon as they are able to use their weapons, they strait gather to themselves three or four stragglers or kern, with whom wandering a while up and down idly the country, taking only meat, he at last falleth into some bad occasion, that shall be offered; which being once made known, he is thenceforth counted a man of worth, in whom there is courage.

philosophers, the sage elevates himself above every accident of life; and securely placed in the temple of wisdom, looks down on inferior mortals engaged in pursuit of honours, riches, reputation, and every frivolous enjoyment. These pretensions, no doubt, when stretched to the utmost, are by far too magnificent for human nature. They carry, however, a grandeur with them, which seizes the spectator, and strikes him with admiration. And the nearer we can approach in practice to this sublime tranquillity and indifference (for we must distinguish it from a stupid insensibility), the more secure enjoyment shall we attain within ourselves, and the more greatness of mind shall we discover to the world. The philosophical tranquillity may, indeed, be considered only as a branch of magnanimity.

Who admires not Socrates; his perpetual serenity and contentment, amidst the greatest poverty and domestic vexations; his resolute contempt of riches, and his magnanimous care of preserving liberty, while he refused all assistance from his friends and disciples, and avoided even the dependence of an obligation? Epictetus had not so much as a door to his little house or hovel; and therefore, soon lost his iron lamp, the only furniture which he had worth taking. But resolving to disappoint all robbers for the future, he supplied its place with an earthen lamp, of which he very peacefully kept possession ever after.

Among the ancients, the heroes in philosophy, as well as those in war and patriotism, have a grandeur and force of sentiment, which astonishes our narrow souls, and is rashly rejected as extravagant and supernatural. They, in their turn, I allow, would have had equal reason to consider as romantic and incredible, the degree of humanity, clemency, order, tranquillity, and other social virtues, to which, in the administration of government, we have attained in modern times, had any one been then able to have made a fair representation of them. Such is the compensation, which nature, or rather education, has made in the distribution of excellencies and virtues, in those different ages.

207. The merit of benevolence, arising from its utility, and its tendency to promote the good of mankind has been already explained, and is, no doubt, the source of a *considerable* part of that esteem, which is so universally paid to it. But it will also be allowed, that the very softness and tenderness of the sentiment, its

engaging endearments, its fond expressions, its delicate attentions, and all that flow of mutual confidence and regard, which enters into a warm attachment of love and friendship: it will be allowed, I say, that these feelings, being delightful in themselves, are necessarily communicated to the spectators, and melt them into the same fondness and delicacy. The tear naturally starts in our eye on the apprehension of a warm sentiment of this nature: our breast heaves, our heart is agitated, and every humane tender principle of our frame is set in motion, and gives us the purest and most satisfactory enjoyment.

When poets form descriptions of Elysian fields, where the blessed inhabitants stand in no need of each other's assistance, they yet represent them as maintaining a constant intercourse of love and friendship, and sooth our fancy with the pleasing image of these soft and gentle passions. The idea of tender tranquillity in a pastoral Arcadia is agreeable from a like principle, as has been observed above.*

Who would live amidst perpetual wrangling, and scolding, and mutual reproaches? The roughness and harshness of these emotions disturb and displease us: we suffer by contagion and sympathy; nor can we remain indifferent spectators, even though certain that no pernicious consequences would ever follow from such angry passions.

208. As a certain proof that the whole merit of benevolence is not derived from its usefulness, we may observe, that in a kind way of blame, we say, a person is *too good*; when he exceeds his part in society, and carries his attention for others beyond the proper bounds. In like manner, we say, a man is *too high-spirited*, *too intrepid*, *too indifferent about fortune*: reproaches, which really, at bottom, imply more esteem than many panegyrics. Being accustomed to rate the merit and demerit of characters chiefly by their useful or pernicious tendencies, we cannot forbear applying the epithet of blame, when we discover a sentiment, which rises to a degree, that is hurtful; but it may happen, at the same time, that its noble elevation, or its engaging tenderness so seizes the heart, as rather to increase our friendship and concern for the person.†

* Section 5, Part 2.

† Cheerfulness could scarce admit of blame from its excess, were it not that dissolute mirth, without a proper cause or subject, is a sure symptom and characteristic of folly, and on that account disgustful.

The amours and attachments of Harry IV of France, during the civil wars of the league, frequently hurt his interest and his cause; but all the young, at least, and amorous, who can sympathize with the tender passions, will allow that this very weakness, for they will readily call it such, chiefly endears that hero, and interests them in his fortunes.

The excessive bravery and resolute inflexibility of Charles XII ruined his own country, and infested all his neighbours; but have such splendour and greatness in their appearance, as strikes us with admiration; and they might, in some degree, be even approved of, if they betrayed not sometimes too evident symptoms of madness and disorder.

209. The Athenians pretended to the first invention of agriculture and of laws: and always valued themselves extremely on the benefit thereby procured to the whole race of mankind. They also boasted, and with reason, of their warlike enterprises; particularly against those innumerable fleets and armies of Persians, which invaded Greece during the reigns of Darius and Xerxes. But though there be no comparison in point of utility, between these peaceful and military honours; yet we find, that the orators, who have writ such elaborate panegyrics on that famous city, have chiefly triumphed in displaying the warlike achievements. Lysias, Thucydides, Plato, and Isocrates discover, all of them, the same partiality; which, though condemned by calm reason and reflection, appears so natural in the mind of man.

It is observable, that the great charm of poetry consists in lively pictures of the sublime passions, magnanimity, courage, disdain of fortune; or those of the tender affections, love and friendship; which warm the heart, and diffuse over it similar sentiments and emotions. And though all kinds of passion, even the most disagreeable, such as grief and anger, are observed, when excited by poetry, to convey a satisfaction, from a mechanism of nature, not easy to be explained: yet those more elevated or softer affections have a peculiar influence, and please from more than one cause or principle. Not to mention that they alone interest us in the fortune of the persons represented, or communicate any esteem and affection for their character.

And can it possibly be doubted, that this talent itself of poets, to move the passions, this pathetic and sublime of sentiment, is a very considerable merit; and being enhanced by its extreme rarity, may exalt the person possessed of it, above every character of the age in which he lives? The prudence, address, steadiness, and benign government of Augustus, adorned with all the splendour of his noble birth and imperial crown, render him but an unequal competitor for fame with Virgil, who lays nothing into the opposite scale but the divine beauties of his poetical genius.

The very sensibility to these beauties, or a delicacy of taste, is itself a beauty in any character; as conveying the purest, the most durable, and most innocent of all enjoyments.

210. These are some instances of the several species of merit, that are valued for the immediate pleasure which they communicate to the person possessed of them. No views of utility or of future beneficial consequences enter into this sentiment of approbation; yet is it of a kind similar to that other sentiment, which arises from views of a public or private utility. The same social sympathy, we may observe, or fellow-feeling with human happiness or misery, gives rise to both; and this analogy, in all the parts of the present theory, may justly be regarded as a confirmation of it.

SECTION EIGHT
*Of qualities immediately agreeable to others**

211. As the mutual shocks, in *society*, and the oppositions of interest and self-love have constrained mankind to establish the laws of *justice*, in order to preserve the advantages of mutual assistance and protection: in like manner, the eternal contrarieties, in *company*, of men's pride and self-conceit, have introduced the rules of Good Manners or Politeness, in order to facilitate the intercourse of minds, and an undisturbed commerce and conversation. Among well-bred people, a mutual deference is affected; contempt of others disguised; authority concealed; attention given to each in his turn; and an easy stream of conversation maintained, without vehemence, without interruption, without eagerness for victory, and without any airs of superiority. These attentions and regards are immediately *agreeable* to others, abstracted from any consideration of utility or beneficial tendencies: they conciliate affection, promote esteem, and extremely enhance the merit of the person who regulates his behaviour by them.

Many of the forms of breeding are arbitrary and casual; but the thing expressed by them is still the same. A Spaniard goes out of his own house before his guest, to signify that he leaves him master of all. In other countries, the landlord walks out last, as a common mark of deference and regard.

212. But, in order to render a man perfect *good company*, he must have Wit and Ingenuity as well as good manners. What wit is, it may not be easy to define; but it is easy surely to determine that it is a quality immediately *agreeable* to others, and communicating, on its first appearance, a lively joy and satisfaction to every one who has any comprehension of it. The most profound metaphysics, indeed,

---

* It is the nature and, indeed, the definition of virtue, that it is *a quality of the mind agreeable to or approved by every one who considers or contemplates it.* But some qualities produce pleasure, because they are useful to society, or useful or agreeable to the person himself; others produce it more immediately, which is the case with the class of virtues here considered.

might be employed in explaining the various kinds and species of wit; and many classes of it, which are now received on the sole testimony of taste and sentiment, might, perhaps, be resolved into more general principles. But this is sufficient for our present purpose, that it does affect taste and sentiment, and bestowing an immediate enjoyment, is a sure source of approbation and affection.

In countries where men pass most of their time in conversation, and visits, and assemblies, these *companionable* qualities, so to speak, are of high estimation, and form a chief part of personal merit. In countries where men live a more domestic life, and either are employed in business, or amuse themselves in a narrower circle of acquaintance, the more solid qualities are chiefly regarded. Thus, I have often observed, that, among the French, the first questions with regard to a stranger are, *Is he polite? Has he wit?* In our own country, the chief praise bestowed is always that of a *good-natured, sensible fellow.*

In conversation, the lively spirit of dialogue is *agreeable,* even to those who desire not to have any share in the discourse: hence the teller of long stories, or the pompous declaimer, is very little approved of. But most men desire likewise their turn in the conversation, and regard, with a very evil eye, that *loquacity* which deprives them of a right they are naturally so jealous of.

There is a sort of harmless *liars,* frequently to be met with in company, who deal much in the marvellous. Their usual intention is to please and entertain; but as men are most delighted with what they conceive to be truth, these people mistake extremely the means of pleasing, and incur universal blame. Some indulgence, however, to lying or fiction is given in *humorous* stories; because it is there really agreeable and entertaining, and truth is not of any importance.

Eloquence, genius of all kinds, even good sense, and sound reasoning, when it rises to an eminent degree, and is employed upon subjects of any considerable dignity and nice discernment; all these endowments seem immediately agreeable, and have a merit distinct from their usefulness. Rarity, likewise, which so much enhances the price of every thing, must set an additional value on these noble talents of the human mind.

213. Modesty may be understood in different senses, even abstracted from chastity, which has been already treated of. It

sometimes means that tenderness and nicety of honour, that apprehension of blame, that dread of intrusion or injury towards others, that Pudor, which is the proper guardian of every kind of virtue, and a sure preservative against vice and corruption. But its most usual meaning is when it is opposed to *impudence* and *arrogance*, and expresses a diffidence of our own judgement, and a due attention and regard for others. In young men chiefly, this quality is a sure sign of good sense; and is also the certain means of augmenting that endowment, by preserving their ears open to instruction, and making them still grasp after new attainments. But it has a further charm to every spectator; by flattering every man's vanity, and presenting the appearance of a docile pupil, who receives, with proper attention and respect, every word they utter.

Men have, in general, a much greater propensity to over-value than undervalue themselves; notwithstanding the opinion of Aristotle.* This makes us more jealous of the excess on the former side, and causes us to regard, with a peculiar indulgence, all tendency to modesty and self-diffidence; as esteeming the danger less of falling into any vicious extreme of that nature. It is thus in countries where men's bodies are apt to exceed in corpulency, personal beauty is placed in a much greater degree of slenderness, than in countries where that is the most usual defect. Being so often struck with instances of one species of deformity, men think they can never keep at too great a distance from it, and wish always to have a leaning to the opposite side. In like manner, were the door opened to self-praise, and were Montaigne's maxim observed, that one should say as frankly, *I have sense, I have learning, I have courage, beauty, or wit,* as it is sure we often think so; were this the case, I say, every one is sensible that such a flood of impertinence would break in upon us, as would render society wholly intolerable. For this reason custom has established it as a rule, in common societies, that men should not indulge themselves in self-praise, or even speak much of themselves; and it is only among intimate friends or people of very manly behaviour, that one is allowed to do himself justice. Nobody finds fault with Maurice, Prince of Orange, for his reply to one who asked him, whom he esteemed the first general of the age, *The Marquis of Spinola,* said he, *is the second.* Though it is observable, that the

* *Ethic. ad Nicomachum.*

self-praise implied is here better implied, than if it had been directly expressed, without any cover or disguise.

He must be a very superficial thinker, who imagines that all instances of mutual deference are to be understood in earnest, and that a man would be more esteemable for being ignorant of his own merits and accomplishments. A small bias towards modesty, even in the internal sentiment, is favourably regarded, especially in young people; and a strong bias is required in the outward behaviour; but this excludes not a noble pride and spirit, which may openly display itself in its full extent, when one lies under calumny or oppression of any kind. The generous contumacy of Socrates, as Cicero calls it, has been highly celebrated in all ages; and when joined to the usual modesty of his behaviour, forms a shining character. Iphicrates, the Athenian, being accused of betraying the interests of his country, asked his accuser, *Would you*, says he, *have, on a like occasion, been guilty of that crime? By no means*, replied the other. *And can you then imagine*, cried the hero, *that Iphicrates would be guilty?* * – In short, a generous spirit and self-value, well founded, decently disguised, and courageously supported under distress and calumny, is a great excellency, and seems to derive its merit from the noble elevation of its sentiment, or its immediate agreeableness to its possessor. In ordinary characters, we approve of a bias towards modesty, which is a quality immediately agreeable to others: the vicious excess of the former virtue, namely, insolence or haughtiness, is immediately disagreeable to others; the excess of the latter is so to the possessor. Thus are the boundaries of these duties adjusted.

214. A desire of fame, reputation, or a character with others, is so far from being blameable, that it seems inseparable from virtue, genius, capacity, and a generous or noble disposition. An attention even to trivial matters, in order to please, is also expected and demanded by society; and no one is surprised, if he find a man in company to observe a greater elegance of dress and more pleasant flow of conversation, than when he passes his time at home, and with his own family. Wherein, then, consists Vanity, which is so justly regarded as a fault or imperfection. It seems to consist chiefly in such an intemperate display of our advantages, honours, and accomplishments; in such an importunate and open demand of

* Quinctil. lib. v. cap. 12.

praise and admiration, as is offensive to others, and encroaches too
far on *their* secret vanity and ambition. It is besides a sure symptom
of the want of true dignity and elevation of mind, which is so
great an ornament in any character. For why that impatient desire
of applause; as if you were not justly entitled to it, and might
not reasonably expect that it would for ever attend you? Why so
anxious to inform us of the great company which you have kept;
the obliging things which were said to you; the honours, the
distinctions which you met with; as if these were not things of
course, and what we could readily, of ourselves, have imagined,
without being told of them?

215. Decency, or a proper regard to age, sex, character, and
station in the world, may be ranked among the qualities which
are immediately agreeable to others, and which, by that means,
acquire praise and approbation. An effeminate behaviour in a man,
a rough manner in a woman; these are ugly because unsuitable to
each character, and different from the qualities which we expect in
the sexes. It is as if a tragedy abounded in comic beauties, or a
comedy in tragic. The disproportions hurt the eye, and convey a
disagreeable sentiment to the spectators, the source of blame and
disapprobation. This is that *indecorum*, which is explained so much
at large by Cicero in his *Offices*.

Among the other virtues, we may also give Cleanliness a place;
since it naturally renders us agreeable to others, and is no inconsiderable source of love and affection. No one will deny, that a
negligence in this particular is a fault; and as faults are nothing but
smaller vices, and this fault can have no other origin than the
uneasy sensation which it excites in others; we may, in this
instance, seemingly so trivial, clearly discover the origin of moral
distinctions, about which the learned have involved themselves in
such mazes of perplexity and error.

216. But besides all the *agreeable* qualities, the origin of whose
beauty we can, in some degree, explain and account for, there still
remains something mysterious and inexplicable, which conveys an
immediate satisfaction to the spectator, but how, or why, or for
what reason, he cannot pretend to determine. There is a manner,
a grace, an ease, a genteelness, an I-know-not-what, which some
men possess above others, which is very different from external
beauty and comeliness, and which, however, catches our affection

almost as suddenly and powerfully. And though this *manner* be chiefly talked of in the passion between the sexes, where the concealed magic is easily explained, yet surely much of it prevails in all our estimation of characters, and forms no inconsiderable part of personal merit. This class of accomplishments, therefore, must be trusted entirely to the blind, but sure testimony of taste and sentiment; and must be considered as a part of ethics, left by nature to baffle all the pride of philosophy, and make her sensible of her narrow boundaries and slender acquisitions.

We approve of another, because of his wit, politeness, modesty, decency, or any agreeable quality which he possesses; although he be not of our acquaintance, nor has ever given us any entertainment, by means of these accomplishments. The idea, which we form of their effect on his acquaintance, has an agreeable influence on our imagination, and gives us the sentiment of approbation. This principle enters into all the judgements which we form concerning manners and characters.

SECTION NINE
Conclusion

Part 1

217. It may justly appear surprising that any man in so late an age, should find it requisite to prove, by elaborate reasoning, that Personal Merit consists altogether in the possession of mental qualities, *useful* or *agreeable* to the *person himself* or to *others*. It might be expected that this principle would have occurred even to the first rude, unpractised enquirers concerning morals, and been received from its own evidence, without any argument or disputation. Whatever is valuable in any kind, so naturally classes itself under the division of *useful* or *agreeable*, the *utile* or the *dulce*, that it is not easy to imagine why we should ever seek further, or consider the question as a matter of nice research or inquiry. And as every thing useful or agreeable must possess these qualities with regard either to the *person himself* or to *others*, the complete delineation or description of merit seems to be performed as naturally as a shadow is cast by the sun, or an image is reflected upon water. If the ground, on which the shadow is cast, be not broken and uneven; nor the surface from which the image is reflected, disturbed and confused; a just figure is immediately presented, without any art or attention. And it seems a reasonable presumption, that systems and hypotheses have perverted our natural understanding, when a theory, so simple and obvious, could so long have escaped the most elaborate examination.

218. But however the case may have fared with philosophy, in common life these principles are still implicitly maintained; nor is any other topic of praise or blame ever recurred to, when we employ any panegyric or satire, any applause or censure of human action and behaviour. If we observe men, in every intercourse of business or pleasure, in every discourse and conversation, we shall

find them nowhere, except the schools, at any loss upon this subject. What so natural, for instance, as the following dialogue? You are very happy, we shall suppose one to say, addressing himself to another, that you have given your daughter to Cleanthes. He is a man of honour and humanity. Every one, who has any intercourse with him, is sure of *fair* and *kind* treatment.* I congratulate you too, says another, on the promising expectations of this son-in-law; whose assiduous application to the study of the laws, whose quick penetration and early knowledge both of men and business, prognosticate the greatest honours and advancement.† You surprise me, replies a third, when you talk of Cleanthes as a man of business and application. I met him lately in a circle of the gayest company, and he was the very life and soul of our conversation: so much wit with good manners; so much gallantry without affectation; so much ingenious knowledge so genteelly delivered, I have never before observed in any one.‡ You would admire him still more, says a fourth, if you knew him more familiarly. That cheerfulness, which you might remark in him, is not a sudden flash struck out by company: it runs through the whole tenor of his life, and preserves a perpetual serenity on his countenance, and tranquillity in his soul. He has met with severe trials, misfortunes as well as dangers; and by his greatness of mind, was still superior to all of them.§ The image, gentlemen, which you have here delineated of Cleanthes, cried I, is that of accomplished merit. Each of you has given a stroke of the pencil to his figure; and you have unawares exceeded all the pictures drawn by Gratian or Castiglione. A philosopher might select this character as a model of perfect virtue.

219. And as every quality which is useful or agreeable to ourselves or others is, in common life, allowed to be a part of personal merit; so no other will ever be received, where men judge of things by their natural, unprejudiced reason, without the delusive glosses of superstition and false religion. Celibacy, fasting, penance, mortification, self-denial, humility, silence, solitude, and the whole train of monkish virtues; for what reason are they everywhere rejected by men of sense, but because they serve to no manner

---

* Qualities useful to others.
† Qualities useful to the person himself.
‡ Qualities immediately agreeable to others.
§ Qualities immediately agreeable to the person himself.

of purpose; neither advance a man's fortune in the world, nor render him a more valuable member of society; neither qualify him for the entertainment of company, nor increase his power of self-enjoyment? We observe, on the contrary, that they cross all these desirable ends; stupify the understanding and harden the heart, obscure the fancy and sour the temper. We justly, therefore, transfer them to the opposite column, and place them in the catalogue of vices; nor has any superstition force sufficient among men of the world, to pervert entirely these natural sentiments. A gloomy, hair-brained enthusiast, after his death, may have a place in the calendar; but will scarcely ever be admitted, when alive, into intimacy and society, except by those who are as delirious and dismal as himself.

220. It seems a happiness in the present theory, that it enters not into that vulgar dispute concerning the *degrees* of benevolence or self-love, which prevail in human nature; a dispute which is never likely to have any issue, both because men, who have taken part, are not easily convinced, and because the phenomena, which can be produced on either side, are so dispersed, so uncertain, and subject to so many interpretations, that it is scarcely possible accurately to compare them, or draw from them any determinate inference or conclusion. It is sufficient for our present purpose, if it be allowed, what surely, without the greatest absurdity cannot be disputed, that there is some benevolence, however small, infused into our bosom; some spark of friendship for human kind; some particle of the dove kneaded into our frame, along with the elements of the wolf and serpent. Let these generous sentiments be supposed ever so weak; let them be insufficient to move even a hand or finger of our body, they must still direct the determinations of our mind, and where everything else is equal, produce a cool preference of what is useful and serviceable to mankind, above what is pernicious and dangerous. *A moral distinction*, therefore, immediately arises; a general sentiment of blame and approbation; a tendency, however faint, to the objects of the one, and a proportionable aversion to those of the other. Nor will those reasoners, who so earnestly maintain the predominant selfishness of human kind, be any wise scandalized at hearing of the weak sentiments of virtue implanted in our nature. On the contrary, they are found as ready to maintain the one tenet as the other; and their spirit of satire (for such it appears, rather than of

corruption) naturally gives rise to both opinions; which have, indeed, a great and almost an indissoluble connexion together.

221. Avarice, ambition, vanity, and all passions vulgarly, though improperly, comprised under the denomination of *self-love*, are here excluded from our theory concerning the origin of morals, not because they are too weak, but because they have not a proper direction for that purpose. The notion of morals implies some sentiment common to all mankind, which recommends the same object to general approbation, and makes every man, or most men, agree in the same opinion or decision concerning it. It also implies some sentiment, so universal and comprehensive as to extend to all mankind, and render the actions and conduct, even of the persons the most remote, an object of applause or censure, according as they agree or disagree with that rule of right which is established. These two requisite circumstances belong alone to the sentiment of humanity here insisted on. The other passions produce in every breast, many strong sentiments of desire and aversion, affection and hatred; but these neither are felt so much in common, nor are so comprehensive, as to be the foundation of any general system and established theory of blame or approbation.

222. When a man denominates another his *enemy*, his *rival*, his *antagonist*, his *adversary*, he is understood to speak the language of self-love, and to express sentiments, peculiar to himself, and arising from his particular circumstances and situation. But when he bestows on any man the epithets of *vicious* or *odious* or *depraved*, he then speaks another language, and expresses sentiments, in which he expects all his audience are to concur with him. He must here, therefore, depart from his private and particular situation, and must choose a point of view, common to him with others; he must move some universal principle of the human frame, and touch a string to which all mankind have an accord and symphony. If he mean, therefore, to express that this man possesses qualities, whose tendency is pernicious to society, he has chosen this common point of view, and has touched the principle of humanity, in which every man, in some degree, concurs. While the human heart is compounded of the same elements as at present, it will never be wholly indifferent to public good, nor entirely unaffected with the tendency of characters and manners. And though this affection of humanity may not generally be

esteemed so strong as vanity or ambition, yet, being common to all men, it can alone be the foundation of morals, or of any general system of blame or praise. One man's ambition is not another's ambition, nor will the same event or object satisfy both; but the humanity of one man is the humanity of every one, and the same object touches this passion in all human creatures.

223. But the sentiments, which arise from humanity, are not only the same in all human creatures, and produce the same approbation or censure; but they also comprehend all human creatures; nor is there any one whose conduct or character is not, by their means, an object to every one of censure or approbation. On the contrary, those other passions, commonly denominated selfish, both produce different sentiments in each individual, according to his particular situation; and also contemplate the greater part of mankind with the utmost indifference and unconcern. Whoever has a high regard and esteem for me flatters my vanity; whoever expresses contempt mortifies and displeases me; but as my name is known but to a small part of mankind, there are few who come within the sphere of this passion, or excite, on its account, either my affection or disgust. But if you represent a tyrannical, insolent, or barbarous behaviour, in any country or in any age of the world, I soon carry my eye to the pernicious tendency of such a conduct, and feel the sentiment of repugnance and displeasure towards it. No character can be so remote as to be, in this light, wholly indifferent to me. What is beneficial to society or to the person himself must still be preferred. And every quality or action, of every human being, must, by this means, be ranked under some class or denomination, expressive of general censure or applause.

What more, therefore, can we ask to distinguish the sentiments, dependent on humanity, from those connected with any other passion, or to satisfy us, why the former are the origin of morals, not the latter? Whatever conduct gains my approbation, by touching my humanity, procures also the applause of all mankind, by affecting the same principle in them; but what serves my avarice or ambition pleases these passions in me alone, and affects not the avarice and ambition of the rest of mankind. There is no circumstance of conduct in any man, provided it have a beneficial tendency, that is not agreeable to my humanity, however remote the person; but every man, so far removed as neither to cross nor serve my avarice and ambition, is regarded as wholly indifferent by those passions. The distinction, therefore, between these species of sentiment being so great and evident, language must soon be moulded upon it, and must invent a peculiar set of terms, in order to express those universal sentiments of censure or approbation, which arise from humanity, or from views of general usefulness and its contrary. Virtue and Vice become then known; morals are recognized; certain general ideas are framed of human conduct and behaviour; such measures are expected from men in such situations. This action is determined to be conformable to our abstract rule; that other, contrary. And by such universal principles are the particular sentiments of self-love frequently controlled and limited.*

224. From instances of popular tumults, seditions, factions, panics, and of all passions, which are shared with a multitude, we may learn the influence of society in exciting and supporting any emotion; while the most ungovernable disorders are raised, we find, by that means, from the slightest and most frivolous occasions. Solon was no very cruel, though, perhaps, an unjust legislator, who punished neuters in civil wars; and few, I believe, would, in such cases, incur the penalty, were their affection and discourse allowed sufficient to absolve them. No selfishness, and scarce any philosophy, have there force sufficient to support a total coolness and indifference; and he must be more or less than man,

---

* It seems certain, both from reason and experience, that a rude, untaught savage regulates chiefly his love and hatred by the ideas of private utility and injury, and has but faint conceptions of a general rule or system of behaviour. The man who stands opposite to him in battle, he hates heartily, not only for the present moment, which is almost unavoidable, but for ever after; nor is he satisfied without the most extreme punishment and vengeance. But we, accustomed to society, and to more enlarged reflections, consider, that this man is serving his own country and community; that any man, in the same situation, would do the same; that we ourselves, in like circumstances, observe a like conduct; that; in general, human society is best supported on such maxims: and by these suppositions and views, we correct, in some measure, our ruder and narrower positions. And though much of our friendship and enemity be still regulated by private considerations of benefit and harm, we pay, at least, this homage to general rules, which we are accustomed to respect, that we commonly pervert our adversary's conduct, by imputing malice or injustice to him, in order to give vent to those passions, which arise from self-love and private interest. When the heart is full of rage, it never wants pretences of this nature; though sometimes as frivolous, as those from which Horace, being almost crushed by the fall of a tree, effects to accuse of parricide the first planter of it.

who kindles not in the common blaze. What wonder then, that moral sentiments are found of such influence in life; though springing from principles, which may appear, at first sight, somewhat small and delicate? But these principles, we must remark, are social and universal; they form, in a manner, the *party* of humankind against vice or disorder, its common enemy. And as the benevolent concern for others is diffused, in a greater or less degree, over all men, and is the same in all, it occurs more frequently in discourse, is cherished by society and conversation, and the blame and approbation, consequent on it, are thereby roused from that lethargy into which they are probably lulled, in solitary and uncultivated nature. Other passions, though perhaps originally stronger, yet being selfish and private, are often overpowered by its force, and yield the dominion of our breast to those social and public principles.

225. Another spring of our constitution, that brings a great addition of force to moral sentiments, is the love of fame; which rules, with such uncontrolled authority, in all generous minds, and is often the grand object of all their designs and undertakings. By our continual and earnest pursuit of a character, a name, a reputation in the world, we bring our own deportment and conduct frequently in review, and consider how they appear in the eyes of those who approach and regard us. This constant habit of surveying ourselves, as it were, in reflection, keeps alive all the sentiments of right and wrong, and begets, in noble natures, a certain reverence for themselves as well as others, which is the surest guardian of every virtue. The animal conveniencies and pleasures sink gradually in their value; while every inward beauty and moral grace is studiously acquired, and the mind is accomplished in every perfection, which can adorn or embellish a rational creature.

Here is the most perfect morality with which we are acquainted: here is displayed the force of many sympathies. Our moral sentiment is itself a feeling chiefly of that nature, and our regard to a character with others seems to arise only from a care of preserving a character with ourselves; and in order to attain this end, we find it necessary to prop our tottering judgement on the correspondent approbation of mankind.

226. But, that we may accommodate matters, and remove if possible every difficulty, let us allow all these reasonings to be

false. Let us allow that, when we resolve the pleasure, which arises from views of utility, into the sentiments of humanity and sympathy, we have embraced a wrong hypothesis. Let us confess it necessary to find some other explication of that applause, which is paid to objects, whether inanimate, animate, or rational, if they have a tendency to promote the welfare and advantage of mankind. However difficult it be to conceive that an object is approved of on account of its tendency to a certain end, while the end itself is totally indifferent: let us swallow this absurdity, and consider what are the consequences. The preceding delineation or definition of Personal Merit must still retain its evidence and authority: it must still be allowed that every quality of the mind, which is *useful* or *agreeable* to the *person himself* or to *others*, communicates a pleasure to the spectator, engages his esteem, and is admitted under the honourable denomination of virtue or merit. Are not justice, fidelity, honour, veracity, allegiance, chastity, esteemed solely on account of their tendency to promote the good of society? Is not that tendency inseparable from humanity, benevolence, lenity, generosity, gratitude, moderation, tenderness, friendship, and all the other social virtues? Can it possibly be doubted that industry, discretion, frugality, secrecy, order, perseverance, forethought, judgement, and this whole class of virtues and accomplishments, of which many pages would not contain the catalogue; can it be doubted, I say, that the tendency of these qualities to promote the interest and happiness of their possessor, is the sole foundation of their merit? Who can dispute that a mind, which supports a perpetual serenity and cheerfulness, a noble dignity and undaunted spirit, a tender affection and good-will to all around; as it has more enjoyment within itself, is also a more animating and rejoicing spectacle, than if dejected with melancholy, tormented with anxiety, irritated with rage, or sunk into the most abject baseness and degeneracy? And as to the qualities, immediately *agreeable* to *others*, they speak sufficiently for themselves; and he must be unhappy, indeed, either in his own temper, or in his situation and company, who has never perceived the charms of a facetious wit or flowing affability, of a delicate modesty or decent genteelness of address and manner.

227. I am sensible, that nothing can be more unphilosophical than to be positive or dogmatical on any subject; and that, even if

excessive scepticism could be maintained, it would not be more destructive to all just reasoning and inquiry. I am convinced that, where men are the most sure and arrogant, they are commonly the most mistaken, and have there given reins to passion, without that proper deliberation and suspense, which can alone secure them from the grossest absurdities. Yet, I must confess, that this enumeration puts the matter in so strong a light, that I cannot, *at present*, be more assured of any truth, which I learn from reasoning and argument, than that personal merit consists entirely in the usefulness or agreeableness of qualities to the person himself possessed of them, or to others, who have any intercourse with him. But when I reflect that, though the bulk and figure of the earth have been measured and delineated, though the motions of the tides have been accounted for, the order and economy of the heavenly bodies subjected to their proper laws, and Infinite itself reduced to calculation; yet men still dispute concerning the foundation of their moral duties. When I reflect on this, I say, I fall back into diffidence and scepticism, and suspect that an hypothesis, so obvious, had it been a true one, would, long ere now, have been received by the unanimous suffrage and consent of mankind.

Part 2

Having explained the moral *approbation* attending merit or virtue, there remains nothing but briefly to consider our interested *obligation* to it, and to inquire whether every man, who has any regard to his own happiness and welfare, will not best find his account in the practice of every moral duty. If this can be clearly ascertained from the foregoing theory, we shall have the satisfaction to reflect, that we have advanced principles, which not only, it is hoped, will stand the test of reasoning and inquiry, but may contribute to the amendment of men's lives, and their improvement in morality and social virtue. And though the philosophical truth of any proposition by no means depends on its tendency to promote the interests of society; yet a man has but a bad grace, who delivers a theory, however true, which, he must confess, leads to a practice dangerous and pernicious. Why rake into those corners of nature which spread a nuisance all around? Why dig up the pestilence from the pit in which it is buried? The ingenuity of your researches may be admired, but your systems will be detested; and mankind will agree, if they cannot refute them, to sink them, at least, in eternal silence and oblivion. Truths which are *pernicious* to society, if any such there be, will yield to errors which are salutary and *advantageous*.

But what philosophical truths can be more advantageous to society, than those here delivered, which represent virtue in all her genuine and most engaging charms, and makes us approach her with ease, familiarity, and affection? The dismal dress falls off, with which many divines, and some philosophers, have covered her; and nothing appears but gentleness, humanity, beneficence, affability; nay, even at proper intervals, play, frolic, and gaiety. She talks not of useless austerities and rigours, suffering and self-denial. She declares that her sole purpose is to make her votaries and all mankind, during every instant of their existence, if possible, cheerful and happy; nor does she ever willingly part with any pleasure but in hopes of ample compensation in some other period of their lives. The sole trouble which she demands, is that of just calculation, and a steady preference of the greater happiness. And if any austere pretenders approach her, enemies to joy and pleasure, she either rejects them as hypocrites and deceivers; or, if she admit them in her train, they are ranked, however, among the least favoured of her votaries.

And, indeed, to drop all figurative expression, what hopes can we ever have of engaging mankind to a practice which we confess full of austerity and rigour? Or what theory of morals can ever serve any useful purpose, unless it can show, by a particular detail, that all the duties which it recommends, are also the true interest of each individual? The peculiar advantage of the foregoing system seems to be, that it furnishes proper mediums for that purpose.

229. That the virtues which are immediately *useful* or *agreeable* to the person possessed of them, are desirable in a view to self-interest, it would surely be superfluous to prove. Moralists, indeed, may spare themselves all the pains which they often take in recommending these duties. To what purpose collect arguments to evince that temperance is advantageous, and the excesses of pleasure hurtful, when it appears that these excesses are only denominated such, because they are hurtful; and that, if the unlimited use of strong liquors, for instance, no more impaired health or the

faculties of mind and body than the use of air or water, it would not be a whit more vicious or blameable?

It seems equally superfluous to prove, that the *companionable* virtues of good manners and wit, decency and genteelness, are more desirable than the contrary qualities. Vanity alone, without any other consideration, is a sufficient motive to make us wish for the possession of these accomplishments. No man was ever willingly deficient in this particular. All our failures here proceed from bad education, want of capacity, or a perverse and unpliable disposition. Would you have your company coveted, admired, followed; rather than hated, despised, avoided? Can any one seriously deliberate in the case? As no enjoyment is sincere, without some reference to company and society; so no society can be agreeable, or even tolerable, where a man feels his presence unwelcome, and discovers all around him symptoms of disgust and aversion.

230. But why, in the greater society or confederacy of mankind, should not the case be the same as in particular clubs and companies? Why is it more doubtful, that the enlarged virtues of humanity, generosity, beneficence, are desirable with a view of happiness and self-interest, than the limited endowments of ingenuity and politeness? Are we apprehensive lest those social affections interfere, in a greater and more immediate degree than any other pursuits, with private utility, and cannot be gratified, without some important sacrifice of honour and advantage? If so, we are but ill-instructed in the nature of the human passions, and are more influenced by verbal distinctions than by real differences.

Whatever contradiction may vulgarly be supposed between the *selfish* and *social* sentiments or dispositions, they are really no more opposite than selfish and ambitious, selfish and revengeful, selfish and vain. It is requisite that there be an original propensity of some kind, in order to be a basis to self-love, by giving a relish to the objects of its pursuit; and none more fit for this purpose than benevolence or humanity. The goods of fortune are spent in one gratification or another: the miser who accumulates his annual income, and lends it out at interest, has really spent it in the gratification of his avarice. And it would be difficult to show why a man is more a loser by a generous action, than by any other method of expense; since the utmost which he can attain by the most elaborate selfishness, is the indulgence of some affection.

231. Now if life, without passion, must be altogether insipid and tiresome; let a man suppose that he has full power of modelling his own disposition, and let him deliberate what appetite or desire he would choose for the foundation of his happiness and enjoyment. Every affection, he would observe, when gratified by success, gives a satisfaction proportioned to its force and violence; but besides this advantage, common to all, the immediate feeling of benevolence and friendship, humanity and kindness, is sweet, smooth, tender, and agreeable, independent of all fortune and accidents. These virtues are besides attended with a pleasing consciousness or remembrance, and keep us in humour with ourselves as well as others; while we retain the agreeable reflection of having done our part towards mankind and society. And though all men show a jealousy of our success in the pursuits of avarice and ambition; yet are we almost sure of their good-will and good wishes, so long as we persevere in the paths of virtue, and employ ourselves in the execution of generous plans and purposes. What other passion is there where we shall find so many advantages united; an agreeable sentiment, a pleasing consciousness, a good reputation? But of these truths, we may observe, men are, of themselves, pretty much convinced; nor are they deficient in their duty to society, because they would not wish to be generous, friendly, and humane; but because they do not feel themselves such.

232. Treating vice with the greatest candour, and making it all possible concessions, we must acknowledge that there is not, in any instance, the smallest pretext for giving it the preference above virtue, with a view of self-interest; except, perhaps, in the case of justice, where a man, taking things in a certain light, may often seem to be a loser by his integrity. And though it is allowed that, without a regard to property, no society could subsist; yet according to the imperfect way in which human affairs are conducted, a sensible knave, in particular incidents, may think that an act of iniquity or infidelity will make a considerable addition to his fortune, without causing any considerable breach in the social union and confederacy. That *honesty is the best policy*, may be a good general rule, but is liable to many exceptions; and he, it may perhaps be thought, conducts himself with most wisdom, who observes the general rule, and takes advantage of all the exceptions.

233. I must confess that, if a man think that this reasoning much requires an answer, it would be a little difficult to find any which will to him appear satisfactory and convincing. If his heart rebel not against such pernicious maxims, if he feel no reluctance to the thoughts of villainy or baseness, he has indeed lost a considerable motive to virtue; and we may expect that this practice will be answerable to his speculation. But in all ingenuous natures, the antipathy to treachery and roguery is too strong to be counter-balanced by any views of profit or pecuniary advantage. Inward peace of mind, consciousness of integrity, a satisfactory review of our own conduct; these are circumstances, very requisite to happiness, and will be cherished and cultivated by every honest man, who feels the importance of them.

Such a one has, besides, the frequent satisfaction of seeing knaves, with all their pretended cunning and abilities, betrayed by their own maxims; and while they purpose to cheat with moderation and secrecy, a tempting incident occurs, nature is frail, and they give into the snare; whence they can never extricate themselves, without a total loss of reputation, and the forfeiture of all future trust and confidence with mankind.

But were they ever so secret and successful, the honest man, if he has any tincture of philosophy, or even common observation and reflection, will discover that they themselves are, in the end, the greatest dupes, and have sacrificed the invaluable enjoyment of a character, with themselves at least, for the acquisition of worthless toys and gewgaws. How little is requisite to supply the *necessities* of nature? And in a view to *pleasure*, what comparison between the unbought satisfaction of conversation, society, study, even health and the common beauties of nature, but above all the peaceful reflection on one's own conduct; what comparison, I say, between these and the feverish, empty amusements of luxury and expense? These natural pleasures, indeed, are really without price; both because they are below all price in their attainment, and above it in their enjoyment.

APPENDIX ONE

Concerning moral sentiment

234. If the foregoing hypothesis be received, it will now be easy for us to determine the question first started,* concerning the general principles of morals; and though we postponed the decision of that question, lest it should then involve us in intricate speculations, which are unfit for moral discourses, we may resume it at present, and examine how far either *reason* or *sentiment* enters into all decisions of praise or censure.

One principal foundation of moral praise being supposed to lie in the usefulness of any quality or action, it is evident that *reason* must enter for a considerable share in all decisions of this kind; since nothing but that faculty can instruct us in the tendency of qualities and actions, and point out their beneficial consequences to society and to their possessor. In many cases this is an affair liable to great controversy: doubts may arise; opposite interests may occur; and a preference must be given to one side, from very nice views, and a small overbalance of utility. This is particularly remarkable in questions with regard to justice; as is, indeed, natural to suppose, from that species of utility which attends this virtue.† Were every single instance of justice, like that of benevolence, useful to society; this would be a more simple state of the case, and seldom liable to great controversy. But as single instances of justice are often pernicious in their first and immediate tendency, and as the advantage to society results only from the observance of the general rule, and from the concurrence and combination of several persons in the same equitable conduct; the case here becomes more intricate and involved. The various circumstances of society; the various consequences of any practice; the various interests which may be

* Section 1.
† See Appendix 3.

proposed; these, on many occasions, are doubtful, and subject to great discussion and inquiry. The object of municipal laws is to fix all the questions with regard to justice: the debates of civilians; the reflections of politicians; the precedents of history and public records, are all directed to the same purpose. And a very accurate *reason* or *judgement* is often requisite, to give the true determination, amidst such intricate doubts arising from obscure or opposite utilities.

235. But though reason, when fully assisted and improved, be sufficient to instruct us in the pernicious or useful tendency of qualities and actions; it is not alone sufficient to produce any moral blame or approbation. Utility is only a tendency to a certain end; and were the end totally indifferent to us, we should feel the same indifference towards the means. It is requisite a *sentiment* should here display itself, in order to give a preference to the useful above the pernicious tendencies. This sentiment can be no other than a feeling for the happiness of mankind, and a resentment of their misery; since these are the different ends which virtue and vice have a tendency to promote. Here therefore *reason* instructs us in the several tendencies of actions, and *humanity* makes a distinction in favour of those which are useful and beneficial.

236. This partition between the faculties of understanding and sentiment, in all moral decisions, seems clear from the preceding hypothesis. But I shall suppose that hypothesis false: it will then be requisite to look out for some other theory that may be satisfactory; and I dare venture to affirm that none such will ever be found, so long as we suppose reason to be the sole source of morals. To prove this, it will be proper to weigh the five following considerations.

I. It is easy for a false hypothesis to maintain some appearance of truth, while it keeps wholly in generals, makes use of undefined terms, and employs comparisons, instead of instances. This is particularly remarkable in that philosophy, which ascribes the discernment of all moral distinctions to reason alone, without the concurrence of sentiment. It is impossible that, in any particular instance, this hypothesis can so much as be rendered intelligible, whatever specious figure it may make in general declamations and discourses. Examine the crime of *ingratitude*, for instance; which has place, wherever we observe good-will, expressed and known, together with good-offices performed, on the one side, and a return of ill-will or indifference, with ill-offices or neglect on the other: anatomize all these circumstances, and examine, by your reason alone, in what consists the demerit or blame. You never will come to any issue or conclusion.

237. Reason judges either of *matter of fact* or of *relations*. Enquire then, *first*, where is that matter of fact which we here call *crime*; point it out; determine the time of its existence; describe its essence or nature; explain the sense or faculty to which it discovers itself. It resides in the mind of the person who is ungrateful. He must, therefore, feel it, and be conscious of it. But nothing is there, except the passion of ill-will or absolute indifference. You cannot say that these, of themselves, always, and in all circumstances, are crimes. No, they are only crimes when directed towards persons who have before expressed and displayed good-will towards us. Consequently, we may infer, that the crime of ingratitude is not any particular individual *fact*; but arises from a complication of circumstances, which, being presented to the spectator, excites the *sentiment* of blame, by the particular structure and fabric of his mind.

238. This representation, you say, is false. Crime, indeed, consists not in a particular *fact*, of whose reality we are assured by *reason*; but it consists in certain *moral relations*, discovered by reason, in the same manner as we discover by reason the truths of geometry or algebra. But what are the relations, I ask, of which you here talk? In the case stated above, I see first good-will and good-offices in one person; then ill-will and ill-offices in the other. Between these, there is a relation of *contrariety*. Does the crime consist in that relation? But suppose a person bore me ill-will or did me ill-offices; and I, in return, were indifferent towards him, or did him good offices. Here is the same relation of *contrariety*; and yet my conduct is often highly laudable. Twist and turn this matter as much as you will, you can never rest the morality on relation; but must have recourse to the decisions of sentiment.

When it is affirmed that two and three are equal to the half of ten, this relation of equality I understand perfectly. I conceive, that if ten be divided into two parts, of which one has as many units as the other; and if any of these parts be compared to two added to three, it will contain as many units as that compound number. But when you draw thence a comparison to moral relations, I own that I am altogether at a loss to understand you. A moral action, a crime, such as ingratitude, is a complicated object. Does the morality consist in the relation of its parts to each other? How? After what manner? Specify the relation: be more particular and explicit in your propositions, and you will easily see their falsehood.

239. No, say you, the morality consists in the relation of actions to the rule of right; and they are denominated good or ill, according as they agree or disagree with it. What then is this rule of right? In what does it consist? How is it determined? By reason, you say, which examines the moral relations of actions. So that moral relations are determined by the comparison of action to a rule. And that rule is determined by considering the moral relations of objects. Is not this fine reasoning?

All this is metaphysics, you cry. That is enough; there needs nothing more to give a strong presumption of falsehood. Yes, reply I, here are metaphysics surely; but they are all on your side, who advance an abstruse hypothesis, which can never be made intelligible, nor quadrate with any particular instance or illustration. The hypothesis which we embrace is plain. It maintains that morality is determined by sentiment. It defines virtue to be *whatever mental action or quality gives to a spectator the pleasing sentiment of approbation;* and vice the contrary. We then proceed to examine a plain matter of fact, to wit, what actions have this influence. We consider all the circumstances in which these actions agree, and thence endeavour to extract some general observations with regard to these sentiments. If you call this metaphysics, and find anything abstruse here, you need only conclude that your turn of mind is not suited to the moral sciences.

240. II. When a man, at any time, deliberates concerning his own conduct (as, whether he had better, in a particular emergence, assist a brother or a benefactor), he must consider these separate relations, with all the circumstances and situations of the persons, in order to determine the superior duty and obligation; and in order to determine the proportion of lines in any triangle, it is necessary to examine the nature of that figure, and the relation which its several parts bear to each other. But notwithstanding this appearing similarity in the two cases, there is, at bottom, an extreme difference between them. A speculative reasoner concerning triangles or

circles considers the several known and given relations of the parts of these figures; and thence infers some unknown relation, which is dependent on the former. But in moral deliberations we must be acquainted beforehand with all the objects, and all their relations to each other; and from a comparison of the whole, fix our choice or approbation. No new fact to be ascertained; no new relation to be discovered. All the circumstances of the case are supposed to be laid before us, ere we can fix any sentence of blame or approbation. If any material circumstance be yet unknown or doubtful, we must first employ our inquiry or intellectual faculties to assure us of it; and must suspend for a time all moral decision or sentiment. While we are ignorant whether a man were aggressor or not, how can we determine whether the person who killed him be criminal or innocent? But after every circumstance, every relation is known, the understanding has no further room to operate, nor any object on which it could employ itself. The approbation or blame which then ensues, cannot be the work of the judgement, but of the heart; and is not a speculative proposition or affirmation, but an active feeling or sentiment. In the disquisitions of the understanding, from known circumstances and relations, we infer some new and unknown. In moral decisions, all the circumstances and relations must be previously known; and the mind, from the contemplation of the whole, feels some new impression of affection or disgust, esteem or contempt, approbation or blame.

241. Hence the great difference between a mistake of *fact* and one of *right*; and hence the reason why the one is commonly criminal and not the other. When Oedipus killed Laius, he was ignorant of the relation, and from circumstances, innocent and involuntary, formed erroneous opinions concerning the action which he committed. But when Nero killed Agrippina, all the relations between himself and the person, and all the circumstances of the fact, were previously known to him; but the motive of revenge, or fear, or interest, prevailed in his savage heart over the sentiments of duty and humanity. And when we express that detestation against him to which he himself, in a little time, became insensible, it is not that we see any relations, of which he was ignorant; but that, for the rectitude of our disposition, we feel sentiments against which he was hardened from flattery and a long perseverance in the most enormous crimes. In these sentiments

then, not in a discovery of relations of any kind, do all moral determinations consist. Before we can pretend to form any decision of this kind, everything must be known and ascertained on the side of the object or action. Nothing remains but to feel, on our part, some sentiment of blame or approbation; whence we pronounce the action criminal or virtuous.

242. III. This doctrine will become still more evident, if we compare moral beauty with natural, to which in many particulars it bears so near a resemblance. It is on the proportion, relation, and position of parts, that all natural beauty depends; but it would be absurd thence to infer, that the perception of beauty, like that of truth in geometrical problems, consists wholly in the perception of relations, and was performed entirely by the understanding or intellectual faculties. In all the sciences, our mind from the known relations investigates the unknown. But in all decisions of taste or external beauty, all the relations are beforehand obvious to the eye; and we thence proceed to feel a sentiment of complacency or disgust, according to the nature of the object, and disposition of our organs.

Euclid has fully explained all the qualities of the circle; but has not in any proposition said a word of its beauty. The reason is evident. The beauty is not a quality of the circle. It lies not in any part of the line, whose parts are equally distant from a common centre. It is only the effect which that figure produces upon the mind, whose peculiar fabric or structure renders it susceptible of such sentiments. In vain would you look for it in the circle, or seek it, either by your senses or by mathematical reasoning, in all the properties of that figure.

Attend to Palladio and Perrault, while they explain all the parts and proportions of a pillar. They talk of the cornice, and frieze, and base, and entablature, and shaft, and architrave; and give the description and position of each of these members. But should you ask the description and position of its beauty, they would readily reply, that the beauty is not in any of the parts or members of a pillar, but results from the whole, when that complicated figure is presented to an intelligent mind, susceptible to those finer sensations. Till such a spectator appear, there is nothing but a figure of such particular dimensions and proportions: from his sentiments alone arise its elegance and beauty.

Again; attend to Cicero, while he paints the crimes of a Verres or a Catiline. You must acknowledge that the moral turpitude results, in the same manner, from the contemplation of the whole, when presented to a being whose organs have such a particular structure and formation. The orator may paint rage, insolence, barbarity on the one side; meekness, suffering, sorrow, innocence on the other. But if you feel no indignation or compassion arise in you from this complication of circumstances, you would in vain ask him, in what consists the crime or villainy, which he so vehemently exclaims against? At what time, or on what subject it first began to exist? And what has a few months afterwards become of it, when every disposition and thought of all the actors is totally altered or annihilated? No satisfactory answer can be given to any of these questions, upon the abstract hypothesis of morals; and we must at last acknowledge, that the crime or immorality is no particular fact or relation, which can be the object of the understanding, but arises entirely from the sentiment of disapprobation, which, by the structure of human nature, we unavoidably feel on the apprehension of barbarity or treachery.

243. IV. Inanimate objects may bear to each other all the same relations which we observe in moral agents; though the former can never be the object of love or hatred, nor are consequently susceptible of merit or iniquity. A young tree, which over-tops and destroys its parent, stands in all the same relations with Nero, when he murdered Agrippina; and if morality consisted merely in relations, would no doubt be equally criminal.

244. V. It appears evident that the ultimate ends of human actions can never, in any case, be accounted for by *reason*, but recommend themselves entirely to the sentiments and affections of mankind, without any dependence on the intellectual faculties. Ask a man *why he uses exercise*; he will answer, *because he desires to keep his health*. If you then enquire, *why he desires health*, he will readily reply, *because sickness is painful*. If you push your enquiries farther, and desire a reason *why he hates pain*, it is impossible he can ever give any. This is an ultimate end, and is never referred to any other object.

Perhaps to your second question, *why he desires health*, he may also reply, that *it is necessary for the exercise of his calling*. If you ask, *why he is anxious on that head*, he will answer, *because he desires to get money.* If you demand *Why? It is the instrument of pleasure,* says he. And beyond this it is an absurdity to ask for a reason. It is impossible there can be a progress *in infinitum;* and that one thing can always be a reason why another is desired. Something must be desirable on its own account, and because of its immediate accord or agreement with human sentiment and affection.

245. Now as virtue is an end, and is desirable on its own account, without fee and reward, merely for the immediate satisfaction which it conveys; it is requisite that there should be some sentiment which it touches, some internal taste or feeling, or whatever you may please to call it, which distinguishes moral good and evil, and which embraces the one and rejects the other.

246. Thus the distinct boundaries and offices of *reason* and of *taste* are easily ascertained. The former conveys the knowledge of truth and falsehood: the latter gives the sentiment of beauty and deformity, vice and virtue. The one discovers objects as they really stand in nature, without addition and diminution: the other has a productive faculty, and gilding or staining all natural objects with the colours, borrowed from internal sentiment, raises in a manner a new creation. Reason being cool and disengaged, is no motive to action, and directs only the impulse received from appetite or inclination, by showing us the means of attaining happiness or avoiding misery: Taste, as it gives pleasure or pain, and thereby constitutes happiness or misery, becomes a motive to action, and is the first spring or impulse to desire and volition. From circumstances and relations, known or supposed, the former leads us to the discovery of the concealed and unknown: after all circumstances and relations are laid before us, the latter makes us feel from the whole a new sentiment of blame or approbation. The standard of the one, being founded on the nature of things, is eternal and inflexible, even by the will of the Supreme Being: the standard of the other arising from the eternal frame and constitution of animals, is ultimately derived from that Supreme Will, which bestowed on each being its peculiar nature, and arranged the several classes and orders of existence.

Of self-love

247. There is a principle, supposed to prevail among many, which is utterly incompatible with all virtue or moral sentiment; and as it can proceed from nothing but the most depraved disposition, so in its turn it tends still further to encourage that depravity. This principle is, that all *benevolence* is mere hypocrisy, friendship a cheat, public spirit a farce, fidelity a snare to procure trust and confidence; and that while all of us, at bottom, pursue only our private interest, we wear these fair disguises, in order to put others off their guard, and expose them the more to our wiles and machinations. What heart one must be possessed of who possesses such principles, and who feels no internal sentiment that belies so pernicious a theory, it is easy to imagine: and also what degree of affection and benevolence he can bear to a species whom he represents under such odious colours, and supposes so little susceptible of gratitude or any return of affection. Or if we should not ascribe these principles wholly to a corrupted heart, we must at least account for them from the most careless and precipitate examination. Superficial reasoners, indeed, observing many false pretences among mankind, and feeling, perhaps, no very strong restraint in their own disposition, might draw a general and a hasty conclusion that all is equally corrupted, and that men, different from all other animals, and indeed from all other species of existence, admit of no degrees of good or bad, but are, in every instance, the same creatures under different disguises and appearances.

248. There is another principle, somewhat resembling the former; which has been much insisted on by philosophers, and has been the foundation of many a system; that, whatever affection one may feel, or imagine he feels for others, no passion is, or can be disinterested; that the most generous friendship, however

sincere, is a modification of self-love; and that, even unknown to ourselves, we seek only our own gratification, while we appear the most deeply engaged in schemes for the liberty and happiness of mankind. By a turn of imagination, by a refinement of reflection, by an enthusiasm of passion, we seem to take part in the interests of others, and imagine ourselves divested of all selfish considerations: but, at bottom, the most generous patriot and most niggardly miser, the bravest hero and most abject coward, have, in every action, an equal regard to their own happiness and welfare.

Whoever concludes from the seeming tendency of this opinion, that those, who make profession of it, cannot possibly feel the true sentiments of benevolence, or have any regard for genuine virtue, will often find himself, in practice, very much mistaken. Probity and honour were no strangers to Epicurus and his sect. Atticus and Horace seem to have enjoyed from nature, and cultivated by reflection, as generous and friendly dispositions as any disciple of the austerer schools. And among the modern, Hobbes and Locke, who maintained the selfish system of morals, lived irreproachable lives; though the former lay not under any restraint of religion which might supply the defects of his philosophy.

249. An Epicurean or a Hobbist readily allows, that there is such a thing as friendship in the world, without hypocrisy or disguise; though he may attempt, by a philosophical chemistry, to resolve the elements of this passion, if I may so speak, into those of another, and explain every affection to be self-love, twisted and moulded, by a particular turn of imagination, into a variety of appearances. But as the same turn of imagination prevails not in every man, nor gives the same direction to the original passion; this is sufficient even according to the selfish system to make the widest difference in human characters, and denominate one man virtuous and humane, another vicious and meanly interested. I esteem the man whose self-love, by whatever means, is so directed as to give him a concern for others, and render him serviceable to society: as I hate or despise him, who has no regard to any thing beyond his own gratifications and enjoyments. In vain would you suggest that these characters, though seemingly opposite, are at bottom the same, and that a very inconsiderable turn of thought forms the whole

difference between them. Each character, notwithstanding these inconsiderable differences, appears to me, in practice, pretty durable and untransmutable. And I find not in this more than in other subjects, that the natural sentiments arising from the general appearances of things are easily destroyed by subtile reflections concerning the minute origin of these appearances. Does not the lively, cheerful colour of a countenance inspire me with complacency and pleasure; even though I learn from philosophy that all difference of complexion arises from the most minute differences of thickness, in the most minute parts of the skin; by means of which a superficies is qualified to reflect one of the original colours of light, and absorb the others?

250. But though the question concerning the universal or partial selfishness of man be not so material as is usually imagined to morality and practice, it is certainly of consequence in the speculative science of human nature, and is a proper object of curiosity and enquiry. It may not, therefore, be unsuitable, in this place, to bestow a few reflections upon it.*

The most obvious objection to the selfish hypothesis is, that, as it is contrary to common feeling and our most unprejudiced notions, there is required the highest stretch of philosophy to establish so extraordinary a paradox. To the most careless observer there appear to be such dispositions as benevolence and generosity; such affections as love, friendship, compassion, gratitude. These sentiments have their causes, effects, objects, and operations, marked by common language and observation, and plainly distinguished from those of the selfish passions. And as this is the obvious appearance of things, it must be admitted, till some hypothesis be discovered, which by penetrating deeper into human nature, may prove the former affections to be nothing but modifications of the

---

* Benevolence naturally divides into two kinds, the *general* and the *particular*. The first is, where we have no friendship or connexion or esteem for the person, but feel only a general sympathy with him or a compassion for his pains, and a congratulation with his pleasures. The other species of benevolence is founded on an opinion of virtue, on services done us, or on some particular connexions. Both these sentiments must be allowed real in human nature: but whether they will resolve into some nice considerations of self-love, is a question more curious than important. The former sentiment, to wit, that of general benevolence, or humanity, or sympathy, we shall have occasion frequently to treat of in the course of this inquiry; and I assume it as real, from general experience, without any other proof.

latter. All attempts of this kind have hitherto proved fruitless, and seem to have proceeded entirely from that love of *simplicity* which has been the source of much false reasoning in philosophy. I shall not here enter into any detail on the present subject. Many able philosophers have shown the insufficiency of these systems. And I shall take for granted what, I believe, the smallest reflection will make evident to every impartial enquirer.

251. But the nature of the subject furnishes the strongest presumption, that no better system will ever, for the future, be invented, in order to account for the origin of the benevolent from the selfish affections, and reduce all the various emotions of the human mind to a perfect simplicity. The case is not the same in this species of philosophy as in physics. Many an hypothesis in nature, contrary to first appearances, has been found, on more accurate scrutiny, solid and satisfactory. Instances of this kind are so frequent that a judicious, as well as witty philosopher,* has ventured to affirm, if there be more than one way in which any phenomenon may be produced, that there is general presumption for its arising from the causes which are the least obvious and familiar. But the presumption always lies on the other side, in all enquiries concerning the origin of our passions, and of the internal operations of the human mind. The simplest and most obvious cause which can there be assigned for any phenomenon, is probably the true one. When a philosopher, in the explication of his system, is obliged to have recourse to some very intricate and refined reflections, and to suppose them essential to the production of any passion or emotion, we have reason to be extremely on our guard against so fallacious an hypothesis. The affections are not susceptible of any impression from the refinements of reason or imagination; and it is always found that a vigorous exertion of the latter faculties, necessarily, from the narrow capacity of the human mind, destroys all activity in the former. Our predominant motive or intention is, indeed, frequently concealed from ourselves when it is mingled and confounded with other motives which the mind, from vanity or self-conceit, is desirous of supposing more prevalent: but there is no instance that a concealment of this nature has ever arisen from the abstruseness and intricacy of the motive. A man that has lost a

---

* Mons. Fontenelle.

friend and patron may flatter himself that all his grief arises from generous sentiments, without any mixture of narrow or interested considerations: but a man that grieves for a valuable friend, who needed his patronage and protection; how can we suppose, that his passionate tenderness arises from some metaphysical regards to a self-interest, which has no foundation or reality? We may as well imagine that minute wheels and springs, like those of a watch, give motion to a loaded waggon, as account for the origin of passion from such abstruse reflections.

252. Animals are found susceptible of kindness, both to their own species and to ours; nor is there, in this case, the least suspicion of disguise or artifice. Shall we account for all *their* sentiments, too, from refined deductions of self-interest? Or if we admit a disinterested benevolence in the inferior species, by what rule of analogy can we refuse it in the superior?

Love between the sexes begets a complacency and good-will, very distinct from the gratification of an appetite. Tenderness to their offspring, in all sensible beings, is commonly able alone to counter-balance the strongest motives of self-love, and has no manner of dependence on that affection. What interest can a fond mother have in view, who loses her health by assiduous attendance on her sick child, and afterwards languishes and dies of grief, when freed, by its death, from the slavery of that attendance?

Is gratitude no affection of the human breast, or is that a word merely, without any meaning or reality? Have we no satisfaction in one man's company above another's, and no desire of the welfare of our friend, even though absence or death should prevent us from all participation in it? Or what is it commonly, that gives us any participation in it, even while alive and present, but our affection and regard to him?

These and a thousand other instances are marks of a general benevolence in human nature, where no *real* interest binds us to the object. And how an *imaginary* interest known and avowed for such, can be the origin of any passion or emotion, seems difficult to explain. No satisfactory hypothesis of this kind has yet been discovered; nor is there the smallest probability that the future industry of men will ever be attended with more favourable success.

253. But farther, if we consider rightly of the matter, we shall find that the hypothesis which allows of a disinterested benevolence, distinct from self-love, has really more *simplicity* in it, and is more conformable to the analogy of nature than that which pretends to resolve all friendship and humanity into this latter principle. There are bodily wants or appetites acknowledged by every one, which necessarily precede all sensual enjoyment, and carry us directly to seek possession of the object. Thus, hunger and thirst have eating and drinking for their end; and from the gratification of these primary appetites arises a pleasure, which may become the object of another species of desire or inclination that is secondary and interested. In the same manner there are mental passions by which we are impelled immediately to seek particular objects, such as fame or power, or vengeance without any regard to interest; and when these objects are attained a pleasing enjoyment ensues, as the consequence of our indulged affections. Nature must, by the internal frame and constitution of the mind, give an original propensity to fame, ere we can reap any pleasure from that acquisition, or pursue it from motives of self-love, and desire of happiness. If I have no vanity, I take no delight in praise: if I be void of ambition, power gives me no enjoyment: if I be not angry, the punishment of an adversary is totally indifferent to me. In all these cases there is a passion which points immediately to the object, and constitutes it our good or happiness; as there are other secondary passions which afterwards arise, and pursue it as a part of our happiness, when once it is constituted such by our original affections. Were there no appetite of any kind antecedent to self-love, that propensity could scarcely ever exert itself; because we should, in that case, have felt few and slender pains or pleasures, and have little misery or happiness to avoid or to pursue.

254. Now where is the difficulty in conceiving, that this may likewise be the case with benevolence and friendship, and that, from the original frame of our temper, we may feel a desire of another's happiness or good, which, by means of that affection, becomes our own good, and is afterwards pursued, from the combined motives of benevolence and self-enjoyments? Who sees not that vengeance, from the force alone of passion, may be so eagerly pursued, as to make us knowingly neglect every consideration of ease, interest, or safety; and, like some vindictive animals,

infuse our very souls into the wounds we give an enemy;[*] and what a malignant philosophy must it be, that will not allow to humanity and friendship the same privileges which are undisputably granted to the darker passions of enmity and resentment; such a philosophy is more like a satyr than a true delineation or description of human nature; and may be a good foundation for paradoxical wit and raillery, but is a very bad one for any serious argument or reasoning.

---

[*] Animasque in vulnere ponunt. Virg. Dum alteri noceat, sui negligens, says Seneca of Anger. *De Ira*, 1. i.

APPENDIX THREE
Some farther considerations with regard to justice

255. The intention of this Appendix is to give some more particular explication of the origin and nature of Justice, and to mark some differences between it and the other virtues.

The social virtues of humanity and benevolence exert their influence immediately by a direct tendency or instinct, which chiefly keeps in view the simple object, moving the affections, and comprehends not any scheme or system, nor the consequences resulting from the concurrence, imitation, or example of others. A parent flies to the relief of his child; transported by that natural sympathy which actuates him, and which affords no leisure to reflect on the sentiments or conduct of the rest of mankind in like circumstances. A generous man cheerfully embraces an opportunity of serving his friend; because he then feels himself under the dominion of the beneficent affections, nor is he concerned whether any other person in the universe were ever before actuated by such noble motives, or will ever afterwards prove their influence. In all these cases the social passions have in view a single individual object, and pursue the safety or happiness alone of the person loved and esteemed. With this they are satisfied: in this they acquiesce. And as the good, resulting from their benign influence, is in itself complete and entire, it also excites the moral sentiment of approbation, without any reflection on farther consequences, and without any more enlarged views of the concurrence or imitation of the other members of society. On the contrary, were the generous friend or disinterested patriot to stand alone in the practice of beneficence, this would rather enhance his value in our eyes, and join the praise of rarity and novelty to his other more exalted merits.

256. The case is not the same with the social virtues of justice and fidelity. They are highly useful, or indeed absolutely necessary

to the well-being of mankind: but the benefit resulting from them is not the consequence of every individual single act; but arises from the whole scheme or system concurred in by the whole, or the greater part of the society. General peace and order are the attendants of justice or a general abstinence from the possessions of others; but a particular regard to the particular right of one individual citizen may frequently, considered in itself, be productive of pernicious consequences. The result of the individual acts is here, in many instances, directly opposite to that of the whole system of actions; and the former may be extremely hurtful, while the latter is, to the highest degree, advantageous. Riches, inherited from a parent, are, in a bad man's hand, the instrument of mischief. The right of succession may, in one instance, be hurtful. Its benefit arises only from the observance of the general rule; and it is sufficient, if compensation be thereby made for all the ills and inconveniences which flow from particular characters and situations.

Cyrus, young and unexperienced, considered only the individual case before him, and reflected on a limited fitness and convenience, when he assigned the long coat to the tall boy, and the short coat to the other of smaller size. His governor instructed him better, while he pointed out more enlarged views and consequences, and informed his pupil of the general, inflexible rules, necessary to support general peace and order in society.

The happiness and prosperity of mankind, arising from the social virtue of benevolence and its subdivisions, may be compared to a wall, built by many hands, which still rises by each stone that is heaped upon it, and receives increase proportional to the diligence and care of each workman. The same happiness, raised by the social virtue of justice and its subdivisions, may be compared to the building of a vault, where each individual stone would, of itself, fall to the ground; nor is the whole fabric supported but by the mutual assistance and combination of its corresponding parts.

All the laws of nature, which regulate property, as well as all civil laws, are general, and regard alone some essential circumstances of the case, without taking into consideration the characters, situations, and connexions of the person concerned, or any particular consequences which may result from the determination of these laws in any particular case which offers. They deprive, without scruple, a beneficent man of all his possessions, if acquired by mistake, without a good title; in order to bestow them on a selfish miser, who has already heaped up immense stores of superfluous riches. Public utility requires that property should be regulated by general inflexible rules; and though such rules are adopted as best serve the same end of public utility, it is impossible for them to prevent all particular hardships, or make beneficial consequences result from every individual case. It is sufficient, if the whole plan or scheme be necessary to the support of civil society, and if the balance of good, in the main, do thereby preponderate much above that of evil. Even the general laws of the universe, though planned by infinite wisdom, cannot exclude all evil or inconvenience in every particular operation.

257. It has been asserted by some, that justice arises from Human Conventions, and proceeds from the voluntary choice, consent, or combination of mankind. If by *convention* be here meant a *promise* (which is the most usual sense of the word) nothing can be more absurd than this position. The observance of promises is itself one of the most considerable parts of justice, and we are not surely bound to keep our word because we have given our word to keep it. But if by convention be meant a sense of common interest, which sense each man feels in his own breast, which he remarks in his fellows, and which carries him, in concurrence with others, into a general plan or system of actions, which tends to public utility; it must be owned, that, in this sense, justice arises from human conventions. For if it be allowed (what is, indeed, evident) that the particular consequences of a particular act of justice may be hurtful to the public as well as to individuals; it follows that every man, in embracing that virtue, must have an eye to the whole plan or system, and must expect the concurrence of his fellows in the same conduct and behaviour. Did all his views terminate in the consequences of each act of his own, his benevolence and humanity, as well as his self-love, might often prescribe to him measures of conduct very different from those which are agreeable to the strict rules of right and justice.

Thus, two men pull the oars of a boat by common convention for common interest, without any promise or contract; thus gold and silver are made the measures of exchange; thus speech and words and language are fixed by human convention and agreement. Whatever is advantageous to two or more persons, if all perform their part; but what loses all advantage if only one perform, can arise from no other principle There would otherwise be no motive for any one of them to enter into that scheme of conduct.*

258. The word *natural* is commonly taken in so many senses and is of so loose a signification, that it seems vain to dispute whether justice be natural or not. If self-love, if benevolence be natural to man; if reason and forethought be also natural; then may the same epithet be applied to justice, order, fidelity, property, society. Men's inclination, their necessities, lead them to combine; their understanding and experience tell them that this combination is impossible where each governs himself by no rule, and pays no regard to the possessions of others: and from these passions and reflections conjoined, as soon as we observe like passions and reflections in others, the sentiment of justice, throughout all ages, has infallibly and certainly had place to some degree or other in every individual of the human species. In so sagacious an animal, what necessarily arises from the exertion of his intellectual faculties may justly be esteemed natural.†

* This theory concerning the origin of property, and consequently of justice, is, in the main, the same with that hinted at and adopted by Grotius. 'Hinc discimus, quae fuerit causa, ob quam a primaeva communione rerum primo mobilium, deinde et immobilium discessum est: nimirum quod cum non contenti homines vesci sponte natis, antra habitare, corpore aut nudo agere, aut corticibus arborum ferarumve pellibus vestito, vitae genus exquisitius delegissent, industria opus fuit, quam singuli rebus singulis adhiberent. Quo minus autem fructus in commune conferrentur, primum obstitit locorum, in quae homines discesserunt, distantia, deinde justitiae et amoris defectus, per quem fiebat, ut nec in labore, nec in consumtione fructuum, quae debebat, aequalitas servaretur. Simul discimus, quomodo res in proprietatem iverint; non animi actu solo, neque enim scire alii poterant, quid alii suum esse vellent, ut eo abstinerent, et idem velle plures poterant; sed pacto quodam aut expresso, ut per divisionem, aut tacito, ut per occupationem.' *De jure belli et pacis*, lib. ii. cap. 2. sec. 2. art. 4 and 5.

† Natural may be opposed, either to what is *unusual*, *miraculous* or *artificial*. In the two former senses, justice and property are undoubtedly natural. But as they suppose reason, forethought, design, and a social union and confederacy among men, perhaps that epithet cannot strictly, in the last sense, be applied to them. Had men lived without society, property had never been known, and neither justice nor injustice had ever existed. But society among human creatures had been impossible without reason and forethought. Inferior animals, that unite, are guided by instinct, which supplies the place for reason. But all these disputes are merely verbal.

259. Among all civilized nations it has been the constant endeavour to remove everything arbitrary and partial from the decision of property, and to fix the sentence of judges by such general views and considerations as may be equal to every member of society. For besides, that nothing could be more dangerous than to accustom the bench, even in the smallest instance, to regard private friendship or enmity; it is certain, that men, where they imagine that there was no other reason for the preference of their adversary but personal favour, are apt to entertain the strongest ill-will against the magistrates and judges. When natural reason, therefore, points out no fixed view of public utility by which a controversy of property can be decided, positive laws are often framed to supply its place, and direct the procedure of all courts of judicature. Where these too fail, as often happens, precedents are called for; and a former decision, though given itself without any sufficient reason, justly becomes a sufficient reason for a new decision. If direct laws and precedents be wanting, imperfect and indirect ones are brought in aid; and the controverted case is ranged under them by analogical reasonings and comparisons, and similitudes, and correspondencies, which are often more fanciful than real. In general, it may safely be affirmed that jurisprudence is, in this respect, different from all the sciences; and that in many of its nicer questions, there cannot properly be said to be truth or falsehood on either side. If one pleader bring the case under any former law or precedent, by a refined analogy or comparison; the opposite pleader is not at a loss to find an opposite analogy or comparison: and the preference given by the judge is often founded more on taste and imagination than on any solid argument. Public utility is the general object of all courts of judicature; and this utility too requires a stable rule in all controversies: but where several rules, nearly equal and indifferent, present themselves, it is a very slight turn of thought which fixes the decision in favour of either party.*

---

* That there be a separation or distinction of possessions, and that this separation be steady and constant; this is absolutely required by the interests of society, and hence the origin of justice and property. What possessions are assigned to particular persons; this is, generally speaking, pretty indifferent; and is often determined by very frivolous views and considerations. We shall mention a few particulars.

Were a society formed among several independent members, the most obvious rule, which could be agreed on, would be to annex property to *present* possession, and leave every one a right to what he at present enjoys. The relation of possession, which takes place between the person and the object, naturally draws on the relation of property.

260. We may just observe, before we conclude this subject, that after the laws of justice are fixed by views of general utility, the injury, the hardship, the harm, which result to any individual from a violation of them, enter very much into consideration, and are a

---

For a like reason, occupation or first possession becomes the foundation of property.

Where a man bestows labour and industry upon any object, which before belonged to no body; as in cutting down and shaping a tree, in cultivating a field, &c., the alterations, which he produces, causes a relation between him and the object, and naturally engages us to annex it to him by the new relation of property. This cause here concurs with the public utility, which consists in the encouragement given to industry and labour.

Perhaps too, private humanity towards the possessor concurs, in this instance, with the other motives, and engages us to leave with him what he has acquired by his sweat and labour; and what he has flattered himself in the constant enjoyment of. For though private humanity can, by no means, be the origin of justice; since the latter virtue so often contradicts the former; yet when the rule of separate and constant possession is once formed by the indispensable necessities of society, private humanity, and an aversion to the doing a hardship to another, may, in a particular instance, give rise to a particular rule of property.

I am much inclined to think, that the right succession or inheritance much depends on those connexions of the imagination, and that the relation to a former proprietor begetting a relation to the object, is the cause why the property is transferred to a man after the death of his kinsman. It is true; industry is more encouraged by the transference of possession to children or near relations: but this consideration will only have place in a cultivated society; whereas the right of succession is regarded even among the greatest Barbarians.

Acquisition of property by *accession* can be explained no way but by having recourse to the relations and connexions of the imaginations.

The property of rivers, by the laws of most nations, and by the natural turn of our thoughts, is attributed to the proprietors of their banks, excepting such vast rivers as the Rhine or the Danube, which seem too large to follow as an accession to the property of the neighbouring fields. Yet even these rivers are considered as the property of that nation, through whose dominions they run; the idea of a nation being of a suitable bulk to correspond with them, and bear them such a relation in the fancy.

The accessions, which are made to land, bordering upon rivers, follow the land, say the civilians, provided it be made by what they call *alluvion*, that is, insensibly and imperceptibly; which are circumstances, that assist the imagination in the conjunction.

Where there is any considerable portion torn at once from one bank and added to another, it becomes not *his* property, whose land it falls on, till it unite with the land, and till the trees and plants have spread their roots into both. Before that, the thought does not sufficiently join them.

In short, we must ever distinguish between the necessity of a separation and constancy in men's possession, and the rules, which assign particular objects to particular persons. The first necessity is obvious, strong, and invincible: the latter may depend on a public utility more light and frivolous, on the sentiment of private humanity and aversion to private hardship, on positive laws, on precedents, analogies, and very fine connexions and turns of the imagination.

great source of that universal blame which attends every wrong or iniquity. By the laws of society, this coat, this horse is mine, and *ought* to remain perpetually in my possession: I reckon on the secure enjoyment of it: by depriving me of it, you disappoint my expectations, and doubly displease me, and offend every by-stander. It is a public wrong, so far as the rules of equity are violated: it is a private harm, so far as an individual is injured. And though the second consideration could have no place, were not the former previously established: for otherwise the distinction of *mine* and *thine* would be unknown in society: yet there is no question but the regard to general good is much enforced by the respect to particular. What injures the community, without hurting any individual, is often more lightly thought of. But where the greatest public wrong is also conjoined with a consider-able private one, no wonder the highest disapprobation attends so iniquitous a behaviour.

Of some verbal disputes

261. Nothing is more usual than for philosophers to encroach upon the province of grammarians; and to engage in disputes of words, while they imagine that they are handling controversies of the deepest importance and concern. It was in order to avoid altercations, so frivolous and endless, that I endeavoured to state with the utmost caution the object of our present enquiry; and proposed simply to collect, on the one hand, a list of those mental qualities which are the object of love or esteem, and form a part of personal merit; and on the other hand, a catalogue of those qualities which are the object of censure or reproach, and which detract from the character of the person possessed of them; subjoining some reflections concerning the origin of these sentiments of praise or blame. On all occasions, where there might arise the least hesitation, I avoided the terms *virtue* and *vice*; because some of those qualities, which I classed among the objects of praise, receive, in the English language, the appellation of *talents*, rather than of virtues; as some of the blameable or censurable qualities are often called *defects*, rather than vices. It may now, perhaps, be expected that before we conclude this moral enquiry, we should exactly separate the one from the other; should mark the precise boundaries of virtues and talents, vices and defects; and should explain the reason and origin of that distinction. But in order to excuse myself from this undertaking, which would, at last, prove only a grammatical enquiry, I shall subjoin the four following reflections, which shall contain all that I intend to say on the present subject.

262. *First*, I do not find that in the English, or any other modern tongue, the boundaries are exactly fixed between virtues and talents, vices and defects, or that a precise definition can be given of the one as contradistinguished from the other. Were we to

say, for instance, that the esteemable qualities alone, which are voluntary, are entitled to the appellations of virtues; we should soon recollect the qualities of courage, equanimity, patience, self-command; with many others, which almost every language classes under this appellation, though they depend little or not at all on our choice. Should we affirm that the qualities alone, which prompt us to act our part in society, are entitled to that honourable distinction; it must immediately occur that these are indeed the most valuable qualities, and are commonly denominated the *social* virtues; but that this very epithet supposes that there are also virtues of another species. Should we lay hold of the distinction between *intellectual* and *moral* endowments, and affirm the last alone to be the real and genuine virtues, because they alone lead to action; we should find that many of those qualities, usually called intellectual virtues, such as prudence, penetration, discernment, discretion, had also a considerable influence on conduct. The distinction between the *heart* and the *head* may also be adopted: the qualities of the first may be defined such as in their immediate exertion are accompanied with a feeling of sentiment; and these alone may be called the genuine virtues: but industry, frugality, temperance, secrecy, perseverance, and many other laudable powers or habits, generally styled virtues are exerted without any immediate sentiment in the person possessed of them, and are only known to him by their effects. It is fortunate, amidst all this seeming perplexity, that the question, being merely verbal, cannot possibly be of any importance. A moral, philosophical discourse needs not enter into all these caprices of language, which are so variable in different dialects, and in different ages of the same dialect. But on the whole, it seems to me, that though it is always allowed, that there are virtues of many different kinds, yet, when a man is called *virtuous*, or is denominated a man of virtue, we chiefly regard his social qualities, which are, indeed, the most valuable. It is, at the same time, certain, that any remarkable defect in courage, temperance, economy, industry, understanding, dignity of mind, would bereave even a very good-natured, honest man of this honourable appellation. Who did ever say, except by way of irony, that such a one was a man of great virtue, but an egregious blockhead?

263. But, *secondly*, it is no wonder that languages should not be very precise in marking the boundaries between virtues and

talents, vices and defects; since there is so little distinction made in our internal estimation of them. It seems indeed certain, that the *sentiment* of conscious worth, the self-satisfaction proceeding from a review of a man's own conduct and character; it seems certain, I say, that this sentiment, which, though the most common of all others, has no proper name in our language,[*] arises from the endowments of courage and capacity, industry and ingenuity, as well as from any other mental excellencies. Who, on the other hand, is not deeply mortified with reflecting on his own folly and dissoluteness, and feels not a secret sting or compunction whenever his memory presents any past occurrence, where he behaved with stupidity or ill-manners? No time can efface the cruel ideas of a man's own foolish conduct, or of affronts, which cowardice or impudence has brought upon him. They still haunt his solitary hours, damp his most aspiring thoughts, and show him, even to himself, in the most contemptible and most odious colours imaginable.

What is there too we are more anxious to conceal from others than such blunders, infirmities, and meannesses, or more dread to have exposed by raillery and satire? And is not the chief object of vanity, our bravery or learning, our wit or breeding, our eloquence or address, our taste or abilities? These we display with care, if not with ostentation; and we commonly show more ambition of excelling in them, than even in the social virtues themselves, which are, in reality, of such superior excellence. Good-nature and honesty, especially the latter, are so indispensably required, that, though the greatest censure attends any violation of these duties, no eminent praise follows such common instances of them, as seem essential to the support of human society. And hence the reason, in my opinion, why, though men often extol so liberally the qualities of their heart, they are shy in commending the endowments of their head: because the latter virtues, being supposed more rare and extra-ordinary, are observed to be the more usual objects of pride

---

[*] The term, pride, is commonly taken in a bad sense; but this sentiment seems indifferent, and may be either good or bad, according as it is well or ill founded, and according to the other circumstances which accompany it. The French express this sentiment by the term, *amour propre*, but as they also express self-love as well as vanity by the same term, there arises thence a great confusion in Rochefoucault, and many of their moral writers.

and self-conceit; and when boasted of, beget a strong suspicion of these sentiments.

264. It is hard to tell, whether you hurt a man's character most by calling him a knave or a coward, and whether a beastly glutton or drunkard be not as odious and contemptible, as a selfish, ungenerous miser. Give me my choice, and I would rather, for my own happiness and self-enjoyment, have a friendly, humane heart, than possess all the other virtues of Demosthenes and Philip united: but I would rather pass with the world for one endowed with extensive genius and intrepid courage, and should thence expect stronger instances of general applause and admiration. The figure which a man makes in life, the reception which he meets with in company, the esteem paid him by his acquaintance; all these advantages depend as much upon his good sense and judgement, as upon any other part of his character. Had a man the best intentions in the world, and were the farthest removed from all injustice and violence, he would never be able to make himself be much regarded, without a moderate share, at least, of parts and understanding.

265. What is it then we can here dispute about? If sense and courage, temperance and industry, wisdom and knowledge confessedly form a considerable part of *personal merit*: if a man, possessed of these qualities, is both better satisfied with himself, and better entitled to the good-will, esteem, and services of others, than one entirely destitute of them; if, in short, the *sentiments* are similar which arise from these endowments and from the social virtues; is there any reason for being so extremely scrupulous about a *word*, or disputing whether they be entitled to the denomination of virtues? It may, indeed, be pretended, that the sentiment of approbation, which those accomplishments produce, besides its being *inferior*, is also somewhat *different* from that which attends the virtues of justice and humanity. But this seems not a sufficient reason for ranking them entirely under different classes and appellations. The character of Caesar and that of Cato, as drawn by Sallust, are both of them virtuous, in the strictest and most limited sense of the word; but in a different way: nor are the sentiments entirely the same which arise from them. The one produces love, the other esteem: the one is amiable, the other awful: we should wish to meet the one character in a

friend; the other we should be ambitious of in ourselves. In like manner the approbation, which attends temperance or industry or frugality, may be somewhat different from that which is paid to the social virtues, without making them entirely of a different species. And, indeed, we may observe, that these endowments, more than the other virtues, produce not, all of them, the same kind of approbation. Good sense and genius beget esteem and regard: wit and humour excite love and affection.[*]

Most people, I believe, will naturally, without premeditation, assent to the definition of the elegant and judicious poet:

> Virtue (for mere good-nature is a fool)
> Is sense and spirit with humanity.[†]

What pretensions has a man to our generous assistance or good offices, who has dissipated his wealth in profuse expenses, idle vanities, chimerical projects, dissolute pleasures or extravagant gaming? These vices (for we scruple not to call them such) bring misery unpitied, and contempt on every one addicted to them.

Achaeus, a wise and prudent prince, fell into a fatal snare, which cost him his crown and life, after having used every reasonable precaution to guard himself against it. On that account, says the historian, he is a just object of regard and compassion: his betrayers alone of hatred and contempt.[‡]

---

[*] Love and esteem are nearly the same passion, and arise from similar causes. The qualities, which produce both, are such as communicate pleasure. But where this pleasure is severe and serious; or where its object is great, and makes a strong impression, or where it produces any degree of humility and awe; in all these cases, the passion, which arises from the pleasure, is more properly denominated esteem than love. Benevolence attends both; but is connected with love in a more eminent degree. There seems to be still a stronger mixture of pride in contempt than of humility in esteem; and the reason would not be difficulty to one, who studied accurately the passions. All these various mixtures and compositions and appearances of sentiment form a very curious subject of speculation, but are wide of our present purpose. Throughout this enquiry, we always consider in general, what qualities are a subject of praise or of censure, without entering into all the minute differences of sentiment, which they excite. It is evident, that whatever is contemned, is also disliked, as well as what is hated; and we here endeavour to take objects, according to their most simple views and appearances. These sciences are but too apt to appear abstract to common readers, even with all the precautions which we can take to clear them from superfluous speculations, and bring them down to every capacity.

[†] *The Art of preserving Health.* Book 4.

[‡] Polybius, lib. viii. cap. 2.

The precipitate flight and improvident negligence of Pompey, at the beginning of the civil wars, appeared such notorious blunders to Cicero, as quite palled his friendship towards that great man. *In the same manner*, says he, *as want of cleanliness, decency, or discretion in a mistress are found to alienate our affections.* For so he expresses himself, where he talks, not in the character of a philosopher, but in that of a statesman and man of the world, to his friend Atticus.*

266. But the same Cicero, in imitation of all the ancient moralists, when he reasons as a philosopher, enlarges very much his ideas of virtue, and comprehends every laudable quality or endowment of the mind, under that honourable appellation. This leads to the *third* reflection, which we proposed to make, to wit, that the ancient moralists, the best models, made no material distinction among the different species of mental endowments and defects, but treated all alike under the appellation of virtues and vices, and made them indiscriminately the object of their moral reasonings. The *prudence* explained in Cicero's *Offices*† is that sagacity, which leads to the discovery of truth, and preserves us from error and mistake. *magnanimity, temperance, decency*, are there also at large discoursed of. And as that eloquent moralist followed the common received division of the four cardinal virtues, our social duties form but one head, in the general distribution of his subject.‡

We need only peruse the titles of chapters in Aristotle's *Ethics* to be convinced that he ranks courage, temperance, magnificence,

---

* Lib. ix. epist. 10.

† Lib. i. cap. 6.

‡ The following passage of Cicero is worth quoting, as being the most clear and express to our purpose, that any thing can be imagined, and, in a dispute, which is chiefly verbal, must, on account of the author, carry an authority, from which there can be no appeal.

'Virtus autem, quae est per se ipsa laudabilis, et sine qua nihil laudari potest, tamen habet plures partes, quarum alia est alia ad laudationem aptior. Sunt enim aliae virtutes, quae videntur in moribus hominum, et quadam comitate ac beneficentia positae: aliae quae in ingenii aliqua facultate, aut animi magnitudine ac robore. Nam clementia, justitia, benignitas, fides, fortitudo in periculis communibus, jucunda est auditu in laudationibus. Omnes enim hae virtutes non tam ipsis, qui eas in se habent, quam generi hominum fructuosae putantur. Sapientia et magnitude animi, qua omnes res humanae tenues et pro nihilo putantur, et in cogitando vis quaedam ingenii, et ipsa eloquentia admirationis habet non minus, jucunditatis minus. Ipsos enim magis videntur, quos laudamus, quam illos, apud quos laudamus, ornare ac tueri: sed tamen in laudenda jungenda sunt etiam haec genera virtutum. Ferunt enim aures hominum, cum illa quae jucunda et grata, tum etiam illa, quae mirabilia sunt in virtute, laudari.' De orat. lib. ii. cap. 89.

magnanimity, modesty, prudence, and a manly openness, among the virtues, as well as justice and friendship.

To *sustain* and to *abstain*, that is, to be patient and continent, appeared to some of the ancients a summary comprehension of all morals.

Epictetus has scarcely ever mentioned the sentiment of humanity and compassion, but in order to put his disciples on their guard against it. The virtue of the *Stoics* seems to consist chiefly in a firm temper and a sound understanding. With them, as with Solomon and the eastern moralists, folly and wisdom are equivalent to vice and virtue.

Men will praise thee, says David,* when thou dost well unto thyself. I hate a wise man, says the Greek poet,† who is not wise to himself. Plutarch is no more cramped by systems in his philosophy than in his history. Where he compares the great men of Greece and Rome, he fairly sets in opposition all their blemishes and accomplishments of whatever kind, and omits nothing considerable, which can either depress or exalt their characters. His moral discourses contain the same free and natural censure of men and manners.

The character of Hannibal, as drawn by Livy,‡ is esteemed partial, but allows him many eminent virtues. Never was there a genius, says the historian, more equally fitted for those opposite offices of commanding and obeying; and it were, therefore, difficult to determine whether he rendered himself *dearer* to the general or to the army. To none would Hasdrubal entrust more willingly the conduct of any dangerous enterprize; under none did the soldiers discover more courage and confidence. Great boldness in facing danger; great prudence in the midst of it. No labour could fatigue his body or subdue his mind. Cold and heat were indifferent to him: meat and drink he sought as supplies to the necessities of nature, not as gratifications of his voluptuous appetites. Waking or rest he used indiscriminately, by night or by day. – These great Virtues were balanced by great Vices; inhuman

---

I suppose, if Cicero were now alive, it would be found difficult to fetter his moral sentiments by narrow systems; or persuade him, that no qualities were to be admitted as *virtues*, or acknowledged to be a part of *personal merit*, but what were recommended by *The Whole Duty of Man*.

* Psalm 49th.

† μισῶ σοφιστὴν ὅστις οὐχ αὑτῷ σοφός. EURIPIDES.

‡ Lib. xxi. cap. 4.

cruelty; perfidy more than *punic*; no truth, no faith, no regard to oaths, promises, or religion.

The character of Alexander the Sixth, to be found in Guicciardin,* is pretty similar, but juster; and is a proof that even the moderns, where they speak naturally, hold the same language with the ancients. In this pope, says he, there was a singular capacity and judgement: admirable prudence; a wonderful talent of persuasion; and in all momentous enterprizes a diligence and dexterity incredible. But these *virtues* were infinitely overbalanced by his *vices*; no faith, no religion, insatiable avarice, exorbitant ambition, and a more than barbarous cruelty.

Polybius,[†] reprehending Timaeus for his partiality against Agathocles, whom he himself allows to be the most cruel and impious of all tyrants, says: if he took refuge in Syracuse, as asserted by that historian, flying the dirt and smoke and toil of his former profession of a potter; and if proceeding from such slender beginnings, he became master, in a little time, of all Sicily; brought the Carthaginian state into the utmost danger; and at last died in old age, and in possession of sovereign dignity: must he not be allowed something prodigious and extraordinary, and to have possessed great talents and capacity for business and action? His historian, therefore, ought not to have alone related what tended to his reproach and infamy; but also what might redound to his Praise and Honour.

267. In general, we may observe, that the distinction of voluntary or involuntary was little regarded by the ancients in their moral reasonings; where they frequently treated the question as very doubtful, *whether virtue could be taught or not?*[‡] They justly considered that cowardice, meanness, levity, anxiety, impatience, folly, and many other qualities of the mind, might appear ridiculous and deformed, contemptible and odious, though independent of the will. Nor could it be supposed, at all times, in every man's power to attain every kind of mental more than of exterior beauty.

268. And here there occurs the *fourth* reflection which I purposed to make, in suggesting the reason why modern philosophers have often followed a course in their moral enquiries so different

---

* Lib. i.

† Lib. xii.

‡ Vid. Plato in Menone, Seneca *de otio sap*. cap. 31. So also Horace, *Virtutem doctrina paret, naturane donet, Epist*. lib. i. ep. 18. Aeschines *Socraticus*, Dial. 1.

from that of the ancients. In later times, philosophy of all kinds, especially ethics, have been more closely united with theology than ever they were observed to be among the heathens; and as this latter science admits of no terms of composition, but bends every branch of knowledge to its own purpose, without much regard to the phenomena of nature, or to the unbiased sentiments of the mind, hence reasoning, and even language, have been warped from their natural course, and distinctions have been endeavoured to be established where the difference of the objects was, in a manner, imperceptible. Philosophers, or rather divines under that disguise, treating all morals as on a like footing with civil laws, guarded by the sanctions of reward and punishment, were necessarily led to render this circumstance, of *voluntary* or *involuntary*, the foundation of their whole theory. Every one may employ *terms* in what sense he pleases: but this, in the mean time, must be allowed, that *sentiments* are every day experienced of blame and praise, which have objects beyond the dominion of the will or choice, and of which it behoves us, if not as moralists, as speculative philosophers at least, to give some satisfactory theory and explication.

A blemish, a fault, a vice, a crime; these expressions seem to denote different degrees of censure and disapprobation; which are, however, all of them, at the bottom, pretty nearly all the same kind of species. The explication of one will easily lead us into a just conception of the others; and it is of greater consequence to attend to things than to verbal appellations. That we owe a duty to ourselves is confessed even in the most vulgar system of morals; and it must be of consequence to examine that duty, in order to see whether it bears any affinity to that which we owe to society. It is probable that the approbation attending the observance of both is of a similar nature, and arises from similar principles, whatever appellation we may give to either of these excellencies.

A DIALOGUE

A DIALOGUE

My friend, Palamedes, who is as great a rambler in his principles as in his person, and who has run over, by study and travel, almost every region of the intellectual and material world, surprized me lately with an account of a nation, with whom, he told me, he had passed a considerable part of his life, and whom, he found, in the main, a people extremely civilized and intelligent.

There is a country, said he, in the world, called Fourli, no matter for its longitude or latitude, whose inhabitants have ways of thinking, in many things, particularly in morals, diametrically opposite to ours. When I came among them, I found that I must submit to double pains; first to learn the meaning of the terms in their language, and then to know the import of those terms, and the praise or blame attached to them. After a word had been explained to me, and a character which it expressed had been described, I concluded, that such an epithet must necessarily be the greatest reproach in the world; and was extremely surprized to find one in a public company, apply it to a person, with whom he lived in the strictest intimacy and friendship. *You fancy*, said I, one day, to an acquaintance, *that* Changuis *is your mortal enemy: I love to extinguish quarrels; and I must, therefore, tell you, that I heard him talk of you in the most obliging manner.* But to my great astonishment, when I repeated Changuis's words, though I had both remembered and understood them perfectly, I found, that they were taken for the most mortal affront, and that I had very innocently rendered the breach between these persons altogether irreparable.

As it was my fortune to come among this people on a very advantageous footing, I was immediately introduced to the best company; and being desired by Alcheic to live with him, I readily accepted of his invitation; as I found him universally esteemed for his personal merit, and indeed regarded by every one in Fourli, as a perfect character.

One evening he invited me, as an amusement, to bear him company in a serenade, which he intended to give to Gulki, with whom, he told me, he was extremely enamoured; and I soon found that his taste was not singular: for we met many of his rivals, who had come on the same errand. I very naturally concluded, that this mistress of his must be one of the finest women in town; and I already felt a secret inclination to see her, and be acquainted with her. But as the moon began to rise, I was much surprized to find that we were in the midst of the university, where Gulki studied: and I was somewhat ashamed for having attended my friend, on such an errand.

I was afterwards told, that Alcheic's choice of Gulki was very much approved of by all the good company in town; and that it was expected, while he gratified his own passion, he would perform to that young man the same good office, which he had himself owed to Elkouf. It seems Alcheic had been very handsome in his youth, had been courted by many lovers; but had bestowed his favours chiefly on the sage Elkouf; to whom he was supposed to owe, in a great measure, the astonishing progress which he had made in philosophy and virtue.

It gave me some surprize that Alcheic's wife (who by-the-by happened also to be his sister) was no wise scandalized at this species of infidelity.

Much about the same time I discovered (for it was not attempted to be kept a secret from me or any body) that Alcheic was a murderer and a parricide, and had put to death an innocent person, the most nearly connected with him, and whom he was bound to protect and defend by all the ties of nature and humanity. When I asked, with all the caution and deference imaginable, what was his motive for this action; he replied coolly, that he was not then so much at ease in his circumstances as he is at present, and that he had acted, in that particular, by the advice of all his friends.

Having heard Alcheic's virtue so extremely celebrated, I pretended to join in the general voice of acclamation, and only asked, by way of curiosity, as a stranger, which of all his noble actions was most highly applauded; and I soon found, that all sentiments were united in giving the preference to the assassination of Usbek. This Usbek had been to the last moment Alcheic's intimate friend, had laid many high obligations upon him, had even saved his life on a certain occasion, and had, by his will, which was found after the murder, made him heir to a considerable part of his fortune. Alcheic, it seems, conspired with about twenty or thirty more, most of them also Usbek's friends; and falling altogether on that unhappy man, when he was not aware, they had torne him with a hundred wounds; and given him that reward for all his past favours and obligations. Usbek, said the general voice of the people, had many great and good qualities: his very vices were shining, magnificent, and generous: but this action of Alcheic's sets him far above Usbek in the eyes of all judges of merit; and is one of the noblest that ever perhaps the sun shone upon.

Another part of Alcheic's conduct, which I also found highly applauded, was his behaviour towards Calish, with whom he was joined in a project or undertaking of some importance. Calish, being a passionate man, gave Alcheic, one day, a sound drubbing; which he took very patiently, waited the return of Calish's good-humour, kept still a fair correspondence with him; and by that means brought the affair, in which they were joined, to a happy issue, and gained to himself immortal honour by his remarkable temper and moderation.

I have lately received a letter from a correspondent in Fourli, by which I learn, that, since my departure, Alcheic, falling into a bad state of health, has fairly hanged himself; and has died universally regretted and applauded in that country. So virtuous and noble a life, says each Fourlian, could not be better crowned than by so noble an end; and Alcheic has proved by this, as well as by all his other actions, what was his constant principle during his life, and what he boasted of near his last moments, that a wise man is scarcely inferior to the great god, Vitzli. This is the name of the supreme deity among the Fourlians.

The notions of this people, continued Palamedes, are as extraordinary with regard to good-manners and sociableness, as with regard to morals. My friend Alcheic formed once a party for my entertainment, composed of all the prime wits and philosophers of Fourli; and each of us brought his mess along with him to the place where we assembled. I observed one of them to be worse provided than the rest, and offered him a share of my mess, which happened to be a roasted pullet: and I could not but remark, that he and all the rest of the company smiled at my simplicity. I was told, that Alcheic had once so much interest with his club as to prevail with them to eat in common, and that he had made use of an artifice for that purpose. He persuaded those, whom he observed to be worst provided, to offer their mess to the company; after which, the others, who had brought more delicate fare, were ashamed not to make the same offer. This is regarded as so extraordinary an event, that it has since, as I learn, been recorded in the history of Alcheic's life, composed by one of the greatest geniuses of Fourli.

Pray, said I, Palamedes, when you were at Fourli, did you also learn the art of turning your friends into ridicule, by telling them strange stories, and then laughing at them, if they believed you? I assure you, replied he, had I been disposed to learn such a lesson, there was no place in the world more proper. My friend, so often mentioned, did nothing, from morning to night, but sneer, and banter, and rally; and you could scarcely ever distinguish whether he were in jest or earnest. But you think, then, that my story is improbable; and that I have used, or rather abused the privilege of a traveller. To be sure, said I, you were but in jest. Such barbarous and savage manners are not only incompatible with a civilized, intelligent people, such as you said these were; but are scarcely compatible with human nature. They exceed all we ever read of, among the Mingelians, and Topinamboues.

Have a care, cried he, have a care! You are not aware that you are speaking blasphemy, and are abusing your favourites, the Greeks, especially the Athenians, whom I have couched, all along, under these bizarre names I employed. If you consider aright, there is not one stroke of the foregoing character, which might not be found in the man of highest merit at Athens, without diminishing in the least from the brightness of his character. The amours of the Greeks, their marriages,* and the exposing of their children cannot but strike you immediately. The death of Usbek is an exact counter-part to that of Caesar.

All to a trifle, said I, interrupting him: you did not mention that Usbek was an usurper.

I did not, replied he; lest you should discover the parallel I aimed at. But even adding this circumstance, we should make no scruple,

---

* The laws of Athens allowed a man to marry his sister by the father. Solon's law forbid pederasty to slaves, as being an act of too grat dignity for such mean persons.

according to our sentiments of morals, to denominate Brutus, and Cassius, ungrateful traitors and assassins: though you know, that they are, perhaps, the highest characters of all antiquity; and the Athenians erected statues to them; which they placed near those of Harmodius and Aristogiton, their own deliverers. And if you think this circumstance, which you mention, so material to absolve these patriots, I shall compensate it by another, not mentioned, which will equally aggravate their crime. A few days before the execution of their fatal purpose, they all swore fealty to Caesar; and protesting to hold his person ever sacred, they touched the altar with those hands, which they had already armed for his destruction.[*]

I need not remind you of the famous and applauded story of Themistocles, and of his patience towards Eurybiades, the Spartan, his commanding officer, who, heated by debate, lifted his cane to him in a council of war (the same thing as if he had cudgelled him). *Strike!* cries the Athenian, *strike! but hear me.*

You are too good a scholar not to discover the ironical Socrates and his Athenian club in my last story; and you will certainly observe, that it is exactly copied from Xenophon, with a variation only of the names.[†] And I think I have fairly made it appear, that an Athenian man of merit might be such a one as with us would pass for incestuous, a parricide, an assassin, an ungrateful, perjured traitor, and something else too abominable to be named; not to mention his rusticity and ill-manners. And having lived in this manner, his death might be entirely suitable: He might conclude the scene by a desperate act of self-murder, and die with the most absurd blasphemies in his mouth. And notwithstanding all this, he shall have statues, if not altars, erected to his memory; poems and orations shall be composed in his praise; great sects shall be proud of calling themselves by his name; and the most distant posterity shall blindly continue their admiration: Though were such a one to arise among themselves, they would justly regard him with horror and execration.

I might have been aware, replied I, of your artifice. You seem to take pleasure in this topic: and are indeed the only man I ever knew, who was well acquainted with the ancients, and did not extremely admire them. But instead of attacking their

[*] Appian, *Bell. Civ.* lib. iii. Suetonius in *Vita Caesaris.*
[†] *Mem. Soc.* lib. iii. sub fine.

philosophy, their eloquence, or poetry, the usual subjects of
controversy between us, you now seem to impeach their morals,
and accuse them of ignorance in a science, which is the only
one, in my opinion, in which they are not surpassed by the
moderns. Geometry, physics, astronomy, anatomy, botany, geography, navigation; in these we justly claim the superiority: But
what have we to oppose to their moralists? Your representation
of things is fallacious. You have no indulgence for the manners
and customs of different ages. Would you try a Greek or Roman
by the common law of England? Hear him defend himself by his
own maxims; and then pronounce.

There are no manners so innocent or reasonable, but may
be rendered odious or ridiculous, if measured by a standard,
unknown to the persons; especially, if you employ a little art or
eloquence, in aggravating some circumstances, and extenuating
others, as best suits the purpose of your discourse. All these artifices
may easily be retorted on you. Could I inform the Athenians, for
instance, that there was a nation, in which adultery, both active and
passive, so to speak, was in the highest vogue and esteem: in which
every man of education chose for his mistress a married woman, the
wife, perhaps, of his friend and companion; and valued himself
upon these infamous conquests, as much as if he had been several
times a conqueror in boxing or wrestling at the Olympic games: in
which every man also took a pride in his tameness and facility with
regard to his own wife, and was glad to make friends or gain interest
by allowing her to prostitute her charms; and even, without any
such motive, gave her full liberty and indulgence: I ask, what
sentiments the Athenians would entertain of such a people; they
who never mentioned the crime of adultery but in conjunction
with robbery and poisoning? Which would they admire most, the
villainy or the meanness of such a conduct?

Should I add, that the same people were as proud of their
slavery and dependance as the Athenians of their liberty; and
though a man among them were oppressed, disgraced, impov-
erished, insulted, or imprisoned by the tyrant, he would still
regard it as the highest merit to love, serve, and obey him; and
even to die for his smallest glory or satisfaction: These noble
Greeks would probably ask me, whether I spoke of a human
society, or of some inferior, servile species.

It was then I might inform my Athenian audience, that these people, however, wanted not spirit and bravery. If a man, say I, though their intimate friend, should throw out, in a private company, a raillery against them, nearly approaching any of those, with which your generals and demagogues every day regale each other, in the face of the whole city, they never can forgive him; but in order to revenge themselves, they oblige him immediately to run them through the body, or be himself murdered. And if a man, who is an absolute stranger to them, should desire them, at the peril of their own life, to cut the throat of their bosom-companion, they immediately obey, and think themselves highly obliged and honoured by the commission. These are their maxims of honour: this is their favourite morality.

But though so ready to draw their sword against their friends and countrymen; no disgrace, no infamy, no pain, no poverty will ever engage these people to turn the point of it against their own breast. A man of rank would row in the galleys, would beg his bread, would languish in prison, would suffer any tortures, and still preserve his wretched life. Rather than escape his enemies by a generous contempt of death, he would infamously receive the same death from his enemies, aggravated by their triumphant insults, and by the most exquisite sufferings.

It is very usual too, continued I, among this people to erect jails, where every art of plaguing and tormenting the unhappy prisoners is carefully studied and practised: and in these jails it is usual for a parent voluntarily to shut up several of his children; in order, that another child, whom he owns to have no greater or rather less merit than the rest, may enjoy his whole fortune, and wallow in every kind of voluptuousness and pleasure. Nothing so virtuous in their opinion as this barbarous partiality.

But what is more singular in this whimsical nation, say I to the Athenians, is, that a frolic of yours during the Saturnalia,* when the slaves are served by their masters, is seriously continued by them throughout the whole year, and throughout the whole course of their lives; accompanied too with some circumstances, which still farther augment the absurdity and ridicule. Your sport

---

* The Greeks kept the feast of Saturn or Chronus, as well as the Romans. See Lucian, *Epist. Saturn.*

only elevates for a few days those, whom fortune has thrown down, and whom she too, in sport, may really elevate for ever above you: But this nation gravely exalts those whom nature has subjected to them, and whose inferiority and infirmities are absolutely incurable. The women, though without virtue, are their masters and sovereigns: these they reverence, praise, and magnify: to these, they pay the highest deference and respect: and in all places and all times, the superiority of the females is readily acknowledged and submitted to by every one who has the least pretensions to education and politeness. Scarce any crime would be so universally detested as an infraction of this rule.

You need go no further, replied Palamedes; I can easily conjecture the people whom you aim at. The strokes, with which you have painted them, are pretty just; and yet you must acknowledge, that scarce any people are to be found, either in ancient or modern times, whose national character is, upon the whole, less liable to exception. But I give you thanks for helping me out with my argument. I had no intention of exalting the moderns at the expense of the ancients. I only meant to represent the uncertainty of all these judgments concerning characters; and to convince you, that fashion, vogue, custom, and law, were the chief foundation of all moral determinations. The Athenians surely, were a civilized, intelligent people, if ever there was one; and yet their man of merit might, in this age, be held in horror and execration. The French are also, without doubt, a very civilized, intelligent people; and yet their man of merit might, with the Athenians, be an object of the highest contempt and ridicule, and even hatred. And what renders the matter more extraordinary: these two people are supposed to be the most similar in their national character of any in ancient and modern times; and while the English flatter themselves that they resemble the Romans, their neighbours on the continent draw the parallel between themselves and those polite Greeks. What wide difference, therefore, in the sentiments of morals, must be found between civilized nations and Barbarians, or between nations whose characters have little in common? How shall we pretend to fix a standard for judgments of this nature?

By tracing matters, replied I, a little higher, and examining the first principles, which each nation establishes, of blame or censure.

The Rhine flows north, the Rhone south; yet both spring from the same mountain, and are also actuated, in their opposite directions, by the same principle of gravity. The different inclinations of the ground on which they run, cause all the difference of their courses.

In how many circumstances would an Athenian and a French man of merit certainly resemble each other? Good sense, knowledge, wit, eloquence, humanity, fidelity, truth, justice, courage, temperance, constancy, dignity of mind: these you have all omitted, in order to insist only on the points in which they may, by accident, differ. Very well: I am willing to comply with you; and shall endeavour to account for these differences from the most universal, established principles of morals.

The Greek loves, I care not to examine more particularly. I shall only observe, that, however blameable, they arose from a very innocent cause, the frequency of the gymnastic exercises among that people; and were recommended, though absurdly, as the source of friendship, sympathy, mutual attachment, and fidelity;* qualities esteemed in all nations and all ages.

The marriage of half-brothers and sisters seems no great difficulty. Love between the nearer relations is contrary to reason and public utility; but the precise point, where we are to stop, can scarcely be determined by natural reason; and is therefore a very proper subject for municipal law or custom. If the Athenians went a little too far on the one side, the canon law has surely pushed matters a great way into the other extreme.†

Had you asked a parent at Athens, why he bereaved his child of that life, which he had so lately given it. It is because I love it, he would reply; and regard the poverty which it must inherit from me, as a greater evil than death, which it is not capable of dreading, feeling, or resenting.‡

How is public liberty, the most valuable of all blessings, to be recovered from the hands of an usurper or tyrant, if his power shields him from public rebellion, and our scruples from private vengeance? That his crime is capital by law, you acknowledge: and must the highest aggravation of his crime, the putting of himself

---

* Plat, *Symp.* p.182, exedit. Ser.
† See Enquiry, Section 4.
‡ Plut. de amore prolis, sub fine.

above law, form his full security? You can reply nothing, but by showing the great inconveniencies of assassination; which could any one have proved clearly to the ancients, he had reformed their sentiments in this particular.

Again, to cast your eye on the picture which I have drawn of modern manners; there is almost as great difficulty, I acknowledge, to justify French as Greek gallantry; except only, that the former is much more natural and agreeable than the latter. But our neighbours, it seems, have resolved to sacrifice some of the domestic to the sociable pleasures; and to prefer ease, freedom, and an open commerce, to a strict fidelity and constancy. These ends are both good, and are somewhat difficult to reconcile; nor need we be surprised, if the customs of nations incline too much, sometimes to the one side, sometimes to the other.

The most inviolable attachment to the laws of our country is every where acknowledged a capital virtue; and where the people are not so happy, as to have any legislature but a single person, the strictest loyalty is, in that case, the truest patriotism.

Nothing surely can be more absurd and barbarous than the practice of duelling; but those, who justify it, say, that it begets civility and good-manners. And a duellist, you may observe, always values himself upon his courage, his sense of honour, his fidelity and friendship; qualities, which are here indeed very oddly directed, but which have been esteemed universally, since the foundation of the world.

Have the gods forbid self-murder? An Athenian allows, that it ought to be forborne. Has the Deity permitted it? A Frenchman allows that death is preferable to pain and infamy.

You see then, continued I, that the principles upon which men reason in morals are always the same; though the conclusions which they draw are often very different. That they all reason aright with regard to this subject, more than with regard to any other, it is not incumbent on any moralist to show. It is sufficient, that the original principles of censure or blame are uniform, and that erroneous conclusions can be corrected by sounder reasoning and larger experience. Though many ages have elapsed since the fall of Greece and Rome; though many changes have arrived in religion, language, laws, and customs; none of these revolutions has ever produced any considerable innovation in the primary sentiments of morals, more than in those of external beauty. Some minute differences, perhaps, may be observed in both. Horace* celebrates a low forehead, and Anacreon joined eyebrows:† But the Apollo and the Venus of antiquity are still our models for male and female beauty; in like manner as the character of Scipio continues our standard for the glory of heroes, and that of Cornelia for the honour of matrons.

It appears, that there never was any quality recommended by any one, as a virtue or moral excellence, but on account of its being *useful*, or *agreeable* to a man *himself*, or to *others*. For what other reason can ever be assigned for praise or approbation? Or where would be the sense of extolling a good character or action, which, at the same time, is allowed to be *good for nothing*? All the differences, therefore, in morals, may be reduced to this one general foundation, and may be accounted for by the different views, which people take of these circumstances.

Sometimes men differ in their judgment about the usefulness of any habit or action: sometimes also the peculiar circumstances of things render one moral quality more useful than others, and give it a peculiar preference.

It is not surprising, that, during a period of war and disorder, the military virtues should be more celebrated than the pacific, and attract more the admiration and attention of mankind. 'How usual is it,' says Tully,‡ 'to find Cimbrians, Celtiberians, and other Barbarians, who bear, with inflexible constancy, all the fatigues and dangers of the field; but are immediately dispirited under the pain and hazard of a languishing distemper: while, on the other hand, the Greeks patiently endure the slow approaches of death, when armed with sickness and disease; but timorously fly his presence, when he attacks them violently with swords and falchions!' So different is even the same virtue of courage among warlike or peaceful nations! And indeed, we may observe, that, as the difference between war and peace is the greatest that arises among nations and public societies, it produces also the greatest variations in moral sentiment, and diversifies the most our ideas of virtue and personal merit.

Sometimes, too, magnanimity, greatness of mind, disdain of slavery, inflexible rigour and integrity, may better suit the circumstances

* *Epist.* lib. i. epist. 7.
† Ode 28. Petronius (cap. 86) joins both these circumstances as beauties.
‡ *Tusc. Quaest.* lib. ii.

of one age than those of another, and have a more kindly influence, both on public affairs, and on a man's own safety and advancement. Our idea of merit, therefore, will also vary a little with these variations; and Labeo, perhaps, be censured for the same qualities, which procured Cato the highest approbation.

A degree of luxury may be ruinous and pernicious in a native of Switzerland, which only fosters the arts, and encourages industry in a Frenchman or Englishman. We are not, therefore, to expect, either the same sentiments, or the same laws in Berne, which prevail in London or Paris.

Different customs have also some influence as well as different utilities; and by giving an early bias to the mind, may produce a superior propensity, either to the useful or the agreeable qualities; to those which regard self, or those which extend to society. These four sources of moral sentiment still subsist; but particular accidents may, at one time, make any one of them flow with greater abundance than at another.

The customs of some nations shut up the women from all social commerce: Those of others make them so essential a part of society and conversation, that, except where business is transacted, the male sex alone are supposed almost wholly incapable of mutual discourse and entertainment. As this difference is the most material that can happen in private life, it must also produce the greatest variation in our moral sentiments.

Of all nations in the world, where polygamy was not allowed, the Greeks seem to have been the most reserved in their commerce with the fair sex, and to have imposed on them the strictest laws of modesty and decency. We have a strong instance of this in an oration of Lysias.* A widow injured, ruined, undone, calls a meeting of a few of her nearest friends and relations; and though never before accustomed, says the orator, to speak in the presence of men, the distress of her circumstances constrained her to lay the case before them. The very opening of her mouth in such company required, it seems, an apology.

When Demosthenes prosecuted his tutors, to make them refund his patrimony, it became necessary for him, in the course of the law-suit, to prove that the marriage of Aphobus's sister with Oneter was entirely fraudulent, and that, notwithstanding her

* *Orat.* 33.

sham marriage, she had lived with her brother at Athens for two years past, ever since her divorce from her former husband. And it is remarkable, that though these were people of the first fortune and distinction in the city, the orator could prove this fact no way, but by calling for her female slaves to be put to the question, and by the evidence of one physician, who had seen her in her brother's house during her illness.* So reserved were Greek manners.

We may be assured, that an extreme purity of manners was the consequence of this reserve. Accordingly we find, that, except the fabulous stories of an Helen and a Clytemnestra, there scarcely is an instance of any event in the Greek history, which proceeded from the intrigues of women. On the other hand, in modern times, particularly in a neighbouring nation, the females enter into all transactions and all management of church and state: and no man can expect success, who takes not care to obtain their good graces. Harry the third, by incurring the displeasure of the fair, endangered his crown, and lost his life, as much as by his indulgence to heresy.

It is needless to dissemble: the consequence of a very free commerce between the sexes, and of their living much together, will often terminate in intrigues and gallantry. We must sacrifice somewhat of the useful, if we be very anxious to obtain all the agreeable qualities; and cannot pretend to reach alike every kind of advantage. Instances of licence, daily multiplying, will weaken the scandal with the one sex, and teach the other, by degrees, to adopt the famous maxim of La Fontaine, with regard to female infidelity, *that if one knows it, it is but a small matter; if one knows it not, it is nothing.*[†]

Some people are inclined to think, that the best way of adjusting all differences, and of keeping the proper medium between the *agreeable* and the *useful* qualities of the sex, is to live with them after the manner of the Romans and the English (for the customs of these two nations seem similar in this respect);[‡] that is, without

---

* *In Oneterem.*

† Quand on le sçait, c'est peu de chose;
  Quand on l'ignore, ce n'est rien.

‡ During the time of the emperors, the Romans seem to have been more given to intrigues and gallantry than the English are at present: and the women of condition, in order to retain their lovers, endeavoured to fix a name of reproach

gallantry, and without jealousy. By a parity of reason, the customs of the Spaniards and of the Italians of an age ago (for the present are very different) must be the worst of any; because they favour both gallantry* and jealousy.

Nor will these different customs of nations affect the one sex only: Their idea of personal merit in the males must also be somewhat different with regard, at least, to conversation, address, and humour. The one nation, where the men live much apart, will naturally more approve of prudence; the other of gaiety. With the one simplicity of manners will be in the highest esteem; with the other, politeness. The one will distinguish themselves by good-sense and judgment; the other, by taste and delicacy. The eloquence of the former will shine most in the senate; that of the other, on the theatre.

These, I say, are the natural effects of such customs. For it must be confessed, that chance has a great influence on national manners; and many events happen in society, which are not to be accounted for by general rules. Who could imagine, for instance, that the Romans, who lived freely with their women, should be very indifferent about music, and esteem dancing infamous: While the Greeks, who never almost saw a woman but in their own houses, were continually piping, singing, and dancing?

The differences of moral sentiment, which naturally arise from a republican or monarchical government, are also very obvious; as well as those which proceed from general riches or poverty, union or faction, ignorance or learning. I shall conclude this long discourse with observing, that different customs and situations vary not the original ideas of merit (however they may, some consequences) in any very essential point, and prevail chiefly with regard to young men, who can aspire to the agreeable qualities, and may attempt to please. The Manner, the Ornaments, the Graces, which succeed in this shape, are more arbitrary and casual: But the merit of riper years is almost every where the same; and consists chiefly in integrity, humanity, ability, knowledge, and the other more solid and useful qualities of the human mind.

---

on those who were addicted to wenching and low amours. They were called Ancillarioli. See Seneca de beneficiis, lib. i. cap. 9. See also Martial, lib. ii. epig. 58.
* The gallantry here meant is that of amours and attachments, not that of complaisance, which is as much paid to the fair sex in England as in any other country.

What you insist on, replied Palamedes, may have some found-ation, when you adhere to the maxims of common life and ordinary conduct. Experience and the practice of the world readily correct any great extravagance on either side. But what say you to artificial lives and manners? How do you reconcile the maxims, on which, in different ages and nations, these are founded?

What do you understand by artificial lives and manners? said I. I explain myself, replied he. You know, that religion had, in ancient times, very little influence on common life, and that, after men had performed their duty in sacrifices and prayers at the temple, they thought, that the gods left the rest of their conduct to themselves, and were little pleased or offended with those virtues or vices, which only affected the peace and happiness of human society. In those ages, it was the business of philosophy alone to regulate men's ordinary behaviour and deportment; and accord-ingly, we may observe, that this being the sole principle, by which a man could elevate himself above his fellows, it acquired a mighty ascendant over many, and produced great singularities of maxims and of conduct. At present, when philosophy has lost the allure-ment of novelty, it has no such extensive influence; but seems to confine itself mostly to speculations in the closet; in the same manner, as the ancient religion was limited to sacrifices in the temple. Its place is now supplied by the modern religion, which inspects our whole conduct, and prescribes an universal rule to our actions, to our words, to our very thoughts and inclinations; a rule so much the more austere, as it is guarded by infinite, though distant, rewards and punishments; and no infraction of it can ever be concealed or disguised.

Diogenes is the most celebrated model of extravagant philosophy. Let us seek a parallel to him in modern times. We shall not disgrace any philosophic name by a comparison with the Dominics or Loyolas, or any canonized monk or friar. Let us compare him to Pascal, a man of parts and genius as well as Diogenes himself; and perhaps too, a man of virtue, had he allowed his virtuous inclin-ations to have exerted and displayed themselves.

The foundation of Diogenes's conduct was an endeavour to render himself an independent being as much as possible, and to confine all his wants and desires and pleasures within himself and his own mind: The aim of Pascal was to keep a perpetual sense of his dependence before his eyes, and never to forget his numberless wants and infirmities. The ancient supported himself by magnanimity, ostentation, pride, and the idea of his own superiority above his fellow-creatures. The modern made constant profession of humility and abasement, of the contempt and hatred of himself; and endeavoured to attain these supposed virtues, as far as they are attainable. The austerities of the Greek were in order to inure himself to hardships, and prevent his ever suffering: Those of the Frenchman were embraced merely for their own sake, and in order to suffer as much as possible. The philosopher indulged himself in the most beastly pleasures, even in public: The saint refused himself the most innocent, even in private. The former thought it his duty to love his friends, and to rail at them, and reprove them, and scold them: The latter endeavoured to be absolutely indifferent towards his nearest relations, and to love and speak well of his enemies. The great object of Diogenes's wit was every kind of superstition, that is every kind of religion known in his time. The mortality of the soul was his standard principle; and even his sentiments of a divine providence seem to have been licentious. The most ridiculous superstitions directed Pascal's faith and practice; and an extreme contempt of this life, in comparison of the future, was the chief foundation of his conduct.

In such a remarkable contrast do these two men stand: yet both of them have met with general admiration in their different ages, and have been proposed as models of imitation. Where then is the universal standard of morals, which you talk of? And what rule shall we establish for the many different, nay contrary sentiments of mankind?

An experiment, said I, which succeeds in the air, will not always succeed in a vacuum. When men depart from the maxims of common reason, and affect these artificial lives, as you call them, no one can answer for what will please or displease them. They are in a different element from the rest of mankind; and the natural principles of their mind play not with the same regularity, as if left to themselves, free from the illusions of religious superstition or philosophical enthusiasm.

MY OWN LIFE

MY OWN LIFE

It is difficult for a man to speak long of himself without Vanity; therefore, I shall be short. It may be thought an instance of vanity that I pretend at all to write my life; but this Narrative shall contain little more than the History of my Writings; as, indeed, almost all my life has been spent in Literary pursuits and occupations. The first success of most of my writings was not such as to be an object of vanity.

I was born the 26th of April 1711, old style, at Edinburgh. I was of a good family, both by father and mother: my father's family is a branch of the Earl of Home's, or Hume's; and my ancestors had been proprietors of the estate, which my brother possesses, for several generations. My mother was daughter of Sir David Falconer, President of the College of Justice: the title of Lord Halkerton came by succession to her brother.

My family, however, was not rich, and being myself a younger brother, my patrimony, according to the mode of my country, was of course very slender. My father, who passed for a man of parts, died when I was an infant, leaving me, with an elder brother and a sister, under the care of our mother, a woman of singular merit, who, though young and handsome, devoted herself entirely to the rearing and educating of her children. I passed through the ordinary course of education with success, and was seized very early with a passion for literature, which has been the ruling passion of my life, and the great source of my enjoyments. My studious disposition, my sobriety, and my industry, gave my family a notion that the law was a proper profession for me; but I found an unsurmountable aversion to everything but the pursuits of philosophy and general learning; and while they fancied I was poring upon Voet and Vinnius, Cicero and Virgil were the authors which I was secretly devouring.

My very slender fortune, however, being unsuitable to this plan of life, and my health being a little broken by my ardent application, I was tempted, or rather forced, to make a very feeble trial for entering into a more active scene of life. In 1734, I went to Bristol, with some recommendations to eminent merchants, but in a few months found that scene totally unsuitable to me. I went over to France, with a view of prosecuting my studies in a country retreat; and I there laid that plan of life, which I have steadily and successfully pursued. I resolved to make a very rigid frugality supply my deficiency of fortune, to maintain unimpaired my independency, and to regard every object as contemptible, except the improvement of my talents in literature.

During my retreat in France, first at Reims, but chiefly at La Flêche, in Anjou, I composed my *Treatise of Human Nature*. After passing three years very agreeably in that country, I came over to London in 1737. In the end of 1738, I published my Treatise, and immediately went down to my mother and my brother, who lived at his country-house, and was employing himself very judiciously and successfully in the improvement of his fortune.

Never literary attempt was more unfortunate than my *Treatise of Human Nature*. It fell *dead-born from the press*, without reaching such distinction, as even to excite a murmur among the zealots. But being naturally of a cheerful and sanguine temper, I very soon recovered [from] the blow, and prosecuted with great ardor my studies in the country. In 1742, I printed at Edinburgh the first part of my *Essays*; the work was favourably received, and soon made me entirely forget my former disappointment. I continued with my mother and brother in the country, and in that time recovered the knowledge of the Greek language, which I had too much neglected in my early youth.

In 1745, I received a letter from the Marquis of Annandale, inviting me to come and live with him in England; I found also, that the friends and family of that young noble man were desirous of putting him under my care and direction, for the state of his mind and health required it. I lived with him a twelvemonth. My appointments during that time made a considerable accession to my small fortune. I then received an invitation from General St Clair to attend him as a secretary to his expedition, which was at 'rst meant against Canada, but ended in an incursion on the coast of France. Next year, to wit, 1747, I received an invitation from the General to attend him in the same station in his military embassy to the courts of Vienna and Turin. I then wore the uniform of an officer, and was introduced at these courts as aid-de-camp to the general, along with Sir Harry Erskine and Captain Grant, now General Grant. These two years were almost the only interruptions which my studies have received during the course of my life: I passed them agreeably, and in good company; and my appointments, with my frugality, had made me reach a fortune, which I called independent, though most of my friends were inclined to smile when I said so; in short, I was now master of near a thousand pounds.

I had always entertained a notion, that my want of success in publishing the *Treatise of Human Nature*, had proceeded more from the manner than the matter, and that I had been guilty of a very usual indiscretion, in going to the press too early. I, therefore, cast the first part of that work anew in *The Enquiry concerning Human Understanding*, which was published while I was at Turin. But this piece was at first little more successful than the *Treatise of Human Nature*. On my return from Italy, I had the mortification to find all England in a ferment, on account of Dr Middleton's *Free Enquiry*, while my performance was entirely overlooked and neglected. A new edition, which had been published at London of my *Essays*, moral and political, met not with a much better reception.

Such is the force of natural temper, that these disappointments made little or no impression on me. I went down in 1749, and lived two years with my brother at his country house, for my mother was now dead. I there composed the second part of my *Essays*, which I called *Political Discourses*, and also my *Enquiry concerning the Principles of Morals*, which is another part of my treatise that I cast anew. Meanwhile, my bookseller, A. Millar, informed me, that my former publications (all but the unfortunate *Treatise*) were beginning to be the subject of conversation; that the sale of them was gradually increasing, and that new editions were demanded. Answers by Reverends, and Right Reverends, came out two or three in a year; and I found, by Dr Warburton's railing, that the books were beginning to be esteemed in good company. However I had fixed a resolution, which I inflexibly maintained, never reply to any body; and not being very irascible in my temper, I have easily kept myself clear of all literary squabbles. These symptoms of a rising reputation gave me encouragement, as I was ever more disposed to see the favourable than unfavourable side of things; a turn of mind which it is more happy to possess, than to be born to an estate of ten thousand a year.

In 1751, I removed from the country to the town, the true scene for a man of letters. In 1752, were published at Edinburgh, where I then lived, my *Political Discourses*, the only work of mine that was successful on the first publication. It was well received abroad and at home. In the same year was published at London, my *Enquiry concerning the Principles of Morals*; which, in my own opinion (who ought not to judge on that subject), is of all my writings, historical, philosophical, or literary, incomparably the best. It came unnoticed and unobserved into the world.

In 1752, the Faculty of Advocates chose me their Librarian, an office from which I received little or no emolument, but which gave me the command of a large library. I then formed the plan of writing the History of England; but being frightened with the notion of continuing a narrative through a period of 1700 years, I commenced with the accession of the House of Stuart, an epoch when, I thought, the misrepresentations of faction began chiefly to take place. I was, I own, sanguine in my expectations of the success of this work. I thought that I was the only historian, that had at once neglected present power, interest, and authority, and the cry of popular prejudices; and as the subject was suited to every capacity, I expected proportional applause. But miserable was my disappointment: I was assailed by one cry of reproach, disapprobation, and even detestation; English, Scotch, and Irish, Whig and Tory, churchman and sectary, freethinker and religionist, patriot and courtier, united in their rage against the man, who had presumed to shed a generous tear for the fate of Charles I and the Earl of Strafford; and after the first ebullitions of their fury were over, what was still more mortifying, the book seemed to sink into oblivion. Mr Millar told me, that in a twelve-month he sold only forty-five copies of it. I scarcely, indeed, heard of one man in the three kingdoms, considerable for rank or letters, that could endure the book. I must only except the primate of England, Dr Herring, and the primate of Ireland, Dr Stone, which seem two odd exceptions. These dignified prelates separately sent me messages not to be discouraged.

I was, however, I confess, discouraged; and had not the war been at that time breaking out between France and England, I had certainly retired to some provincial town of the former kingdom, have changed my name, and never more have returned to my native country. But as this scheme was not now practicable, and the subsequent volume was considerably advanced, I resolved to pick up courage and to persevere.

In this interval, I published at London my *Natural History of Religion*, along with some other small pieces: its public entry was rather obscure, except only that Dr Hurd wrote a pamphlet against it, with all the illiberal petulance, arrogance, and scurrility, which distinguish the Warburtonian school. This pamphlet gave me some consolation for the otherwise indifferent reception of my performance.

In 1756, two years after the fall of the first volume, was published the second volume of my *History*, containing the period from the death of Charles I till the Revolution. This performance happened to give less displeasure to the Whigs, and was better received. It not only rose itself, but helped to buoy up its unfortunate brother.

But though I had been taught by experience, that the Whig party were in possession of bestowing all places, both in the state and in literature, I was so little inclined to yield to their senseless clamour, that in above a hundred alterations, which farther study, reading, or reflection engaged me to make in the reigns of the two first Stuarts, I have made all them invariably to the Tory side. It is ridiculous to consider the English constitution before that period as a regular plan of liberty.

In 1759, I published my *History of the House of Tudor*. The clamour against this performance was almost equal to that against the History of the two first Stuarts. The reign of Elizabeth was particularly obnoxious. But I was now callous against the impressions of public folly, and continued very peaceably and contentedly in my retreat at Edinburgh, to finish, in two volumes, the mor' early part of the *English History*, which I gave to the public 1761, with tolerable, and but tolerable success.

But, notwithstanding this variety of winds and seasons, to which my writings had been exposed, they had still been making such advances, that the copy-money given me by the booksellers, much exceeded anything formerly known in England; I was become not only independent, but opulent. I retired to my native country of Scotland, determined never more to set my foot out of it; and retaining the satisfaction of never having preferred a request to one great man, or even making advances of friendship to any of them. As I was now turned of fifty, I thought of passing all the rest of my life in this philosophical manner, when I received, in 1763, an invitation from the Earl of Hertford, with whom I was not in the least acquainted, to attend him on his embassy to Paris, with a near prospect of being appointed secretary to the embassy; and, in the meanwhile, of performing the functions of that office. This offer, however inviting, I at first declined, both because I was reluctant to begin connexions with the great, and because I was afraid that the civilities and gay company of Paris would prove disagreeable to a person of my age and humour: but on his lordship's repeating the invitation, I accepted of it. I have every reason, both of pleasure and interest, to think myself happy in my connexion with that nobleman, as well as afterwards with his brother, General Conway.

Those who have not seen the strange effects of modes, will never imagine the reception I met with at Paris, from men and women of all ranks and stations. The more I resiled from their excessive civilities, the more I was loaded with them. There is, however, a real satisfaction in living at Paris, from the great number of sensible, knowing, and polite company with which that city abounds above all places in the universe. I thought once of settling there for life.

I was appointed secretary to the embassy; and in summer 1765, Lord Hertford left me, being appointed Lord Lieutenant of Ireland. I was *chargé d'affaires* till the arrival of the Duke of Richmond, towards the end of the year. In the beginning of 1766, I left Paris, and next summer went to Edinburgh, with the same view as formerly, of burying myself in a philosophical retreat. I returned to that place, not richer, but with much more money, and a much larger income, by means of Lord Hertford's friendship, than I left it; I was desirous of trying what superfluity could produce, as I had formerly made an experiment of a competency. But, in 1767, I received from Mr Conway an invitation to be Under-secretary; and this invitation, both the character of the person, and my connexions with Lord Hertford, prevented me from declining. I returned to Edinburgh in 1768, very opulent (for I possessed a revenue of 1000*l.* a year), healthy, and though somewhat stricken in years, with the prospect of enjoying long my ease, and of seeing the increase of my reputation.

In spring 1775, I was struck with a disorder in my bowels, which at first gave me no alarm, but has since, as I apprehend it, become mortal and incurable. I now reckon upon a speedy dissolution. I have suffered very little pain from my disorder; and what is more strange, have, notwithstanding the great decline of my person, never suffered a moment's abatement of my spirits; insomuch, that were I to name the period of my life, which I should most choose to pass over again, I might be tempted to point to this later period. I possess the same ardour as ever in study, and the same gaiety in company. I consider, besides, that a man of sixty-five, by dying, cuts off only a few years of infirmities; and though I see many symptoms of my literary reputation's breaking out at last with additional lustre, I knew that I could have but few years to enjoy it. It is difficult to be more detached from life than I am at present.

To conclude historically with my own character. I am, or rather was (for that is the style I must now use in speaking of myself, which emboldens me the more to speak my sentiments); I was, I say, a man of mild dispositions, of command of temper, of an open, social, and cheerful humour, capable of attachment, but little susceptible of enmity, and of great moderation in all my passions. Even my love of literary fame, my ruling passion, never soured my temper, notwithstanding my frequent disappointments. My company was not unacceptable to the young and careless, as well as to the studious and literary; and as I took a particular pleasure in the company of modest women, I had no reason to be displeased with the reception I met with from them. In a word, though most men any wise eminent, have found reason to complain of calumny, I never was touched, or even attacked by her baleful tooth: and though I wantonly exposed myself to the rage of both civil and religious factions, they seemed to be disarmed in my behalf their wonted fury. My friends never had occasion to vindicate

one circumstance of my character and conduct: not but that the
zealots, we may well suppose, would have been glad to invent and
propagate any story to my disadvantage, but they could never find
any which they thought would wear the face of probability. I
cannot say there is no vanity in making this funeral oration of
myself, but I hope it is not a misplaced one; and this is a matter of
fact which is easily cleared and ascertained.

April 18, 1776